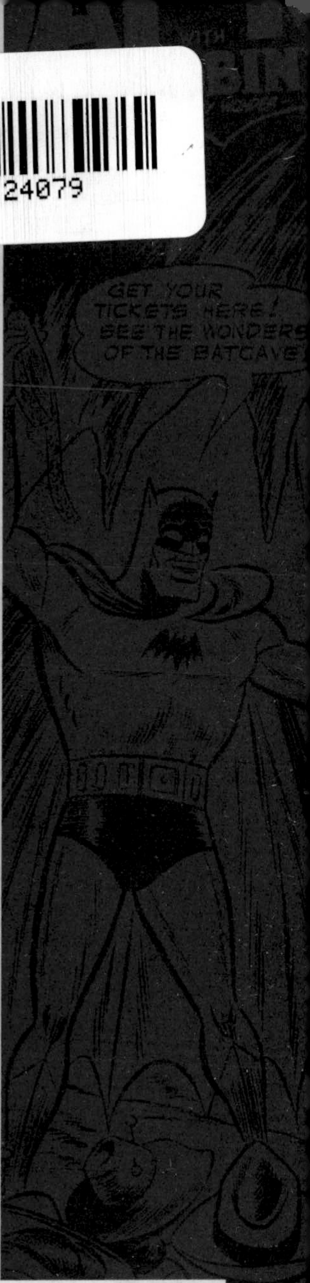
GET YOUR TICKETS HERE! SEE THE WONDERS OF THE BATCAVE!

Table of Contents

TROPHIES OF THE BATCAVE:

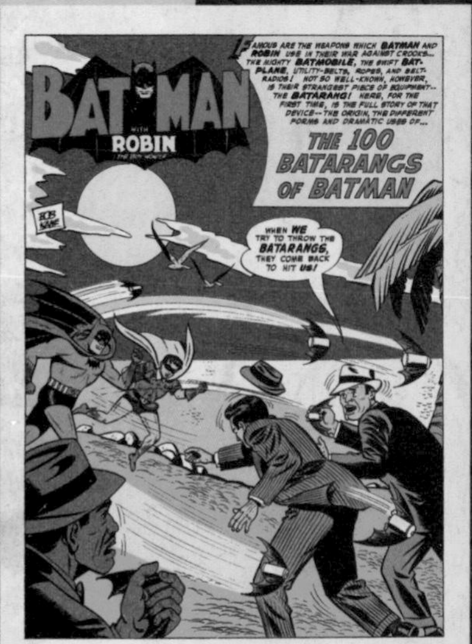
BATMAN
ROBIN
THE 100 BATARANGS OF BATMAN
WHEN WE TRY TO THROW THE BATARANGS, THEY COME BACK TO HIT US!

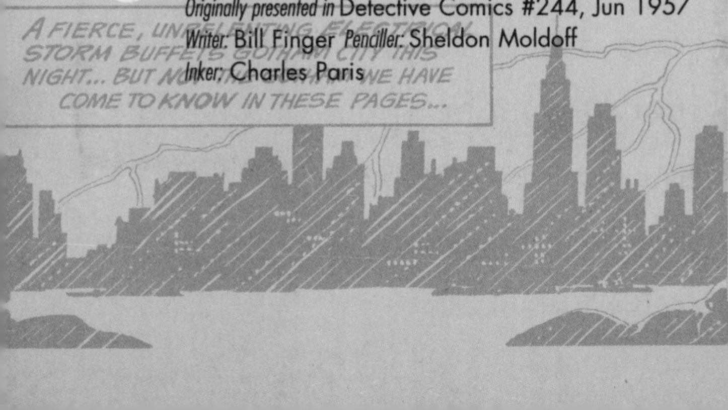
COME TO KNOW IN THESE PAGES...

BEGINNINGS OF THE BATCAVE

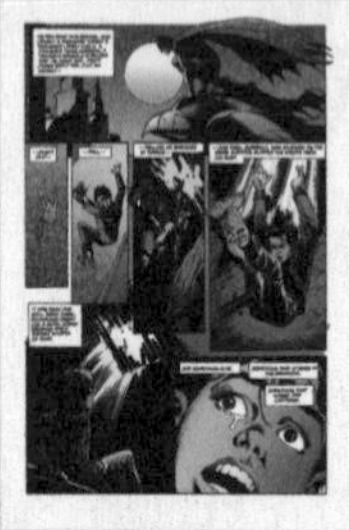

TALES FROM THE BATCAVE

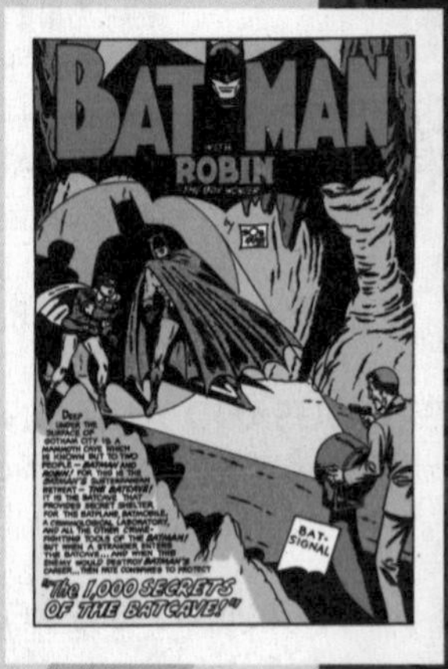

BATMAN
ROBIN
"The 1,000 SECRETS OF THE BATCAVE!"

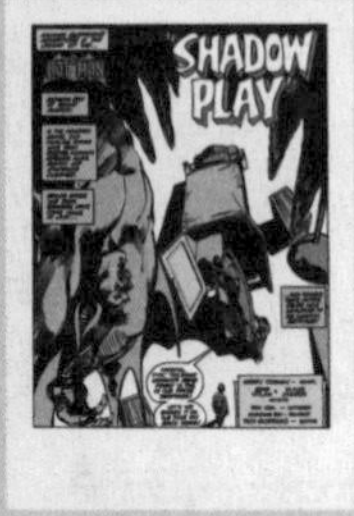

SHADOW PLAY

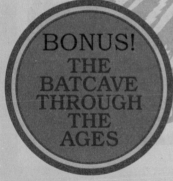

BONUS! THE BATCAVE THROUGH THE AGES

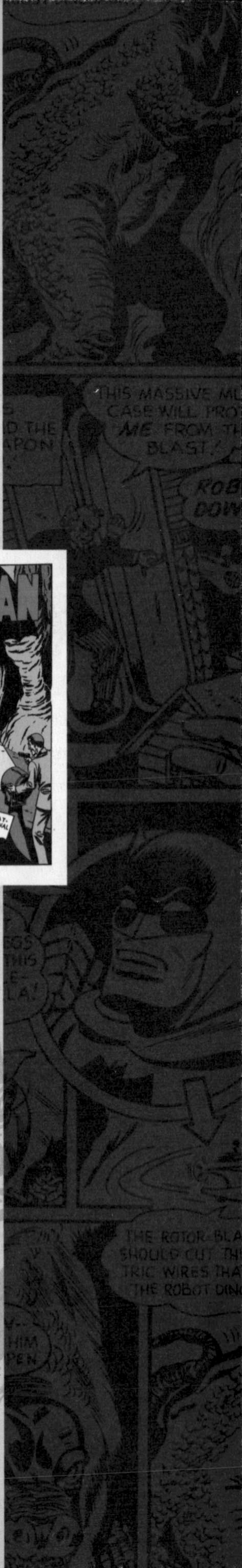

BATCAVE IN THE 40s

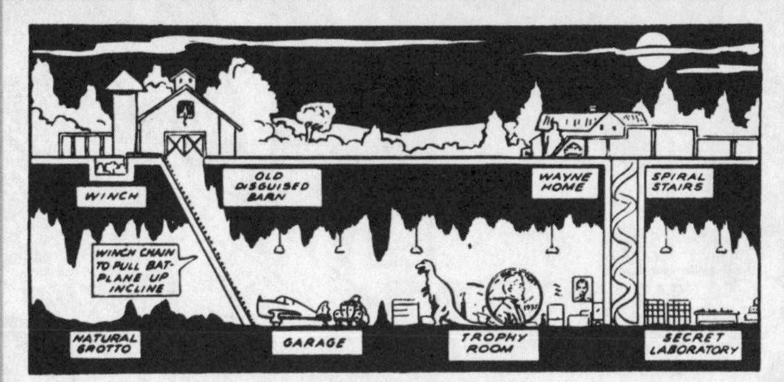
WINCH
OLD DISGUISED BARN
WAYNE HOME
SPIRAL STAIRS
WINCH CHAIN TO PULL BAT-PLANE UP INCLINE
NATURAL GROTTO
GARAGE
TROPHY ROOM
SECRET LABORATORY

Batcave cutaway diagram, 1948 © NPP 1948

From: BATMAN 48 *(1948)*
Art: **JIM MOONEY**

Originally operating out of the old barn on the Wayne property, Batman accidentally discovered the caverns beneath. At first it was used to store his crimefighting equipment and vehicles, but soon it would serve as his base of operations.

BATCAVE IN THE 50s

From: DETECTIVE COMICS 205 *(1954)*
Art: **SHELLY MOLDOFF/CHARLES PARIS**

As the Dynamic Duo's crusade continued, more space would be needed. In the diagram below, which is only a partial view, you can see that Batman began adding a second level.

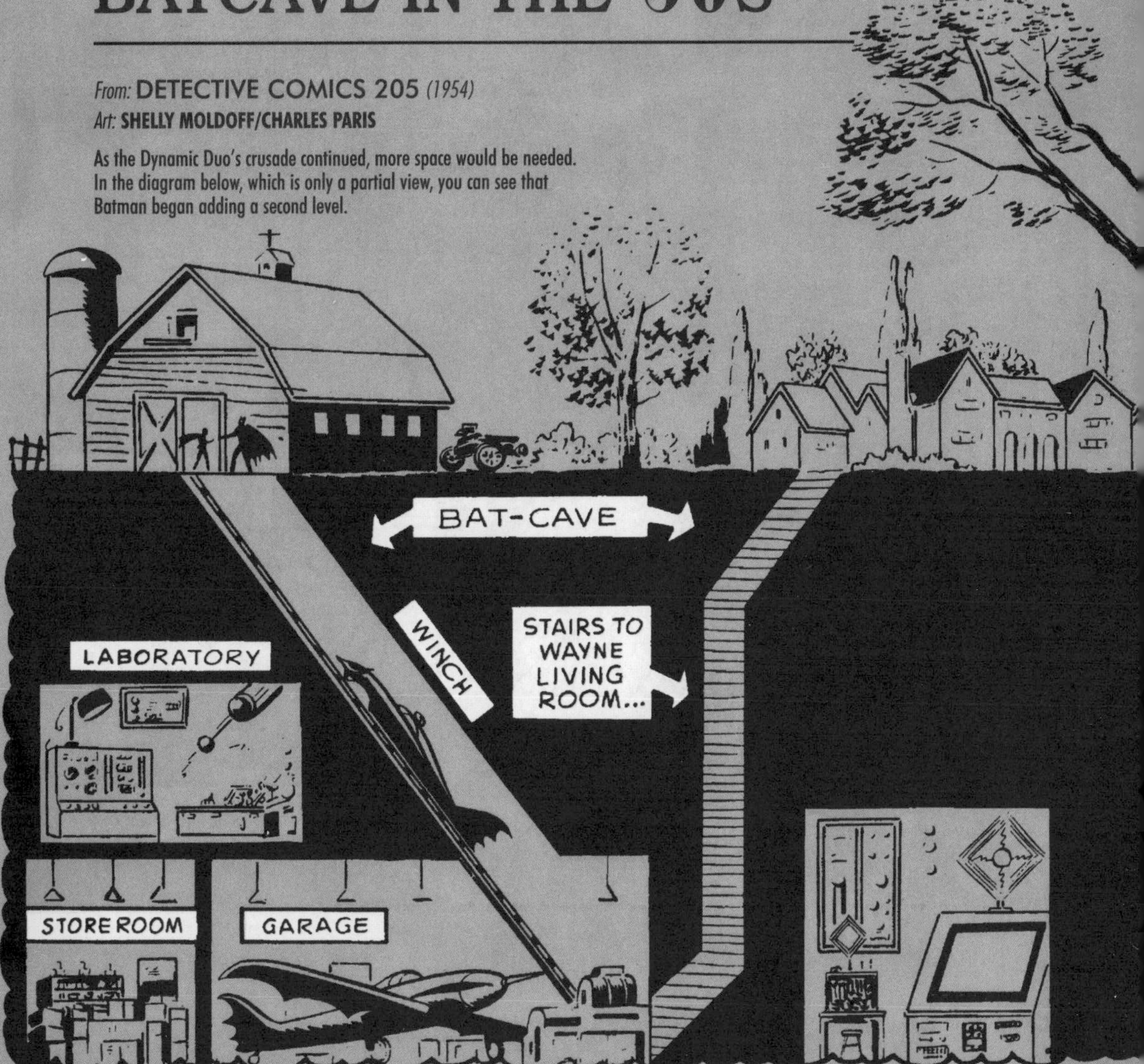
BAT-CAVE
WINCH
STAIRS TO WAYNE LIVING ROOM...
LABORATORY
STOREROOM
GARAGE

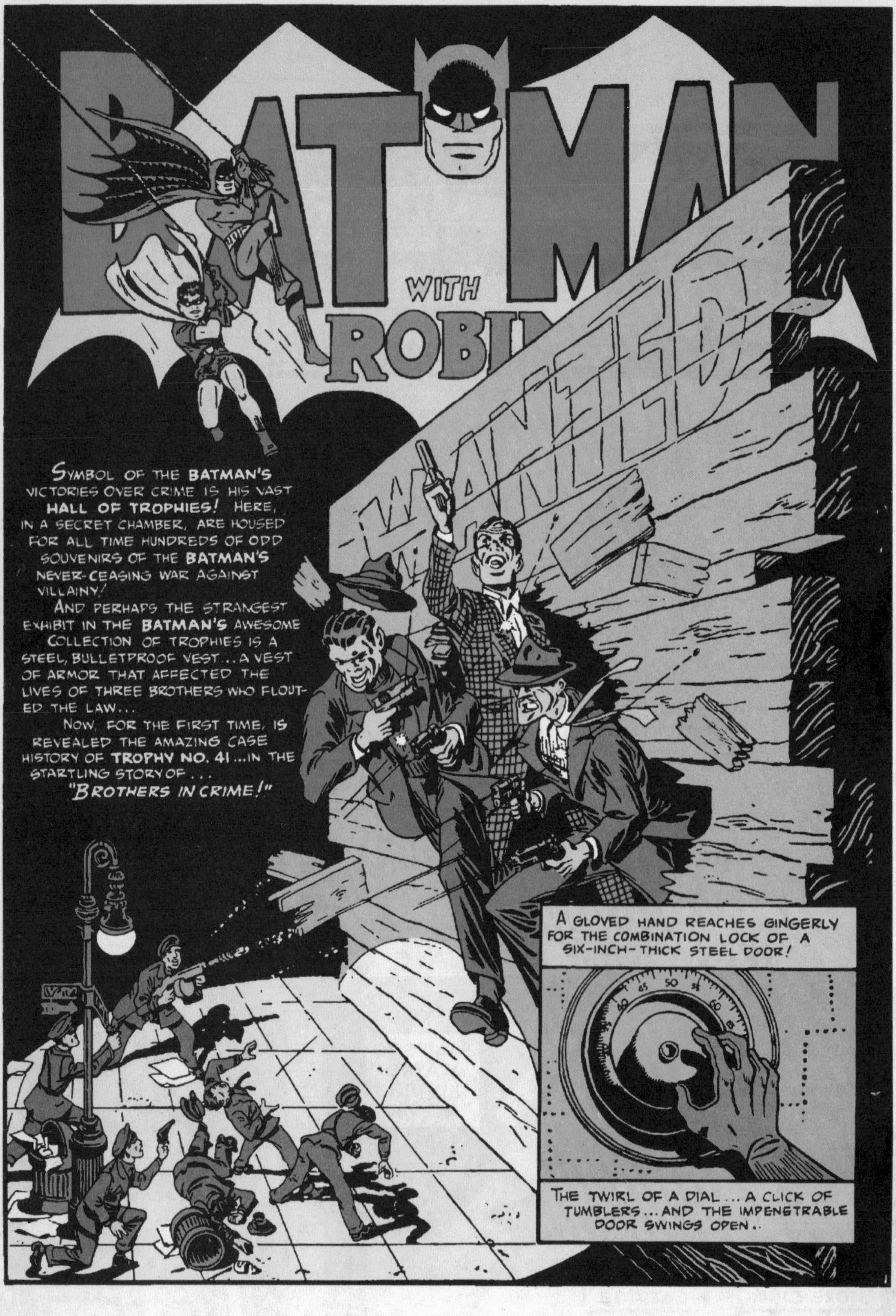
BATMAN
WITH ROBIN
WANTED
SYMBOL OF THE BATMAN'S VICTORIES OVER CRIME IS HIS VAST HALL OF TROPHIES! HERE, IN A SECRET CHAMBER, ARE HOUSED FOR ALL TIME HUNDREDS OF ODD SOUVENIRS OF THE BATMAN'S NEVER-CEASING WAR AGAINST VILLAINY!
AND PERHAPS THE STRANGEST EXHIBIT IN THE BATMAN'S AWESOME COLLECTION OF TROPHIES IS A STEEL, BULLETPROOF VEST... A VEST OF ARMOR THAT AFFECTED THE LIVES OF THREE BROTHERS WHO FLOUTED THE LAW...
NOW, FOR THE FIRST TIME, IS REVEALED THE AMAZING CASE HISTORY OF TROPHY NO. 41 ...IN THE STARTLING STORY OF ...
"BROTHERS IN CRIME!"
A GLOVED HAND REACHES GINGERLY FOR THE COMBINATION LOCK OF A SIX-INCH-THICK STEEL DOOR!
THE TWIRL OF A DIAL ... A CLICK OF TUMBLERS ... AND THE IMPENETRABLE DOOR SWINGS OPEN ..

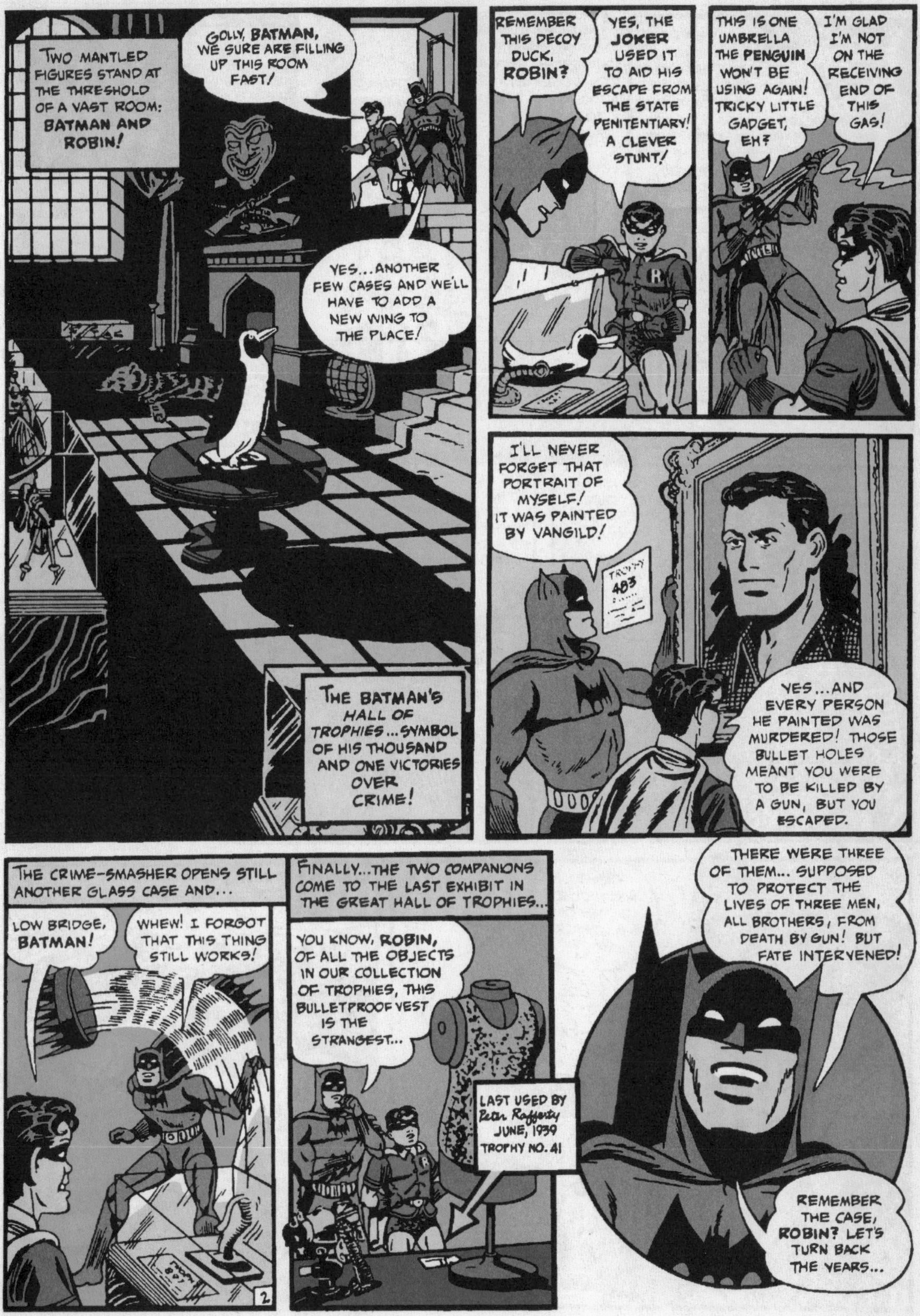
TWO MANTLED FIGURES STAND AT THE THRESHOLD OF A VAST ROOM: BATMAN AND ROBIN!
GOLLY, BATMAN, WE SURE ARE FILLING UP THIS ROOM FAST!
YES...ANOTHER FEW CASES AND WE'LL HAVE TO ADD A NEW WING TO THE PLACE!
THE BATMAN'S HALL OF TROPHIES...SYMBOL OF HIS THOUSAND AND ONE VICTORIES OVER CRIME!
REMEMBER THIS DECOY DUCK, ROBIN?
YES, THE JOKER USED IT TO AID HIS ESCAPE FROM THE STATE PENITENTIARY! A CLEVER STUNT!
THIS IS ONE UMBRELLA THE PENGUIN WON'T BE USING AGAIN! TRICKY LITTLE GADGET, EH?
I'M GLAD I'M NOT ON THE RECEIVING END OF THIS GAS!
I'LL NEVER FORGET THAT PORTRAIT OF MYSELF! IT WAS PAINTED BY VANGILD!
TROPHY 483
YES...AND EVERY PERSON HE PAINTED WAS MURDERED! THOSE BULLET HOLES MEANT YOU WERE TO BE KILLED BY A GUN, BUT YOU ESCAPED.
THE CRIME-SMASHER OPENS STILL ANOTHER GLASS CASE AND...
LOW BRIDGE, BATMAN!
WHEW! I FORGOT THAT THIS THING STILL WORKS!
2
FINALLY...THE TWO COMPANIONS COME TO THE LAST EXHIBIT IN THE GREAT HALL OF TROPHIES...
YOU KNOW, ROBIN, OF ALL THE OBJECTS IN OUR COLLECTION OF TROPHIES, THIS BULLETPROOF VEST IS THE STRANGEST...
LAST USED BY Peter Rafferty JUNE, 1939 TROPHY NO. 41
THERE WERE THREE OF THEM... SUPPOSED TO PROTECT THE LIVES OF THREE MEN, ALL BROTHERS, FROM DEATH BY GUN! BUT FATE INTERVENED!
REMEMBER THE CASE, ROBIN? LET'S TURN BACK THE YEARS...

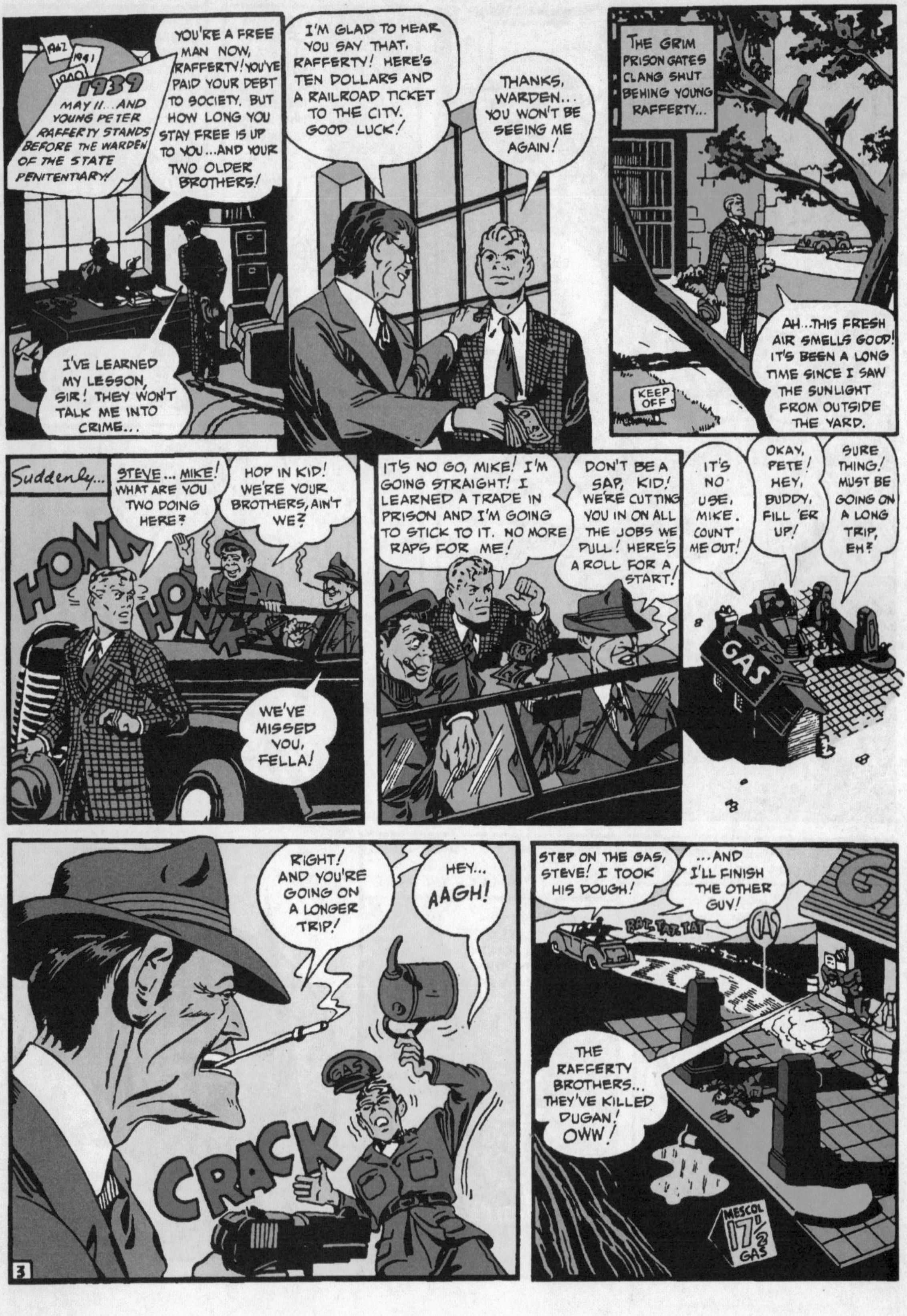
1942
1941
1940
1939
MAY 11... AND YOUNG PETER RAFFERTY STANDS BEFORE THE WARDEN OF THE STATE PENITENTIARY!
YOU'RE A FREE MAN NOW, RAFFERTY! YOU'VE PAID YOUR DEBT TO SOCIETY. BUT HOW LONG YOU STAY FREE IS UP TO YOU... AND YOUR TWO OLDER BROTHERS!
I'VE LEARNED MY LESSON, SIR! THEY WON'T TALK ME INTO CRIME...
I'M GLAD TO HEAR YOU SAY THAT, RAFFERTY! HERE'S TEN DOLLARS AND A RAILROAD TICKET TO THE CITY. GOOD LUCK!
THANKS, WARDEN... YOU WON'T BE SEEING ME AGAIN!
THE GRIM PRISON GATES CLANG SHUT BEHING YOUNG RAFFERTY...
AH... THIS FRESH AIR SMELLS GOOD! IT'S BEEN A LONG TIME SINCE I SAW THE SUNLIGHT FROM OUTSIDE THE YARD.
KEEP OFF
Suddenly...
STEVE... MIKE! WHAT ARE YOU TWO DOING HERE?
HOP IN KID! WE'RE YOUR BROTHERS, AIN'T WE?
HONK HONK
WE'VE MISSED YOU, FELLA!
IT'S NO GO, MIKE! I'M GOING STRAIGHT! I LEARNED A TRADE IN PRISON AND I'M GOING TO STICK TO IT. NO MORE RAPS FOR ME!
DON'T BE A SAP, KID! WE'RE CUTTING YOU IN ON ALL THE JOBS WE PULL! HERE'S A ROLL FOR A START!
IT'S NO USE, MIKE. COUNT ME OUT!
OKAY, PETE! HEY, BUDDY, FILL 'ER UP!
SURE THING! MUST BE GOING ON A LONG TRIP, EH?
GAS
RIGHT! AND YOU'RE GOING ON A LONGER TRIP!
HEY... AAGH!
CRACK
GAS
3
STEP ON THE GAS, STEVE! I TOOK HIS DOUGH!
...AND I'LL FINISH THE OTHER GUY!
RAT TAT TAT
GAS
THE RAFFERTY BROTHERS... THEY'VE KILLED DUGAN! OWW!
MESCOL 17 1/2 GAS

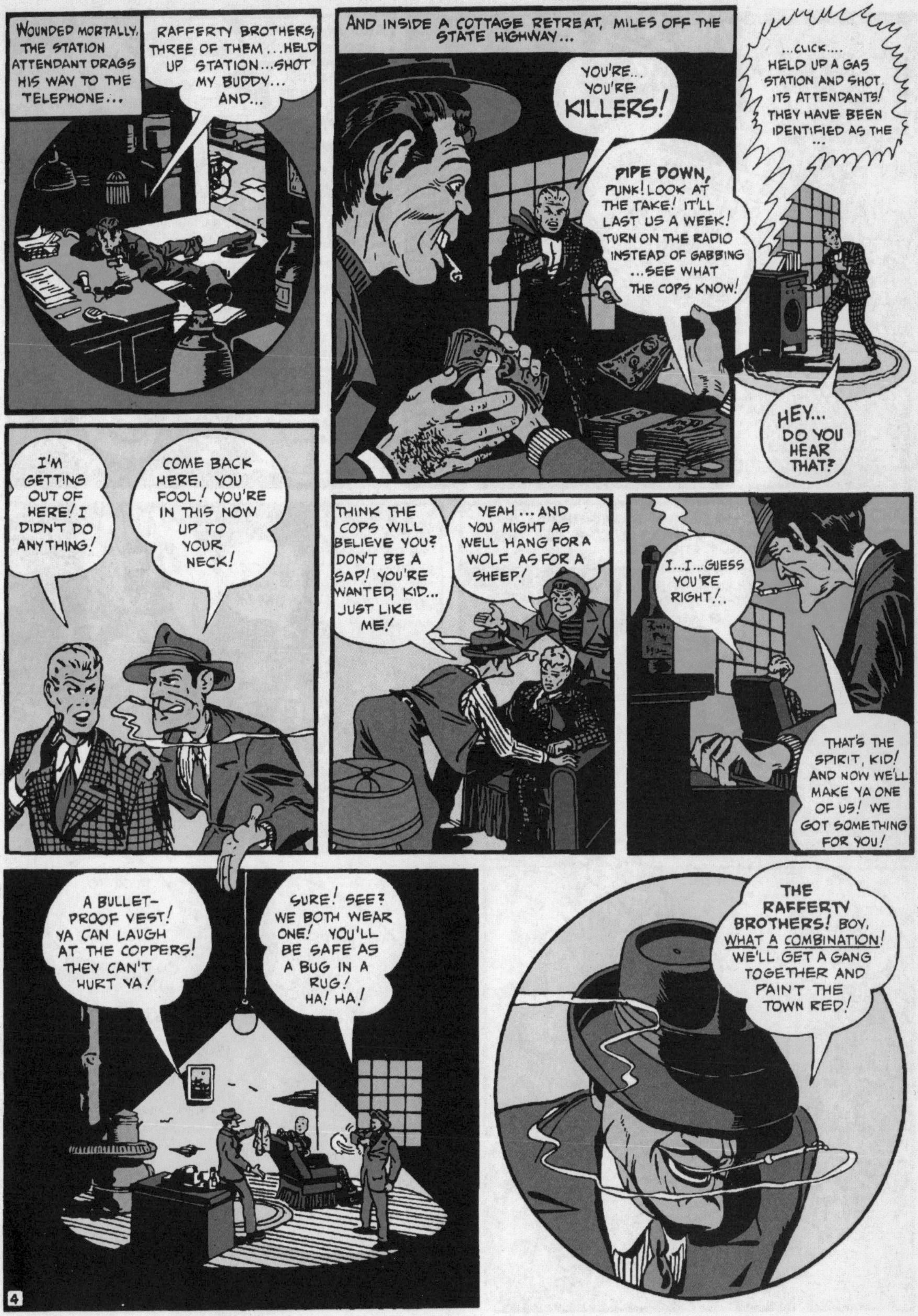
WOUNDED MORTALLY, THE STATION ATTENDANT DRAGS HIS WAY TO THE TELEPHONE...
RAFFERTY BROTHERS, THREE OF THEM...HELD UP STATION...SHOT MY BUDDY... AND...
AND INSIDE A COTTAGE RETREAT, MILES OFF THE STATE HIGHWAY...
YOU'RE... YOU'RE KILLERS!
PIPE DOWN, PUNK! LOOK AT THE TAKE! IT'LL LAST US A WEEK! TURN ON THE RADIO INSTEAD OF GABBING ...SEE WHAT THE COPS KNOW!
...CLICK.... HELD UP A GAS STATION AND SHOT ITS ATTENDANTS! THEY HAVE BEEN IDENTIFIED AS THE ...
HEY... DO YOU HEAR THAT?
I'M GETTING OUT OF HERE! I DIDN'T DO ANYTHING!
COME BACK HERE, YOU FOOL! YOU'RE IN THIS NOW UP TO YOUR NECK!
THINK THE COPS WILL BELIEVE YOU? DON'T BE A SAP! YOU'RE WANTED, KID... JUST LIKE ME!
YEAH ... AND YOU MIGHT AS WELL HANG FOR A WOLF AS FOR A SHEEP!
I...I...GUESS YOU'RE RIGHT!..
THAT'S THE SPIRIT, KID! AND NOW WE'LL MAKE YA ONE OF US! WE GOT SOMETHING FOR YOU!
A BULLET-PROOF VEST! YA CAN LAUGH AT THE COPPERS! THEY CAN'T HURT YA!
SURE! SEE? WE BOTH WEAR ONE! YOU'LL BE SAFE AS A BUG IN A RUG! HA! HA!
THE RAFFERTY BROTHERS! BOY, WHAT A COMBINATION! WE'LL GET A GANG TOGETHER AND PAINT THE TOWN RED!
4

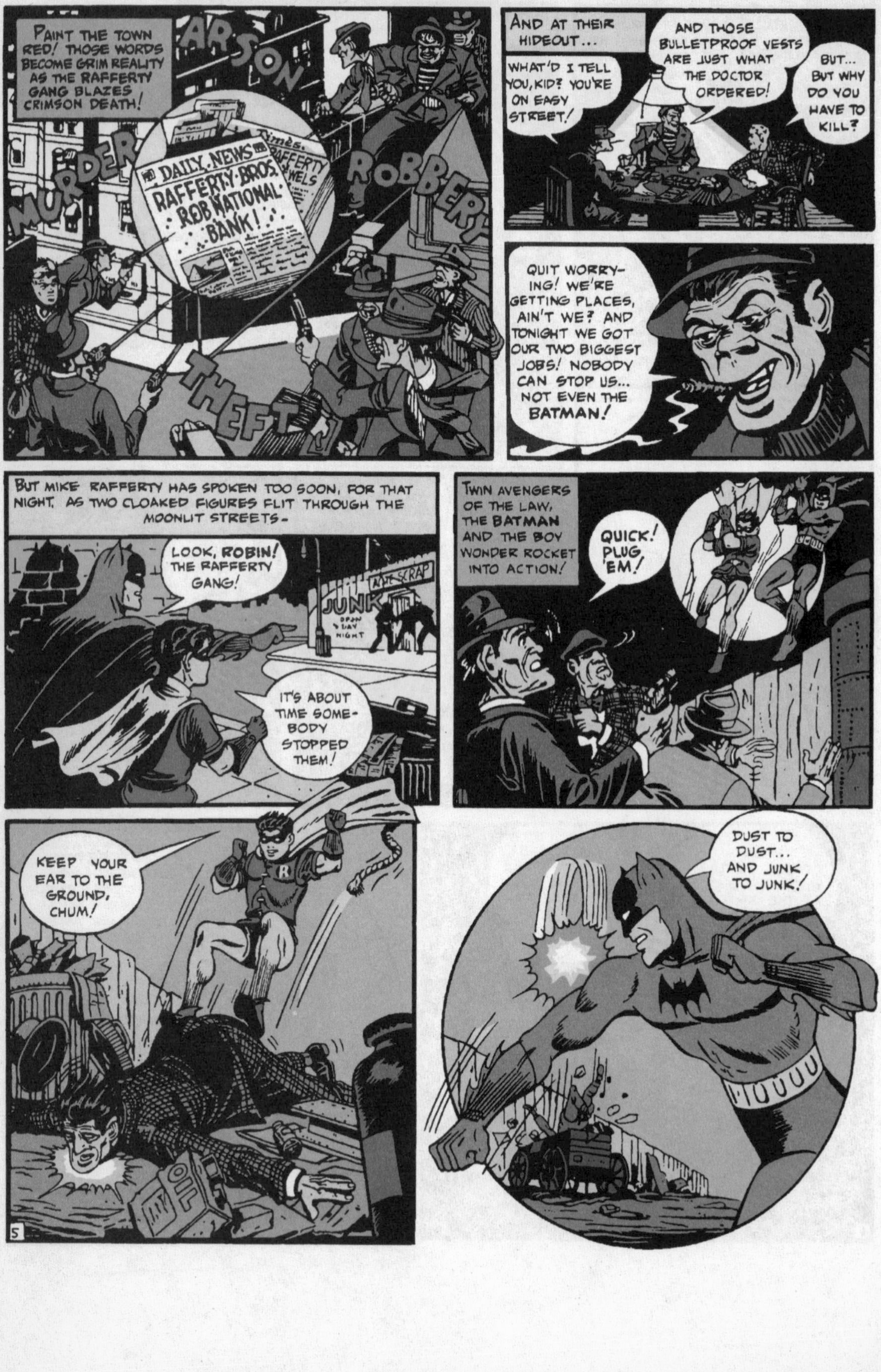

PAINT THE TOWN RED! THOSE WORDS BECOME GRIM REALITY AS THE RAFFERTY GANG BLAZES CRIMSON DEATH!
ARSON
MURDER
DAILY NEWS
RAFFERTY BROS. ROB NATIONAL BANK!
ROBBERY
THEFT
AND AT THEIR HIDEOUT...
WHAT'D I TELL YOU, KID? YOU'RE ON EASY STREET!
AND THOSE BULLETPROOF VESTS ARE JUST WHAT THE DOCTOR ORDERED!
BUT... BUT WHY DO YOU HAVE TO KILL?
QUIT WORRYING! WE'RE GETTING PLACES, AIN'T WE? AND TONIGHT WE GOT OUR TWO BIGGEST JOBS! NOBODY CAN STOP US... NOT EVEN THE BATMAN!
BUT MIKE RAFFERTY HAS SPOKEN TOO SOON, FOR THAT NIGHT, AS TWO CLOAKED FIGURES FLIT THROUGH THE MOONLIT STREETS-
LOOK, ROBIN! THE RAFFERTY GANG!
JUNK
OPEN DAY NIGHT
IT'S ABOUT TIME SOMEBODY STOPPED THEM!
TWIN AVENGERS OF THE LAW, THE BATMAN AND THE BOY WONDER ROCKET INTO ACTION!
QUICK! PLUG 'EM!
KEEP YOUR EAR TO THE GROUND, CHUM!
OIL
DUST TO DUST... AND JUNK TO JUNK!

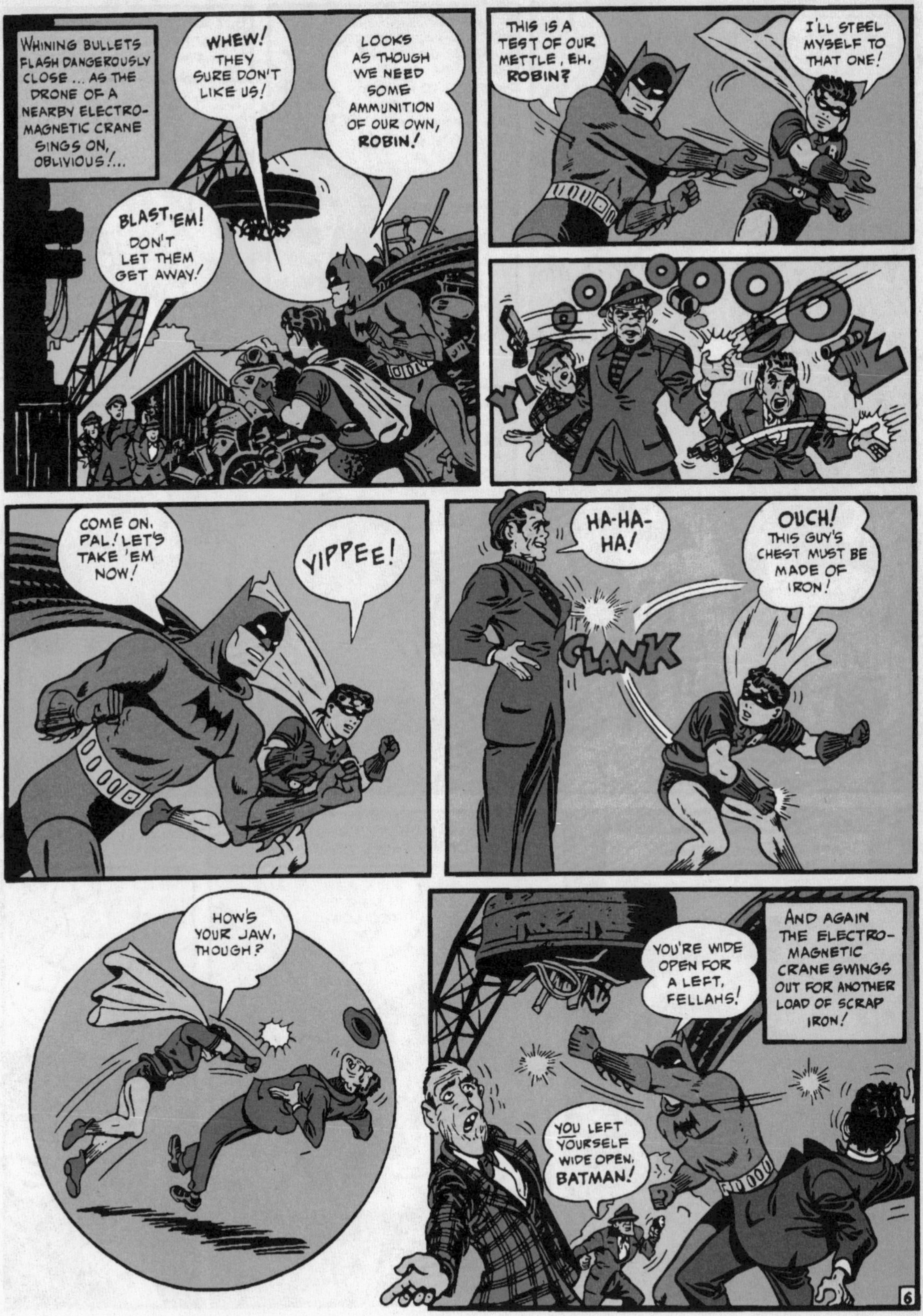
WHINING BULLETS FLASH DANGEROUSLY CLOSE ... AS THE DRONE OF A NEARBY ELECTRO-MAGNETIC CRANE SINGS ON, OBLIVIOUS!...
WHEW! THEY SURE DON'T LIKE US!
LOOKS AS THOUGH WE NEED SOME AMMUNITION OF OUR OWN, ROBIN!
BLAST 'EM! DON'T LET THEM GET AWAY!
THIS IS A TEST OF OUR METTLE, EH, ROBIN?
I'LL STEEL MYSELF TO THAT ONE!
OOOOOOW
YI
COME ON, PAL! LET'S TAKE 'EM NOW!
YIPPEE!
HA-HA-HA!
OUCH! THIS GUY'S CHEST MUST BE MADE OF IRON!
CLANK
HOW'S YOUR JAW, THOUGH?
YOU'RE WIDE OPEN FOR A LEFT, FELLAHS!
AND AGAIN THE ELECTRO-MAGNETIC CRANE SWINGS OUT FOR ANOTHER LOAD OF SCRAP IRON!
YOU LEFT YOURSELF WIDE OPEN, BATMAN!
6

A PERILOUS MOMENT AND JUST AS STEVE RAFFERTY IS ABOUT TO SQUEEZE THE TRIGGER...THE CRANE DIPS DOWN AND...

HELP!

HEY, LOOK AT STEVE!

HE'S MAGNETIZED! THE ELECTRO-MAGNETIC CRANE WON'T LET GO OF HIS METAL VEST. HE'LL BE DROPPED TO HIS DEATH IF THAT OPERATOR CUTS OFF THE CURRENT! I'VE GOT TO SAVE HIM, EVEN IF HE'S A KILLER!

BUT A TREACHEROUS BLOW FROM BEHIND FELLS THE GALLANT DARK KNIGHT!

GOT YOU!

POW

THE CRANE SWINGS OUT...

HELP!

YEEOW

...AND RELEASES ITS LOAD IN THE FREIGHT CAR AND THUS, IRONICALLY, THE GANG LEADER'S OWN HENCHMAN DOOMS HIM!

"SAFE AS A BUG IN A RUG!" VAIN BOAST... FOR STEVE RAFFERTY'S BULLETPROOF VEST HAS BROUGHT HIM DEATH!

MEANWHILE, ROBIN SPRINGS TO THE RESCUE OF HIS DAZED COMPANION...

YOUR AIM IN LIFE IS TOO LOW, RAT!

SUDDENLY, THE SHRIEK BLAST OF A WHISTLE...

THE COPS! LET'S GET OUT OF HERE!

EEEEEEEEEEE

12

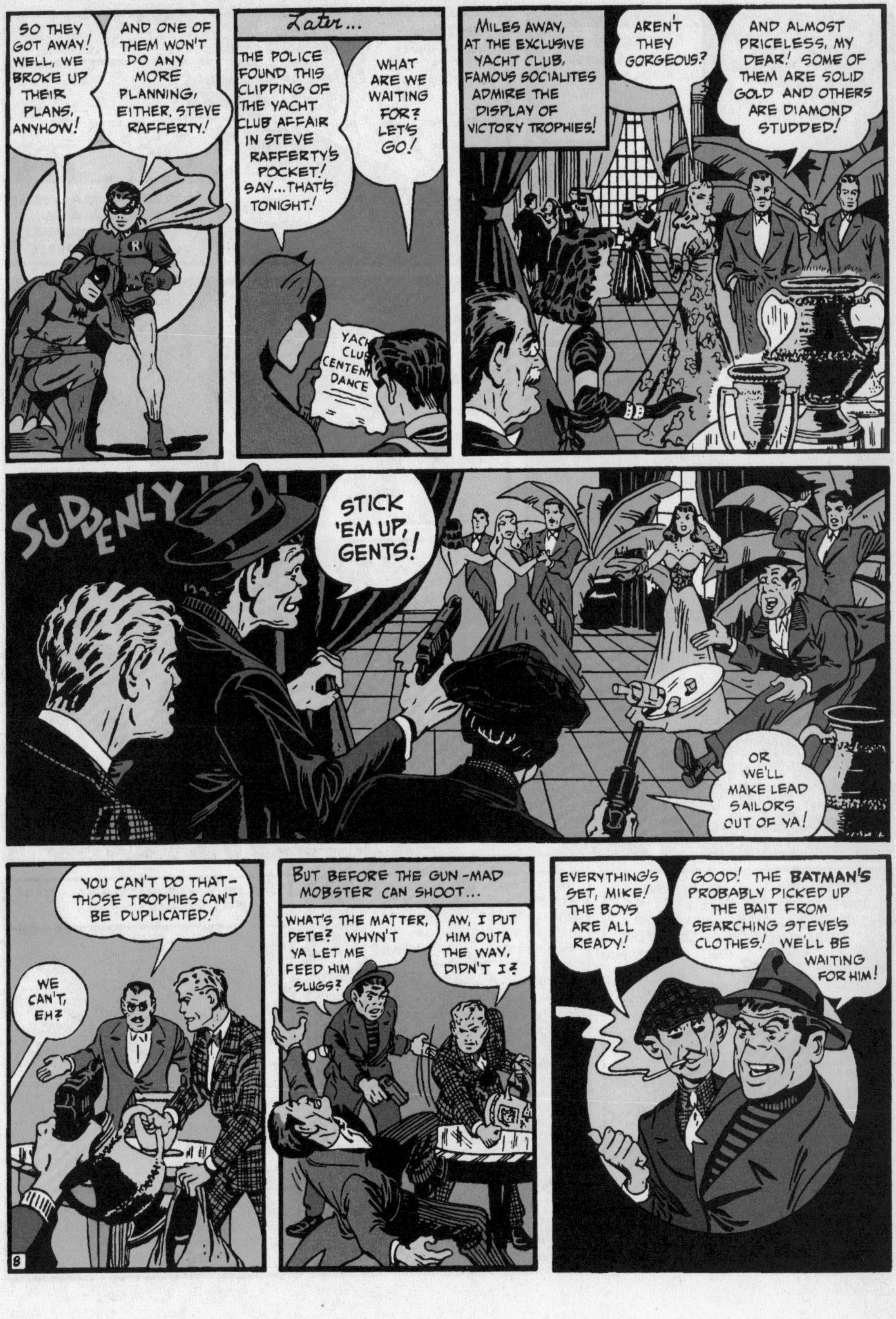
SO THEY GOT AWAY! WELL, WE BROKE UP THEIR PLANS, ANYHOW!
AND ONE OF THEM WON'T DO ANY MORE PLANNING, EITHER, STEVE RAFFERTY!
Later...
THE POLICE FOUND THIS CLIPPING OF THE YACHT CLUB AFFAIR IN STEVE RAFFERTY'S POCKET! SAY...THAT'S TONIGHT!
WHAT ARE WE WAITING FOR? LET'S GO!
MILES AWAY, AT THE EXCLUSIVE YACHT CLUB, FAMOUS SOCIALITES ADMIRE THE DISPLAY OF VICTORY TROPHIES!
AREN'T THEY GORGEOUS?
AND ALMOST PRICELESS, MY DEAR! SOME OF THEM ARE SOLID GOLD AND OTHERS ARE DIAMOND STUDDED!
SUDDENLY
STICK 'EM UP, GENTS!
OR WE'LL MAKE LEAD SAILORS OUT OF YA!
YOU CAN'T DO THAT-THOSE TROPHIES CAN'T BE DUPLICATED!
WE CAN'T, EH?
8
BUT BEFORE THE GUN-MAD MOBSTER CAN SHOOT...
WHAT'S THE MATTER, PETE? WHYN'T YA LET ME FEED HIM SLUGS?
AW, I PUT HIM OUTA THE WAY, DIDN'T I?
EVERYTHING'S SET, MIKE! THE BOYS ARE ALL READY!
GOOD! THE BATMAN'S PROBABLY PICKED UP THE BAIT FROM SEARCHING STEVE'S CLOTHES! WE'LL BE WAITING FOR HIM!

AT THAT MOMENT, THE STREAMLINED BATMOBILE NEARS THE YACHT CLUB AT A MILE-A-MINUTE CLIP...

YACHT CLUB

THEY'RE PULLING UP THE DRAW-BRIDGE!

WE CAN'T STOP! WE'LL HAVE TO GO AHEAD! HOLD TIGHT!

WHO SAID YOU SHOULD NEVER CROSS A BRIDGE BEFORE COMING TO IT?

I DUNNO... BUT WE'RE DOING IT!

ZOOM

ACCELERATING TO FULL SPEED, THE SUPER-CHARGED CAR SHOOTS FORWARD ACROSS EMPTY SPACE.

ZUMP

YEOW! BACK TO THE CLUB HOUSE! WE'LL FIX 'EM!

...AND MAKES A FOUR-WHEEL LANDING!

LAST STOP!

ALL OUT—FOR ACTION!

AS THE POWER-HOUSE PAIR LEAPS TOWARD THE CLUB VERANDA, A HUGE WIRE MESH-NET SWOOPS DOWN FROM ABOVE.

HA! THEY WALKED RIGHT IN-TO IT!

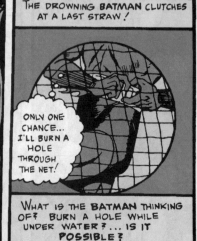

LOOK AT 'EM—THE BATMAN AND ROBIN! SOME CATCH!

HURRY UP! WE'LL TAKE 'EM FOR A NEW KIND OF RIDE!

THEY'LL BE DEAD FISH IN NO TIME!

WELL, I GUESS I'LL MEET THE GANG AT THE HIDEOUT. NO ONE COULD SAVE BATMAN AND ROBIN NOW. NOT EVEN ME!

NOTHING IN MY UTILITY BELT IS SHARP ENOUGH TO CUT THIS WIRE! EXCEPT... MAYBE...

THERE'S NO WAY OF ESCAPE! WE'LL DROWN!

THE DROWNING BATMAN CLUTCHES AT A LAST STRAW!

ONLY ONE CHANCE... I'LL BURN A HOLE THROUGH THE NET!

WHAT IS THE BATMAN THINKING OF? BURN A HOLE WHILE UNDER WATER?... IS IT POSSIBLE?

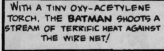

WITH A TINY OXY-ACETYLENE TORCH, THE **BATMAN** SHOOTS A STREAM OF TERRIFIC HEAT AGAINST THE WIRE NET!

LUCKY I REMEMBERED THAT UNDERSEA DIVERS USE THESE IN SALVAGING WRECKED SHIPS!

GEE!

Moments later...

WHEW! FRESH AIR! BOY, THAT TORCH BURNED RIGHT THROUGH WATER!

SILENTLY, THE DYNAMIC DUO INCHES ALONG TOWARD THE REAR OF THE BOAT!...

BIF

BOP

BAM

...AND EXPLODES INTO ACTION!

THE LOOSE WHEEL OF THE BOAT SPINS FREE AND...

LOOK OUT! WE'RE GOING OVER!

UGH... THAT'S THE SECOND DUCKING TODAY!

HELP... GLUB... HELP!

WHAT'S THAT? SOMEBODY IS DROWNING!

BATMAN IS RIGHT! ALONE IN THE DARK, MIKE RAFFERTY.

MY VEST...GLUB... ITS WEIGHING ME DOWN— HELP... AGH!

HEY, MIKE'S DROWNED!

HIS VEST MAY HAVE BEEN BULLETPROOF — BUT IT WASN'T WATER-PROOF! IF HE HADN'T BEEN WEARING IT, HE MIGHT HAVE SAVED HIMSELF!

AND A SECOND BROTHER MEETS DOOM BECAUSE OF A BULLETPROOF VEST!

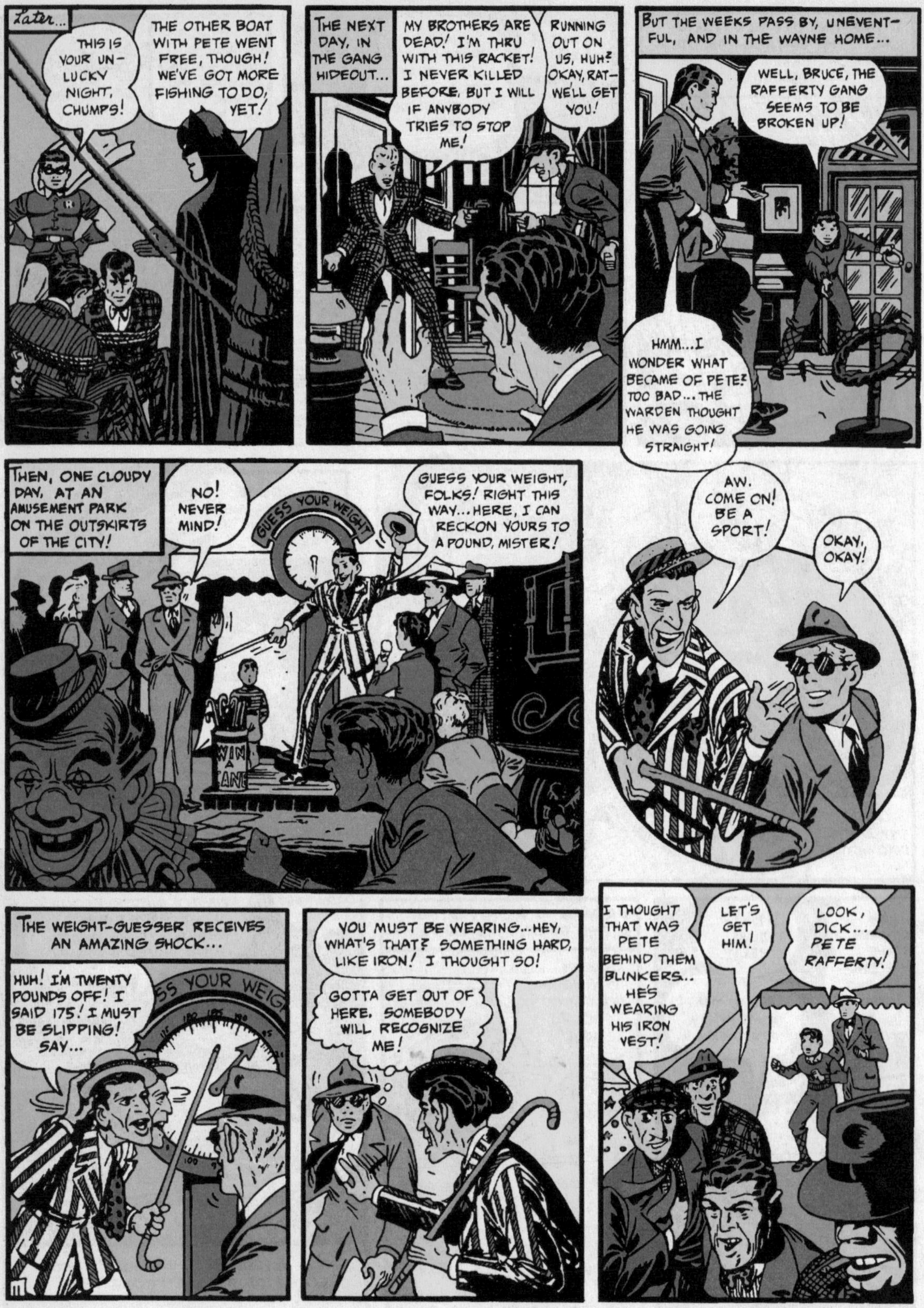
Later...
THIS IS YOUR UN-LUCKY NIGHT, CHUMPS!
THE OTHER BOAT WITH PETE WENT FREE, THOUGH! WE'VE GOT MORE FISHING TO DO, YET!
THE NEXT DAY, IN THE GANG HIDEOUT...
MY BROTHERS ARE DEAD! I'M THRU WITH THIS RACKET! I NEVER KILLED BEFORE, BUT I WILL IF ANYBODY TRIES TO STOP ME!
RUNNING OUT ON US, HUH? OKAY, RAT—WE'LL GET YOU!
BUT THE WEEKS PASS BY, UNEVENTFUL, AND IN THE WAYNE HOME...
WELL, BRUCE, THE RAFFERTY GANG SEEMS TO BE BROKEN UP!
HMM...I WONDER WHAT BECAME OF PETE? TOO BAD... THE WARDEN THOUGHT HE WAS GOING STRAIGHT!
THEN, ONE CLOUDY DAY, AT AN AMUSEMENT PARK ON THE OUTSKIRTS OF THE CITY!
NO! NEVER MIND!
GUESS YOUR WEIGHT
GUESS YOUR WEIGHT, FOLKS! RIGHT THIS WAY... HERE, I CAN RECKON YOURS TO A POUND, MISTER!
AW. COME ON! BE A SPORT!
OKAY, OKAY!
THE WEIGHT-GUESSER RECEIVES AN AMAZING SHOCK...
HUH! I'M TWENTY POUNDS OFF! I SAID 175! I MUST BE SLIPPING! SAY...
YOU MUST BE WEARING...HEY, WHAT'S THAT? SOMETHING HARD, LIKE IRON! I THOUGHT SO!
GOTTA GET OUT OF HERE. SOMEBODY WILL RECOGNIZE ME!
I THOUGHT THAT WAS PETE BEHIND THEM BLINKERS.. HE'S WEARING HIS IRON VEST!
LET'S GET HIM!
LOOK, DICK... PETE RAFFERTY!

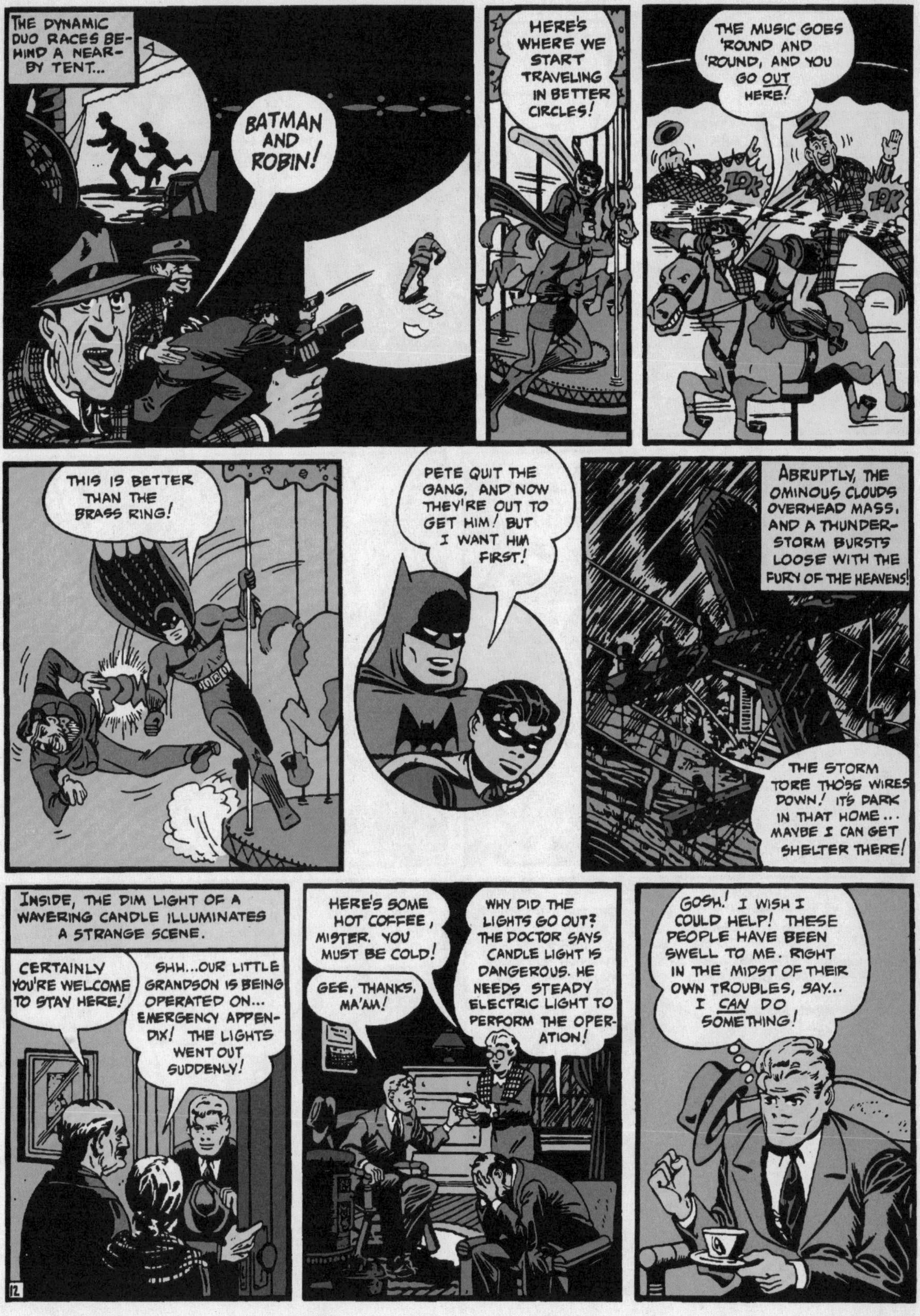
THE DYNAMIC DUO RACES BEHIND A NEARBY TENT...
BATMAN AND ROBIN!
HERE'S WHERE WE START TRAVELING IN BETTER CIRCLES!
THE MUSIC GOES 'ROUND AND 'ROUND, AND YOU GO OUT HERE!
ZOK
ZOK
THIS IS BETTER THAN THE BRASS RING!
PETE QUIT THE GANG, AND NOW THEY'RE OUT TO GET HIM! BUT I WANT HIM FIRST!
ABRUPTLY, THE OMINOUS CLOUDS OVERHEAD MASS, AND A THUNDERSTORM BURSTS LOOSE WITH THE FURY OF THE HEAVENS!
THE STORM TORE THOSE WIRES DOWN! IT'S DARK IN THAT HOME... MAYBE I CAN GET SHELTER THERE!
INSIDE, THE DIM LIGHT OF A WAVERING CANDLE ILLUMINATES A STRANGE SCENE.
CERTAINLY YOU'RE WELCOME TO STAY HERE!
SHH...OUR LITTLE GRANDSON IS BEING OPERATED ON... EMERGENCY APPENDIX! THE LIGHTS WENT OUT SUDDENLY!
12
HERE'S SOME HOT COFFEE, MISTER. YOU MUST BE COLD!
GEE, THANKS, MA'AM!
WHY DID THE LIGHTS GO OUT? THE DOCTOR SAYS CANDLE LIGHT IS DANGEROUS. HE NEEDS STEADY ELECTRIC LIGHT TO PERFORM THE OPERATION!
GOSH! I WISH I COULD HELP! THESE PEOPLE HAVE BEEN SWELL TO ME. RIGHT IN THE MIDST OF THEIR OWN TROUBLES, SAY... I CAN DO SOMETHING!

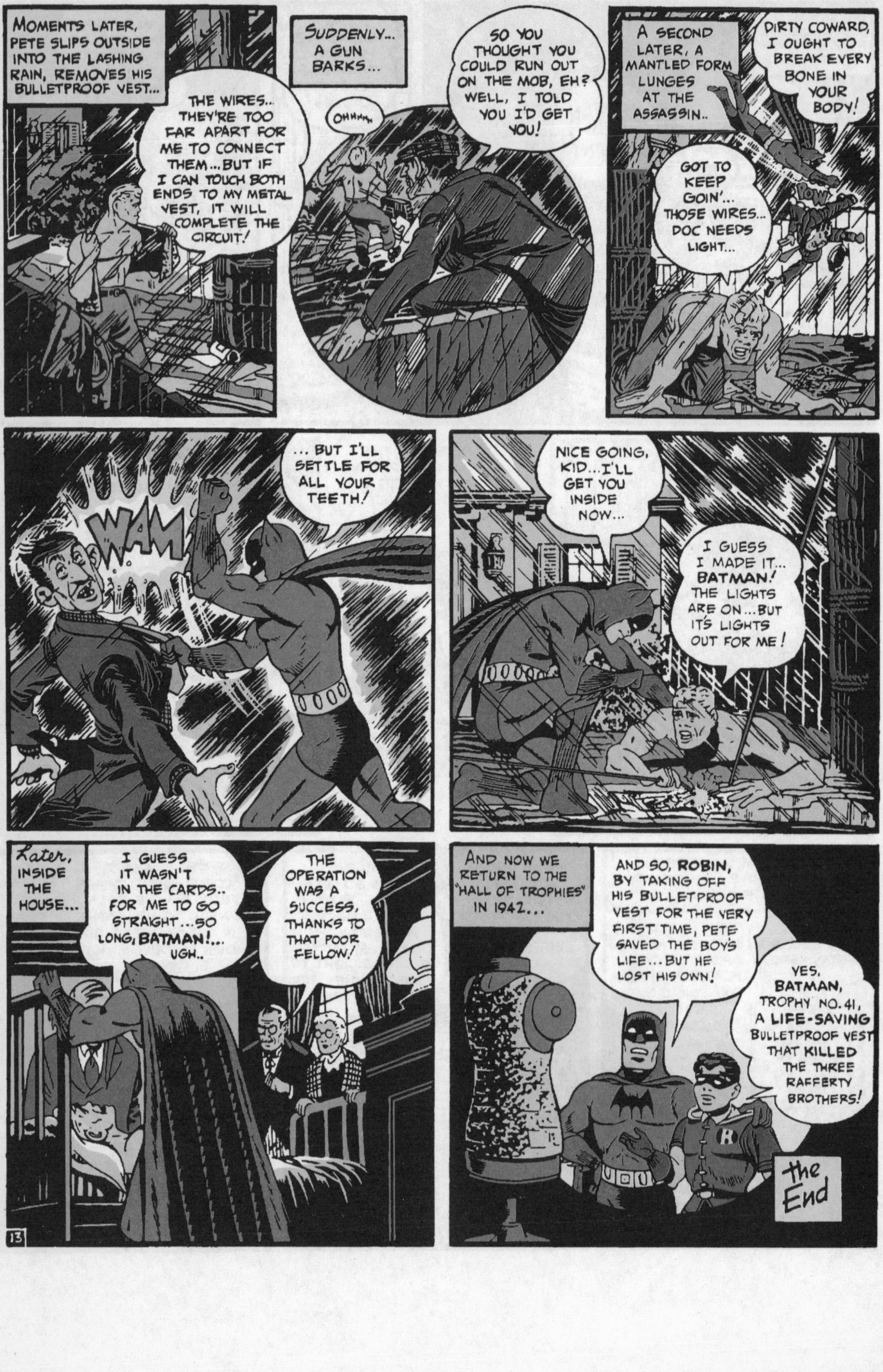
MOMENTS LATER, PETE SLIPS OUTSIDE INTO THE LASHING RAIN, REMOVES HIS BULLETPROOF VEST...
THE WIRES.. THEY'RE TOO FAR APART FOR ME TO CONNECT THEM...BUT IF I CAN TOUCH BOTH ENDS TO MY METAL VEST, IT WILL COMPLETE THE CIRCUIT!
SUDDENLY... A GUN BARKS...
OHHHH..
SO YOU THOUGHT YOU COULD RUN OUT ON THE MOB, EH? WELL, I TOLD YOU I'D GET YOU!
A SECOND LATER, A MANTLED FORM LUNGES AT THE ASSASSIN..
DIRTY COWARD, I OUGHT TO BREAK EVERY BONE IN YOUR BODY!
GOT TO KEEP GOIN'... THOSE WIRES... DOC NEEDS LIGHT...
WAM
... BUT I'LL SETTLE FOR ALL YOUR TEETH!
NICE GOING, KID...I'LL GET YOU INSIDE NOW...
I GUESS I MADE IT... BATMAN! THE LIGHTS ARE ON...BUT IT'S LIGHTS OUT FOR ME!
Later, INSIDE THE HOUSE...
I GUESS IT WASN'T IN THE CARDS.. FOR ME TO GO STRAIGHT...SO LONG, BATMAN!... UGH..
THE OPERATION WAS A SUCCESS, THANKS TO THAT POOR FELLOW!
13
AND NOW WE RETURN TO THE "HALL OF TROPHIES" IN 1942...
AND SO, ROBIN, BY TAKING OFF HIS BULLETPROOF VEST FOR THE VERY FIRST TIME, PETE SAVED THE BOY'S LIFE... BUT HE LOST HIS OWN!
YES, BATMAN, TROPHY NO. 41, A LIFE-SAVING BULLETPROOF VEST THAT KILLED THE THREE RAFFERTY BROTHERS!
the End

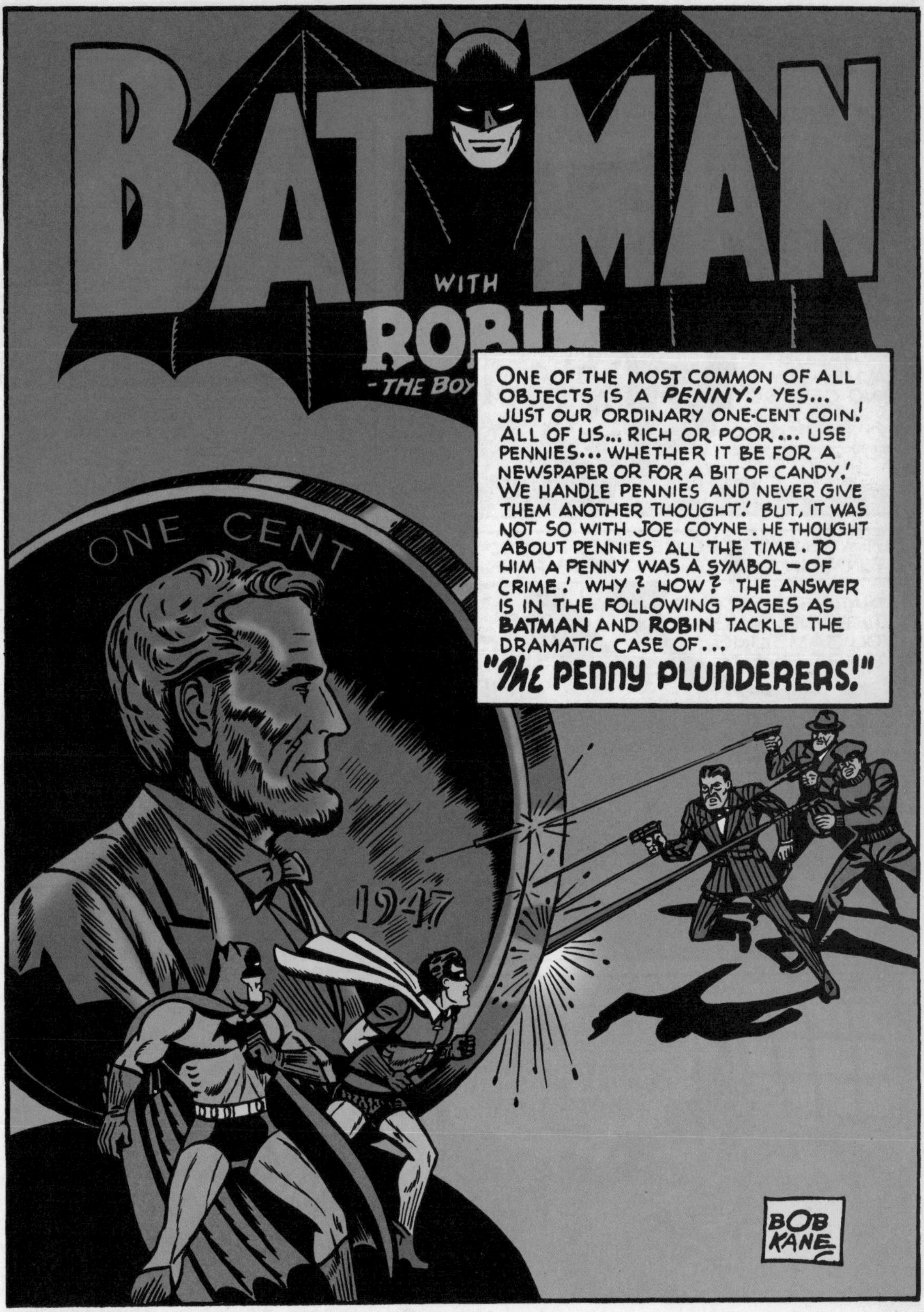
BATMAN
WITH
ROBIN
-THE BOY
ONE OF THE MOST COMMON OF ALL OBJECTS IS A PENNY! YES... JUST OUR ORDINARY ONE-CENT COIN! ALL OF US... RICH OR POOR... USE PENNIES... WHETHER IT BE FOR A NEWSPAPER OR FOR A BIT OF CANDY! WE HANDLE PENNIES AND NEVER GIVE THEM ANOTHER THOUGHT! BUT, IT WAS NOT SO WITH JOE COYNE. HE THOUGHT ABOUT PENNIES ALL THE TIME. TO HIM A PENNY WAS A SYMBOL—OF CRIME! WHY? HOW? THE ANSWER IS IN THE FOLLOWING PAGES AS BATMAN AND ROBIN TACKLE THE DRAMATIC CASE OF...
"The PENNY PLUNDERERS!"
ONE CENT
1947
BOB KANE

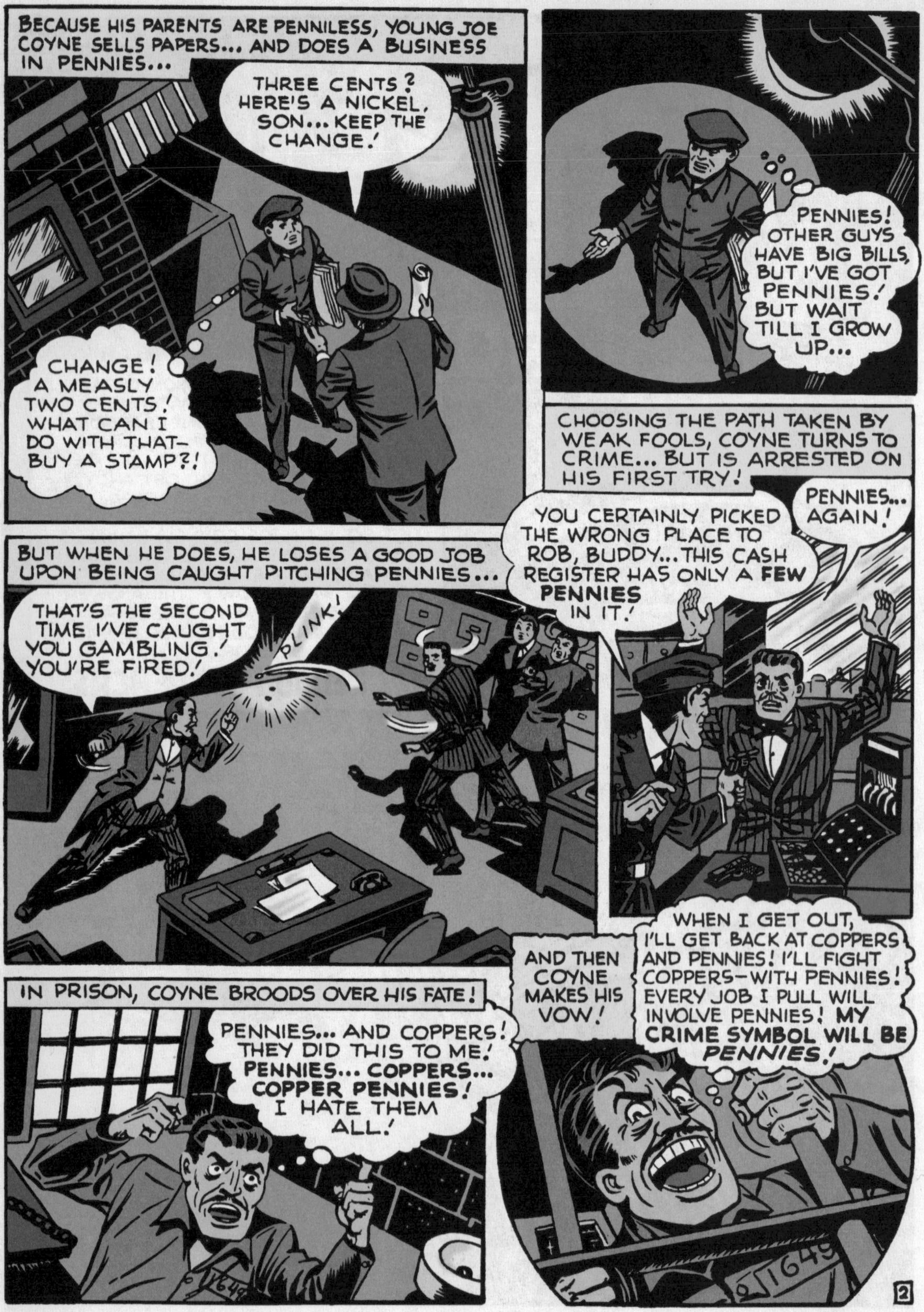

BECAUSE HIS PARENTS ARE PENNILESS, YOUNG JOE COYNE SELLS PAPERS... AND DOES A BUSINESS IN PENNIES...
THREE CENTS? HERE'S A NICKEL, SON... KEEP THE CHANGE!
CHANGE! A MEASLY TWO CENTS! WHAT CAN I DO WITH THAT- BUY A STAMP?!
PENNIES! OTHER GUYS HAVE BIG BILLS, BUT I'VE GOT PENNIES! BUT WAIT TILL I GROW UP...
BUT WHEN HE DOES, HE LOSES A GOOD JOB UPON BEING CAUGHT PITCHING PENNIES...
THAT'S THE SECOND TIME I'VE CAUGHT YOU GAMBLING! YOU'RE FIRED!
PLINK!
CHOOSING THE PATH TAKEN BY WEAK FOOLS, COYNE TURNS TO CRIME... BUT IS ARRESTED ON HIS FIRST TRY!
YOU CERTAINLY PICKED THE WRONG PLACE TO ROB, BUDDY... THIS CASH REGISTER HAS ONLY A **FEW PENNIES** IN IT!
PENNIES... AGAIN!
IN PRISON, COYNE BROODS OVER HIS FATE!
PENNIES... AND COPPERS! THEY DID THIS TO ME! **PENNIES... COPPERS... COPPER PENNIES!** I HATE THEM ALL!
AND THEN COYNE MAKES HIS VOW!
WHEN I GET OUT, I'LL GET BACK AT COPPERS AND PENNIES! I'LL FIGHT COPPERS—WITH PENNIES! EVERY JOB I PULL WILL INVOLVE PENNIES! **MY CRIME SYMBOL WILL BE *PENNIES*!**
2

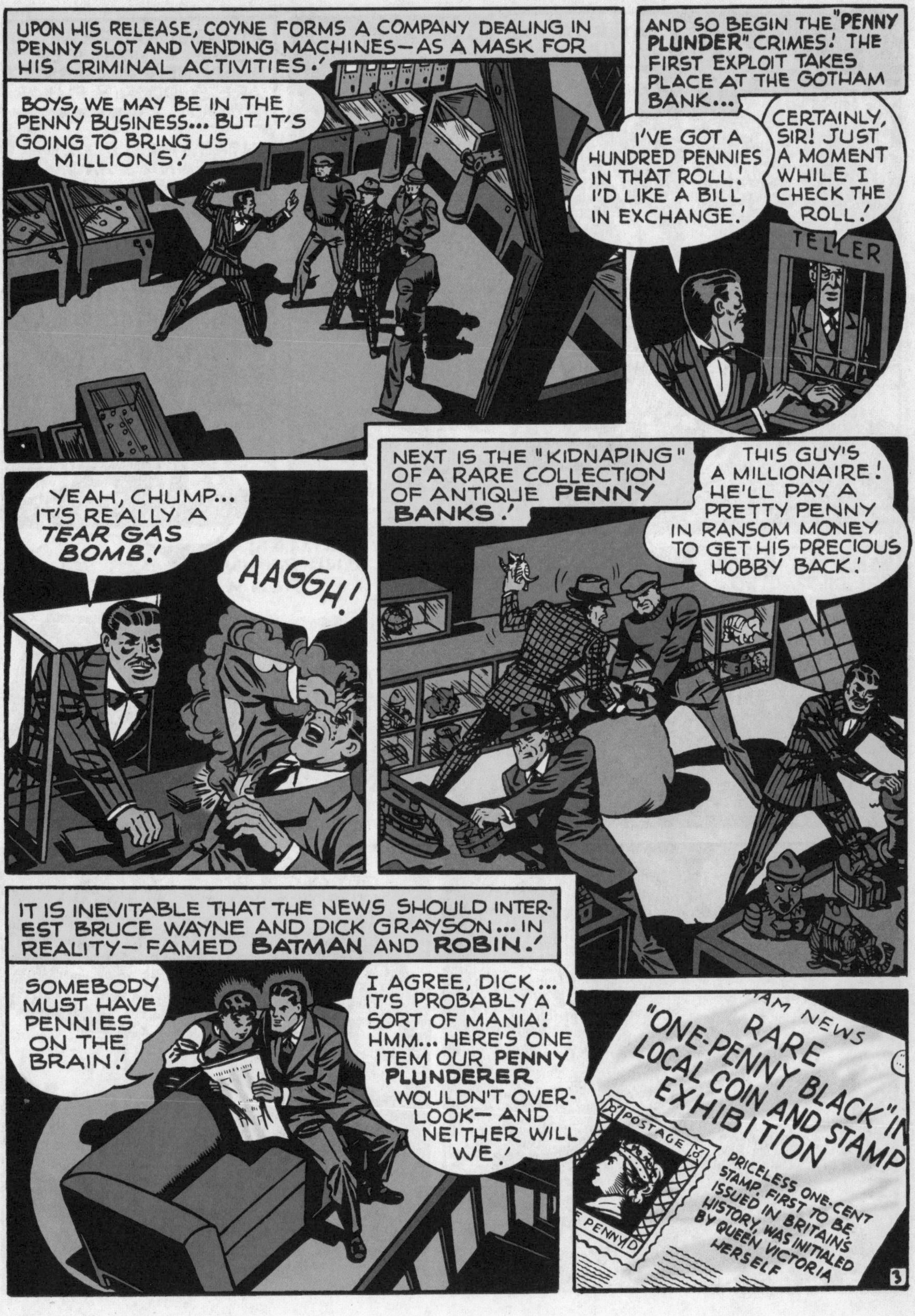
UPON HIS RELEASE, COYNE FORMS A COMPANY DEALING IN PENNY SLOT AND VENDING MACHINES—AS A MASK FOR HIS CRIMINAL ACTIVITIES!
BOYS, WE MAY BE IN THE PENNY BUSINESS... BUT IT'S GOING TO BRING US MILLIONS!
AND SO BEGIN THE "PENNY PLUNDER" CRIMES! THE FIRST EXPLOIT TAKES PLACE AT THE GOTHAM BANK...
I'VE GOT A HUNDRED PENNIES IN THAT ROLL! I'D LIKE A BILL IN EXCHANGE!
CERTAINLY, SIR! JUST A MOMENT WHILE I CHECK THE ROLL!
TELLER
YEAH, CHUMP... IT'S REALLY A TEAR GAS BOMB!
AAGGH!
NEXT IS THE "KIDNAPING" OF A RARE COLLECTION OF ANTIQUE PENNY BANKS!
THIS GUY'S A MILLIONAIRE! HE'LL PAY A PRETTY PENNY IN RANSOM MONEY TO GET HIS PRECIOUS HOBBY BACK!
IT IS INEVITABLE THAT THE NEWS SHOULD INTEREST BRUCE WAYNE AND DICK GRAYSON... IN REALITY—FAMED BATMAN AND ROBIN!
SOMEBODY MUST HAVE PENNIES ON THE BRAIN!
I AGREE, DICK... IT'S PROBABLY A SORT OF MANIA! HMM... HERE'S ONE ITEM OUR PENNY PLUNDERER WOULDN'T OVERLOOK—AND NEITHER WILL WE!
RARE "ONE-PENNY BLACK" IN LOCAL COIN AND STAMP EXHIBITION
POSTAGE
PENNY
PRICELESS ONE-CENT STAMP, FIRST TO BE ISSUED IN BRITAIN'S HISTORY, WAS INITIALED BY QUEEN VICTORIA HERSELF
3

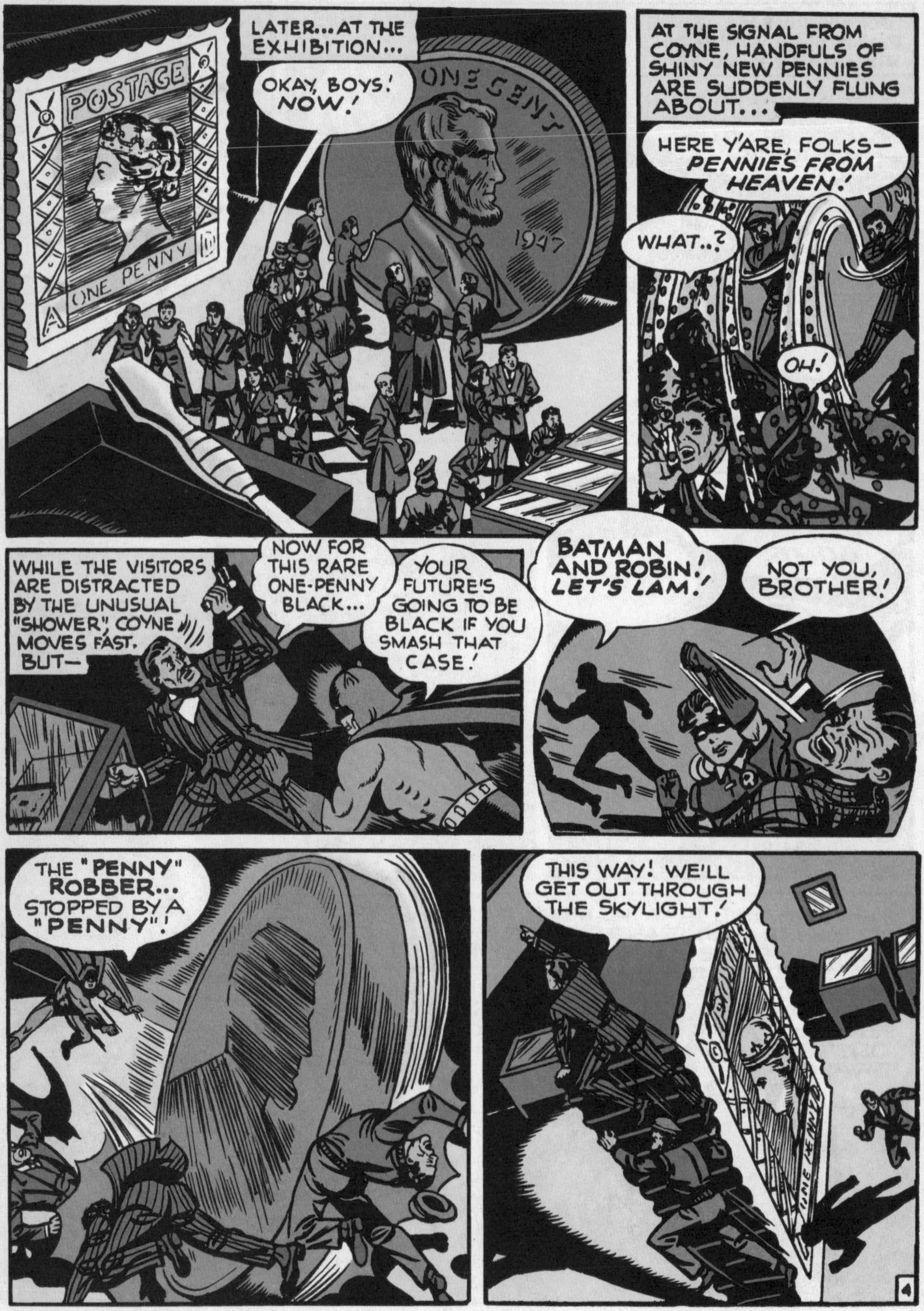
LATER...AT THE EXHIBITION...
OKAY, BOYS! NOW!
POSTAGE
ONE PENNY
ONE CENT
1947
AT THE SIGNAL FROM COYNE, HANDFULS OF SHINY NEW PENNIES ARE SUDDENLY FLUNG ABOUT...
HERE Y'ARE, FOLKS— PENNIES FROM HEAVEN!
WHAT..?
OH!
WHILE THE VISITORS ARE DISTRACTED BY THE UNUSUAL "SHOWER," COYNE MOVES FAST. BUT—
NOW FOR THIS RARE ONE-PENNY BLACK...
YOUR FUTURE'S GOING TO BE BLACK IF YOU SMASH THAT CASE!
BATMAN AND ROBIN! LET'S LAM!
NOT YOU, BROTHER!
THE "PENNY" ROBBER... STOPPED BY A "PENNY"!
THIS WAY! WE'LL GET OUT THROUGH THE SKYLIGHT!
4

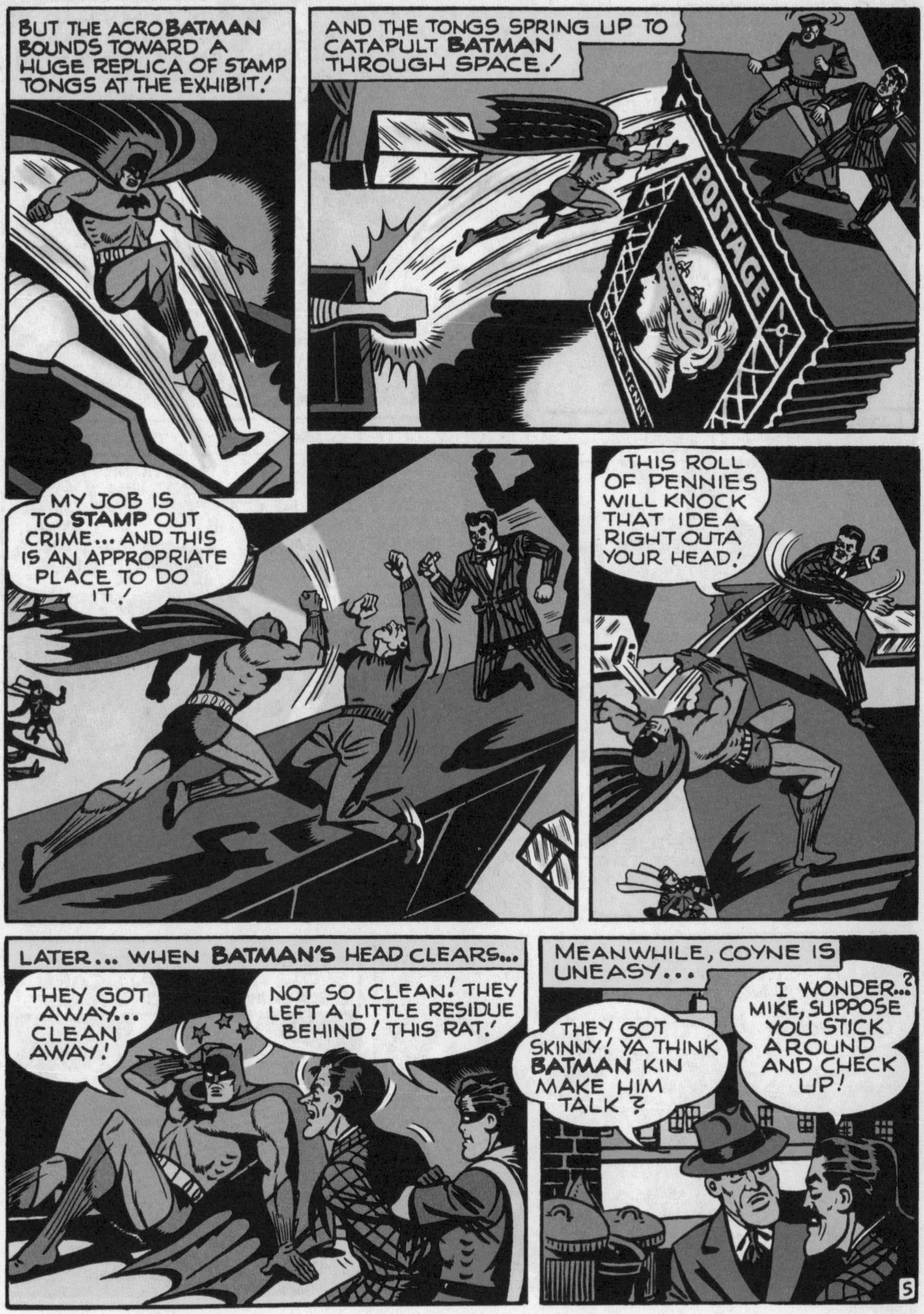
BUT THE ACROBATMAN BOUNDS TOWARD A HUGE REPLICA OF STAMP TONGS AT THE EXHIBIT!
AND THE TONGS SPRING UP TO CATAPULT BATMAN THROUGH SPACE!
POSTAGE
MY JOB IS TO STAMP OUT CRIME... AND THIS IS AN APPROPRIATE PLACE TO DO IT!
THIS ROLL OF PENNIES WILL KNOCK THAT IDEA RIGHT OUTA YOUR HEAD!
LATER... WHEN BATMAN'S HEAD CLEARS...
THEY GOT AWAY... CLEAN AWAY!
NOT SO CLEAN! THEY LEFT A LITTLE RESIDUE BEHIND! THIS RAT!
MEANWHILE, COYNE IS UNEASY...
THEY GOT SKINNY! YA THINK BATMAN KIN MAKE HIM TALK?
I WONDER..? MIKE, SUPPOSE YOU STICK AROUND AND CHECK UP!
5

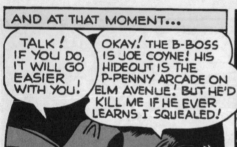

AND AT THAT MOMENT...

TALK! IF YOU DO, IT WILL GO EASIER WITH YOU!

OKAY! THE B-BOSS IS JOE COYNE! HIS HIDEOUT IS THE P-PENNY ARCADE ON ELM AVENUE! BUT HE'D KILL ME IF HE EVER LEARNS I SQUEALED!

NOW I'LL CALL A POLICEMAN TO TAKE YOU TO HEADQUARTERS WHILE ROBIN AND I CALL ON COYNE!

IF I ONLY HAD MY GAT, I COULD KNOCK OFF BATMAN NOW. HMM... I'LL FIX SKINNY FOR SQUEALING!

LATER... AS SKINNY AND THE PATROLMAN TURN A CORNER...

MIKE!

UH!

YEAH, SKINNY... I COME TO RESCUE YOU! AIN'T THAT NICE O' ME?

SOON... AFTER A SHORT-CUT TO THE HIDE-OUT...

WE-ELL, SKINNY... WELCOME HOME! SEE, BOYS... I GOT HIM AWAY FROM THE COPPER! I TAKE CARE OF THE BOYS IN MY MOB... ESPECIALLY A LOYAL BOY LIKE SKINNY!

Y-YEAH-HEH-HEH... TH-THANKS, B-BOSS!

SKINNY, I'M WORRIED ABOUT YOUR HEALTH! YOU BEEN LOSING WEIGHT? LET'S SEE! AND YOU'LL GET YOUR FORTUNE, TOO!

A PENNY DROPPED INTO THE SLOT... AND A SMALL CARD DROPS INTO SHAKING FINGERS!

YOUR FORTUNE
It isn't good! Your future is very dark! The future is always dark for STOOL PIGEONS!

6

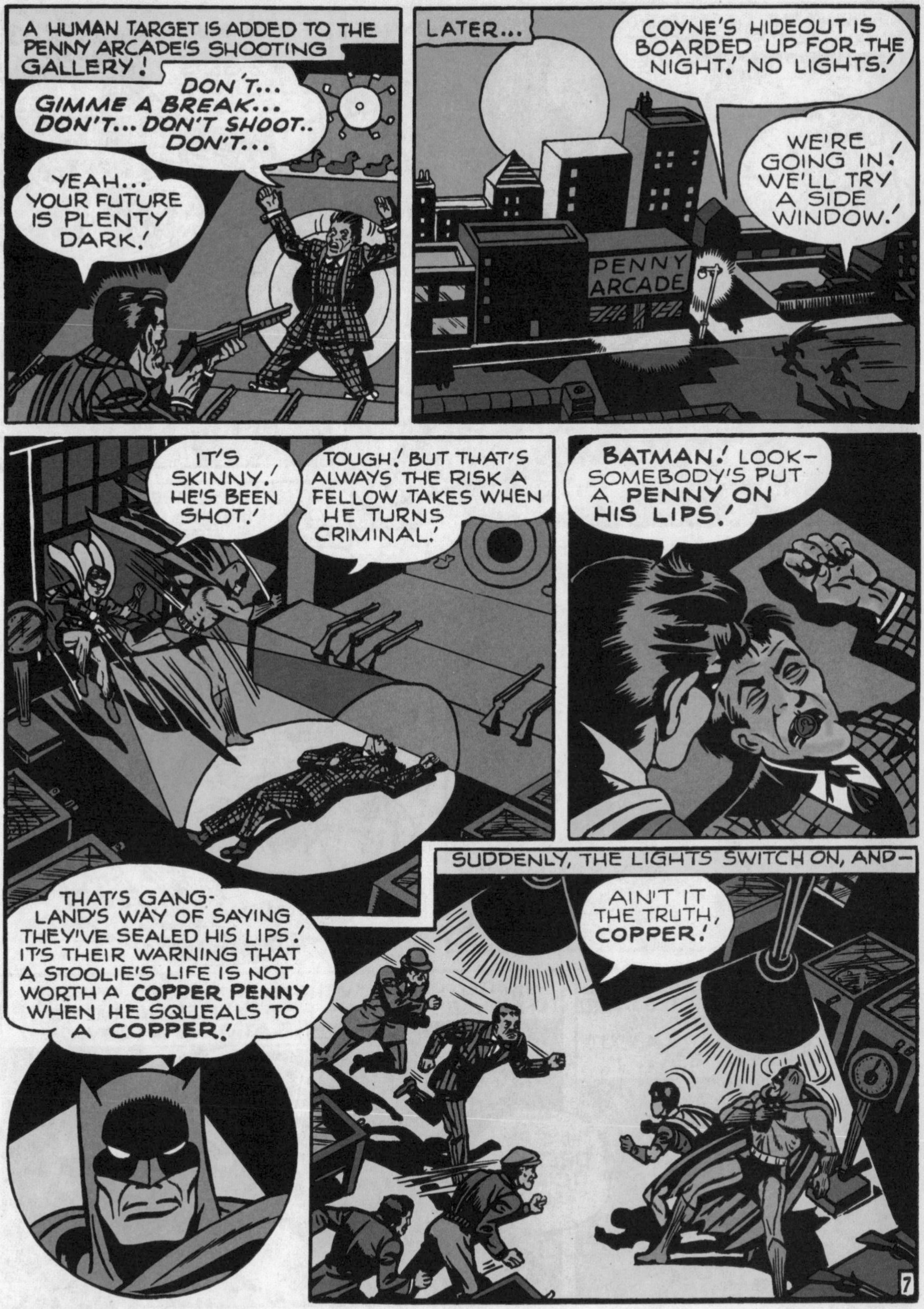
A HUMAN TARGET IS ADDED TO THE PENNY ARCADE'S SHOOTING GALLERY!
DON'T... GIMME A BREAK... DON'T... DON'T SHOOT.. DON'T...
YEAH... YOUR FUTURE IS PLENTY DARK!
LATER...
COYNE'S HIDEOUT IS BOARDED UP FOR THE NIGHT! NO LIGHTS!
WE'RE GOING IN! WE'LL TRY A SIDE WINDOW!
PENNY ARCADE
IT'S SKINNY! HE'S BEEN SHOT!
TOUGH! BUT THAT'S ALWAYS THE RISK A FELLOW TAKES WHEN HE TURNS CRIMINAL!
BATMAN! LOOK— SOMEBODY'S PUT A PENNY ON HIS LIPS!
THAT'S GANGLAND'S WAY OF SAYING THEY'VE SEALED HIS LIPS! IT'S THEIR WARNING THAT A STOOLIE'S LIFE IS NOT WORTH A COPPER PENNY WHEN HE SQUEALS TO A COPPER!
SUDDENLY, THE LIGHTS SWITCH ON, AND—
AIN'T IT THE TRUTH, COPPER!
7

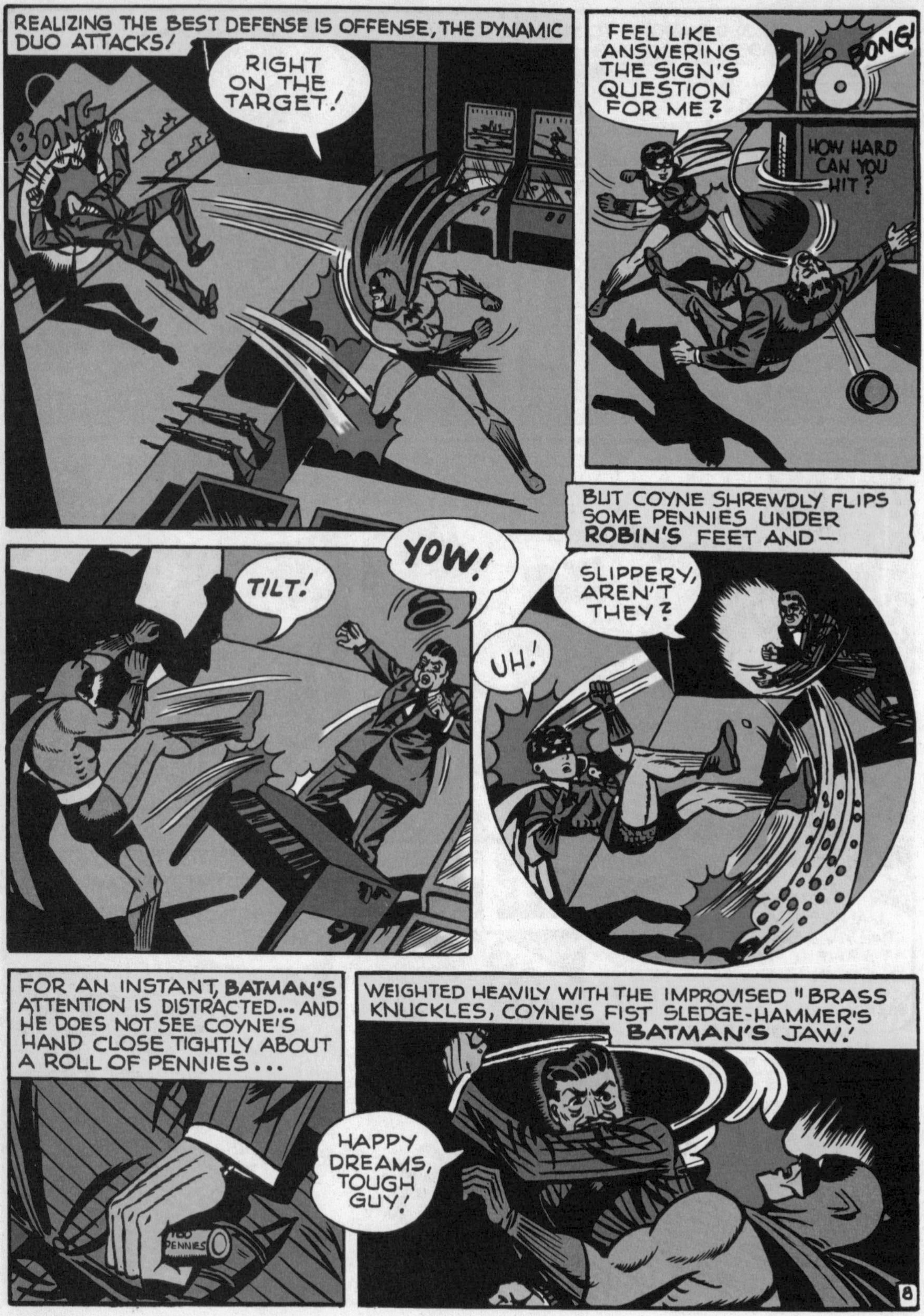

REALIZING THE BEST DEFENSE IS OFFENSE, THE DYNAMIC DUO ATTACKS!
RIGHT ON THE TARGET!
BONG
FEEL LIKE ANSWERING THE SIGN'S QUESTION FOR ME?
BONG!
HOW HARD CAN YOU HIT?
BUT COYNE SHREWDLY FLIPS SOME PENNIES UNDER ROBIN'S FEET AND—
TILT!
YOW!
SLIPPERY, AREN'T THEY?
UH!
FOR AN INSTANT, BATMAN'S ATTENTION IS DISTRACTED... AND HE DOES NOT SEE COYNE'S HAND CLOSE TIGHTLY ABOUT A ROLL OF PENNIES...
100 PENNIES
WEIGHTED HEAVILY WITH THE IMPROVISED "BRASS KNUCKLES, COYNE'S FIST SLEDGE-HAMMER'S BATMAN'S JAW!
HAPPY DREAMS, TOUGH GUY!
8

LATER... AN AWAKENING IN A WINDOWLESS ROOM...

YOU'VE TAKEN OUR UTILITY BELTS!

YEAH! AND I'VE ALSO RIPPED OUT THE TELEPHONE WIRES! NOW ME AND MY BOYS ARE ON OUR WAY...

SO LONG! HERE'S TWO CENTS—THAT'S ALL YOUR LIVES WILL BE WORTH IN A LITTLE WHILE! HA! HA!

FIRST, I'LL NEED SALTED WATER!

I HOPE YOU KNOW WHAT YOU'RE DOING—'CAUSE I DON'T!

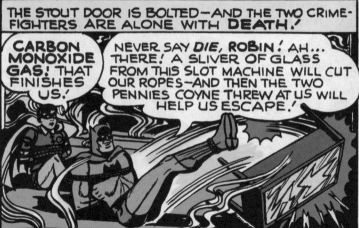

THE STOUT DOOR IS BOLTED—AND THE TWO CRIME-FIGHTERS ARE ALONE WITH DEATH!

CARBON MONOXIDE GAS! THAT FINISHES US!

NEVER SAY DIE, ROBIN! AH... THERE! A SLIVER OF GLASS FROM THIS SLOT MACHINE WILL CUT OUR ROPES—AND THEN THE TWO PENNIES COYNE THREW AT US WILL HELP US ESCAPE!

COYNE DID US A FAVOR BECAUSE HE THREW US ONE OLD COPPER PENNY... AND ONE NEW ZINC-COATED PENNY, OF THE TYPE ISSUED DURING THE WAR!

NOW I PLACE A PIECE OF BLOTTING PAPER BETWEEN THE PENNIES, TIE THEM TOGETHER WITH THIS TELEPHONE WIRE—AND IMMERSE IT IN THE SALT WATER...

ZINC... COPPER... IN SALT WATER! YOU'VE MADE A MIDGET ELECTRIC BATTERY!

YES! IT'S TO SUBSTITUTE FOR THE TELEPHONE-BOX-BATTERY REMOVED BY COYNE! MY BATTERY WILL GENERATE JUST ENOUGH CURRENT FOR ME TO TAP OUT AN S.O.S. ON THE EXPOSED TELEPHONE WIRE WITH MY BATTERY WIRE!

THE BATMAN'S DISTRESS SIGNALS ARE FLASHED TO THE OFFICES OF THE TELEPHONE COMPANY...

MORSE CODE! OHHH!

S.O.S.— PENNY ARCADE ON ELM AVENUE— HURRY— BATMAN—

SHORTLY AFTER, POLICE AXES BREAK DOWN THE DOOR...

(COUGH) BOY, AM I GLAD TO BREATHE FRESH AIR AGAIN!

THANKS FOR THE ASSIST, BOYS... BUT NOW ROBIN AND I WILL TAKE OVER! WE'VE GOT TO LOCATE COYNE!

LATER... IN COYNE'S DESK, A CLUE IS UNEARTHED...

HERE'S SOMETHING! A RENTAL ORDER FROM MILLIONAIRE J.J. WITHERS FOR COIN MACHINES TO BE USED AT A PARTY ON HIS HOUSEBOAT. AND THEY'RE TO BE DELIVERED TONIGHT! IT'S WORTH INVESTIGATING!

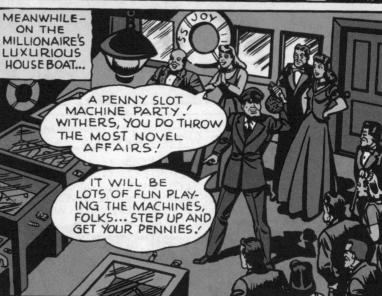

MEANWHILE— ON THE MILLIONAIRE'S LUXURIOUS HOUSEBOAT...

A PENNY SLOT MACHINE PARTY! WITHERS, YOU DO THROW THE MOST NOVEL AFFAIRS!

IT WILL BE LOTS OF FUN PLAYING THE MACHINES, FOLKS... STEP UP AND GET YOUR PENNIES!

BUT THE MACHINES WERE RIGGED BY COYNE, AND AS THE PENNIES ARE INSERTED INTO THE SLOTS, THEY SET OFF TEAR GAS AND SMOKE BOMBS!

AGGH! :COUGH:

:COUGH:

HELP! I CAN'T SEE!

THEN, LIKE MODERN PIRATES, THE PENNY PLUNDERERS BOARD THE HOUSEBOAT!

THIS IS A STICKUP!

EEEK!

WHA-AAT?

10

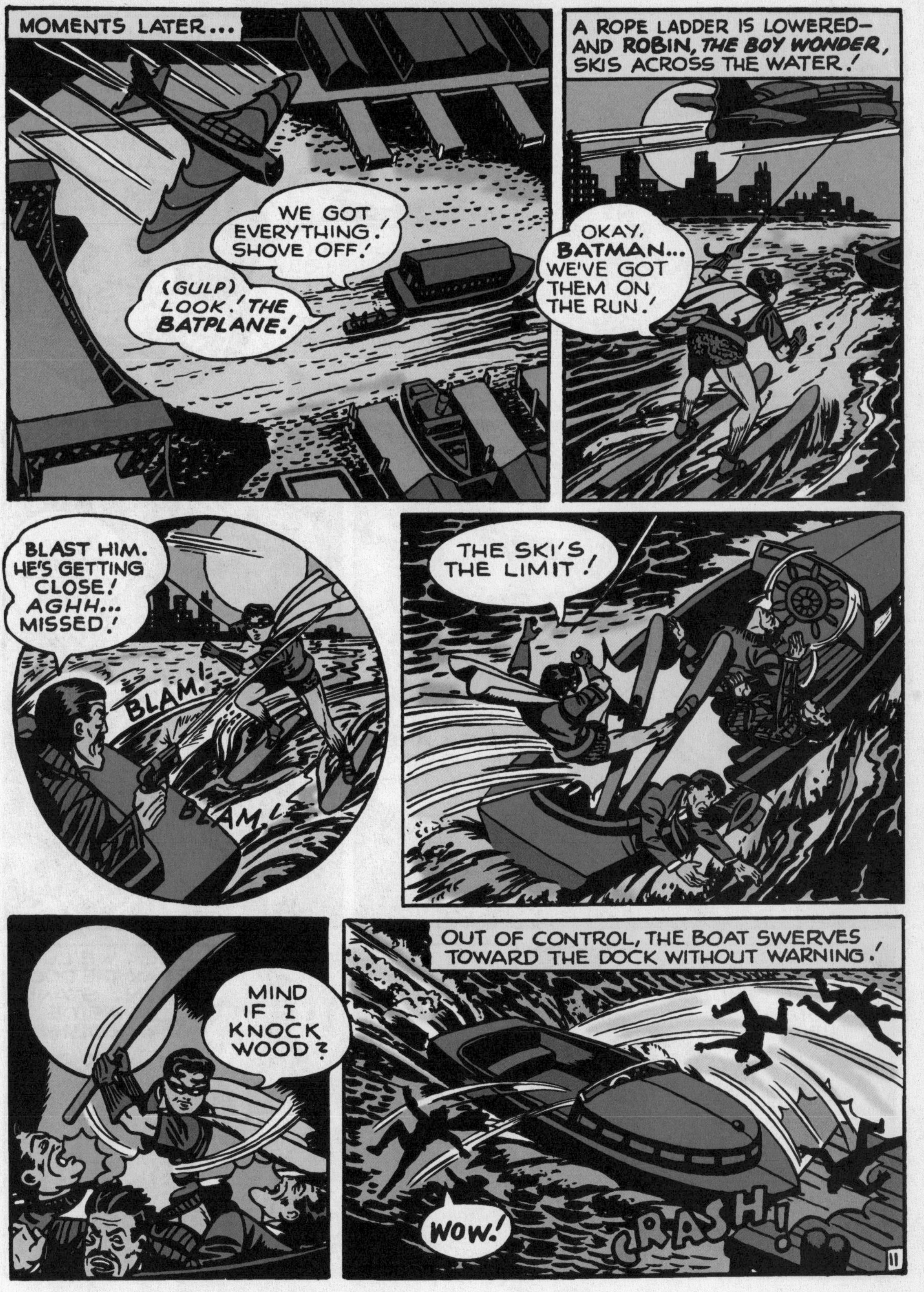
MOMENTS LATER...
WE GOT EVERYTHING! SHOVE OFF!
(GULP) LOOK! THE BATPLANE!
A ROPE LADDER IS LOWERED— AND ROBIN, THE BOY WONDER, SKIS ACROSS THE WATER!
OKAY, BATMAN... WE'VE GOT THEM ON THE RUN!
BLAST HIM. HE'S GETTING CLOSE! AGHH... MISSED!
BLAM!
BLAM!
THE SKI'S THE LIMIT!
MIND IF I KNOCK WOOD?
OUT OF CONTROL, THE BOAT SWERVES TOWARD THE DOCK WITHOUT WARNING!
WOW!
CRASH!
11

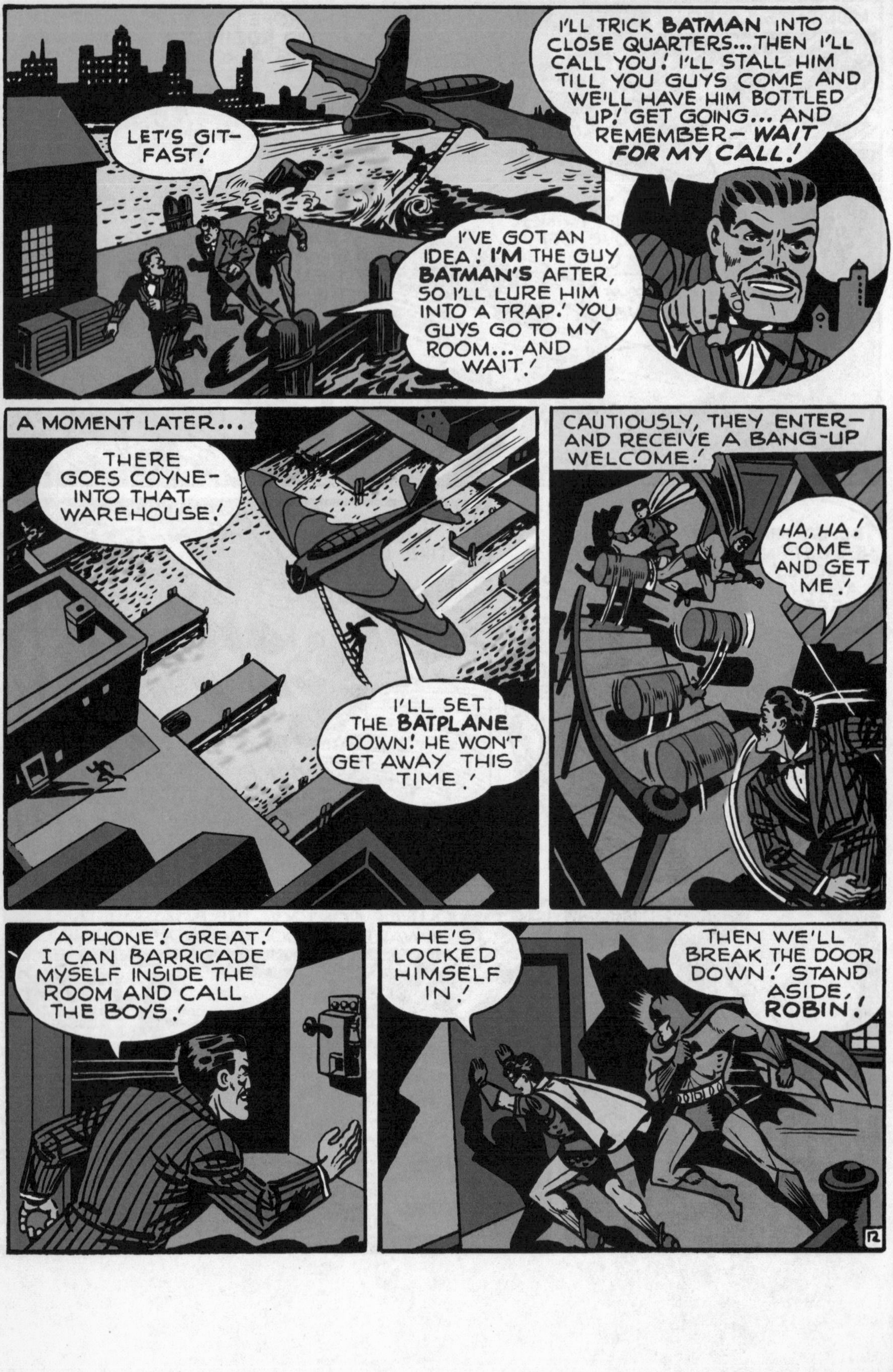
LET'S GIT-FAST!
I'VE GOT AN IDEA! I'M THE GUY BATMAN'S AFTER, SO I'LL LURE HIM INTO A TRAP! YOU GUYS GO TO MY ROOM... AND WAIT!
I'LL TRICK BATMAN INTO CLOSE QUARTERS...THEN I'LL CALL YOU! I'LL STALL HIM TILL YOU GUYS COME AND WE'LL HAVE HIM BOTTLED UP! GET GOING... AND REMEMBER– WAIT FOR MY CALL!
A MOMENT LATER...
THERE GOES COYNE-INTO THAT WAREHOUSE!
I'LL SET THE BATPLANE DOWN! HE WON'T GET AWAY THIS TIME!
CAUTIOUSLY, THEY ENTER-AND RECEIVE A BANG-UP WELCOME!
HA, HA! COME AND GET ME!
A PHONE! GREAT! I CAN BARRICADE MYSELF INSIDE THE ROOM AND CALL THE BOYS!
HE'S LOCKED HIMSELF IN!
THEN WE'LL BREAK THE DOOR DOWN! STAND ASIDE, ROBIN!
12

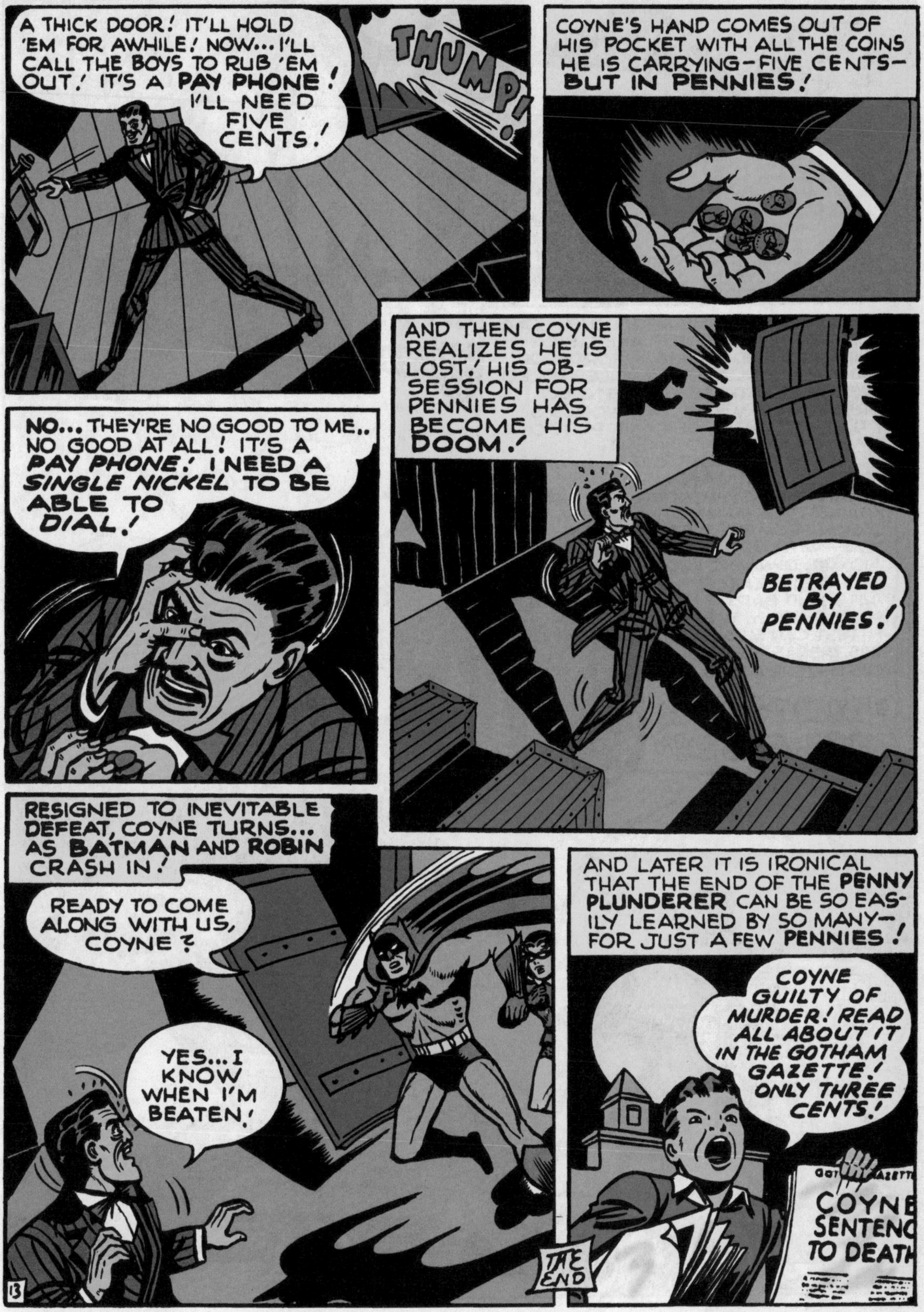
A THICK DOOR! IT'LL HOLD 'EM FOR AWHILE! NOW... I'LL CALL THE BOYS TO RUB 'EM OUT! IT'S A PAY PHONE! I'LL NEED FIVE CENTS!
THUMP!
COYNE'S HAND COMES OUT OF HIS POCKET WITH ALL THE COINS HE IS CARRYING—FIVE CENTS—BUT IN PENNIES!
NO... THEY'RE NO GOOD TO ME.. NO GOOD AT ALL! IT'S A PAY PHONE! I NEED A SINGLE NICKEL TO BE ABLE TO DIAL!
AND THEN COYNE REALIZES HE IS LOST! HIS OBSESSION FOR PENNIES HAS BECOME HIS DOOM!
BETRAYED BY PENNIES!
RESIGNED TO INEVITABLE DEFEAT, COYNE TURNS... AS BATMAN AND ROBIN CRASH IN!
READY TO COME ALONG WITH US, COYNE?
YES... I KNOW WHEN I'M BEATEN!
13
THE END
AND LATER IT IS IRONICAL THAT THE END OF THE PENNY PLUNDERER CAN BE SO EASILY LEARNED BY SO MANY—FOR JUST A FEW PENNIES!
COYNE GUILTY OF MURDER! READ ALL ABOUT IT IN THE GOTHAM GAZETTE! ONLY THREE CENTS!
COYNE SENTENC TO DEATH

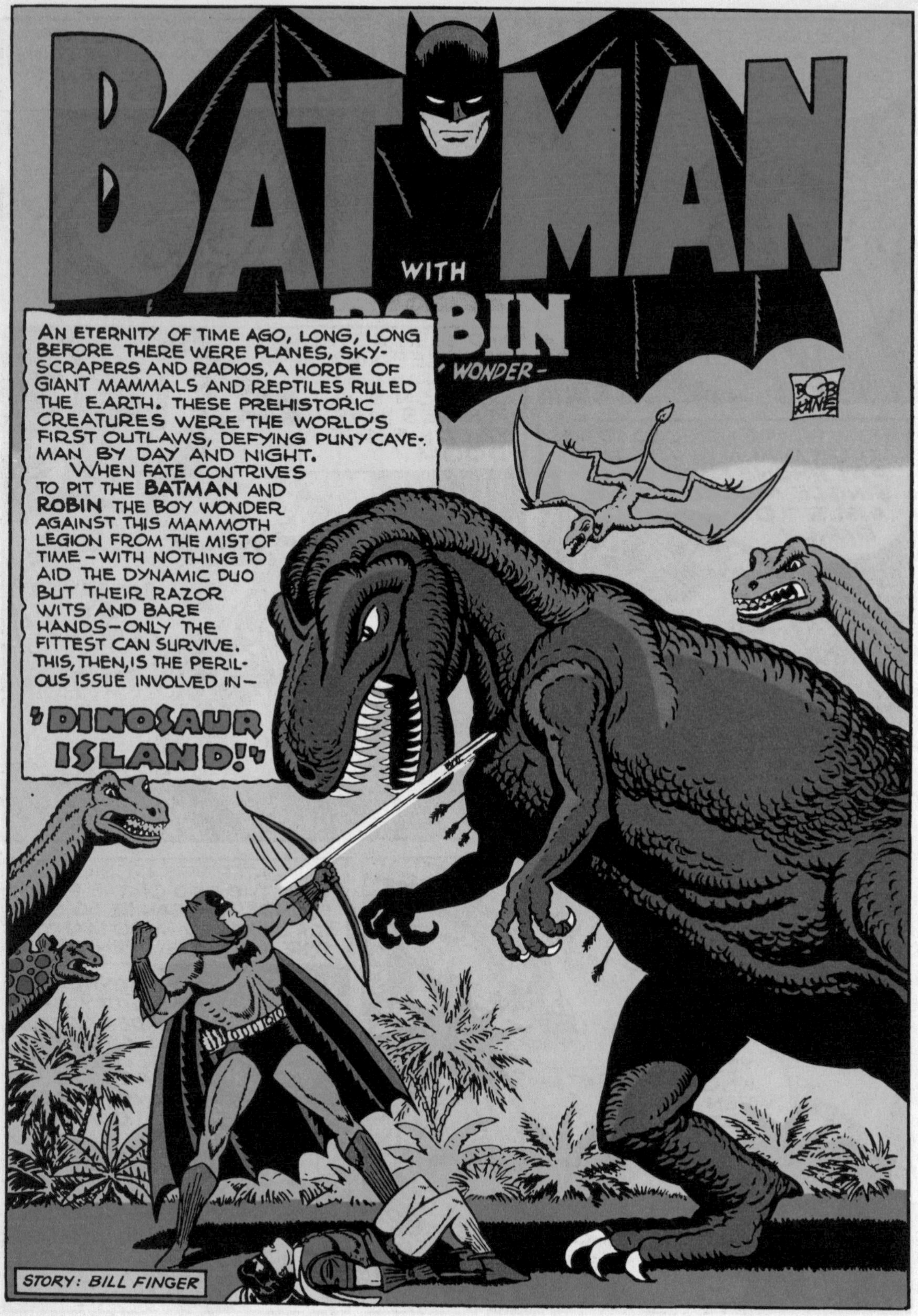
BATMAN
WITH
ROBIN
WONDER-
BOB KANE
AN ETERNITY OF TIME AGO, LONG, LONG BEFORE THERE WERE PLANES, SKY-SCRAPERS AND RADIOS, A HORDE OF GIANT MAMMALS AND REPTILES RULED THE EARTH. THESE PREHISTORIC CREATURES WERE THE WORLD'S FIRST OUTLAWS, DEFYING PUNY CAVE-MAN BY DAY AND NIGHT.
WHEN FATE CONTRIVES TO PIT THE BATMAN AND ROBIN THE BOY WONDER AGAINST THIS MAMMOTH LEGION FROM THE MIST OF TIME - WITH NOTHING TO AID THE DYNAMIC DUO BUT THEIR RAZOR WITS AND BARE HANDS - ONLY THE FITTEST CAN SURVIVE. THIS, THEN, IS THE PERILOUS ISSUE INVOLVED IN -
"DINOSAUR ISLAND!"
STORY: BILL FINGER

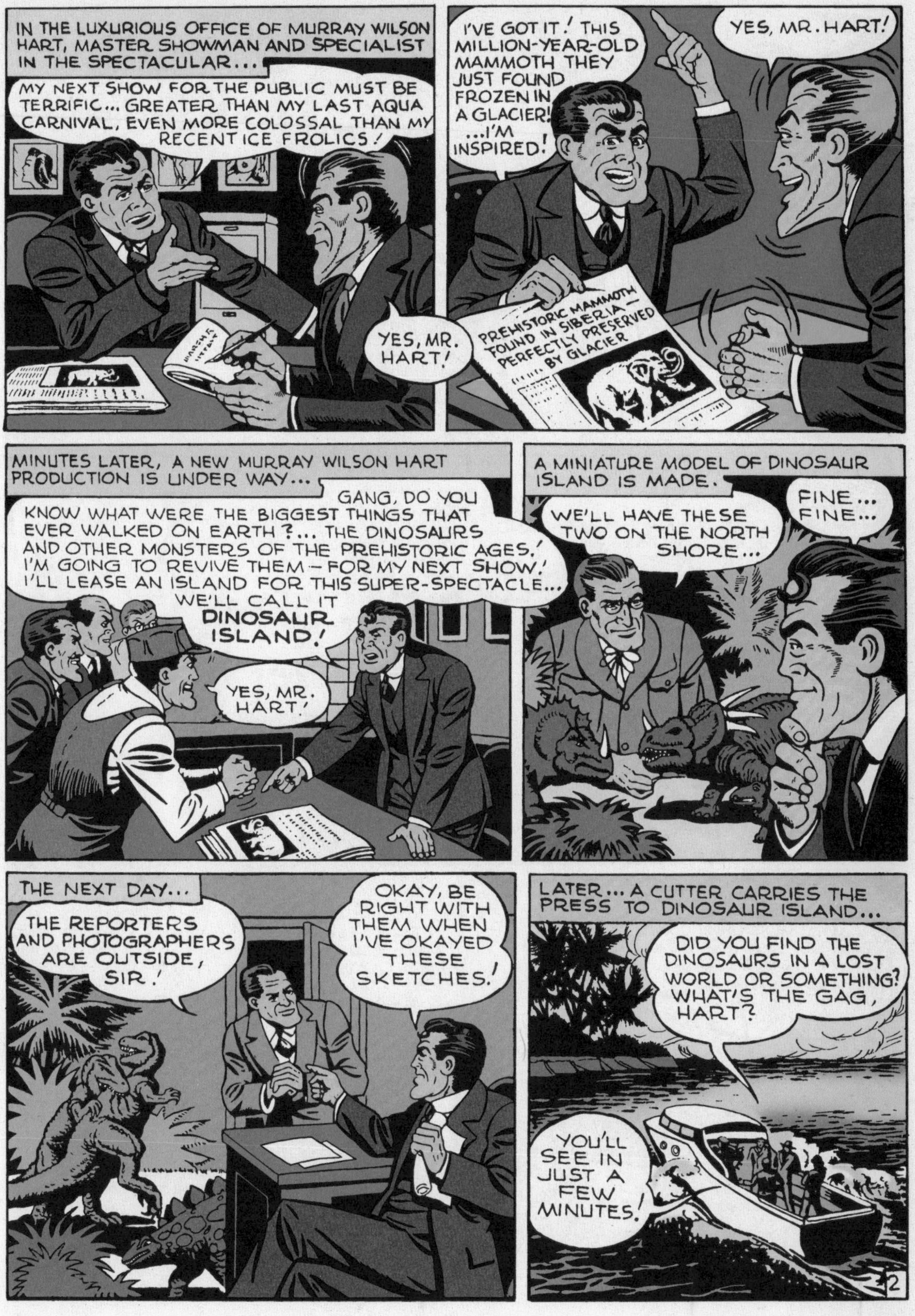
IN THE LUXURIOUS OFFICE OF MURRAY WILSON HART, MASTER SHOWMAN AND SPECIALIST IN THE SPECTACULAR...
MY NEXT SHOW FOR THE PUBLIC MUST BE TERRIFIC... GREATER THAN MY LAST AQUA CARNIVAL, EVEN MORE COLOSSAL THAN MY RECENT ICE FROLICS!
YES, MR. HART!
I'VE GOT IT! THIS MILLION-YEAR-OLD MAMMOTH THEY JUST FOUND FROZEN IN A GLACIER! ...I'M INSPIRED!
YES, MR. HART!
PREHISTORIC MAMMOTH FOUND IN SIBERIA— PERFECTLY PRESERVED BY GLACIER
MINUTES LATER, A NEW MURRAY WILSON HART PRODUCTION IS UNDER WAY...
GANG, DO YOU KNOW WHAT WERE THE BIGGEST THINGS THAT EVER WALKED ON EARTH?... THE DINOSAURS AND OTHER MONSTERS OF THE PREHISTORIC AGES! I'M GOING TO REVIVE THEM — FOR MY NEXT SHOW! I'LL LEASE AN ISLAND FOR THIS SUPER-SPECTACLE... WE'LL CALL IT DINOSAUR ISLAND!
YES, MR. HART!
A MINIATURE MODEL OF DINOSAUR ISLAND IS MADE.
WE'LL HAVE THESE TWO ON THE NORTH SHORE...
FINE... FINE...
THE NEXT DAY...
THE REPORTERS AND PHOTOGRAPHERS ARE OUTSIDE, SIR!
OKAY, BE RIGHT WITH THEM WHEN I'VE OKAYED THESE SKETCHES!
LATER... A CUTTER CARRIES THE PRESS TO DINOSAUR ISLAND...
DID YOU FIND THE DINOSAURS IN A LOST WORLD OR SOMETHING? WHAT'S THE GAG, HART?
YOU'LL SEE IN JUST A FEW MINUTES!
2

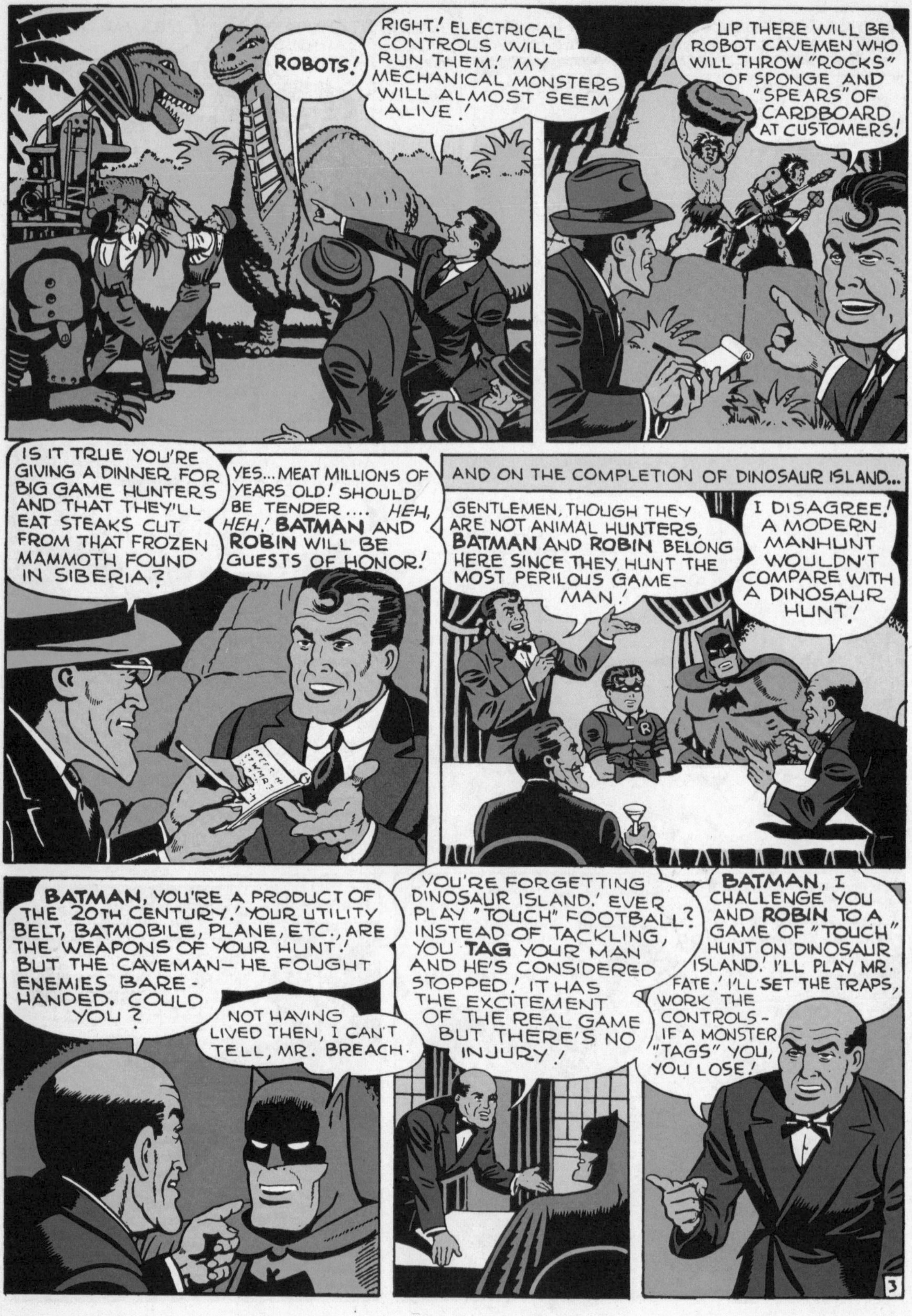
ROBOTS!
RIGHT! ELECTRICAL CONTROLS WILL RUN THEM! MY MECHANICAL MONSTERS WILL ALMOST SEEM ALIVE!
UP THERE WILL BE ROBOT CAVEMEN WHO WILL THROW "ROCKS" OF SPONGE AND "SPEARS" OF CARDBOARD AT CUSTOMERS!
IS IT TRUE YOU'RE GIVING A DINNER FOR BIG GAME HUNTERS AND THAT THEY'LL EAT STEAKS CUT FROM THAT FROZEN MAMMOTH FOUND IN SIBERIA?
YES... MEAT MILLIONS OF YEARS OLD! SHOULD BE TENDER.... HEH, HEH! BATMAN AND ROBIN WILL BE GUESTS OF HONOR!
AND ON THE COMPLETION OF DINOSAUR ISLAND...
GENTLEMEN, THOUGH THEY ARE NOT ANIMAL HUNTERS, BATMAN AND ROBIN BELONG HERE SINCE THEY HUNT THE MOST PERILOUS GAME— MAN!
I DISAGREE! A MODERN MANHUNT WOULDN'T COMPARE WITH A DINOSAUR HUNT!
BATMAN, YOU'RE A PRODUCT OF THE 20TH CENTURY! YOUR UTILITY BELT, BATMOBILE, PLANE, ETC., ARE THE WEAPONS OF YOUR HUNT! BUT THE CAVEMAN— HE FOUGHT ENEMIES BARE-HANDED. COULD YOU?
NOT HAVING LIVED THEN, I CAN'T TELL, MR. BREACH.
YOU'RE FORGETTING DINOSAUR ISLAND! EVER PLAY "TOUCH" FOOTBALL? INSTEAD OF TACKLING, YOU TAG YOUR MAN AND HE'S CONSIDERED STOPPED! IT HAS THE EXCITEMENT OF THE REAL GAME BUT THERE'S NO INJURY!
BATMAN, I CHALLENGE YOU AND ROBIN TO A GAME OF "TOUCH" HUNT ON DINOSAUR ISLAND! I'LL PLAY MR. FATE! I'LL SET THE TRAPS, WORK THE CONTROLS— IF A MONSTER "TAGS" YOU, YOU LOSE!
3

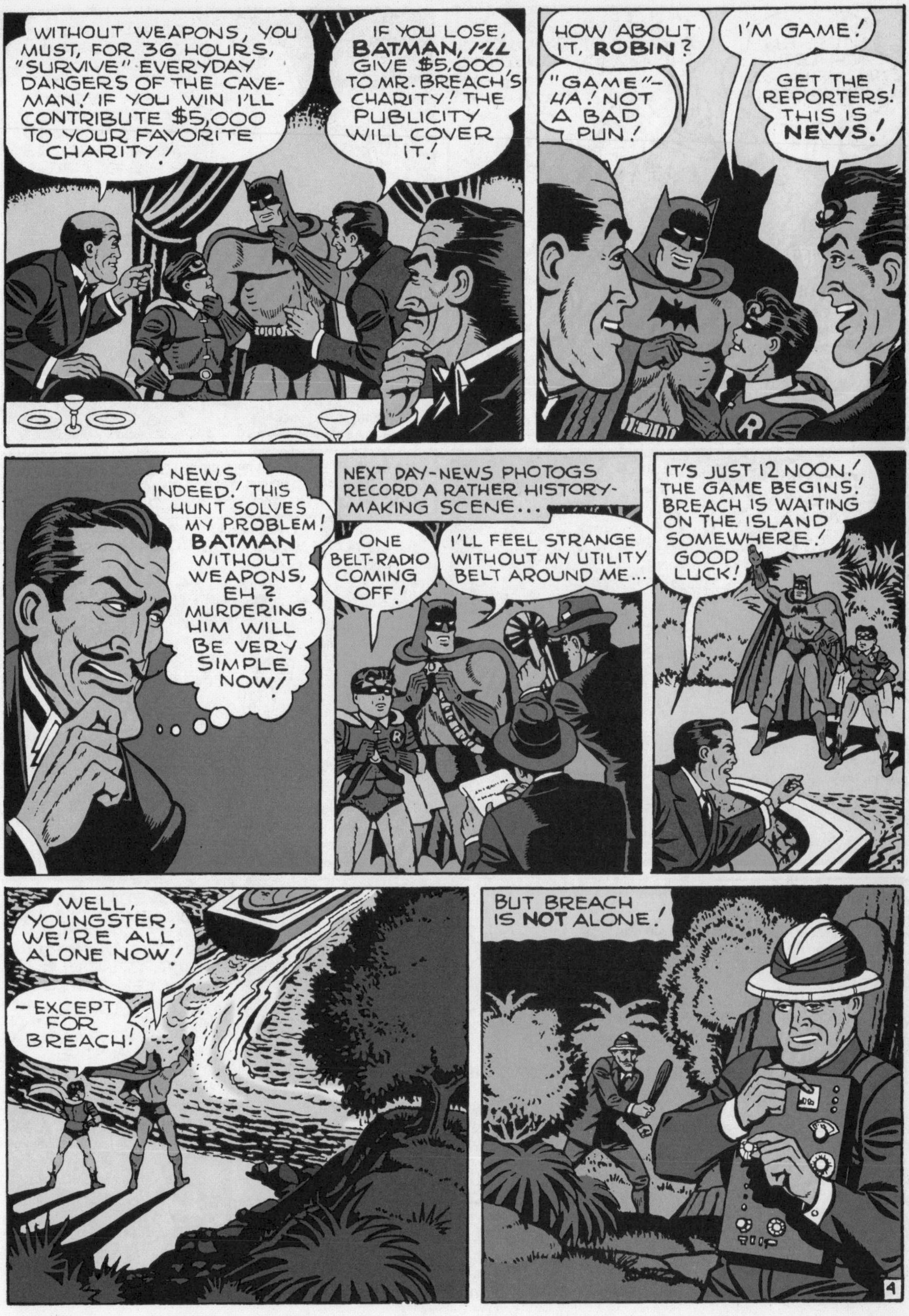
WITHOUT WEAPONS, YOU MUST, FOR 36 HOURS, "SURVIVE" EVERYDAY DANGERS OF THE CAVE-MAN! IF YOU WIN I'LL CONTRIBUTE $5,000 TO YOUR FAVORITE CHARITY!
IF YOU LOSE, BATMAN, I'LL GIVE $5,000 TO MR. BREACH'S CHARITY! THE PUBLICITY WILL COVER IT!
HOW ABOUT IT, ROBIN?
I'M GAME!
"GAME"—HA! NOT A BAD PUN!
GET THE REPORTERS! THIS IS NEWS!
NEWS INDEED! THIS HUNT SOLVES MY PROBLEM! BATMAN WITHOUT WEAPONS, EH? MURDERING HIM WILL BE VERY SIMPLE NOW!
NEXT DAY-NEWS PHOTOGS RECORD A RATHER HISTORY-MAKING SCENE...
ONE BELT-RADIO COMING OFF!
I'LL FEEL STRANGE WITHOUT MY UTILITY BELT AROUND ME...
IT'S JUST 12 NOON! THE GAME BEGINS! BREACH IS WAITING ON THE ISLAND SOMEWHERE! GOOD LUCK!
WELL, YOUNGSTER, WE'RE ALL ALONE NOW!
-EXCEPT FOR BREACH!
BUT BREACH IS NOT ALONE!
4

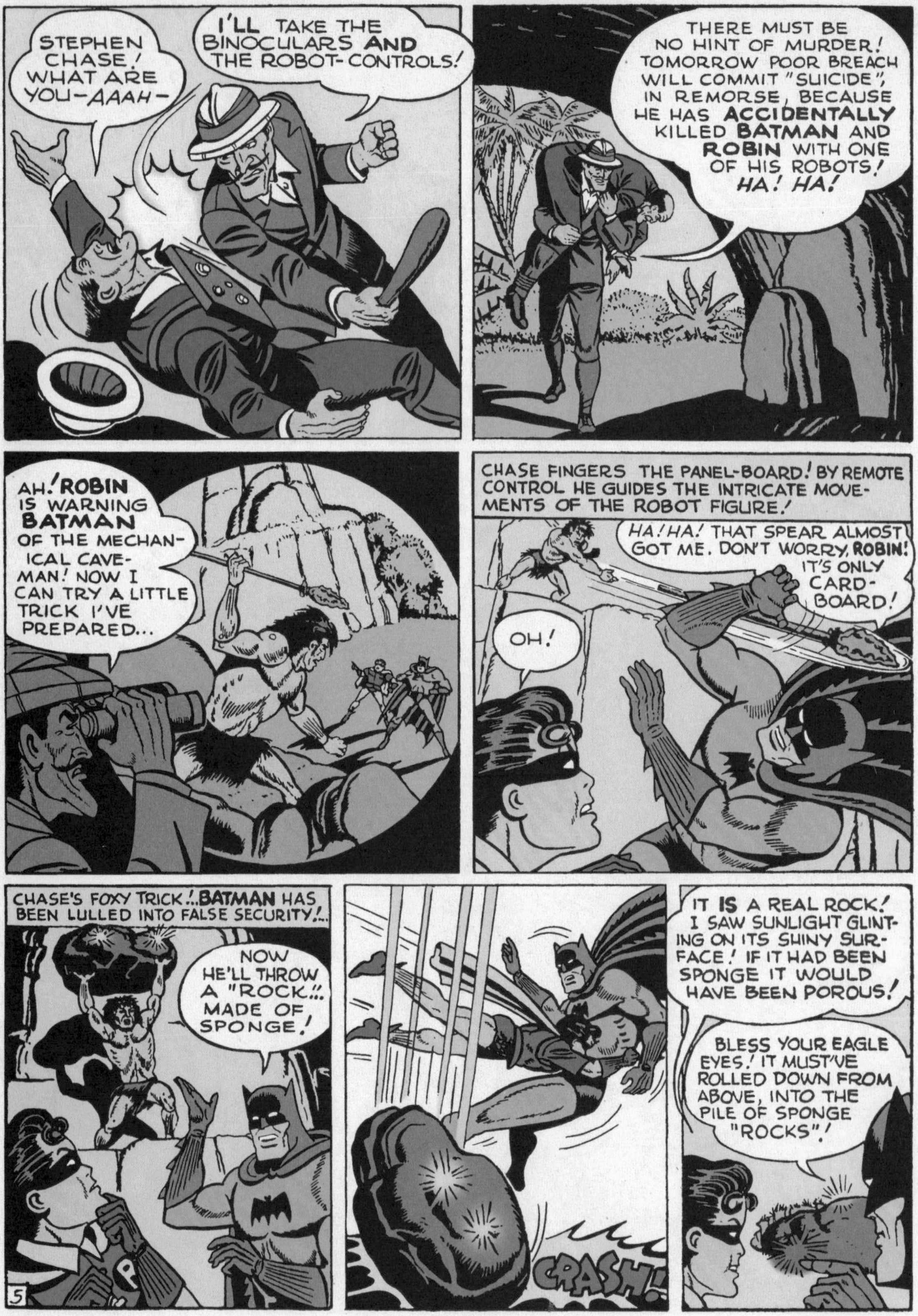
STEPHEN CHASE! WHAT ARE YOU—AAAH—
I'LL TAKE THE BINOCULARS AND THE ROBOT-CONTROLS!
THERE MUST BE NO HINT OF MURDER! TOMORROW POOR BREACH WILL COMMIT "SUICIDE", IN REMORSE, BECAUSE HE HAS ACCIDENTALLY KILLED BATMAN AND ROBIN WITH ONE OF HIS ROBOTS! HA! HA!
AH! ROBIN IS WARNING BATMAN OF THE MECHANICAL CAVEMAN! NOW I CAN TRY A LITTLE TRICK I'VE PREPARED...
CHASE FINGERS THE PANEL-BOARD! BY REMOTE CONTROL HE GUIDES THE INTRICATE MOVEMENTS OF THE ROBOT FIGURE!
HA! HA! THAT SPEAR ALMOST GOT ME. DON'T WORRY, ROBIN! IT'S ONLY CARDBOARD!
OH!
CHASE'S FOXY TRICK!..BATMAN HAS BEEN LULLED INTO FALSE SECURITY!..
NOW HE'LL THROW A "ROCK"!.. MADE OF SPONGE!
5
CRASH!
IT IS A REAL ROCK! I SAW SUNLIGHT GLINTING ON ITS SHINY SURFACE! IF IT HAD BEEN SPONGE IT WOULD HAVE BEEN POROUS!
BLESS YOUR EAGLE EYES! IT MUST'VE ROLLED DOWN FROM ABOVE, INTO THE PILE OF SPONGE "ROCKS"!

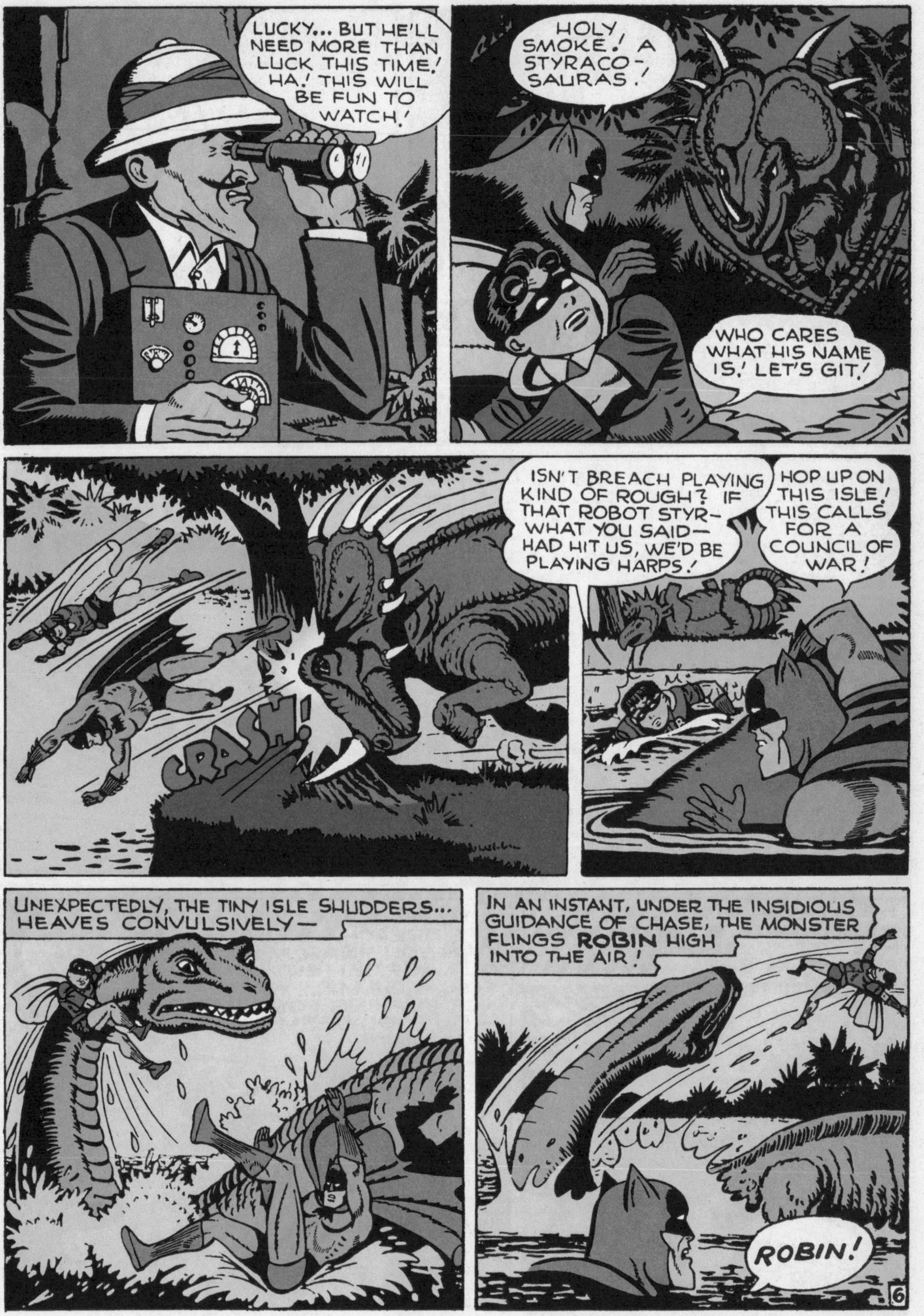
LUCKY... BUT HE'LL NEED MORE THAN LUCK THIS TIME! HA! THIS WILL BE FUN TO WATCH!
HOLY SMOKE! A STYRACO-SAURAS!
WHO CARES WHAT HIS NAME IS! LET'S GIT!
CRASH!
ISN'T BREACH PLAYING KIND OF ROUGH? IF THAT ROBOT STYR-WHAT YOU SAID-HAD HIT US, WE'D BE PLAYING HARPS!
HOP UP ON THIS ISLE! THIS CALLS FOR A COUNCIL OF WAR!
UNEXPECTEDLY, THE TINY ISLE SHUDDERS... HEAVES CONVULSIVELY—
IN AN INSTANT, UNDER THE INSIDIOUS GUIDANCE OF CHASE, THE MONSTER FLINGS ROBIN HIGH INTO THE AIR!
ROBIN!
6

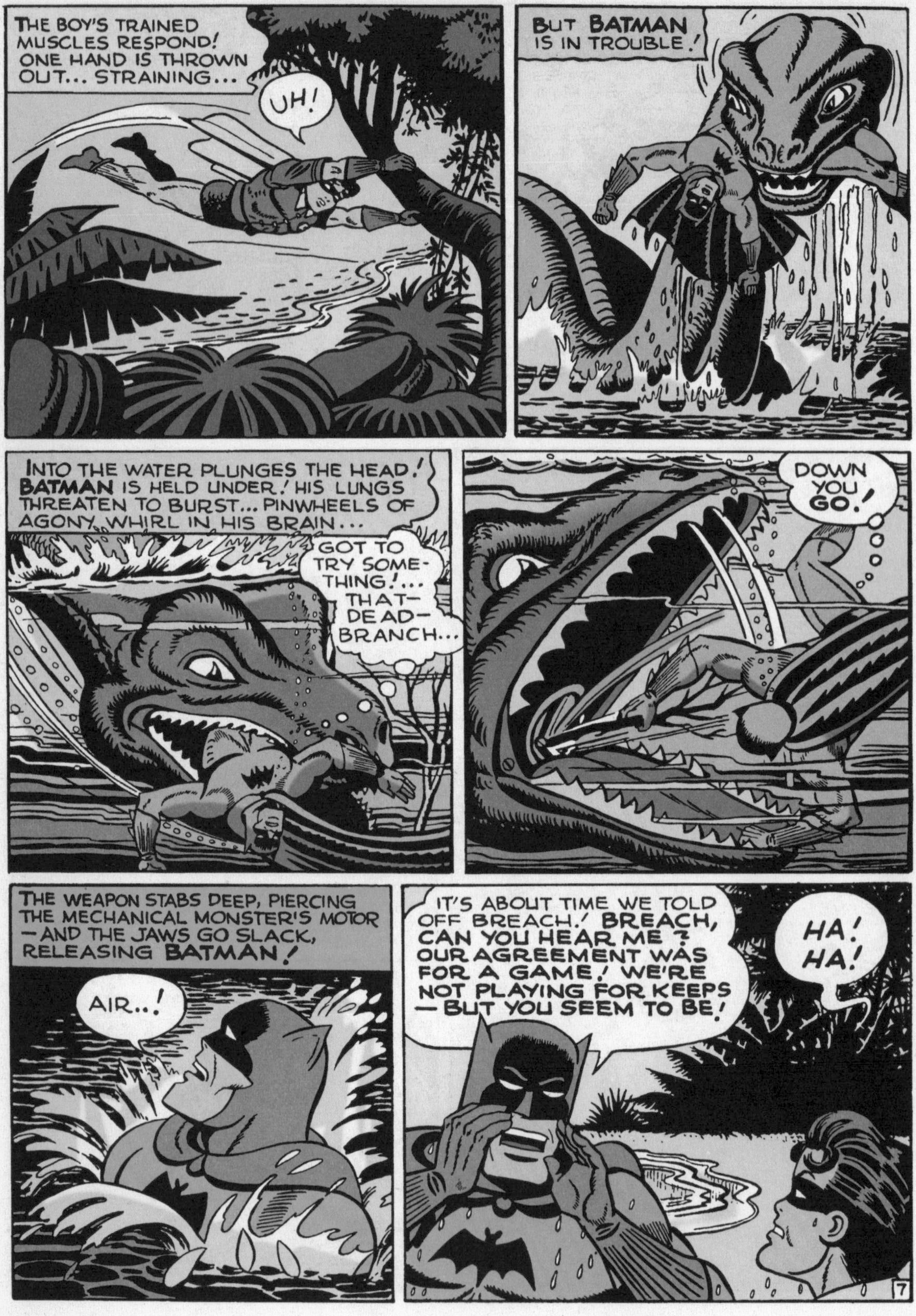
THE BOY'S TRAINED MUSCLES RESPOND! ONE HAND IS THROWN OUT... STRAINING...
UH!
BUT BATMAN IS IN TROUBLE!
INTO THE WATER PLUNGES THE HEAD! BATMAN IS HELD UNDER! HIS LUNGS THREATEN TO BURST... PINWHEELS OF AGONY WHIRL IN HIS BRAIN...
GOT TO TRY SOMETHING!... THAT--DEAD-BRANCH...
DOWN YOU GO!
THE WEAPON STABS DEEP, PIERCING THE MECHANICAL MONSTER'S MOTOR --AND THE JAWS GO SLACK, RELEASING BATMAN!
AIR...!
IT'S ABOUT TIME WE TOLD OFF BREACH! BREACH, CAN YOU HEAR ME? OUR AGREEMENT WAS FOR A GAME! WE'RE NOT PLAYING FOR KEEPS --BUT YOU SEEM TO BE!
HA! HA!
7

THE NAME IS CHASE! WE MET AT THE DINNER, REMEMBER? I'M GOING TO MURDER YOU, BATMAN, AND MAKE YOUR DEATH LOOK ACCI-DENTAL-SO THAT THE UNDERWORLD WILL BE RID OF YOU! TALLY HO, BATMAN!
HA! HA! TALLY HO!
THIS IS NO LONGER A GAME! WE'RE FIGHTING FOR OUR LIVES NOW! WE'LL NEED WEAPONS...
THE ANCIENT CAVEMAN MADE WEAPONS OF ANIMAL SKELETON BONES! WE CAN BORROW A TRICK FROM THEM!
UH-HUH! THESE IRON AND STEEL "BONES" WILL MAKE ARROW HEADS AND KNIVES...
HOW VERY ENERGETIC! PERHAPS I CAN MAKE THEM EXPEND MORE ENERGY! HA! HA! I'M REALLY ENJOY-ING THIS VERY MUCH!
ONCE AGAIN THE CRIMINAL'S FINGERS SNAKE OVER THE CONTROL PANEL—
LOOK!!
ROBOT CAVEMEN!
ROBOT PRIMITIVE AGAINST MODERN MAN! THE MOST BIZARRE BATTLE EVER FOUGHT!
(GULP)... IT'S ALMOST LIKE KILLING A REAL MAN!
BUT THEY'RE NOT REAL MEN! THEY'RE MACHINES!
8

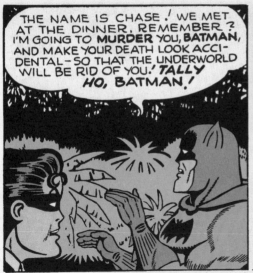

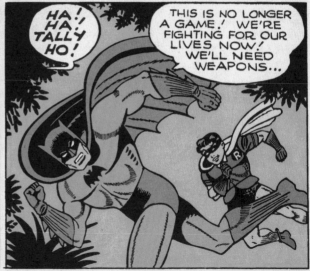

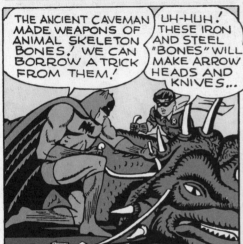

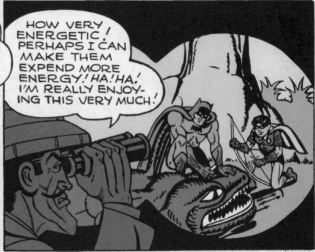

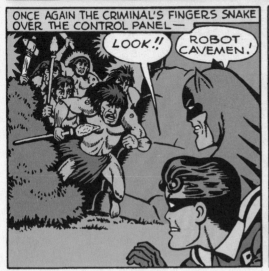

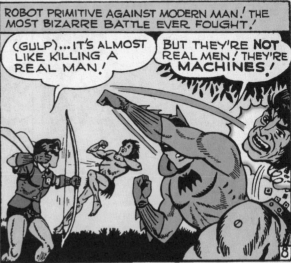

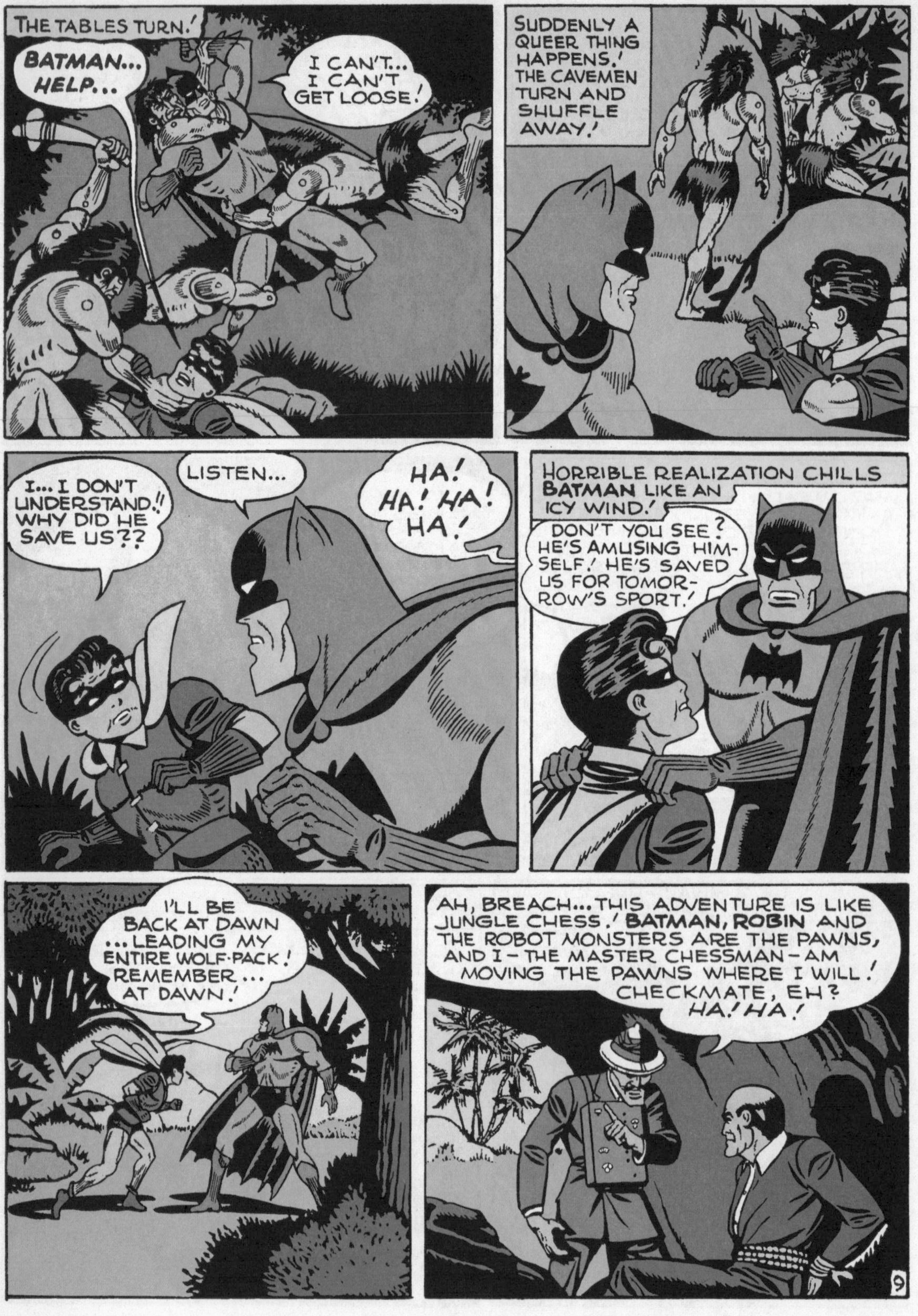
THE TABLES TURN!
BATMAN... HELP...
I CAN'T... I CAN'T GET LOOSE!
SUDDENLY A QUEER THING HAPPENS! THE CAVEMEN TURN AND SHUFFLE AWAY!
I... I DON'T UNDERSTAND!! WHY DID HE SAVE US??
LISTEN...
HA! HA! HA! HA!
HORRIBLE REALIZATION CHILLS BATMAN LIKE AN ICY WIND!
DON'T YOU SEE? HE'S AMUSING HIMSELF! HE'S SAVED US FOR TOMORROW'S SPORT!
I'LL BE BACK AT DAWN ...LEADING MY ENTIRE WOLF-PACK! REMEMBER... AT DAWN!
AH, BREACH... THIS ADVENTURE IS LIKE JUNGLE CHESS! BATMAN, ROBIN AND THE ROBOT MONSTERS ARE THE PAWNS, AND I - THE MASTER CHESSMAN - AM MOVING THE PAWNS WHERE I WILL! CHECKMATE, EH? HA! HA!
9

JUNGLE NIGHT! CHASE SLEEPS—BUT **BATMAN** AND **ROBIN**, LIKE SUDDENLY CAGED WILDLIFE, ARE APPREHENSIVE, RESTLESS...

WISH I COULD SLEEP!... FUNNY, I THOUGHT I'D BE SCARED, BUT I'M NOT!... GUESS WE'RE IN OVER OUR HEADS THIS TIME!... **BATMAN'S** WORRIED ...EVEN THOUGH HE DOESN'T ACT IT!

ROBIN'S TAKING THIS OKAY!... HE'S A GREAT KID... I WON'T LET HIM DOWN! I'LL THINK OF SOMETHING ...I'VE GOT TO!

IF ONLY WE HAD YOUR UTILITY BELT! OR THE BATPLANE...

MAYBE WE HAVE!

WHAT'S THE IDEA OF THE ARROW-LINE?

THOSE MECHANICAL PTERODACTYLS! THEY'RE NOT CONTROLLED BY CHASE'S PANEL-BOARD! THEY FLY AUTOMATICALLY, PROBABLY BY SOME ROBOT CONTROL-STATION THAT WORKS AT SET INTERVALS! WE CAN USE ONE OF THOSE FLYING KITES!

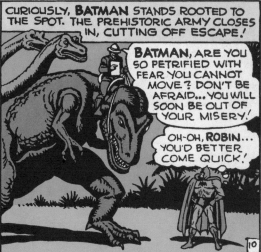

ALL NIGHT LONG, THE TWO LABOR, WORKING AGAINST TIME! AND THEN—THE DAWN!

IT'S ALL FINISHED! **BATMAN**... MAYBE I OUGHT TO BE THE ONE!

NO, **ROBIN**, I'LL HAVE TO BE THE BAIT THAT'LL LURE CHASE TO THE SPOT WE CHOSE! IT'LL HAVE TO WORK—OR ELSE...

ALONE NOW, **BATMAN** WAITS! SOON, LUMBERING THROUGH THE FOREST—A PROCESSION OF THE DAWN WORLD!

CURIOUSLY, **BATMAN** STANDS ROOTED TO THE SPOT. THE PREHISTORIC ARMY CLOSES IN, CUTTING OFF ESCAPE!

BATMAN, ARE YOU SO PETRIFIED WITH FEAR YOU CANNOT MOVE? DON'T BE AFRAID... YOU WILL SOON BE OUT OF YOUR MISERY!

OH-OH, **ROBIN**... YOU'D BETTER COME QUICK!

10

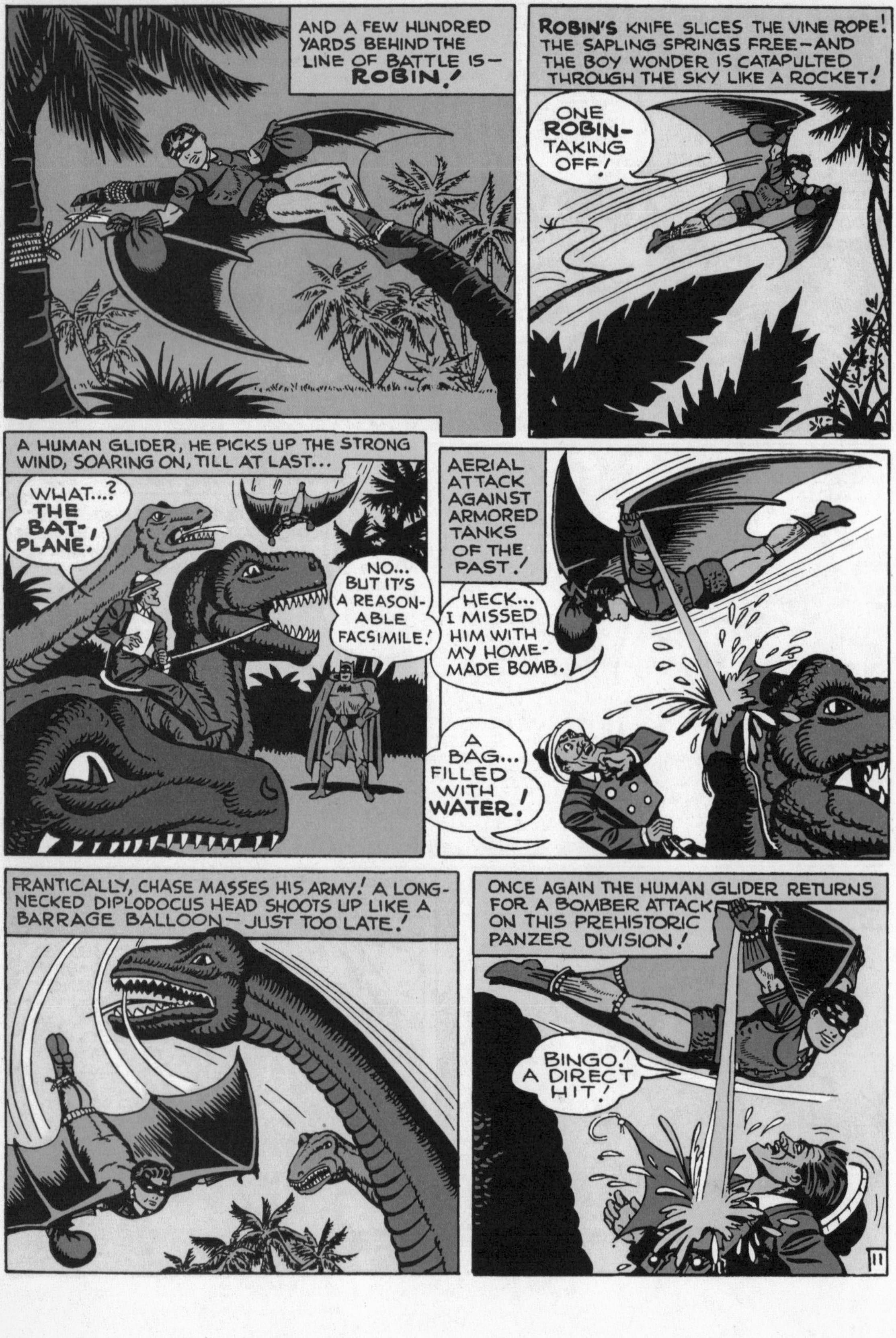
AND A FEW HUNDRED YARDS BEHIND THE LINE OF BATTLE IS— ROBIN!
ROBIN'S KNIFE SLICES THE VINE ROPE! THE SAPLING SPRINGS FREE—AND THE BOY WONDER IS CATAPULTED THROUGH THE SKY LIKE A ROCKET!
ONE ROBIN-TAKING OFF!
A HUMAN GLIDER, HE PICKS UP THE STRONG WIND, SOARING ON, TILL AT LAST...
WHAT...? THE BAT-PLANE!
NO... BUT IT'S A REASON-ABLE FACSIMILE!
AERIAL ATTACK AGAINST ARMORED TANKS OF THE PAST!
HECK... I MISSED HIM WITH MY HOME-MADE BOMB.
A BAG... FILLED WITH WATER!
FRANTICALLY, CHASE MASSES HIS ARMY! A LONG-NECKED DIPLODOCUS HEAD SHOOTS UP LIKE A BARRAGE BALLOON—JUST TOO LATE!
ONCE AGAIN THE HUMAN GLIDER RETURNS FOR A BOMBER ATTACK ON THIS PREHISTORIC PANZER DIVISION!
BINGO! A DIRECT HIT!
11

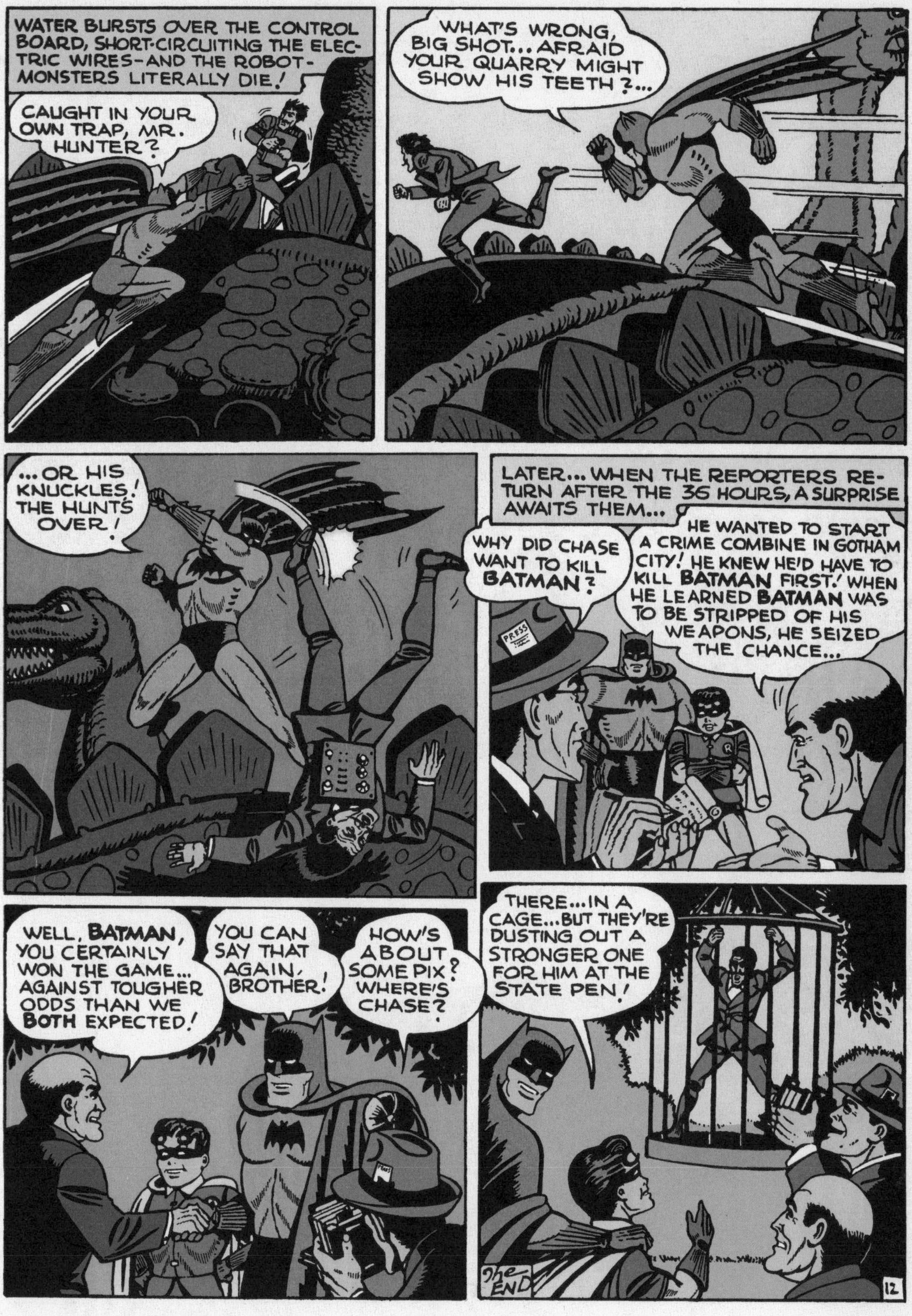
WATER BURSTS OVER THE CONTROL BOARD, SHORT-CIRCUITING THE ELECTRIC WIRES-AND THE ROBOT-MONSTERS LITERALLY DIE!
CAUGHT IN YOUR OWN TRAP, MR. HUNTER?
WHAT'S WRONG, BIG SHOT... AFRAID YOUR QUARRY MIGHT SHOW HIS TEETH?...
...OR HIS KNUCKLES! THE HUNT'S OVER!
LATER... WHEN THE REPORTERS RETURN AFTER THE 36 HOURS, A SURPRISE AWAITS THEM...
WHY DID CHASE WANT TO KILL BATMAN?
HE WANTED TO START A CRIME COMBINE IN GOTHAM CITY! HE KNEW HE'D HAVE TO KILL BATMAN FIRST! WHEN HE LEARNED BATMAN WAS TO BE STRIPPED OF HIS WEAPONS, HE SEIZED THE CHANCE...
PRESS
WELL, BATMAN, YOU CERTAINLY WON THE GAME... AGAINST TOUGHER ODDS THAN WE BOTH EXPECTED!
YOU CAN SAY THAT AGAIN, BROTHER!
HOW'S ABOUT SOME PIX? WHERE'S CHASE?
THERE...IN A CAGE...BUT THEY'RE DUSTING OUT A STRONGER ONE FOR HIM AT THE STATE PEN!
The END
12

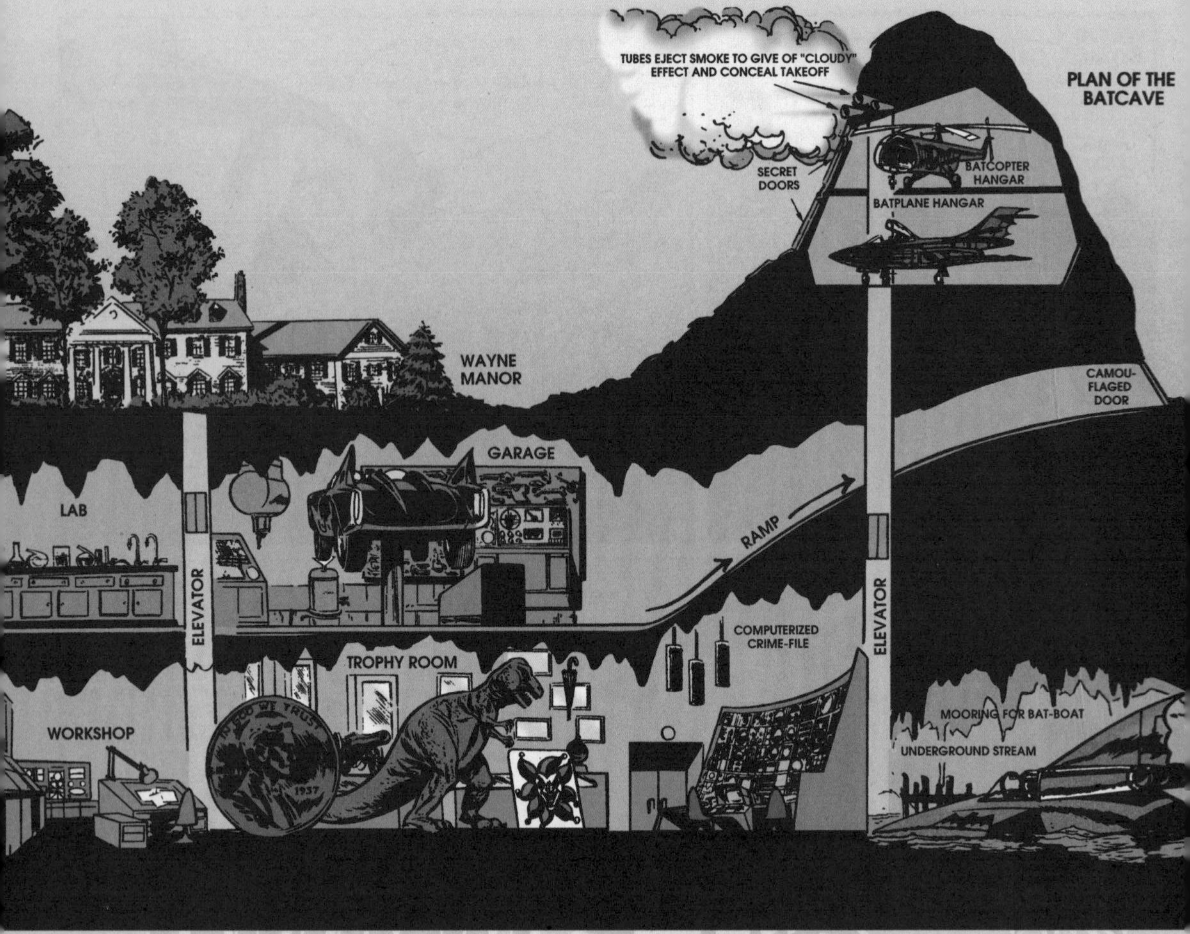
TUBES EJECT SMOKE TO GIVE OF "CLOUDY" EFFECT AND CONCEAL TAKEOFF
PLAN OF THE BATCAVE
SECRET DOORS
BATCOPTER HANGAR
BATPLANE HANGAR
WAYNE MANOR
CAMOU-FLAGED DOOR
GARAGE
LAB
RAMP
ELEVATOR
ELEVATOR
TROPHY ROOM
COMPUTERIZED CRIME-FILE
WORKSHOP
MOORING FOR BAT-BOAT
UNDERGROUND STREAM
1937

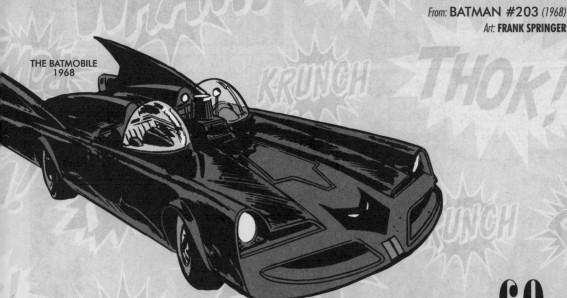

From: BATMAN #203 *(1968)*

Art: **FRANK SPRINGER**

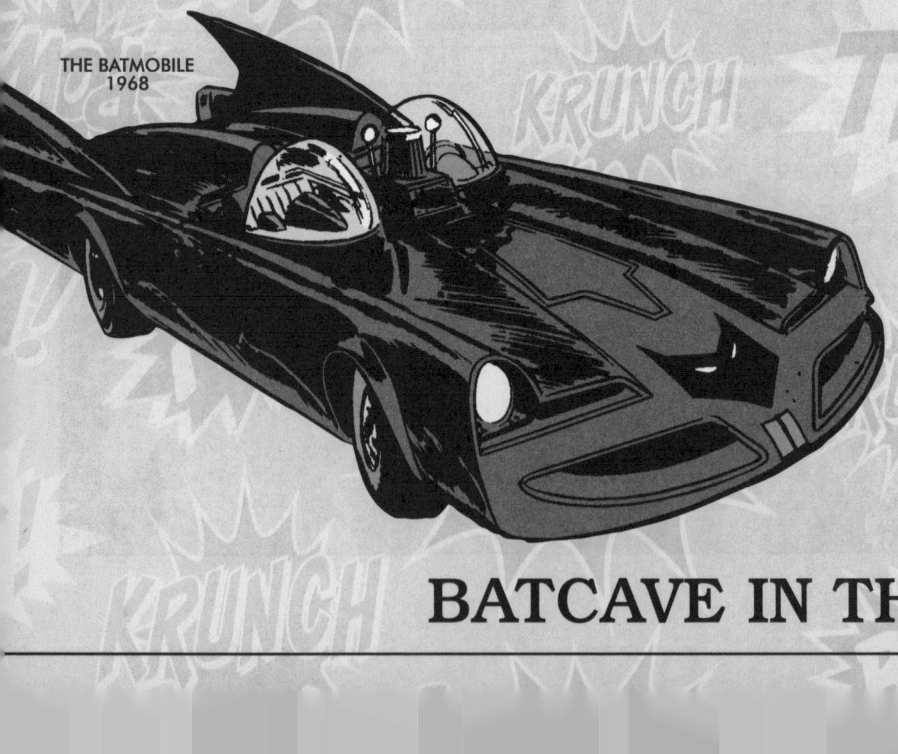
THE BATMOBILE 1968

BATCAVE IN THE 60s

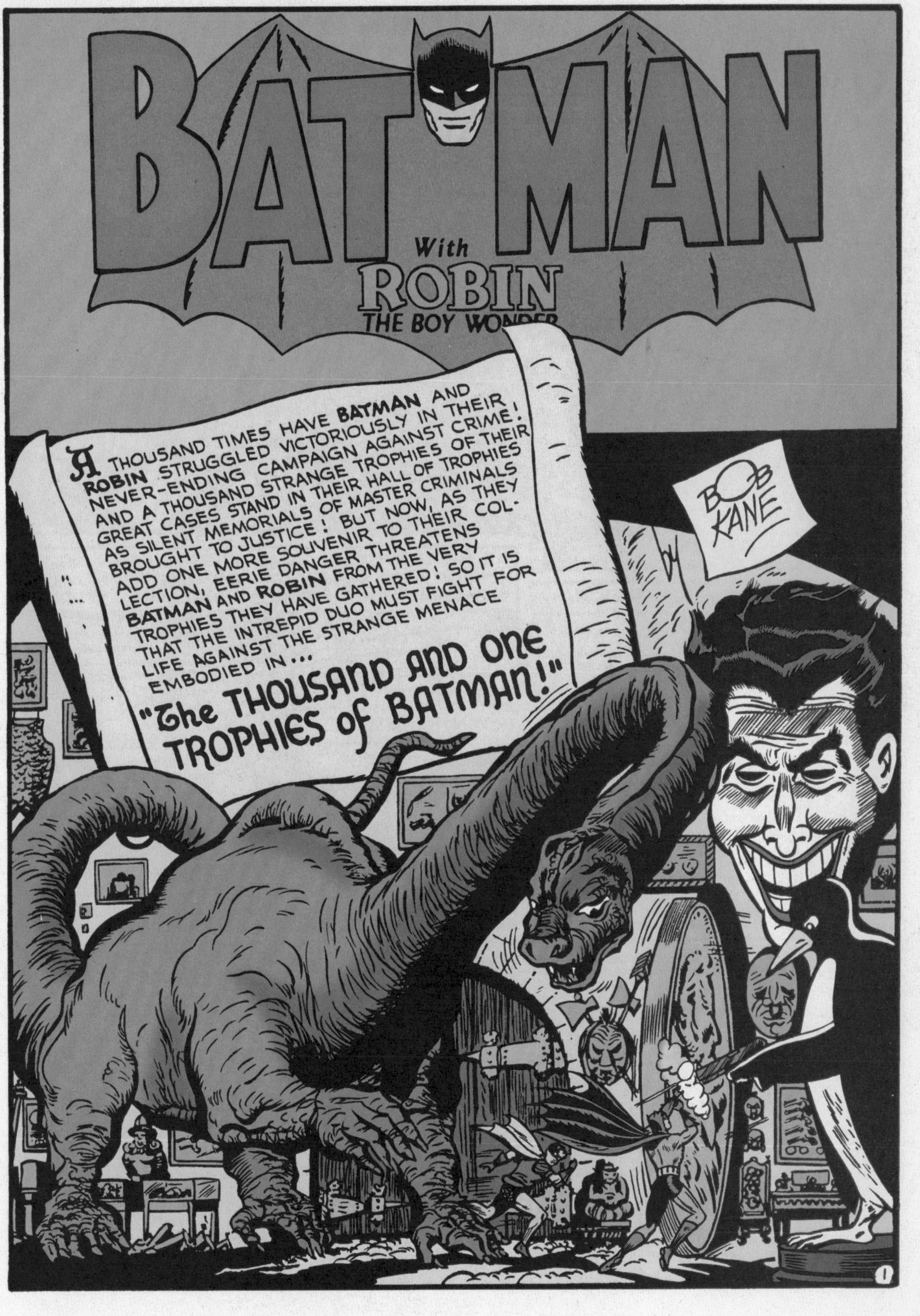
BATMAN
With
ROBIN
THE BOY WONDER
A THOUSAND TIMES HAVE BATMAN AND ROBIN STRUGGLED VICTORIOUSLY IN THEIR NEVER-ENDING CAMPAIGN AGAINST CRIME! AND A THOUSAND STRANGE TROPHIES OF THEIR GREAT CASES STAND IN THEIR HALL OF TROPHIES AS SILENT MEMORIALS OF MASTER CRIMINALS BROUGHT TO JUSTICE! BUT NOW, AS THEY ADD ONE MORE SOUVENIR TO THEIR COLLECTION, EERIE DANGER THREATENS BATMAN AND ROBIN FROM THE VERY TROPHIES THEY HAVE GATHERED! SO IT IS THAT THE INTREPID DUO MUST FIGHT FOR LIFE AGAINST THE STRANGE MENACE EMBODIED IN...
"The THOUSAND AND ONE TROPHIES of BATMAN!"
BOB KANE
1

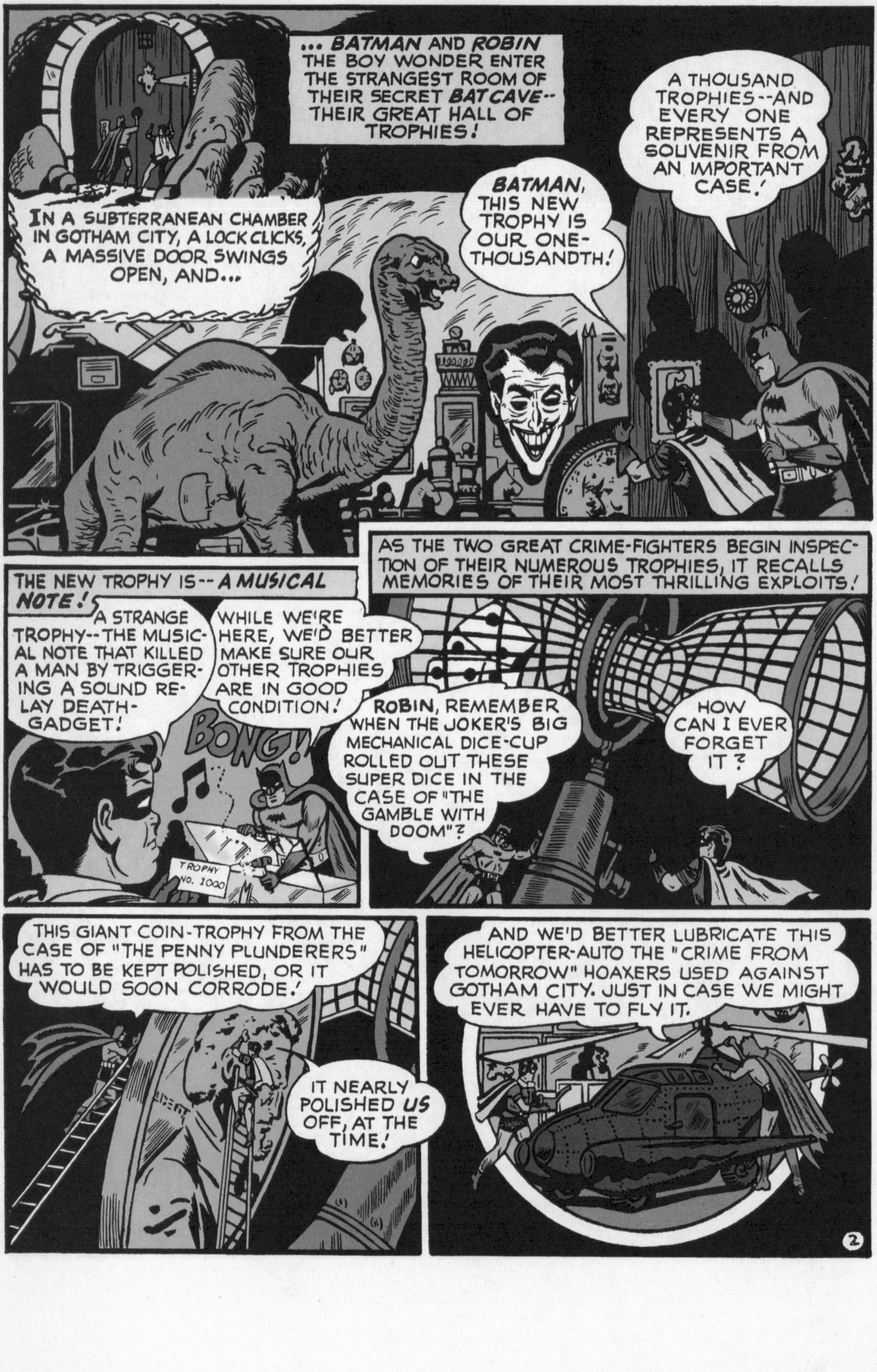
... BATMAN AND ROBIN THE BOY WONDER ENTER THE STRANGEST ROOM OF THEIR SECRET BATCAVE-- THEIR GREAT HALL OF TROPHIES!
IN A SUBTERRANEAN CHAMBER IN GOTHAM CITY, A LOCK CLICKS, A MASSIVE DOOR SWINGS OPEN, AND...
BATMAN, THIS NEW TROPHY IS OUR ONE-THOUSANDTH!
A THOUSAND TROPHIES--AND EVERY ONE REPRESENTS A SOUVENIR FROM AN IMPORTANT CASE!
THE NEW TROPHY IS--A MUSICAL NOTE!
A STRANGE TROPHY--THE MUSICAL NOTE THAT KILLED A MAN BY TRIGGERING A SOUND RELAY DEATH-GADGET!
WHILE WE'RE HERE, WE'D BETTER MAKE SURE OUR OTHER TROPHIES ARE IN GOOD CONDITION!
BONG!
TROPHY NO. 1000
AS THE TWO GREAT CRIME-FIGHTERS BEGIN INSPECTION OF THEIR NUMEROUS TROPHIES, IT RECALLS MEMORIES OF THEIR MOST THRILLING EXPLOITS!
ROBIN, REMEMBER WHEN THE JOKER'S BIG MECHANICAL DICE-CUP ROLLED OUT THESE SUPER DICE IN THE CASE OF "THE GAMBLE WITH DOOM"?
HOW CAN I EVER FORGET IT?
THIS GIANT COIN-TROPHY FROM THE CASE OF "THE PENNY PLUNDERERS" HAS TO BE KEPT POLISHED, OR IT WOULD SOON CORRODE!
IT NEARLY POLISHED US OFF, AT THE TIME!
AND WE'D BETTER LUBRICATE THIS HELICOPTER-AUTO THE "CRIME FROM TOMORROW" HOAXERS USED AGAINST GOTHAM CITY. JUST IN CASE WE MIGHT EVER HAVE TO FLY IT.
2

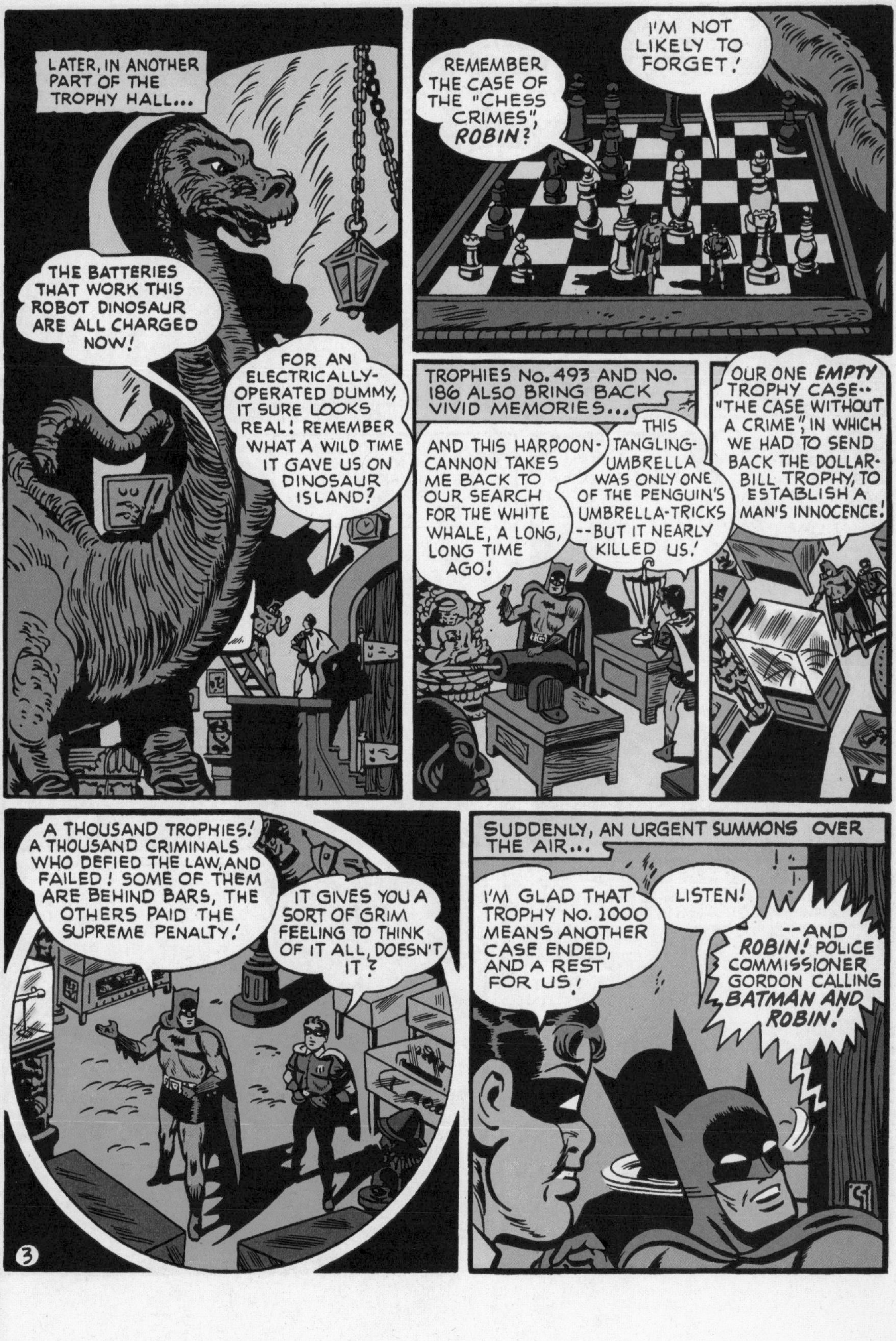
LATER, IN ANOTHER PART OF THE TROPHY HALL...
THE BATTERIES THAT WORK THIS ROBOT DINOSAUR ARE ALL CHARGED NOW!
FOR AN ELECTRICALLY-OPERATED DUMMY, IT SURE LOOKS REAL! REMEMBER WHAT A WILD TIME IT GAVE US ON DINOSAUR ISLAND?
REMEMBER THE CASE OF THE "CHESS CRIMES", ROBIN?
I'M NOT LIKELY TO FORGET!
TROPHIES No. 493 AND No. 186 ALSO BRING BACK VIVID MEMORIES...
AND THIS HARPOON-CANNON TAKES ME BACK TO OUR SEARCH FOR THE WHITE WHALE, A LONG, LONG TIME AGO!
THIS TANGLING-UMBRELLA WAS ONLY ONE OF THE PENGUIN'S UMBRELLA-TRICKS --BUT IT NEARLY KILLED US!
OUR ONE EMPTY TROPHY CASE-- "THE CASE WITHOUT A CRIME", IN WHICH WE HAD TO SEND BACK THE DOLLAR-BILL TROPHY, TO ESTABLISH A MAN'S INNOCENCE!
A THOUSAND TROPHIES! A THOUSAND CRIMINALS WHO DEFIED THE LAW, AND FAILED! SOME OF THEM ARE BEHIND BARS, THE OTHERS PAID THE SUPREME PENALTY!
IT GIVES YOU A SORT OF GRIM FEELING TO THINK OF IT ALL, DOESN'T IT?
3
SUDDENLY, AN URGENT SUMMONS OVER THE AIR...
I'M GLAD THAT TROPHY No. 1000 MEANS ANOTHER CASE ENDED, AND A REST FOR US!
LISTEN!
--AND ROBIN! POLICE COMMISSIONER GORDON CALLING BATMAN AND ROBIN!

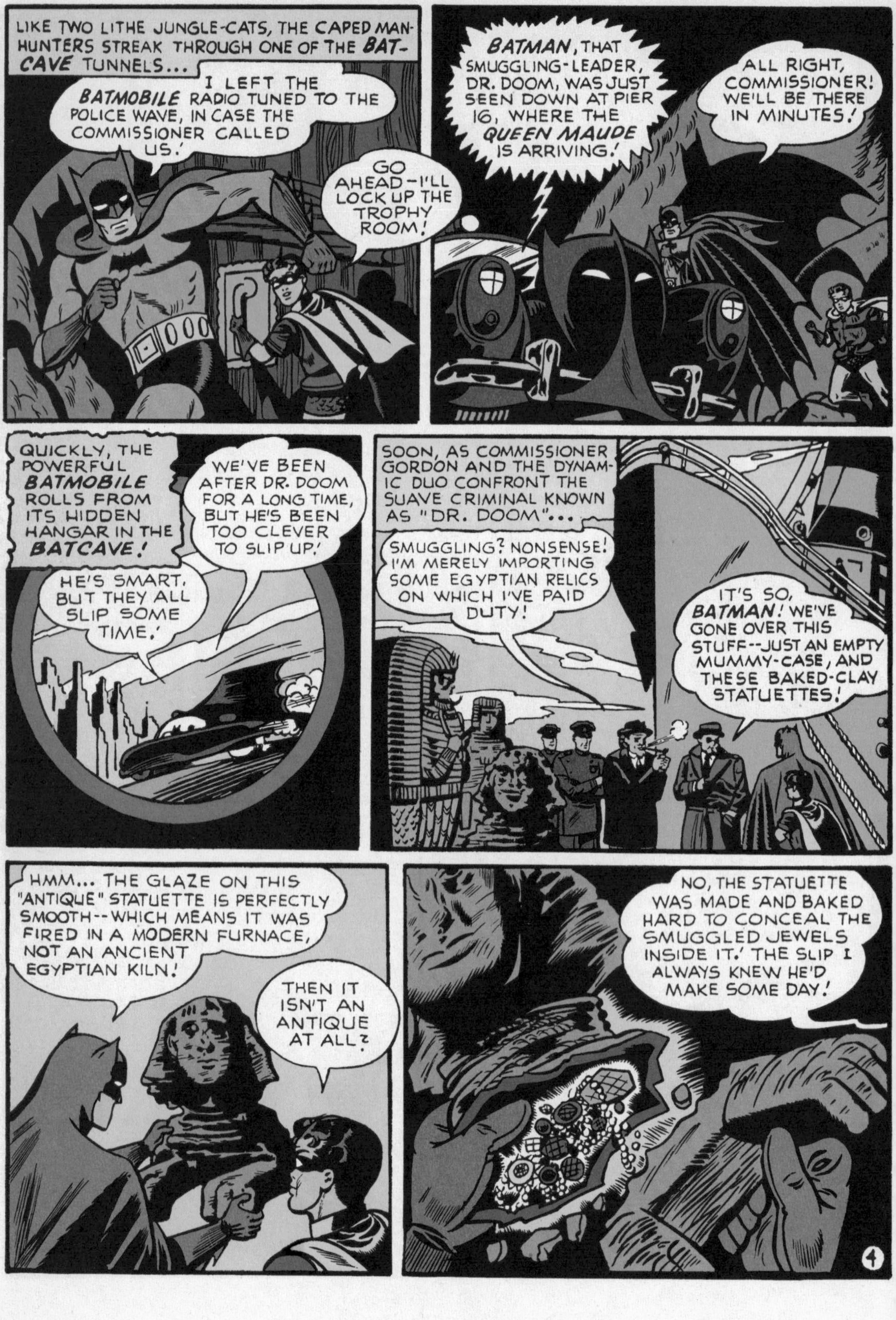
LIKE TWO LITHE JUNGLE-CATS, THE CAPED MAN-HUNTERS STREAK THROUGH ONE OF THE BAT-CAVE TUNNELS...
I LEFT THE BATMOBILE RADIO TUNED TO THE POLICE WAVE, IN CASE THE COMMISSIONER CALLED US!
GO AHEAD--I'LL LOCK UP THE TROPHY ROOM!
BATMAN, THAT SMUGGLING-LEADER, DR. DOOM, WAS JUST SEEN DOWN AT PIER 16, WHERE THE QUEEN MAUDE IS ARRIVING!
ALL RIGHT, COMMISSIONER! WE'LL BE THERE IN MINUTES!
QUICKLY, THE POWERFUL BATMOBILE ROLLS FROM ITS HIDDEN HANGAR IN THE BATCAVE!
WE'VE BEEN AFTER DR. DOOM FOR A LONG TIME, BUT HE'S BEEN TOO CLEVER TO SLIP UP!
HE'S SMART, BUT THEY ALL SLIP SOME TIME!
SOON, AS COMMISSIONER GORDON AND THE DYNAMIC DUO CONFRONT THE SUAVE CRIMINAL KNOWN AS "DR. DOOM"...
SMUGGLING? NONSENSE! I'M MERELY IMPORTING SOME EGYPTIAN RELICS ON WHICH I'VE PAID DUTY!
IT'S SO, BATMAN! WE'VE GONE OVER THIS STUFF--JUST AN EMPTY MUMMY-CASE, AND THESE BAKED-CLAY STATUETTES!
HMM... THE GLAZE ON THIS "ANTIQUE" STATUETTE IS PERFECTLY SMOOTH--WHICH MEANS IT WAS FIRED IN A MODERN FURNACE, NOT AN ANCIENT EGYPTIAN KILN!
THEN IT ISN'T AN ANTIQUE AT ALL?
NO, THE STATUETTE WAS MADE AND BAKED HARD TO CONCEAL THE SMUGGLED JEWELS INSIDE IT! THE SLIP I ALWAYS KNEW HE'D MAKE SOME DAY!
4

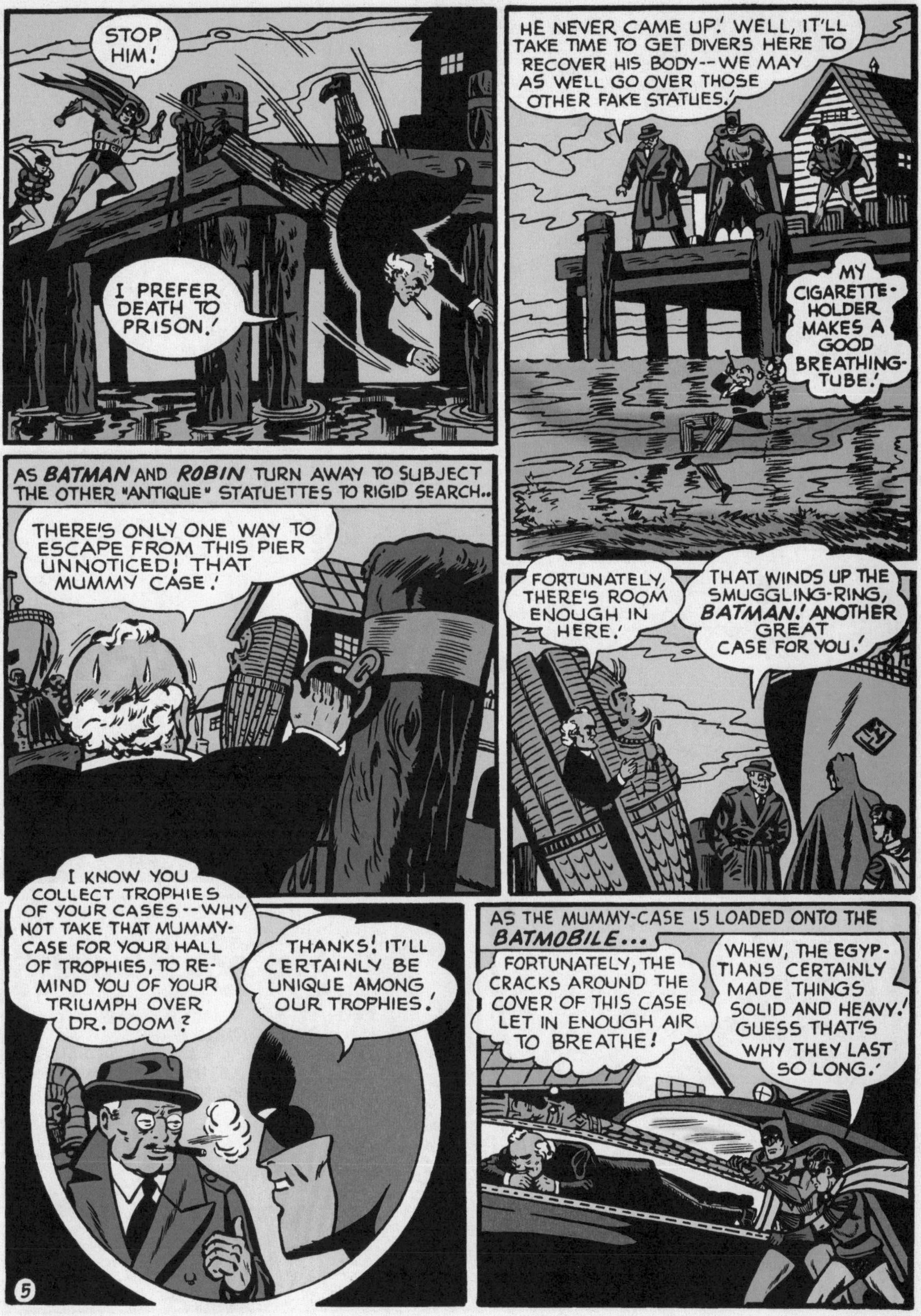
STOP HIM!
I PREFER DEATH TO PRISON!
HE NEVER CAME UP! WELL, IT'LL TAKE TIME TO GET DIVERS HERE TO RECOVER HIS BODY--WE MAY AS WELL GO OVER THOSE OTHER FAKE STATUES!
MY CIGARETTE-HOLDER MAKES A GOOD BREATHING-TUBE!
AS BATMAN AND ROBIN TURN AWAY TO SUBJECT THE OTHER "ANTIQUE" STATUETTES TO RIGID SEARCH..
THERE'S ONLY ONE WAY TO ESCAPE FROM THIS PIER UNNOTICED! THAT MUMMY CASE!
FORTUNATELY, THERE'S ROOM ENOUGH IN HERE!
THAT WINDS UP THE SMUGGLING-RING, BATMAN! ANOTHER GREAT CASE FOR YOU!
I KNOW YOU COLLECT TROPHIES OF YOUR CASES--WHY NOT TAKE THAT MUMMY-CASE FOR YOUR HALL OF TROPHIES, TO RE-MIND YOU OF YOUR TRIUMPH OVER DR. DOOM?
THANKS! IT'LL CERTAINLY BE UNIQUE AMONG OUR TROPHIES!
5
AS THE MUMMY-CASE IS LOADED ONTO THE BATMOBILE...
FORTUNATELY, THE CRACKS AROUND THE COVER OF THIS CASE LET IN ENOUGH AIR TO BREATHE!
WHEW, THE EGYP-TIANS CERTAINLY MADE THINGS SOLID AND HEAVY! GUESS THAT'S WHY THEY LAST SO LONG!

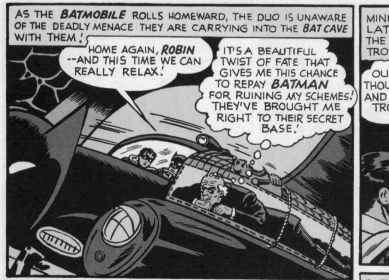

AS THE *BATMOBILE* ROLLS HOMEWARD, THE DUO IS UNAWARE OF THE DEADLY MENACE THEY ARE CARRYING INTO THE *BAT CAVE* WITH THEM!

HOME AGAIN, *ROBIN* --AND THIS TIME WE CAN REALLY RELAX!

IT'S A BEAUTIFUL TWIST OF FATE THAT GIVES ME THIS CHANCE TO REPAY *BATMAN* FOR RUINING MY SCHEMES! THEY'VE BROUGHT ME RIGHT TO THEIR SECRET BASE!

MINUTES LATER, IN THE HALL OF TROPHIES...

OUR THOUSAND AND FIRST TROPHY!

AND THE MOST ANCIENT OF ALL! BUT COME ON-- IT'LL BE A RELIEF TO GET OUT OF COSTUME!

TROPHY NO. 1001

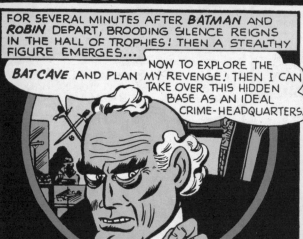

FOR SEVERAL MINUTES AFTER *BATMAN* AND *ROBIN* DEPART, BROODING SILENCE REIGNS IN THE HALL OF TROPHIES! THEN A STEALTHY FIGURE EMERGES...

NOW TO EXPLORE THE *BAT CAVE* AND PLAN MY REVENGE! THEN I CAN TAKE OVER THIS HIDDEN BASE AS AN IDEAL CRIME-HEADQUARTERS!

BUT *BATMAN* AND *ROBIN* LEAVE LITTLE TO CHANCE!

THE DOOR--LOCKED! THEN IF I CAN'T GET OUT OF THIS HALL OF TROPHIES, I'LL HAVE TO SET MY DEATH-TRAP FOR THEM *HERE!*

PRESENTLY...

IT'S IRONIC -- I'M FIXING THINGS SO THAT THEIR OWN TROPHIES OF THEIR PAST TRIUMPHS WILL DESTROY THEM!

USING ALL HIS CRIMINAL GENIUS TO RIG THE GREAT TROPHIES...

THIS FINISHES MY LITTLE AMBUSH! NOW TO CALL THE VICTIMS TO THEIR DOOM! SHORT-CIRCUITING THE ELECTRIC PROWLER-ALARM OUGHT TO DO IT!

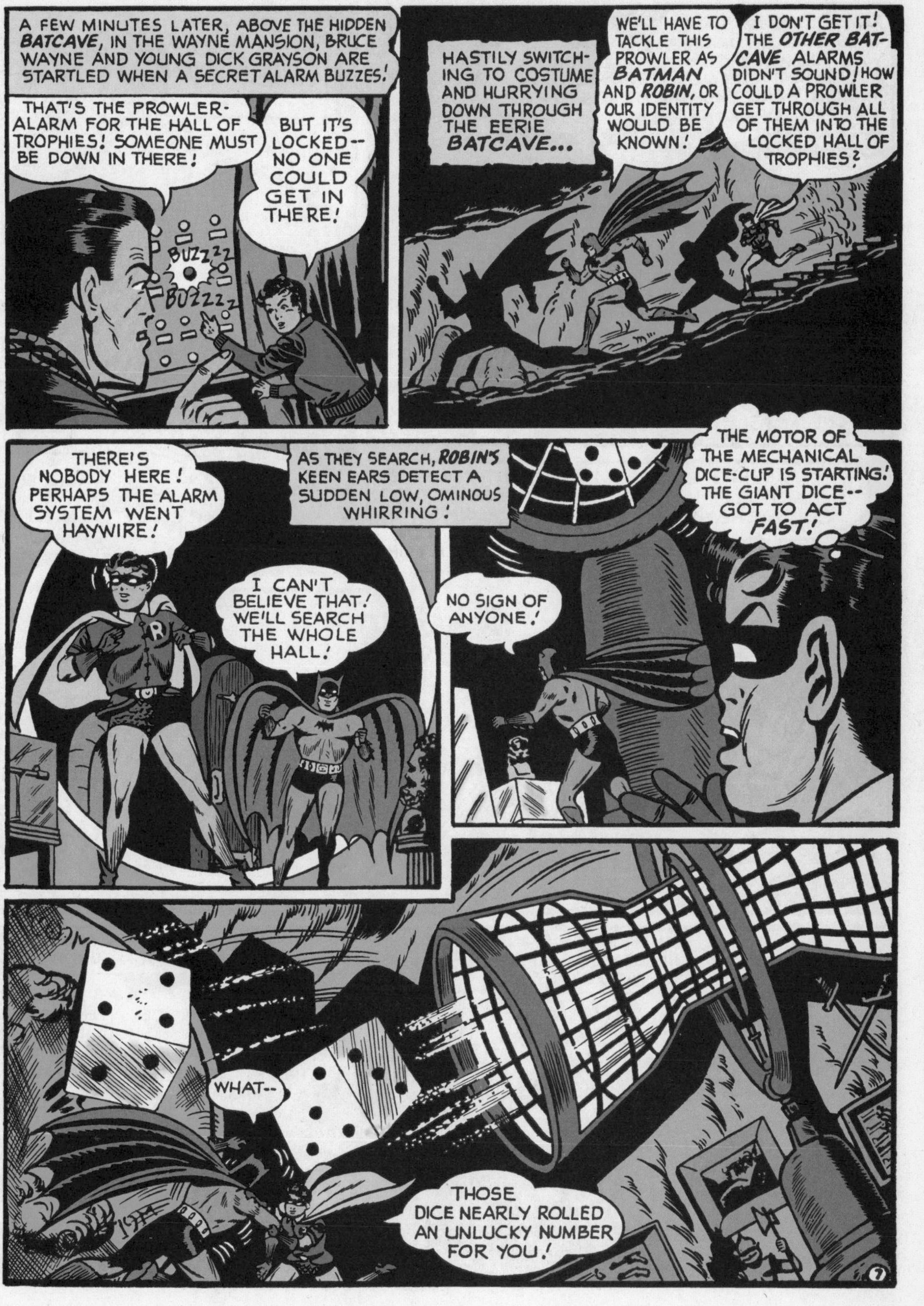
A FEW MINUTES LATER, ABOVE THE HIDDEN BATCAVE, IN THE WAYNE MANSION, BRUCE WAYNE AND YOUNG DICK GRAYSON ARE STARTLED WHEN A SECRET ALARM BUZZES!
THAT'S THE PROWLER-ALARM FOR THE HALL OF TROPHIES! SOMEONE MUST BE DOWN IN THERE!
BUT IT'S LOCKED-- NO ONE COULD GET IN THERE!
BUZZZZ
BUZZZZZ
HASTILY SWITCHING TO COSTUME AND HURRYING DOWN THROUGH THE EERIE BATCAVE...
WE'LL HAVE TO TACKLE THIS PROWLER AS BATMAN AND ROBIN, OR OUR IDENTITY WOULD BE KNOWN!
I DON'T GET IT! THE OTHER BAT-CAVE ALARMS DIDN'T SOUND! HOW COULD A PROWLER GET THROUGH ALL OF THEM INTO THE LOCKED HALL OF TROPHIES?
THERE'S NOBODY HERE! PERHAPS THE ALARM SYSTEM WENT HAYWIRE!
AS THEY SEARCH, ROBIN'S KEEN EARS DETECT A SUDDEN LOW, OMINOUS WHIRRING!
I CAN'T BELIEVE THAT! WE'LL SEARCH THE WHOLE HALL!
NO SIGN OF ANYONE!
THE MOTOR OF THE MECHANICAL DICE-CUP IS STARTING! THE GIANT DICE-- GOT TO ACT FAST!
WHAT--
THOSE DICE NEARLY ROLLED AN UNLUCKY NUMBER FOR YOU!
7

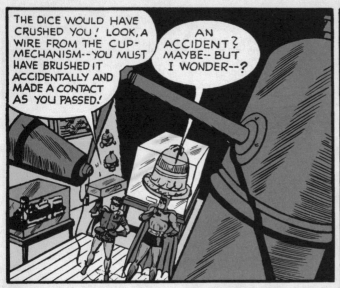

THE DICE WOULD HAVE CRUSHED YOU! LOOK, A WIRE FROM THE CUP-MECHANISM--YOU MUST HAVE BRUSHED IT ACCIDENTALLY AND MADE A CONTACT AS YOU PASSED!

AN ACCIDENT? MAYBE-- BUT I WONDER--?

AS THE GRIM SEARCH GOES ON...

NO PROWLER BACK HERE!

IT'S FALLING ON ME! A BACK-FLIP IS MY ONLY CHANCE!

INSTANTLY USING HIS SUPREME ACROBATIC SKILL, ROBIN DODGES THE MONSTER COIN WITH A BACK FLIP...

CRASH

ONE CENT UNITED STATES OF AMERICA

ROBIN, ARE YOU--?

BUT AT THAT INSTANT THE DEADLY HARPOON-CANNON FIRES!

BATMAN-- DOWN!

MOMENTS LATER, THE SHAKEN MANHUNTERS INSPECT TROPHIES THAT HAVE TURNED INTO A MURDEROUS MENACE!

THAT HARPOON-CANNON'S TRIGGER WAS SET TO JAR OFF AT THE SLIGHT-EST VIBRATION! I SAW THE TRIGGER-CORD JERKING AND DROPPED INSTANTLY!

AND THE GIANT PENNY WAS BALANCED SO THAT ANY-ONE WALKING CLOSE TO IT BROUGHT IT CRASHING DOWN!

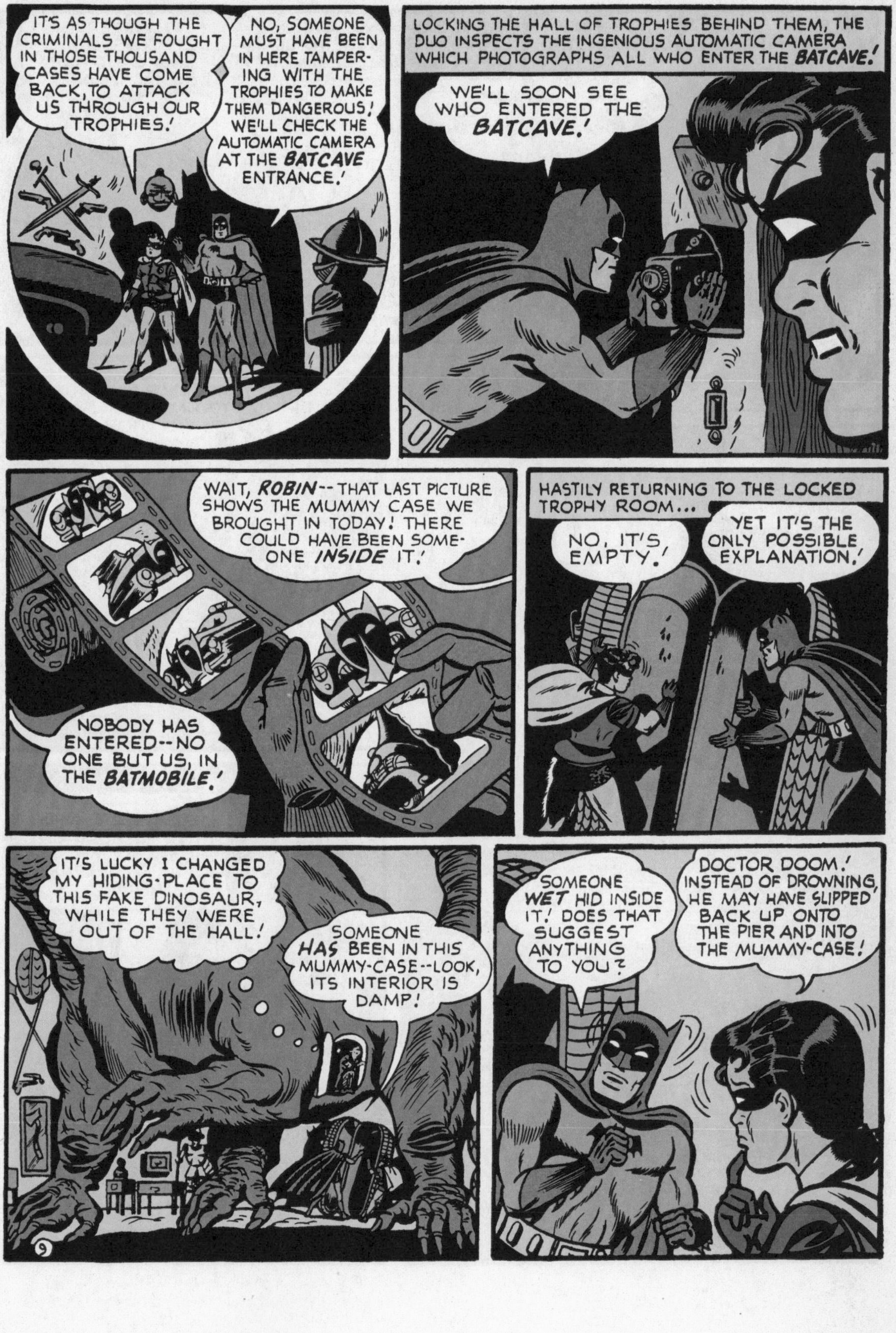
IT'S AS THOUGH THE CRIMINALS WE FOUGHT IN THOSE THOUSAND CASES HAVE COME BACK, TO ATTACK US THROUGH OUR TROPHIES!
NO, SOMEONE MUST HAVE BEEN IN HERE TAMPERING WITH THE TROPHIES TO MAKE THEM DANGEROUS! WE'LL CHECK THE AUTOMATIC CAMERA AT THE BATCAVE ENTRANCE!
LOCKING THE HALL OF TROPHIES BEHIND THEM, THE DUO INSPECTS THE INGENIOUS AUTOMATIC CAMERA WHICH PHOTOGRAPHS ALL WHO ENTER THE BATCAVE!
WE'LL SOON SEE WHO ENTERED THE BATCAVE!
WAIT, ROBIN--THAT LAST PICTURE SHOWS THE MUMMY CASE WE BROUGHT IN TODAY! THERE COULD HAVE BEEN SOMEONE INSIDE IT!
NOBODY HAS ENTERED--NO ONE BUT US, IN THE BATMOBILE!
HASTILY RETURNING TO THE LOCKED TROPHY ROOM...
NO, IT'S EMPTY!
YET IT'S THE ONLY POSSIBLE EXPLANATION!
IT'S LUCKY I CHANGED MY HIDING-PLACE TO THIS FAKE DINOSAUR, WHILE THEY WERE OUT OF THE HALL!
SOMEONE HAS BEEN IN THIS MUMMY-CASE--LOOK, ITS INTERIOR IS DAMP!
SOMEONE WET HID INSIDE IT! DOES THAT SUGGEST ANYTHING TO YOU?
DOCTOR DOOM! INSTEAD OF DROWNING, HE MAY HAVE SLIPPED BACK UP ONTO THE PIER AND INTO THE MUMMY-CASE!
9

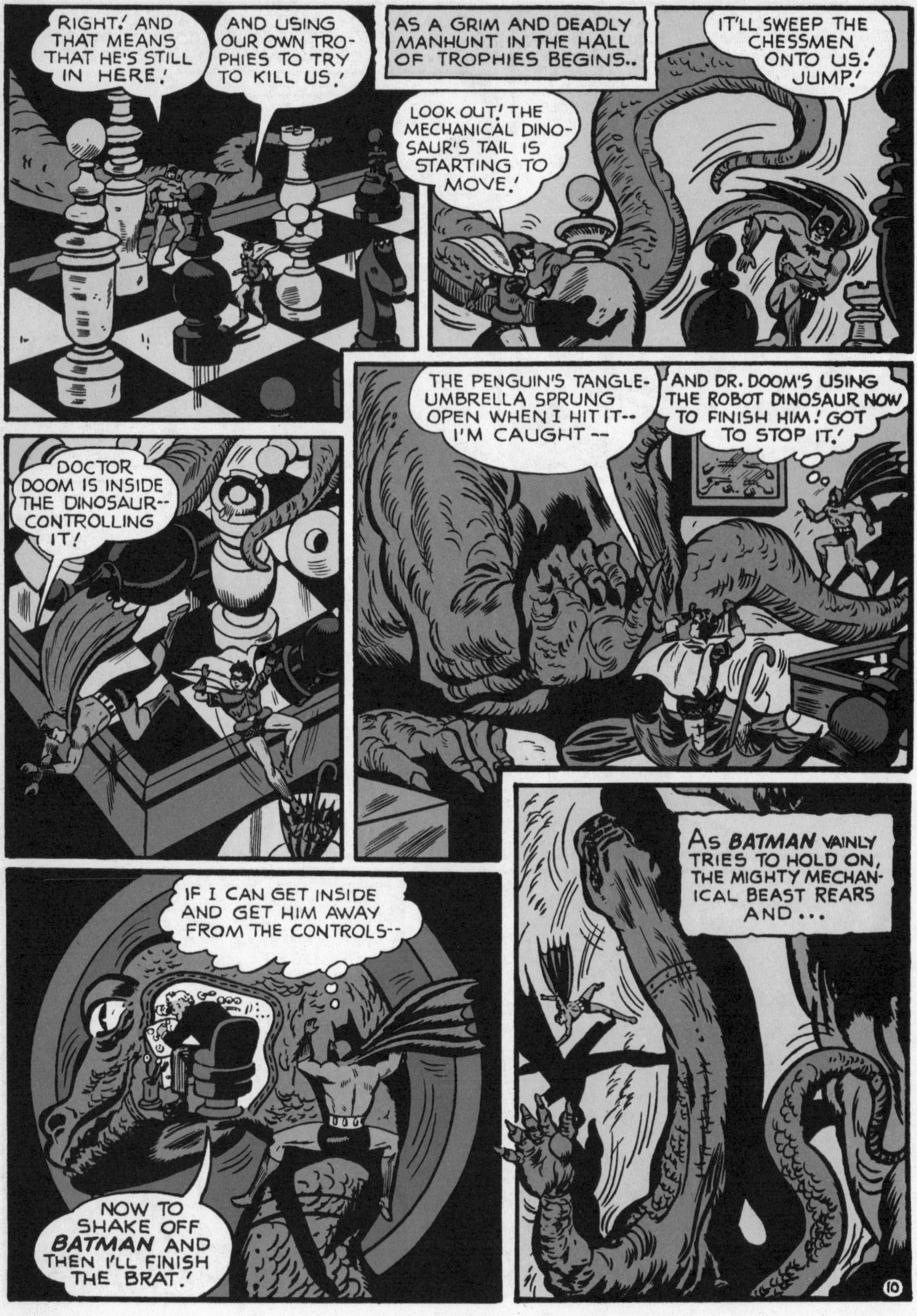
RIGHT! AND THAT MEANS THAT HE'S STILL IN HERE!
AND USING OUR OWN TROPHIES TO TRY TO KILL US!
AS A GRIM AND DEADLY MANHUNT IN THE HALL OF TROPHIES BEGINS..
LOOK OUT! THE MECHANICAL DINOSAUR'S TAIL IS STARTING TO MOVE!
IT'LL SWEEP THE CHESSMEN ONTO US! JUMP!
DOCTOR DOOM IS INSIDE THE DINOSAUR--CONTROLLING IT!
THE PENGUIN'S TANGLE-UMBRELLA SPRUNG OPEN WHEN I HIT IT--I'M CAUGHT--
AND DR. DOOM'S USING THE ROBOT DINOSAUR NOW TO FINISH HIM! GOT TO STOP IT!
IF I CAN GET INSIDE AND GET HIM AWAY FROM THE CONTROLS--
NOW TO SHAKE OFF BATMAN AND THEN I'LL FINISH THE BRAT!
AS BATMAN VAINLY TRIES TO HOLD ON, THE MIGHTY MECHANICAL BEAST REARS AND...
10

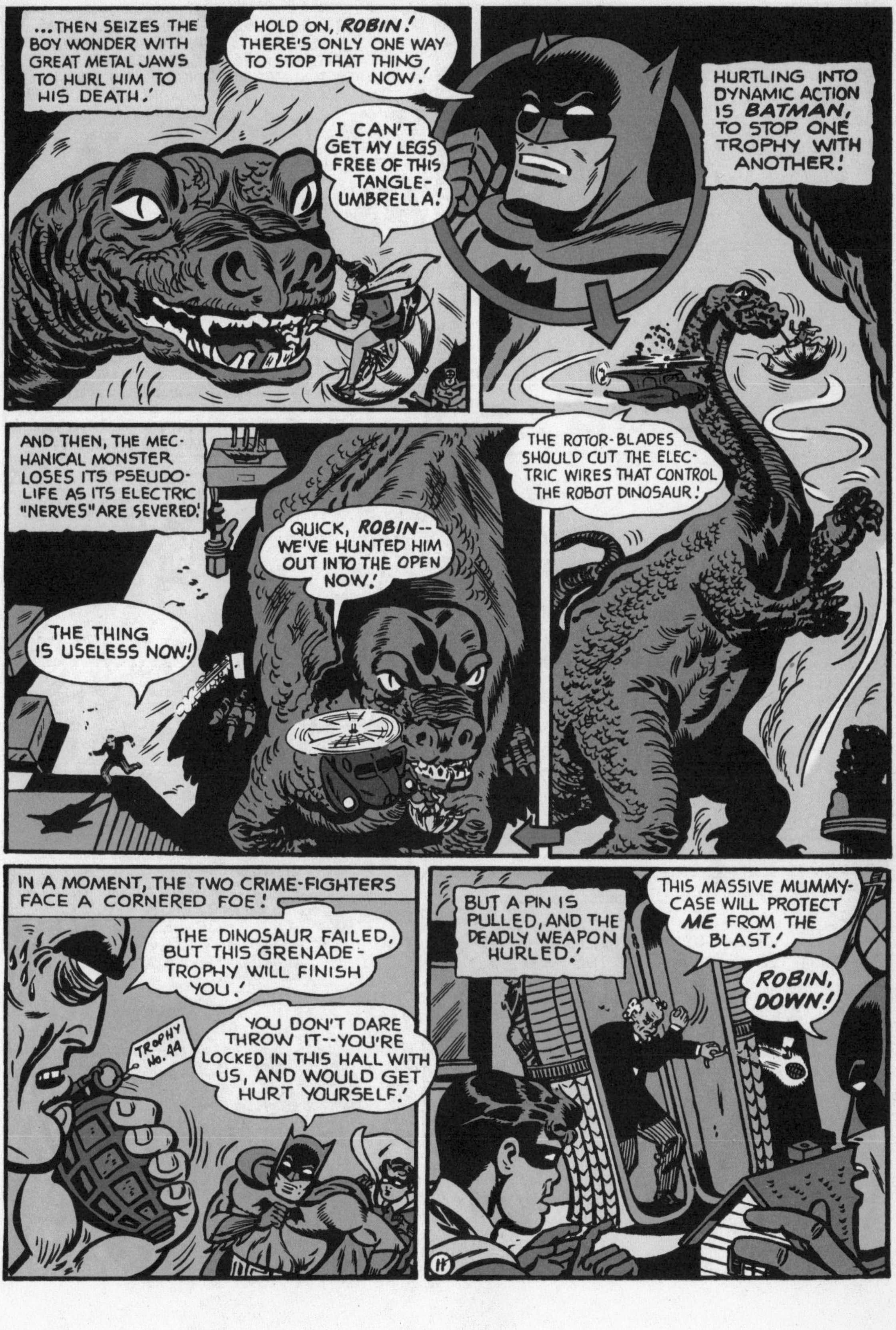
...THEN SEIZES THE BOY WONDER WITH GREAT METAL JAWS TO HURL HIM TO HIS DEATH!
HOLD ON, ROBIN! THERE'S ONLY ONE WAY TO STOP THAT THING NOW!
I CAN'T GET MY LEGS FREE OF THIS TANGLE-UMBRELLA!
HURTLING INTO DYNAMIC ACTION IS BATMAN, TO STOP ONE TROPHY WITH ANOTHER!
AND THEN, THE MECHANICAL MONSTER LOSES ITS PSEUDO-LIFE AS ITS ELECTRIC "NERVES" ARE SEVERED!
THE ROTOR-BLADES SHOULD CUT THE ELECTRIC WIRES THAT CONTROL THE ROBOT DINOSAUR!
QUICK, ROBIN-- WE'VE HUNTED HIM OUT INTO THE OPEN NOW!
THE THING IS USELESS NOW!
IN A MOMENT, THE TWO CRIME-FIGHTERS FACE A CORNERED FOE!
THE DINOSAUR FAILED, BUT THIS GRENADE-TROPHY WILL FINISH YOU!
TROPHY No. 44
YOU DON'T DARE THROW IT--YOU'RE LOCKED IN THIS HALL WITH US, AND WOULD GET HURT YOURSELF!
BUT A PIN IS PULLED, AND THE DEADLY WEAPON HURLED!
THIS MASSIVE MUMMY-CASE WILL PROTECT ME FROM THE BLAST!
ROBIN, DOWN!
11

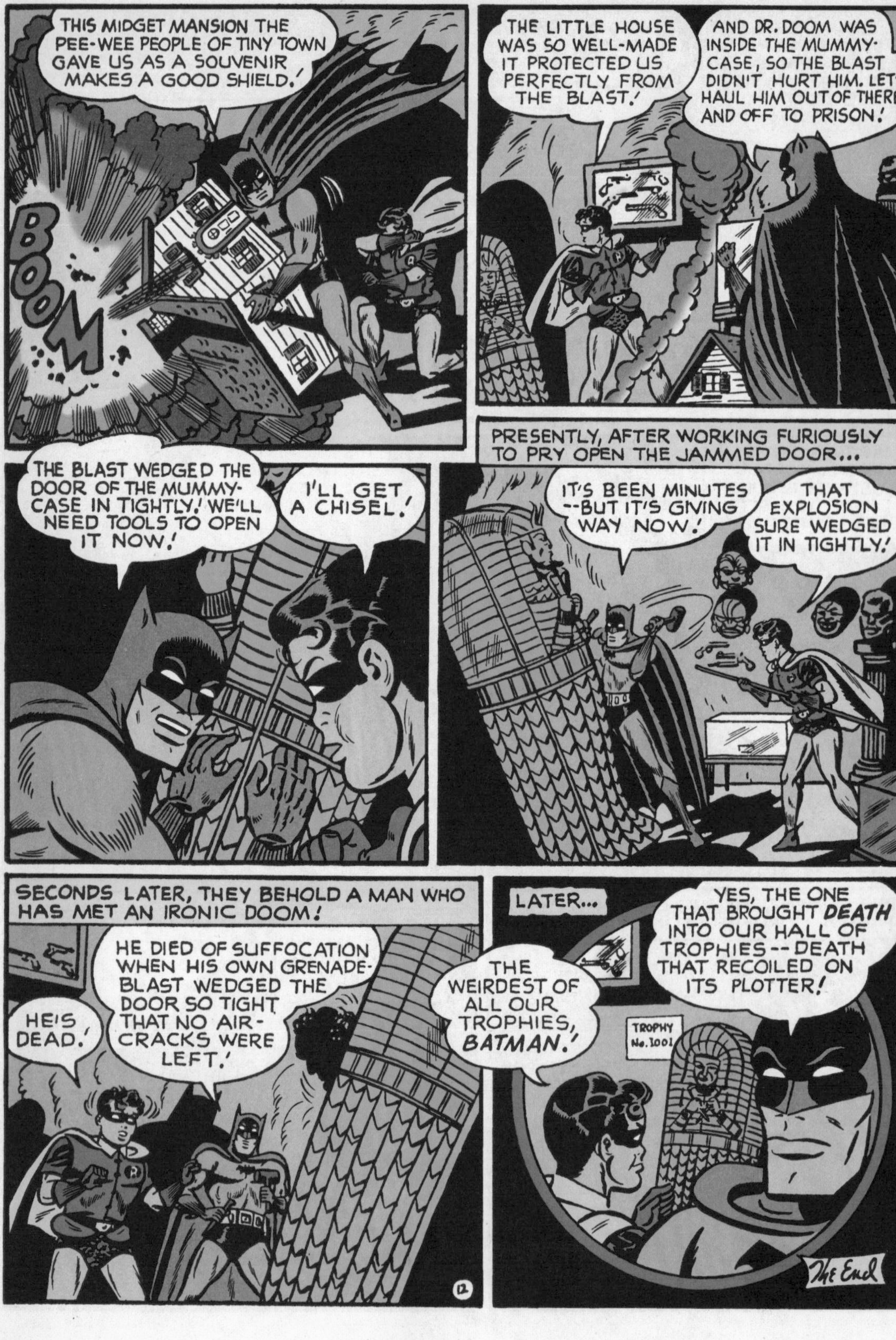
THIS MIDGET MANSION THE PEE-WEE PEOPLE OF TINY TOWN GAVE US AS A SOUVENIR MAKES A GOOD SHIELD!
BOOM
THE LITTLE HOUSE WAS SO WELL-MADE IT PROTECTED US PERFECTLY FROM THE BLAST!
AND DR. DOOM WAS INSIDE THE MUMMY-CASE, SO THE BLAST DIDN'T HURT HIM. LET'S HAUL HIM OUT OF THERE, AND OFF TO PRISON!
THE BLAST WEDGED THE DOOR OF THE MUMMY-CASE IN TIGHTLY! WE'LL NEED TOOLS TO OPEN IT NOW!
I'LL GET A CHISEL!
PRESENTLY, AFTER WORKING FURIOUSLY TO PRY OPEN THE JAMMED DOOR...
IT'S BEEN MINUTES --BUT IT'S GIVING WAY NOW!
THAT EXPLOSION SURE WEDGED IT IN TIGHTLY!
SECONDS LATER, THEY BEHOLD A MAN WHO HAS MET AN IRONIC DOOM!
HE'S DEAD!
HE DIED OF SUFFOCATION WHEN HIS OWN GRENADE-BLAST WEDGED THE DOOR SO TIGHT THAT NO AIR-CRACKS WERE LEFT!
12
LATER...
THE WEIRDEST OF ALL OUR TROPHIES, BATMAN!
YES, THE ONE THAT BROUGHT DEATH INTO OUR HALL OF TROPHIES -- DEATH THAT RECOILED ON ITS PLOTTER!
TROPHY No. 1001
The End

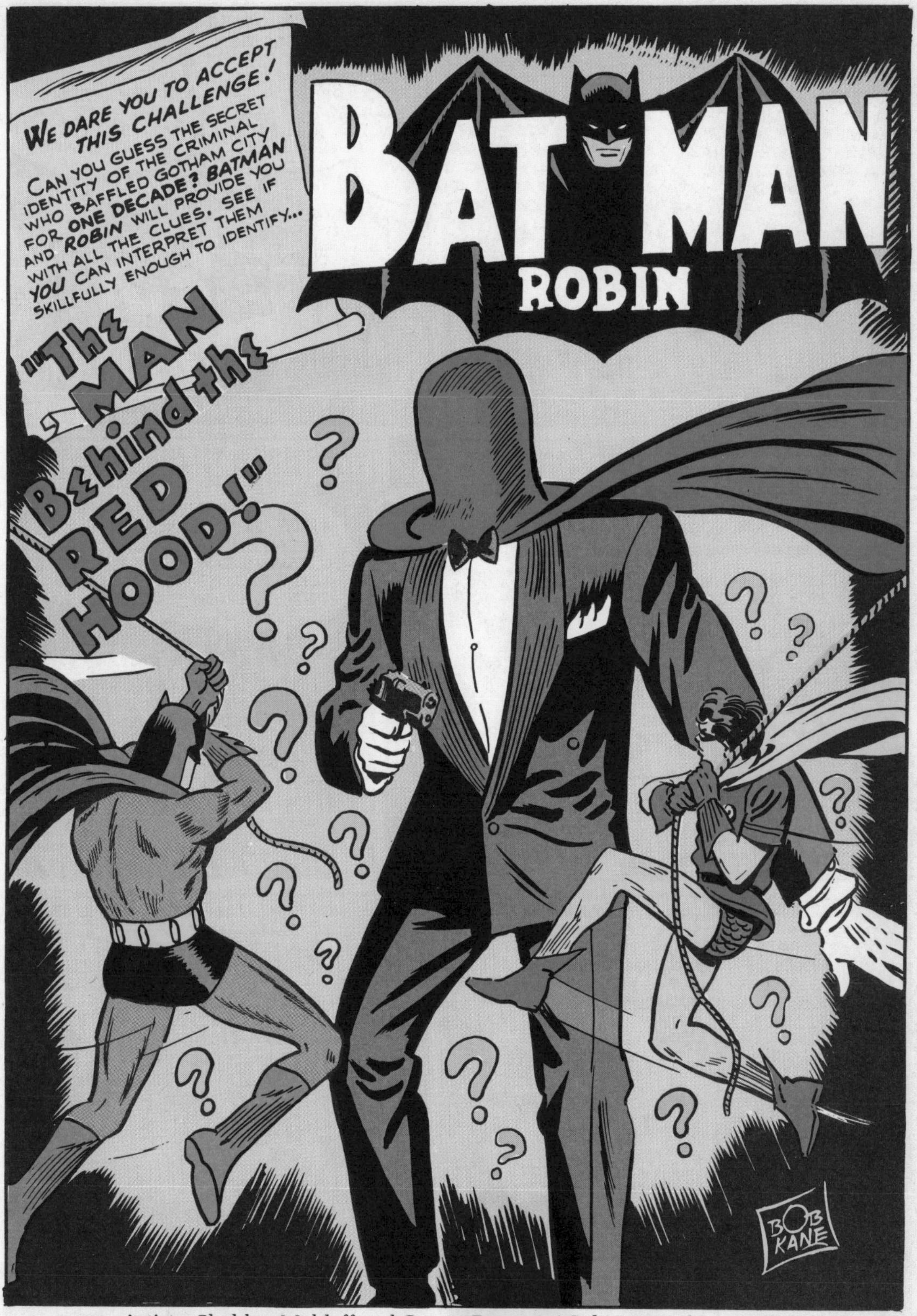
WE DARE YOU TO ACCEPT THIS CHALLENGE!
CAN YOU GUESS THE SECRET IDENTITY OF THE CRIMINAL WHO BAFFLED GOTHAM CITY FOR ONE DECADE? BATMAN AND ROBIN WILL PROVIDE YOU WITH ALL THE CLUES. SEE IF YOU CAN INTERPRET THEM SKILLFULLY ENOUGH TO IDENTIFY...
BATMAN
ROBIN
"The MAN Behind the RED HOOD!"
BOB KANE

Artists: Sheldon Moldoff and George Roussos / Colorist: Anthony Tollin

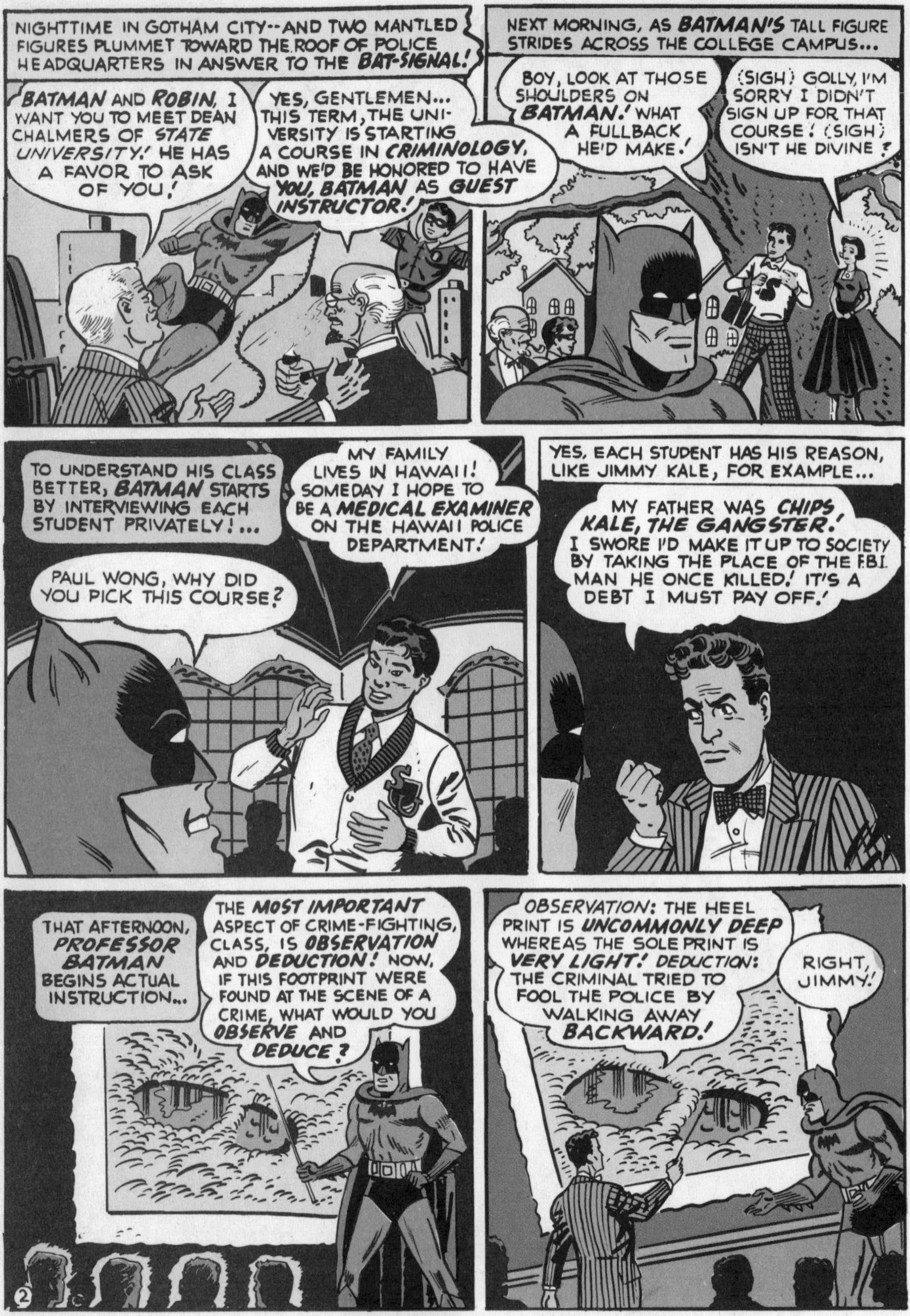

NIGHTTIME IN GOTHAM CITY--AND TWO MANTLED FIGURES PLUMMET TOWARD THE ROOF OF POLICE HEADQUARTERS IN ANSWER TO THE BAT-SIGNAL!
BATMAN AND ROBIN, I WANT YOU TO MEET DEAN CHALMERS OF STATE UNIVERSITY! HE HAS A FAVOR TO ASK OF YOU!
YES, GENTLEMEN... THIS TERM, THE UNIVERSITY IS STARTING A COURSE IN CRIMINOLOGY, AND WE'D BE HONORED TO HAVE YOU, BATMAN AS GUEST INSTRUCTOR!
NEXT MORNING, AS BATMAN'S TALL FIGURE STRIDES ACROSS THE COLLEGE CAMPUS...
BOY, LOOK AT THOSE SHOULDERS ON BATMAN! WHAT A FULLBACK HE'D MAKE!
(SIGH) GOLLY, I'M SORRY I DIDN'T SIGN UP FOR THAT COURSE! (SIGH) ISN'T HE DIVINE?
TO UNDERSTAND HIS CLASS BETTER, BATMAN STARTS BY INTERVIEWING EACH STUDENT PRIVATELY!...
PAUL WONG, WHY DID YOU PICK THIS COURSE?
MY FAMILY LIVES IN HAWAII! SOMEDAY I HOPE TO BE A MEDICAL EXAMINER ON THE HAWAII POLICE DEPARTMENT!
YES, EACH STUDENT HAS HIS REASON, LIKE JIMMY KALE, FOR EXAMPLE...
MY FATHER WAS CHIPS KALE, THE GANGSTER! I SWORE I'D MAKE IT UP TO SOCIETY BY TAKING THE PLACE OF THE F.B.I. MAN HE ONCE KILLED! IT'S A DEBT I MUST PAY OFF!
THAT AFTERNOON, PROFESSOR BATMAN BEGINS ACTUAL INSTRUCTION...
THE MOST IMPORTANT ASPECT OF CRIME-FIGHTING, CLASS, IS OBSERVATION AND DEDUCTION! NOW, IF THIS FOOTPRINT WERE FOUND AT THE SCENE OF A CRIME, WHAT WOULD YOU OBSERVE AND DEDUCE?
2
OBSERVATION: THE HEEL PRINT IS UNCOMMONLY DEEP WHEREAS THE SOLE PRINT IS VERY LIGHT! DEDUCTION: THE CRIMINAL TRIED TO FOOL THE POLICE BY WALKING AWAY BACKWARD!
RIGHT, JIMMY!

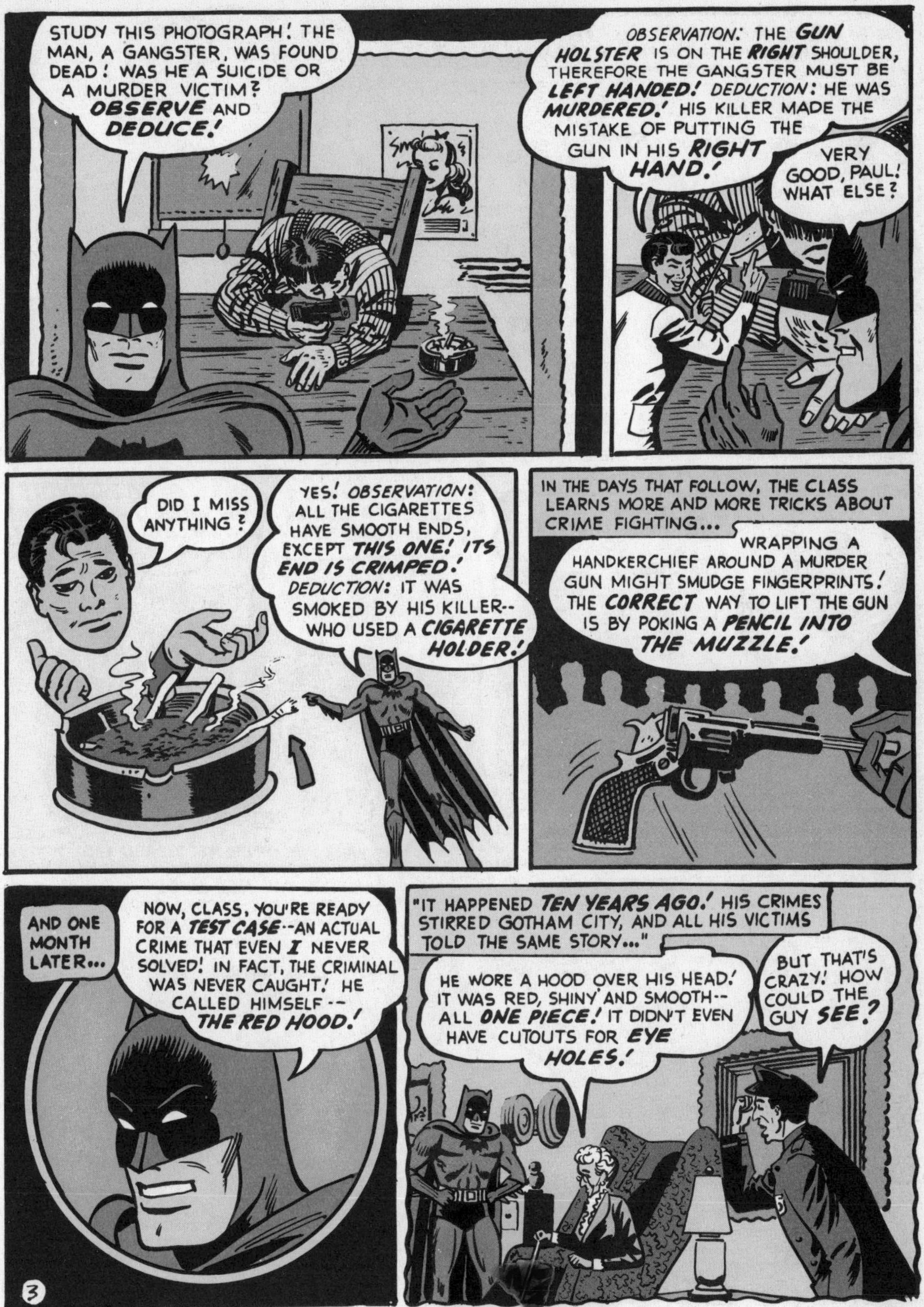
STUDY THIS PHOTOGRAPH! THE MAN, A GANGSTER, WAS FOUND DEAD! WAS HE A SUICIDE OR A MURDER VICTIM? OBSERVE AND DEDUCE!
OBSERVATION: THE GUN HOLSTER IS ON THE RIGHT SHOULDER, THEREFORE THE GANGSTER MUST BE LEFT HANDED! DEDUCTION: HE WAS MURDERED! HIS KILLER MADE THE MISTAKE OF PUTTING THE GUN IN HIS RIGHT HAND!
VERY GOOD, PAUL! WHAT ELSE?
DID I MISS ANYTHING?
YES! OBSERVATION: ALL THE CIGARETTES HAVE SMOOTH ENDS, EXCEPT THIS ONE! ITS END IS CRIMPED! DEDUCTION: IT WAS SMOKED BY HIS KILLER-- WHO USED A CIGARETTE HOLDER!
IN THE DAYS THAT FOLLOW, THE CLASS LEARNS MORE AND MORE TRICKS ABOUT CRIME FIGHTING...
WRAPPING A HANDKERCHIEF AROUND A MURDER GUN MIGHT SMUDGE FINGERPRINTS! THE CORRECT WAY TO LIFT THE GUN IS BY POKING A PENCIL INTO THE MUZZLE!
AND ONE MONTH LATER...
NOW, CLASS, YOU'RE READY FOR A TEST CASE--AN ACTUAL CRIME THAT EVEN I NEVER SOLVED! IN FACT, THE CRIMINAL WAS NEVER CAUGHT! HE CALLED HIMSELF -- THE RED HOOD!
3
"IT HAPPENED TEN YEARS AGO! HIS CRIMES STIRRED GOTHAM CITY, AND ALL HIS VICTIMS TOLD THE SAME STORY..."
HE WORE A HOOD OVER HIS HEAD! IT WAS RED, SHINY AND SMOOTH-- ALL ONE PIECE! IT DIDN'T EVEN HAVE CUTOUTS FOR EYE HOLES!
BUT THAT'S CRAZY! HOW COULD THE GUY SEE?

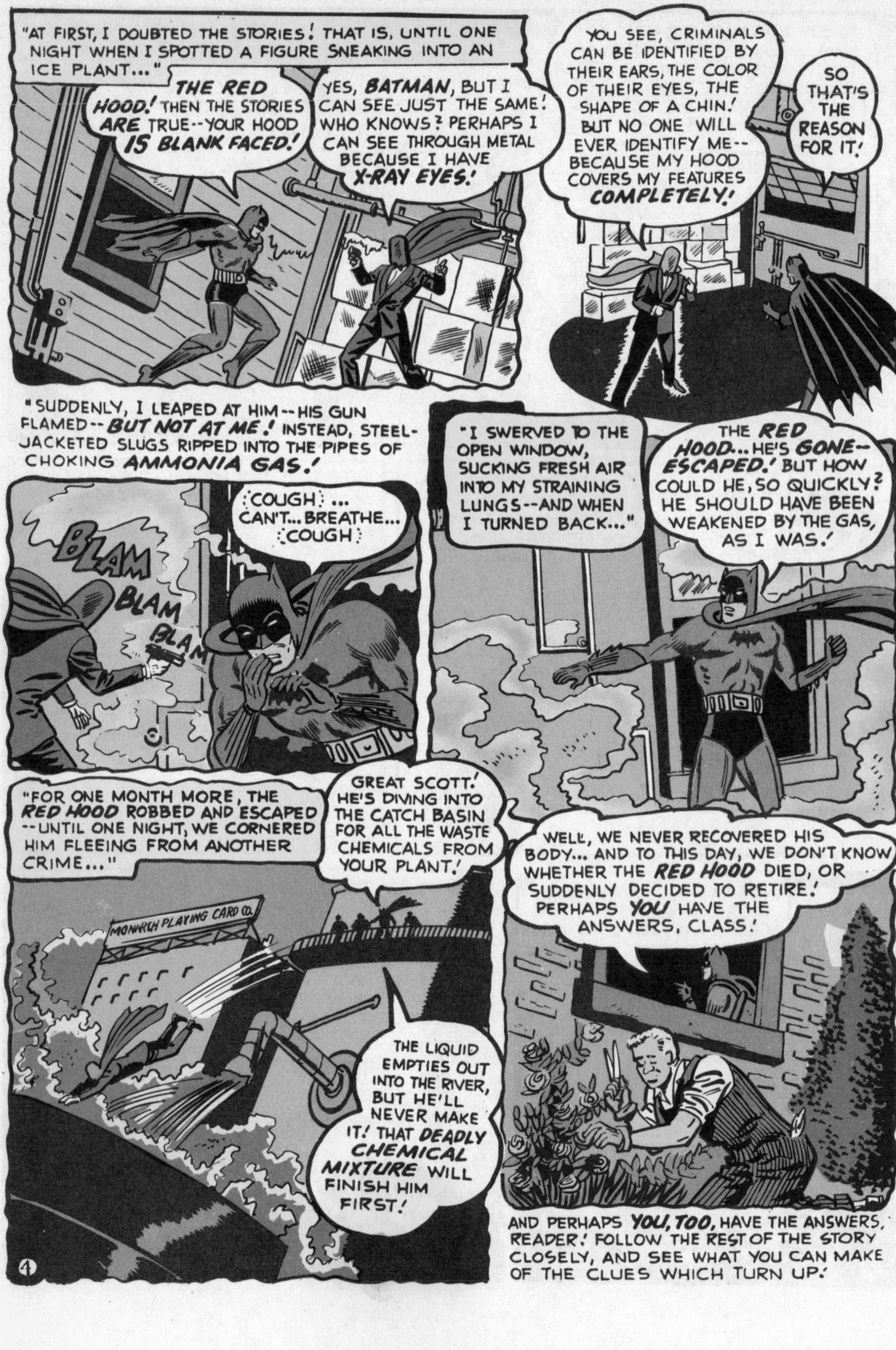
"AT FIRST, I DOUBTED THE STORIES! THAT IS, UNTIL ONE NIGHT WHEN I SPOTTED A FIGURE SNEAKING INTO AN ICE PLANT..."
THE RED HOOD! THEN THE STORIES ARE TRUE--YOUR HOOD IS BLANK FACED!
YES, BATMAN, BUT I CAN SEE JUST THE SAME! WHO KNOWS? PERHAPS I CAN SEE THROUGH METAL BECAUSE I HAVE X-RAY EYES!
YOU SEE, CRIMINALS CAN BE IDENTIFIED BY THEIR EARS, THE COLOR OF THEIR EYES, THE SHAPE OF A CHIN! BUT NO ONE WILL EVER IDENTIFY ME--BECAUSE MY HOOD COVERS MY FEATURES COMPLETELY!
SO THAT'S THE REASON FOR IT!
"SUDDENLY, I LEAPED AT HIM--HIS GUN FLAMED--BUT NOT AT ME! INSTEAD, STEEL-JACKETED SLUGS RIPPED INTO THE PIPES OF CHOKING AMMONIA GAS!
BLAM
BLAM
BLAM
COUGH ... CAN'T... BREATHE... COUGH
"I SWERVED TO THE OPEN WINDOW, SUCKING FRESH AIR INTO MY STRAINING LUNGS--AND WHEN I TURNED BACK..."
THE RED HOOD... HE'S GONE--ESCAPED! BUT HOW COULD HE, SO QUICKLY? HE SHOULD HAVE BEEN WEAKENED BY THE GAS, AS I WAS!
"FOR ONE MONTH MORE, THE RED HOOD ROBBED AND ESCAPED--UNTIL ONE NIGHT, WE CORNERED HIM FLEEING FROM ANOTHER CRIME..."
GREAT SCOTT! HE'S DIVING INTO THE CATCH BASIN FOR ALL THE WASTE CHEMICALS FROM YOUR PLANT!
MONARCH PLAYING CARD CO.
THE LIQUID EMPTIES OUT INTO THE RIVER, BUT HE'LL NEVER MAKE IT! THAT DEADLY CHEMICAL MIXTURE WILL FINISH HIM FIRST!
4
WELL, WE NEVER RECOVERED HIS BODY... AND TO THIS DAY, WE DON'T KNOW WHETHER THE RED HOOD DIED, OR SUDDENLY DECIDED TO RETIRE! PERHAPS YOU HAVE THE ANSWERS, CLASS!
AND PERHAPS YOU, TOO, HAVE THE ANSWERS, READER! FOLLOW THE REST OF THE STORY CLOSELY, AND SEE WHAT YOU CAN MAKE OF THE CLUES WHICH TURN UP!

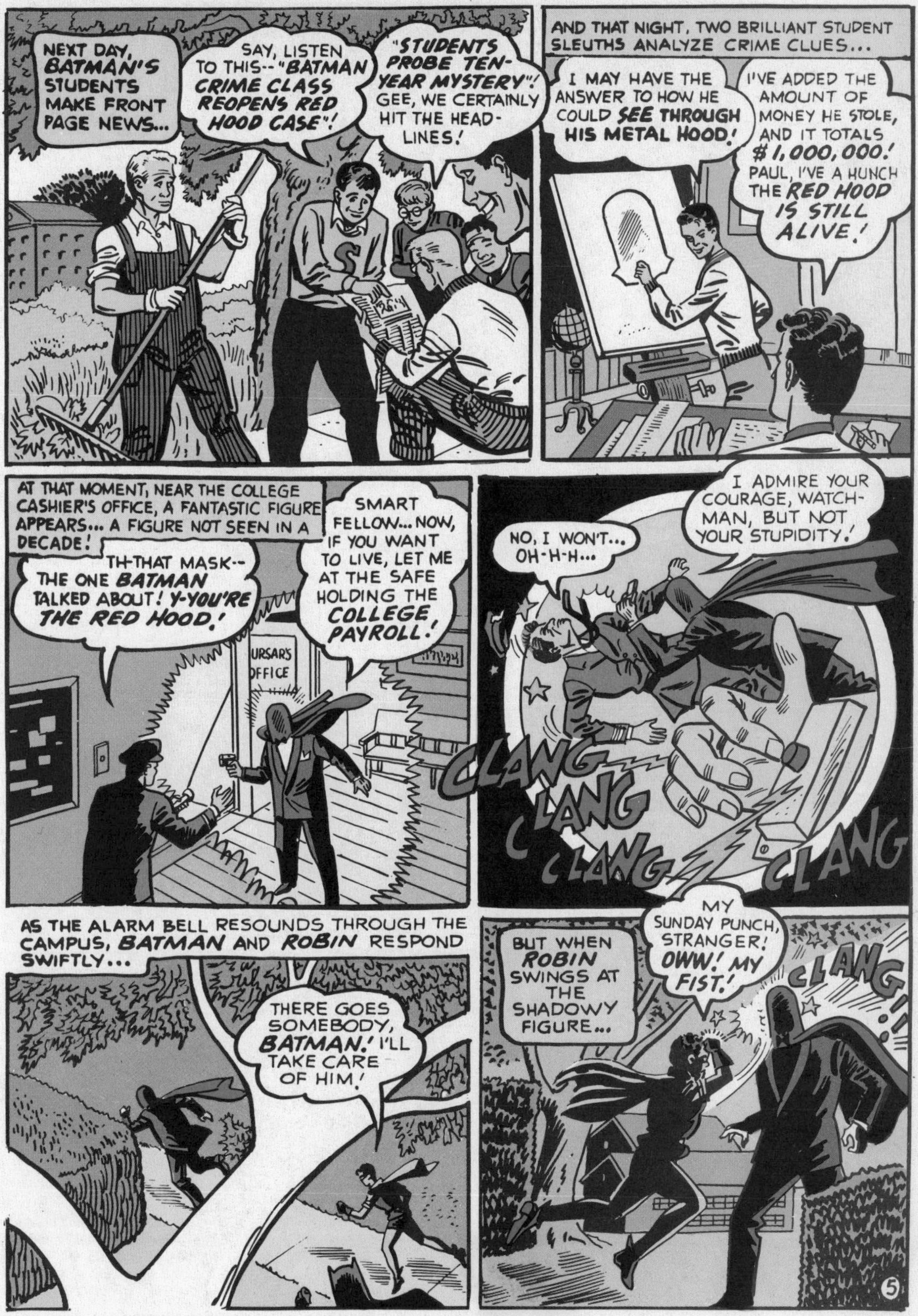
NEXT DAY, BATMAN'S STUDENTS MAKE FRONT PAGE NEWS...
SAY, LISTEN TO THIS-- "BATMAN CRIME CLASS REOPENS RED HOOD CASE"!
"STUDENTS PROBE TEN-YEAR MYSTERY"! GEE, WE CERTAINLY HIT THE HEADLINES!
AND THAT NIGHT, TWO BRILLIANT STUDENT SLEUTHS ANALYZE CRIME CLUES...
I MAY HAVE THE ANSWER TO HOW HE COULD SEE THROUGH HIS METAL HOOD!
I'VE ADDED THE AMOUNT OF MONEY HE STOLE, AND IT TOTALS $1,000,000! PAUL, I'VE A HUNCH THE RED HOOD IS STILL ALIVE!
AT THAT MOMENT, NEAR THE COLLEGE CASHIER'S OFFICE, A FANTASTIC FIGURE APPEARS... A FIGURE NOT SEEN IN A DECADE!
TH-THAT MASK-- THE ONE BATMAN TALKED ABOUT! Y-YOU'RE THE RED HOOD!
SMART FELLOW... NOW, IF YOU WANT TO LIVE, LET ME AT THE SAFE HOLDING THE COLLEGE PAYROLL!
URSAR'S OFFICE
NO, I WON'T... OH-H-H...
I ADMIRE YOUR COURAGE, WATCHMAN, BUT NOT YOUR STUPIDITY!
CLANG CLANG CLANG CLANG
AS THE ALARM BELL RESOUNDS THROUGH THE CAMPUS, BATMAN AND ROBIN RESPOND SWIFTLY...
THERE GOES SOMEBODY, BATMAN! I'LL TAKE CARE OF HIM!
BUT WHEN ROBIN SWINGS AT THE SHADOWY FIGURE...
MY SUNDAY PUNCH, STRANGER! OWW! MY FIST!
CLANG!!
5

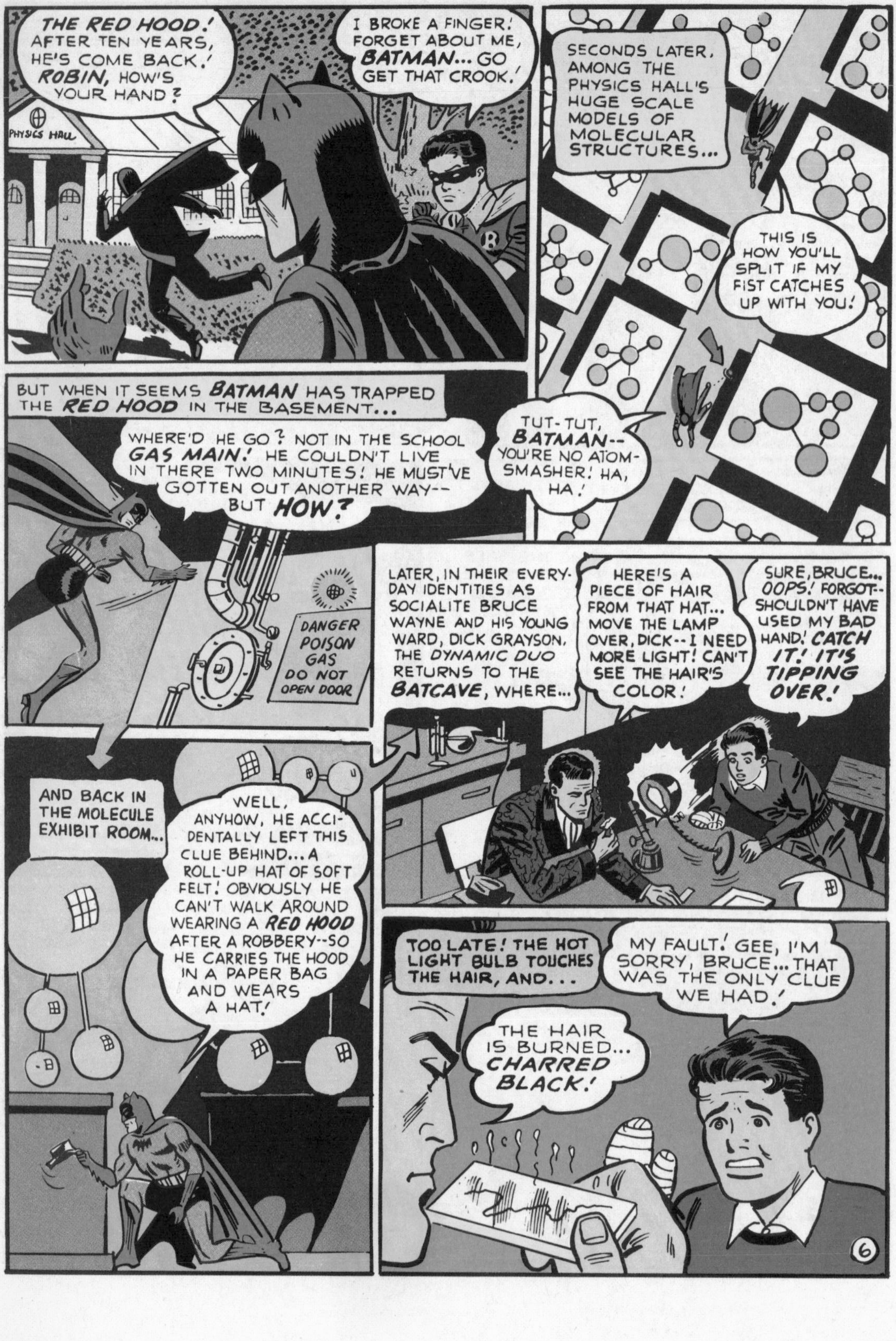

THE RED HOOD! AFTER TEN YEARS, HE'S COME BACK! ROBIN, HOW'S YOUR HAND?
PHYSICS HALL
I BROKE A FINGER! FORGET ABOUT ME, BATMAN... GO GET THAT CROOK!
SECONDS LATER, AMONG THE PHYSICS HALL'S HUGE SCALE MODELS OF MOLECULAR STRUCTURES...
THIS IS HOW YOU'LL SPLIT IF MY FIST CATCHES UP WITH YOU!
TUT-TUT, BATMAN-- YOU'RE NO ATOM-SMASHER! HA, HA!
BUT WHEN IT SEEMS BATMAN HAS TRAPPED THE RED HOOD IN THE BASEMENT...
WHERE'D HE GO? NOT IN THE SCHOOL GAS MAIN! HE COULDN'T LIVE IN THERE TWO MINUTES! HE MUST'VE GOTTEN OUT ANOTHER WAY-- BUT HOW?
DANGER POISON GAS DO NOT OPEN DOOR
AND BACK IN THE MOLECULE EXHIBIT ROOM...
WELL, ANYHOW, HE ACCIDENTALLY LEFT THIS CLUE BEHIND... A ROLL-UP HAT OF SOFT FELT! OBVIOUSLY HE CAN'T WALK AROUND WEARING A RED HOOD AFTER A ROBBERY--SO HE CARRIES THE HOOD IN A PAPER BAG AND WEARS A HAT!
LATER, IN THEIR EVERY-DAY IDENTITIES AS SOCIALITE BRUCE WAYNE AND HIS YOUNG WARD, DICK GRAYSON, THE DYNAMIC DUO RETURNS TO THE BATCAVE, WHERE...
HERE'S A PIECE OF HAIR FROM THAT HAT... MOVE THE LAMP OVER, DICK-- I NEED MORE LIGHT! CAN'T SEE THE HAIR'S COLOR!
SURE, BRUCE... OOPS! FORGOT-- SHOULDN'T HAVE USED MY BAD HAND! CATCH IT! IT'S TIPPING OVER!
TOO LATE! THE HOT LIGHT BULB TOUCHES THE HAIR, AND...
MY FAULT! GEE, I'M SORRY, BRUCE... THAT WAS THE ONLY CLUE WE HAD!
THE HAIR IS BURNED... CHARRED BLACK!
6

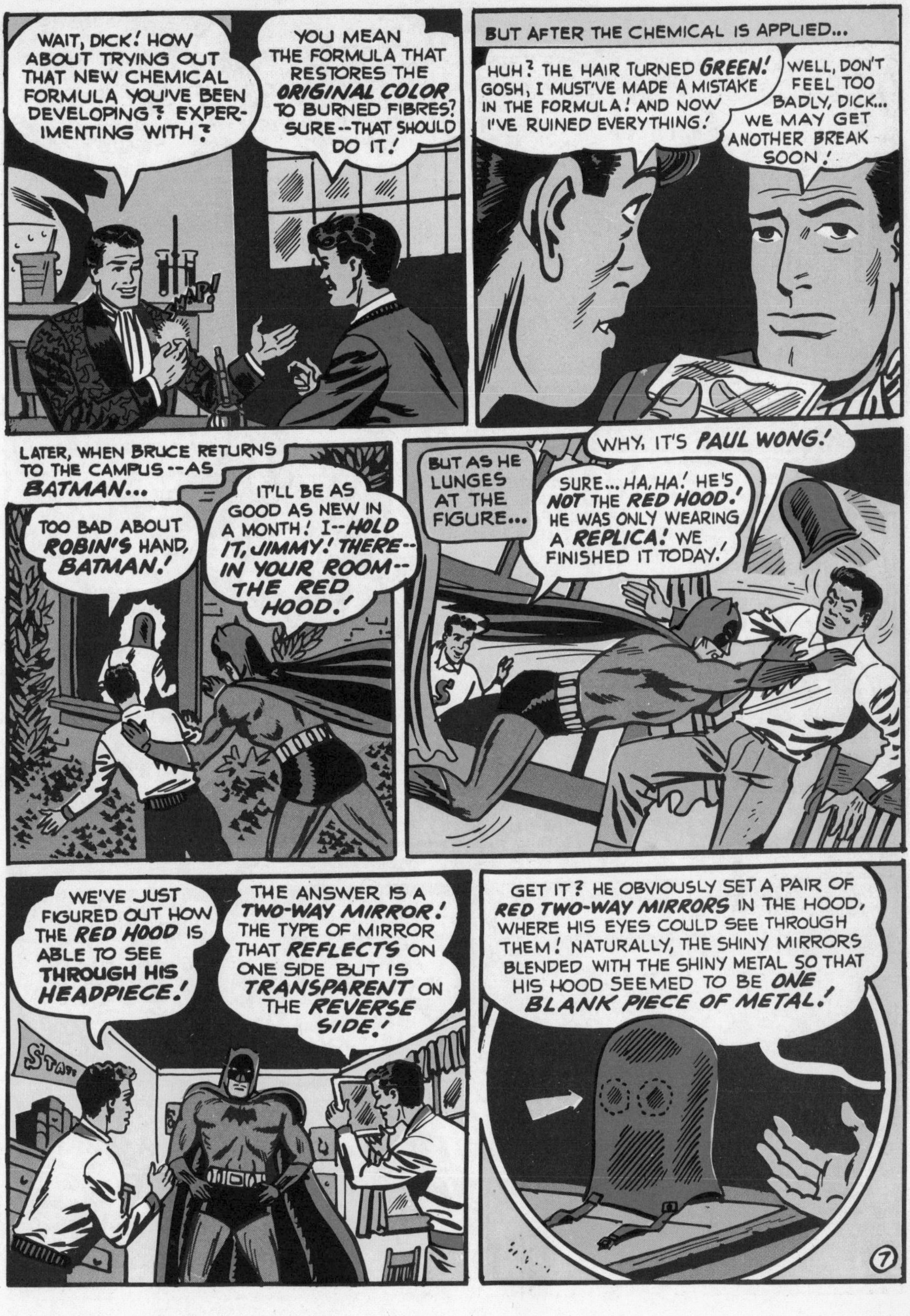
WAIT, DICK! HOW ABOUT TRYING OUT THAT NEW CHEMICAL FORMULA YOU'VE BEEN DEVELOPING? EXPERIMENTING WITH?
YOU MEAN THE FORMULA THAT RESTORES THE ORIGINAL COLOR TO BURNED FIBRES? SURE--THAT SHOULD DO IT!
SNAP!
BUT AFTER THE CHEMICAL IS APPLIED...
HUH? THE HAIR TURNED GREEN! GOSH, I MUST'VE MADE A MISTAKE IN THE FORMULA! AND NOW I'VE RUINED EVERYTHING!
WELL, DON'T FEEL TOO BADLY, DICK... WE MAY GET ANOTHER BREAK SOON!
LATER, WHEN BRUCE RETURNS TO THE CAMPUS--AS BATMAN...
TOO BAD ABOUT ROBIN'S HAND, BATMAN!
IT'LL BE AS GOOD AS NEW IN A MONTH! I--HOLD IT, JIMMY! THERE--IN YOUR ROOM--THE RED HOOD!
BUT AS HE LUNGES AT THE FIGURE...
WHY, IT'S PAUL WONG!
SURE... HA, HA! HE'S NOT THE RED HOOD! HE WAS ONLY WEARING A REPLICA! WE FINISHED IT TODAY!
WE'VE JUST FIGURED OUT HOW THE RED HOOD IS ABLE TO SEE THROUGH HIS HEADPIECE!
THE ANSWER IS A TWO-WAY MIRROR! THE TYPE OF MIRROR THAT REFLECTS ON ONE SIDE BUT IS TRANSPARENT ON THE REVERSE SIDE!
GET IT? HE OBVIOUSLY SET A PAIR OF RED TWO-WAY MIRRORS IN THE HOOD, WHERE HIS EYES COULD SEE THROUGH THEM! NATURALLY, THE SHINY MIRRORS BLENDED WITH THE SHINY METAL SO THAT HIS HOOD SEEMED TO BE ONE BLANK PIECE OF METAL!
7

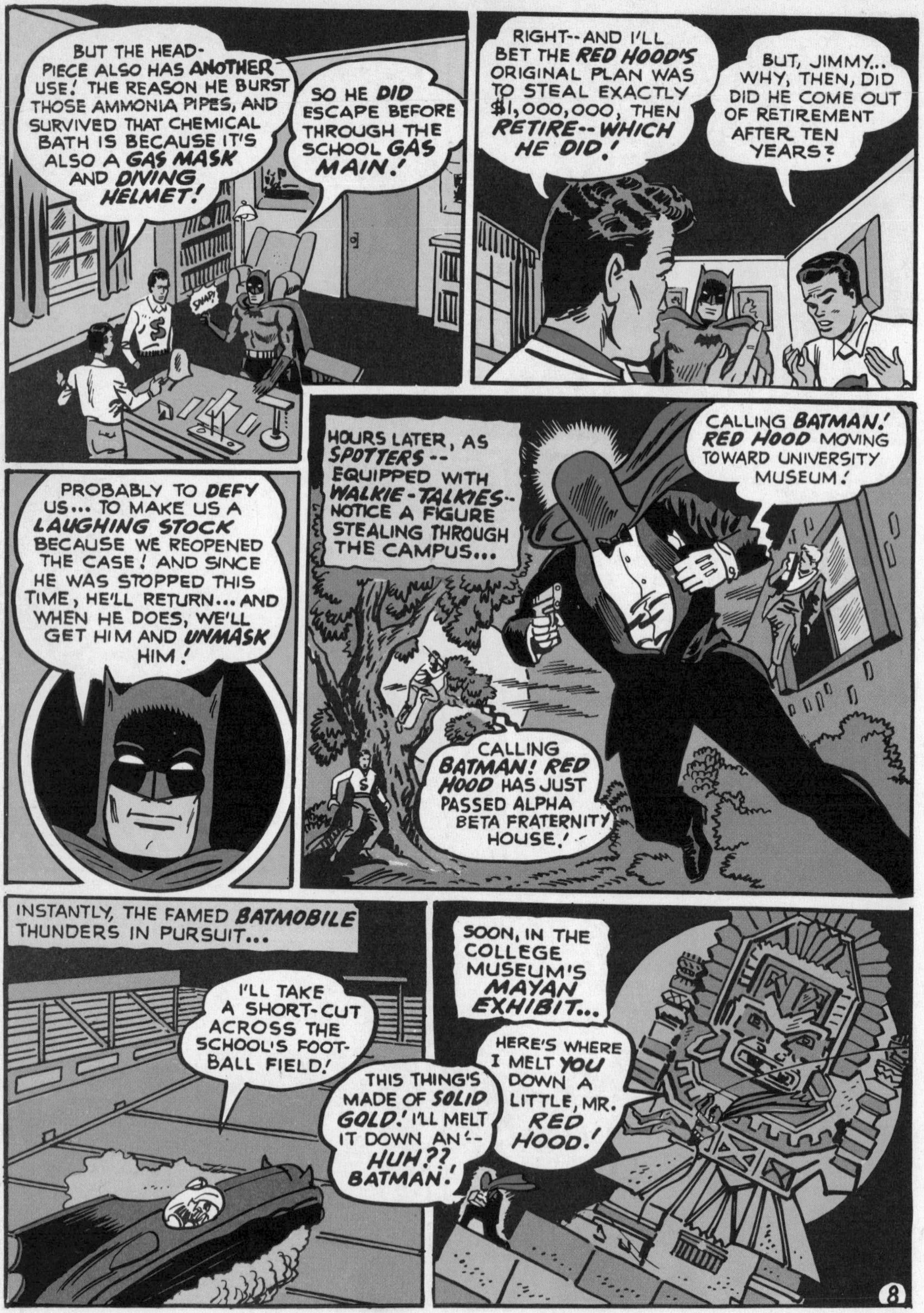

BUT THE HEAD-PIECE ALSO HAS ANOTHER USE! THE REASON HE BURST THOSE AMMONIA PIPES, AND SURVIVED THAT CHEMICAL BATH IS BECAUSE IT'S ALSO A GAS MASK AND DIVING HELMET!
SO HE DID ESCAPE BEFORE THROUGH THE SCHOOL GAS MAIN!
SNAP!
RIGHT--AND I'LL BET THE RED HOOD'S ORIGINAL PLAN WAS TO STEAL EXACTLY $1,000,000, THEN RETIRE--WHICH HE DID!
BUT, JIMMY... WHY, THEN, DID HE COME OUT OF RETIREMENT AFTER TEN YEARS?
PROBABLY TO DEFY US... TO MAKE US A LAUGHING STOCK BECAUSE WE REOPENED THE CASE! AND SINCE HE WAS STOPPED THIS TIME, HE'LL RETURN... AND WHEN HE DOES, WE'LL GET HIM AND UNMASK HIM!
HOURS LATER, AS SPOTTERS -- EQUIPPED WITH WALKIE-TALKIES -- NOTICE A FIGURE STEALING THROUGH THE CAMPUS...
CALLING BATMAN! RED HOOD MOVING TOWARD UNIVERSITY MUSEUM!
CALLING BATMAN! RED HOOD HAS JUST PASSED ALPHA BETA FRATERNITY HOUSE!
INSTANTLY, THE FAMED BATMOBILE THUNDERS IN PURSUIT...
I'LL TAKE A SHORT-CUT ACROSS THE SCHOOL'S FOOT-BALL FIELD!
SOON, IN THE COLLEGE MUSEUM'S MAYAN EXHIBIT...
THIS THING'S MADE OF SOLID GOLD! I'LL MELT IT DOWN AN'-- HUH?? BATMAN!
HERE'S WHERE I MELT YOU DOWN A LITTLE, MR. RED HOOD!
8

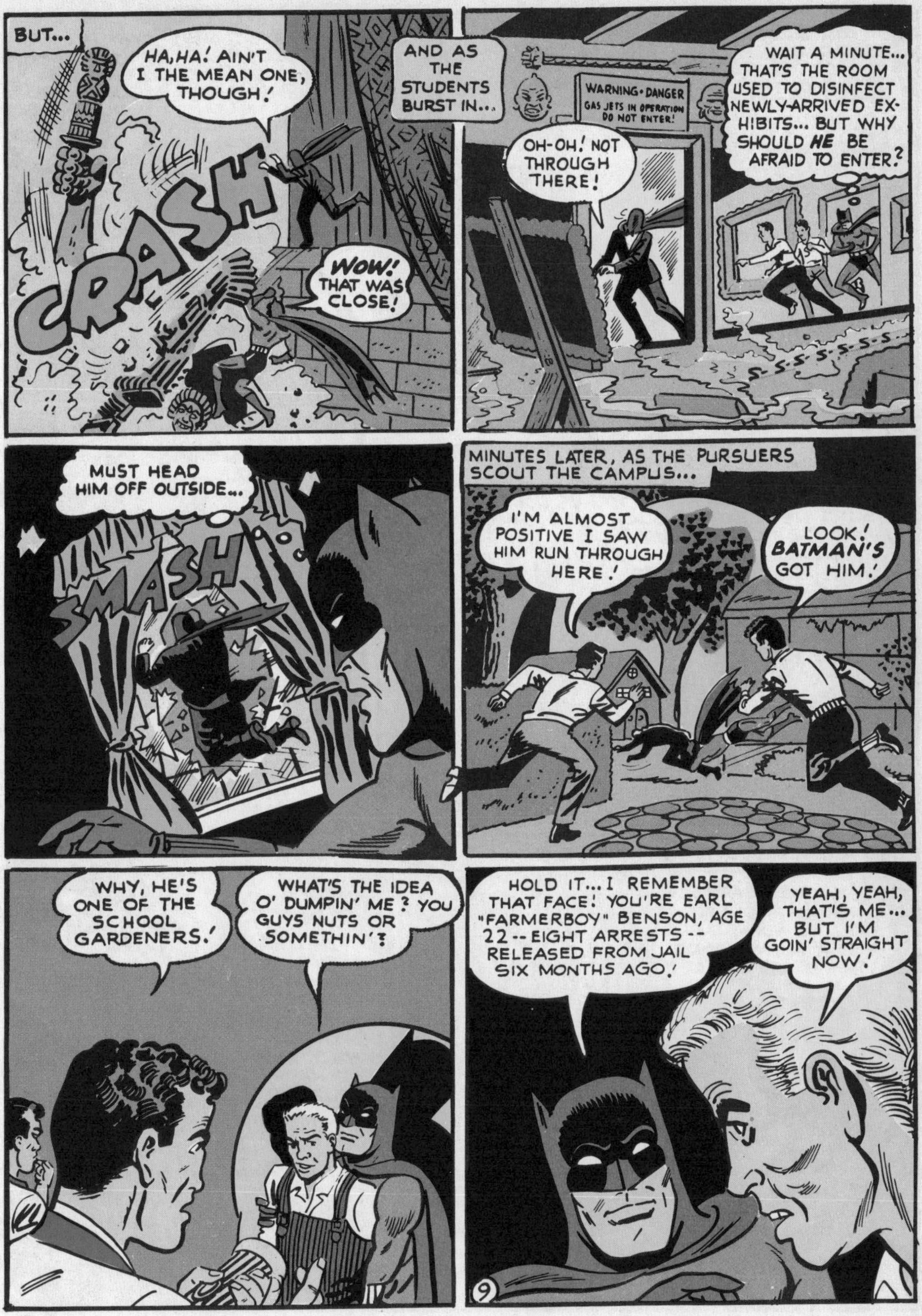
BUT...
HA, HA! AIN'T I THE MEAN ONE, THOUGH!
CRASH
WOW! THAT WAS CLOSE!
AND AS THE STUDENTS BURST IN...
WARNING • DANGER GAS JETS IN OPERATION DO NOT ENTER!
OH-OH! NOT THROUGH THERE!
WAIT A MINUTE... THAT'S THE ROOM USED TO DISINFECT NEWLY-ARRIVED EXHIBITS... BUT WHY SHOULD HE BE AFRAID TO ENTER?
S-S-S-S-S-S-S
MUST HEAD HIM OFF OUTSIDE...
SMASH
MINUTES LATER, AS THE PURSUERS SCOUT THE CAMPUS...
I'M ALMOST POSITIVE I SAW HIM RUN THROUGH HERE!
LOOK! BATMAN'S GOT HIM!
WHY, HE'S ONE OF THE SCHOOL GARDENERS!
WHAT'S THE IDEA O' DUMPIN' ME? YOU GUYS NUTS OR SOMETHIN'?
HOLD IT... I REMEMBER THAT FACE! YOU'RE EARL "FARMERBOY" BENSON, AGE 22 -- EIGHT ARRESTS -- RELEASED FROM JAIL SIX MONTHS AGO!
YEAH, YEAH, THAT'S ME... BUT I'M GOIN' STRAIGHT NOW!
9

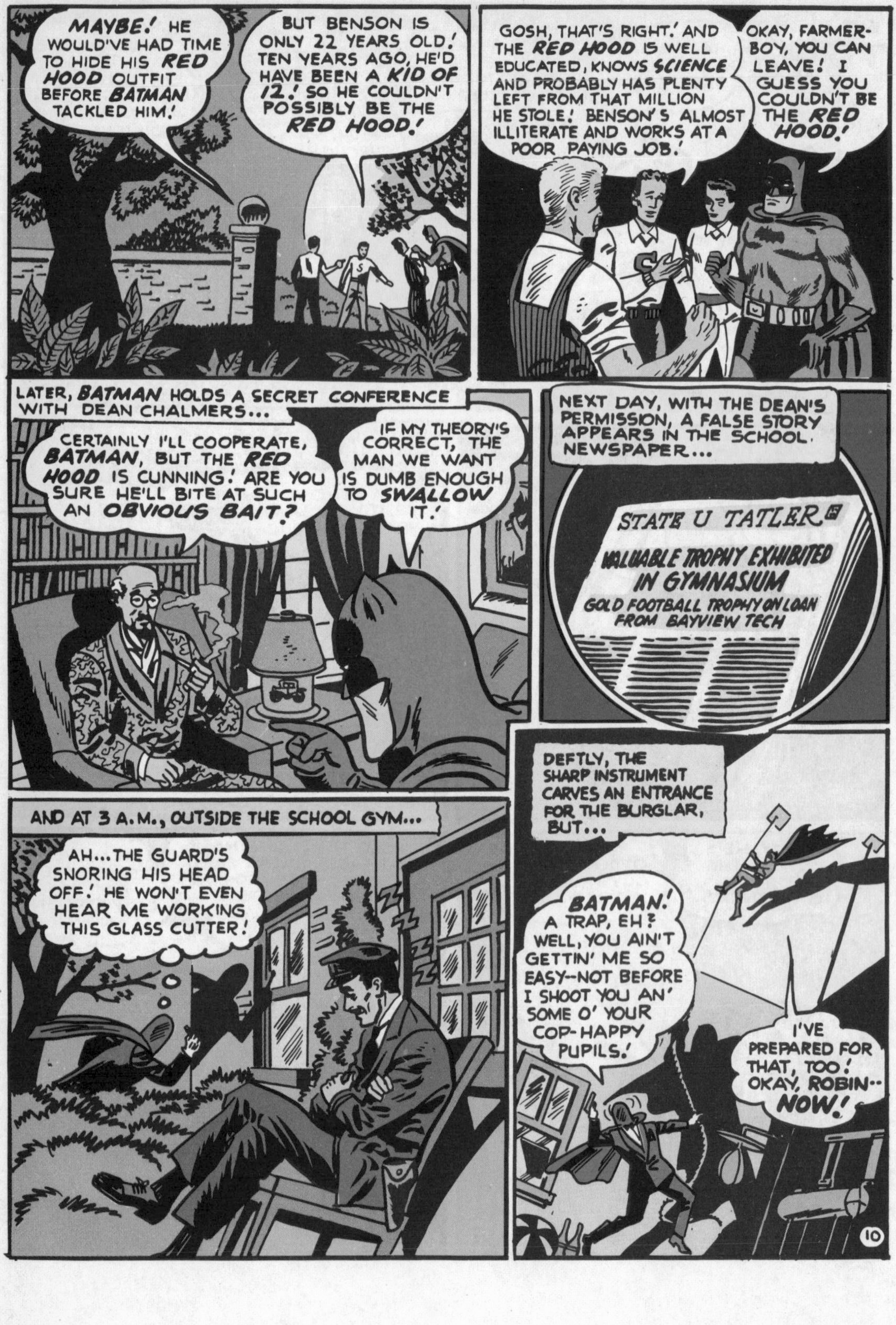
MAYBE! HE WOULD'VE HAD TIME TO HIDE HIS RED HOOD OUTFIT BEFORE BATMAN TACKLED HIM!
BUT BENSON IS ONLY 22 YEARS OLD! TEN YEARS AGO, HE'D HAVE BEEN A KID OF 12! SO HE COULDN'T POSSIBLY BE THE RED HOOD!
GOSH, THAT'S RIGHT! AND THE RED HOOD IS WELL EDUCATED, KNOWS SCIENCE AND PROBABLY HAS PLENTY LEFT FROM THAT MILLION HE STOLE! BENSON'S ALMOST ILLITERATE AND WORKS AT A POOR PAYING JOB!
OKAY, FARMER-BOY, YOU CAN LEAVE! I GUESS YOU COULDN'T BE THE RED HOOD!
LATER, BATMAN HOLDS A SECRET CONFERENCE WITH DEAN CHALMERS...
CERTAINLY I'LL COOPERATE, BATMAN, BUT THE RED HOOD IS CUNNING! ARE YOU SURE HE'LL BITE AT SUCH AN OBVIOUS BAIT?
IF MY THEORY'S CORRECT, THE MAN WE WANT IS DUMB ENOUGH TO SWALLOW IT!
NEXT DAY, WITH THE DEAN'S PERMISSION, A FALSE STORY APPEARS IN THE SCHOOL NEWSPAPER...
STATE U TATLER
VALUABLE TROPHY EXHIBITED IN GYMNASIUM
GOLD FOOTBALL TROPHY ON LOAN FROM BAYVIEW TECH
AND AT 3 A.M., OUTSIDE THE SCHOOL GYM...
AH...THE GUARD'S SNORING HIS HEAD OFF! HE WON'T EVEN HEAR ME WORKING THIS GLASS CUTTER!
DEFTLY, THE SHARP INSTRUMENT CARVES AN ENTRANCE FOR THE BURGLAR, BUT...
BATMAN! A TRAP, EH? WELL, YOU AIN'T GETTIN' ME SO EASY--NOT BEFORE I SHOOT YOU AN' SOME O' YOUR COP-HAPPY PUPILS!
I'VE PREPARED FOR THAT, TOO! OKAY, ROBIN-- NOW!
10

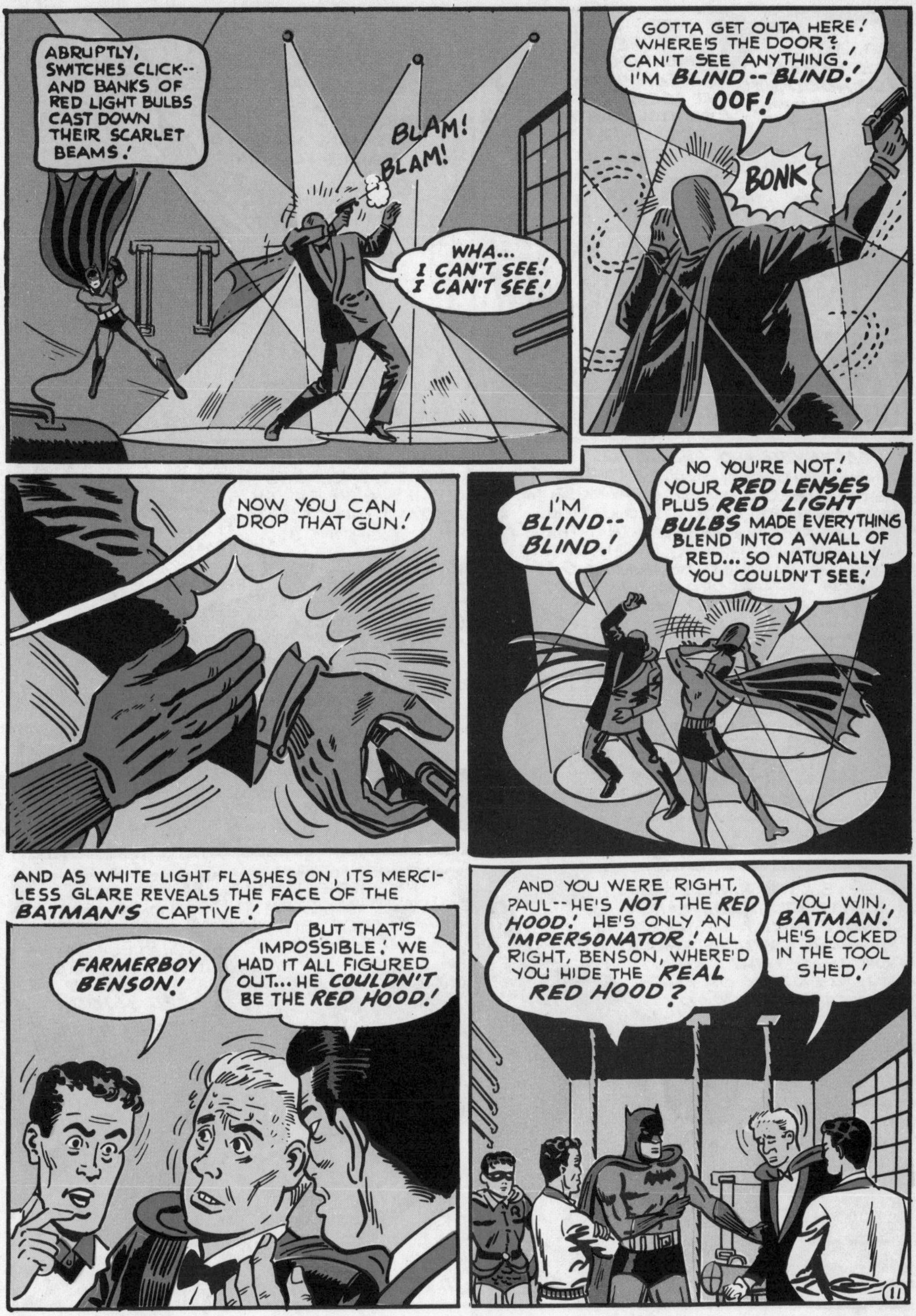
ABRUPTLY, SWITCHES CLICK-- AND BANKS OF RED LIGHT BULBS CAST DOWN THEIR SCARLET BEAMS!
BLAM! BLAM!
WHA... I CAN'T SEE! I CAN'T SEE!
GOTTA GET OUTA HERE! WHERE'S THE DOOR? CAN'T SEE ANYTHING! I'M BLIND -- BLIND! OOF!
BONK
NOW YOU CAN DROP THAT GUN!
I'M BLIND-- BLIND!
NO YOU'RE NOT! YOUR RED LENSES PLUS RED LIGHT BULBS MADE EVERYTHING BLEND INTO A WALL OF RED... SO NATURALLY YOU COULDN'T SEE!
AND AS WHITE LIGHT FLASHES ON, ITS MERCILESS GLARE REVEALS THE FACE OF THE BATMAN'S CAPTIVE!
FARMERBOY BENSON!
BUT THAT'S IMPOSSIBLE! WE HAD IT ALL FIGURED OUT... HE COULDN'T BE THE RED HOOD!
AND YOU WERE RIGHT, PAUL--HE'S NOT THE RED HOOD! HE'S ONLY AN IMPERSONATOR! ALL RIGHT, BENSON, WHERE'D YOU HIDE THE REAL RED HOOD?
YOU WIN, BATMAN! HE'S LOCKED IN THE TOOL SHED!
11

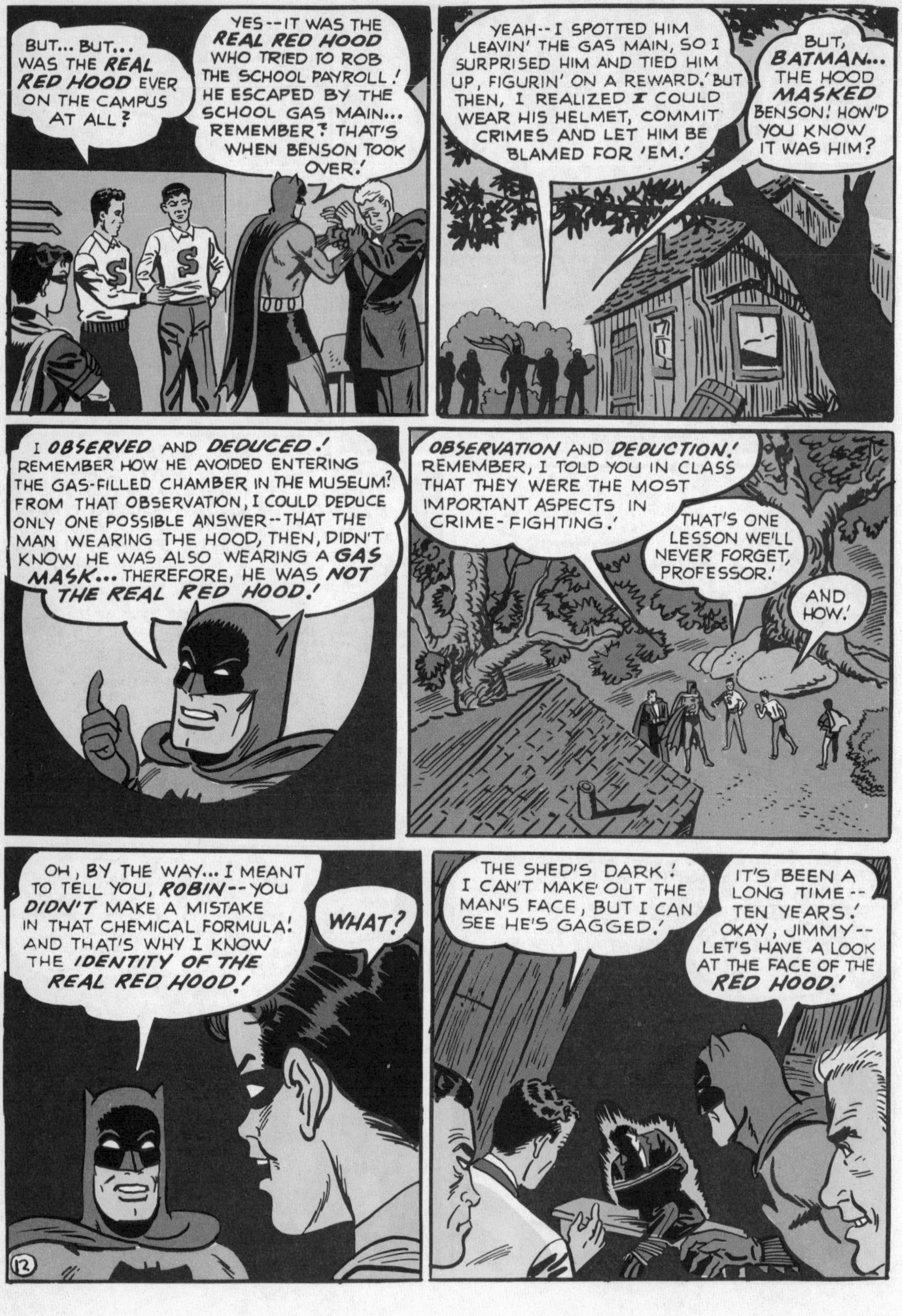
BUT... BUT... WAS THE REAL RED HOOD EVER ON THE CAMPUS AT ALL?
YES--IT WAS THE REAL RED HOOD WHO TRIED TO ROB THE SCHOOL PAYROLL! HE ESCAPED BY THE SCHOOL GAS MAIN... REMEMBER? THAT'S WHEN BENSON TOOK OVER!
YEAH--I SPOTTED HIM LEAVIN' THE GAS MAIN, SO I SURPRISED HIM AND TIED HIM UP, FIGURIN' ON A REWARD! BUT THEN, I REALIZED I COULD WEAR HIS HELMET, COMMIT CRIMES AND LET HIM BE BLAMED FOR 'EM!
BUT, BATMAN... THE HOOD MASKED BENSON! HOW'D YOU KNOW IT WAS HIM?
I OBSERVED AND DEDUCED! REMEMBER HOW HE AVOIDED ENTERING THE GAS-FILLED CHAMBER IN THE MUSEUM? FROM THAT OBSERVATION, I COULD DEDUCE ONLY ONE POSSIBLE ANSWER--THAT THE MAN WEARING THE HOOD, THEN, DIDN'T KNOW HE WAS ALSO WEARING A GAS MASK... THEREFORE, HE WAS NOT THE REAL RED HOOD!
OBSERVATION AND DEDUCTION! REMEMBER, I TOLD YOU IN CLASS THAT THEY WERE THE MOST IMPORTANT ASPECTS IN CRIME-FIGHTING!
THAT'S ONE LESSON WE'LL NEVER FORGET, PROFESSOR!
AND HOW!
OH, BY THE WAY... I MEANT TO TELL YOU, ROBIN--YOU DIDN'T MAKE A MISTAKE IN THAT CHEMICAL FORMULA! AND THAT'S WHY I KNOW THE IDENTITY OF THE REAL RED HOOD!
WHAT?
12
THE SHED'S DARK! I CAN'T MAKE OUT THE MAN'S FACE, BUT I CAN SEE HE'S GAGGED!
IT'S BEEN A LONG TIME--TEN YEARS! OKAY, JIMMY--LET'S HAVE A LOOK AT THE FACE OF THE RED HOOD!

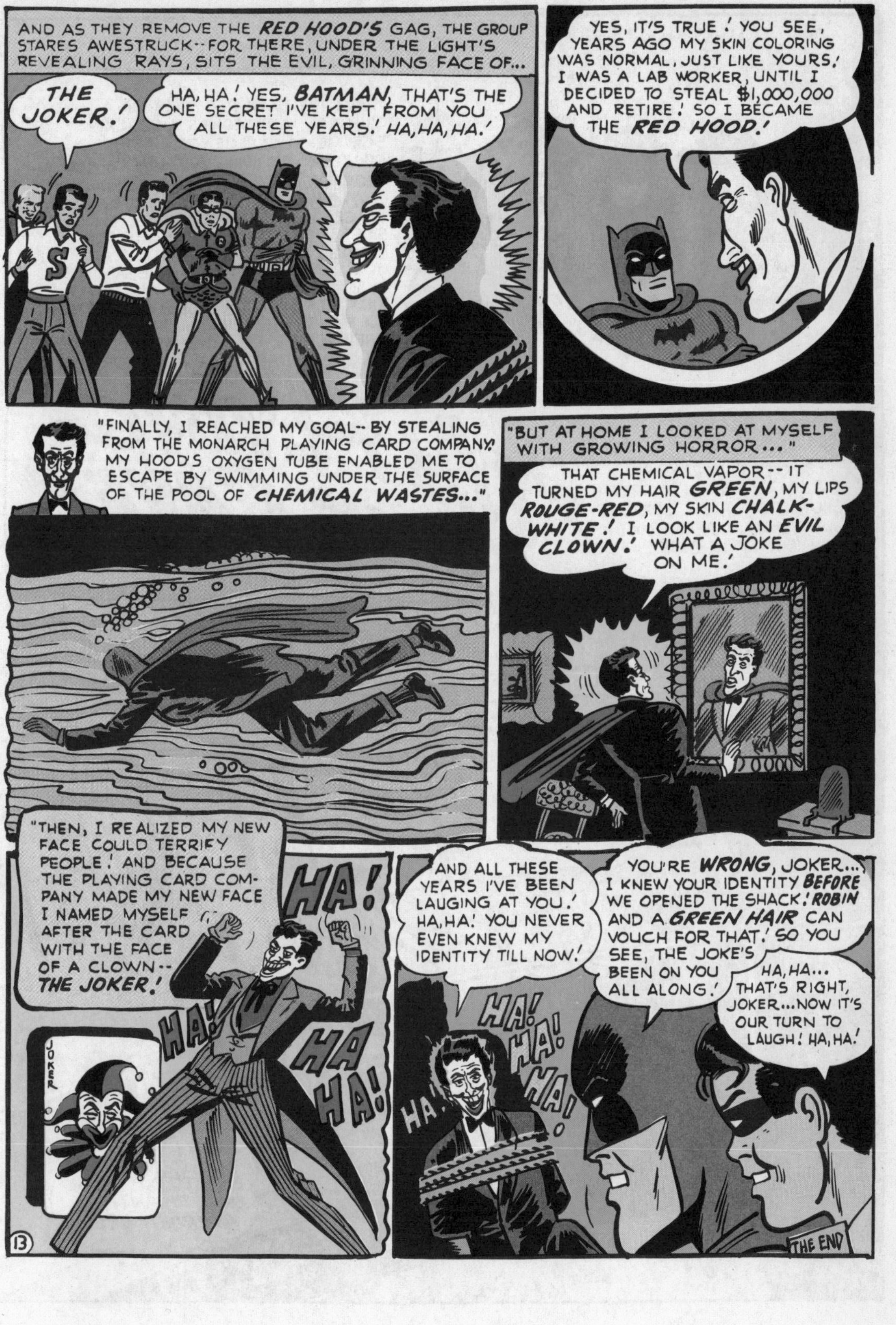
AND AS THEY REMOVE THE RED HOOD'S GAG, THE GROUP STARES AWESTRUCK--FOR THERE, UNDER THE LIGHT'S REVEALING RAYS, SITS THE EVIL, GRINNING FACE OF...
THE JOKER!
HA, HA! YES, BATMAN, THAT'S THE ONE SECRET I'VE KEPT FROM YOU ALL THESE YEARS! HA, HA, HA!
YES, IT'S TRUE! YOU SEE, YEARS AGO MY SKIN COLORING WAS NORMAL, JUST LIKE YOURS! I WAS A LAB WORKER, UNTIL I DECIDED TO STEAL $1,000,000 AND RETIRE! SO I BECAME THE RED HOOD!
"FINALLY, I REACHED MY GOAL-- BY STEALING FROM THE MONARCH PLAYING CARD COMPANY! MY HOOD'S OXYGEN TUBE ENABLED ME TO ESCAPE BY SWIMMING UNDER THE SURFACE OF THE POOL OF CHEMICAL WASTES..."
"BUT AT HOME I LOOKED AT MYSELF WITH GROWING HORROR..."
THAT CHEMICAL VAPOR-- IT TURNED MY HAIR GREEN, MY LIPS ROUGE-RED, MY SKIN CHALK-WHITE! I LOOK LIKE AN EVIL CLOWN! WHAT A JOKE ON ME!
"THEN, I REALIZED MY NEW FACE COULD TERRIFY PEOPLE! AND BECAUSE THE PLAYING CARD COMPANY MADE MY NEW FACE I NAMED MYSELF AFTER THE CARD WITH THE FACE OF A CLOWN-- THE JOKER!
HA! HA! HA HA HA!
JOKER
13
AND ALL THESE YEARS I'VE BEEN LAUGHING AT YOU! HA, HA! YOU NEVER EVEN KNEW MY IDENTITY TILL NOW!
YOU'RE WRONG, JOKER... I KNEW YOUR IDENTITY BEFORE WE OPENED THE SHACK! ROBIN AND A GREEN HAIR CAN VOUCH FOR THAT! SO YOU SEE, THE JOKE'S BEEN ON YOU ALL ALONG!
HA, HA... THAT'S RIGHT, JOKER... NOW IT'S OUR TURN TO LAUGH! HA, HA!
HA! HA! HA! HA!
THE END

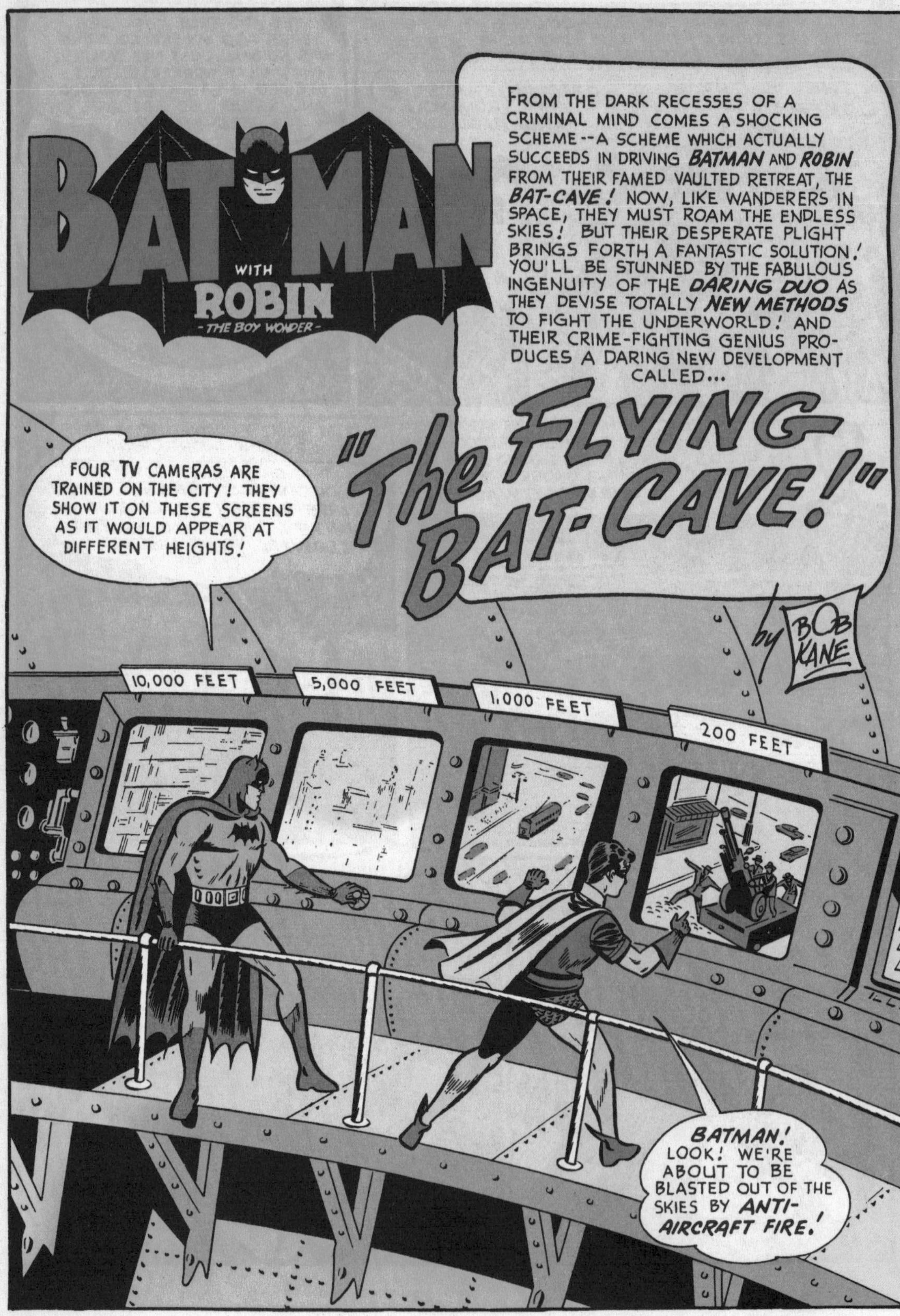
BATMAN WITH ROBIN -THE BOY WONDER-
FROM THE DARK RECESSES OF A CRIMINAL MIND COMES A SHOCKING SCHEME--A SCHEME WHICH ACTUALLY SUCCEEDS IN DRIVING BATMAN AND ROBIN FROM THEIR FAMED VAULTED RETREAT, THE BAT-CAVE! NOW, LIKE WANDERERS IN SPACE, THEY MUST ROAM THE ENDLESS SKIES! BUT THEIR DESPERATE PLIGHT BRINGS FORTH A FANTASTIC SOLUTION! YOU'LL BE STUNNED BY THE FABULOUS INGENUITY OF THE DARING DUO AS THEY DEVISE TOTALLY NEW METHODS TO FIGHT THE UNDERWORLD! AND THEIR CRIME-FIGHTING GENIUS PRODUCES A DARING NEW DEVELOPMENT CALLED...
"The FLYING BAT-CAVE!"
by BOB KANE
FOUR TV CAMERAS ARE TRAINED ON THE CITY! THEY SHOW IT ON THESE SCREENS AS IT WOULD APPEAR AT DIFFERENT HEIGHTS!
10,000 FEET
5,000 FEET
1,000 FEET
200 FEET
BATMAN! LOOK! WE'RE ABOUT TO BE BLASTED OUT OF THE SKIES BY ANTI-AIRCRAFT FIRE!

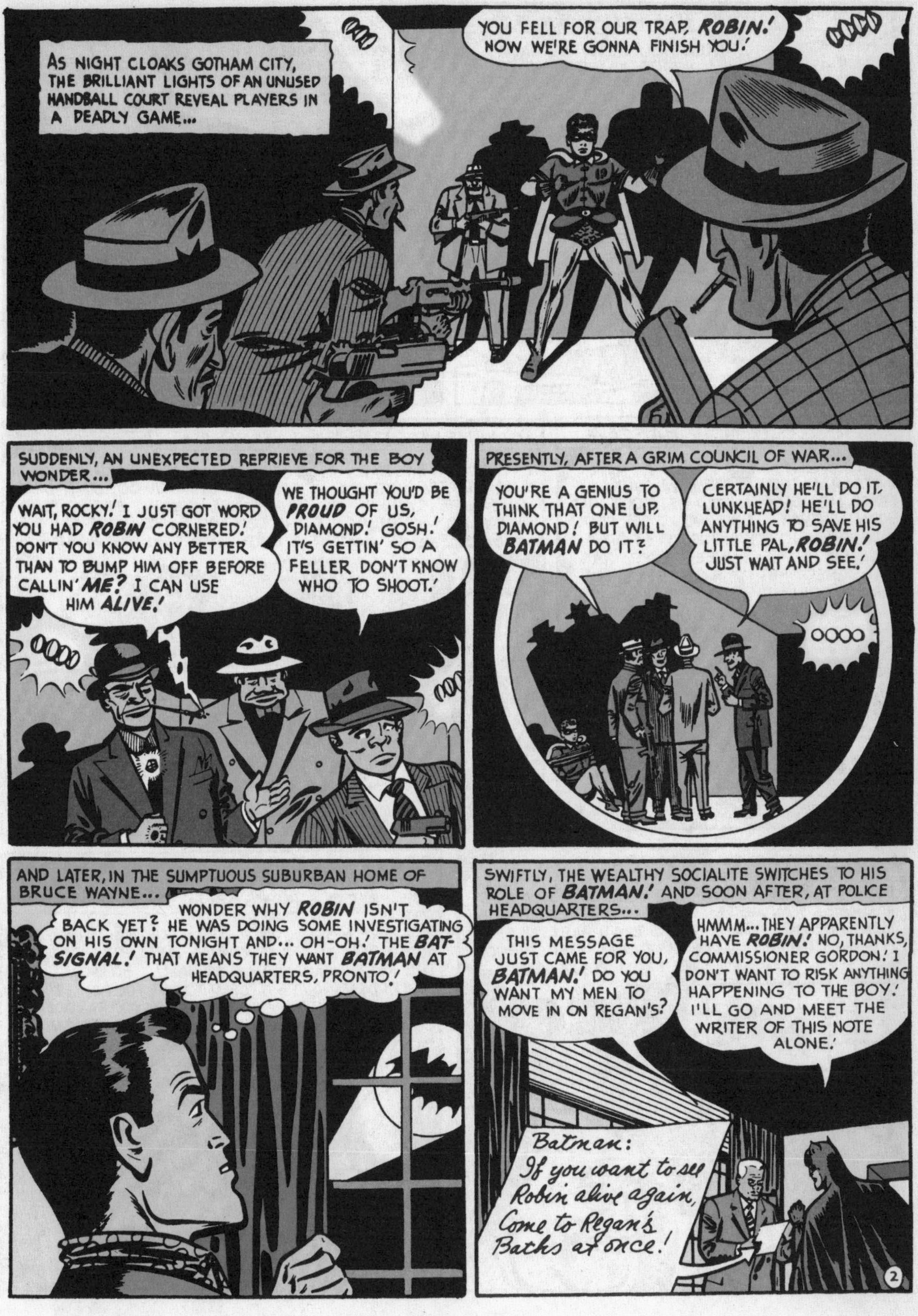
AS NIGHT CLOAKS GOTHAM CITY, THE BRILLIANT LIGHTS OF AN UNUSED HANDBALL COURT REVEAL PLAYERS IN A DEADLY GAME...
YOU FELL FOR OUR TRAP, ROBIN! NOW WE'RE GONNA FINISH YOU!
SUDDENLY, AN UNEXPECTED REPRIEVE FOR THE BOY WONDER...
WAIT, ROCKY! I JUST GOT WORD YOU HAD ROBIN CORNERED! DON'T YOU KNOW ANY BETTER THAN TO BUMP HIM OFF BEFORE CALLIN' ME? I CAN USE HIM ALIVE!
WE THOUGHT YOU'D BE PROUD OF US, DIAMOND! GOSH! IT'S GETTIN' SO A FELLER DON'T KNOW WHO TO SHOOT!
PRESENTLY, AFTER A GRIM COUNCIL OF WAR...
YOU'RE A GENIUS TO THINK THAT ONE UP, DIAMOND! BUT WILL BATMAN DO IT?
CERTAINLY HE'LL DO IT, LUNKHEAD! HE'LL DO ANYTHING TO SAVE HIS LITTLE PAL, ROBIN! JUST WAIT AND SEE!
AND LATER, IN THE SUMPTUOUS SUBURBAN HOME OF BRUCE WAYNE...
WONDER WHY ROBIN ISN'T BACK YET? HE WAS DOING SOME INVESTIGATING ON HIS OWN TONIGHT AND... OH-OH! THE BAT-SIGNAL! THAT MEANS THEY WANT BATMAN AT HEADQUARTERS, PRONTO!
SWIFTLY, THE WEALTHY SOCIALITE SWITCHES TO HIS ROLE OF BATMAN! AND SOON AFTER, AT POLICE HEADQUARTERS...
THIS MESSAGE JUST CAME FOR YOU, BATMAN! DO YOU WANT MY MEN TO MOVE IN ON REGAN'S?
HMMM... THEY APPARENTLY HAVE ROBIN! NO, THANKS, COMMISSIONER GORDON! I DON'T WANT TO RISK ANYTHING HAPPENING TO THE BOY! I'LL GO AND MEET THE WRITER OF THIS NOTE ALONE!
Batman: If you want to see Robin alive again, Come to Regan's Baths at once!
2

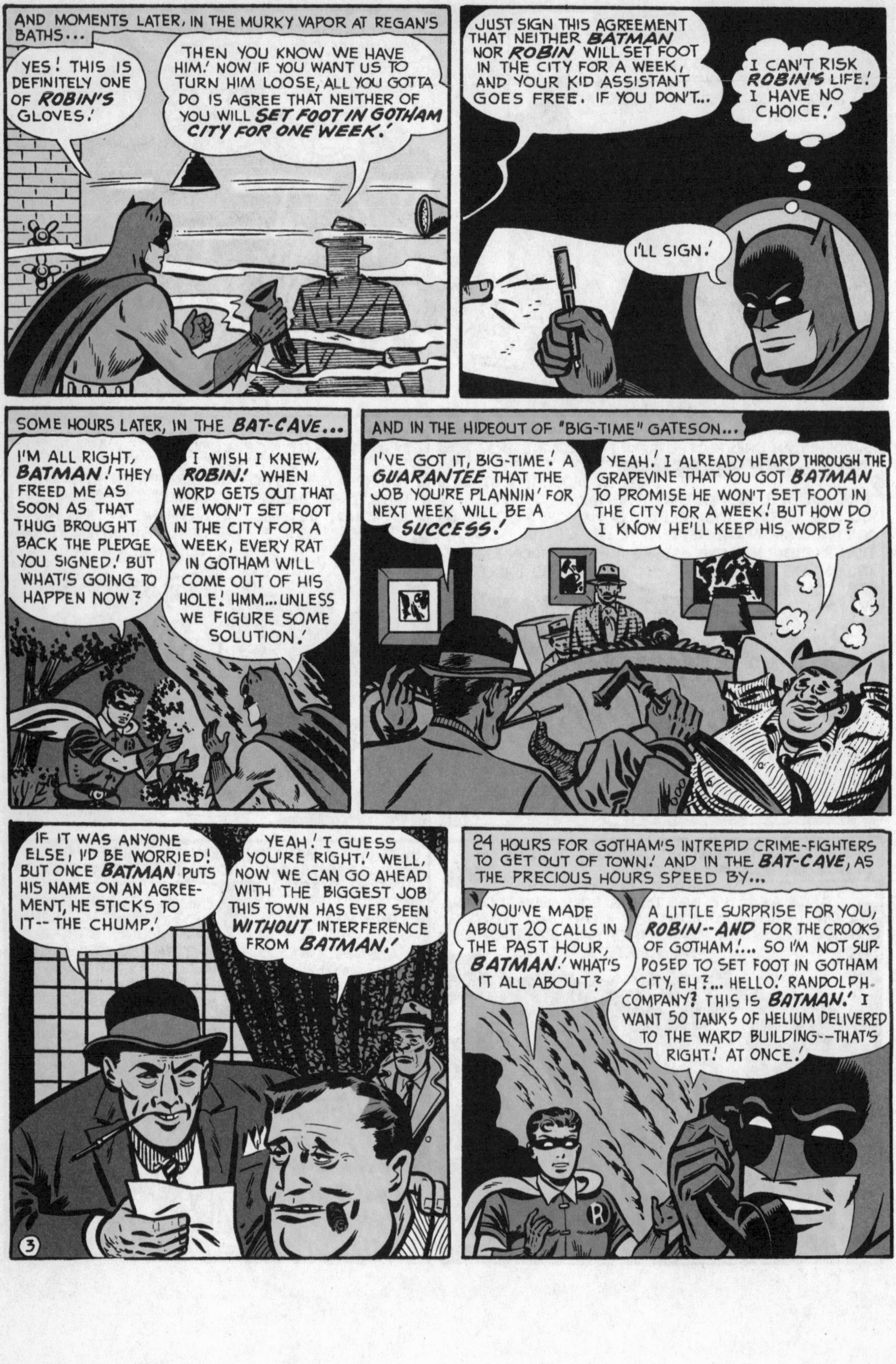
AND MOMENTS LATER, IN THE MURKY VAPOR AT REGAN'S BATHS...
YES! THIS IS DEFINITELY ONE OF ROBIN'S GLOVES!
THEN YOU KNOW WE HAVE HIM! NOW IF YOU WANT US TO TURN HIM LOOSE, ALL YOU GOTTA DO IS AGREE THAT NEITHER OF YOU WILL SET FOOT IN GOTHAM CITY FOR ONE WEEK!
JUST SIGN THIS AGREEMENT THAT NEITHER BATMAN NOR ROBIN WILL SET FOOT IN THE CITY FOR A WEEK, AND YOUR KID ASSISTANT GOES FREE. IF YOU DON'T...
I CAN'T RISK ROBIN'S LIFE! I HAVE NO CHOICE!
I'LL SIGN!
SOME HOURS LATER, IN THE BAT-CAVE...
I'M ALL RIGHT, BATMAN! THEY FREED ME AS SOON AS THAT THUG BROUGHT BACK THE PLEDGE YOU SIGNED! BUT WHAT'S GOING TO HAPPEN NOW?
I WISH I KNEW, ROBIN! WHEN WORD GETS OUT THAT WE WON'T SET FOOT IN THE CITY FOR A WEEK, EVERY RAT IN GOTHAM WILL COME OUT OF HIS HOLE! HMM...UNLESS WE FIGURE SOME SOLUTION!
AND IN THE HIDEOUT OF "BIG-TIME" GATESON...
I'VE GOT IT, BIG-TIME! A GUARANTEE THAT THE JOB YOU'RE PLANNIN' FOR NEXT WEEK WILL BE A SUCCESS!
YEAH! I ALREADY HEARD THROUGH THE GRAPEVINE THAT YOU GOT BATMAN TO PROMISE HE WON'T SET FOOT IN THE CITY FOR A WEEK! BUT HOW DO I KNOW HE'LL KEEP HIS WORD?
IF IT WAS ANYONE ELSE, I'D BE WORRIED! BUT ONCE BATMAN PUTS HIS NAME ON AN AGREEMENT, HE STICKS TO IT-- THE CHUMP!
YEAH! I GUESS YOU'RE RIGHT! WELL, NOW WE CAN GO AHEAD WITH THE BIGGEST JOB THIS TOWN HAS EVER SEEN WITHOUT INTERFERENCE FROM BATMAN!
3
24 HOURS FOR GOTHAM'S INTREPID CRIME-FIGHTERS TO GET OUT OF TOWN! AND IN THE BAT-CAVE, AS THE PRECIOUS HOURS SPEED BY...
YOU'VE MADE ABOUT 20 CALLS IN THE PAST HOUR, BATMAN! WHAT'S IT ALL ABOUT?
A LITTLE SURPRISE FOR YOU, ROBIN--AND FOR THE CROOKS OF GOTHAM!... SO I'M NOT SUPPOSED TO SET FOOT IN GOTHAM CITY, EH?... HELLO! RANDOLPH COMPANY? THIS IS BATMAN! I WANT 50 TANKS OF HELIUM DELIVERED TO THE WARD BUILDING--THAT'S RIGHT! AT ONCE!

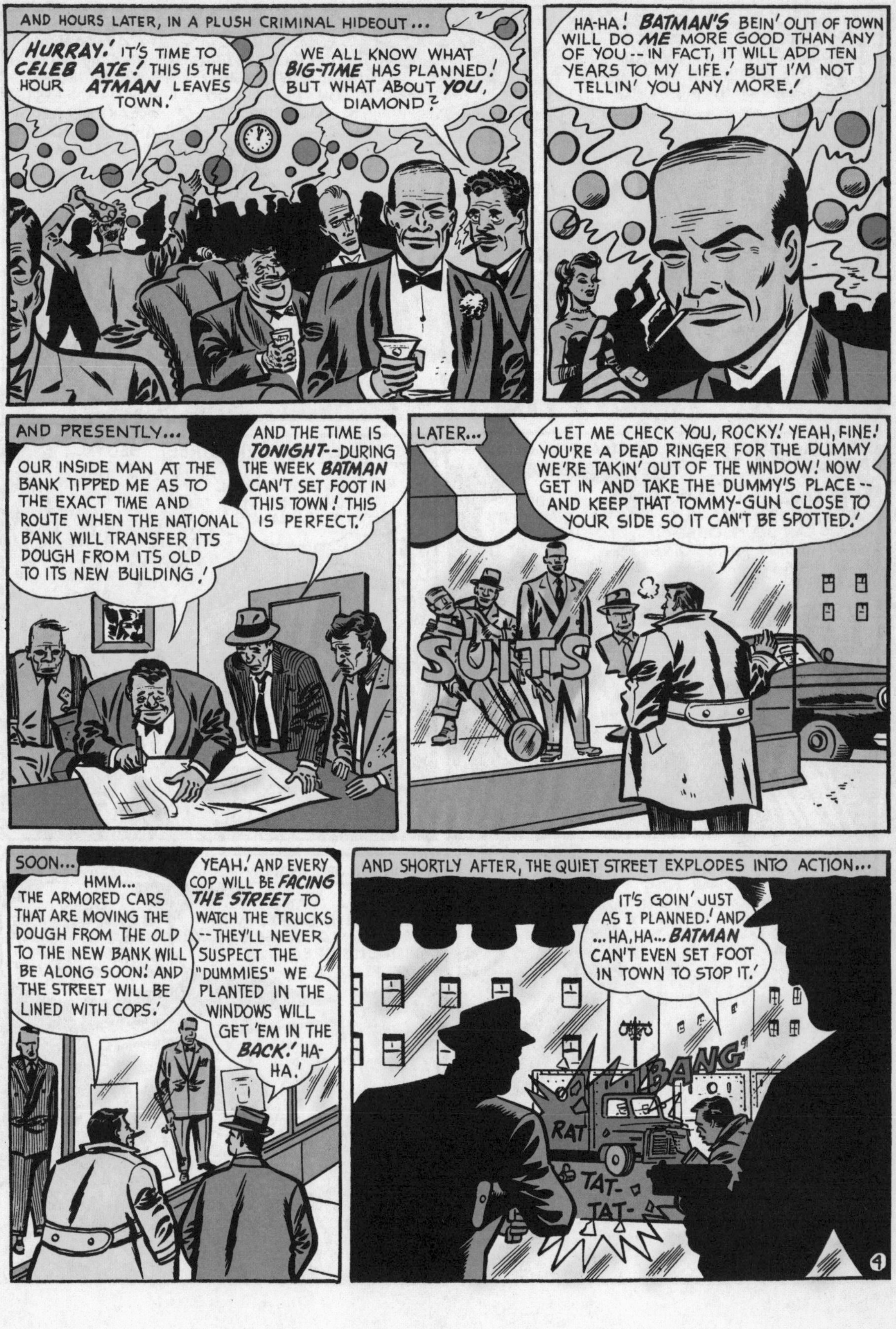
AND HOURS LATER, IN A PLUSH CRIMINAL HIDEOUT...
HURRAY! IT'S TIME TO CELEB ATE! THIS IS THE HOUR ATMAN LEAVES TOWN!
WE ALL KNOW WHAT BIG-TIME HAS PLANNED! BUT WHAT ABOUT YOU, DIAMOND?
HA-HA! BATMAN'S BEIN' OUT OF TOWN WILL DO ME MORE GOOD THAN ANY OF YOU -- IN FACT, IT WILL ADD TEN YEARS TO MY LIFE! BUT I'M NOT TELLIN' YOU ANY MORE!
AND PRESENTLY...
OUR INSIDE MAN AT THE BANK TIPPED ME AS TO THE EXACT TIME AND ROUTE WHEN THE NATIONAL BANK WILL TRANSFER ITS DOUGH FROM ITS OLD TO ITS NEW BUILDING!
AND THE TIME IS TONIGHT--DURING THE WEEK BATMAN CAN'T SET FOOT IN THIS TOWN! THIS IS PERFECT!
LATER...
LET ME CHECK YOU, ROCKY! YEAH, FINE! YOU'RE A DEAD RINGER FOR THE DUMMY WE'RE TAKIN' OUT OF THE WINDOW! NOW GET IN AND TAKE THE DUMMY'S PLACE -- AND KEEP THAT TOMMY-GUN CLOSE TO YOUR SIDE SO IT CAN'T BE SPOTTED!
SUITS
SOON...
HMM... THE ARMORED CARS THAT ARE MOVING THE DOUGH FROM THE OLD TO THE NEW BANK WILL BE ALONG SOON! AND THE STREET WILL BE LINED WITH COPS!
YEAH! AND EVERY COP WILL BE FACING THE STREET TO WATCH THE TRUCKS -- THEY'LL NEVER SUSPECT THE "DUMMIES" WE PLANTED IN THE WINDOWS WILL GET 'EM IN THE BACK! HA-HA!
AND SHORTLY AFTER, THE QUIET STREET EXPLODES INTO ACTION...
IT'S GOIN' JUST AS I PLANNED! AND ...HA, HA... BATMAN CAN'T EVEN SET FOOT IN TOWN TO STOP IT!
BANG
RAT
TAT-TAT-
4

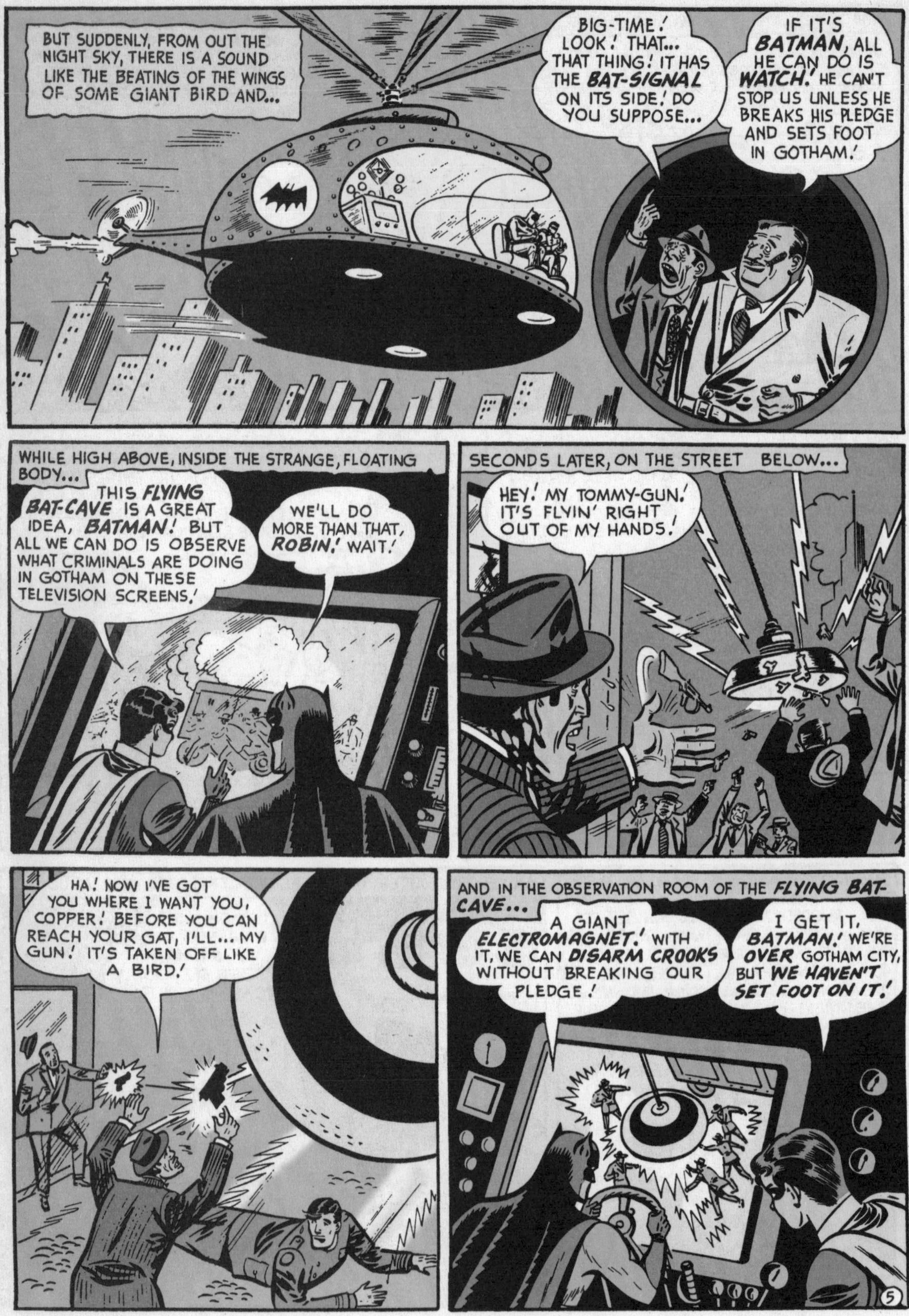
BUT SUDDENLY, FROM OUT THE NIGHT SKY, THERE IS A SOUND LIKE THE BEATING OF THE WINGS OF SOME GIANT BIRD AND...
BIG-TIME! LOOK! THAT... THAT THING! IT HAS THE BAT-SIGNAL ON ITS SIDE! DO YOU SUPPOSE...
IF IT'S BATMAN, ALL HE CAN DO IS WATCH! HE CAN'T STOP US UNLESS HE BREAKS HIS PLEDGE AND SETS FOOT IN GOTHAM!
WHILE HIGH ABOVE, INSIDE THE STRANGE, FLOATING BODY...
THIS FLYING BAT-CAVE IS A GREAT IDEA, BATMAN! BUT ALL WE CAN DO IS OBSERVE WHAT CRIMINALS ARE DOING IN GOTHAM ON THESE TELEVISION SCREENS!
WE'LL DO MORE THAN THAT, ROBIN! WAIT!
SECONDS LATER, ON THE STREET BELOW...
HEY! MY TOMMY-GUN! IT'S FLYIN' RIGHT OUT OF MY HANDS!
HA! NOW I'VE GOT YOU WHERE I WANT YOU, COPPER! BEFORE YOU CAN REACH YOUR GAT, I'LL... MY GUN! IT'S TAKEN OFF LIKE A BIRD!
AND IN THE OBSERVATION ROOM OF THE FLYING BAT-CAVE...
A GIANT ELECTROMAGNET! WITH IT, WE CAN DISARM CROOKS WITHOUT BREAKING OUR PLEDGE!
I GET IT, BATMAN! WE'RE OVER GOTHAM CITY, BUT WE HAVEN'T SET FOOT ON IT!
5

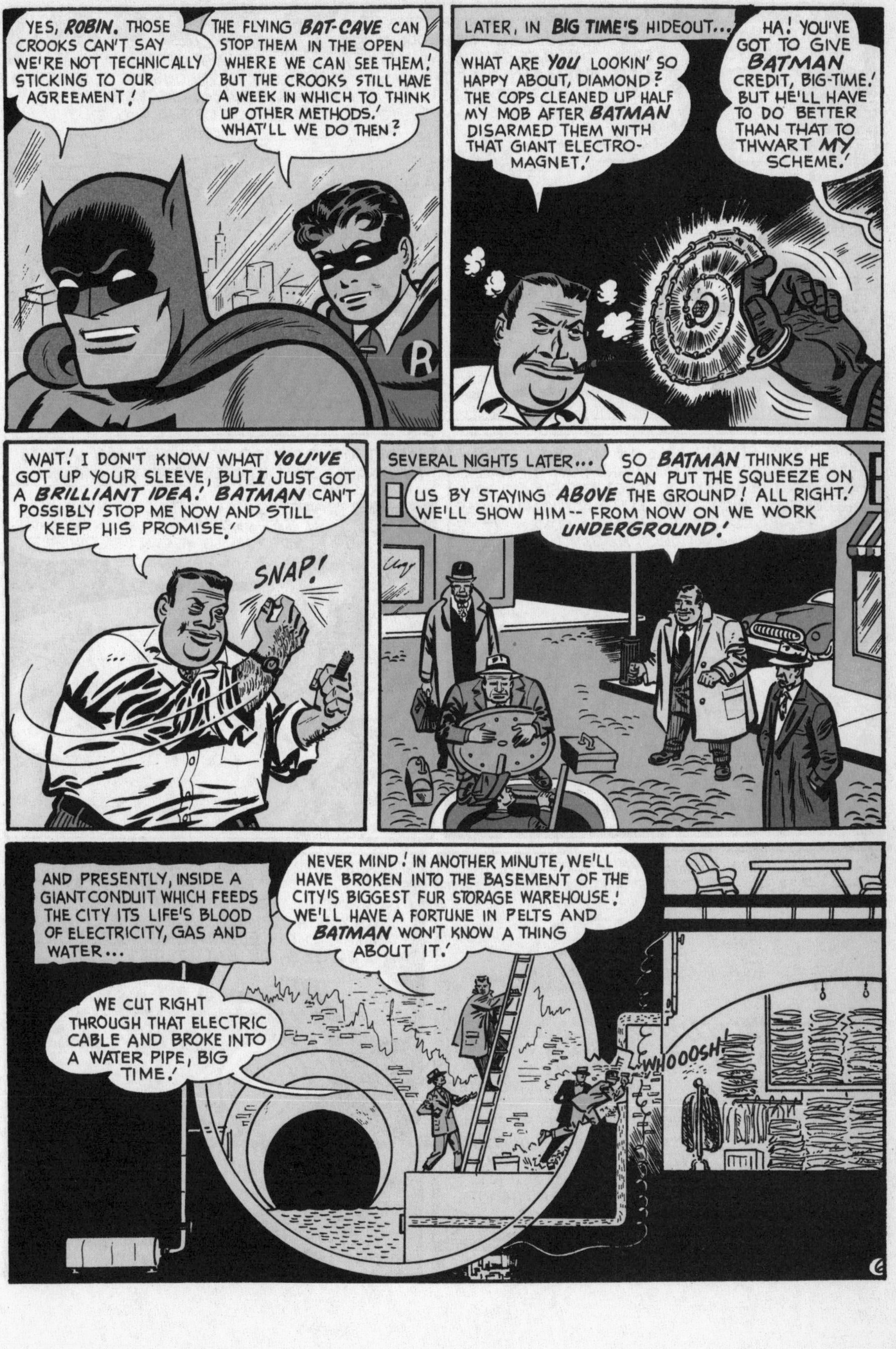

YES, ROBIN. THOSE CROOKS CAN'T SAY WE'RE NOT TECHNICALLY STICKING TO OUR AGREEMENT!
THE FLYING BAT-CAVE CAN STOP THEM IN THE OPEN WHERE WE CAN SEE THEM! BUT THE CROOKS STILL HAVE A WEEK IN WHICH TO THINK UP OTHER METHODS! WHAT'LL WE DO THEN?
LATER, IN BIG TIME'S HIDEOUT...
WHAT ARE YOU LOOKIN' SO HAPPY ABOUT, DIAMOND? THE COPS CLEANED UP HALF MY MOB AFTER BATMAN DISARMED THEM WITH THAT GIANT ELECTRO-MAGNET!
HA! YOU'VE GOT TO GIVE BATMAN CREDIT, BIG-TIME! BUT HE'LL HAVE TO DO BETTER THAN THAT TO THWART MY SCHEME!
WAIT! I DON'T KNOW WHAT YOU'VE GOT UP YOUR SLEEVE, BUT I JUST GOT A BRILLIANT IDEA! BATMAN CAN'T POSSIBLY STOP ME NOW AND STILL KEEP HIS PROMISE!
SNAP!
SEVERAL NIGHTS LATER...
SO BATMAN THINKS HE CAN PUT THE SQUEEZE ON US BY STAYING ABOVE THE GROUND! ALL RIGHT! WE'LL SHOW HIM-- FROM NOW ON WE WORK UNDERGROUND!
AND PRESENTLY, INSIDE A GIANT CONDUIT WHICH FEEDS THE CITY ITS LIFE'S BLOOD OF ELECTRICITY, GAS AND WATER...
NEVER MIND! IN ANOTHER MINUTE, WE'LL HAVE BROKEN INTO THE BASEMENT OF THE CITY'S BIGGEST FUR STORAGE WAREHOUSE! WE'LL HAVE A FORTUNE IN PELTS AND BATMAN WON'T KNOW A THING ABOUT IT!
WE CUT RIGHT THROUGH THAT ELECTRIC CABLE AND BROKE INTO A WATER PIPE, BIG TIME!
WHOOOSH!
6

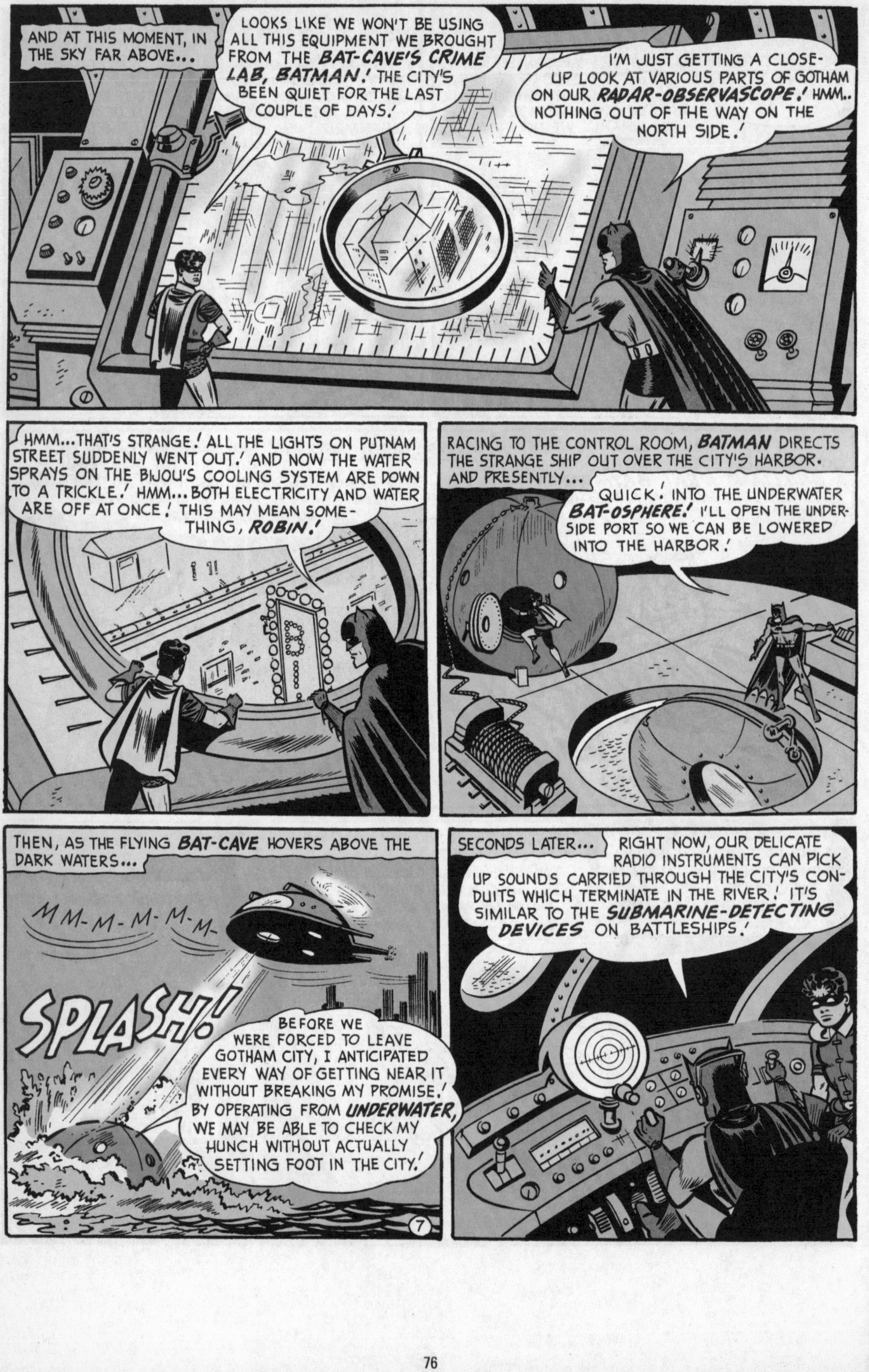
AND AT THIS MOMENT, IN THE SKY FAR ABOVE...
LOOKS LIKE WE WON'T BE USING ALL THIS EQUIPMENT WE BROUGHT FROM THE BAT-CAVE'S CRIME LAB, BATMAN! THE CITY'S BEEN QUIET FOR THE LAST COUPLE OF DAYS!
I'M JUST GETTING A CLOSE-UP LOOK AT VARIOUS PARTS OF GOTHAM ON OUR RADAR-OBSERVASCOPE! HMM.. NOTHING OUT OF THE WAY ON THE NORTH SIDE!
HMM...THAT'S STRANGE! ALL THE LIGHTS ON PUTNAM STREET SUDDENLY WENT OUT! AND NOW THE WATER SPRAYS ON THE BIJOU'S COOLING SYSTEM ARE DOWN TO A TRICKLE! HMM...BOTH ELECTRICITY AND WATER ARE OFF AT ONCE! THIS MAY MEAN SOME-THING, ROBIN!
RACING TO THE CONTROL ROOM, BATMAN DIRECTS THE STRANGE SHIP OUT OVER THE CITY'S HARBOR. AND PRESENTLY...
QUICK! INTO THE UNDERWATER BAT-OSPHERE! I'LL OPEN THE UNDER-SIDE PORT SO WE CAN BE LOWERED INTO THE HARBOR!
THEN, AS THE FLYING BAT-CAVE HOVERS ABOVE THE DARK WATERS...
MM-M-M-M-M-
SPLASH!
BEFORE WE WERE FORCED TO LEAVE GOTHAM CITY, I ANTICIPATED EVERY WAY OF GETTING NEAR IT WITHOUT BREAKING MY PROMISE! BY OPERATING FROM UNDERWATER, WE MAY BE ABLE TO CHECK MY HUNCH WITHOUT ACTUALLY SETTING FOOT IN THE CITY!
7
SECONDS LATER...
RIGHT NOW, OUR DELICATE RADIO INSTRUMENTS CAN PICK UP SOUNDS CARRIED THROUGH THE CITY'S CON-DUITS WHICH TERMINATE IN THE RIVER! IT'S SIMILAR TO THE SUBMARINE-DETECTING DEVICES ON BATTLESHIPS!

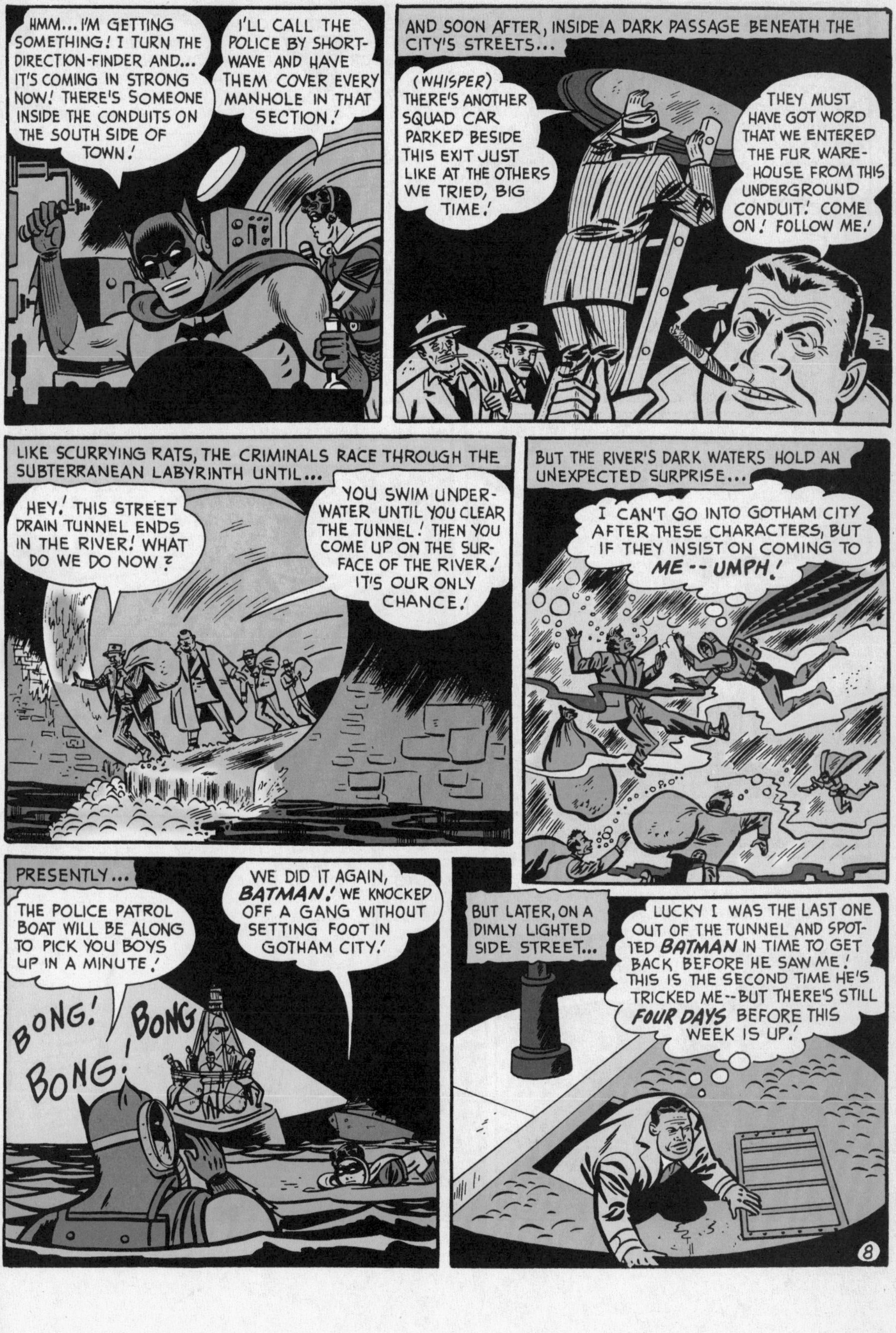

HMM... I'M GETTING SOMETHING! I TURN THE DIRECTION-FINDER AND... IT'S COMING IN STRONG NOW! THERE'S SOMEONE INSIDE THE CONDUITS ON THE SOUTH SIDE OF TOWN!
I'LL CALL THE POLICE BY SHORT-WAVE AND HAVE THEM COVER EVERY MANHOLE IN THAT SECTION!
AND SOON AFTER, INSIDE A DARK PASSAGE BENEATH THE CITY'S STREETS...
(WHISPER) THERE'S ANOTHER SQUAD CAR PARKED BESIDE THIS EXIT JUST LIKE AT THE OTHERS WE TRIED, BIG TIME!
THEY MUST HAVE GOT WORD THAT WE ENTERED THE FUR WARE-HOUSE FROM THIS UNDERGROUND CONDUIT! COME ON! FOLLOW ME!
LIKE SCURRYING RATS, THE CRIMINALS RACE THROUGH THE SUBTERRANEAN LABYRINTH UNTIL...
HEY! THIS STREET DRAIN TUNNEL ENDS IN THE RIVER! WHAT DO WE DO NOW?
YOU SWIM UNDER-WATER UNTIL YOU CLEAR THE TUNNEL! THEN YOU COME UP ON THE SUR-FACE OF THE RIVER! IT'S OUR ONLY CHANCE!
BUT THE RIVER'S DARK WATERS HOLD AN UNEXPECTED SURPRISE...
I CAN'T GO INTO GOTHAM CITY AFTER THESE CHARACTERS, BUT IF THEY INSIST ON COMING TO ME -- UMPH!
PRESENTLY...
THE POLICE PATROL BOAT WILL BE ALONG TO PICK YOU BOYS UP IN A MINUTE!
WE DID IT AGAIN, BATMAN! WE KNOCKED OFF A GANG WITHOUT SETTING FOOT IN GOTHAM CITY!
BONG! BONG! BONG!
BUT LATER, ON A DIMLY LIGHTED SIDE STREET...
LUCKY I WAS THE LAST ONE OUT OF THE TUNNEL AND SPOT-TED BATMAN IN TIME TO GET BACK BEFORE HE SAW ME! THIS IS THE SECOND TIME HE'S TRICKED ME--BUT THERE'S STILL FOUR DAYS BEFORE THIS WEEK IS UP!
8

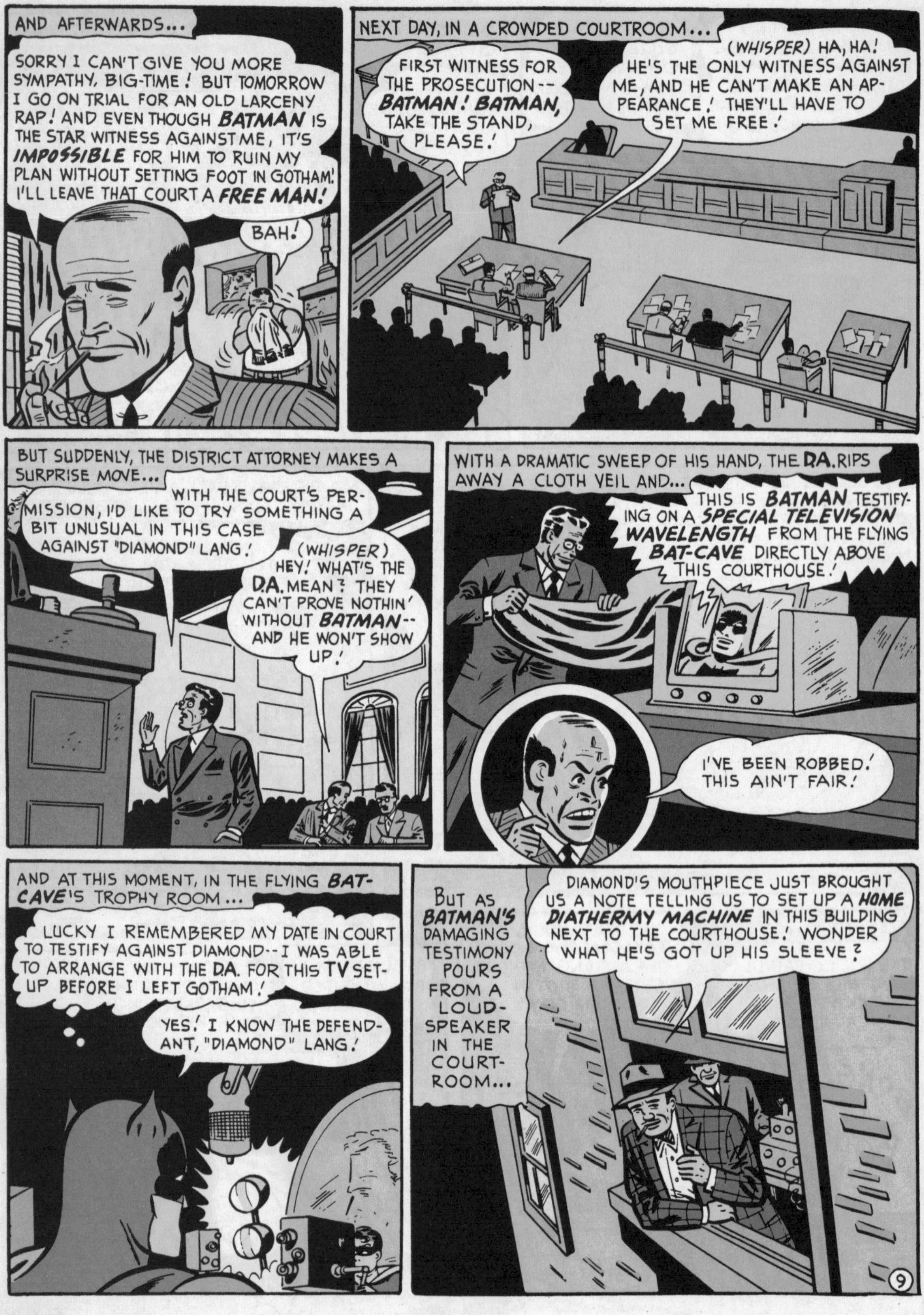
AND AFTERWARDS...
SORRY I CAN'T GIVE YOU MORE SYMPATHY, BIG-TIME! BUT TOMORROW I GO ON TRIAL FOR AN OLD LARCENY RAP! AND EVEN THOUGH BATMAN IS THE STAR WITNESS AGAINST ME, IT'S IMPOSSIBLE FOR HIM TO RUIN MY PLAN WITHOUT SETTING FOOT IN GOTHAM! I'LL LEAVE THAT COURT A FREE MAN!
BAH!
NEXT DAY, IN A CROWDED COURTROOM...
FIRST WITNESS FOR THE PROSECUTION -- BATMAN! BATMAN, TAKE THE STAND, PLEASE!
(WHISPER) HA, HA! HE'S THE ONLY WITNESS AGAINST ME, AND HE CAN'T MAKE AN APPEARANCE! THEY'LL HAVE TO SET ME FREE!
BUT SUDDENLY, THE DISTRICT ATTORNEY MAKES A SURPRISE MOVE...
WITH THE COURT'S PERMISSION, I'D LIKE TO TRY SOMETHING A BIT UNUSUAL IN THIS CASE AGAINST "DIAMOND" LANG!
(WHISPER) HEY! WHAT'S THE D.A. MEAN? THEY CAN'T PROVE NOTHIN' WITHOUT BATMAN -- AND HE WON'T SHOW UP!
WITH A DRAMATIC SWEEP OF HIS HAND, THE D.A. RIPS AWAY A CLOTH VEIL AND...
THIS IS BATMAN TESTIFYING ON A SPECIAL TELEVISION WAVELENGTH FROM THE FLYING BAT-CAVE DIRECTLY ABOVE THIS COURTHOUSE!
I'VE BEEN ROBBED! THIS AIN'T FAIR!
AND AT THIS MOMENT, IN THE FLYING BAT-CAVE'S TROPHY ROOM...
LUCKY I REMEMBERED MY DATE IN COURT TO TESTIFY AGAINST DIAMOND -- I WAS ABLE TO ARRANGE WITH THE D.A. FOR THIS TV SET-UP BEFORE I LEFT GOTHAM!
YES! I KNOW THE DEFENDANT, "DIAMOND" LANG!
BUT AS BATMAN'S DAMAGING TESTIMONY POURS FROM A LOUD-SPEAKER IN THE COURTROOM...
DIAMOND'S MOUTHPIECE JUST BROUGHT US A NOTE TELLING US TO SET UP A HOME DIATHERMY MACHINE IN THIS BUILDING NEXT TO THE COURTHOUSE! WONDER WHAT HE'S GOT UP HIS SLEEVE?
9

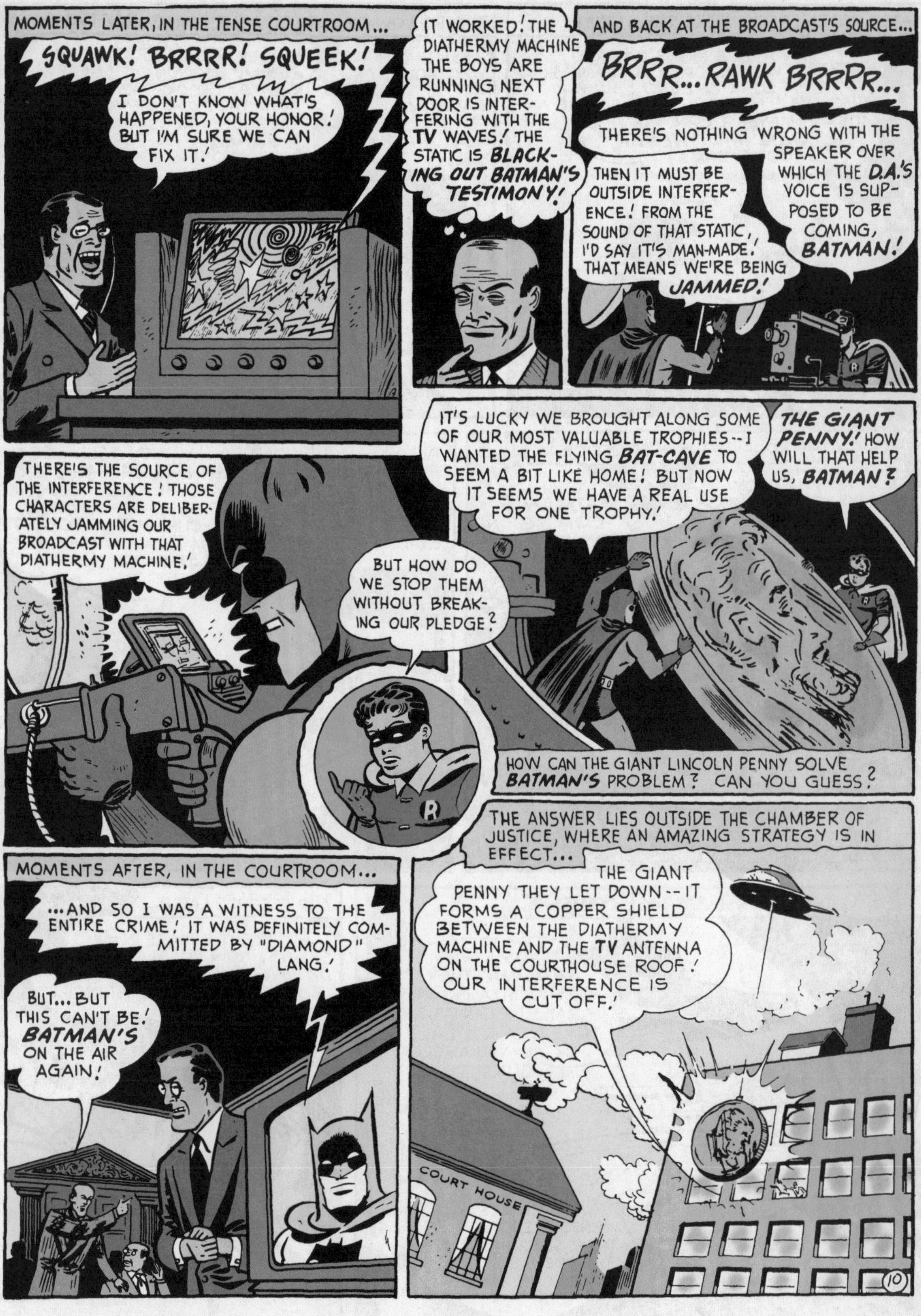

MOMENTS LATER, IN THE TENSE COURTROOM...
SQUAWK! BRRRR! SQUEEK!
I DON'T KNOW WHAT'S HAPPENED, YOUR HONOR! BUT I'M SURE WE CAN FIX IT!
IT WORKED! THE DIATHERMY MACHINE THE BOYS ARE RUNNING NEXT DOOR IS INTERFERING WITH THE TV WAVES! THE STATIC IS BLACKING OUT BATMAN'S TESTIMONY!
AND BACK AT THE BROADCAST'S SOURCE...
BRRR...RAWK BRRRR...
THERE'S NOTHING WRONG WITH THE SPEAKER OVER WHICH THE D.A.'S VOICE IS SUPPOSED TO BE COMING, BATMAN!
THEN IT MUST BE OUTSIDE INTERFERENCE! FROM THE SOUND OF THAT STATIC, I'D SAY IT'S MAN-MADE! THAT MEANS WE'RE BEING JAMMED!
THERE'S THE SOURCE OF THE INTERFERENCE! THOSE CHARACTERS ARE DELIBERATELY JAMMING OUR BROADCAST WITH THAT DIATHERMY MACHINE!
BUT HOW DO WE STOP THEM WITHOUT BREAKING OUR PLEDGE?
IT'S LUCKY WE BROUGHT ALONG SOME OF OUR MOST VALUABLE TROPHIES--I WANTED THE FLYING BAT-CAVE TO SEEM A BIT LIKE HOME! BUT NOW IT SEEMS WE HAVE A REAL USE FOR ONE TROPHY!
THE GIANT PENNY! HOW WILL THAT HELP US, BATMAN?
HOW CAN THE GIANT LINCOLN PENNY SOLVE BATMAN'S PROBLEM? CAN YOU GUESS?
MOMENTS AFTER, IN THE COURTROOM...
...AND SO I WAS A WITNESS TO THE ENTIRE CRIME! IT WAS DEFINITELY COMMITTED BY "DIAMOND" LANG!
BUT...BUT THIS CAN'T BE! BATMAN'S ON THE AIR AGAIN!
THE ANSWER LIES OUTSIDE THE CHAMBER OF JUSTICE, WHERE AN AMAZING STRATEGY IS IN EFFECT...
THE GIANT PENNY THEY LET DOWN--IT FORMS A COPPER SHIELD BETWEEN THE DIATHERMY MACHINE AND THE TV ANTENNA ON THE COURTHOUSE ROOF! OUR INTERFERENCE IS CUT OFF!
COURT HOUSE
10

LATER, AS BIG-TIME WALKS THE STREETS OF GOTHAM CITY...

ONE MORE DAY AND *BATMAN* WILL BE BACK IN TOWN! SO FAR, MY SCORE IS ZERO! HMM... THAT WAR MEMORIAL GIVES ME AN IDEA! MAYBE I CAN FIX IT SO *BATMAN* WILL *NEVER* COME BACK!

THE FOLLOWING NIGHT, IN THE FLYING *BAT-CAVE*...

LESS THAN TWO MORE HOURS AND OUR "EXILE" IS OVER, *BATMAN*! I'LL CERTAINLY BE GLAD WHEN--

BUT OUR *TROUBLES* AREN'T OVER, *ROBIN!* LOOK ON THE *OBSERVA-SCOPE!* CROOKS ARE ESCAPING FROM THE *POST OFFICE* OVER THE ROOF! I'M GUIDING THE *BAT-CAVE* IN FOR A CLOSER LOOK!

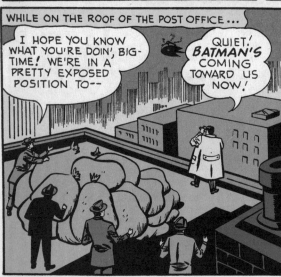

WHILE ON THE ROOF OF THE POST OFFICE...

I HOPE YOU KNOW WHAT YOU'RE DOIN', BIG-TIME! WE'RE IN A PRETTY EXPOSED POSITION TO--

QUIET! *BATMAN'S* COMING TOWARD US NOW!

ALL RIGHT! THROW OFF THE MAIL BAG CAMOUFLAGE! TURN ON THE SEARCH-LIGHTS! STAND BY TO FIRE!

HA, HA! WHAT A SURPRISE WHEN *BATMAN* RUNS INTO *FLAK!* HE NEVER USES GUNS, SO THERE'S NO WAY HE CAN STOP OUR *ANTI-AIRCRAFT* FROM KNOCKIN' THE FLYING *BAT-CAVE* OUT OF THE SKY!

THEN, AS THE SURPRISE BARRAGE OPENS UP...

AKK
AK-K
BAM
AK

IT WAS A TRAP, *BATMAN!* THEY WEREN'T STEALING SACKS OF MAIL--THE CANVAS BAGS WERE A CAMOUFLAGE FOR THE ANTI-AIRCRAFT GUNS!

ZZZING

WE'RE PINPOINTED IN THEIR SEARCHLIGHTS! THEY'RE SURE OF A DIRECT HIT SOON!

AND SECONDS LATER...

AH! RIGHT SQUARE IN MY SIGHTS! NOW I'LL BLAST THE *DARING DUO* AND THEIR FLYING *BAT-CAVE* OUT OF EXISTENCE!

11

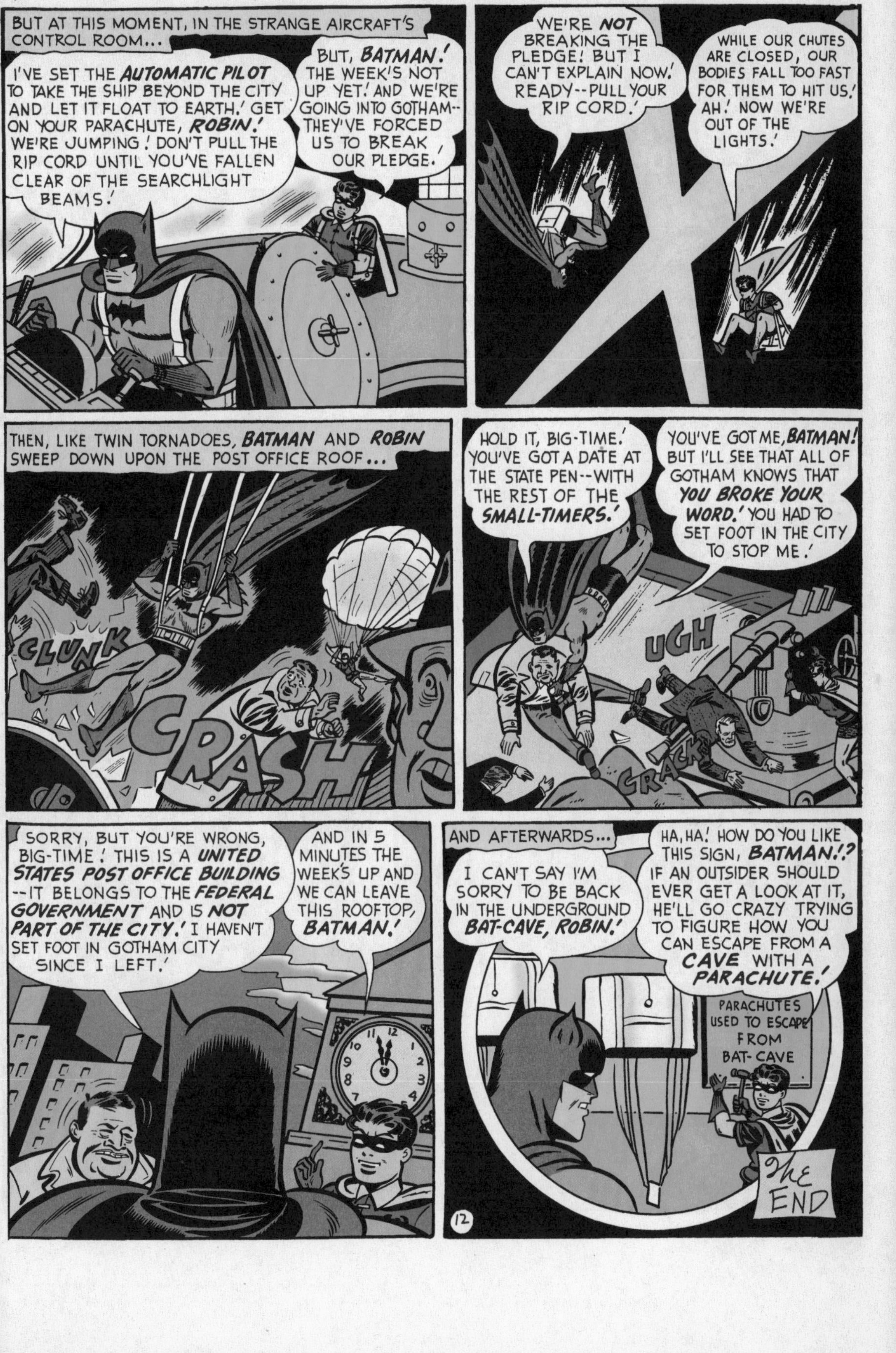
BUT AT THIS MOMENT, IN THE STRANGE AIRCRAFT'S CONTROL ROOM...
I'VE SET THE AUTOMATIC PILOT TO TAKE THE SHIP BEYOND THE CITY AND LET IT FLOAT TO EARTH.! GET ON YOUR PARACHUTE, ROBIN.! WE'RE JUMPING! DON'T PULL THE RIP CORD UNTIL YOU'VE FALLEN CLEAR OF THE SEARCHLIGHT BEAMS.!
BUT, BATMAN.! THE WEEK'S NOT UP YET.! AND WE'RE GOING INTO GOTHAM--THEY'VE FORCED US TO BREAK OUR PLEDGE.!
WE'RE NOT BREAKING THE PLEDGE! BUT I CAN'T EXPLAIN NOW.! READY--PULL YOUR RIP CORD.!
WHILE OUR CHUTES ARE CLOSED, OUR BODIES FALL TOO FAST FOR THEM TO HIT US.! AH.! NOW WE'RE OUT OF THE LIGHTS.!
THEN, LIKE TWIN TORNADOES, BATMAN AND ROBIN SWEEP DOWN UPON THE POST OFFICE ROOF...
CLUNK
CRASH
HOLD IT, BIG-TIME.! YOU'VE GOT A DATE AT THE STATE PEN--WITH THE REST OF THE SMALL-TIMERS.!
YOU'VE GOT ME, BATMAN! BUT I'LL SEE THAT ALL OF GOTHAM KNOWS THAT YOU BROKE YOUR WORD.! YOU HAD TO SET FOOT IN THE CITY TO STOP ME.!
UGH
CRACK
SORRY, BUT YOU'RE WRONG, BIG-TIME! THIS IS A UNITED STATES POST OFFICE BUILDING --IT BELONGS TO THE FEDERAL GOVERNMENT AND IS NOT PART OF THE CITY.! I HAVEN'T SET FOOT IN GOTHAM CITY SINCE I LEFT.!
AND IN 5 MINUTES THE WEEK'S UP AND WE CAN LEAVE THIS ROOFTOP, BATMAN.!
12
AND AFTERWARDS...
I CAN'T SAY I'M SORRY TO BE BACK IN THE UNDERGROUND BAT-CAVE, ROBIN.!
HA, HA! HOW DO YOU LIKE THIS SIGN, BATMAN.!? IF AN OUTSIDER SHOULD EVER GET A LOOK AT IT, HE'LL GO CRAZY TRYING TO FIGURE HOW YOU CAN ESCAPE FROM A CAVE WITH A PARACHUTE.!
PARACHUTES USED TO ESCAPE FROM BAT-CAVE
THE END

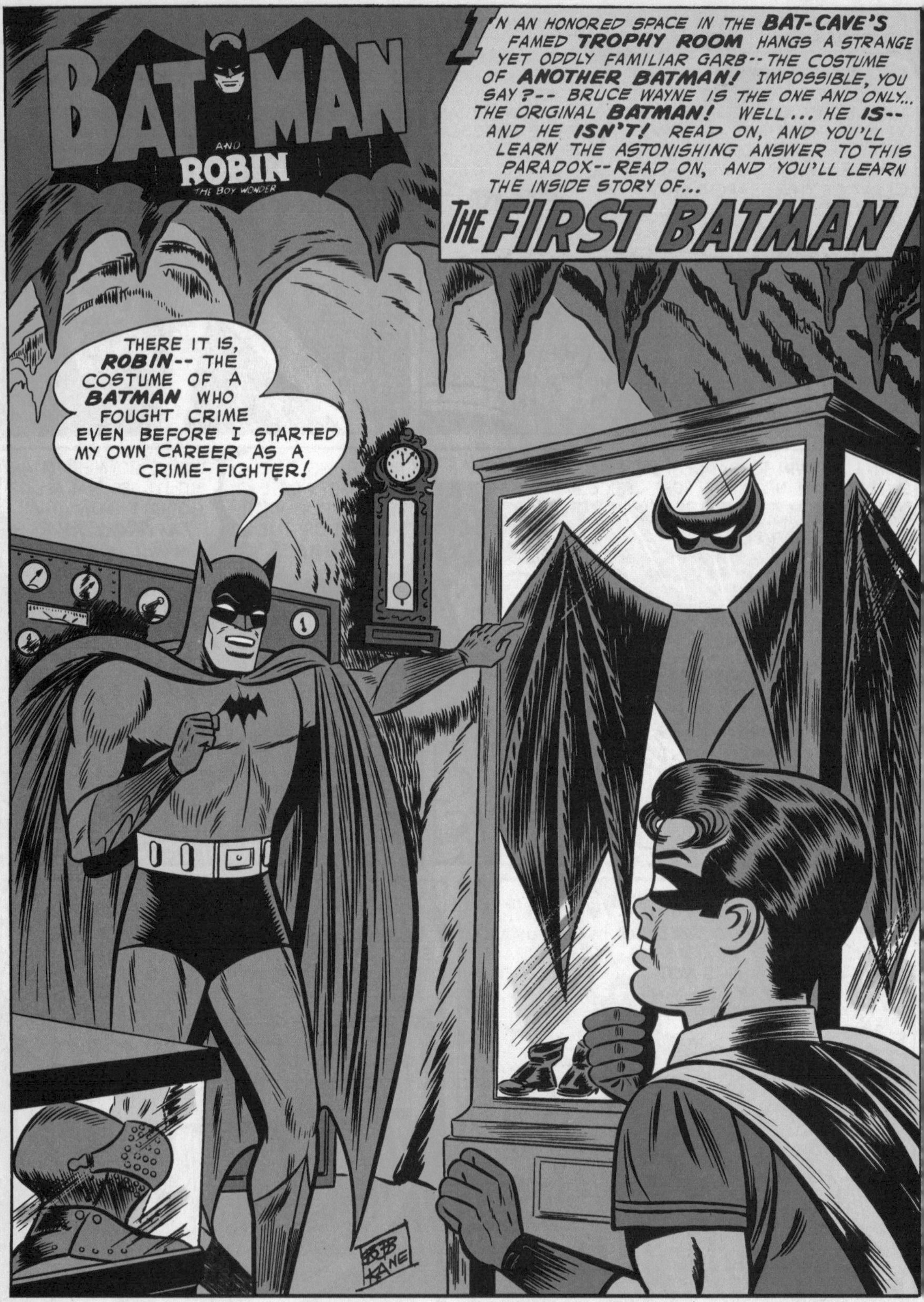
BATMAN AND ROBIN THE BOY WONDER
IN AN HONORED SPACE IN THE BAT-CAVE'S FAMED TROPHY ROOM HANGS A STRANGE YET ODDLY FAMILIAR GARB--THE COSTUME OF ANOTHER BATMAN! IMPOSSIBLE, YOU SAY?-- BRUCE WAYNE IS THE ONE AND ONLY... THE ORIGINAL BATMAN! WELL... HE IS-- AND HE ISN'T! READ ON, AND YOU'LL LEARN THE ASTONISHING ANSWER TO THIS PARADOX--READ ON, AND YOU'LL LEARN THE INSIDE STORY OF...
THE FIRST BATMAN
THERE IT IS, ROBIN-- THE COSTUME OF A BATMAN WHO FOUGHT CRIME EVEN BEFORE I STARTED MY OWN CAREER AS A CRIME-FIGHTER!
BOB KANE

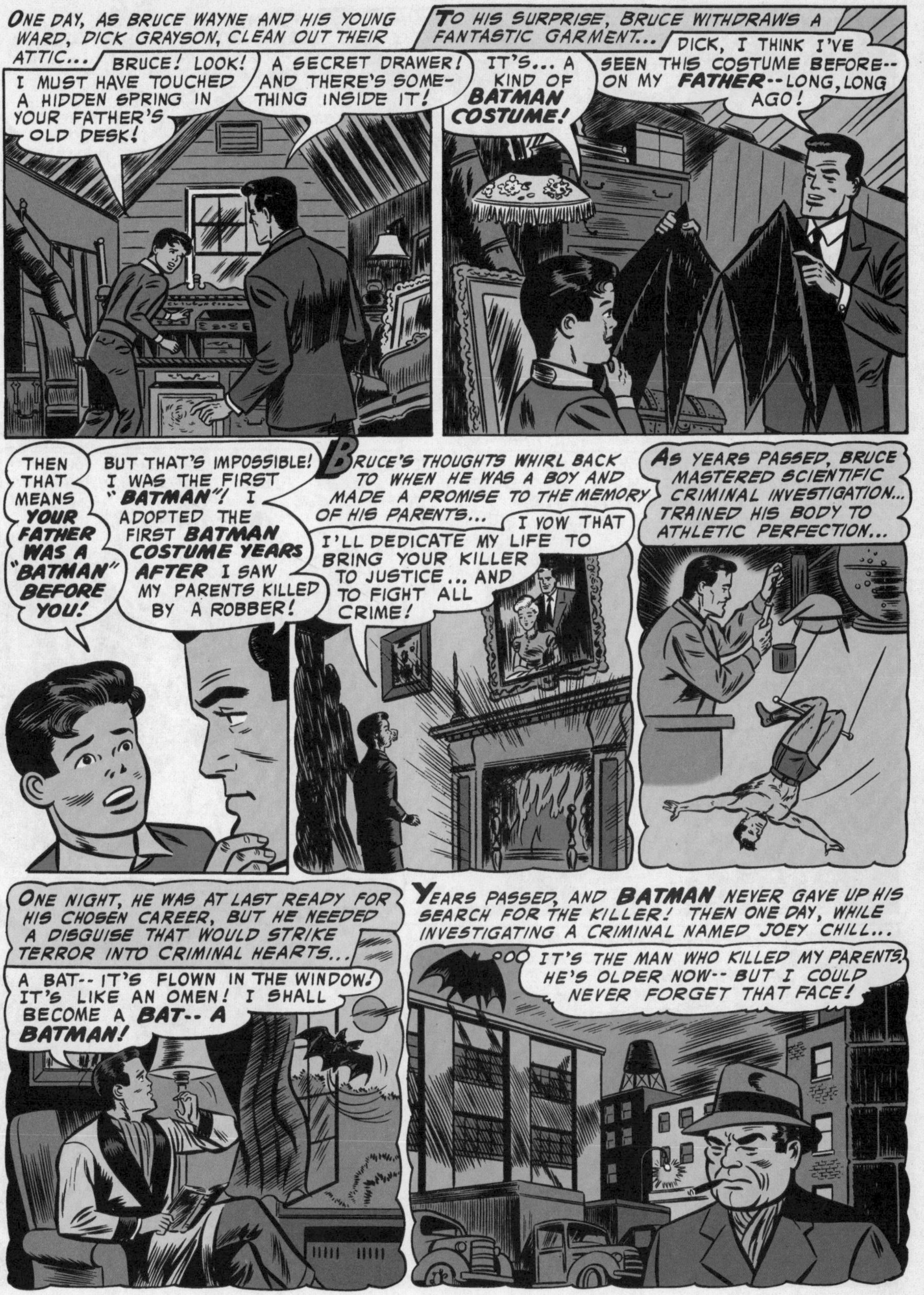

ONE DAY, AS BRUCE WAYNE AND HIS YOUNG WARD, DICK GRAYSON, CLEAN OUT THEIR ATTIC...
BRUCE! LOOK! I MUST HAVE TOUCHED A HIDDEN SPRING IN YOUR FATHER'S OLD DESK!
A SECRET DRAWER! AND THERE'S SOMETHING INSIDE IT!
TO HIS SURPRISE, BRUCE WITHDRAWS A FANTASTIC GARMENT...
IT'S... A KIND OF BATMAN COSTUME!
DICK, I THINK I'VE SEEN THIS COSTUME BEFORE-- ON MY FATHER--LONG, LONG AGO!
THEN THAT MEANS YOUR FATHER WAS A "BATMAN" BEFORE YOU!
BUT THAT'S IMPOSSIBLE! I WAS THE FIRST "BATMAN"! I ADOPTED THE FIRST BATMAN COSTUME YEARS AFTER I SAW MY PARENTS KILLED BY A ROBBER!
BRUCE'S THOUGHTS WHIRL BACK TO WHEN HE WAS A BOY AND MADE A PROMISE TO THE MEMORY OF HIS PARENTS...
I VOW THAT I'LL DEDICATE MY LIFE TO BRING YOUR KILLER TO JUSTICE... AND TO FIGHT ALL CRIME!
AS YEARS PASSED, BRUCE MASTERED SCIENTIFIC CRIMINAL INVESTIGATION... TRAINED HIS BODY TO ATHLETIC PERFECTION...
ONE NIGHT, HE WAS AT LAST READY FOR HIS CHOSEN CAREER, BUT HE NEEDED A DISGUISE THAT WOULD STRIKE TERROR INTO CRIMINAL HEARTS...
A BAT-- IT'S FLOWN IN THE WINDOW! IT'S LIKE AN OMEN! I SHALL BECOME A BAT-- A BATMAN!
YEARS PASSED, AND BATMAN NEVER GAVE UP HIS SEARCH FOR THE KILLER! THEN ONE DAY, WHILE INVESTIGATING A CRIMINAL NAMED JOEY CHILL...
IT'S THE MAN WHO KILLED MY PARENTS! HE'S OLDER NOW-- BUT I COULD NEVER FORGET THAT FACE!

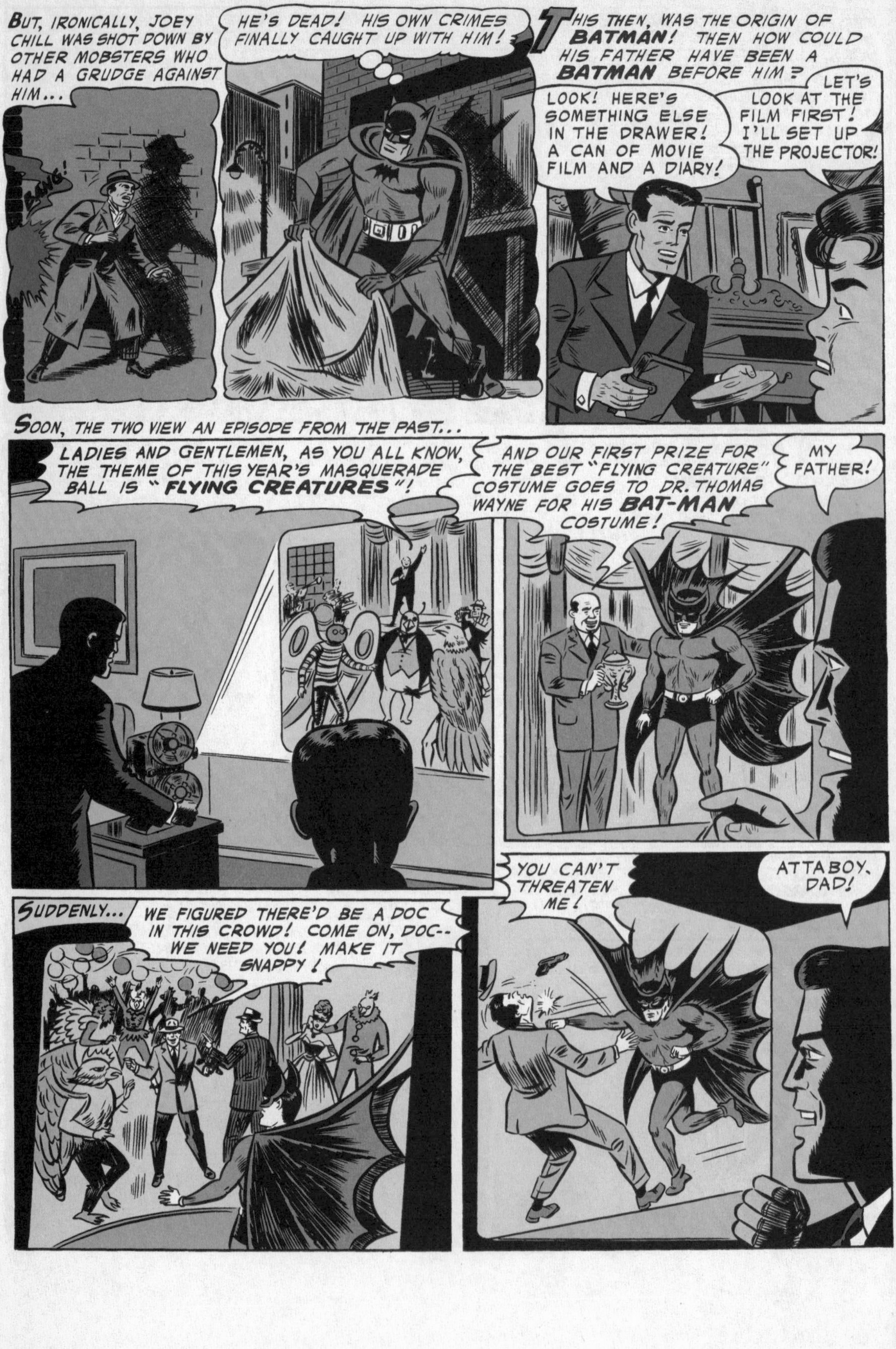

BUT, IRONICALLY, JOEY CHILL WAS SHOT DOWN BY OTHER MOBSTERS WHO HAD A GRUDGE AGAINST HIM...
BANG!
HE'S DEAD! HIS OWN CRIMES FINALLY CAUGHT UP WITH HIM!
THIS THEN, WAS THE ORIGIN OF BATMAN! THEN HOW COULD HIS FATHER HAVE BEEN A BATMAN BEFORE HIM?
LOOK! HERE'S SOMETHING ELSE IN THE DRAWER! A CAN OF MOVIE FILM AND A DIARY!
LET'S LOOK AT THE FILM FIRST! I'LL SET UP THE PROJECTOR!
SOON, THE TWO VIEW AN EPISODE FROM THE PAST...
LADIES AND GENTLEMEN, AS YOU ALL KNOW, THE THEME OF THIS YEAR'S MASQUERADE BALL IS "FLYING CREATURES"!
AND OUR FIRST PRIZE FOR THE BEST "FLYING CREATURE" COSTUME GOES TO DR. THOMAS WAYNE FOR HIS BAT-MAN COSTUME!
MY FATHER!
SUDDENLY...
WE FIGURED THERE'D BE A DOC IN THIS CROWD! COME ON, DOC-- WE NEED YOU! MAKE IT SNAPPY!
YOU CAN'T THREATEN ME!
ATTABOY, DAD!

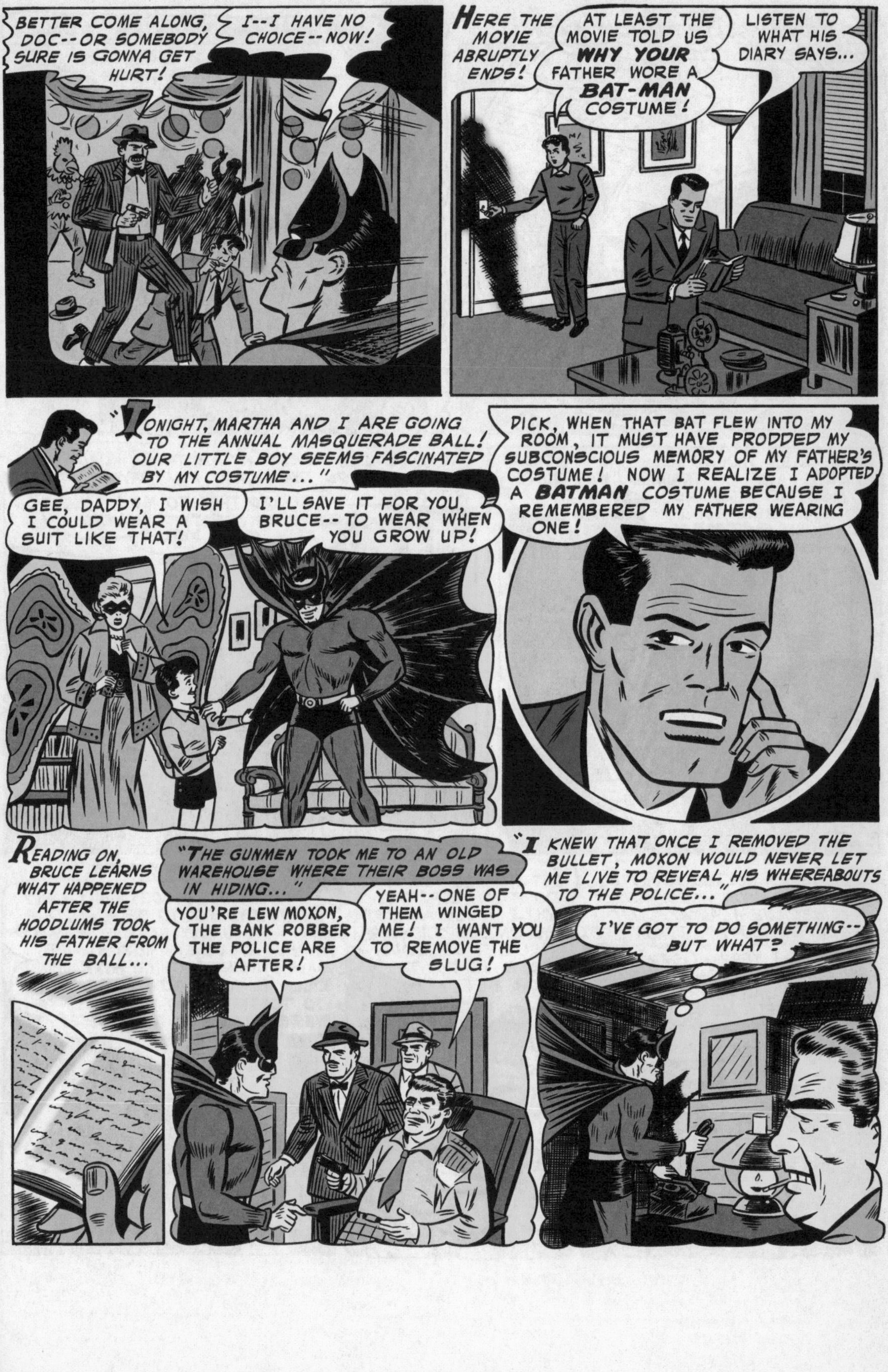
BETTER COME ALONG, DOC--OR SOMEBODY SURE IS GONNA GET HURT!
I--I HAVE NO CHOICE--NOW!
HERE THE MOVIE ABRUPTLY ENDS!
AT LEAST THE MOVIE TOLD US WHY YOUR FATHER WORE A BAT-MAN COSTUME!
LISTEN TO WHAT HIS DIARY SAYS...
"TONIGHT, MARTHA AND I ARE GOING TO THE ANNUAL MASQUERADE BALL! OUR LITTLE BOY SEEMS FASCINATED BY MY COSTUME..."
GEE, DADDY, I WISH I COULD WEAR A SUIT LIKE THAT!
I'LL SAVE IT FOR YOU, BRUCE--TO WEAR WHEN YOU GROW UP!
DICK, WHEN THAT BAT FLEW INTO MY ROOM, IT MUST HAVE PRODDED MY SUBCONSCIOUS MEMORY OF MY FATHER'S COSTUME! NOW I REALIZE I ADOPTED A BATMAN COSTUME BECAUSE I REMEMBERED MY FATHER WEARING ONE!
READING ON, BRUCE LEARNS WHAT HAPPENED AFTER THE HOODLUMS TOOK HIS FATHER FROM THE BALL...
"THE GUNMEN TOOK ME TO AN OLD WAREHOUSE WHERE THEIR BOSS WAS IN HIDING..."
YOU'RE LEW MOXON, THE BANK ROBBER THE POLICE ARE AFTER!
YEAH--ONE OF THEM WINGED ME! I WANT YOU TO REMOVE THE SLUG!
"I KNEW THAT ONCE I REMOVED THE BULLET, MOXON WOULD NEVER LET ME LIVE TO REVEAL HIS WHEREABOUTS TO THE POLICE..."
I'VE GOT TO DO SOMETHING--BUT WHAT?

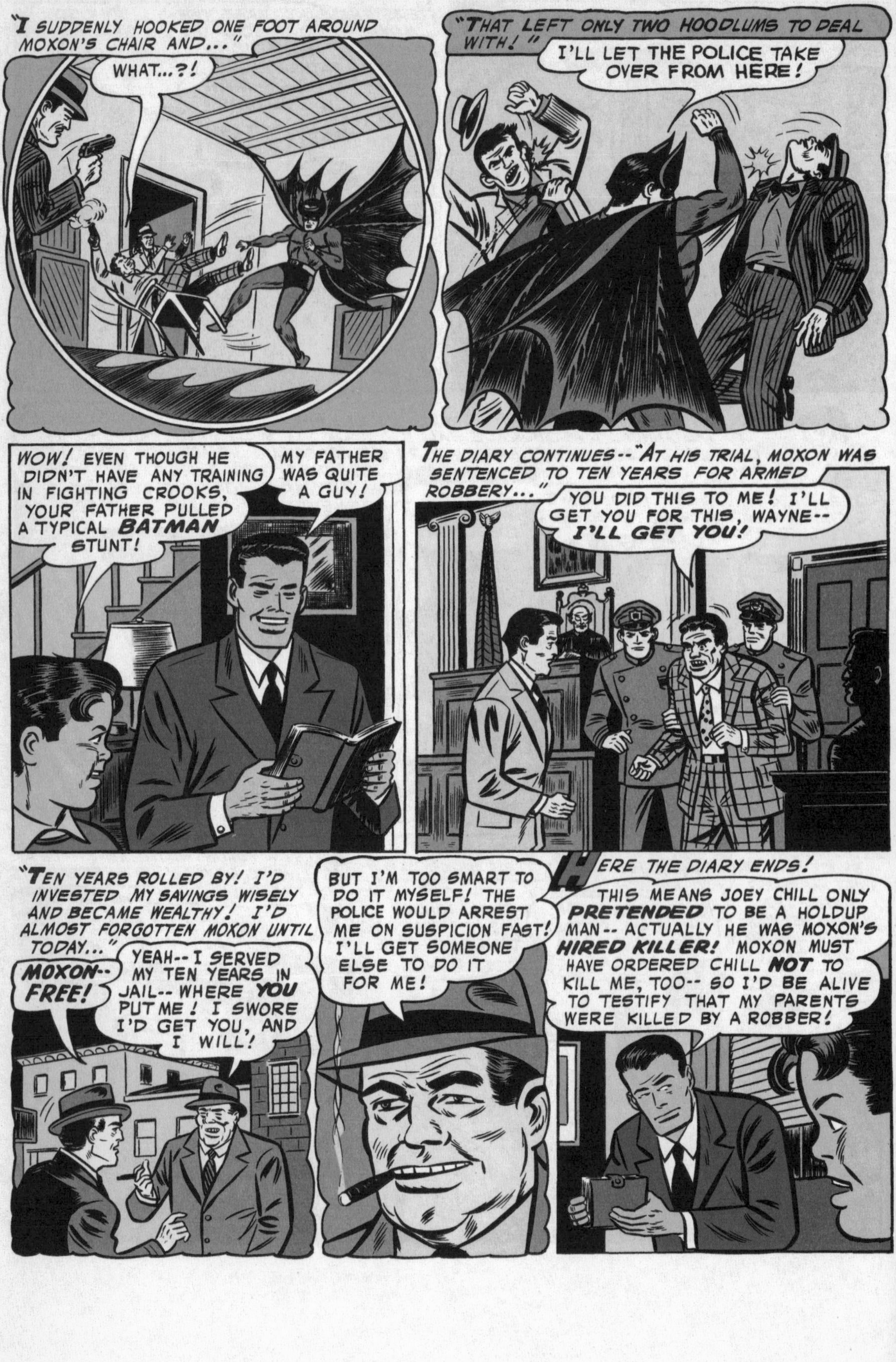
"I SUDDENLY HOOKED ONE FOOT AROUND MOXON'S CHAIR AND..."
WHAT...?!
"THAT LEFT ONLY TWO HOODLUMS TO DEAL WITH!"
I'LL LET THE POLICE TAKE OVER FROM HERE!
WOW! EVEN THOUGH HE DIDN'T HAVE ANY TRAINING IN FIGHTING CROOKS, YOUR FATHER PULLED A TYPICAL BATMAN STUNT!
MY FATHER WAS QUITE A GUY!
THE DIARY CONTINUES--"AT HIS TRIAL, MOXON WAS SENTENCED TO TEN YEARS FOR ARMED ROBBERY..."
YOU DID THIS TO ME! I'LL GET YOU FOR THIS, WAYNE-- I'LL GET YOU!
"TEN YEARS ROLLED BY! I'D INVESTED MY SAVINGS WISELY AND BECAME WEALTHY! I'D ALMOST FORGOTTEN MOXON UNTIL TODAY..."
MOXON-- FREE!
YEAH-- I SERVED MY TEN YEARS IN JAIL-- WHERE YOU PUT ME! I SWORE I'D GET YOU, AND I WILL!
BUT I'M TOO SMART TO DO IT MYSELF! THE POLICE WOULD ARREST ME ON SUSPICION FAST! I'LL GET SOMEONE ELSE TO DO IT FOR ME!
HERE THE DIARY ENDS!
THIS MEANS JOEY CHILL ONLY PRETENDED TO BE A HOLDUP MAN-- ACTUALLY HE WAS MOXON'S HIRED KILLER! MOXON MUST HAVE ORDERED CHILL NOT TO KILL ME, TOO-- SO I'D BE ALIVE TO TESTIFY THAT MY PARENTS WERE KILLED BY A ROBBER!

GOSH, BRUCE-- MOXON USED **YOU** AS HIS **ALIBI!**

HE USED ME AS A COVERUP FOR HIS DELIBERATE MURDER OF MY PARENTS! PUT ON YOUR COSTUME, DICK-- **WE'VE JUST REOPENED THE WAYNE MURDER CASE!**

LATER, IN THE OFFICE OF POLICE COMMISSIONER GORDON...

COMMISSIONER, I'D LIKE TO KNOW THE WHEREABOUTS OF LEW MOXON!

I'LL HAVE THIS TELE-PHOTOED TO EVERY POLICE DEPARTMENT IN THE COUNTRY!

AND WHEN THE INFORMATION COMES...

MOXON IS NOW IN THE **BILLBOARD BLIMP** BUSINESS OUT WEST-- IN COASTAL CITY!

SOON AFTER, THE SLEEK **BATPLANE** RACES THROUGH THE SKIES...

WHY DID YOU HAVE ME BRING ALONG YOUR FATHER'S COSTUME, **BATMAN?**

IT GIVES ME THE FEELING THAT MY FATHER IS WITH ME ON THIS CASE!

HOURS LATER, AT THEIR DESTINATION, TWO FIGURES MOVE LIKE SHADOWS TOWARDS A BLIMP HANGAR...

MOXON SKY-HI ADVERTISING CO.

BUT, IN THE DARKNESS, **ROBIN'S** FOOT KICKS A MISPLACED GASOLINE CAN...

CLANK

BATMAN AND ROBIN! GET 'EM!

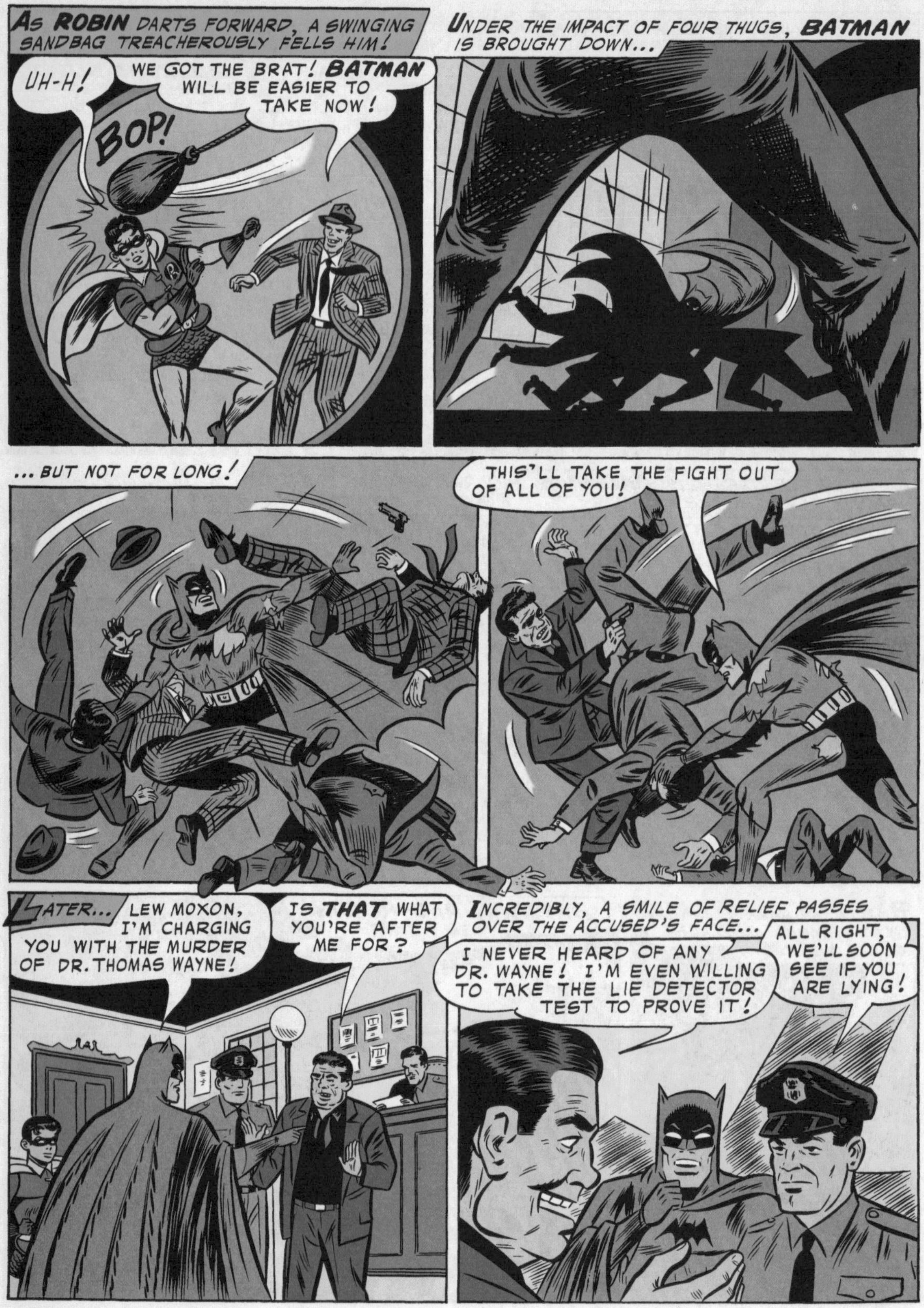

AS ROBIN DARTS FORWARD, A SWINGING SANDBAG TREACHEROUSLY FELLS HIM!
UH-H!
WE GOT THE BRAT! BATMAN WILL BE EASIER TO TAKE NOW!
BOP!
UNDER THE IMPACT OF FOUR THUGS, BATMAN IS BROUGHT DOWN...
... BUT NOT FOR LONG!
THIS'LL TAKE THE FIGHT OUT OF ALL OF YOU!
LATER... LEW MOXON, I'M CHARGING YOU WITH THE MURDER OF DR. THOMAS WAYNE!
IS THAT WHAT YOU'RE AFTER ME FOR?
INCREDIBLY, A SMILE OF RELIEF PASSES OVER THE ACCUSED'S FACE...
I NEVER HEARD OF ANY DR. WAYNE! I'M EVEN WILLING TO TAKE THE LIE DETECTOR TEST TO PROVE IT!
ALL RIGHT, WE'LL SOON SEE IF YOU ARE LYING!

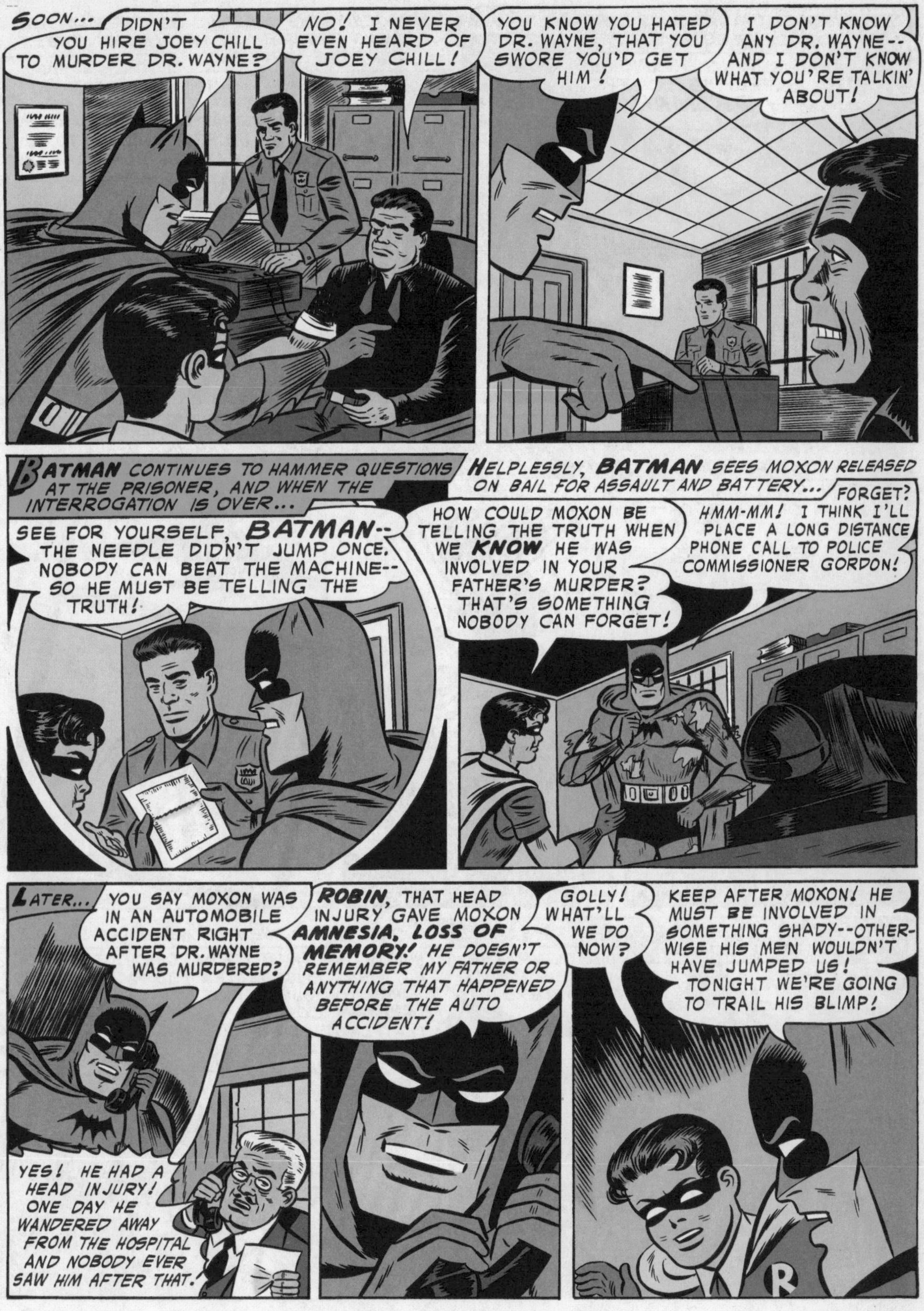
SOON...
DIDN'T YOU HIRE JOEY CHILL TO MURDER DR. WAYNE?
NO! I NEVER EVEN HEARD OF JOEY CHILL!
YOU KNOW YOU HATED DR. WAYNE, THAT YOU SWORE YOU'D GET HIM!
I DON'T KNOW ANY DR. WAYNE-- AND I DON'T KNOW WHAT YOU'RE TALKIN' ABOUT!
BATMAN CONTINUES TO HAMMER QUESTIONS AT THE PRISONER, AND WHEN THE INTERROGATION IS OVER...
SEE FOR YOURSELF, BATMAN-- THE NEEDLE DIDN'T JUMP ONCE. NOBODY CAN BEAT THE MACHINE-- SO HE MUST BE TELLING THE TRUTH!
HELPLESSLY, BATMAN SEES MOXON RELEASED ON BAIL FOR ASSAULT AND BATTERY...
HOW COULD MOXON BE TELLING THE TRUTH WHEN WE KNOW HE WAS INVOLVED IN YOUR FATHER'S MURDER? THAT'S SOMETHING NOBODY CAN FORGET!
FORGET? HMM-MM! I THINK I'LL PLACE A LONG DISTANCE PHONE CALL TO POLICE COMMISSIONER GORDON!
LATER...
YOU SAY MOXON WAS IN AN AUTOMOBILE ACCIDENT RIGHT AFTER DR. WAYNE WAS MURDERED?
YES! HE HAD A HEAD INJURY! ONE DAY HE WANDERED AWAY FROM THE HOSPITAL AND NOBODY EVER SAW HIM AFTER THAT.
ROBIN, THAT HEAD INJURY GAVE MOXON AMNESIA, LOSS OF MEMORY! HE DOESN'T REMEMBER MY FATHER OR ANYTHING THAT HAPPENED BEFORE THE AUTO ACCIDENT!
GOLLY! WHAT'LL WE DO NOW?
KEEP AFTER MOXON! HE MUST BE INVOLVED IN SOMETHING SHADY--OTHERWISE HIS MEN WOULDN'T HAVE JUMPED US! TONIGHT WE'RE GOING TO TRAIL HIS BLIMP!

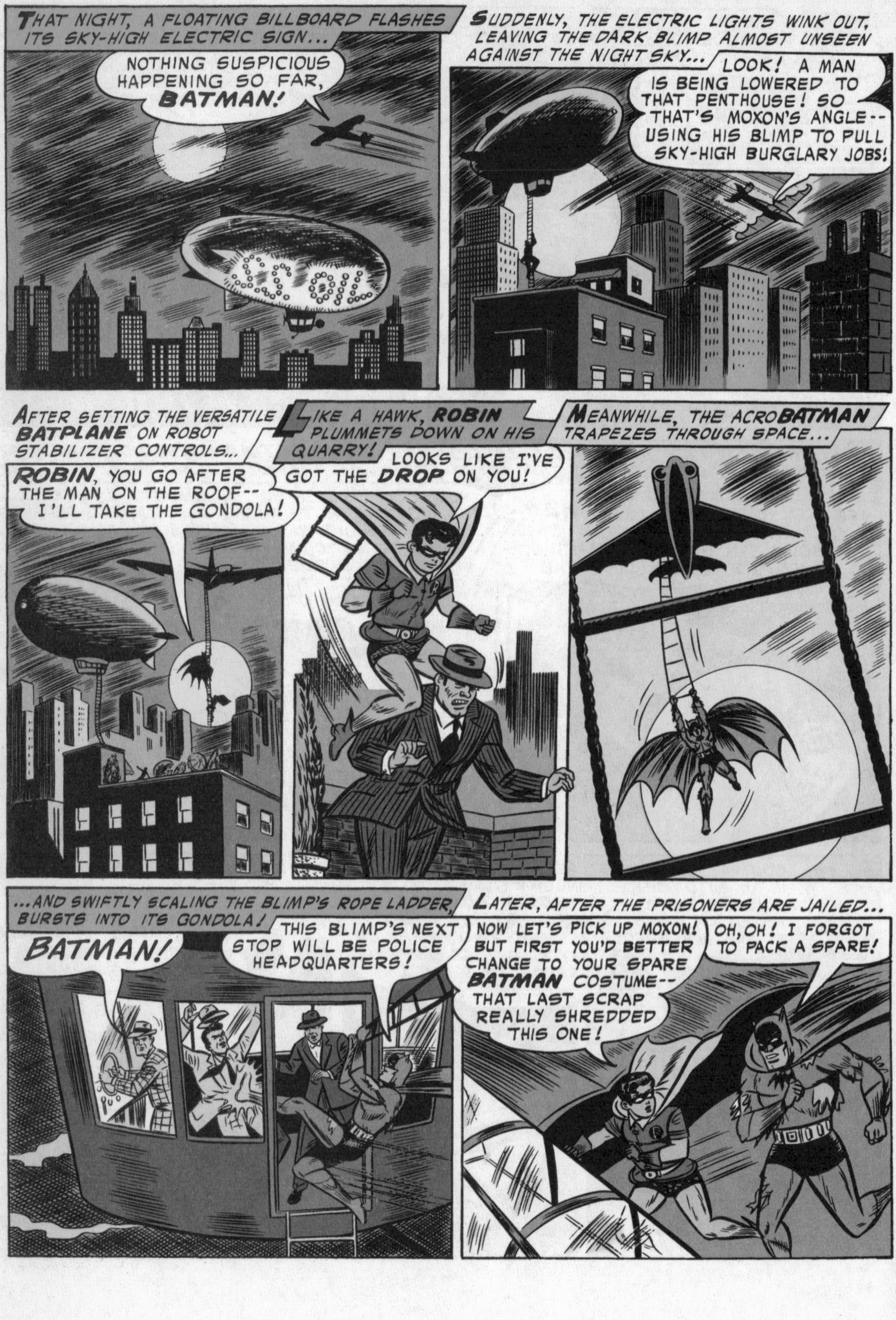
THAT NIGHT, A FLOATING BILLBOARD FLASHES ITS SKY-HIGH ELECTRIC SIGN...
NOTHING SUSPICIOUS HAPPENING SO FAR, BATMAN!
SUDDENLY, THE ELECTRIC LIGHTS WINK OUT, LEAVING THE DARK BLIMP ALMOST UNSEEN AGAINST THE NIGHT SKY...
LOOK! A MAN IS BEING LOWERED TO THAT PENTHOUSE! SO THAT'S MOXON'S ANGLE-- USING HIS BLIMP TO PULL SKY-HIGH BURGLARY JOBS!
AFTER SETTING THE VERSATILE BATPLANE ON ROBOT STABILIZER CONTROLS...
ROBIN, YOU GO AFTER THE MAN ON THE ROOF-- I'LL TAKE THE GONDOLA!
LIKE A HAWK, ROBIN PLUMMETS DOWN ON HIS QUARRY!
LOOKS LIKE I'VE GOT THE DROP ON YOU!
MEANWHILE, THE ACROBATMAN TRAPEZES THROUGH SPACE...
...AND SWIFTLY SCALING THE BLIMP'S ROPE LADDER, BURSTS INTO ITS GONDOLA!
BATMAN!
THIS BLIMP'S NEXT STOP WILL BE POLICE HEADQUARTERS!
LATER, AFTER THE PRISONERS ARE JAILED...
NOW LET'S PICK UP MOXON! BUT FIRST YOU'D BETTER CHANGE TO YOUR SPARE BATMAN COSTUME-- THAT LAST SCRAP REALLY SHREDDED THIS ONE!
OH, OH! I FORGOT TO PACK A SPARE!

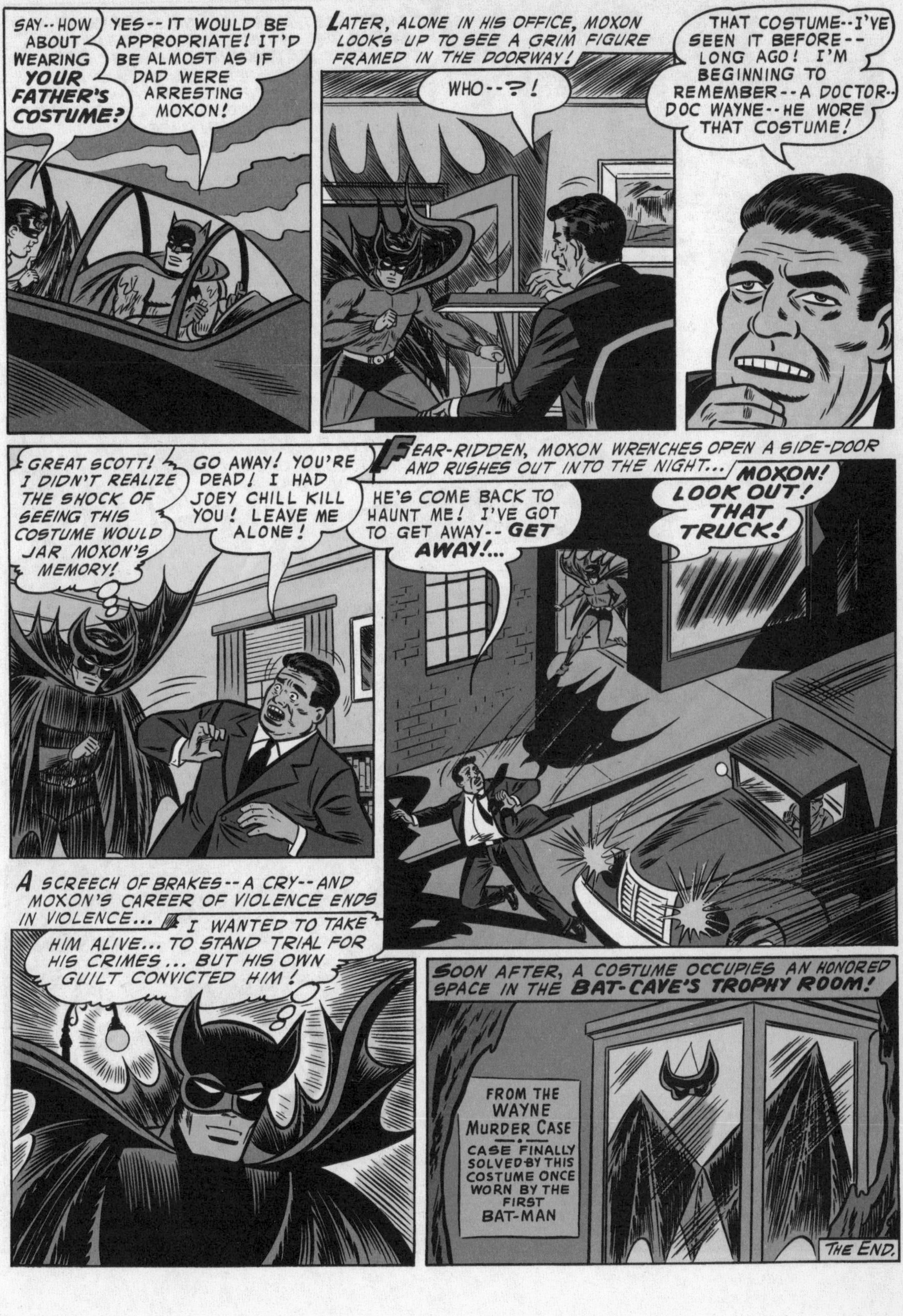
SAY--HOW ABOUT WEARING YOUR FATHER'S COSTUME?
YES--IT WOULD BE APPROPRIATE! IT'D BE ALMOST AS IF DAD WERE ARRESTING MOXON!
LATER, ALONE IN HIS OFFICE, MOXON LOOKS UP TO SEE A GRIM FIGURE FRAMED IN THE DOORWAY!
WHO--?!
THAT COSTUME--I'VE SEEN IT BEFORE--LONG AGO! I'M BEGINNING TO REMEMBER--A DOCTOR--DOC WAYNE--HE WORE THAT COSTUME!
GREAT SCOTT! I DIDN'T REALIZE THE SHOCK OF SEEING THIS COSTUME WOULD JAR MOXON'S MEMORY!
GO AWAY! YOU'RE DEAD! I HAD JOEY CHILL KILL YOU! LEAVE ME ALONE!
FEAR-RIDDEN, MOXON WRENCHES OPEN A SIDE-DOOR AND RUSHES OUT INTO THE NIGHT...
HE'S COME BACK TO HAUNT ME! I'VE GOT TO GET AWAY--GET AWAY!...
MOXON! LOOK OUT! THAT TRUCK!
A SCREECH OF BRAKES--A CRY--AND MOXON'S CAREER OF VIOLENCE ENDS IN VIOLENCE...
I WANTED TO TAKE HIM ALIVE... TO STAND TRIAL FOR HIS CRIMES... BUT HIS OWN GUILT CONVICTED HIM!
SOON AFTER, A COSTUME OCCUPIES AN HONORED SPACE IN THE BAT-CAVE'S TROPHY ROOM!
FROM THE WAYNE MURDER CASE
CASE FINALLY SOLVED BY THIS COSTUME ONCE WORN BY THE FIRST BAT-MAN
THE END.

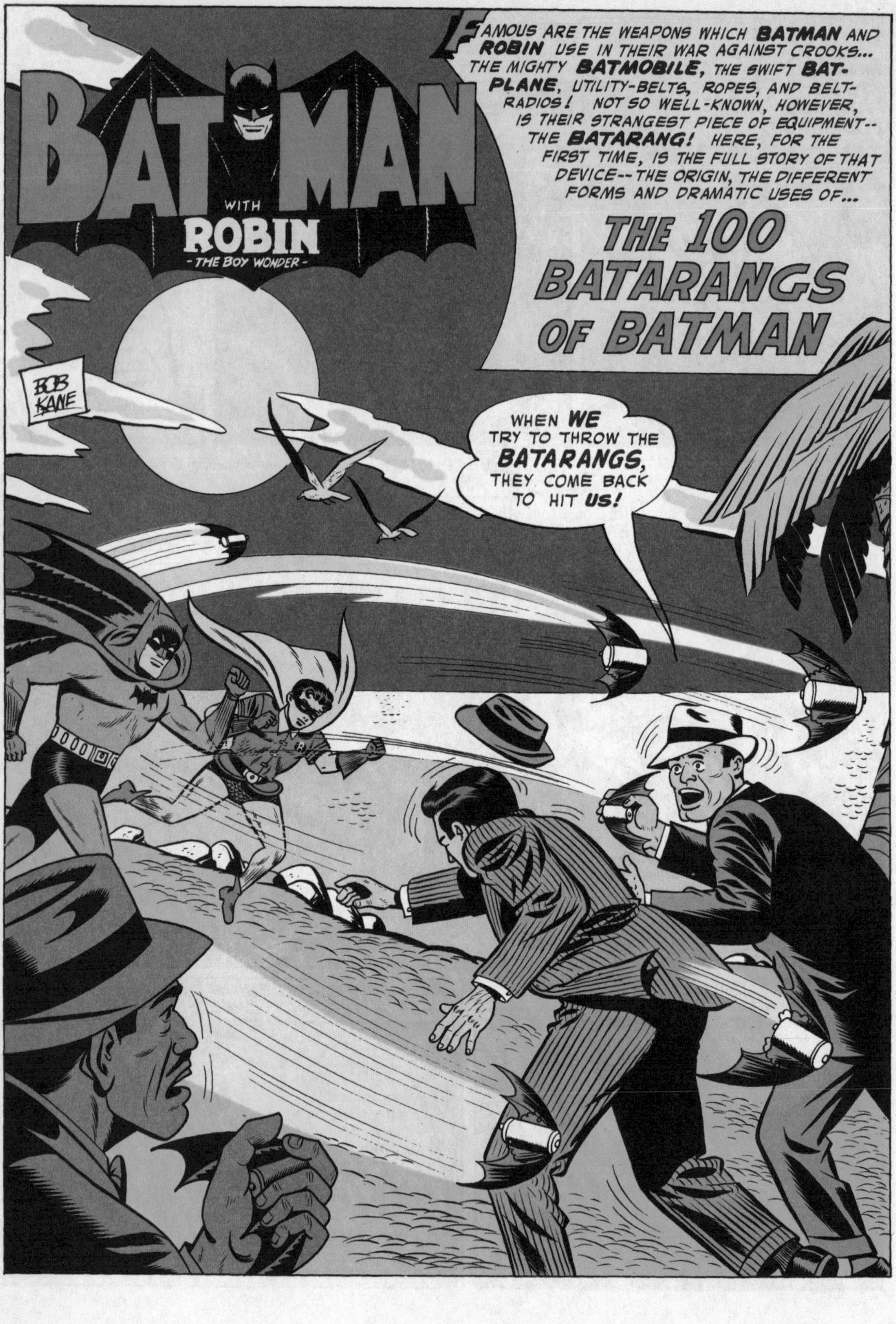
BATMAN
WITH
ROBIN
-THE BOY WONDER-
FAMOUS ARE THE WEAPONS WHICH BATMAN AND ROBIN USE IN THEIR WAR AGAINST CROOKS... THE MIGHTY BATMOBILE, THE SWIFT BAT-PLANE, UTILITY-BELTS, ROPES, AND BELT-RADIOS! NOT SO WELL-KNOWN, HOWEVER, IS THEIR STRANGEST PIECE OF EQUIPMENT-- THE BATARANG! HERE, FOR THE FIRST TIME, IS THE FULL STORY OF THAT DEVICE-- THE ORIGIN, THE DIFFERENT FORMS AND DRAMATIC USES OF...
THE 100 BATARANGS OF BATMAN
BOB KANE
WHEN WE TRY TO THROW THE BATARANGS, THEY COME BACK TO HIT US!

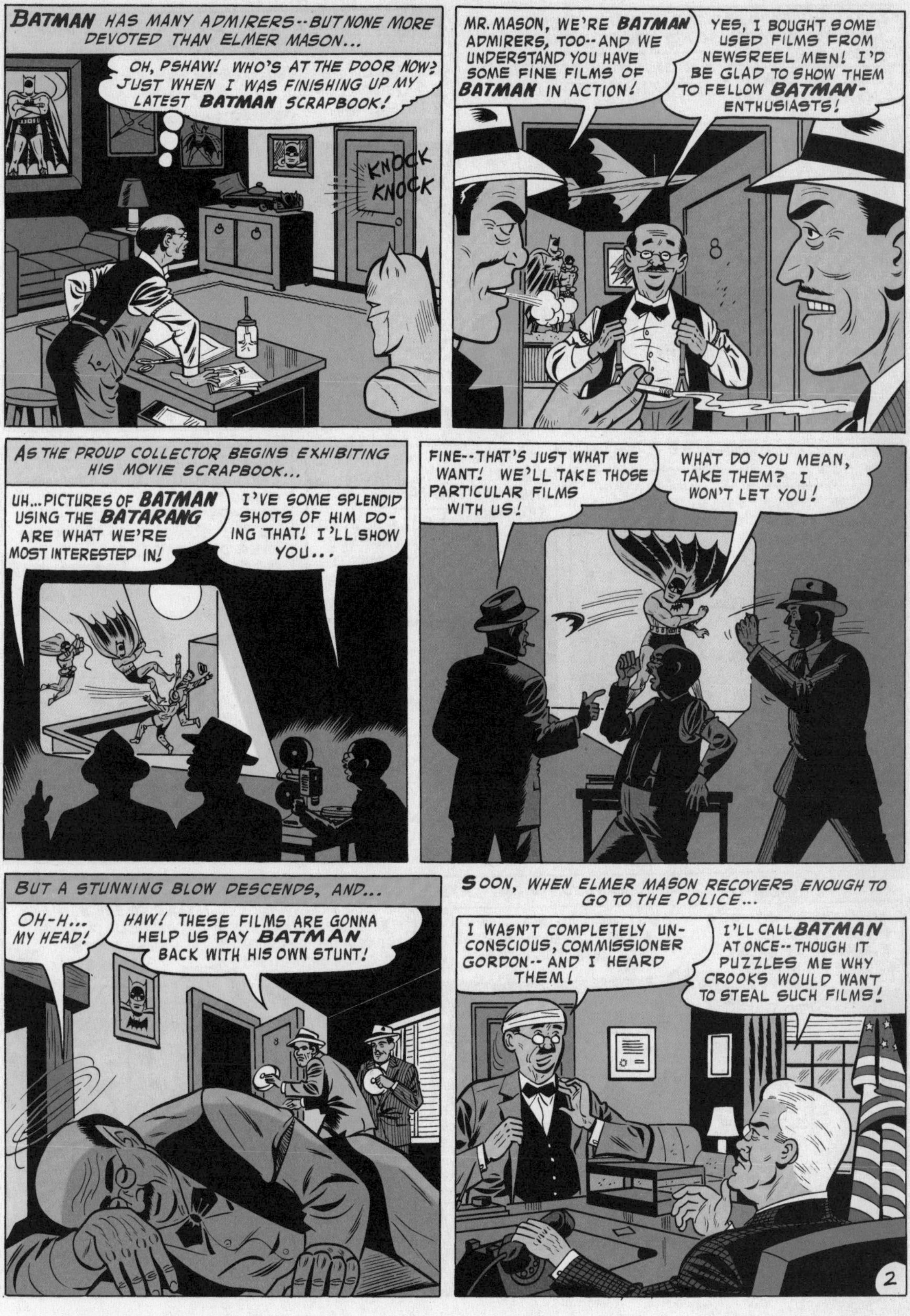
BATMAN HAS MANY ADMIRERS--BUT NONE MORE DEVOTED THAN ELMER MASON...
OH, PSHAW! WHO'S AT THE DOOR NOW? JUST WHEN I WAS FINISHING UP MY LATEST BATMAN SCRAPBOOK!
KNOCK KNOCK
MR. MASON, WE'RE BATMAN ADMIRERS, TOO--AND WE UNDERSTAND YOU HAVE SOME FINE FILMS OF BATMAN IN ACTION!
YES, I BOUGHT SOME USED FILMS FROM NEWSREEL MEN! I'D BE GLAD TO SHOW THEM TO FELLOW BATMAN-ENTHUSIASTS!
AS THE PROUD COLLECTOR BEGINS EXHIBITING HIS MOVIE SCRAPBOOK...
UH...PICTURES OF BATMAN USING THE BATARANG ARE WHAT WE'RE MOST INTERESTED IN!
I'VE SOME SPLENDID SHOTS OF HIM DOING THAT! I'LL SHOW YOU...
FINE--THAT'S JUST WHAT WE WANT! WE'LL TAKE THOSE PARTICULAR FILMS WITH US!
WHAT DO YOU MEAN, TAKE THEM? I WON'T LET YOU!
BUT A STUNNING BLOW DESCENDS, AND...
OH-H... MY HEAD!
HAW! THESE FILMS ARE GONNA HELP US PAY BATMAN BACK WITH HIS OWN STUNT!
SOON, WHEN ELMER MASON RECOVERS ENOUGH TO GO TO THE POLICE...
I WASN'T COMPLETELY UNCONSCIOUS, COMMISSIONER GORDON-- AND I HEARD THEM!
I'LL CALL BATMAN AT ONCE-- THOUGH IT PUZZLES ME WHY CROOKS WOULD WANT TO STEAL SUCH FILMS!
2

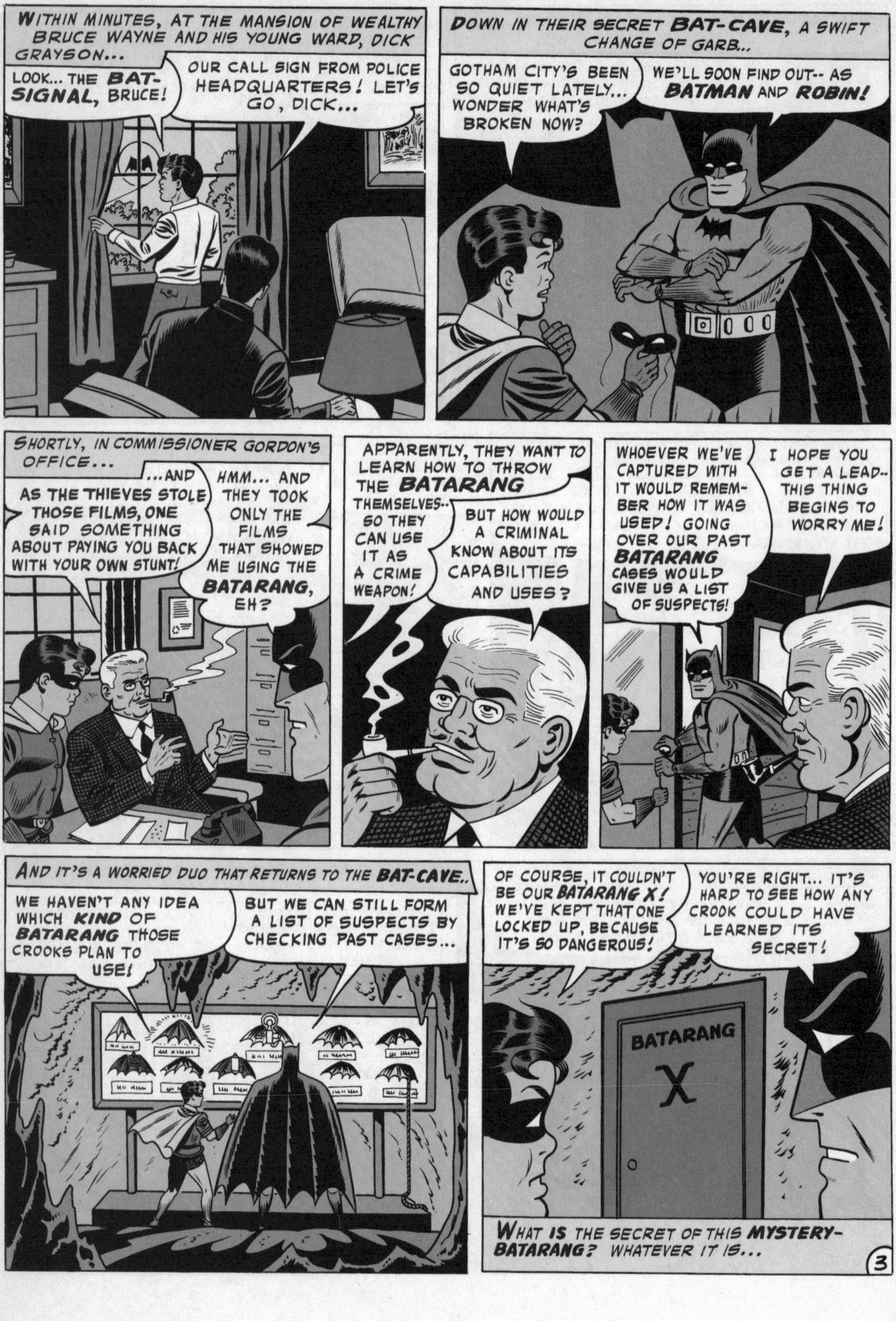
WITHIN MINUTES, AT THE MANSION OF WEALTHY BRUCE WAYNE AND HIS YOUNG WARD, DICK GRAYSON...
LOOK... THE BAT-SIGNAL, BRUCE!
OUR CALL SIGN FROM POLICE HEADQUARTERS! LET'S GO, DICK...
DOWN IN THEIR SECRET BAT-CAVE, A SWIFT CHANGE OF GARB...
GOTHAM CITY'S BEEN SO QUIET LATELY... WONDER WHAT'S BROKEN NOW?
WE'LL SOON FIND OUT-- AS BATMAN AND ROBIN!
SHORTLY, IN COMMISSIONER GORDON'S OFFICE...
...AND AS THE THIEVES STOLE THOSE FILMS, ONE SAID SOMETHING ABOUT PAYING YOU BACK WITH YOUR OWN STUNT!
HMM... AND THEY TOOK ONLY THE FILMS THAT SHOWED ME USING THE BATARANG, EH?
APPARENTLY, THEY WANT TO LEARN HOW TO THROW THE BATARANG THEMSELVES.. SO THEY CAN USE IT AS A CRIME WEAPON!
BUT HOW WOULD A CRIMINAL KNOW ABOUT ITS CAPABILITIES AND USES?
WHOEVER WE'VE CAPTURED WITH IT WOULD REMEMBER HOW IT WAS USED! GOING OVER OUR PAST BATARANG CASES WOULD GIVE US A LIST OF SUSPECTS!
I HOPE YOU GET A LEAD-- THIS THING BEGINS TO WORRY ME!
AND IT'S A WORRIED DUO THAT RETURNS TO THE BAT-CAVE..
WE HAVEN'T ANY IDEA WHICH KIND OF BATARANG THOSE CROOKS PLAN TO USE!
BUT WE CAN STILL FORM A LIST OF SUSPECTS BY CHECKING PAST CASES...
OF COURSE, IT COULDN'T BE OUR BATARANG X! WE'VE KEPT THAT ONE LOCKED UP, BECAUSE IT'S SO DANGEROUS!
YOU'RE RIGHT... IT'S HARD TO SEE HOW ANY CROOK COULD HAVE LEARNED ITS SECRET!
BATARANG X
WHAT IS THE SECRET OF THIS MYSTERY-BATARANG? WHATEVER IT IS...
3

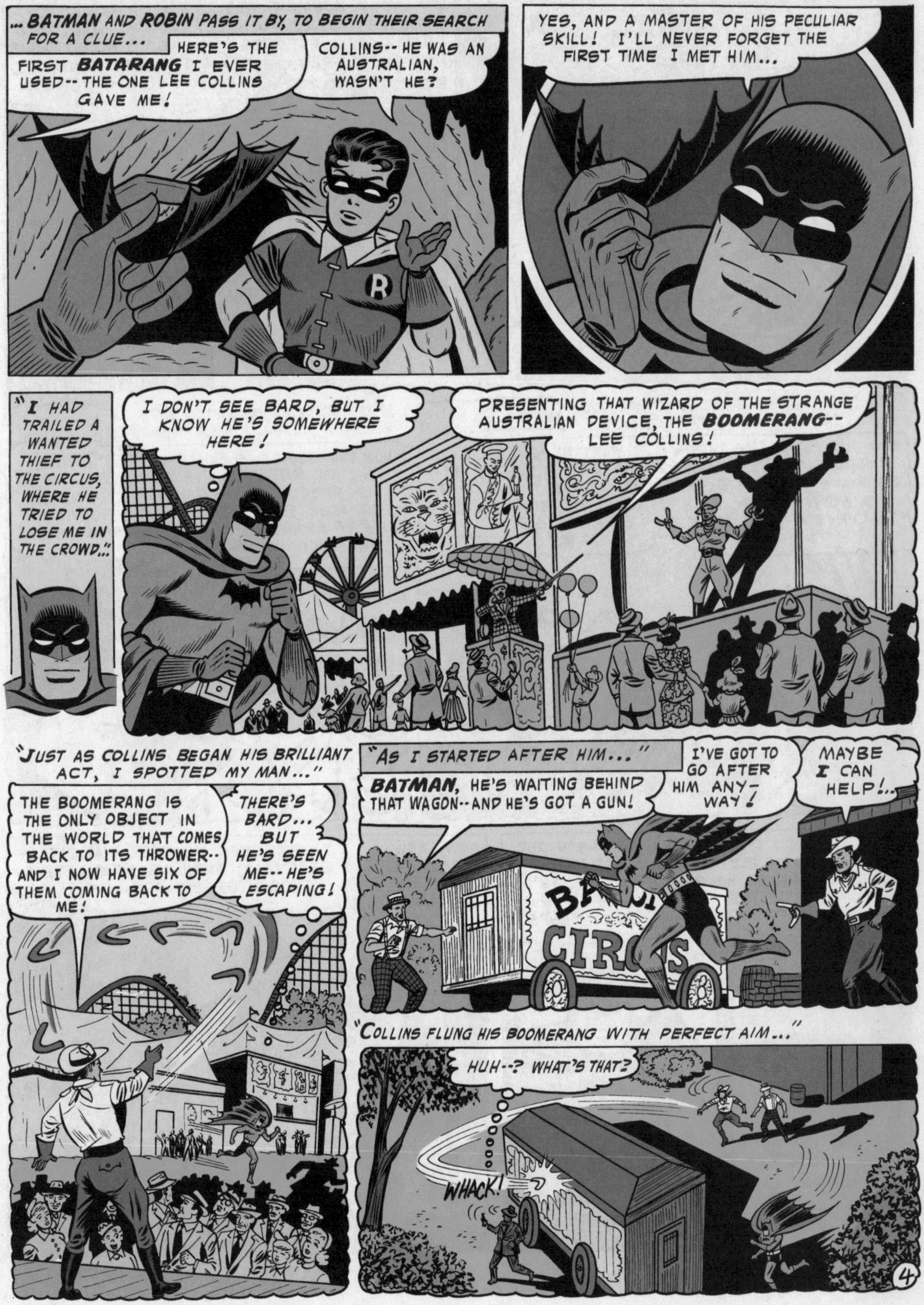
...BATMAN AND ROBIN PASS IT BY, TO BEGIN THEIR SEARCH FOR A CLUE...
HERE'S THE FIRST BATARANG I EVER USED-- THE ONE LEE COLLINS GAVE ME!
COLLINS-- HE WAS AN AUSTRALIAN, WASN'T HE?
YES, AND A MASTER OF HIS PECULIAR SKILL! I'LL NEVER FORGET THE FIRST TIME I MET HIM...
"I HAD TRAILED A WANTED THIEF TO THE CIRCUS, WHERE HE TRIED TO LOSE ME IN THE CROWD..."
I DON'T SEE BARD, BUT I KNOW HE'S SOMEWHERE HERE!
PRESENTING THAT WIZARD OF THE STRANGE AUSTRALIAN DEVICE, THE BOOMERANG-- LEE COLLINS!
"JUST AS COLLINS BEGAN HIS BRILLIANT ACT, I SPOTTED MY MAN..."
THE BOOMERANG IS THE ONLY OBJECT IN THE WORLD THAT COMES BACK TO ITS THROWER-- AND I NOW HAVE SIX OF THEM COMING BACK TO ME!
THERE'S BARD... BUT HE'S SEEN ME-- HE'S ESCAPING!
"AS I STARTED AFTER HIM..."
BATMAN, HE'S WAITING BEHIND THAT WAGON-- AND HE'S GOT A GUN!
I'VE GOT TO GO AFTER HIM ANY-WAY!
MAYBE I CAN HELP!..
"COLLINS FLUNG HIS BOOMERANG WITH PERFECT AIM..."
HUH--? WHAT'S THAT?
WHACK!
4

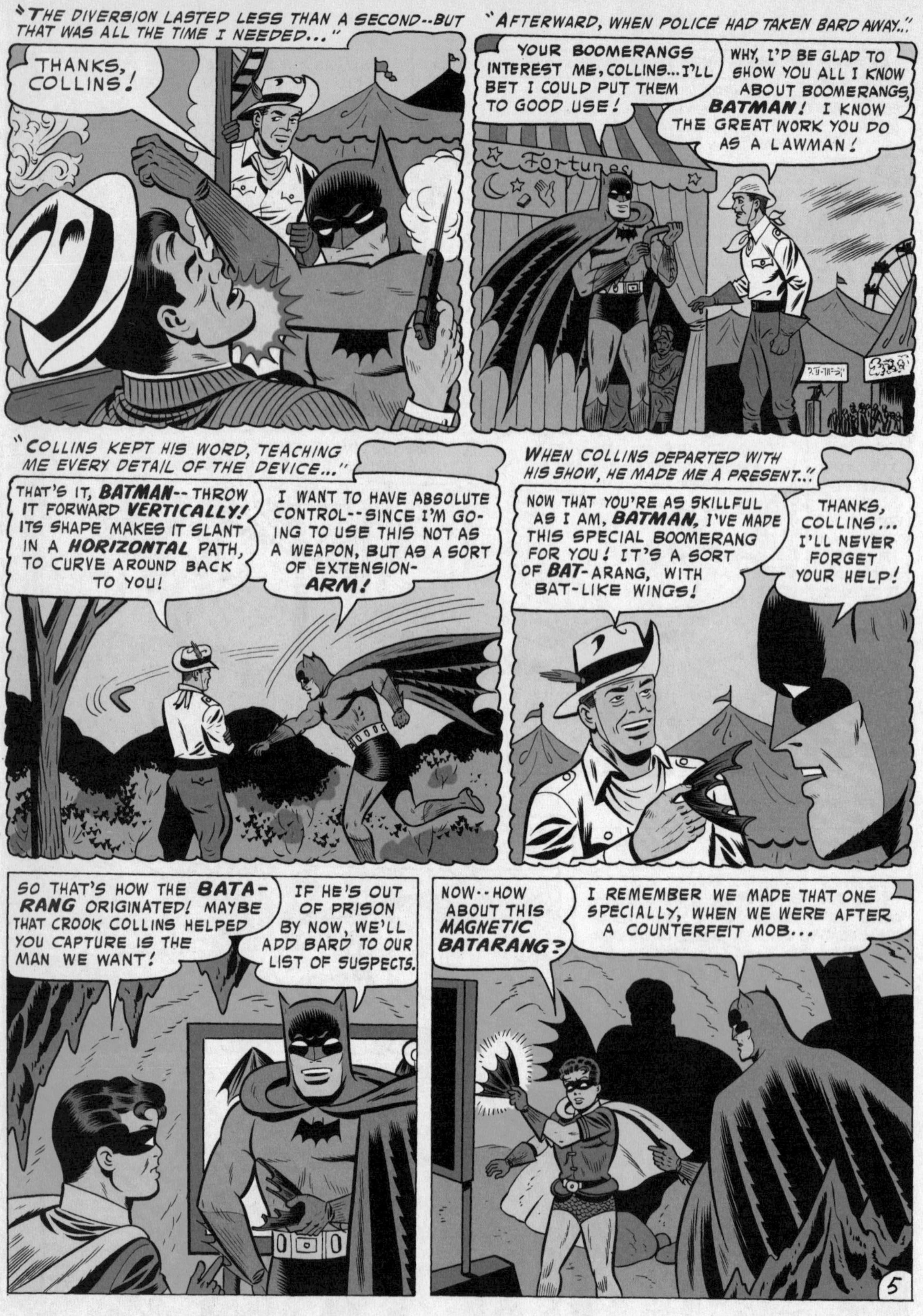
"THE DIVERSION LASTED LESS THAN A SECOND--BUT THAT WAS ALL THE TIME I NEEDED..."
THANKS, COLLINS!
"AFTERWARD, WHEN POLICE HAD TAKEN BARD AWAY..."
YOUR BOOMERANGS INTEREST ME, COLLINS... I'LL BET I COULD PUT THEM TO GOOD USE!
WHY, I'D BE GLAD TO SHOW YOU ALL I KNOW ABOUT BOOMERANGS, BATMAN! I KNOW THE GREAT WORK YOU DO AS A LAWMAN!
Fortunes
"COLLINS KEPT HIS WORD, TEACHING ME EVERY DETAIL OF THE DEVICE..."
THAT'S IT, BATMAN-- THROW IT FORWARD VERTICALLY! ITS SHAPE MAKES IT SLANT IN A HORIZONTAL PATH, TO CURVE AROUND BACK TO YOU!
I WANT TO HAVE ABSOLUTE CONTROL--SINCE I'M GOING TO USE THIS NOT AS A WEAPON, BUT AS A SORT OF EXTENSION-ARM!
WHEN COLLINS DEPARTED WITH HIS SHOW, HE MADE ME A PRESENT..."
NOW THAT YOU'RE AS SKILLFUL AS I AM, BATMAN, I'VE MADE THIS SPECIAL BOOMERANG FOR YOU! IT'S A SORT OF BAT-ARANG, WITH BAT-LIKE WINGS!
THANKS, COLLINS... I'LL NEVER FORGET YOUR HELP!
SO THAT'S HOW THE BATARANG ORIGINATED! MAYBE THAT CROOK COLLINS HELPED YOU CAPTURE IS THE MAN WE WANT!
IF HE'S OUT OF PRISON BY NOW, WE'LL ADD BARD TO OUR LIST OF SUSPECTS.
NOW--HOW ABOUT THIS MAGNETIC BATARANG?
I REMEMBER WE MADE THAT ONE SPECIALLY, WHEN WE WERE AFTER A COUNTERFEIT MOB...
5

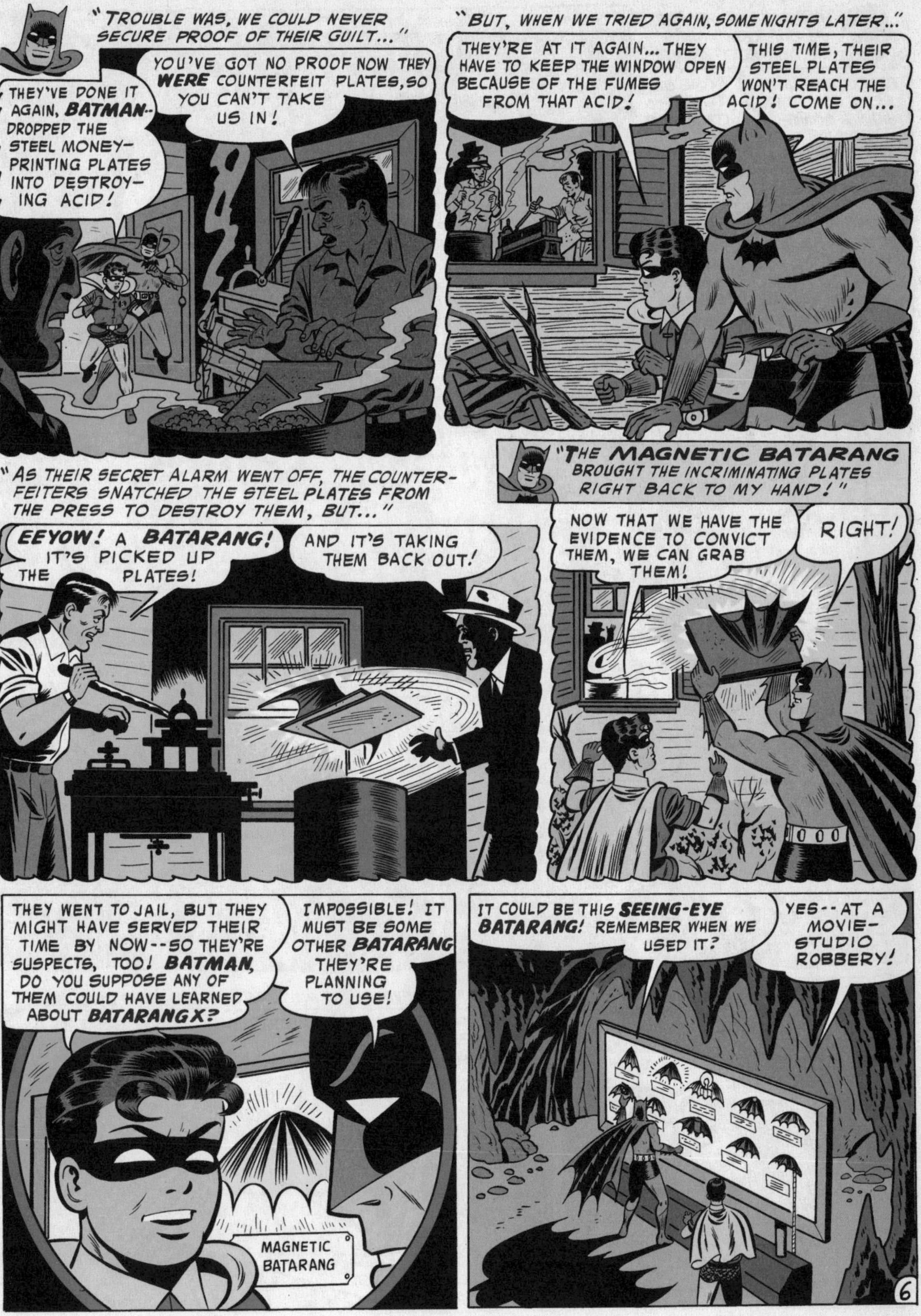

"TROUBLE WAS, WE COULD NEVER SECURE PROOF OF THEIR GUILT..."
THEY'VE DONE IT AGAIN, BATMAN-- DROPPED THE STEEL MONEY-PRINTING PLATES INTO DESTROYING ACID!
YOU'VE GOT NO PROOF NOW THEY WERE COUNTERFEIT PLATES, SO YOU CAN'T TAKE US IN!
"BUT, WHEN WE TRIED AGAIN, SOME NIGHTS LATER..."
THEY'RE AT IT AGAIN... THEY HAVE TO KEEP THE WINDOW OPEN BECAUSE OF THE FUMES FROM THAT ACID!
THIS TIME, THEIR STEEL PLATES WON'T REACH THE ACID! COME ON...
"AS THEIR SECRET ALARM WENT OFF, THE COUNTERFEITERS SNATCHED THE STEEL PLATES FROM THE PRESS TO DESTROY THEM, BUT..."
EEYOW! A BATARANG! IT'S PICKED UP THE PLATES!
AND IT'S TAKING THEM BACK OUT!
"THE MAGNETIC BATARANG BROUGHT THE INCRIMINATING PLATES RIGHT BACK TO MY HAND!"
NOW THAT WE HAVE THE EVIDENCE TO CONVICT THEM, WE CAN GRAB THEM!
RIGHT!
THEY WENT TO JAIL, BUT THEY MIGHT HAVE SERVED THEIR TIME BY NOW--SO THEY'RE SUSPECTS, TOO! BATMAN, DO YOU SUPPOSE ANY OF THEM COULD HAVE LEARNED ABOUT BATARANG X?
IMPOSSIBLE! IT MUST BE SOME OTHER BATARANG THEY'RE PLANNING TO USE!
MAGNETIC BATARANG
IT COULD BE THIS SEEING-EYE BATARANG! REMEMBER WHEN WE USED IT?
YES--AT A MOVIE-STUDIO ROBBERY!
6

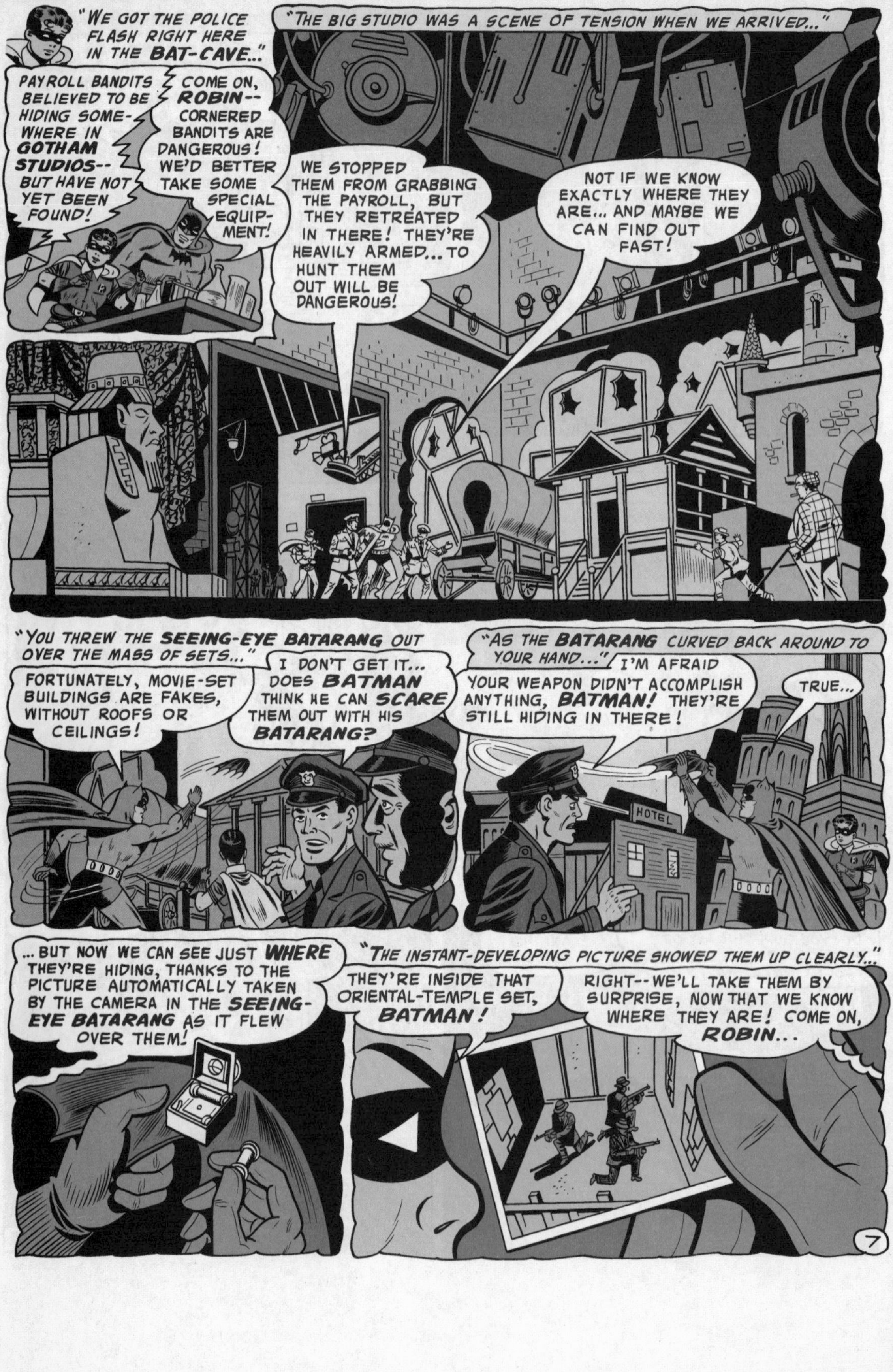
"WE GOT THE POLICE FLASH RIGHT HERE IN THE BAT-CAVE..."
PAYROLL BANDITS BELIEVED TO BE HIDING SOMEWHERE IN GOTHAM STUDIOS-- BUT HAVE NOT YET BEEN FOUND!
COME ON, ROBIN-- CORNERED BANDITS ARE DANGEROUS! WE'D BETTER TAKE SOME SPECIAL EQUIPMENT!
"THE BIG STUDIO WAS A SCENE OF TENSION WHEN WE ARRIVED..."
WE STOPPED THEM FROM GRABBING THE PAYROLL, BUT THEY RETREATED IN THERE! THEY'RE HEAVILY ARMED... TO HUNT THEM OUT WILL BE DANGEROUS!
NOT IF WE KNOW EXACTLY WHERE THEY ARE... AND MAYBE WE CAN FIND OUT FAST!
"YOU THREW THE SEEING-EYE BATARANG OUT OVER THE MASS OF SETS..."
FORTUNATELY, MOVIE-SET BUILDINGS ARE FAKES, WITHOUT ROOFS OR CEILINGS!
I DON'T GET IT... DOES BATMAN THINK HE CAN SCARE THEM OUT WITH HIS BATARANG?
"AS THE BATARANG CURVED BACK AROUND TO YOUR HAND..."
I'M AFRAID YOUR WEAPON DIDN'T ACCOMPLISH ANYTHING, BATMAN! THEY'RE STILL HIDING IN THERE!
TRUE...
HOTEL
... BUT NOW WE CAN SEE JUST WHERE THEY'RE HIDING, THANKS TO THE PICTURE AUTOMATICALLY TAKEN BY THE CAMERA IN THE SEEING-EYE BATARANG AS IT FLEW OVER THEM!
"THE INSTANT-DEVELOPING PICTURE SHOWED THEM UP CLEARLY..."
THEY'RE INSIDE THAT ORIENTAL-TEMPLE SET, BATMAN!
RIGHT--WE'LL TAKE THEM BY SURPRISE, NOW THAT WE KNOW WHERE THEY ARE! COME ON, ROBIN...
7

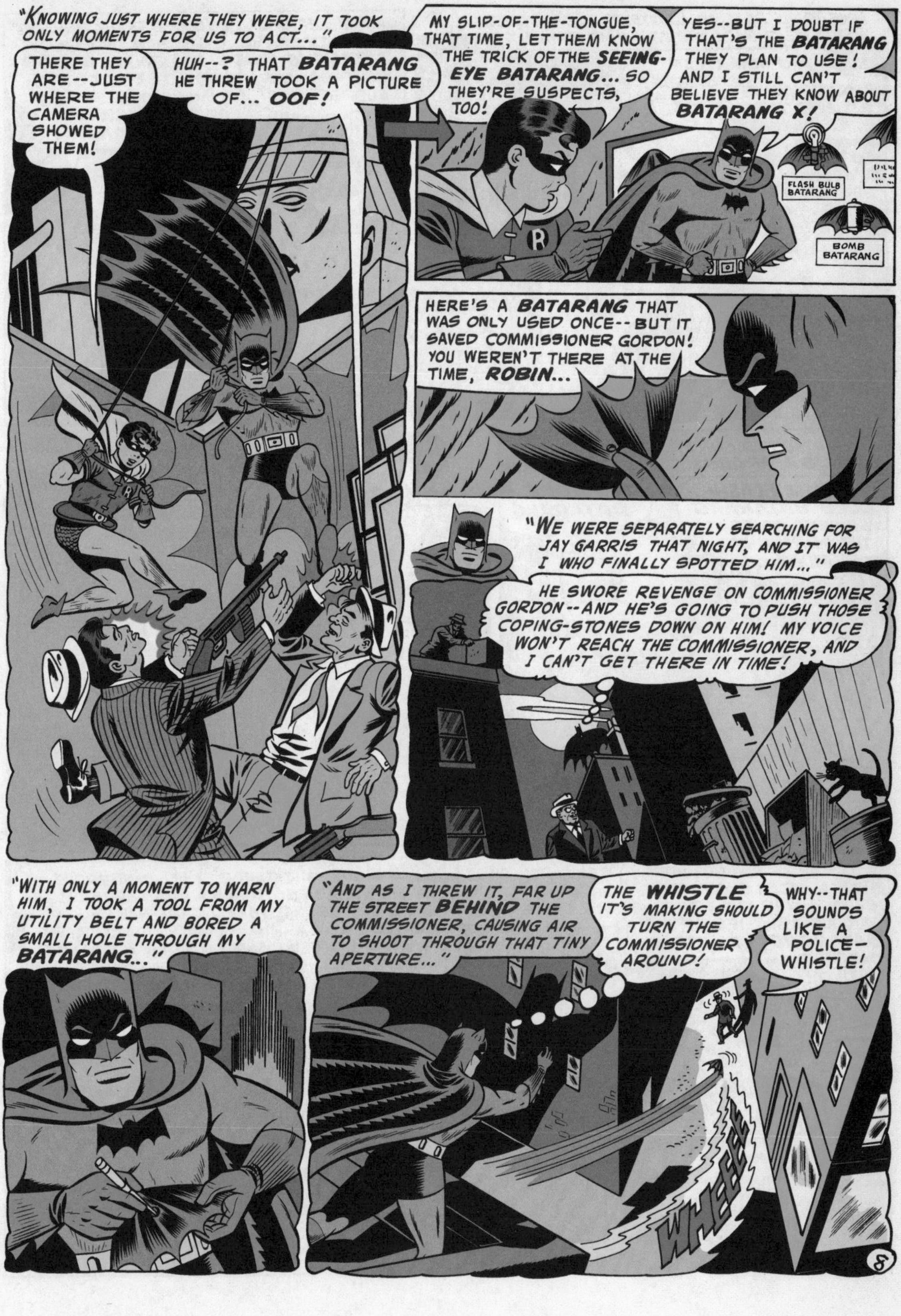
"KNOWING JUST WHERE THEY WERE, IT TOOK ONLY MOMENTS FOR US TO ACT..."
THERE THEY ARE--JUST WHERE THE CAMERA SHOWED THEM!
HUH--? THAT BATARANG HE THREW TOOK A PICTURE OF... OOF!
MY SLIP-OF-THE-TONGUE, THAT TIME, LET THEM KNOW THE TRICK OF THE SEEING-EYE BATARANG... SO THEY'RE SUSPECTS, TOO!
YES--BUT I DOUBT IF THAT'S THE BATARANG THEY PLAN TO USE! AND I STILL CAN'T BELIEVE THEY KNOW ABOUT BATARANG X!
FLASH BULB BATARANG
BOMB BATARANG
HERE'S A BATARANG THAT WAS ONLY USED ONCE--BUT IT SAVED COMMISSIONER GORDON! YOU WEREN'T THERE AT THE TIME, ROBIN...
"WE WERE SEPARATELY SEARCHING FOR JAY GARRIS THAT NIGHT, AND IT WAS I WHO FINALLY SPOTTED HIM..."
HE SWORE REVENGE ON COMMISSIONER GORDON--AND HE'S GOING TO PUSH THOSE COPING-STONES DOWN ON HIM! MY VOICE WON'T REACH THE COMMISSIONER, AND I CAN'T GET THERE IN TIME!
"WITH ONLY A MOMENT TO WARN HIM, I TOOK A TOOL FROM MY UTILITY BELT AND BORED A SMALL HOLE THROUGH MY BATARANG..."
"AND AS I THREW IT, FAR UP THE STREET BEHIND THE COMMISSIONER, CAUSING AIR TO SHOOT THROUGH THAT TINY APERTURE..."
THE WHISTLE IT'S MAKING SHOULD TURN THE COMMISSIONER AROUND!
WHY--THAT SOUNDS LIKE A POLICE-WHISTLE!
WHEEEE
8

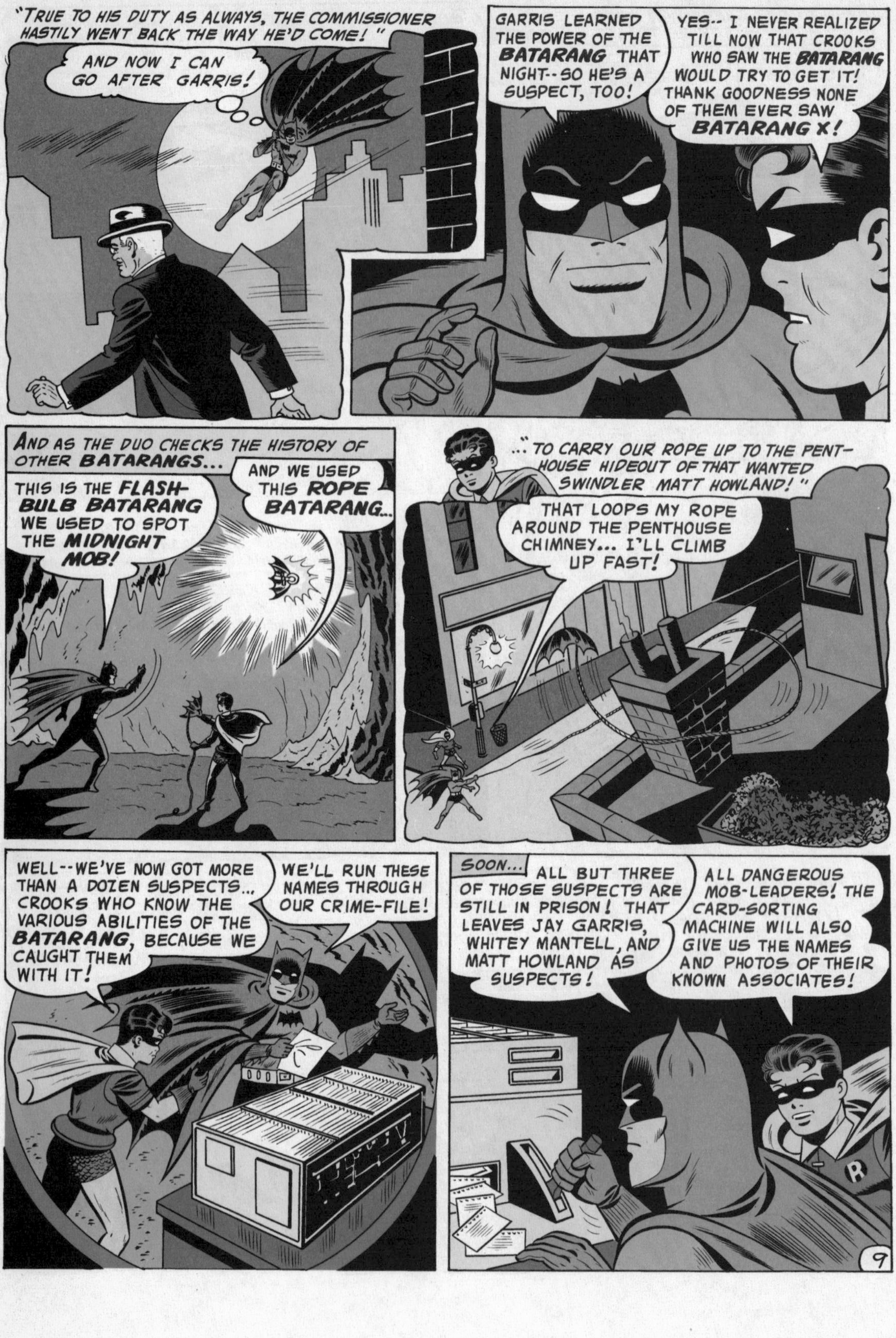
"TRUE TO HIS DUTY AS ALWAYS, THE COMMISSIONER HASTILY WENT BACK THE WAY HE'D COME!"
AND NOW I CAN GO AFTER GARRIS!
GARRIS LEARNED THE POWER OF THE BATARANG THAT NIGHT-- SO HE'S A SUSPECT, TOO!
YES-- I NEVER REALIZED TILL NOW THAT CROOKS WHO SAW THE BATARANG WOULD TRY TO GET IT! THANK GOODNESS NONE OF THEM EVER SAW BATARANG X!
AND AS THE DUO CHECKS THE HISTORY OF OTHER BATARANGS...
THIS IS THE FLASH-BULB BATARANG WE USED TO SPOT THE MIDNIGHT MOB!
AND WE USED THIS ROPE BATARANG...
..."TO CARRY OUR ROPE UP TO THE PENT-HOUSE HIDEOUT OF THAT WANTED SWINDLER MATT HOWLAND!"
THAT LOOPS MY ROPE AROUND THE PENTHOUSE CHIMNEY... I'LL CLIMB UP FAST!
WELL--WE'VE NOW GOT MORE THAN A DOZEN SUSPECTS... CROOKS WHO KNOW THE VARIOUS ABILITIES OF THE BATARANG, BECAUSE WE CAUGHT THEM WITH IT!
WE'LL RUN THESE NAMES THROUGH OUR CRIME-FILE!
SOON...
ALL BUT THREE OF THOSE SUSPECTS ARE STILL IN PRISON! THAT LEAVES JAY GARRIS, WHITEY MANTELL, AND MATT HOWLAND AS SUSPECTS!
ALL DANGEROUS MOB-LEADERS! THE CARD-SORTING MACHINE WILL ALSO GIVE US THE NAMES AND PHOTOS OF THEIR KNOWN ASSOCIATES!
9

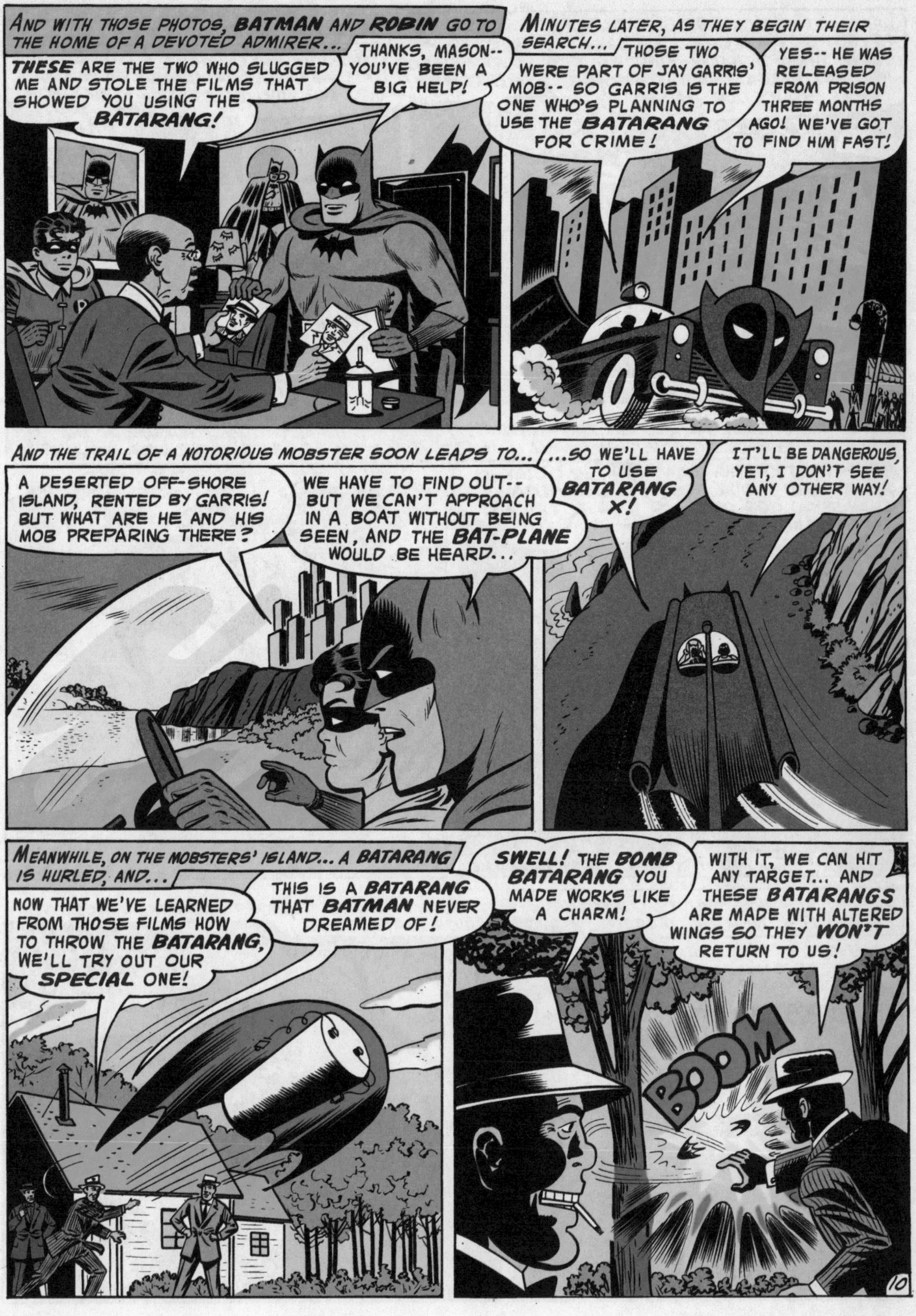
AND WITH THOSE PHOTOS, BATMAN AND ROBIN GO TO THE HOME OF A DEVOTED ADMIRER...
THESE ARE THE TWO WHO SLUGGED ME AND STOLE THE FILMS THAT SHOWED YOU USING THE BATARANG!
THANKS, MASON-- YOU'VE BEEN A BIG HELP!
MINUTES LATER, AS THEY BEGIN THEIR SEARCH...
THOSE TWO WERE PART OF JAY GARRIS' MOB-- SO GARRIS IS THE ONE WHO'S PLANNING TO USE THE BATARANG FOR CRIME!
YES-- HE WAS RELEASED FROM PRISON THREE MONTHS AGO! WE'VE GOT TO FIND HIM FAST!
AND THE TRAIL OF A NOTORIOUS MOBSTER SOON LEADS TO...
A DESERTED OFF-SHORE ISLAND, RENTED BY GARRIS! BUT WHAT ARE HE AND HIS MOB PREPARING THERE?
WE HAVE TO FIND OUT-- BUT WE CAN'T APPROACH IN A BOAT WITHOUT BEING SEEN, AND THE BAT-PLANE WOULD BE HEARD...
...SO WE'LL HAVE TO USE BATARANG X!
IT'LL BE DANGEROUS, YET, I DON'T SEE ANY OTHER WAY!
MEANWHILE, ON THE MOBSTERS' ISLAND... A BATARANG IS HURLED, AND...
NOW THAT WE'VE LEARNED FROM THOSE FILMS HOW TO THROW THE BATARANG, WE'LL TRY OUT OUR SPECIAL ONE!
THIS IS A BATARANG THAT BATMAN NEVER DREAMED OF!
SWELL! THE BOMB BATARANG YOU MADE WORKS LIKE A CHARM!
WITH IT, WE CAN HIT ANY TARGET... AND THESE BATARANGS ARE MADE WITH ALTERED WINGS SO THEY WON'T RETURN TO US!
BOOM
10

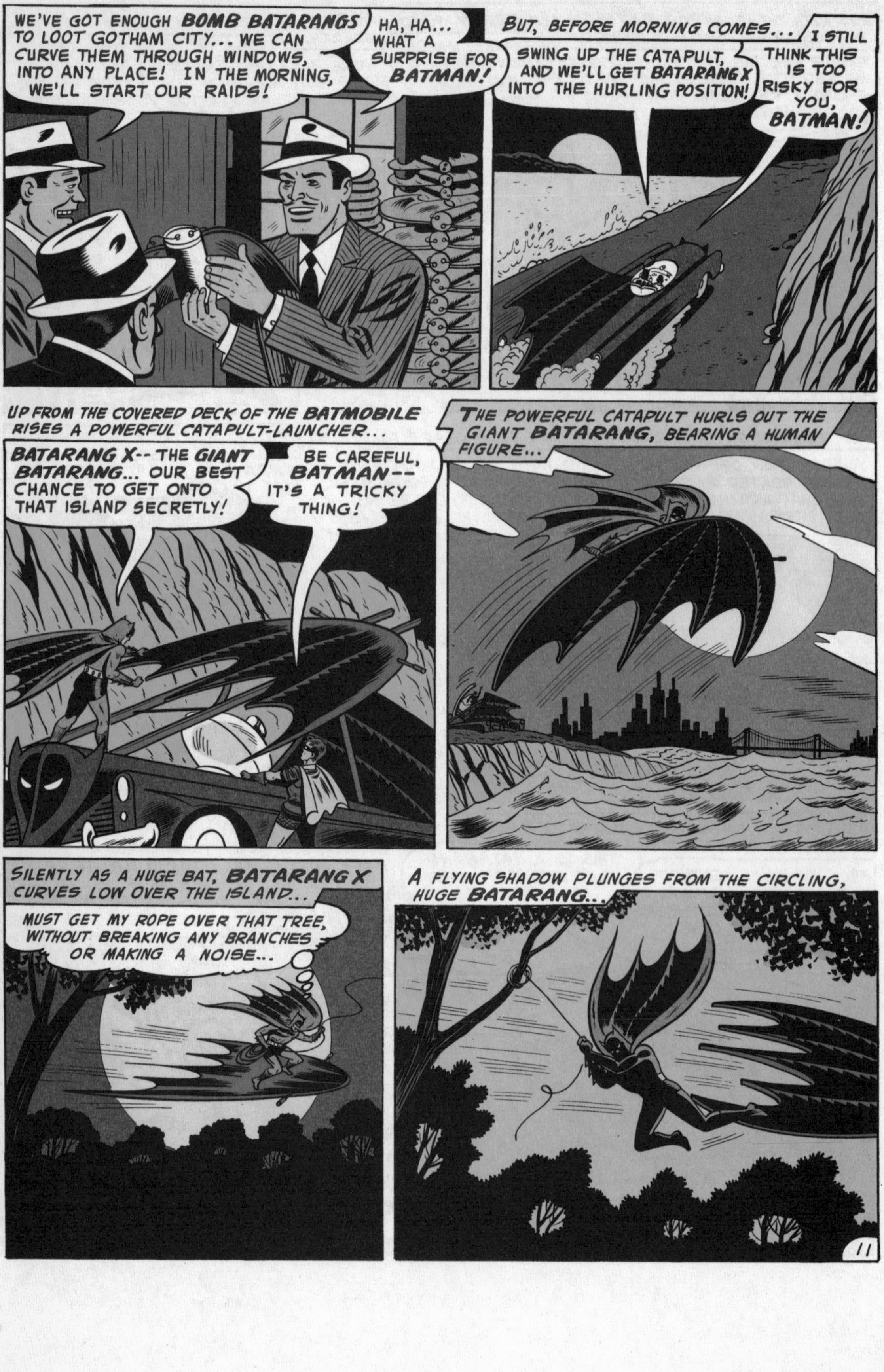
WE'VE GOT ENOUGH BOMB BATARANGS TO LOOT GOTHAM CITY... WE CAN CURVE THEM THROUGH WINDOWS, INTO ANY PLACE! IN THE MORNING, WE'LL START OUR RAIDS!
HA, HA... WHAT A SURPRISE FOR BATMAN!
BUT, BEFORE MORNING COMES...
SWING UP THE CATAPULT, AND WE'LL GET BATARANG X INTO THE HURLING POSITION!
I STILL THINK THIS IS TOO RISKY FOR YOU, BATMAN!
UP FROM THE COVERED DECK OF THE BATMOBILE RISES A POWERFUL CATAPULT-LAUNCHER...
BATARANG X-- THE GIANT BATARANG... OUR BEST CHANCE TO GET ONTO THAT ISLAND SECRETLY!
BE CAREFUL, BATMAN-- IT'S A TRICKY THING!
THE POWERFUL CATAPULT HURLS OUT THE GIANT BATARANG, BEARING A HUMAN FIGURE...
SILENTLY AS A HUGE BAT, BATARANG X CURVES LOW OVER THE ISLAND...
MUST GET MY ROPE OVER THAT TREE, WITHOUT BREAKING ANY BRANCHES OR MAKING A NOISE...
A FLYING SHADOW PLUNGES FROM THE CIRCLING, HUGE BATARANG...
11

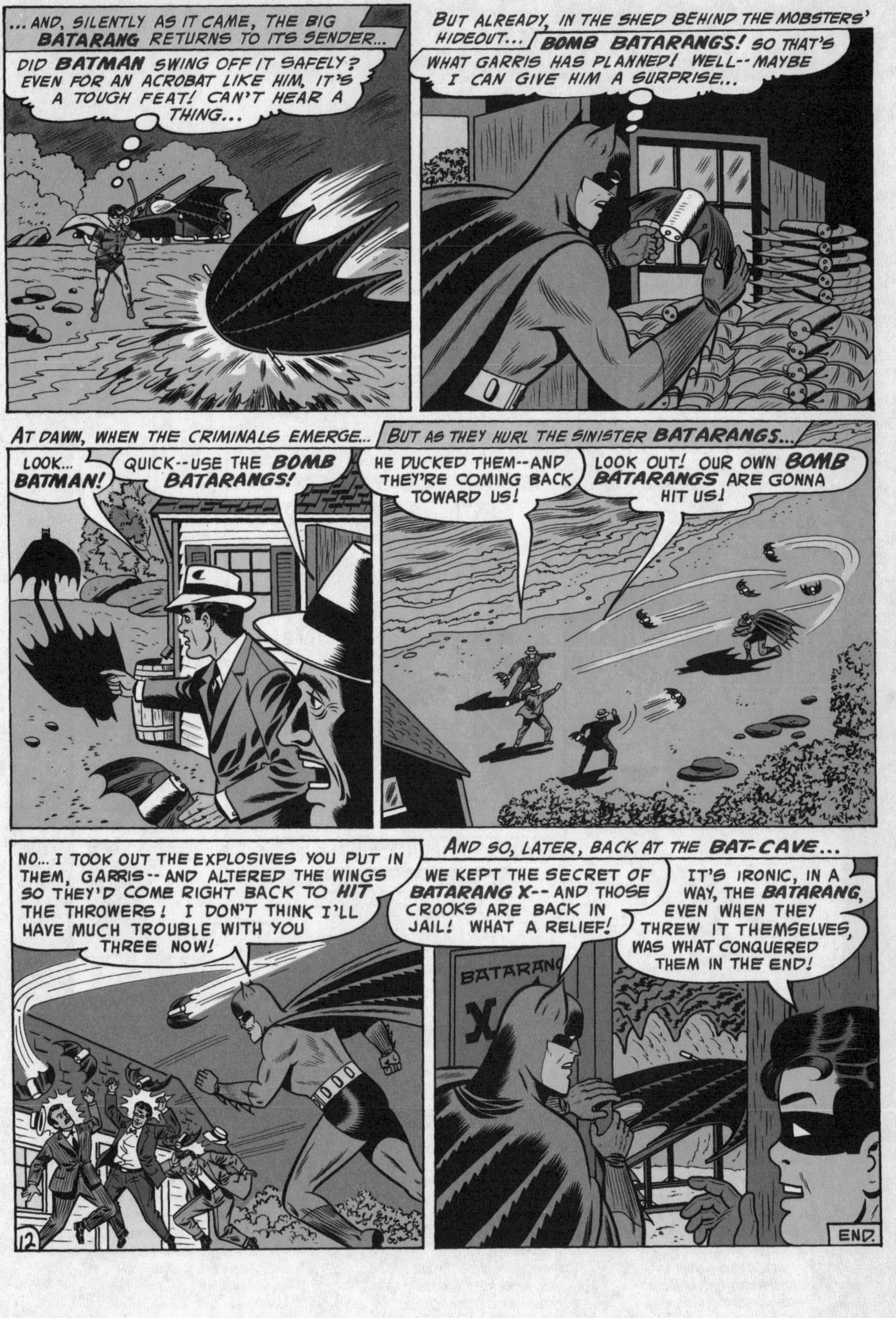

... AND, SILENTLY AS IT CAME, THE BIG BATARANG RETURNS TO IT'S SENDER...
DID BATMAN SWING OFF IT SAFELY? EVEN FOR AN ACROBAT LIKE HIM, IT'S A TOUGH FEAT! CAN'T HEAR A THING...
BUT ALREADY, IN THE SHED BEHIND THE MOBSTERS' HIDEOUT...
BOMB BATARANGS! SO THAT'S WHAT GARRIS HAS PLANNED! WELL-- MAYBE I CAN GIVE HIM A SURPRISE...
AT DAWN, WHEN THE CRIMINALS EMERGE...
LOOK... BATMAN!
QUICK--USE THE BOMB BATARANGS!
BUT AS THEY HURL THE SINISTER BATARANGS...
HE DUCKED THEM--AND THEY'RE COMING BACK TOWARD US!
LOOK OUT! OUR OWN BOMB BATARANGS ARE GONNA HIT US!
NO... I TOOK OUT THE EXPLOSIVES YOU PUT IN THEM, GARRIS-- AND ALTERED THE WINGS SO THEY'D COME RIGHT BACK TO HIT THE THROWERS! I DON'T THINK I'LL HAVE MUCH TROUBLE WITH YOU THREE NOW!
12
AND SO, LATER, BACK AT THE BAT-CAVE...
WE KEPT THE SECRET OF BATARANG X-- AND THOSE CROOKS ARE BACK IN JAIL! WHAT A RELIEF!
IT'S IRONIC, IN A WAY, THE BATARANG, EVEN WHEN THEY THREW IT THEMSELVES, WAS WHAT CONQUERED THEM IN THE END!
BATARANG
X
END.

BATCAVE IN THE 70s

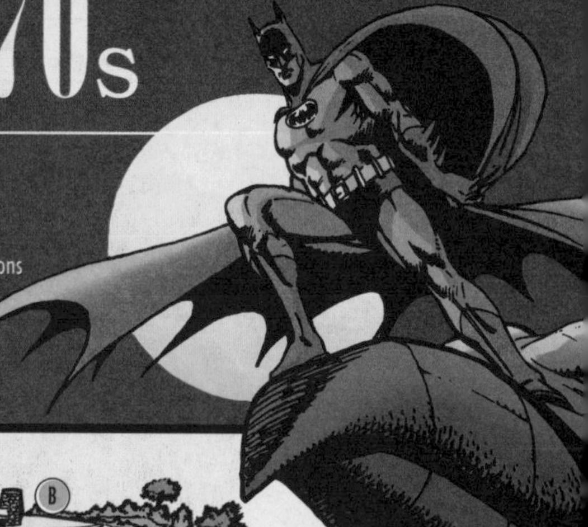

From: LIMITED COLLECTORS EDITION C-44 *(1976)*
Art: **TERRY AUSTIN**

With Dick Grayson off to college, Bruce Wayne decided to move his base of operations to the center of Gotham City. Living in the penthouse of the Wayne Foundation building, Batman moved the contents of the Batcave into a secret sub-basement which became his headquarters for a decade. Eventually the base and all of its equipment would move back to Wayne Manor.

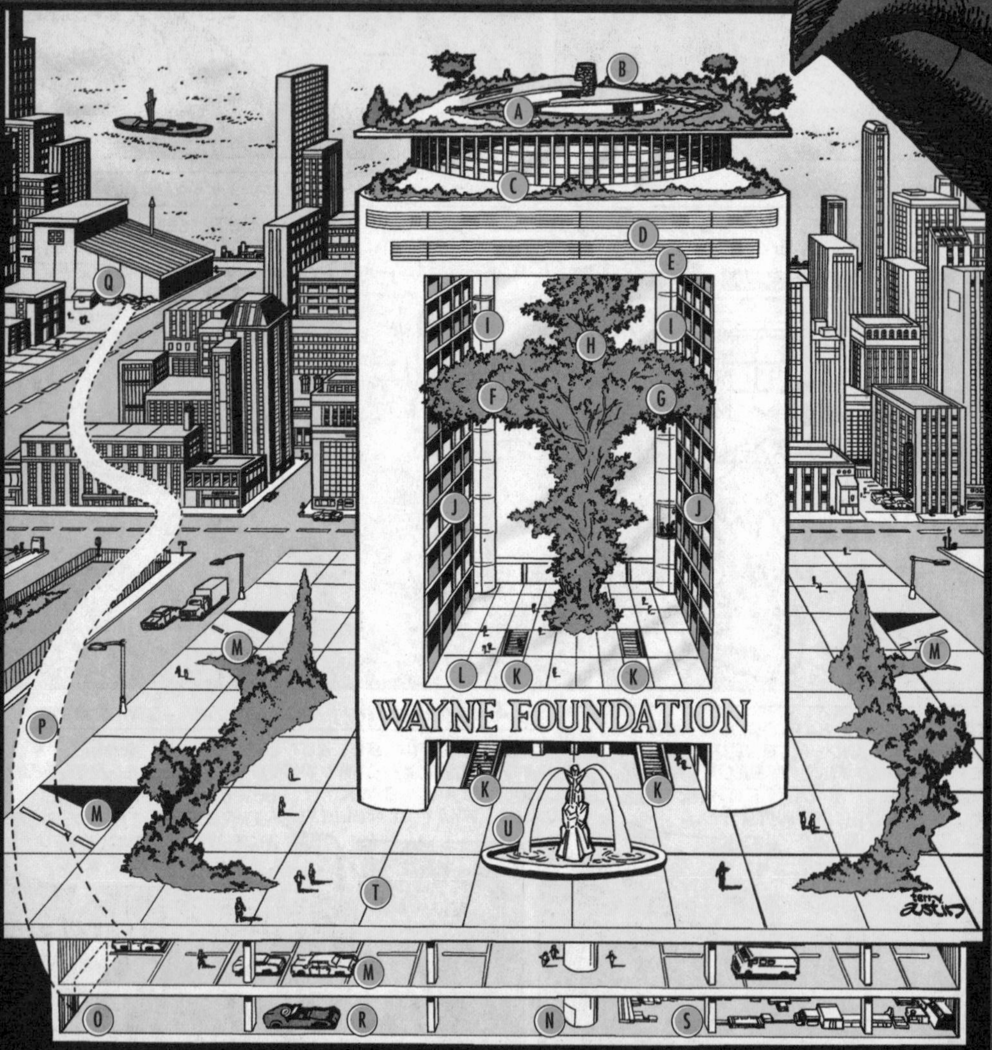

WAYNE FOUNDATION

- A. Bruce Wayne's penthouse.
- B. Fake chimney conceals upper part of secret elevator shaft.
- C. Carousel Restaurant revolves around center pole which conceals secret elevator.
- D. Gymnasium.
- E. Executive offices.
- F. Communications center and maintenance for mechanism which makes restaurant rotate.
- G. Secret communications center for the Batman. Secret elevator opens this side only.
- H. Decorative foliage conceals secret elevator shaft.
- I. Public elevators.
- J. General offices.
- K. Escalators.
- L. Mall surrounded on three sides by shops; fourth side is enclosed by special shatter-proof glass.
- M. Underground parking for public, with ramps to street.
- N. Lower end of secret elevator shaft.
- O. Secret exit for Batmobile in hidden sub-basement.
- P. Secret tunnel under streets leads to...
- Q. ...sealed "unused" warehouse owned by Bruce Wayne, where Batmobile can exit on little-used side-street.
- R. Secret garage for Batmobile.
- S. Batman's secret lab.
- T. Wayne Plaza.
- U. Thomas Wayne Memorial Fountain.

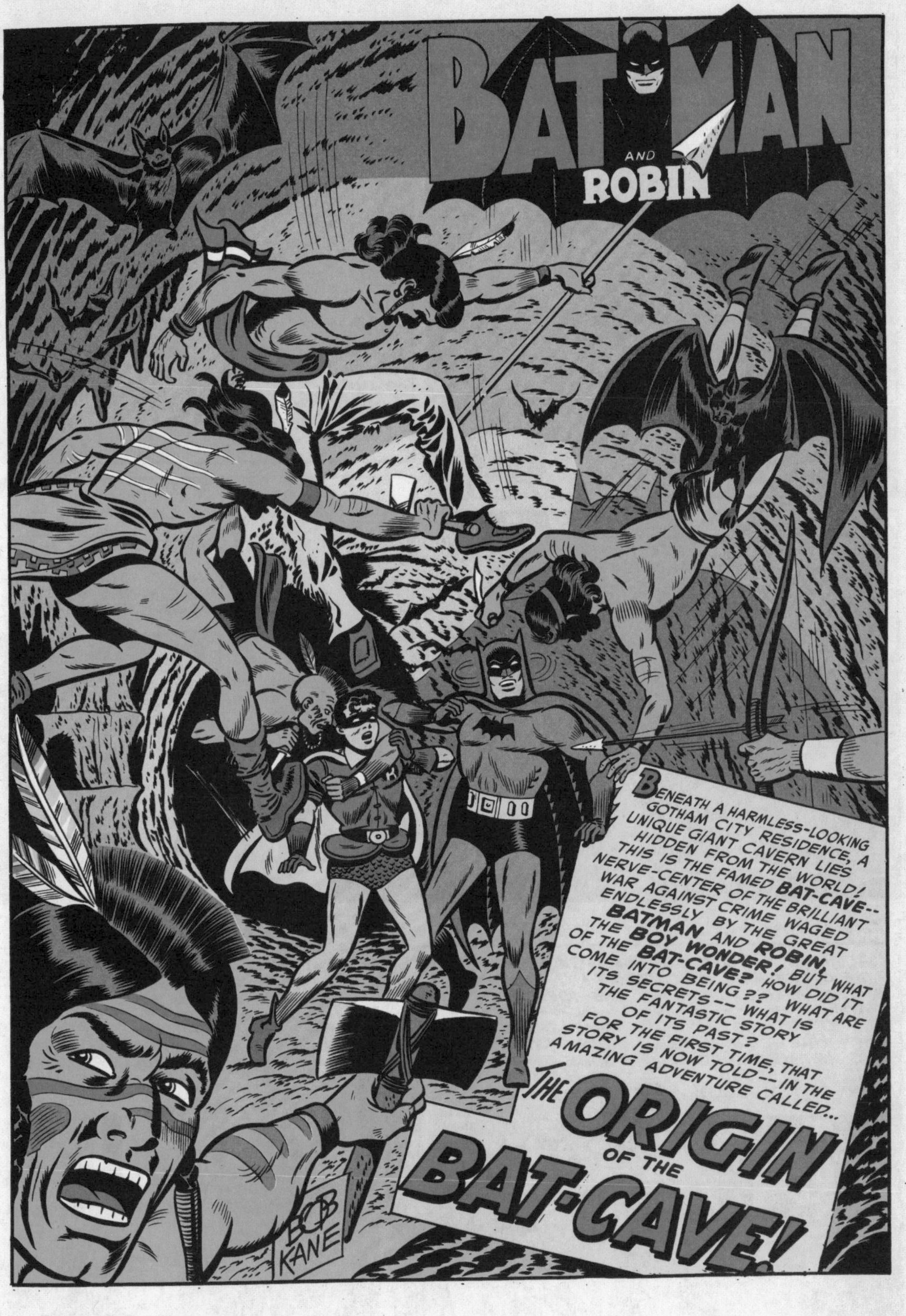
BATMAN
AND
ROBIN
BENEATH A HARMLESS-LOOKING GOTHAM CITY RESIDENCE, A UNIQUE GIANT CAVERN LIES HIDDEN FROM THE WORLD! THIS IS THE FAMED BAT-CAVE-- NERVE-CENTER OF THE BRILLIANT WAR AGAINST CRIME WAGED ENDLESSLY BY THE GREAT BATMAN AND ROBIN, THE BOY WONDER! BUT WHAT OF THE BAT-CAVE? HOW DID IT COME INTO BEING?? WHAT ARE ITS SECRETS-- WHAT IS THE FANTASTIC STORY OF ITS PAST? FOR THE FIRST TIME, THAT STORY IS NOW TOLD-- IN THE AMAZING ADVENTURE CALLED...
THE ORIGIN OF THE BAT-CAVE!
BOB KANE

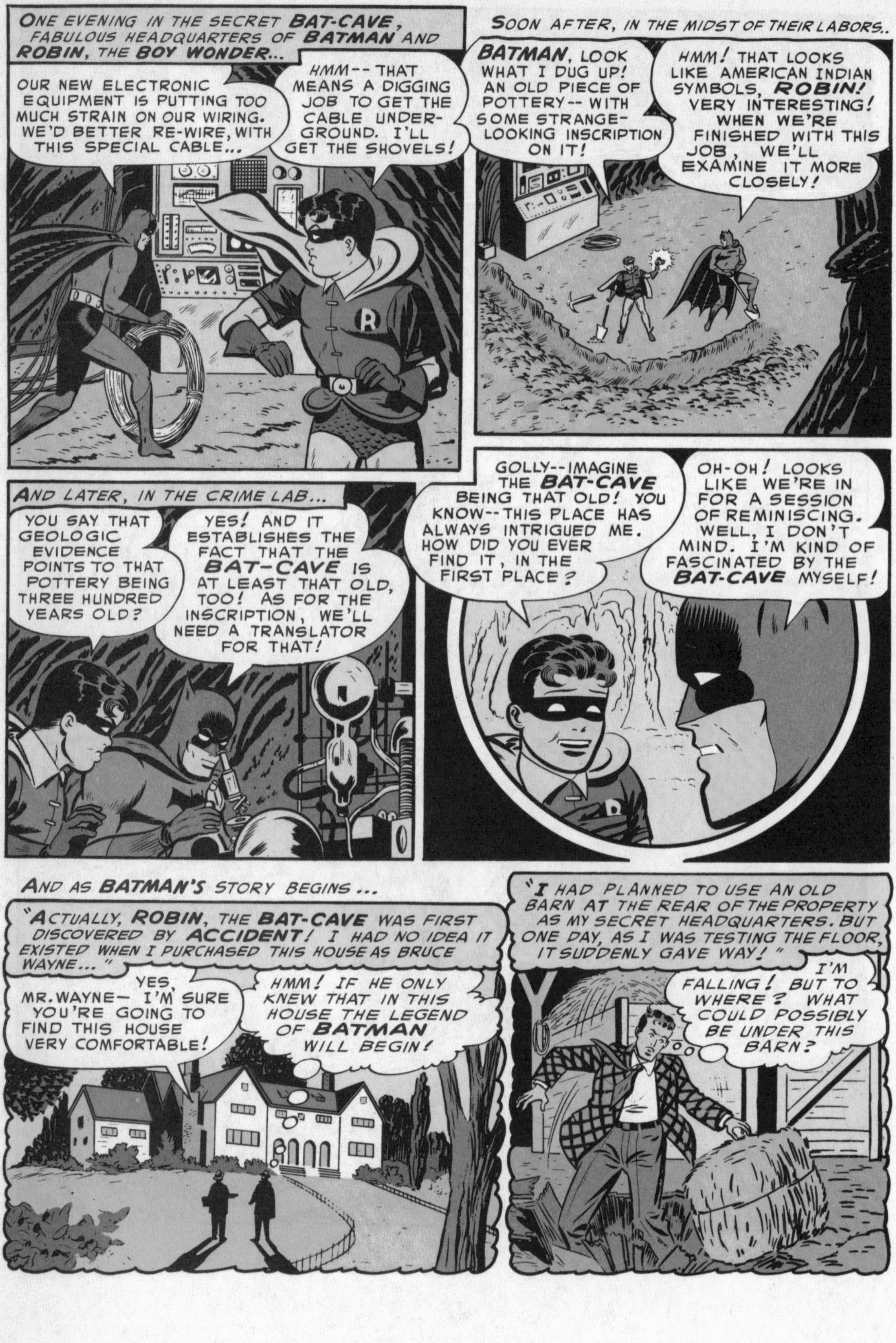
ONE EVENING IN THE SECRET BAT-CAVE, FABULOUS HEADQUARTERS OF BATMAN AND ROBIN, THE BOY WONDER...
OUR NEW ELECTRONIC EQUIPMENT IS PUTTING TOO MUCH STRAIN ON OUR WIRING. WE'D BETTER RE-WIRE, WITH THIS SPECIAL CABLE...
HMM-- THAT MEANS A DIGGING JOB TO GET THE CABLE UNDER-GROUND. I'LL GET THE SHOVELS!
SOON AFTER, IN THE MIDST OF THEIR LABORS..
BATMAN, LOOK WHAT I DUG UP! AN OLD PIECE OF POTTERY-- WITH SOME STRANGE-LOOKING INSCRIPTION ON IT!
HMM! THAT LOOKS LIKE AMERICAN INDIAN SYMBOLS, ROBIN! VERY INTERESTING! WHEN WE'RE FINISHED WITH THIS JOB, WE'LL EXAMINE IT MORE CLOSELY!
AND LATER, IN THE CRIME LAB...
YOU SAY THAT GEOLOGIC EVIDENCE POINTS TO THAT POTTERY BEING THREE HUNDRED YEARS OLD?
YES! AND IT ESTABLISHES THE FACT THAT THE BAT-CAVE IS AT LEAST THAT OLD, TOO! AS FOR THE INSCRIPTION, WE'LL NEED A TRANSLATOR FOR THAT!
GOLLY--IMAGINE THE BAT-CAVE BEING THAT OLD! YOU KNOW--THIS PLACE HAS ALWAYS INTRIGUED ME. HOW DID YOU EVER FIND IT, IN THE FIRST PLACE?
OH-OH! LOOKS LIKE WE'RE IN FOR A SESSION OF REMINISCING. WELL, I DON'T MIND. I'M KIND OF FASCINATED BY THE BAT-CAVE MYSELF!
AND AS BATMAN'S STORY BEGINS ...
"ACTUALLY, ROBIN, THE BAT-CAVE WAS FIRST DISCOVERED BY ACCIDENT! I HAD NO IDEA IT EXISTED WHEN I PURCHASED THIS HOUSE AS BRUCE WAYNE..."
YES, MR. WAYNE-- I'M SURE YOU'RE GOING TO FIND THIS HOUSE VERY COMFORTABLE!
HMM! IF HE ONLY KNEW THAT IN THIS HOUSE THE LEGEND OF BATMAN WILL BEGIN!
"I HAD PLANNED TO USE AN OLD BARN AT THE REAR OF THE PROPERTY AS MY SECRET HEADQUARTERS. BUT ONE DAY, AS I WAS TESTING THE FLOOR, IT SUDDENLY GAVE WAY!"
I'M FALLING! BUT TO WHERE? WHAT COULD POSSIBLY BE UNDER THIS BARN?

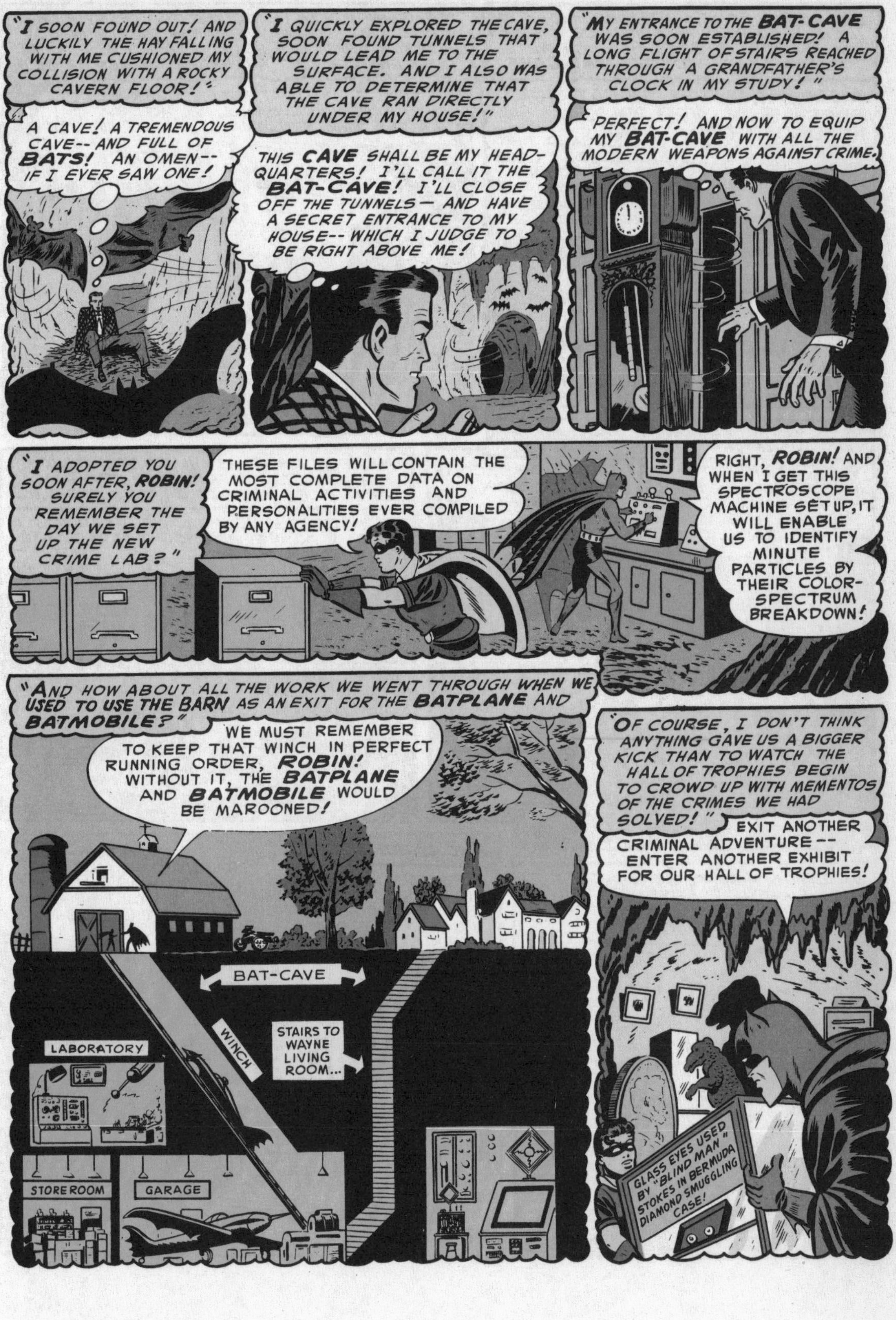
"I SOON FOUND OUT! AND LUCKILY THE HAY FALLING WITH ME CUSHIONED MY COLLISION WITH A ROCKY CAVERN FLOOR!"
A CAVE! A TREMENDOUS CAVE-- AND FULL OF BATS! AN OMEN-- IF I EVER SAW ONE!
"I QUICKLY EXPLORED THE CAVE, SOON FOUND TUNNELS THAT WOULD LEAD ME TO THE SURFACE. AND I ALSO WAS ABLE TO DETERMINE THAT THE CAVE RAN DIRECTLY UNDER MY HOUSE!"
THIS CAVE SHALL BE MY HEAD-QUARTERS! I'LL CALL IT THE BAT-CAVE! I'LL CLOSE OFF THE TUNNELS— AND HAVE A SECRET ENTRANCE TO MY HOUSE-- WHICH I JUDGE TO BE RIGHT ABOVE ME!
"MY ENTRANCE TO THE BAT-CAVE WAS SOON ESTABLISHED! A LONG FLIGHT OF STAIRS REACHED THROUGH A GRANDFATHER'S CLOCK IN MY STUDY!"
PERFECT! AND NOW TO EQUIP MY BAT-CAVE WITH ALL THE MODERN WEAPONS AGAINST CRIME.
"I ADOPTED YOU SOON AFTER, ROBIN! SURELY YOU REMEMBER THE DAY WE SET UP THE NEW CRIME LAB?"
THESE FILES WILL CONTAIN THE MOST COMPLETE DATA ON CRIMINAL ACTIVITIES AND PERSONALITIES EVER COMPILED BY ANY AGENCY!
RIGHT, ROBIN! AND WHEN I GET THIS SPECTROSCOPE MACHINE SET UP, IT WILL ENABLE US TO IDENTIFY MINUTE PARTICLES BY THEIR COLOR-SPECTRUM BREAKDOWN!
"AND HOW ABOUT ALL THE WORK WE WENT THROUGH WHEN WE USED TO USE THE BARN AS AN EXIT FOR THE BATPLANE AND BATMOBILE?"
WE MUST REMEMBER TO KEEP THAT WINCH IN PERFECT RUNNING ORDER, ROBIN! WITHOUT IT, THE BATPLANE AND BATMOBILE WOULD BE MAROONED!
BAT-CAVE
WINCH
STAIRS TO WAYNE LIVING ROOM...
LABORATORY
STOREROOM
GARAGE
"OF COURSE, I DON'T THINK ANYTHING GAVE US A BIGGER KICK THAN TO WATCH THE HALL OF TROPHIES BEGIN TO CROWD UP WITH MEMENTOS OF THE CRIMES WE HAD SOLVED!"
EXIT ANOTHER CRIMINAL ADVENTURE-- ENTER ANOTHER EXHIBIT FOR OUR HALL OF TROPHIES!
GLASS EYES USED BY "BLIND MAN" STOKES IN BERMUDA DIAMOND SMUGGLING CASE!

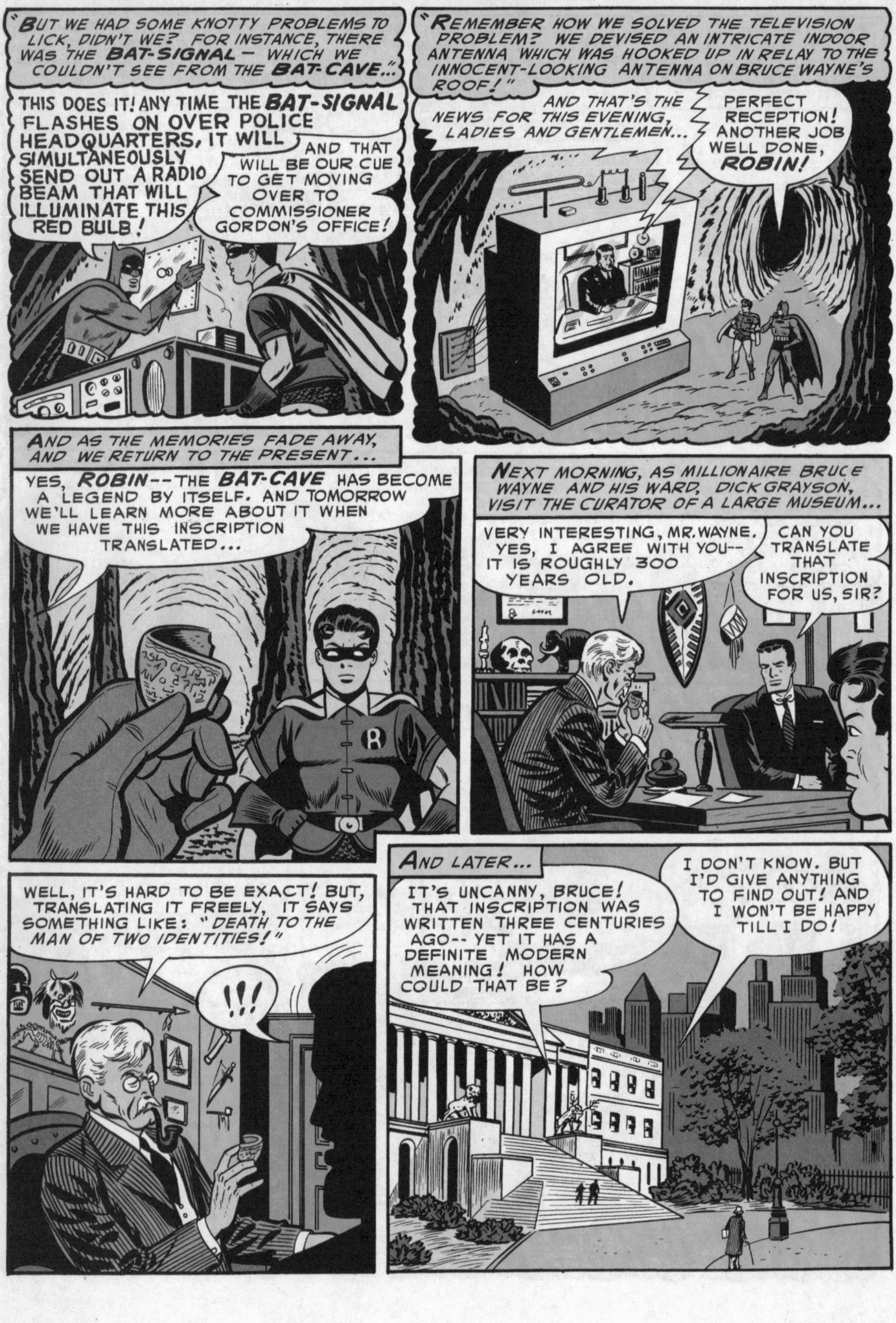
"BUT WE HAD SOME KNOTTY PROBLEMS TO LICK, DIDN'T WE? FOR INSTANCE, THERE WAS THE BAT-SIGNAL-- WHICH WE COULDN'T SEE FROM THE BAT-CAVE..."
THIS DOES IT! ANY TIME THE BAT-SIGNAL FLASHES ON OVER POLICE HEADQUARTERS, IT WILL SIMULTANEOUSLY SEND OUT A RADIO BEAM THAT WILL ILLUMINATE THIS RED BULB!
AND THAT WILL BE OUR CUE TO GET MOVING OVER TO COMMISSIONER GORDON'S OFFICE!
"REMEMBER HOW WE SOLVED THE TELEVISION PROBLEM? WE DEVISED AN INTRICATE INDOOR ANTENNA WHICH WAS HOOKED UP IN RELAY TO THE INNOCENT-LOOKING ANTENNA ON BRUCE WAYNE'S ROOF!"
AND THAT'S THE NEWS FOR THIS EVENING, LADIES AND GENTLEMEN...
PERFECT RECEPTION! ANOTHER JOB WELL DONE, ROBIN!
AND AS THE MEMORIES FADE AWAY, AND WE RETURN TO THE PRESENT...
YES, ROBIN--THE BAT-CAVE HAS BECOME A LEGEND BY ITSELF. AND TOMORROW WE'LL LEARN MORE ABOUT IT WHEN WE HAVE THIS INSCRIPTION TRANSLATED...
NEXT MORNING, AS MILLIONAIRE BRUCE WAYNE AND HIS WARD, DICK GRAYSON, VISIT THE CURATOR OF A LARGE MUSEUM...
VERY INTERESTING, MR. WAYNE. YES, I AGREE WITH YOU-- IT IS ROUGHLY 300 YEARS OLD.
CAN YOU TRANSLATE THAT INSCRIPTION FOR US, SIR?
WELL, IT'S HARD TO BE EXACT! BUT, TRANSLATING IT FREELY, IT SAYS SOMETHING LIKE: "DEATH TO THE MAN OF TWO IDENTITIES!"
!!!
AND LATER...
IT'S UNCANNY, BRUCE! THAT INSCRIPTION WAS WRITTEN THREE CENTURIES AGO-- YET IT HAS A DEFINITE MODERN MEANING! HOW COULD THAT BE?
I DON'T KNOW. BUT I'D GIVE ANYTHING TO FIND OUT! AND I WON'T BE HAPPY TILL I DO!

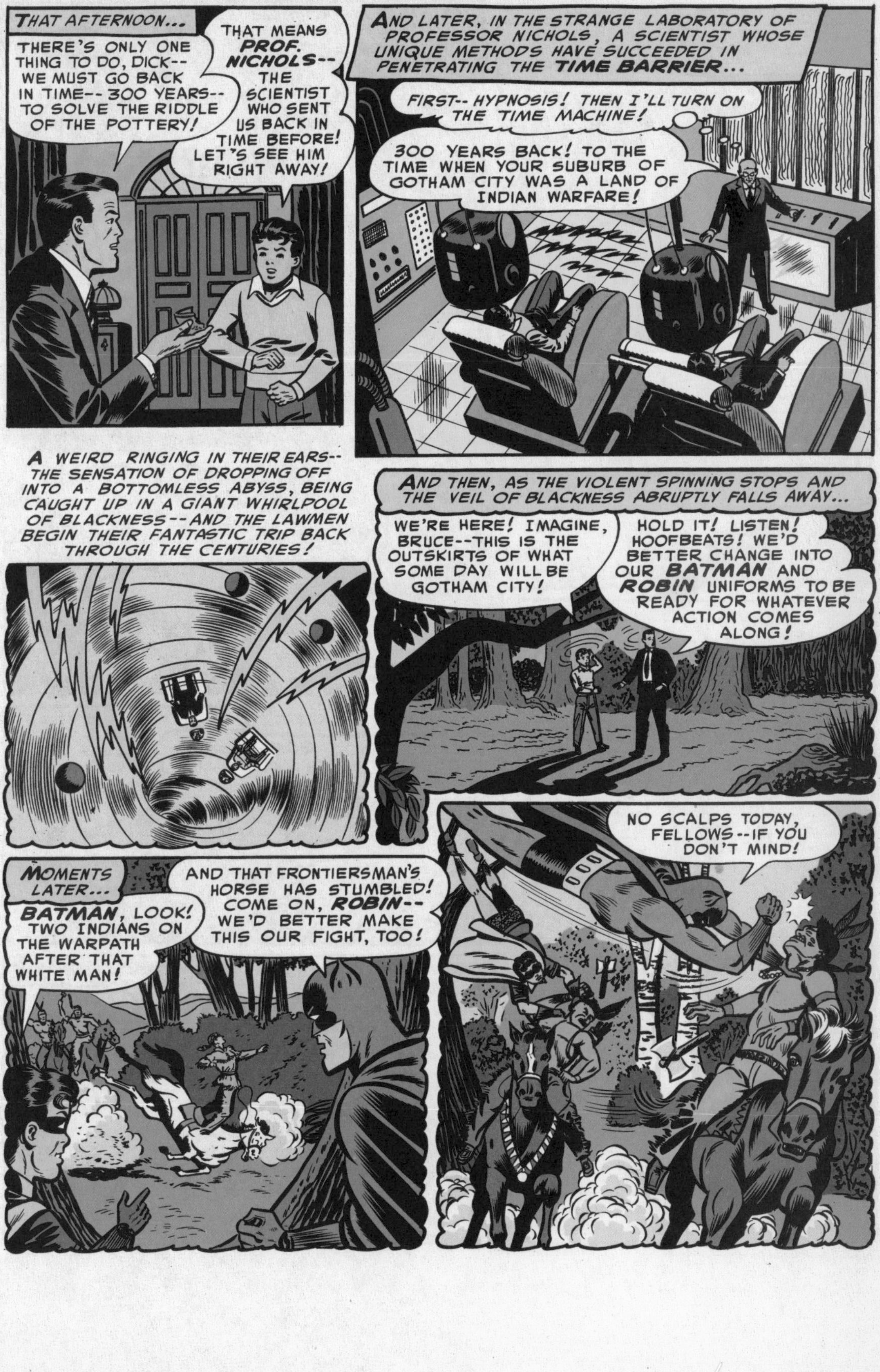
THAT AFTERNOON...
THERE'S ONLY ONE THING TO DO, DICK-- WE MUST GO BACK IN TIME-- 300 YEARS-- TO SOLVE THE RIDDLE OF THE POTTERY!
THAT MEANS PROF. NICHOLS-- THE SCIENTIST WHO SENT US BACK IN TIME BEFORE! LET'S SEE HIM RIGHT AWAY!
AND LATER, IN THE STRANGE LABORATORY OF PROFESSOR NICHOLS, A SCIENTIST WHOSE UNIQUE METHODS HAVE SUCCEEDED IN PENETRATING THE TIME BARRIER...
FIRST-- HYPNOSIS! THEN I'LL TURN ON THE TIME MACHINE!
300 YEARS BACK! TO THE TIME WHEN YOUR SUBURB OF GOTHAM CITY WAS A LAND OF INDIAN WARFARE!
A WEIRD RINGING IN THEIR EARS-- THE SENSATION OF DROPPING OFF INTO A BOTTOMLESS ABYSS, BEING CAUGHT UP IN A GIANT WHIRLPOOL OF BLACKNESS-- AND THE LAWMEN BEGIN THEIR FANTASTIC TRIP BACK THROUGH THE CENTURIES!
AND THEN, AS THE VIOLENT SPINNING STOPS AND THE VEIL OF BLACKNESS ABRUPTLY FALLS AWAY...
WE'RE HERE! IMAGINE, BRUCE--THIS IS THE OUTSKIRTS OF WHAT SOME DAY WILL BE GOTHAM CITY!
HOLD IT! LISTEN! HOOFBEATS! WE'D BETTER CHANGE INTO OUR BATMAN AND ROBIN UNIFORMS TO BE READY FOR WHATEVER ACTION COMES ALONG!
MOMENTS LATER...
BATMAN, LOOK! TWO INDIANS ON THE WARPATH AFTER THAT WHITE MAN!
AND THAT FRONTIERSMAN'S HORSE HAS STUMBLED! COME ON, ROBIN-- WE'D BETTER MAKE THIS OUR FIGHT, TOO!
NO SCALPS TODAY, FELLOWS--IF YOU DON'T MIND!

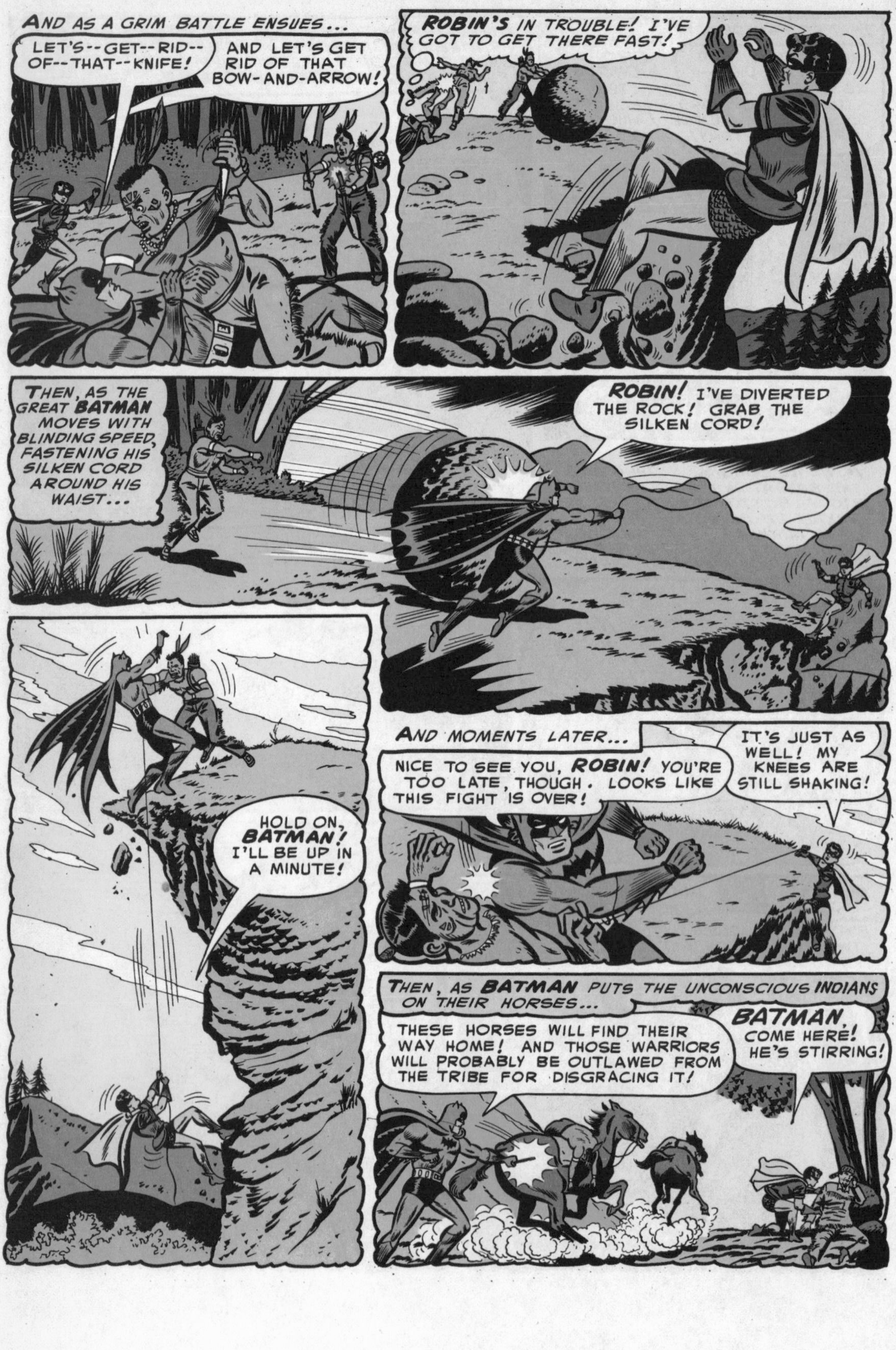
AND AS A GRIM BATTLE ENSUES...
LET'S--GET--RID--OF--THAT--KNIFE!
AND LET'S GET RID OF THAT BOW-AND-ARROW!
ROBIN'S IN TROUBLE! I'VE GOT TO GET THERE FAST!
THEN, AS THE GREAT BATMAN MOVES WITH BLINDING SPEED, FASTENING HIS SILKEN CORD AROUND HIS WAIST...
ROBIN! I'VE DIVERTED THE ROCK! GRAB THE SILKEN CORD!
HOLD ON, BATMAN! I'LL BE UP IN A MINUTE!
AND MOMENTS LATER...
NICE TO SEE YOU, ROBIN! YOU'RE TOO LATE, THOUGH. LOOKS LIKE THIS FIGHT IS OVER!
IT'S JUST AS WELL! MY KNEES ARE STILL SHAKING!
THEN, AS BATMAN PUTS THE UNCONSCIOUS INDIANS ON THEIR HORSES...
THESE HORSES WILL FIND THEIR WAY HOME! AND THOSE WARRIORS WILL PROBABLY BE OUTLAWED FROM THE TRIBE FOR DISGRACING IT!
BATMAN, COME HERE! HE'S STIRRING!

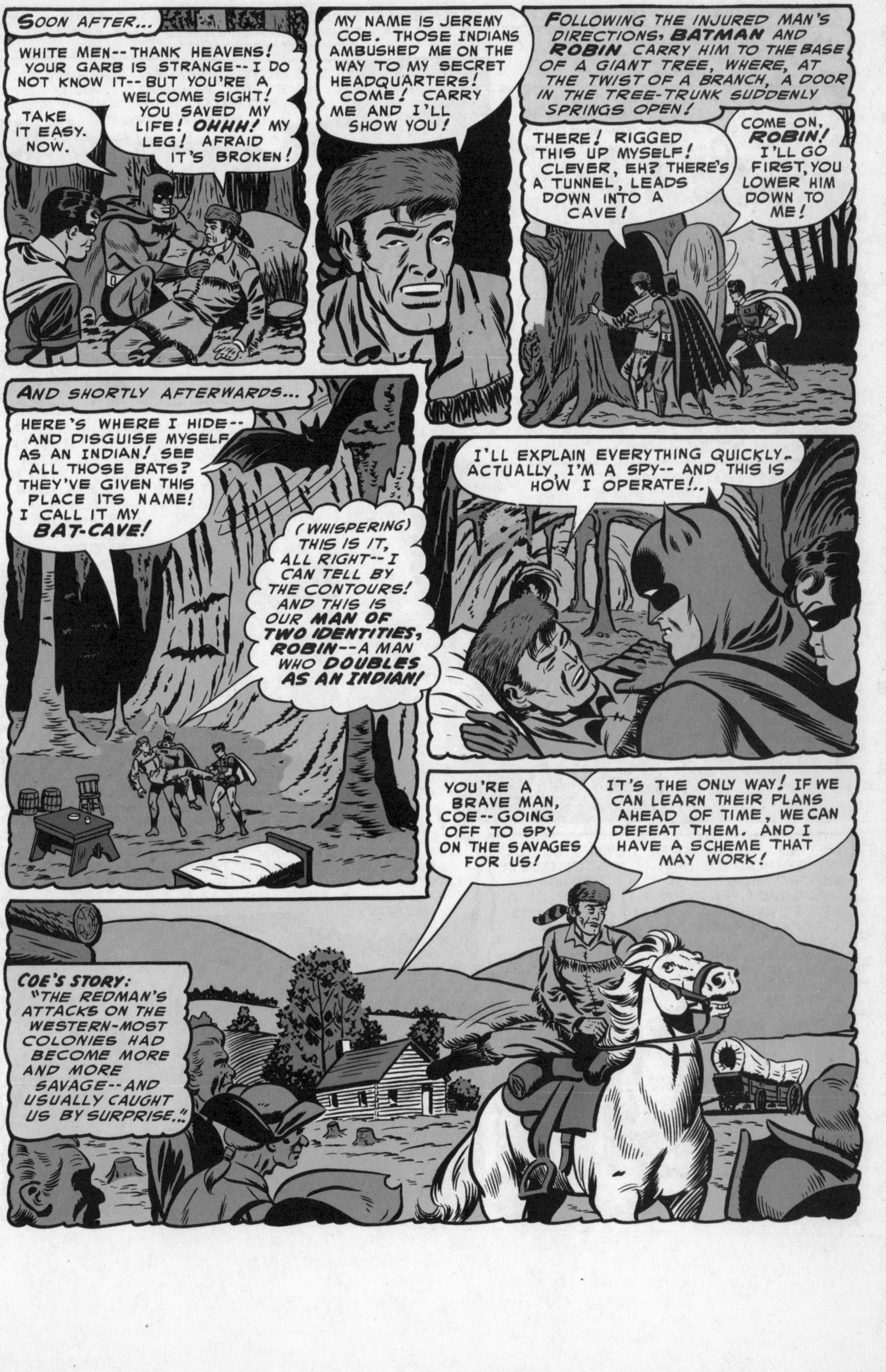
SOON AFTER...
WHITE MEN--THANK HEAVENS! YOUR GARB IS STRANGE--I DO NOT KNOW IT--BUT YOU'RE A WELCOME SIGHT! YOU SAVED MY LIFE! OHHH! MY LEG! AFRAID IT'S BROKEN!
TAKE IT EASY. NOW.
MY NAME IS JEREMY COE. THOSE INDIANS AMBUSHED ME ON THE WAY TO MY SECRET HEADQUARTERS! COME! CARRY ME AND I'LL SHOW YOU!
FOLLOWING THE INJURED MAN'S DIRECTIONS, BATMAN AND ROBIN CARRY HIM TO THE BASE OF A GIANT TREE, WHERE, AT THE TWIST OF A BRANCH, A DOOR IN THE TREE-TRUNK SUDDENLY SPRINGS OPEN!
THERE! RIGGED THIS UP MYSELF! CLEVER, EH? THERE'S A TUNNEL, LEADS DOWN INTO A CAVE!
COME ON, ROBIN! I'LL GO FIRST, YOU LOWER HIM DOWN TO ME!
AND SHORTLY AFTERWARDS...
HERE'S WHERE I HIDE--AND DISGUISE MYSELF AS AN INDIAN! SEE ALL THOSE BATS? THEY'VE GIVEN THIS PLACE ITS NAME! I CALL IT MY BAT-CAVE!
(WHISPERING) THIS IS IT, ALL RIGHT--I CAN TELL BY THE CONTOURS! AND THIS IS OUR MAN OF TWO IDENTITIES, ROBIN--A MAN WHO DOUBLES AS AN INDIAN!
I'LL EXPLAIN EVERYTHING QUICKLY.. ACTUALLY, I'M A SPY--AND THIS IS HOW I OPERATE!..
YOU'RE A BRAVE MAN, COE--GOING OFF TO SPY ON THE SAVAGES FOR US!
IT'S THE ONLY WAY! IF WE CAN LEARN THEIR PLANS AHEAD OF TIME, WE CAN DEFEAT THEM. AND I HAVE A SCHEME THAT MAY WORK!
COE'S STORY: "THE REDMAN'S ATTACKS ON THE WESTERN-MOST COLONIES HAD BECOME MORE AND MORE SAVAGE--AND USUALLY CAUGHT US BY SURPRISE.."

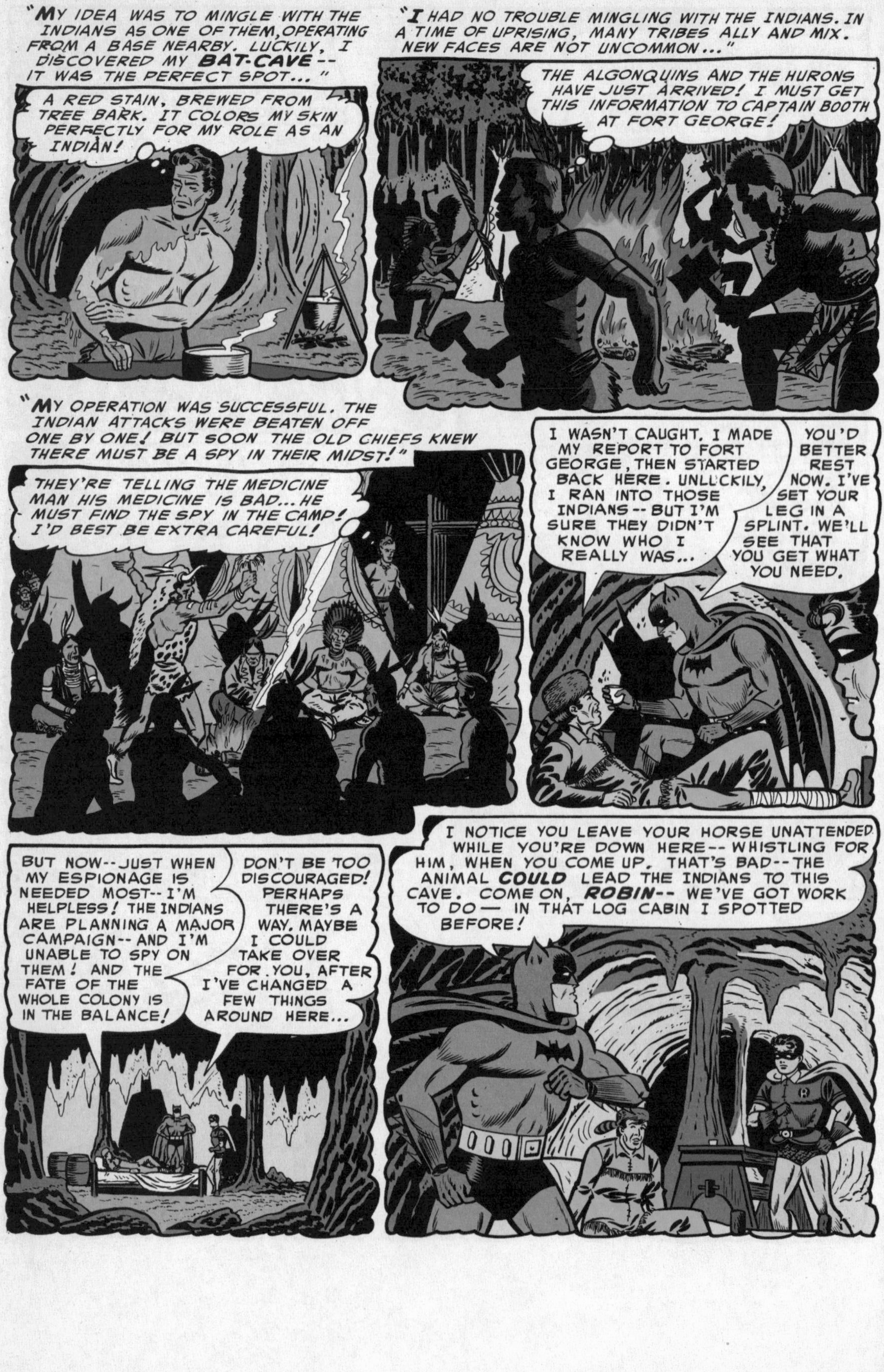
"MY IDEA WAS TO MINGLE WITH THE INDIANS AS ONE OF THEM, OPERATING FROM A BASE NEARBY. LUCKILY, I DISCOVERED MY BAT-CAVE -- IT WAS THE PERFECT SPOT..."
A RED STAIN, BREWED FROM TREE BARK. IT COLORS MY SKIN PERFECTLY FOR MY ROLE AS AN INDIAN!
"I HAD NO TROUBLE MINGLING WITH THE INDIANS. IN A TIME OF UPRISING, MANY TRIBES ALLY AND MIX. NEW FACES ARE NOT UNCOMMON..."
THE ALGONQUINS AND THE HURONS HAVE JUST ARRIVED! I MUST GET THIS INFORMATION TO CAPTAIN BOOTH AT FORT GEORGE!
"MY OPERATION WAS SUCCESSFUL. THE INDIAN ATTACKS WERE BEATEN OFF ONE BY ONE! BUT SOON THE OLD CHIEFS KNEW THERE MUST BE A SPY IN THEIR MIDST!"
THEY'RE TELLING THE MEDICINE MAN HIS MEDICINE IS BAD...HE MUST FIND THE SPY IN THE CAMP! I'D BEST BE EXTRA CAREFUL!
I WASN'T CAUGHT. I MADE MY REPORT TO FORT GEORGE, THEN STARTED BACK HERE. UNLUCKILY, I RAN INTO THOSE INDIANS -- BUT I'M SURE THEY DIDN'T KNOW WHO I REALLY WAS...
YOU'D BETTER REST NOW. I'VE SET YOUR LEG IN A SPLINT. WE'LL SEE THAT YOU GET WHAT YOU NEED.
BUT NOW--JUST WHEN MY ESPIONAGE IS NEEDED MOST--I'M HELPLESS! THE INDIANS ARE PLANNING A MAJOR CAMPAIGN--AND I'M UNABLE TO SPY ON THEM! AND THE FATE OF THE WHOLE COLONY IS IN THE BALANCE!
DON'T BE TOO DISCOURAGED! PERHAPS THERE'S A WAY. MAYBE I COULD TAKE OVER FOR YOU, AFTER I'VE CHANGED A FEW THINGS AROUND HERE...
I NOTICE YOU LEAVE YOUR HORSE UNATTENDED WHILE YOU'RE DOWN HERE-- WHISTLING FOR HIM, WHEN YOU COME UP. THAT'S BAD--THE ANIMAL COULD LEAD THE INDIANS TO THIS CAVE. COME ON, ROBIN-- WE'VE GOT WORK TO DO— IN THAT LOG CABIN I SPOTTED BEFORE!

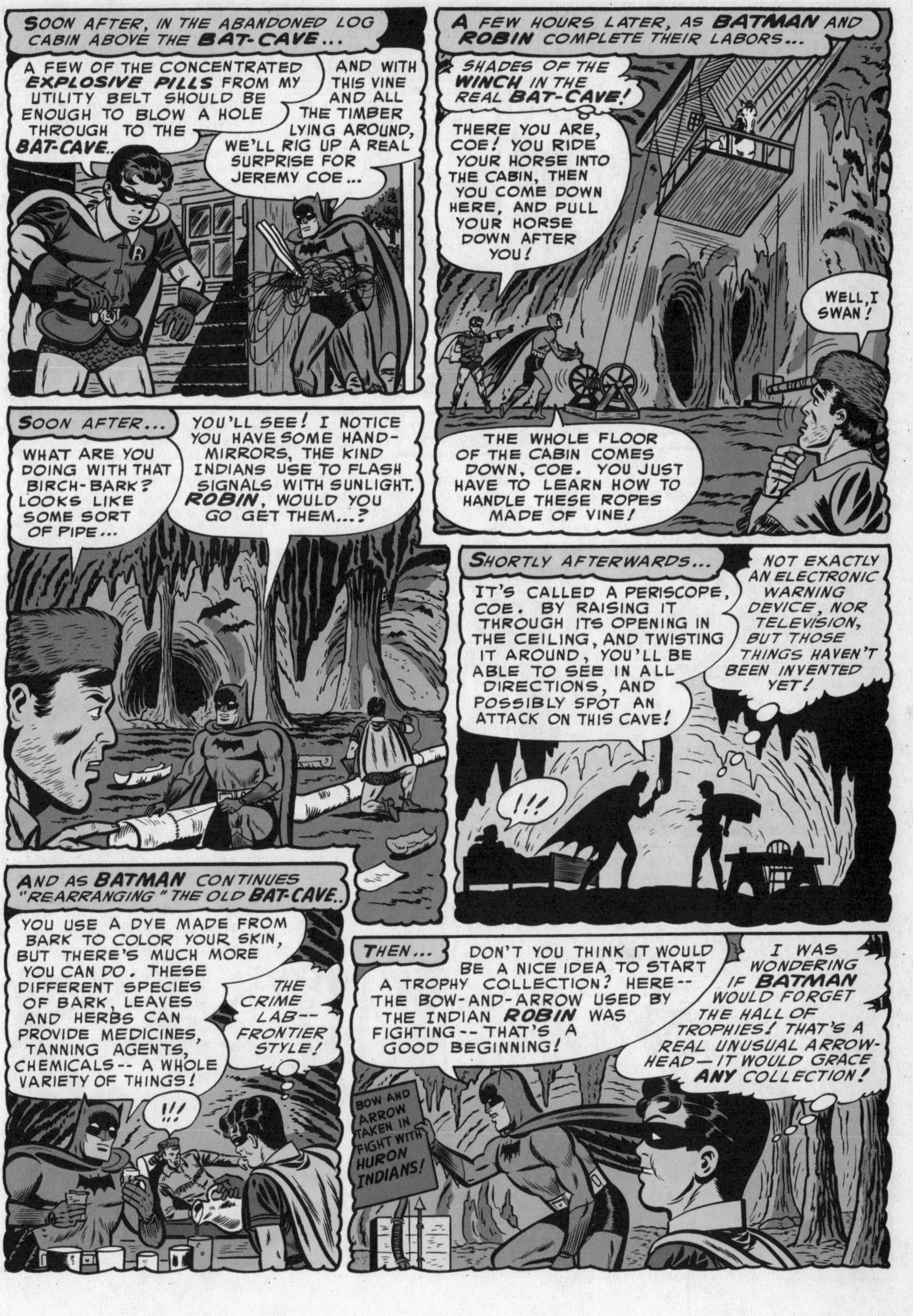
SOON AFTER, IN THE ABANDONED LOG CABIN ABOVE THE BAT-CAVE...
A FEW OF THE CONCENTRATED EXPLOSIVE PILLS FROM MY UTILITY BELT SHOULD BE ENOUGH TO BLOW A HOLE THROUGH TO THE BAT-CAVE..
AND WITH THIS VINE AND ALL THE TIMBER LYING AROUND, WE'LL RIG UP A REAL SURPRISE FOR JEREMY COE...
A FEW HOURS LATER, AS BATMAN AND ROBIN COMPLETE THEIR LABORS...
SHADES OF THE WINCH IN THE REAL BAT-CAVE!
THERE YOU ARE, COE! YOU RIDE YOUR HORSE INTO THE CABIN, THEN YOU COME DOWN HERE, AND PULL YOUR HORSE DOWN AFTER YOU!
WELL, I SWAN!
THE WHOLE FLOOR OF THE CABIN COMES DOWN, COE. YOU JUST HAVE TO LEARN HOW TO HANDLE THESE ROPES MADE OF VINE!
SOON AFTER...
WHAT ARE YOU DOING WITH THAT BIRCH-BARK? LOOKS LIKE SOME SORT OF PIPE...
YOU'LL SEE! I NOTICE YOU HAVE SOME HAND-MIRRORS, THE KIND INDIANS USE TO FLASH SIGNALS WITH SUNLIGHT. ROBIN, WOULD YOU GO GET THEM...?
SHORTLY AFTERWARDS...
IT'S CALLED A PERISCOPE, COE. BY RAISING IT THROUGH ITS OPENING IN THE CEILING, AND TWISTING IT AROUND, YOU'LL BE ABLE TO SEE IN ALL DIRECTIONS, AND POSSIBLY SPOT AN ATTACK ON THIS CAVE!
NOT EXACTLY AN ELECTRONIC WARNING DEVICE, NOR TELEVISION, BUT THOSE THINGS HAVEN'T BEEN INVENTED YET!
!!!
AND AS BATMAN CONTINUES "REARRANGING" THE OLD BAT-CAVE..
YOU USE A DYE MADE FROM BARK TO COLOR YOUR SKIN, BUT THERE'S MUCH MORE YOU CAN DO. THESE DIFFERENT SPECIES OF BARK, LEAVES AND HERBS CAN PROVIDE MEDICINES, TANNING AGENTS, CHEMICALS-- A WHOLE VARIETY OF THINGS!
THE CRIME LAB-- FRONTIER STYLE!
!!!
THEN...
DON'T YOU THINK IT WOULD BE A NICE IDEA, TO START A TROPHY COLLECTION? HERE-- THE BOW-AND-ARROW USED BY THE INDIAN ROBIN WAS FIGHTING-- THAT'S A GOOD BEGINNING!
I WAS WONDERING IF BATMAN WOULD FORGET THE HALL OF TROPHIES! THAT'S A REAL UNUSUAL ARROW-HEAD—IT WOULD GRACE ANY COLLECTION!
BOW AND ARROW TAKEN IN FIGHT WITH HURON INDIANS!

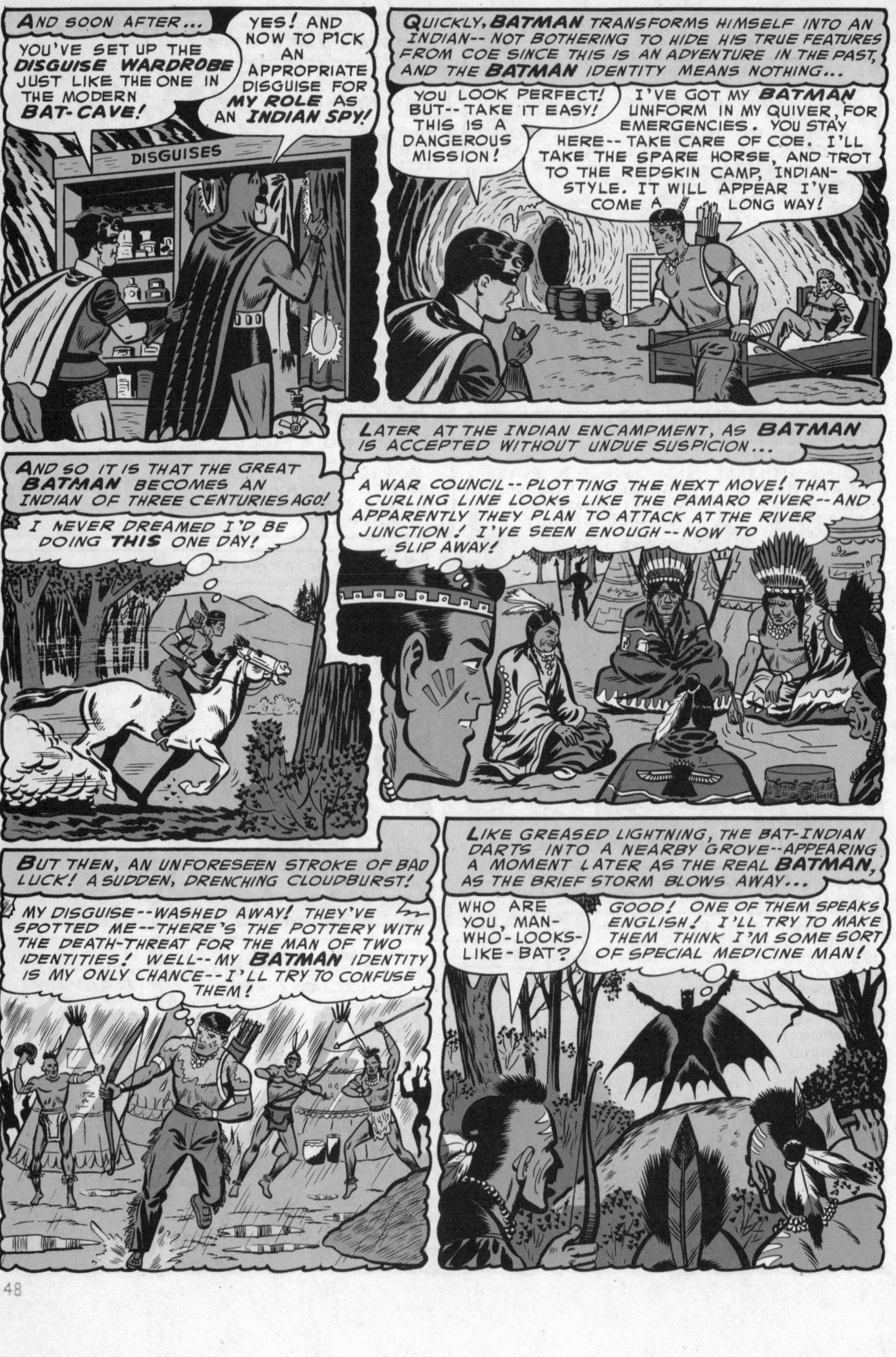
AND SOON AFTER...
YOU'VE SET UP THE DISGUISE WARDROBE JUST LIKE THE ONE IN THE MODERN BAT-CAVE!
YES! AND NOW TO PICK AN APPROPRIATE DISGUISE FOR MY ROLE AS AN INDIAN SPY!
DISGUISES
QUICKLY, BATMAN TRANSFORMS HIMSELF INTO AN INDIAN-- NOT BOTHERING TO HIDE HIS TRUE FEATURES FROM COE SINCE THIS IS AN ADVENTURE IN THE PAST, AND THE BATMAN IDENTITY MEANS NOTHING...
YOU LOOK PERFECT! BUT--TAKE IT EASY! THIS IS A DANGEROUS MISSION!
I'VE GOT MY BATMAN UNIFORM IN MY QUIVER, FOR EMERGENCIES. YOU STAY HERE--TAKE CARE OF COE. I'LL TAKE THE SPARE HORSE, AND TROT TO THE REDSKIN CAMP, INDIAN-STYLE. IT WILL APPEAR I'VE COME A LONG WAY!
AND SO IT IS THAT THE GREAT BATMAN BECOMES AN INDIAN OF THREE CENTURIES AGO!
I NEVER DREAMED I'D BE DOING THIS ONE DAY!
LATER AT THE INDIAN ENCAMPMENT, AS BATMAN IS ACCEPTED WITHOUT UNDUE SUSPICION...
A WAR COUNCIL--PLOTTING THE NEXT MOVE! THAT CURLING LINE LOOKS LIKE THE PAMARO RIVER--AND APPARENTLY THEY PLAN TO ATTACK AT THE RIVER JUNCTION! I'VE SEEN ENOUGH--NOW TO SLIP AWAY!
BUT THEN, AN UNFORESEEN STROKE OF BAD LUCK! A SUDDEN, DRENCHING CLOUDBURST!
MY DISGUISE--WASHED AWAY! THEY'VE SPOTTED ME--THERE'S THE POTTERY WITH THE DEATH-THREAT FOR THE MAN OF TWO IDENTITIES! WELL--MY BATMAN IDENTITY IS MY ONLY CHANCE--I'LL TRY TO CONFUSE THEM!
LIKE GREASED LIGHTNING, THE BAT-INDIAN DARTS INTO A NEARBY GROVE--APPEARING A MOMENT LATER AS THE REAL BATMAN, AS THE BRIEF STORM BLOWS AWAY...
WHO ARE YOU, MAN-WHO-LOOKS-LIKE-BAT?
GOOD! ONE OF THEM SPEAKS ENGLISH! I'LL TRY TO MAKE THEM THINK I'M SOME SORT OF SPECIAL MEDICINE MAN!
48

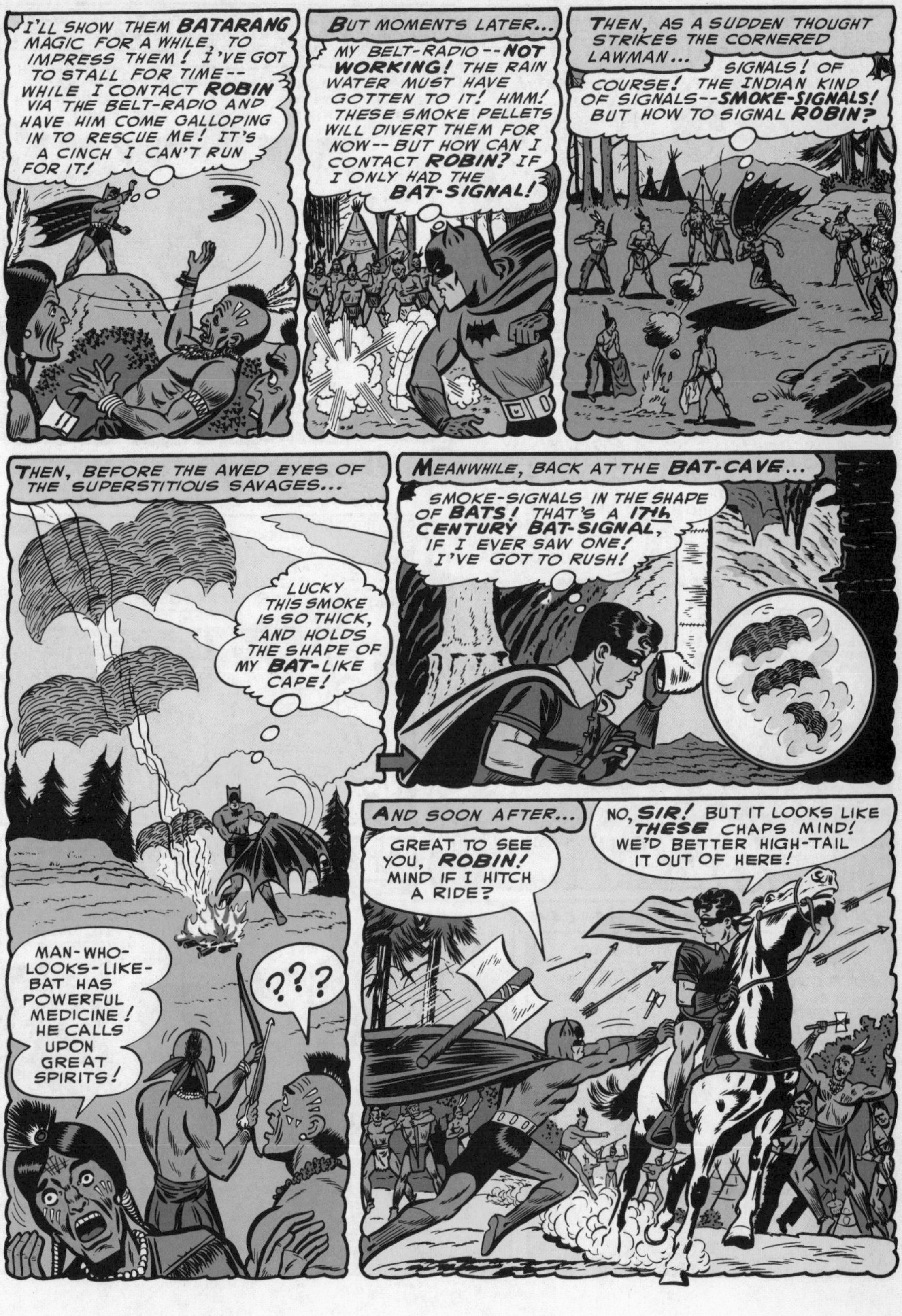
I'LL SHOW THEM BATARANG MAGIC FOR A WHILE, TO IMPRESS THEM! I'VE GOT TO STALL FOR TIME-- WHILE I CONTACT ROBIN VIA THE BELT-RADIO AND HAVE HIM COME GALLOPING IN TO RESCUE ME! IT'S A CINCH I CAN'T RUN FOR IT!
BUT MOMENTS LATER...
MY BELT-RADIO--NOT WORKING! THE RAIN WATER MUST HAVE GOTTEN TO IT! HMM! THESE SMOKE PELLETS WILL DIVERT THEM FOR NOW--BUT HOW CAN I CONTACT ROBIN? IF I ONLY HAD THE BAT-SIGNAL!
THEN, AS A SUDDEN THOUGHT STRIKES THE CORNERED LAWMAN...
SIGNALS! OF COURSE! THE INDIAN KIND OF SIGNALS--SMOKE-SIGNALS! BUT HOW TO SIGNAL ROBIN?
THEN, BEFORE THE AWED EYES OF THE SUPERSTITIOUS SAVAGES...
LUCKY THIS SMOKE IS SO THICK, AND HOLDS THE SHAPE OF MY BAT-LIKE CAPE!
MAN-WHO-LOOKS-LIKE-BAT HAS POWERFUL MEDICINE! HE CALLS UPON GREAT SPIRITS!
???
MEANWHILE, BACK AT THE BAT-CAVE...
SMOKE-SIGNALS IN THE SHAPE OF BATS! THAT'S A 17th CENTURY BAT-SIGNAL, IF I EVER SAW ONE! I'VE GOT TO RUSH!
AND SOON AFTER...
GREAT TO SEE YOU, ROBIN! MIND IF I HITCH A RIDE?
NO, SIR! BUT IT LOOKS LIKE THESE CHAPS MIND! WE'D BETTER HIGH-TAIL IT OUT OF HERE!

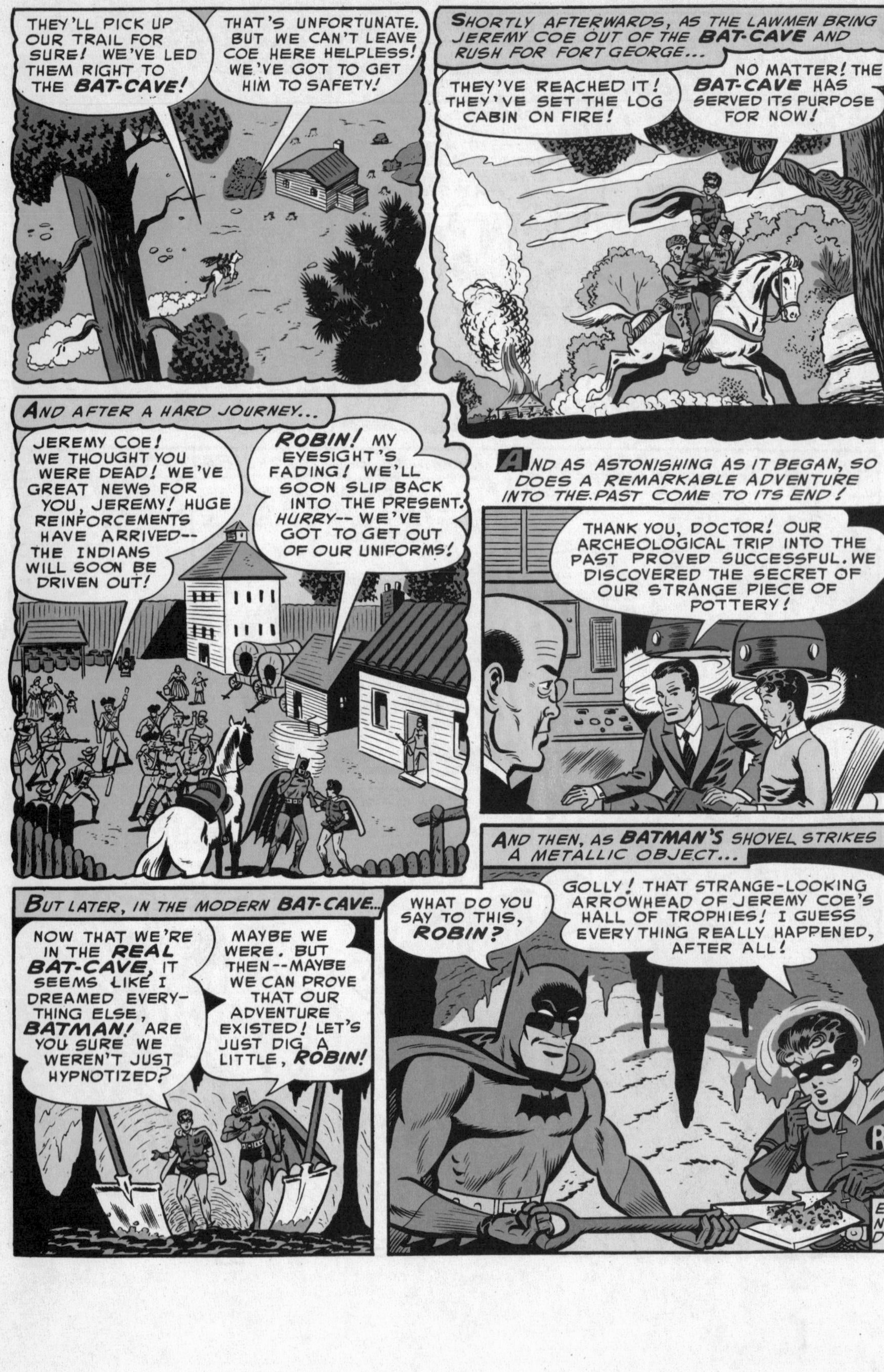
THEY'LL PICK UP OUR TRAIL FOR SURE! WE'VE LED THEM RIGHT TO THE BAT-CAVE!
THAT'S UNFORTUNATE. BUT WE CAN'T LEAVE COE HERE HELPLESS! WE'VE GOT TO GET HIM TO SAFETY!
SHORTLY AFTERWARDS, AS THE LAWMEN BRING JEREMY COE OUT OF THE BAT-CAVE AND RUSH FOR FORT GEORGE...
THEY'VE REACHED IT! THEY'VE SET THE LOG CABIN ON FIRE!
NO MATTER! THE BAT-CAVE HAS SERVED ITS PURPOSE FOR NOW!
AND AFTER A HARD JOURNEY...
JEREMY COE! WE THOUGHT YOU WERE DEAD! WE'VE GREAT NEWS FOR YOU, JEREMY! HUGE REINFORCEMENTS HAVE ARRIVED-- THE INDIANS WILL SOON BE DRIVEN OUT!
ROBIN! MY EYESIGHT'S FADING! WE'LL SOON SLIP BACK INTO THE PRESENT. HURRY-- WE'VE GOT TO GET OUT OF OUR UNIFORMS!
AND AS ASTONISHING AS IT BEGAN, SO DOES A REMARKABLE ADVENTURE INTO THE PAST COME TO ITS END!
THANK YOU, DOCTOR! OUR ARCHEOLOGICAL TRIP INTO THE PAST PROVED SUCCESSFUL. WE DISCOVERED THE SECRET OF OUR STRANGE PIECE OF POTTERY!
BUT LATER, IN THE MODERN BAT-CAVE...
NOW THAT WE'RE IN THE REAL BAT-CAVE, IT SEEMS LIKE I DREAMED EVERYTHING ELSE, BATMAN! ARE YOU SURE WE WEREN'T JUST HYPNOTIZED?
MAYBE WE WERE. BUT THEN--MAYBE WE CAN PROVE THAT OUR ADVENTURE EXISTED! LET'S JUST DIG A LITTLE, ROBIN!
AND THEN, AS BATMAN'S SHOVEL STRIKES A METALLIC OBJECT...
WHAT DO YOU SAY TO THIS, ROBIN?
GOLLY! THAT STRANGE-LOOKING ARROWHEAD OF JEREMY COE'S HALL OF TROPHIES! I GUESS EVERYTHING REALLY HAPPENED, AFTER ALL!
END

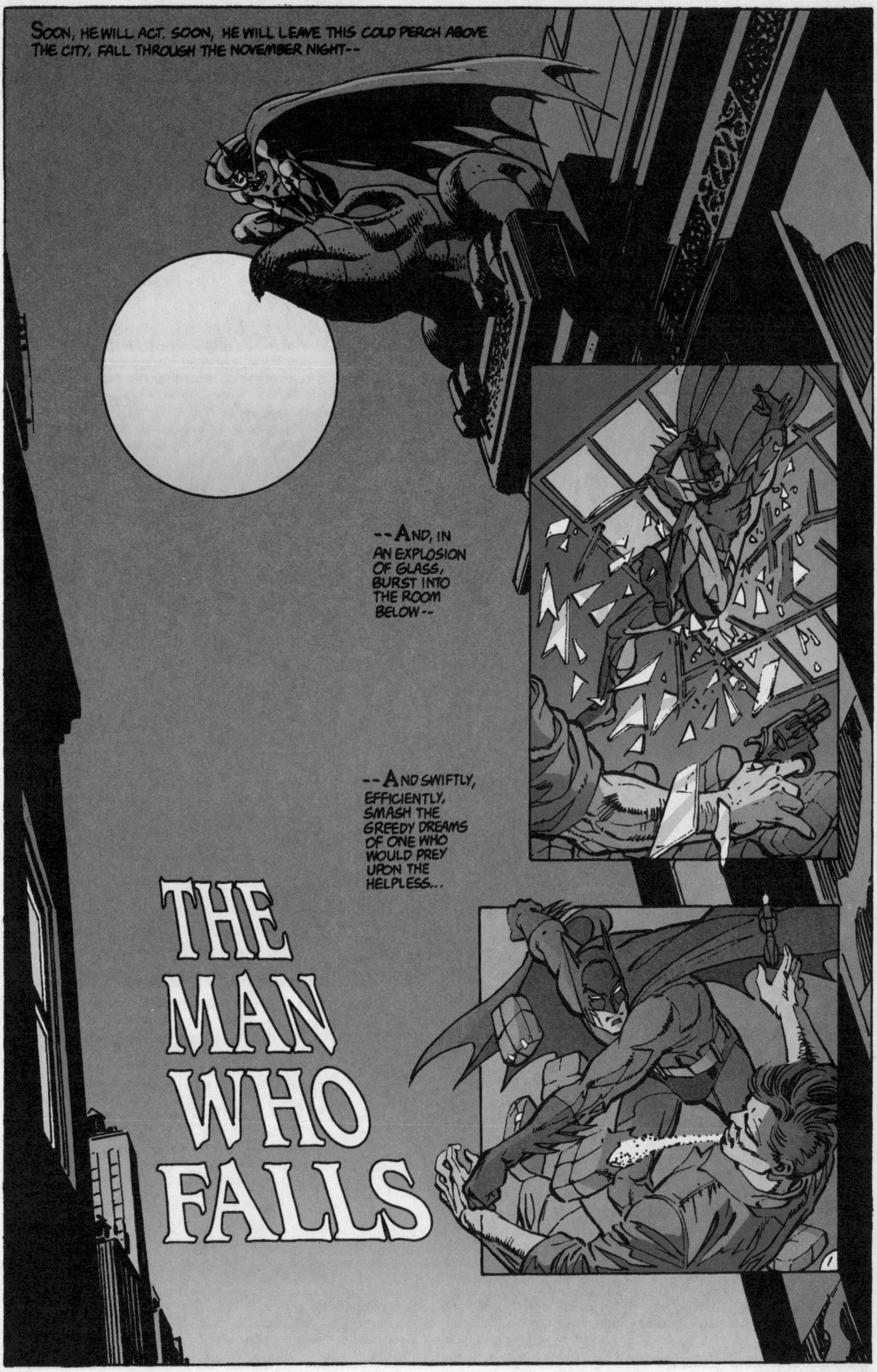
SOON, HE WILL ACT. SOON, HE WILL LEAVE THIS COLD PERCH ABOVE THE CITY, FALL THROUGH THE NOVEMBER NIGHT--
--AND, IN AN EXPLOSION OF GLASS, BURST INTO THE ROOM BELOW--
--AND SWIFTLY, EFFICIENTLY, SMASH THE GREEDY DREAMS OF ONE WHO WOULD PREY UPON THE HELPLESS...
THE MAN WHO FALLS

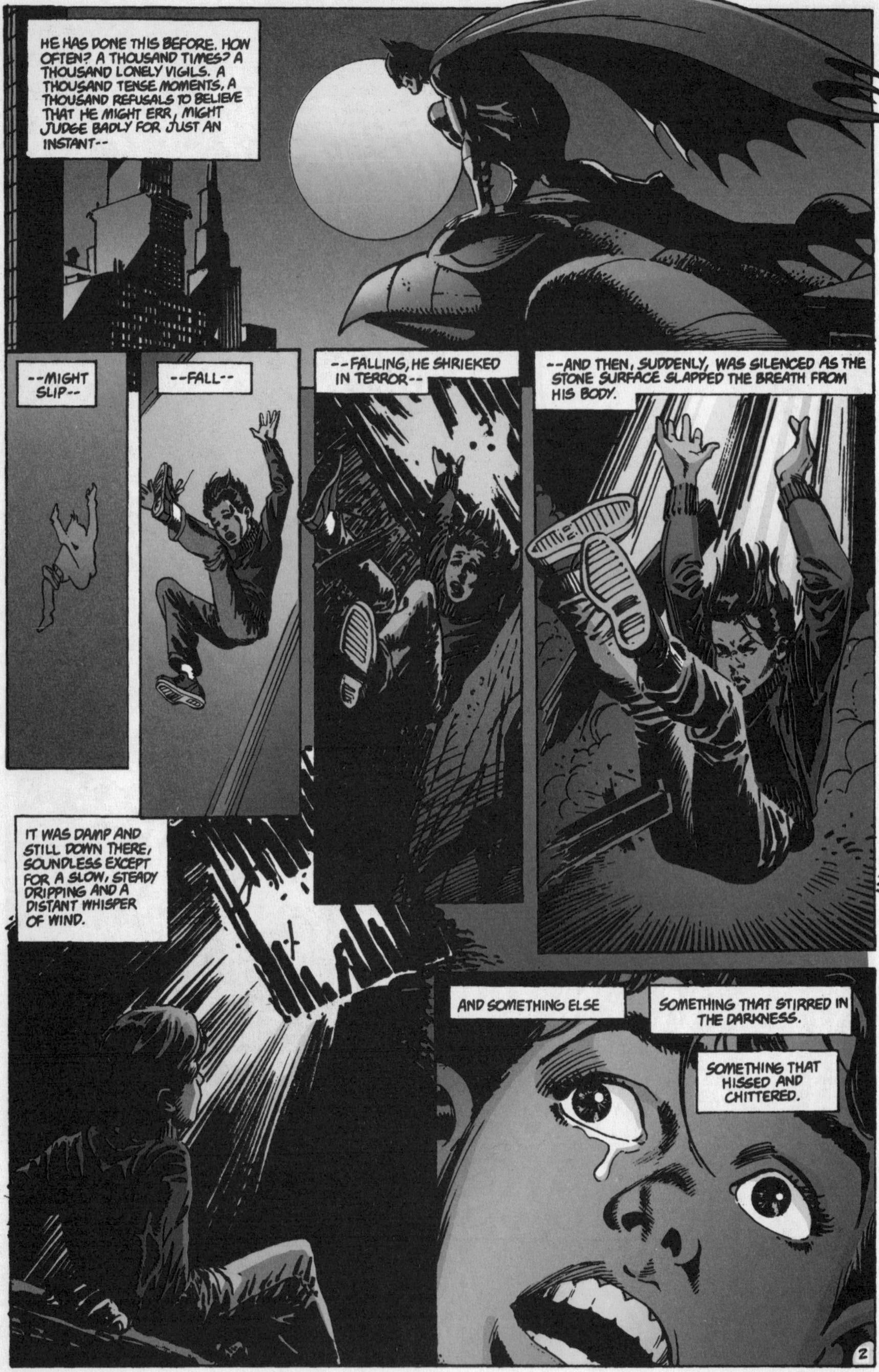
HE HAS DONE THIS BEFORE. HOW OFTEN? A THOUSAND TIMES? A THOUSAND LONELY VIGILS. A THOUSAND TENSE MOMENTS, A THOUSAND REFUSALS TO BELIEVE THAT HE MIGHT ERR, MIGHT JUDGE BADLY FOR JUST AN INSTANT--
--MIGHT SLIP--
--FALL--
--FALLING, HE SHRIEKED IN TERROR--
--AND THEN, SUDDENLY, WAS SILENCED AS THE STONE SURFACE SLAPPED THE BREATH FROM HIS BODY.
IT WAS DAMP AND STILL DOWN THERE, SOUNDLESS EXCEPT FOR A SLOW, STEADY DRIPPING AND A DISTANT WHISPER OF WIND.
AND SOMETHING ELSE
SOMETHING THAT STIRRED IN THE DARKNESS.
SOMETHING THAT HISSED AND CHITTERED.
2

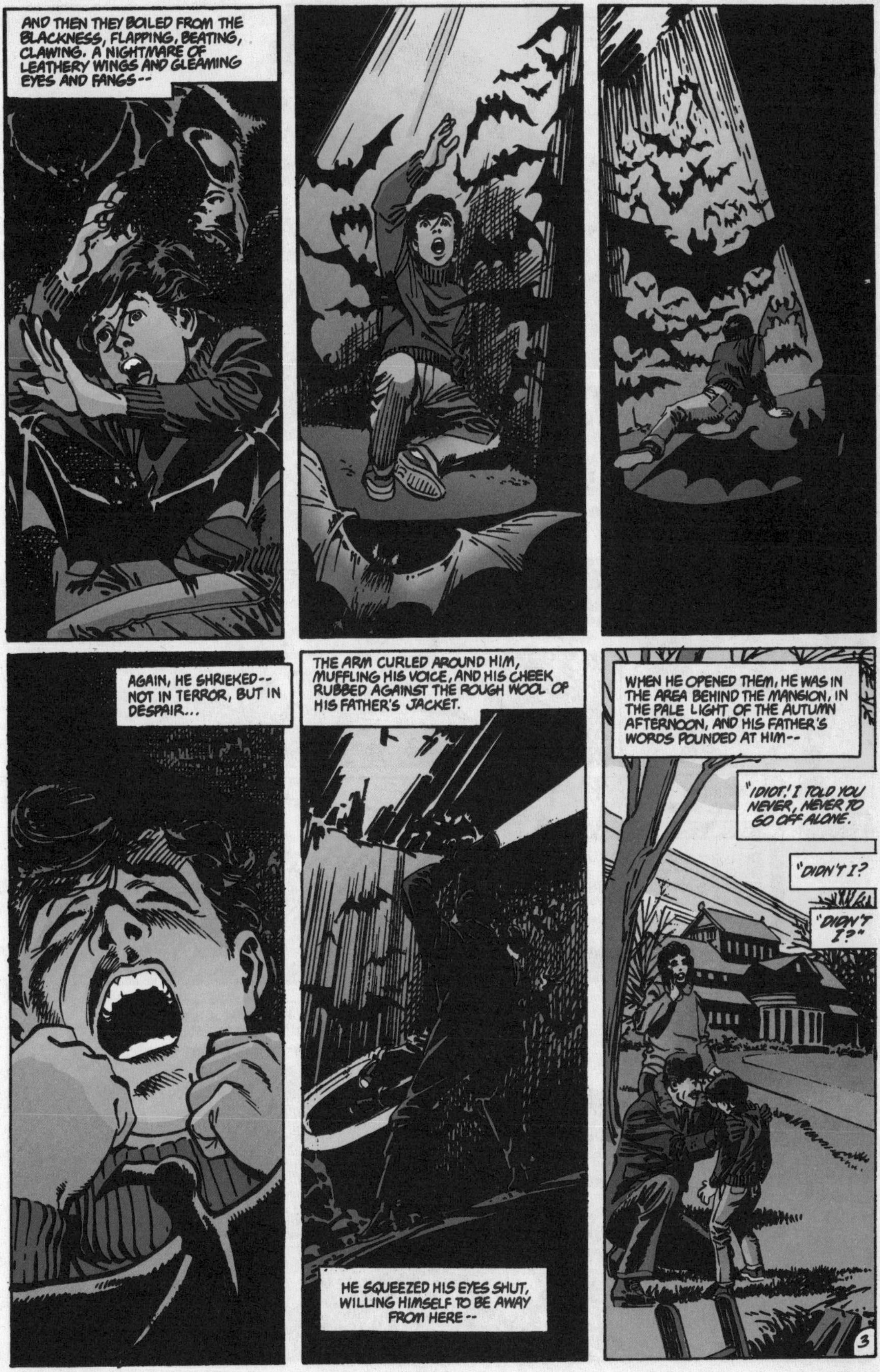
AND THEN THEY BOILED FROM THE BLACKNESS, FLAPPING, BEATING, CLAWING. A NIGHTMARE OF LEATHERY WINGS AND GLEAMING EYES AND FANGS--
AGAIN, HE SHRIEKED--NOT IN TERROR, BUT IN DESPAIR...
THE ARM CURLED AROUND HIM, MUFFLING HIS VOICE, AND HIS CHEEK RUBBED AGAINST THE ROUGH WOOL OF HIS FATHER'S JACKET.
HE SQUEEZED HIS EYES SHUT, WILLING HIMSELF TO BE AWAY FROM HERE--
WHEN HE OPENED THEM, HE WAS IN THE AREA BEHIND THE MANSION, IN THE PALE LIGHT OF THE AUTUMN AFTERNOON, AND HIS FATHER'S WORDS POUNDED AT HIM--
"IDIOT! I TOLD YOU NEVER, NEVER TO GO OFF ALONE.
"DIDN'T I?
"DIDN'T I?"
3

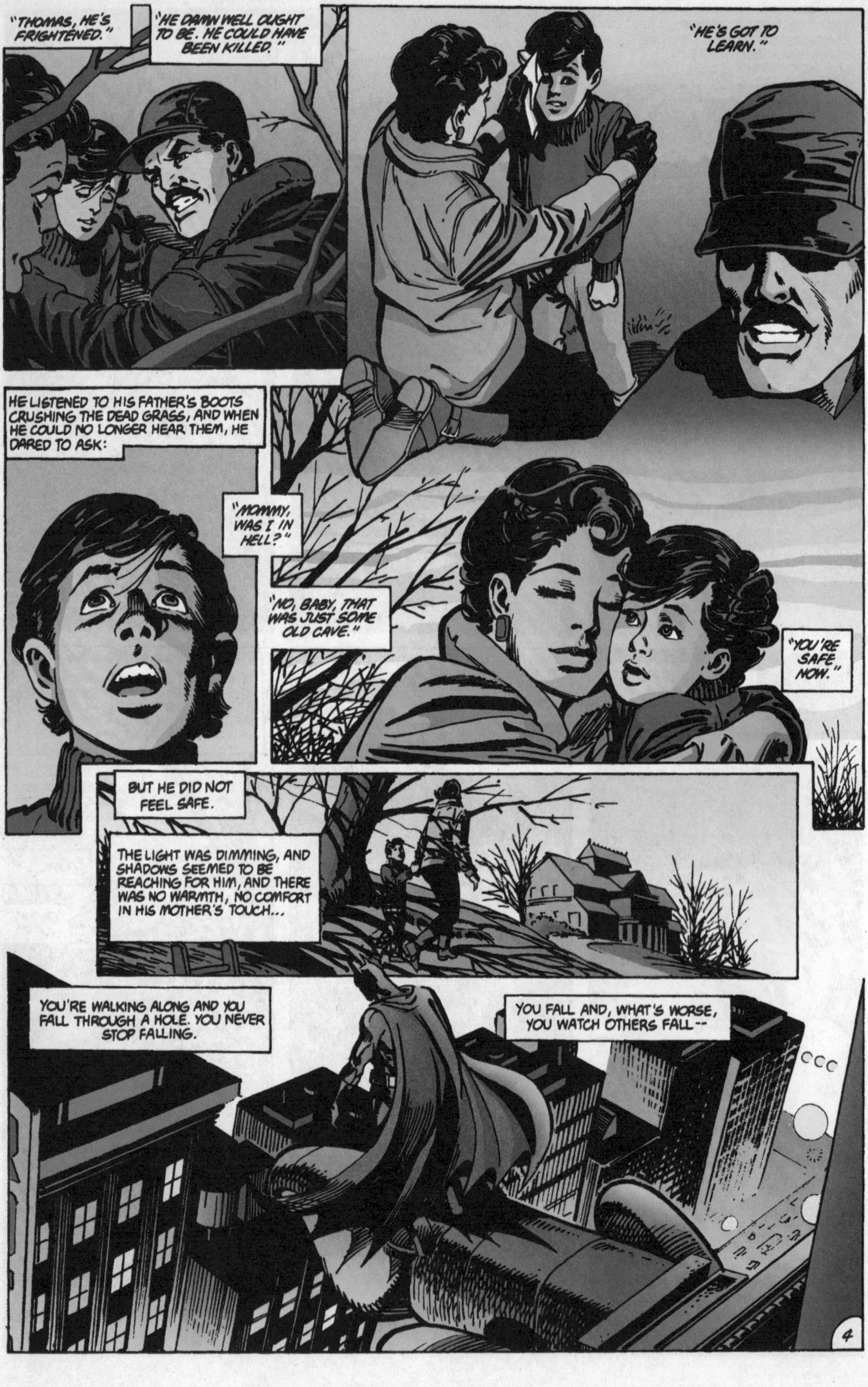

"THOMAS, HE'S FRIGHTENED."
"HE DAMN WELL OUGHT TO BE. HE COULD HAVE BEEN KILLED."
"HE'S GOT TO LEARN."
HE LISTENED TO HIS FATHER'S BOOTS CRUSHING THE DEAD GRASS, AND WHEN HE COULD NO LONGER HEAR THEM, HE DARED TO ASK:
"MOMMY, WAS I IN HELL?"
"NO, BABY, THAT WAS JUST SOME OLD CAVE."
"YOU'RE SAFE NOW."
BUT HE DID NOT FEEL SAFE.
THE LIGHT WAS DIMMING, AND SHADOWS SEEMED TO BE REACHING FOR HIM, AND THERE WAS NO WARMTH, NO COMFORT IN HIS MOTHER'S TOUCH...
YOU'RE WALKING ALONG AND YOU FALL THROUGH A HOLE. YOU NEVER STOP FALLING.
YOU FALL AND, WHAT'S WORSE, YOU WATCH OTHERS FALL--
4

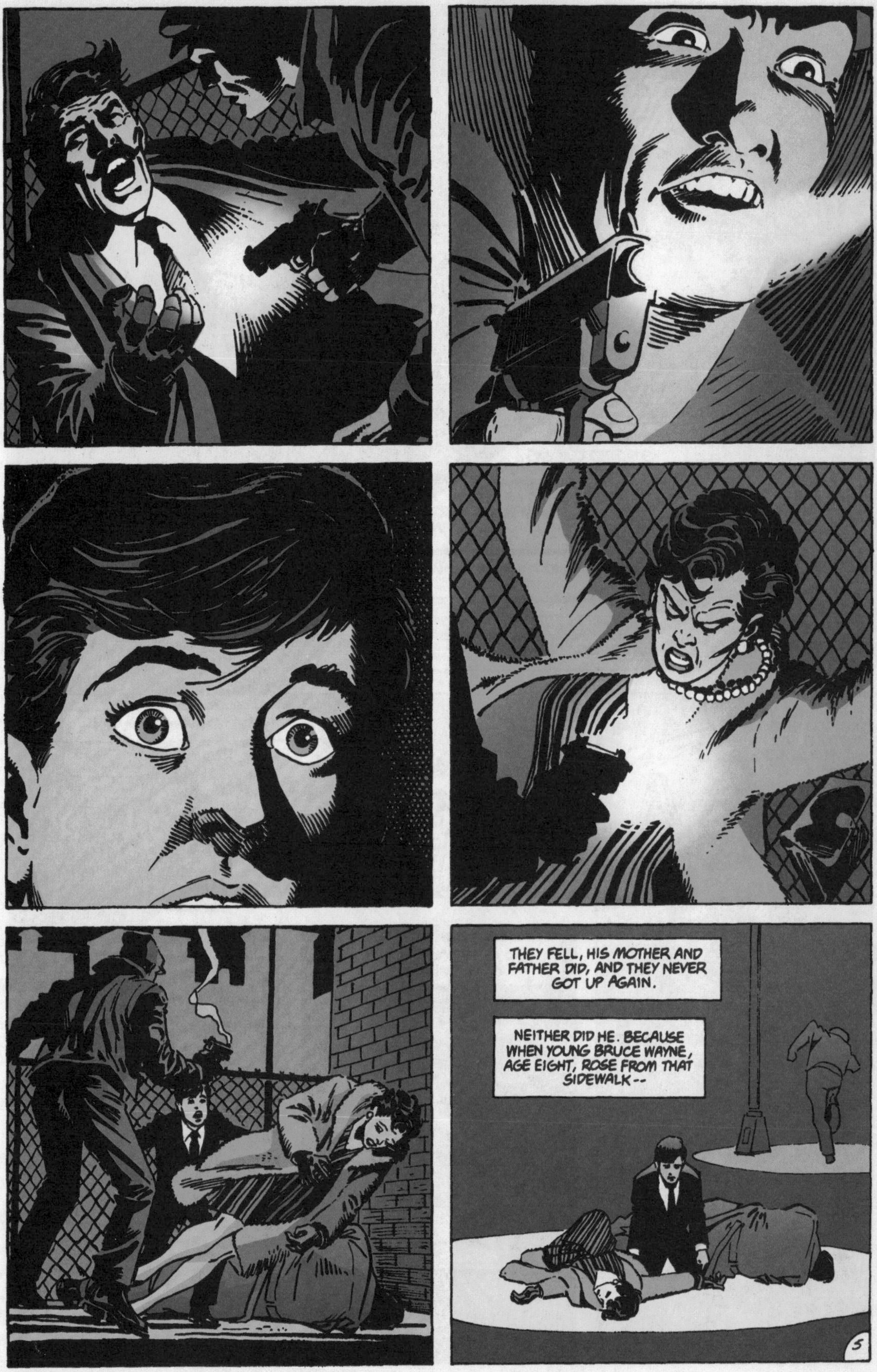
THEY FELL, HIS MOTHER AND FATHER DID, AND THEY NEVER GOT UP AGAIN.
NEITHER DID HE. BECAUSE WHEN YOUNG BRUCE WAYNE, AGE EIGHT, ROSE FROM THAT SIDEWALK --
5

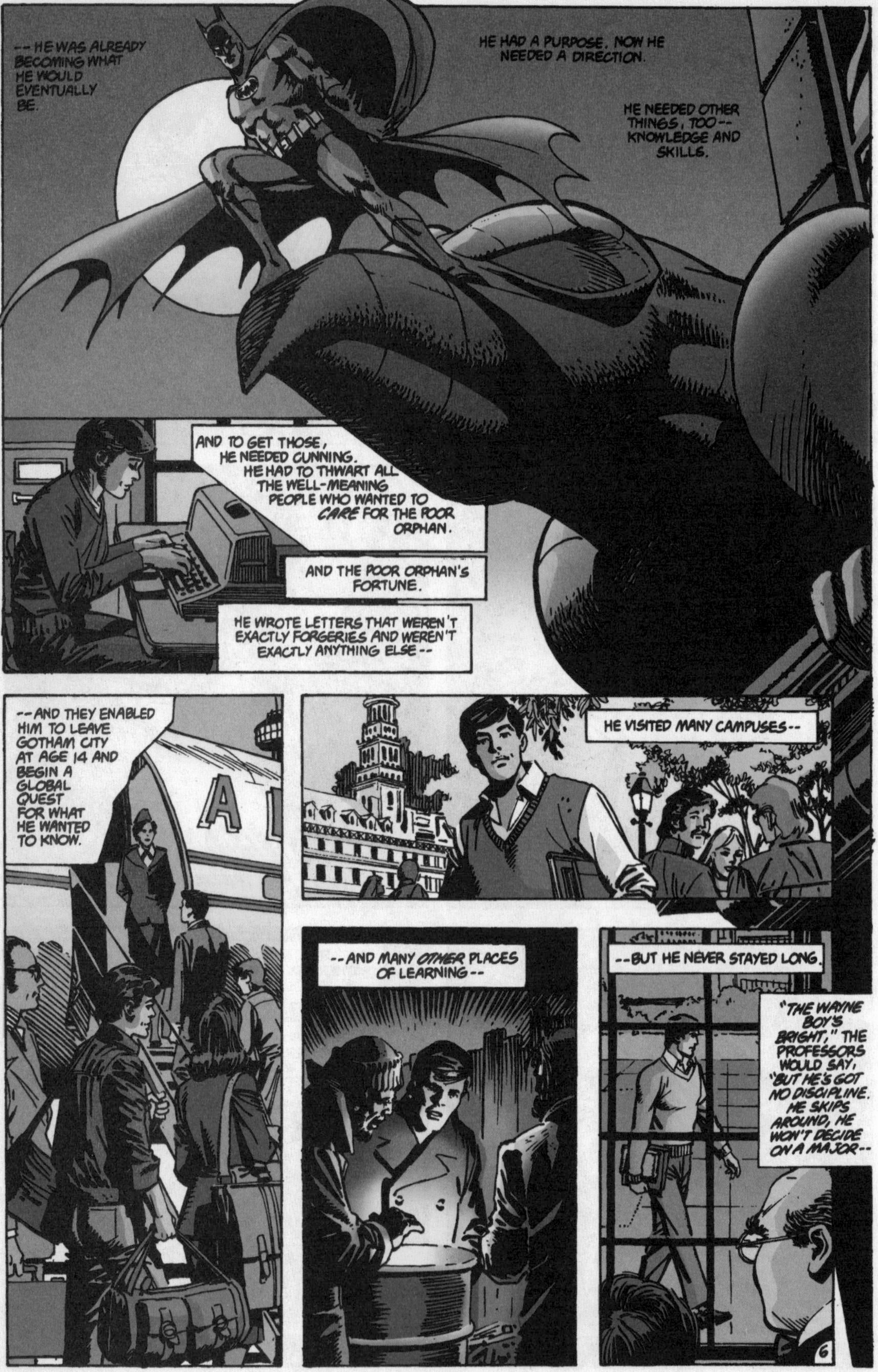
--HE WAS ALREADY BECOMING WHAT HE WOULD EVENTUALLY BE.
HE HAD A PURPOSE. NOW HE NEEDED A DIRECTION.
HE NEEDED OTHER THINGS, TOO-- KNOWLEDGE AND SKILLS.
AND TO GET THOSE, HE NEEDED CUNNING. HE HAD TO THWART ALL THE WELL-MEANING PEOPLE WHO WANTED TO CARE FOR THE POOR ORPHAN.
AND THE POOR ORPHAN'S FORTUNE.
HE WROTE LETTERS THAT WEREN'T EXACTLY FORGERIES AND WEREN'T EXACTLY ANYTHING ELSE--
--AND THEY ENABLED HIM TO LEAVE GOTHAM CITY AT AGE 14 AND BEGIN A GLOBAL QUEST FOR WHAT HE WANTED TO KNOW.
HE VISITED MANY CAMPUSES--
--AND MANY OTHER PLACES OF LEARNING--
--BUT HE NEVER STAYED LONG.
"THE WAYNE BOY'S BRIGHT," THE PROFESSORS WOULD SAY, "BUT HE'S GOT NO DISCIPLINE. HE SKIPS AROUND, HE WON'T DECIDE ON A MAJOR--
6

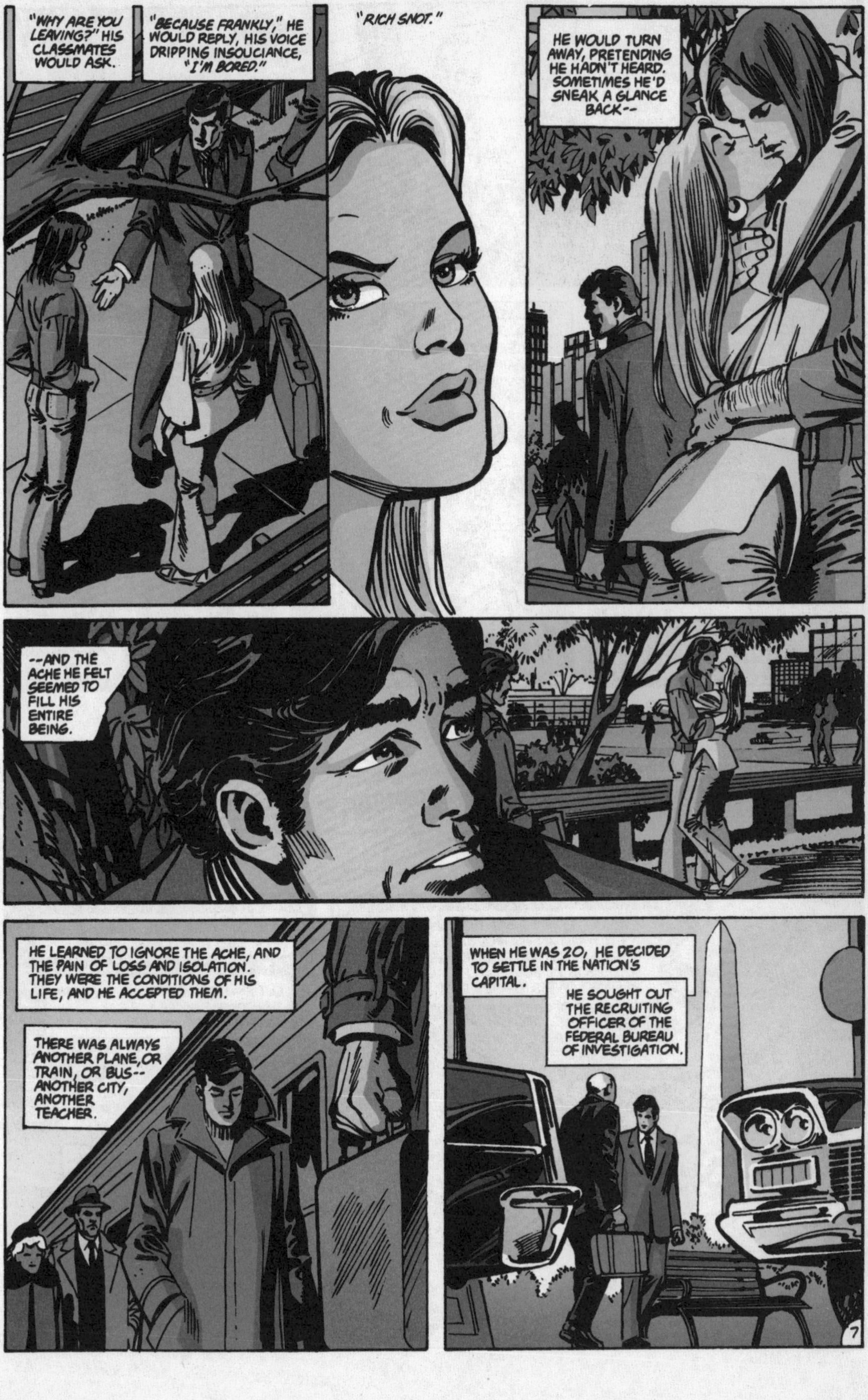
"WHY ARE YOU LEAVING?" HIS CLASSMATES WOULD ASK.
"BECAUSE FRANKLY," HE WOULD REPLY, HIS VOICE DRIPPING INSOUCIANCE, "I'M BORED."
"RICH SNOT."
HE WOULD TURN AWAY, PRETENDING HE HADN'T HEARD. SOMETIMES HE'D SNEAK A GLANCE BACK--
--AND THE ACHE HE FELT SEEMED TO FILL HIS ENTIRE BEING.
HE LEARNED TO IGNORE THE ACHE, AND THE PAIN OF LOSS AND ISOLATION. THEY WERE THE CONDITIONS OF HIS LIFE, AND HE ACCEPTED THEM.
THERE WAS ALWAYS ANOTHER PLANE, OR TRAIN, OR BUS-- ANOTHER CITY, ANOTHER TEACHER.
WHEN HE WAS 20, HE DECIDED TO SETTLE IN THE NATION'S CAPITAL.
HE SOUGHT OUT THE RECRUITING OFFICER OF THE FEDERAL BUREAU OF INVESTIGATION.
7

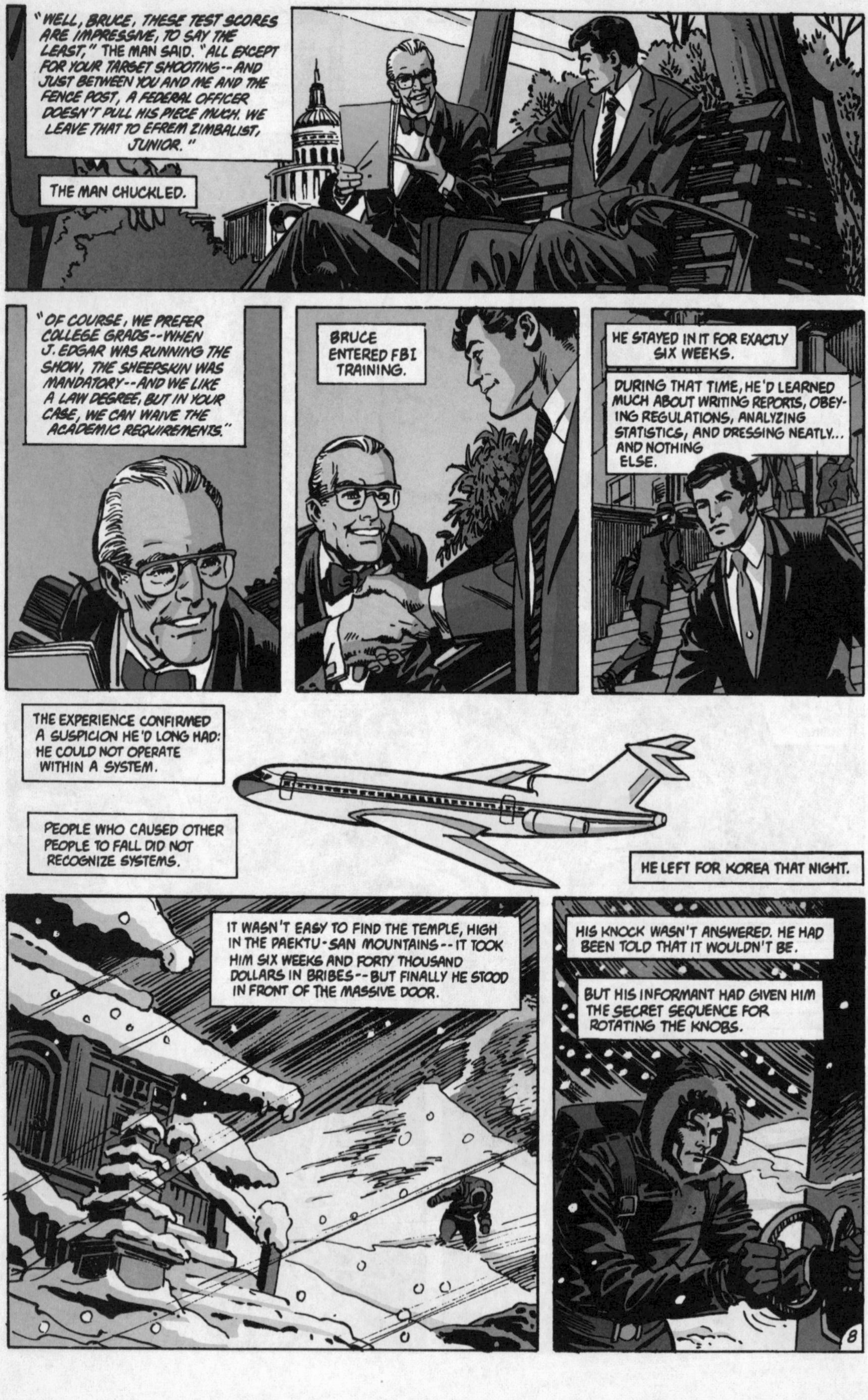
"WELL, BRUCE, THESE TEST SCORES ARE IMPRESSIVE, TO SAY THE LEAST," THE MAN SAID. "ALL EXCEPT FOR YOUR TARGET SHOOTING--AND JUST BETWEEN YOU AND ME AND THE FENCE POST, A FEDERAL OFFICER DOESN'T PULL HIS PIECE MUCH. WE LEAVE THAT TO EFREM ZIMBALIST, JUNIOR."
THE MAN CHUCKLED.
"OF COURSE, WE PREFER COLLEGE GRADS--WHEN J. EDGAR WAS RUNNING THE SHOW, THE SHEEPSKIN WAS MANDATORY--AND WE LIKE A LAW DEGREE, BUT IN YOUR CASE, WE CAN WAIVE THE ACADEMIC REQUIREMENTS."
BRUCE ENTERED FBI TRAINING.
HE STAYED IN IT FOR EXACTLY SIX WEEKS.
DURING THAT TIME, HE'D LEARNED MUCH ABOUT WRITING REPORTS, OBEYING REGULATIONS, ANALYZING STATISTICS, AND DRESSING NEATLY... AND NOTHING ELSE.
THE EXPERIENCE CONFIRMED A SUSPICION HE'D LONG HAD: HE COULD NOT OPERATE WITHIN A SYSTEM.
PEOPLE WHO CAUSED OTHER PEOPLE TO FALL DID NOT RECOGNIZE SYSTEMS.
HE LEFT FOR KOREA THAT NIGHT.
IT WASN'T EASY TO FIND THE TEMPLE, HIGH IN THE PAEKTU-SAN MOUNTAINS--IT TOOK HIM SIX WEEKS AND FORTY THOUSAND DOLLARS IN BRIBES--BUT FINALLY HE STOOD IN FRONT OF THE MASSIVE DOOR.
HIS KNOCK WASN'T ANSWERED. HE HAD BEEN TOLD THAT IT WOULDN'T BE.
BUT HIS INFORMANT HAD GIVEN HIM THE SECRET SEQUENCE FOR ROTATING THE KNOBS.
8

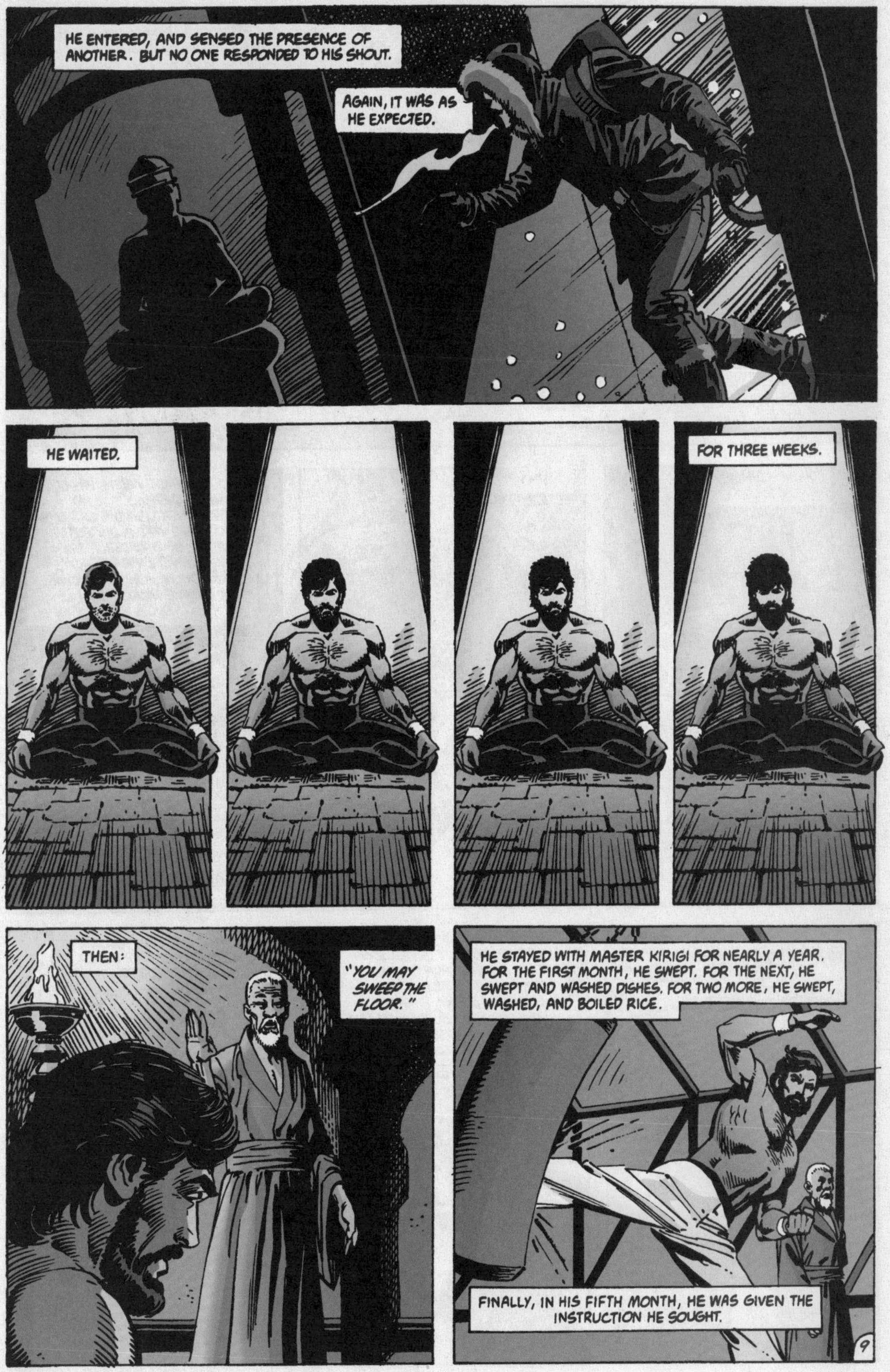
HE ENTERED, AND SENSED THE PRESENCE OF ANOTHER. BUT NO ONE RESPONDED TO HIS SHOUT.
AGAIN, IT WAS AS HE EXPECTED.
HE WAITED.
FOR THREE WEEKS.
THEN:
"YOU MAY SWEEP THE FLOOR."
HE STAYED WITH MASTER KIRIGI FOR NEARLY A YEAR. FOR THE FIRST MONTH, HE SWEPT. FOR THE NEXT, HE SWEPT AND WASHED DISHES. FOR TWO MORE, HE SWEPT, WASHED, AND BOILED RICE.
FINALLY, IN HIS FIFTH MONTH, HE WAS GIVEN THE INSTRUCTION HE SOUGHT.
9

THE ELEVENTH MONTH:

THE MASTER'S VOICE WAS SOMBRE: "NATURE HAS BEEN KIND TO YOU. YOU ARE OF EXCEPTIONAL INTELLIGENCE AND YOUR PHYSIQUE IS EXTRAORDINARY. REFLEXES, VISION, STRENGTH -- ALL ARE ALMOST PERFECT."

"HOW TERRIBLE FOR YOU."

"WHY?"

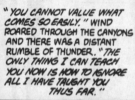

"YOU CANNOT VALUE WHAT COMES SO EASILY." WIND ROARED THROUGH THE CANYONS AND THERE WAS A DISTANT RUMBLE OF THUNDER. "THE ONLY THING I CAN TEACH YOU NOW IS HOW TO IGNORE ALL I HAVE TAUGHT YOU THUS FAR."

"I DO NOT UNDERSTAND."

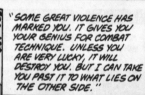

"SOME GREAT VIOLENCE HAS MARKED YOU. IT GIVES YOU YOUR GENIUS FOR COMBAT TECHNIQUE. UNLESS YOU ARE VERY LUCKY, IT WILL DESTROY YOU. BUT I CAN TAKE YOU PAST IT TO WHAT LIES ON THE OTHER SIDE."

"I WILL REQUIRE ANOTHER TWENTY YEARS," MASTER KIRIGI CONCLUDED.

"I DON'T HAVE TWENTY YEARS," BRUCE REPLIED, "AND I DON'T WANT TO FORGET WHAT I'VE LEARNED FROM YOU."

10

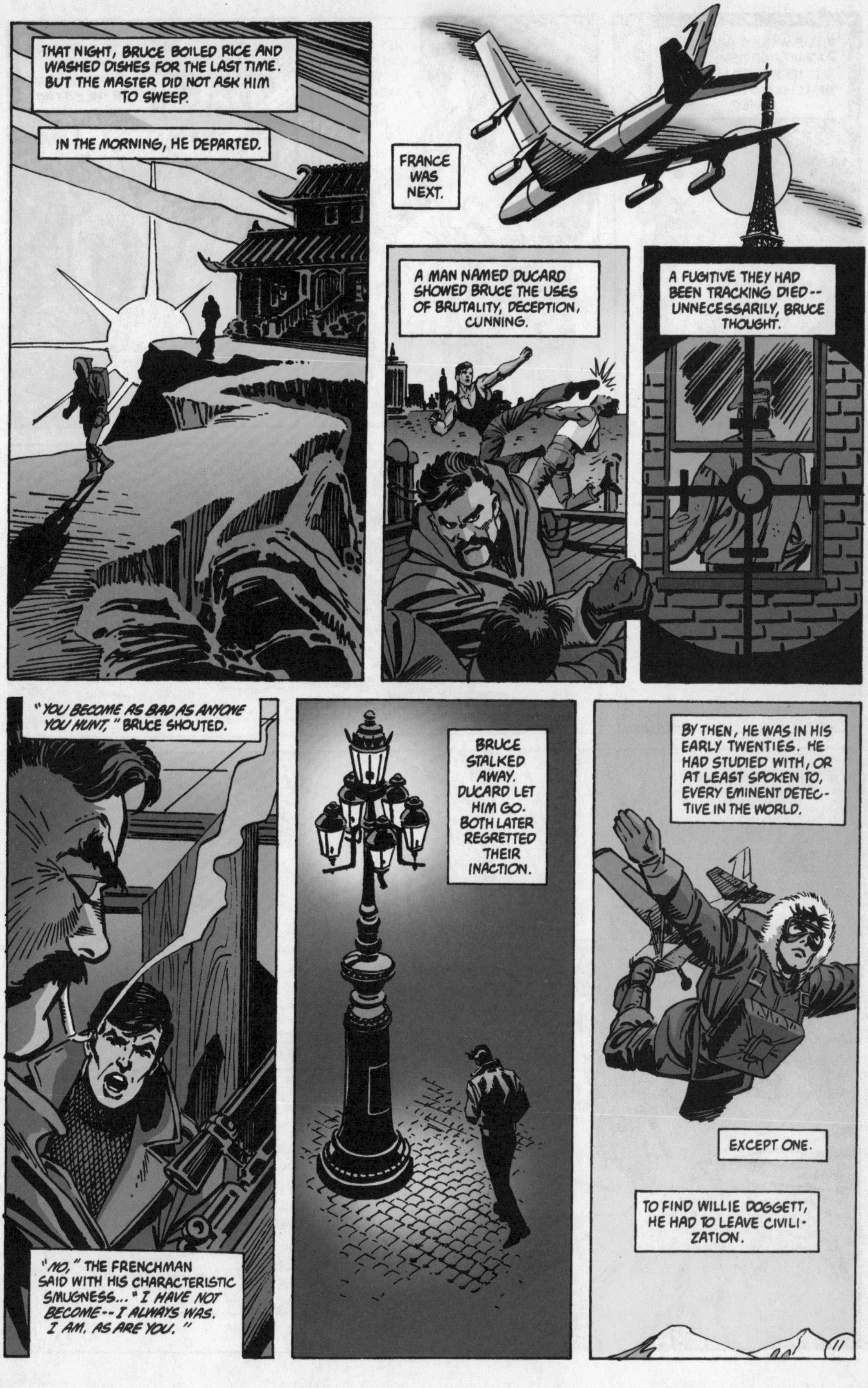
THAT NIGHT, BRUCE BOILED RICE AND WASHED DISHES FOR THE LAST TIME. BUT THE MASTER DID NOT ASK HIM TO SWEEP.
IN THE MORNING, HE DEPARTED.
FRANCE WAS NEXT.
A MAN NAMED DUCARD SHOWED BRUCE THE USES OF BRUTALITY, DECEPTION, CUNNING.
A FUGITIVE THEY HAD BEEN TRACKING DIED-- UNNECESSARILY, BRUCE THOUGHT.
"YOU BECOME AS BAD AS ANYONE YOU HUNT," BRUCE SHOUTED.
"NO," THE FRENCHMAN SAID WITH HIS CHARACTERISTIC SMUGNESS... "I HAVE NOT BECOME-- I ALWAYS WAS. I AM. AS ARE YOU."
BRUCE STALKED AWAY. DUCARD LET HIM GO. BOTH LATER REGRETTED THEIR INACTION.
BY THEN, HE WAS IN HIS EARLY TWENTIES. HE HAD STUDIED WITH, OR AT LEAST SPOKEN TO, EVERY EMINENT DETECTIVE IN THE WORLD.
EXCEPT ONE.
TO FIND WILLIE DOGGETT, HE HAD TO LEAVE CIVILIZATION.
11

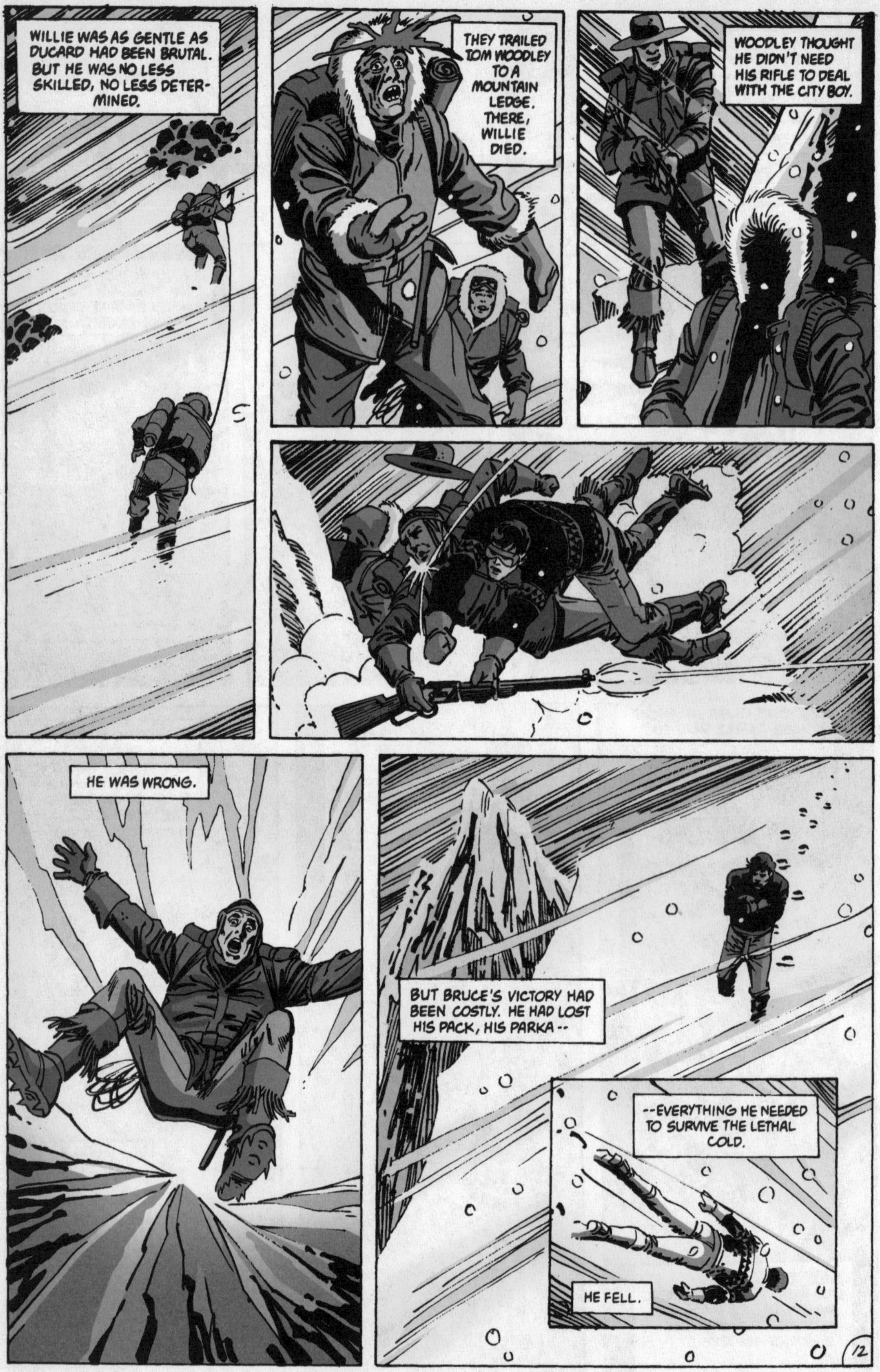
WILLIE WAS AS GENTLE AS DUCARD HAD BEEN BRUTAL. BUT HE WAS NO LESS SKILLED, NO LESS DETERMINED.
THEY TRAILED TOM WOODLEY TO A MOUNTAIN LEDGE. THERE, WILLIE DIED.
WOODLEY THOUGHT HE DIDN'T NEED HIS RIFLE TO DEAL WITH THE CITY BOY.
HE WAS WRONG.
BUT BRUCE'S VICTORY HAD BEEN COSTLY. HE HAD LOST HIS PACK, HIS PARKA --
--EVERYTHING HE NEEDED TO SURVIVE THE LETHAL COLD.
HE FELL.
12

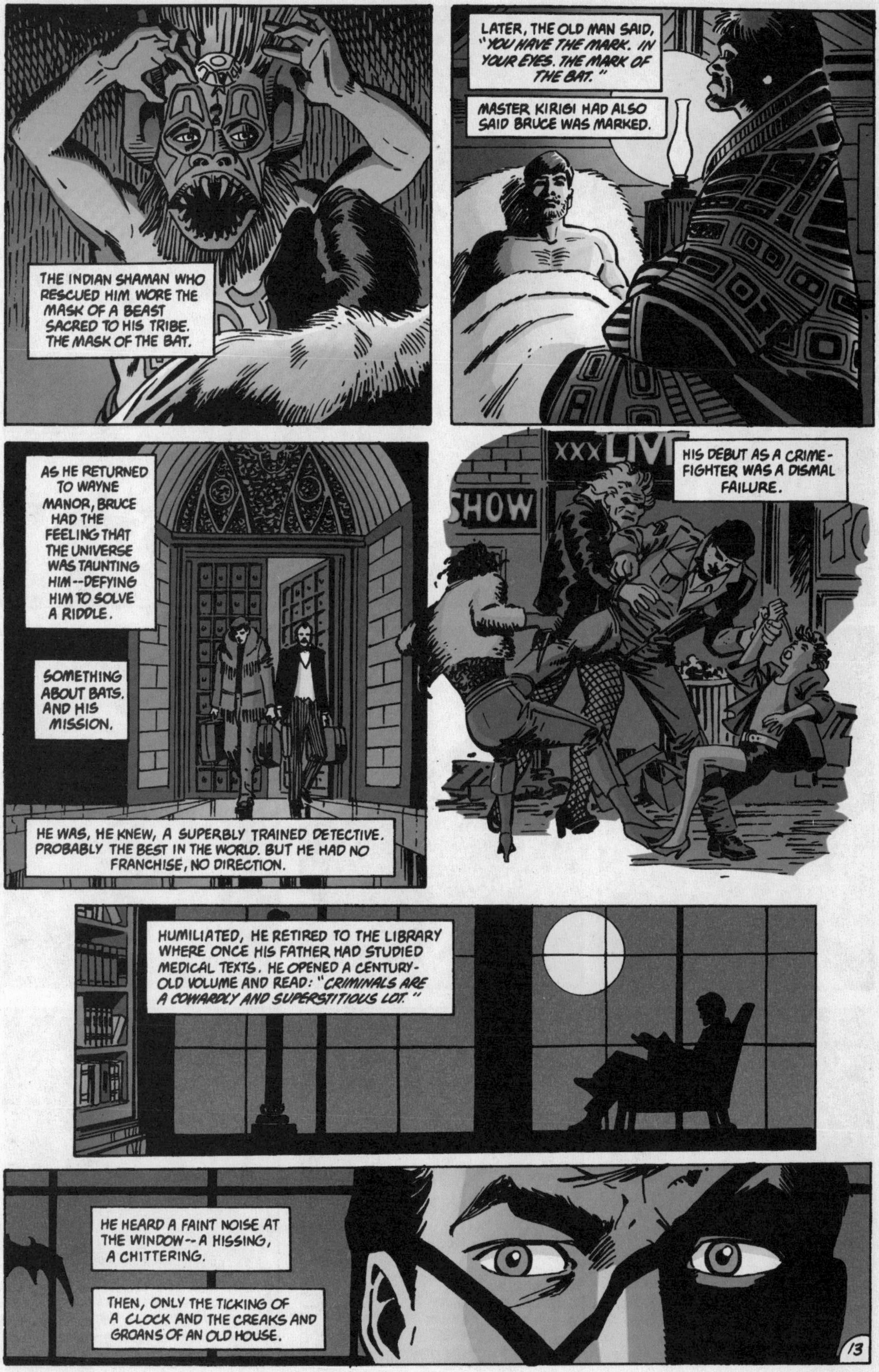
THE INDIAN SHAMAN WHO RESCUED HIM WORE THE MASK OF A BEAST SACRED TO HIS TRIBE. THE MASK OF THE BAT.
LATER, THE OLD MAN SAID, "YOU HAVE THE MARK. IN YOUR EYES. THE MARK OF THE BAT."
MASTER KIRIGI HAD ALSO SAID BRUCE WAS MARKED.
AS HE RETURNED TO WAYNE MANOR, BRUCE HAD THE FEELING THAT THE UNIVERSE WAS TAUNTING HIM--DEFYING HIM TO SOLVE A RIDDLE.
SOMETHING ABOUT BATS. AND HIS MISSION.
HE WAS, HE KNEW, A SUPERBLY TRAINED DETECTIVE. PROBABLY THE BEST IN THE WORLD. BUT HE HAD NO FRANCHISE, NO DIRECTION.
SHOW
HIS DEBUT AS A CRIME-FIGHTER WAS A DISMAL FAILURE.
HUMILIATED, HE RETIRED TO THE LIBRARY WHERE ONCE HIS FATHER HAD STUDIED MEDICAL TEXTS. HE OPENED A CENTURY-OLD VOLUME AND READ: "CRIMINALS ARE A COWARDLY AND SUPERSTITIOUS LOT."
HE HEARD A FAINT NOISE AT THE WINDOW--A HISSING, A CHITTERING.
THEN, ONLY THE TICKING OF A CLOCK AND THE CREAKS AND GROANS OF AN OLD HOUSE.
13

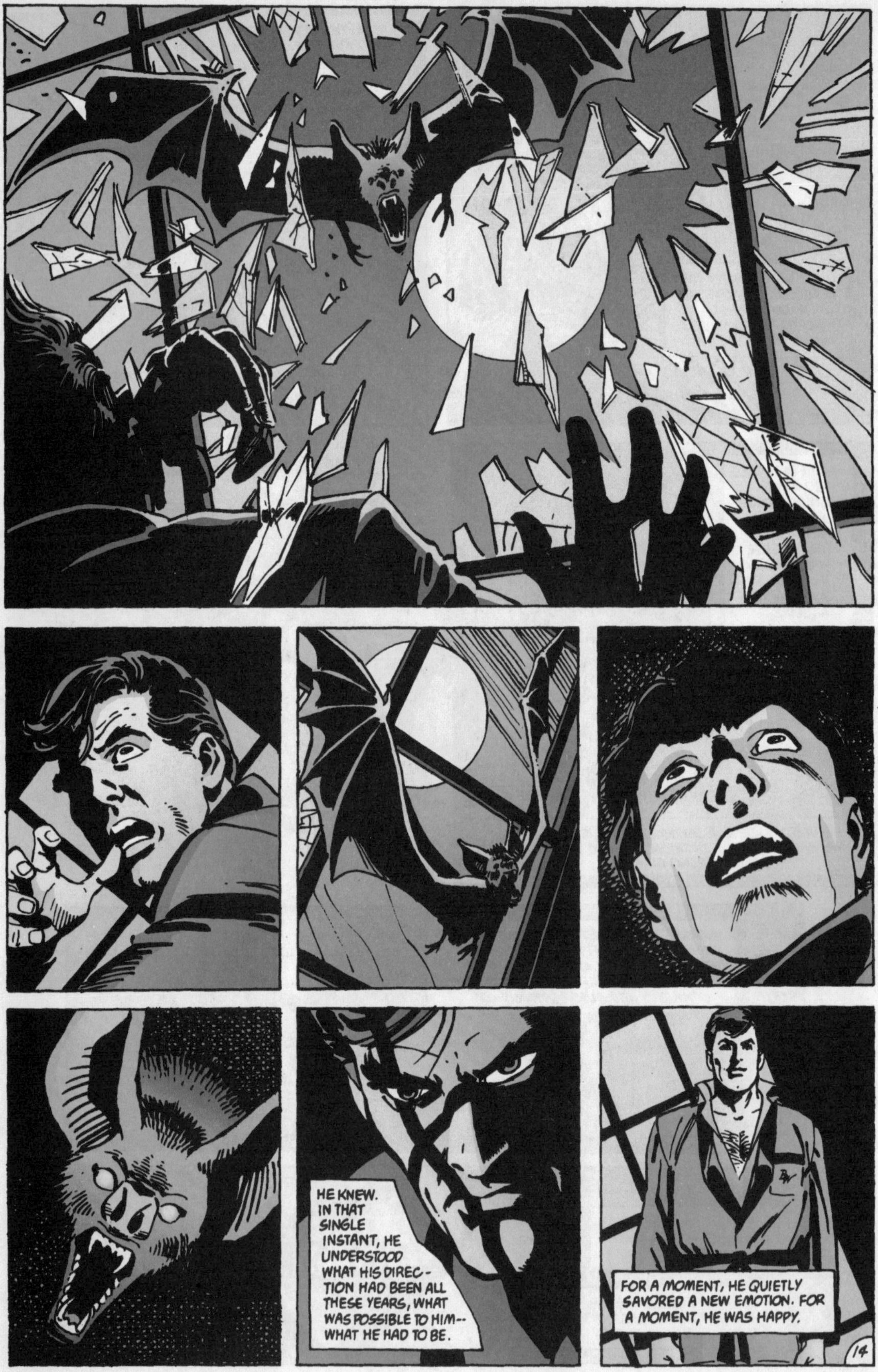
HE KNEW. IN THAT SINGLE INSTANT, HE UNDERSTOOD WHAT HIS DIREC-TION HAD BEEN ALL THESE YEARS, WHAT WAS POSSIBLE TO HIM-- WHAT HE HAD TO BE.
FOR A MOMENT, HE QUIETLY SAVORED A NEW EMOTION. FOR A MOMENT, HE WAS HAPPY.
14

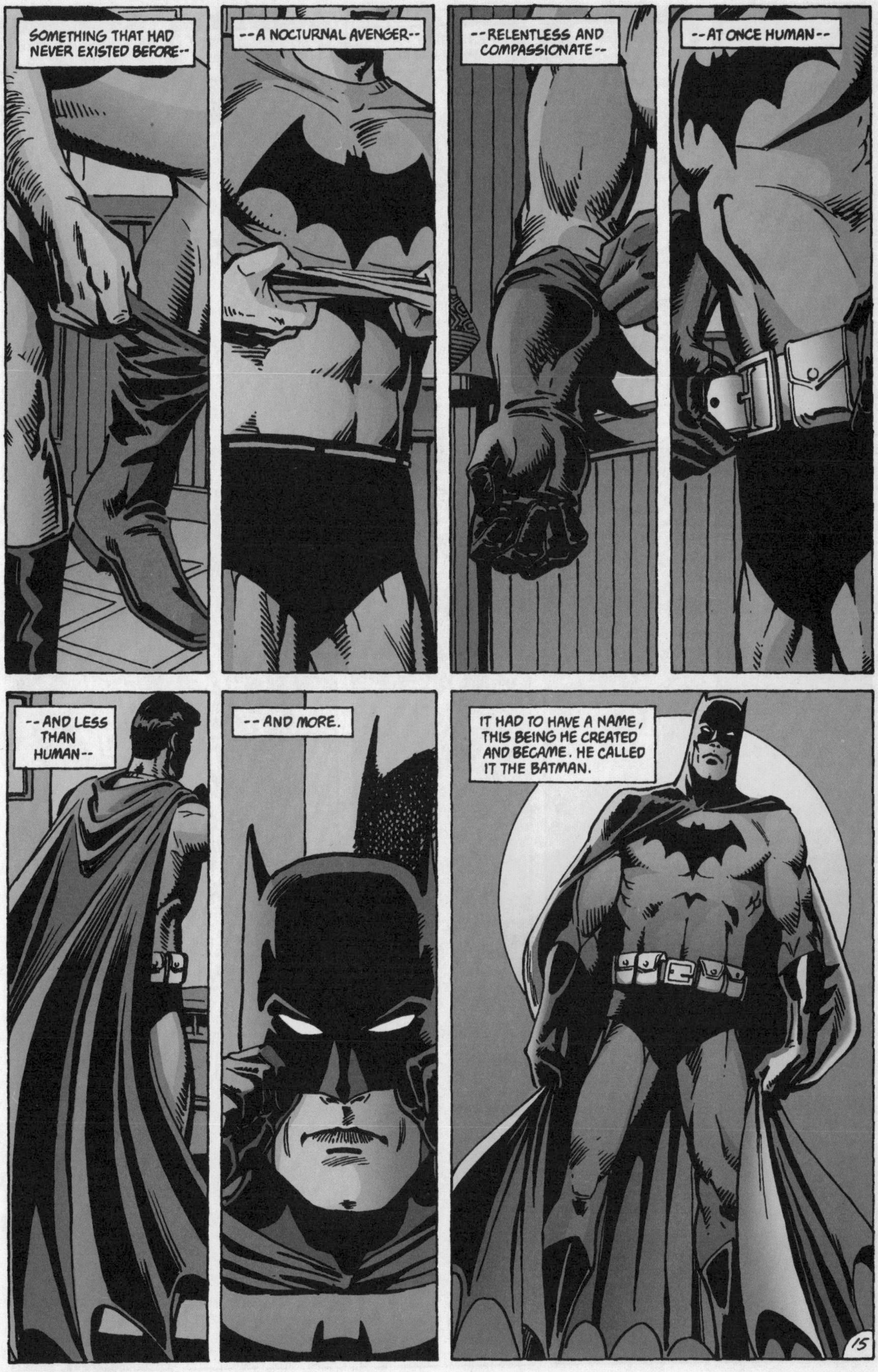
SOMETHING THAT HAD NEVER EXISTED BEFORE--
--A NOCTURNAL AVENGER--
--RELENTLESS AND COMPASSIONATE--
--AT ONCE HUMAN--
--AND LESS THAN HUMAN--
--AND MORE.
IT HAD TO HAVE A NAME, THIS BEING HE CREATED AND BECAME. HE CALLED IT THE BATMAN.
15

HE STANDS, TENSES, RELAXES. THE TIME HAS COME.

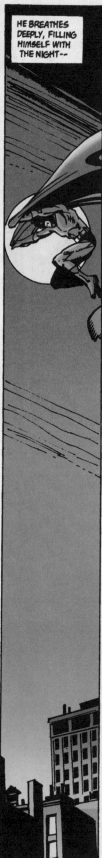

HE BREATHES DEEPLY, FILLING HIMSELF WITH THE NIGHT--

-- AND STEPS FORWARD AND FALLS--

-- AS HE FELL WHEN HE WAS A CHILD--

-- AS HE WILL FALL FOR THE REST OF HIS LIFE...

END

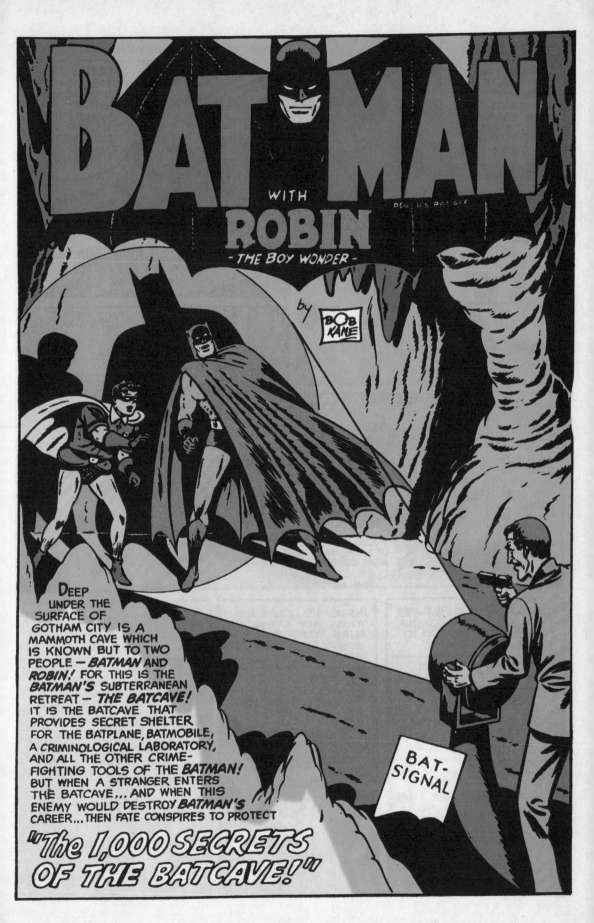

BATMAN

WITH

ROBIN
- THE BOY WONDER -

by BOB KANE

DEEP UNDER THE SURFACE OF GOTHAM CITY IS A MAMMOTH CAVE WHICH IS KNOWN BUT TO TWO PEOPLE — *BATMAN* AND *ROBIN!* FOR THIS IS THE *BATMAN'S* SUBTERRANEAN RETREAT — *THE BATCAVE!* IT IS THE BATCAVE THAT PROVIDES SECRET SHELTER FOR THE BATPLANE, BATMOBILE, A CRIMINOLOGICAL LABORATORY, AND ALL THE OTHER CRIME-FIGHTING TOOLS OF THE *BATMAN!* BUT WHEN A STRANGER ENTERS THE BATCAVE... AND WHEN THIS ENEMY WOULD DESTROY *BATMAN'S* CAREER... THEN FATE CONSPIRES TO PROTECT

BAT-SIGNAL

"The 1,000 SECRETS OF THE BATCAVE!"

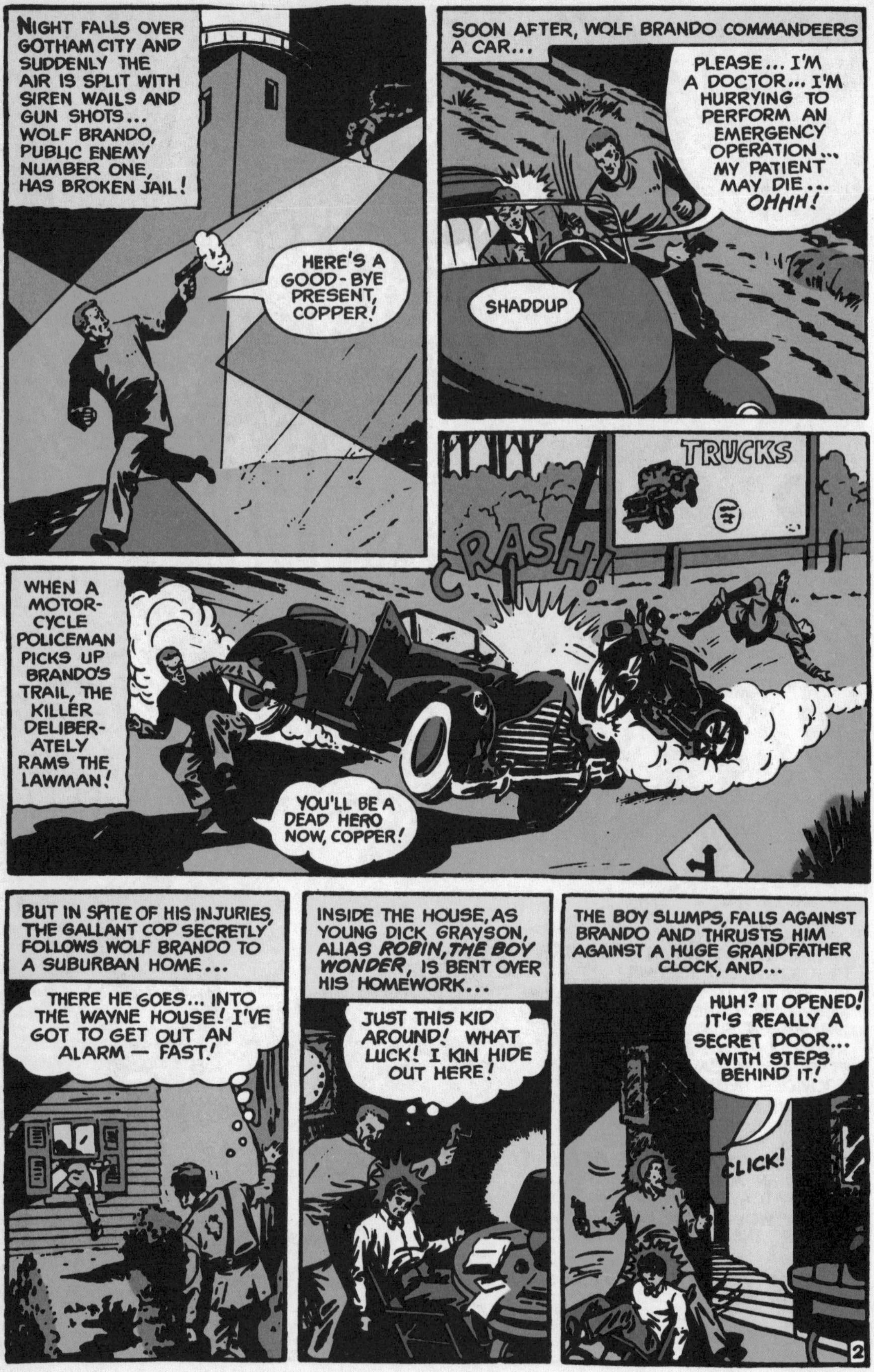
NIGHT FALLS OVER GOTHAM CITY AND SUDDENLY THE AIR IS SPLIT WITH SIREN WAILS AND GUN SHOTS... WOLF BRANDO, PUBLIC ENEMY NUMBER ONE, HAS BROKEN JAIL!
HERE'S A GOOD-BYE PRESENT, COPPER!
SOON AFTER, WOLF BRANDO COMMANDEERS A CAR...
PLEASE... I'M A DOCTOR... I'M HURRYING TO PERFORM AN EMERGENCY OPERATION... MY PATIENT MAY DIE... OHHH!
SHADDUP
TRUCKS
CRASH!
WHEN A MOTOR-CYCLE POLICEMAN PICKS UP BRANDO'S TRAIL, THE KILLER DELIBER-ATELY RAMS THE LAWMAN!
YOU'LL BE A DEAD HERO NOW, COPPER!
BUT IN SPITE OF HIS INJURIES, THE GALLANT COP SECRETLY FOLLOWS WOLF BRANDO TO A SUBURBAN HOME...
THERE HE GOES... INTO THE WAYNE HOUSE! I'VE GOT TO GET OUT AN ALARM — FAST!
INSIDE THE HOUSE, AS YOUNG DICK GRAYSON, ALIAS ROBIN, THE BOY WONDER, IS BENT OVER HIS HOMEWORK...
JUST THIS KID AROUND! WHAT LUCK! I KIN HIDE OUT HERE!
THE BOY SLUMPS, FALLS AGAINST BRANDO AND THRUSTS HIM AGAINST A HUGE GRANDFATHER CLOCK, AND...
HUH? IT OPENED! IT'S REALLY A SECRET DOOR... WITH STEPS BEHIND IT!
CLICK!
2

UPON EXPLORING THE STAIRS, WOLF BRANDO FINDS HIMSELF IN A NATURAL MAMMOTH CAVERN...

WHAT KIND O' PLACE IS THIS? THERE'S A SCIENCE LAB DOWN HERE! HEY—THERE'S A PICTURE... *BATMAN* AND *ROBIN!*

AND THERE'S THE *BATPLANE* AND THE *BATMOBILE!* OHH... I GET IT NOW! I FOUND WHAT EVERY TRIGGER MAN HAS BEEN LOOKIN' FOR! YEAH... I *FOUND BATMAN'S HIDEOUT!*

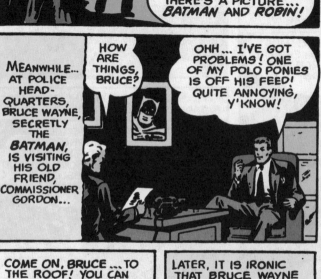

MEANWHILE... AT POLICE HEAD-QUARTERS, BRUCE WAYNE, SECRETLY THE *BATMAN,* IS VISITING HIS OLD FRIEND, COMMISSIONER GORDON...

HOW ARE THINGS, BRUCE?

OHH... I'VE GOT PROBLEMS! ONE OF MY POLO PONIES IS OFF HIS FEED! QUITE ANNOYING, Y'KNOW!

HMPHH! RICH MAN'S TROUBLES! EH... WHAT'S UP, REILLY?

ONE OF OUR BOYS SPOTTED WOLF BRANDO! HE WAS SEEN SNEAKING INTO MR. WAYNE'S HOUSE!

MY HOUSE?

COME ON, BRUCE... TO THE ROOF! YOU CAN HELP ME PAGE SOMEONE WHO CAN HELP US CAPTURE WOLF BRANDO — *THE BATMAN!*

BATMAN?!! BUT *I'M BATMAN!* WHAT A SPOT!

LATER, IT IS IRONIC THAT BRUCE WAYNE HIMSELF HAS TO FLASH THE EERIE SIGNAL THAT IS A SUMMONS FOR THE *BATMAN!*

ODD... HE SHOULD'VE BEEN HERE BY NOW!

I'VE GOT TO GET AWAY SO I CAN RE-APPEAR AS *BATMAN!* HMM... I'VE GOT AN IDEA!

3

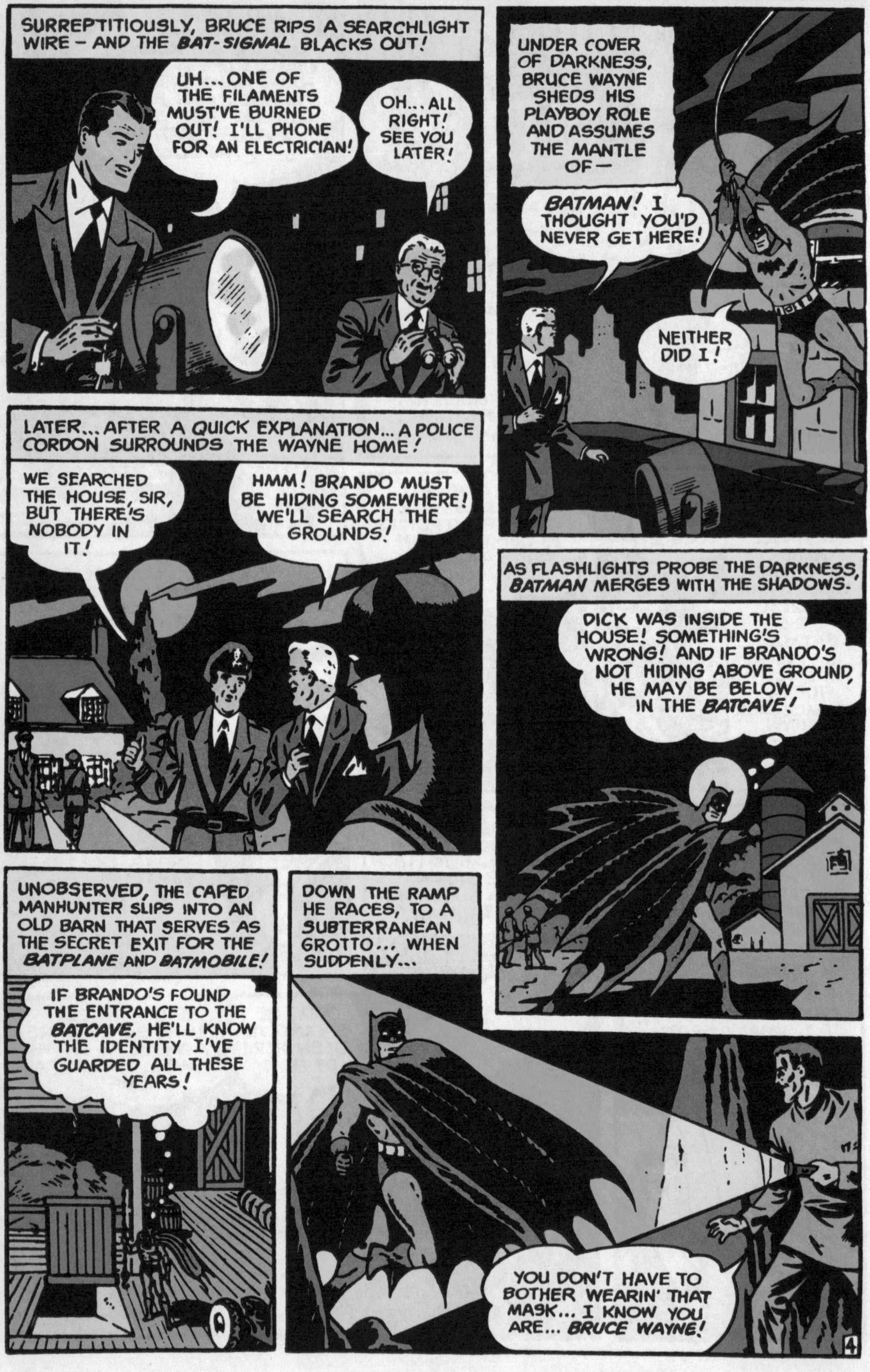
SURREPTITIOUSLY, BRUCE RIPS A SEARCHLIGHT WIRE – AND THE BAT-SIGNAL BLACKS OUT!
UH... ONE OF THE FILAMENTS MUST'VE BURNED OUT! I'LL PHONE FOR AN ELECTRICIAN!
OH... ALL RIGHT! SEE YOU LATER!
UNDER COVER OF DARKNESS, BRUCE WAYNE SHEDS HIS PLAYBOY ROLE AND ASSUMES THE MANTLE OF–
BATMAN! I THOUGHT YOU'D NEVER GET HERE!
NEITHER DID I!
LATER... AFTER A QUICK EXPLANATION... A POLICE CORDON SURROUNDS THE WAYNE HOME!
WE SEARCHED THE HOUSE, SIR, BUT THERE'S NOBODY IN IT!
HMM! BRANDO MUST BE HIDING SOMEWHERE! WE'LL SEARCH THE GROUNDS!
AS FLASHLIGHTS PROBE THE DARKNESS, BATMAN MERGES WITH THE SHADOWS.
DICK WAS INSIDE THE HOUSE! SOMETHING'S WRONG! AND IF BRANDO'S NOT HIDING ABOVE GROUND, HE MAY BE BELOW– IN THE BATCAVE!
UNOBSERVED, THE CAPED MANHUNTER SLIPS INTO AN OLD BARN THAT SERVES AS THE SECRET EXIT FOR THE BATPLANE AND BATMOBILE!
IF BRANDO'S FOUND THE ENTRANCE TO THE BATCAVE, HE'LL KNOW THE IDENTITY I'VE GUARDED ALL THESE YEARS!
DOWN THE RAMP HE RACES, TO A SUBTERRANEAN GROTTO... WHEN SUDDENLY...
YOU DON'T HAVE TO BOTHER WEARIN' THAT MASK... I KNOW YOU ARE... BRUCE WAYNE!
4

AND NOW *BATMAN* FACES THE CRIMINAL WHO HAS STUMBLED UPON ONE OF THE MOST CLOSELY GUARDED SECRETS IN THE WORLD!

WELL, WELL... WHO'D HAVE THOUGHT THE MUCH PHOTOGRAPHED PLAYBOY WAS REALLY *BATMAN* ALL THE TIME! YOU FOOLED EVERYBODY!

ALL RIGHT ...SO YOU KNOW! NOW WHAT?

I WANT YOUR *BATMAN* COSTUME! BY DISGUISING MYSELF AS YOU, I CAN PASS THE COPS! DO THAT FOR ME AND I'LL KEEP YOUR SECRET!

I NEVER MAKE DEALS WITH CRIMINALS! YOU'RE A KILLER, AND I'M BRINGING YOU IN EVEN IF YOU DO REVEAL MY IDENTITY!

CRIMINE FILES

BE SMART, *BATMAN*... OR DICK GRAYSON WILL NEVER WEAR HIS *ROBIN* COSTUME AGAIN!

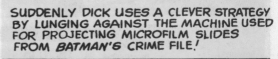

SUDDENLY DICK USES A CLEVER STRATEGY BY LUNGING AGAINST THE MACHINE USED FOR PROJECTING MICROFILM SLIDES FROM *BATMAN'S* CRIME FILE!

WHAT?

CLICK!

AND BRANDO'S EYES ARE DISTRACTED BY THE BIZARRE FACE OF *BATMAN'S* OLD ENEMY— TWO-FACE!

UHH... THAT FACE!

5

THIS IS *ONE* TIME I'M INDEBTED TO *TWO-FACE!*

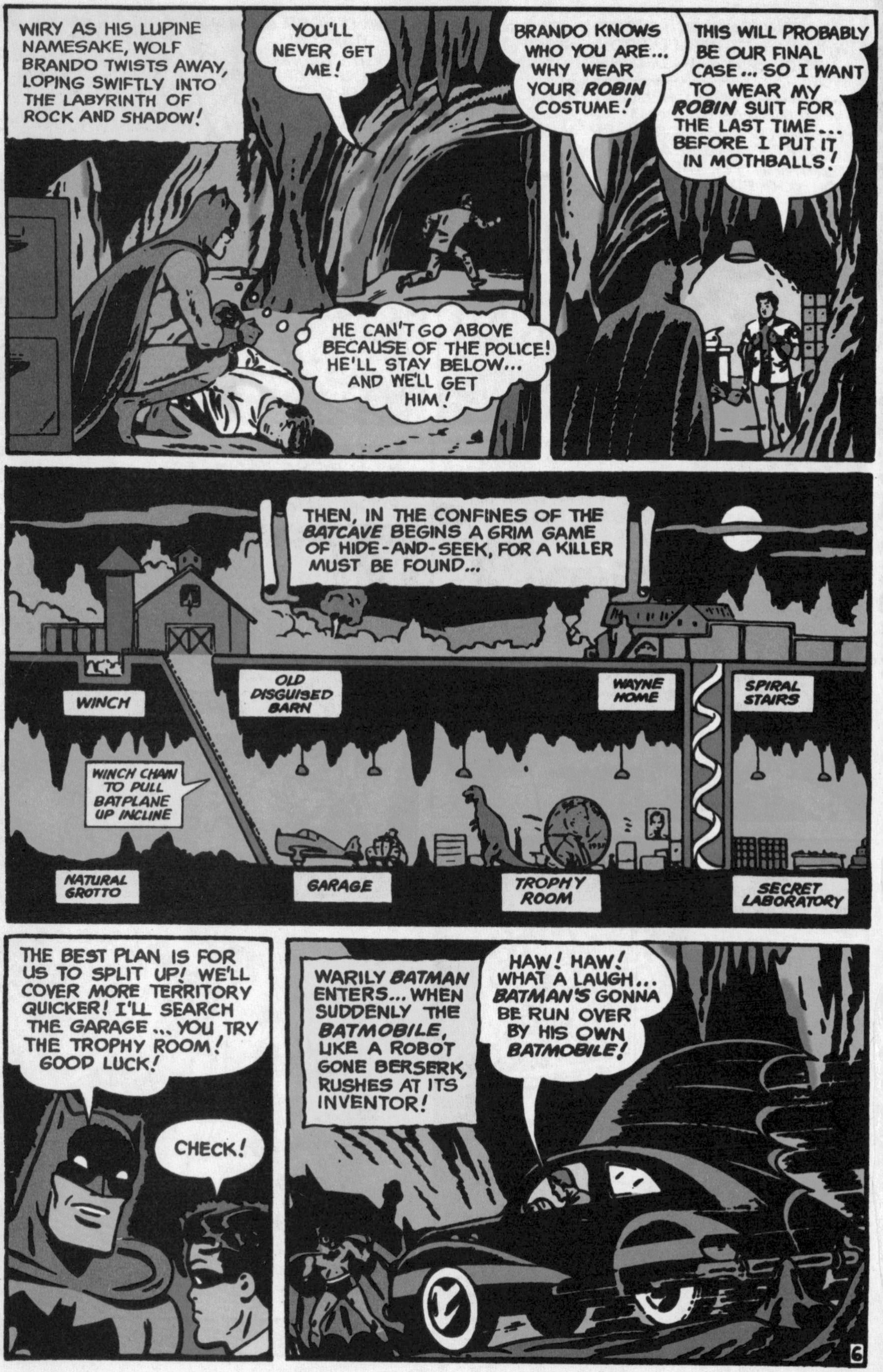
WIRY AS HIS LUPINE NAMESAKE, WOLF BRANDO TWISTS AWAY, LOPING SWIFTLY INTO THE LABYRINTH OF ROCK AND SHADOW!
YOU'LL NEVER GET ME!
HE CAN'T GO ABOVE BECAUSE OF THE POLICE! HE'LL STAY BELOW... AND WE'LL GET HIM!
BRANDO KNOWS WHO YOU ARE... WHY WEAR YOUR ROBIN COSTUME!
THIS WILL PROBABLY BE OUR FINAL CASE... SO I WANT TO WEAR MY ROBIN SUIT FOR THE LAST TIME... BEFORE I PUT IT IN MOTHBALLS!
THEN, IN THE CONFINES OF THE BATCAVE BEGINS A GRIM GAME OF HIDE-AND-SEEK, FOR A KILLER MUST BE FOUND...
WINCH
OLD DISGUISED BARN
WAYNE HOME
SPIRAL STAIRS
WINCH CHAIN TO PULL BATPLANE UP INCLINE
NATURAL GROTTO
GARAGE
TROPHY ROOM
SECRET LABORATORY
THE BEST PLAN IS FOR US TO SPLIT UP! WE'LL COVER MORE TERRITORY QUICKER! I'LL SEARCH THE GARAGE... YOU TRY THE TROPHY ROOM! GOOD LUCK!
CHECK!
WARILY BATMAN ENTERS... WHEN SUDDENLY THE BATMOBILE, LIKE A ROBOT GONE BERSERK, RUSHES AT ITS INVENTOR!
HAW! HAW! WHAT A LAUGH... BATMAN'S GONNA BE RUN OVER BY HIS OWN BATMOBILE!
6

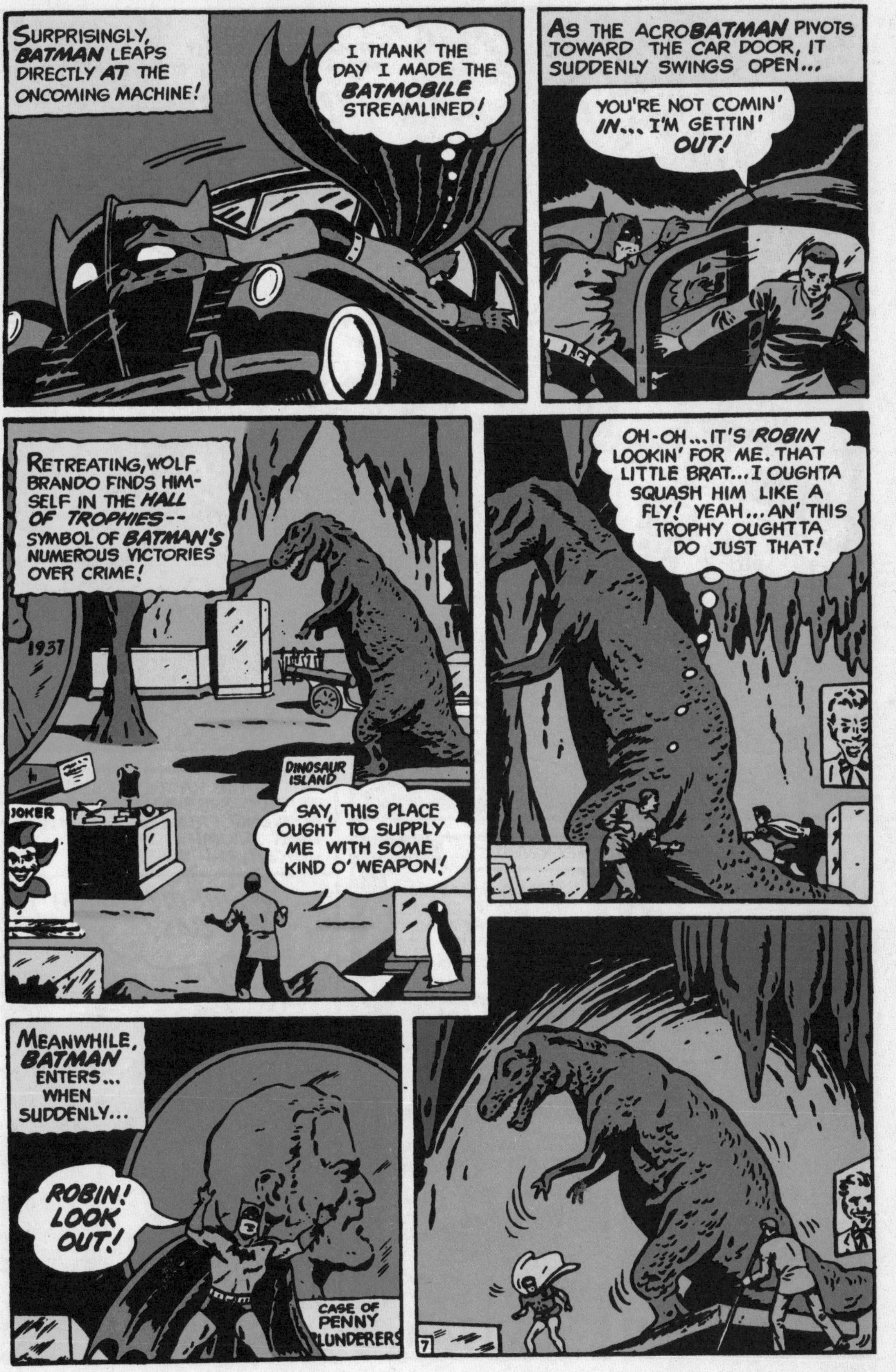
SURPRISINGLY, BATMAN LEAPS DIRECTLY AT THE ONCOMING MACHINE!
I THANK THE DAY I MADE THE BATMOBILE STREAMLINED!
AS THE ACROBATMAN PIVOTS TOWARD THE CAR DOOR, IT SUDDENLY SWINGS OPEN...
YOU'RE NOT COMIN' IN... I'M GETTIN' OUT!
RETREATING, WOLF BRANDO FINDS HIMSELF IN THE HALL OF TROPHIES-- SYMBOL OF BATMAN'S NUMEROUS VICTORIES OVER CRIME!
1937
DINOSAUR ISLAND
JOKER
SAY, THIS PLACE OUGHT TO SUPPLY ME WITH SOME KIND O' WEAPON!
OH-OH... IT'S ROBIN LOOKIN' FOR ME. THAT LITTLE BRAT... I OUGHTA SQUASH HIM LIKE A FLY! YEAH... AN' THIS TROPHY OUGHTTA DO JUST THAT!
MEANWHILE, BATMAN ENTERS... WHEN SUDDENLY...
ROBIN! LOOK OUT!
CASE OF PENNY PLUNDERERS
7

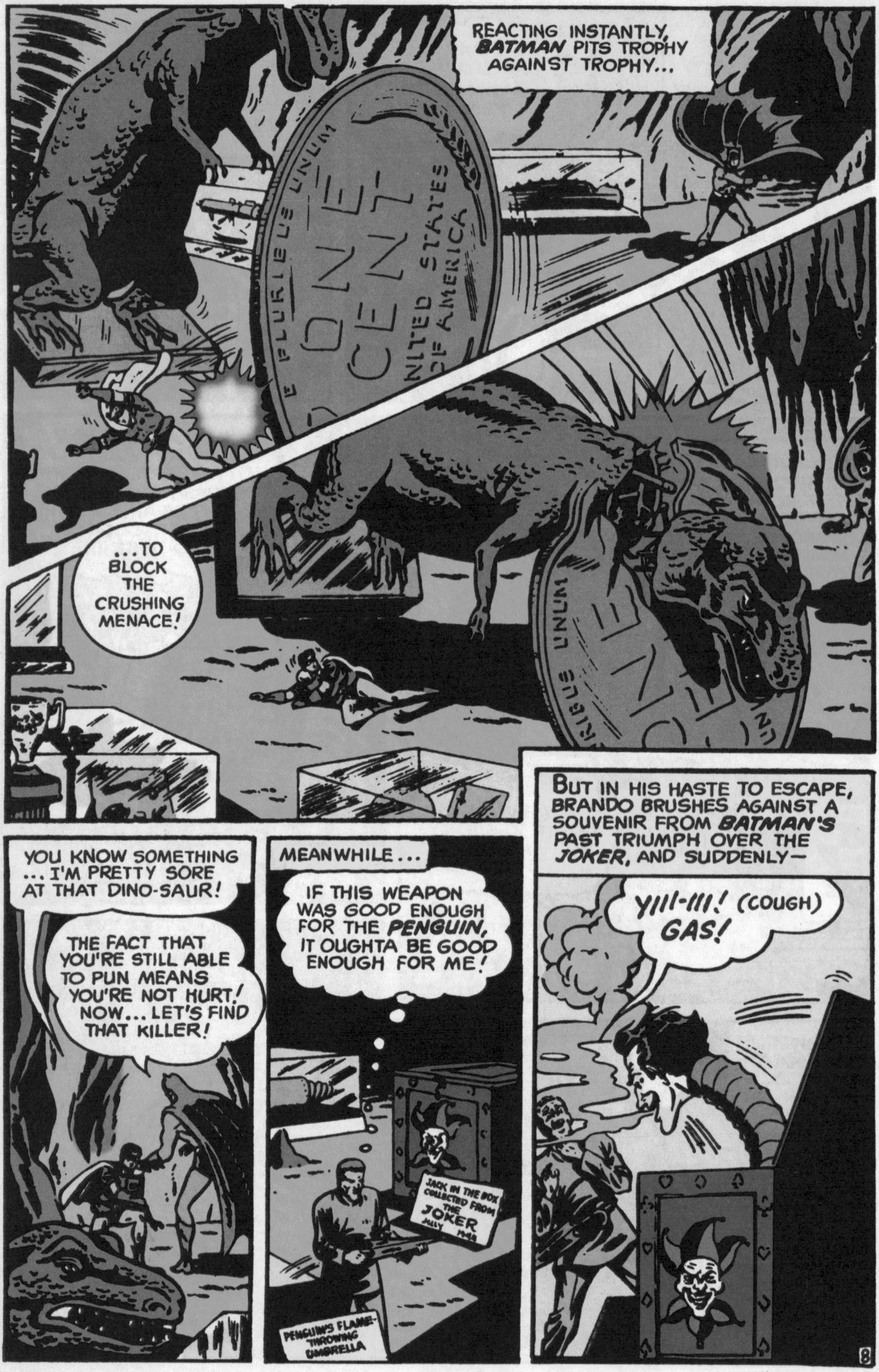

REACTING INSTANTLY, BATMAN PITS TROPHY AGAINST TROPHY...
E PLURIBUS UNUM
ONE CENT
UNITED STATES OF AMERICA
...TO BLOCK THE CRUSHING MENACE!
BUT IN HIS HASTE TO ESCAPE, BRANDO BRUSHES AGAINST A SOUVENIR FROM BATMAN'S PAST TRIUMPH OVER THE JOKER, AND SUDDENLY—
YOU KNOW SOMETHING ... I'M PRETTY SORE AT THAT DINO-SAUR!
THE FACT THAT YOU'RE STILL ABLE TO PUN MEANS YOU'RE NOT HURT! NOW... LET'S FIND THAT KILLER!
MEANWHILE...
IF THIS WEAPON WAS GOOD ENOUGH FOR THE PENGUIN, IT OUGHTA BE GOOD ENOUGH FOR ME!
JACK IN THE BOX COLLECTED FROM THE JOKER JULY 1948
PENGUIN'S FLAME-THROWING UMBRELLA
YIII-III! (COUGH) GAS!
8

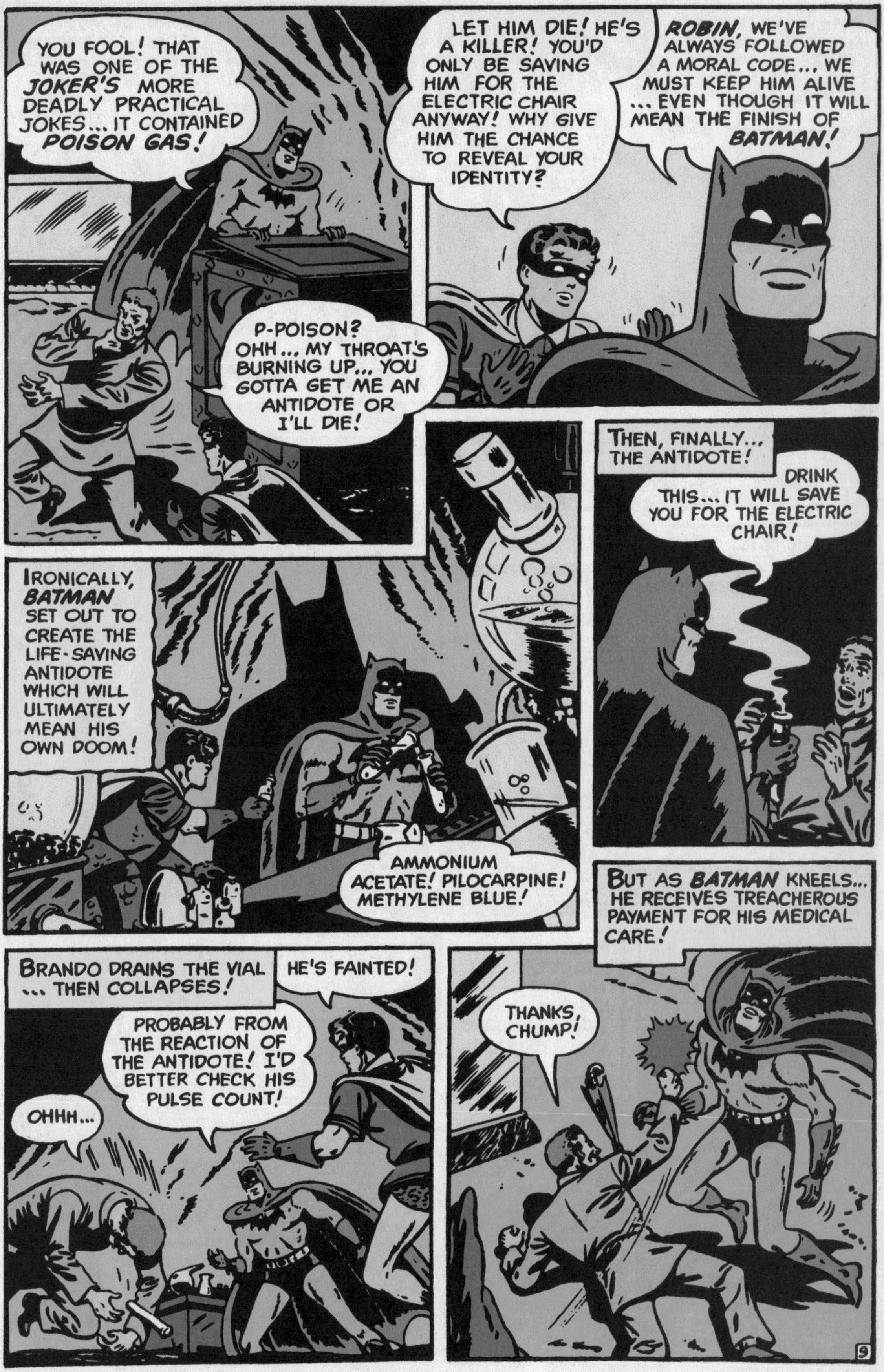
YOU FOOL! THAT WAS ONE OF THE JOKER'S MORE DEADLY PRACTICAL JOKES... IT CONTAINED POISON GAS!
P-POISON? OHH..., MY THROAT'S BURNING UP... YOU GOTTA GET ME AN ANTIDOTE OR I'LL DIE!
LET HIM DIE! HE'S A KILLER! YOU'D ONLY BE SAVING HIM FOR THE ELECTRIC CHAIR ANYWAY! WHY GIVE HIM THE CHANCE TO REVEAL YOUR IDENTITY?
ROBIN, WE'VE ALWAYS FOLLOWED A MORAL CODE..., WE MUST KEEP HIM ALIVE ... EVEN THOUGH IT WILL MEAN THE FINISH OF BATMAN!
IRONICALLY, BATMAN SET OUT TO CREATE THE LIFE-SAVING ANTIDOTE WHICH WILL ULTIMATELY MEAN HIS OWN DOOM!
AMMONIUM ACETATE! PILOCARPINE! METHYLENE BLUE!
THEN, FINALLY... THE ANTIDOTE!
DRINK THIS... IT WILL SAVE YOU FOR THE ELECTRIC CHAIR!
BRANDO DRAINS THE VIAL ... THEN COLLAPSES!
HE'S FAINTED!
PROBABLY FROM THE REACTION OF THE ANTIDOTE! I'D BETTER CHECK HIS PULSE COUNT!
OHHH...
BUT AS BATMAN KNEELS... HE RECEIVES TREACHEROUS PAYMENT FOR HIS MEDICAL CARE!
THANKS, CHUMP!
9

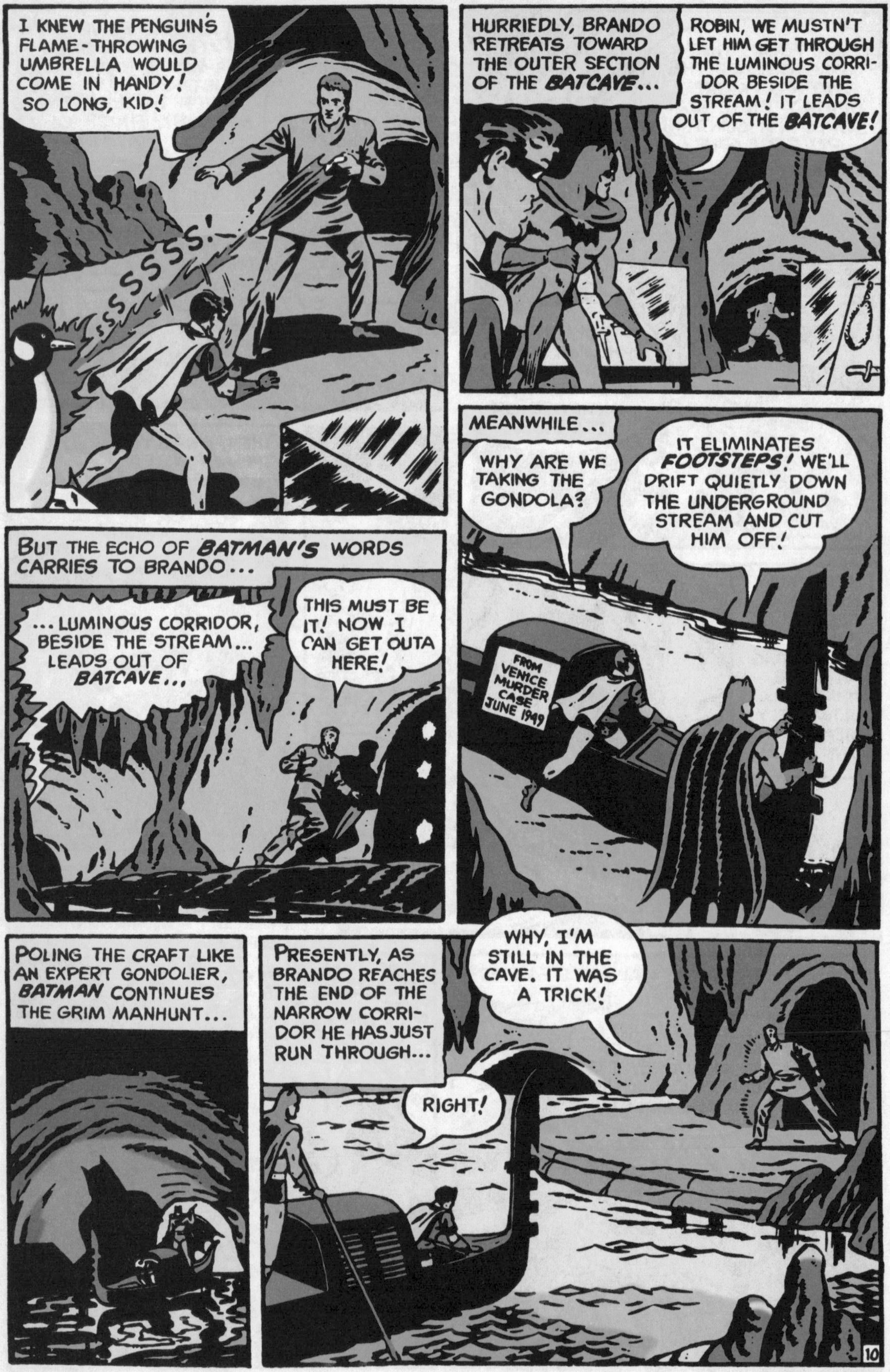
I KNEW THE PENGUIN'S FLAME-THROWING UMBRELLA WOULD COME IN HANDY! SO LONG, KID!
SSSSSS!
HURRIEDLY, BRANDO RETREATS TOWARD THE OUTER SECTION OF THE BATCAVE...
ROBIN, WE MUSTN'T LET HIM GET THROUGH THE LUMINOUS CORRIDOR BESIDE THE STREAM! IT LEADS OUT OF THE BATCAVE!
BUT THE ECHO OF BATMAN'S WORDS CARRIES TO BRANDO...
...LUMINOUS CORRIDOR, BESIDE THE STREAM... LEADS OUT OF BATCAVE...
THIS MUST BE IT! NOW I CAN GET OUTA HERE!
MEANWHILE...
WHY ARE WE TAKING THE GONDOLA?
IT ELIMINATES FOOTSTEPS! WE'LL DRIFT QUIETLY DOWN THE UNDERGROUND STREAM AND CUT HIM OFF!
FROM VENICE MURDER CASE JUNE 1949
POLING THE CRAFT LIKE AN EXPERT GONDOLIER, BATMAN CONTINUES THE GRIM MANHUNT...
PRESENTLY, AS BRANDO REACHES THE END OF THE NARROW CORRIDOR HE HAS JUST RUN THROUGH...
WHY, I'M STILL IN THE CAVE. IT WAS A TRICK!
RIGHT!
10

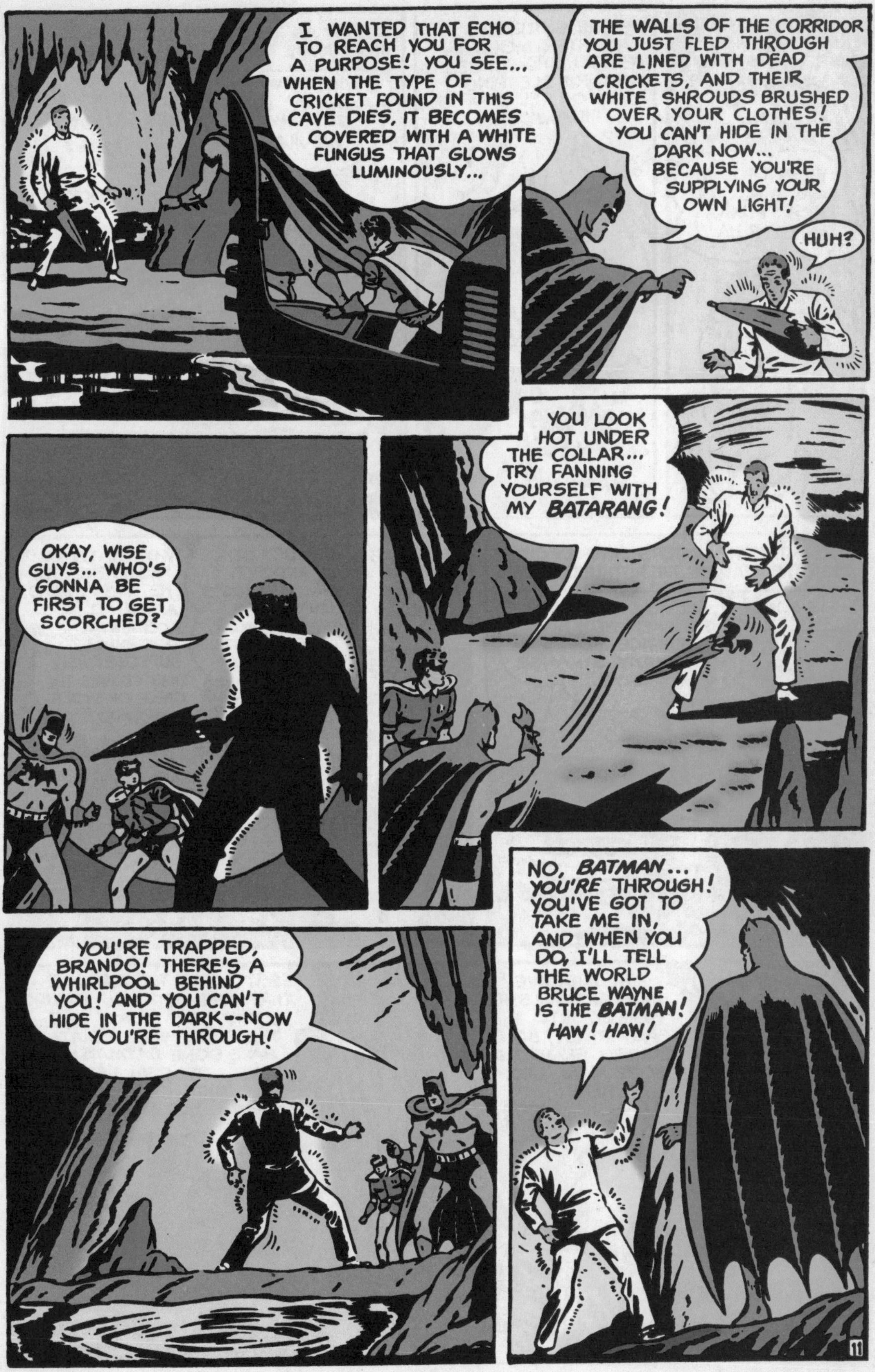
I WANTED THAT ECHO TO REACH YOU FOR A PURPOSE! YOU SEE... WHEN THE TYPE OF CRICKET FOUND IN THIS CAVE DIES, IT BECOMES COVERED WITH A WHITE FUNGUS THAT GLOWS LUMINOUSLY...
THE WALLS OF THE CORRIDOR YOU JUST FLED THROUGH ARE LINED WITH DEAD CRICKETS, AND THEIR WHITE SHROUDS BRUSHED OVER YOUR CLOTHES! YOU CAN'T HIDE IN THE DARK NOW... BECAUSE YOU'RE SUPPLYING YOUR OWN LIGHT!
HUH?
OKAY, WISE GUYS... WHO'S GONNA BE FIRST TO GET SCORCHED?
YOU LOOK HOT UNDER THE COLLAR... TRY FANNING YOURSELF WITH MY BATARANG!
YOU'RE TRAPPED, BRANDO! THERE'S A WHIRLPOOL BEHIND YOU! AND YOU CAN'T HIDE IN THE DARK--NOW YOU'RE THROUGH!
NO, BATMAN... YOU'RE THROUGH! YOU'VE GOT TO TAKE ME IN, AND WHEN YOU DO, I'LL TELL THE WORLD BRUCE WAYNE IS THE BATMAN! HAW! HAW!
11

HAW! HAW! HAW!

EVEN THOUGH YOU WIN... YOU LOSE! FUNNY, ISN'T IT? HAW!

AS THE SHRIEKING LAUGHTER MOUNTS, ITS PIERCING ECHOES DISTURB SLEEPING BATS ON THE ROOF OF THE *BATCAVE*...

HAW! HAW! HAW! HAW! HAW! HAW!

... AND AS THEY FLAP THEIR WINGS TO INVESTIGATE THE SOURCE OF THE NOISE...

I WIN! HAW! HAW! H... AGHHH! BATS! GET AWAY! YA-AAA!

LOOK OUT! THE WHIRLPOOL!

TOO LATE! THE WATERS SWIFTLY CLOSE OVER THE HEAD OF THE RUTHLESS KILLER!

HE'S GONE!

AND MY SECRET HAS PERISHED WITH HIM! JUSTICE MOVES IN MANY STRANGE WAYS...

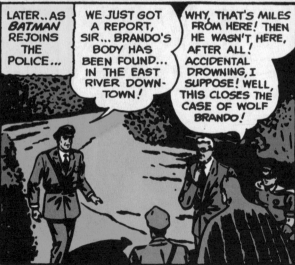

LATER... AS *BATMAN* REJOINS THE POLICE...

WE JUST GOT A REPORT, SIR... BRANDO'S BODY HAS BEEN FOUND... IN THE EAST RIVER DOWNTOWN!

WHY, THAT'S MILES FROM HERE! THEN HE WASN'T HERE, AFTER ALL! ACCIDENTAL DROWNING, I SUPPOSE! WELL, THIS CLOSES THE CASE OF WOLF BRANDO!

AFTERWARD...

THE *BATCAVE* UNDERGROUND STREAM EMPTIES INTO THE EAST RIVER, SO IT CARRIED BRANDO'S BODY AWAY FROM HERE!

YES... IT WAS THE *BATCAVE* THAT DEFEATED WOLF BRANDO ... AND THEN IT CAST OUT THE ENEMY WHO WOULD HAVE DONE *BATMAN* HARM! YES... THE REAL HERO OF THIS CASE WAS *THE BATCAVE*!

The END

BATCAVE IN THE 80s

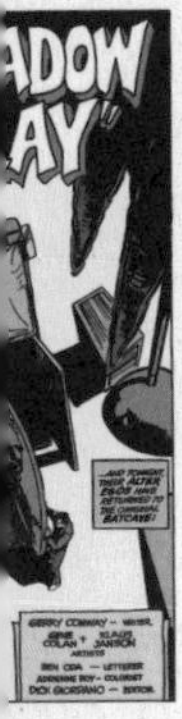

From: WHO'S WHO #2 *(1985)*
Writers: **VARIOUS** *Penciller:* **HOWARD BENDER** *Inker:* **GARY MARTIN**

Located beneath the sprawling grounds of Wayne Manor, the Batcave is the ultra-secret sanctum sanctorum of the Dark Knight Detective called the Batman.

The Cavern was discovered by Bruce Wayne quite by accident, when he fell through the rotted flooring of the old manor barn he had intended to use as his headquarters. Taking the tremendous bat-filled cave as an omen, Wayne determined to make the cave his own.

To this end, Wayne sealed off the limestone cavern's tributary tunnels, then proceeded to equip the main cave with the foremost in scientific apparatus.

Today the Batcave contains the world's most sophisticated computerized crime-lab, an exhaustive computerized file on all known criminals and their methods of operation, a complex workshop where the Batman continues to improve and update the contents of his utility belt, an automotive repair shop, and appropriate housing for his Batmobile, Batplane and Batboat.

Perhaps the Batcave's most famous attraction is the Hall of Trophies, containing mementos from the Batman's greatest cases, foremost among these being the giant penny, the robot dinosaur, and the monstrous Joker playing card that hangs from the ceiling.

Access to the Batcave can be gained only through the camouflaged doors which allow entry and exit for the Batplane, Batboat and Batmobile, or through the secret door behind the stately grandfather clock, which stands in Bruce Wayne's study and leads to a winding staircase down to the cave itself. At various times Wayne has also used an elevator to reach the Batcave, but has apparently abandoned it in recent years due to mechanical difficulties.

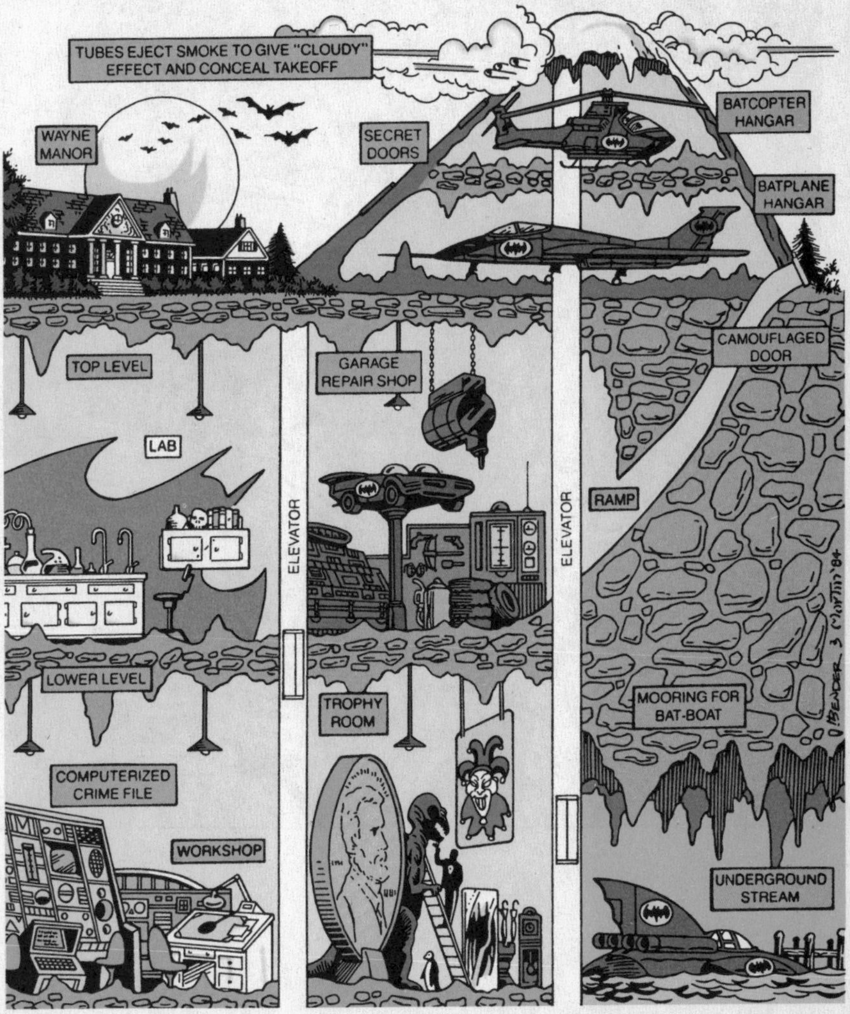

TUBES EJECT SMOKE TO GIVE "CLOUDY" EFFECT AND CONCEAL TAKEOFF
WAYNE MANOR
SECRET DOORS
BATCOPTER HANGAR
BATPLANE HANGAR
CAMOUFLAGED DOOR
TOP LEVEL
GARAGE REPAIR SHOP
LAB
ELEVATOR
ELEVATOR
RAMP
LOWER LEVEL
TROPHY ROOM
MOORING FOR BAT-BOAT
COMPUTERIZED CRIME FILE
WORKSHOP
UNDERGROUND STREAM

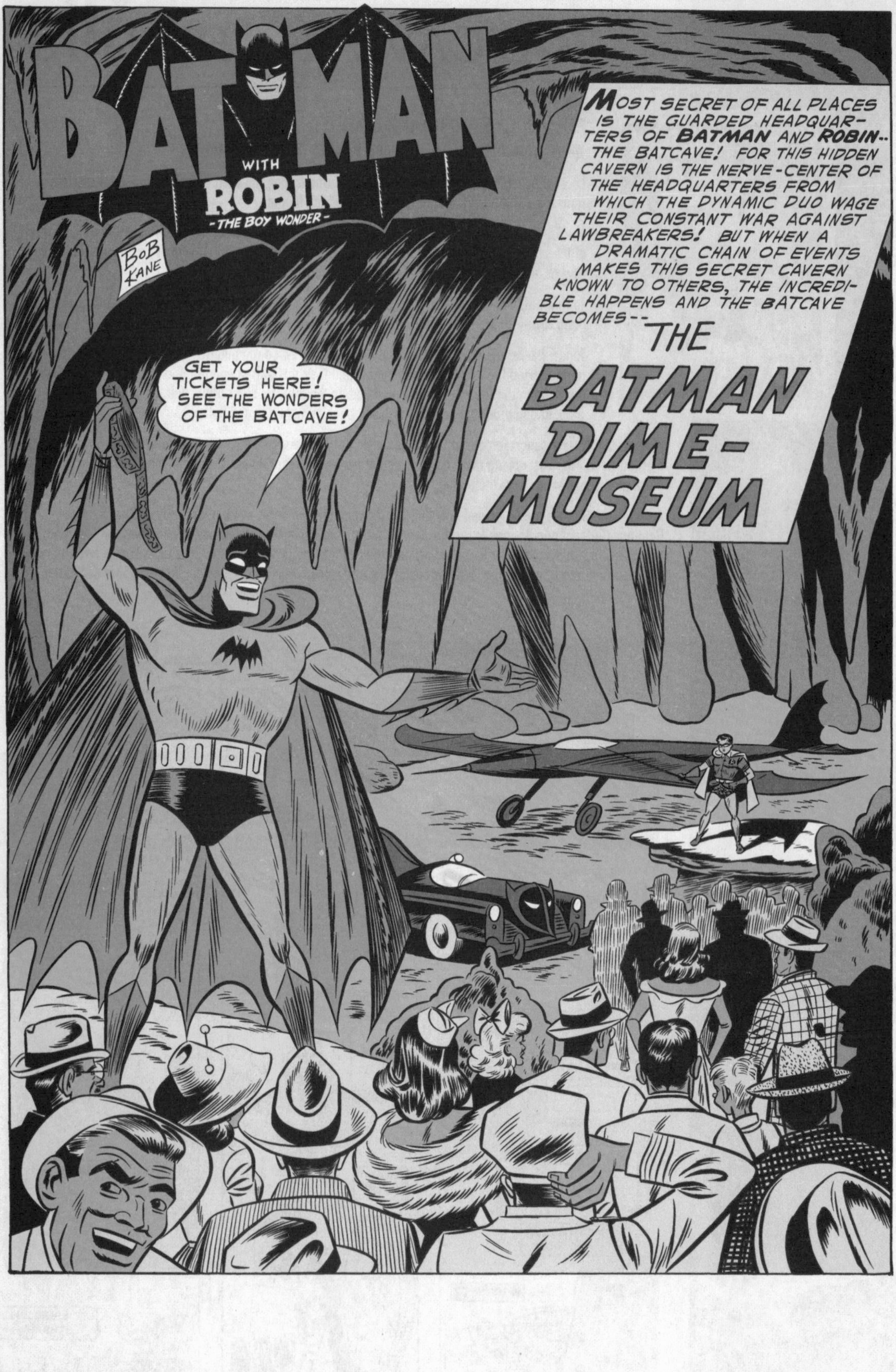
BATMAN
WITH
ROBIN
-THE BOY WONDER-
BOB KANE
MOST SECRET OF ALL PLACES IS THE GUARDED HEADQUARTERS OF BATMAN AND ROBIN.. THE BATCAVE! FOR THIS HIDDEN CAVERN IS THE NERVE-CENTER OF THE HEADQUARTERS FROM WHICH THE DYNAMIC DUO WAGE THEIR CONSTANT WAR AGAINST LAWBREAKERS! BUT WHEN A DRAMATIC CHAIN OF EVENTS MAKES THIS SECRET CAVERN KNOWN TO OTHERS, THE INCREDIBLE HAPPENS AND THE BATCAVE BECOMES--
THE BATMAN DIME-MUSEUM
GET YOUR TICKETS HERE! SEE THE WONDERS OF THE BATCAVE!

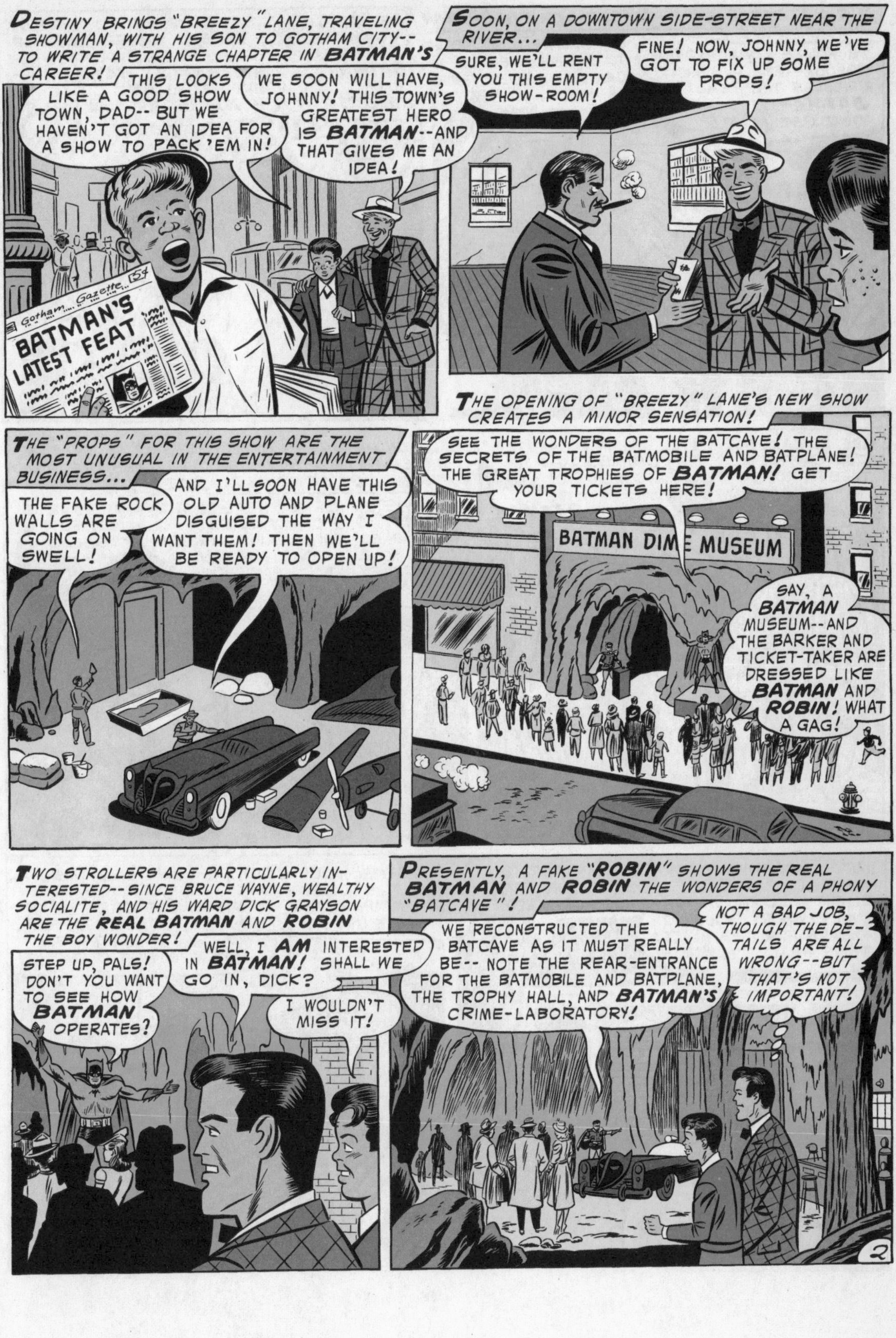

DESTINY BRINGS "BREEZY" LANE, TRAVELING SHOWMAN, WITH HIS SON TO GOTHAM CITY-- TO WRITE A STRANGE CHAPTER IN BATMAN'S CAREER!
THIS LOOKS LIKE A GOOD SHOW TOWN, DAD-- BUT WE HAVEN'T GOT AN IDEA FOR A SHOW TO PACK 'EM IN!
WE SOON WILL HAVE, JOHNNY! THIS TOWN'S GREATEST HERO IS BATMAN--AND THAT GIVES ME AN IDEA!
Gotham Gazette 15¢
BATMAN'S LATEST FEAT
SOON, ON A DOWNTOWN SIDE-STREET NEAR THE RIVER...
SURE, WE'LL RENT YOU THIS EMPTY SHOW-ROOM!
FINE! NOW, JOHNNY, WE'VE GOT TO FIX UP SOME PROPS!
THE "PROPS" FOR THIS SHOW ARE THE MOST UNUSUAL IN THE ENTERTAINMENT BUSINESS...
THE FAKE ROCK WALLS ARE GOING ON SWELL!
AND I'LL SOON HAVE THIS OLD AUTO AND PLANE DISGUISED THE WAY I WANT THEM! THEN WE'LL BE READY TO OPEN UP!
THE OPENING OF "BREEZY" LANE'S NEW SHOW CREATES A MINOR SENSATION!
SEE THE WONDERS OF THE BATCAVE! THE SECRETS OF THE BATMOBILE AND BATPLANE! THE GREAT TROPHIES OF BATMAN! GET YOUR TICKETS HERE!
BATMAN DIME MUSEUM
SAY, A BATMAN MUSEUM--AND THE BARKER AND TICKET-TAKER ARE DRESSED LIKE BATMAN AND ROBIN! WHAT A GAG!
TWO STROLLERS ARE PARTICULARLY INTERESTED--SINCE BRUCE WAYNE, WEALTHY SOCIALITE, AND HIS WARD DICK GRAYSON ARE THE REAL BATMAN AND ROBIN THE BOY WONDER!
STEP UP, PALS! DON'T YOU WANT TO SEE HOW BATMAN OPERATES?
WELL, I AM INTERESTED IN BATMAN! SHALL WE GO IN, DICK?
I WOULDN'T MISS IT!
PRESENTLY, A FAKE "ROBIN" SHOWS THE REAL BATMAN AND ROBIN THE WONDERS OF A PHONY "BATCAVE"!
WE RECONSTRUCTED THE BATCAVE AS IT MUST REALLY BE-- NOTE THE REAR-ENTRANCE FOR THE BATMOBILE AND BATPLANE, THE TROPHY HALL, AND BATMAN'S CRIME-LABORATORY!
NOT A BAD JOB, THOUGH THE DETAILS ARE ALL WRONG--BUT THAT'S NOT IMPORTANT!
2

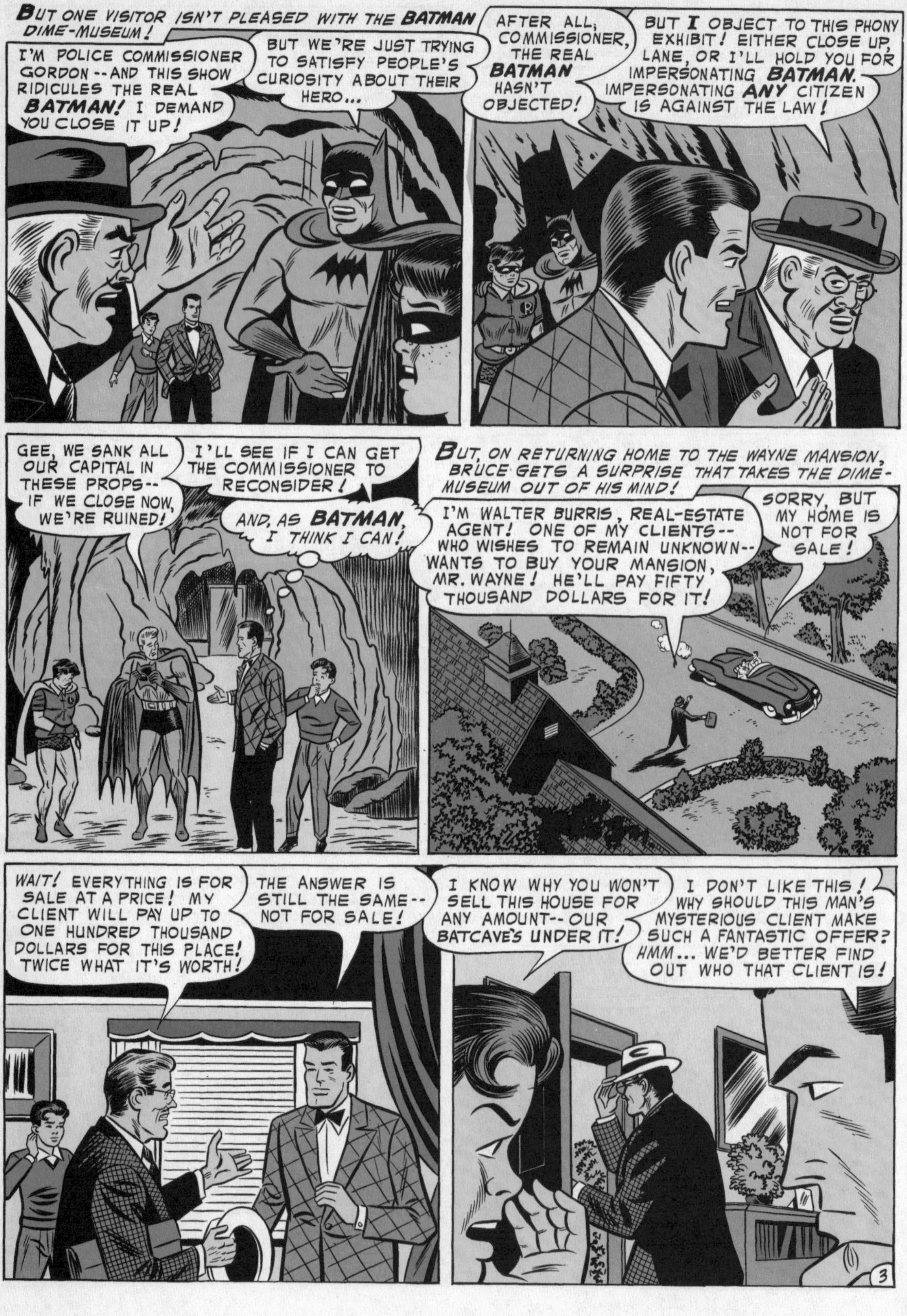
BUT ONE VISITOR ISN'T PLEASED WITH THE BATMAN DIME-MUSEUM!
I'M POLICE COMMISSIONER GORDON -- AND THIS SHOW RIDICULES THE REAL BATMAN! I DEMAND YOU CLOSE IT UP!
BUT WE'RE JUST TRYING TO SATISFY PEOPLE'S CURIOSITY ABOUT THEIR HERO...
AFTER ALL, COMMISSIONER, THE REAL BATMAN HASN'T OBJECTED!
BUT I OBJECT TO THIS PHONY EXHIBIT! EITHER CLOSE UP, LANE, OR I'LL HOLD YOU FOR IMPERSONATING BATMAN. IMPERSONATING ANY CITIZEN IS AGAINST THE LAW!
GEE, WE SANK ALL OUR CAPITAL IN THESE PROPS-- IF WE CLOSE NOW, WE'RE RUINED!
I'LL SEE IF I CAN GET THE COMMISSIONER TO RECONSIDER!
AND, AS BATMAN, I THINK I CAN!
BUT, ON RETURNING HOME TO THE WAYNE MANSION, BRUCE GETS A SURPRISE THAT TAKES THE DIME-MUSEUM OUT OF HIS MIND!
I'M WALTER BURRIS, REAL-ESTATE AGENT! ONE OF MY CLIENTS-- WHO WISHES TO REMAIN UNKNOWN-- WANTS TO BUY YOUR MANSION, MR. WAYNE! HE'LL PAY FIFTY THOUSAND DOLLARS FOR IT!
SORRY, BUT MY HOME IS NOT FOR SALE!
WAIT! EVERYTHING IS FOR SALE AT A PRICE! MY CLIENT WILL PAY UP TO ONE HUNDRED THOUSAND DOLLARS FOR THIS PLACE! TWICE WHAT IT'S WORTH!
THE ANSWER IS STILL THE SAME-- NOT FOR SALE!
I KNOW WHY YOU WON'T SELL THIS HOUSE FOR ANY AMOUNT-- OUR BATCAVE'S UNDER IT!
I DON'T LIKE THIS! WHY SHOULD THIS MAN'S MYSTERIOUS CLIENT MAKE SUCH A FANTASTIC OFFER? HMM... WE'D BETTER FIND OUT WHO THAT CLIENT IS!
3

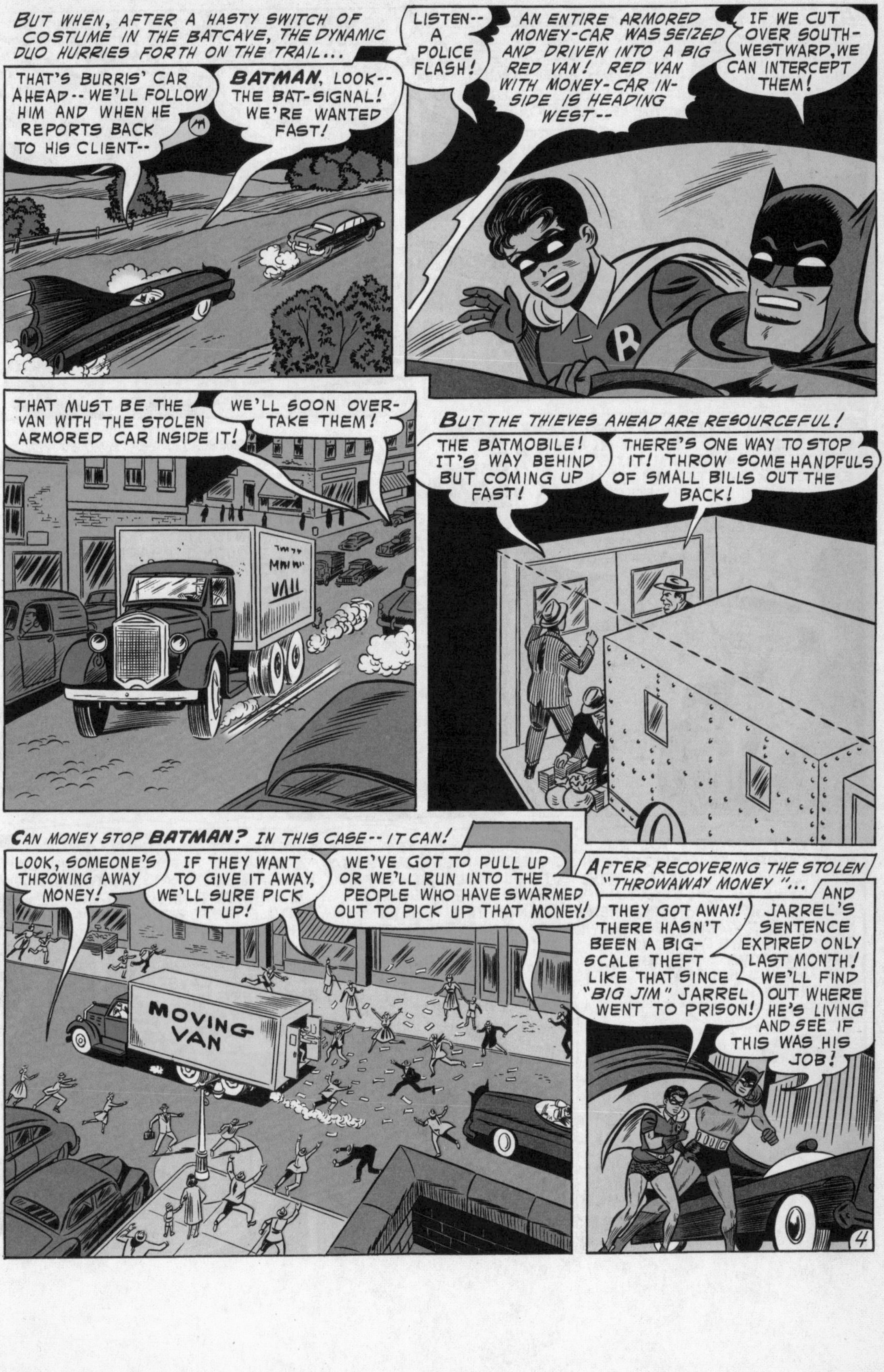
BUT WHEN, AFTER A HASTY SWITCH OF COSTUME IN THE BATCAVE, THE DYNAMIC DUO HURRIES FORTH ON THE TRAIL...
THAT'S BURRIS' CAR AHEAD-- WE'LL FOLLOW HIM AND WHEN HE REPORTS BACK TO HIS CLIENT--
BATMAN, LOOK-- THE BAT-SIGNAL! WE'RE WANTED FAST!
LISTEN-- A POLICE FLASH!
AN ENTIRE ARMORED MONEY-CAR WAS SEIZED AND DRIVEN INTO A BIG RED VAN! RED VAN WITH MONEY-CAR INSIDE IS HEADING WEST--
IF WE CUT OVER SOUTH-WESTWARD, WE CAN INTERCEPT THEM!
THAT MUST BE THE VAN WITH THE STOLEN ARMORED CAR INSIDE IT!
WE'LL SOON OVER-TAKE THEM!
BUT THE THIEVES AHEAD ARE RESOURCEFUL!
THE BATMOBILE! IT'S WAY BEHIND BUT COMING UP FAST!
THERE'S ONE WAY TO STOP IT! THROW SOME HANDFULS OF SMALL BILLS OUT THE BACK!
CAN MONEY STOP BATMAN? IN THIS CASE-- IT CAN!
LOOK, SOMEONE'S THROWING AWAY MONEY!
IF THEY WANT TO GIVE IT AWAY, WE'LL SURE PICK IT UP!
WE'VE GOT TO PULL UP OR WE'LL RUN INTO THE PEOPLE WHO HAVE SWARMED OUT TO PICK UP THAT MONEY!
MOVING VAN
AFTER RECOVERING THE STOLEN "THROWAWAY MONEY"...
THEY GOT AWAY! THERE HASN'T BEEN A BIG-SCALE THEFT LIKE THAT SINCE "BIG JIM" JARREL WENT TO PRISON!
AND JARREL'S SENTENCE EXPIRED ONLY LAST MONTH! WE'LL FIND OUT WHERE HE'S LIVING AND SEE IF THIS WAS HIS JOB!
4

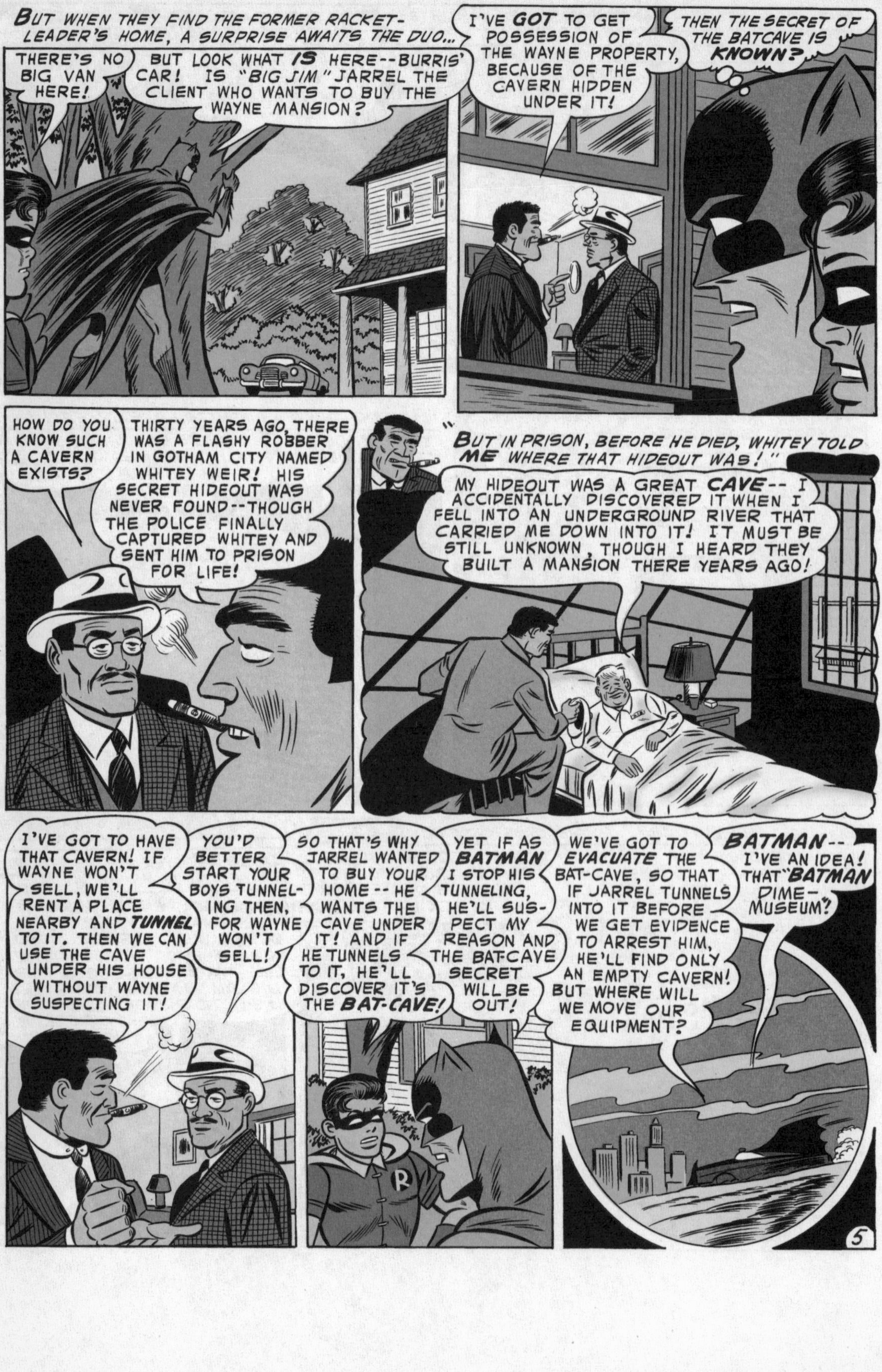
BUT WHEN THEY FIND THE FORMER RACKET-LEADER'S HOME, A SURPRISE AWAITS THE DUO...
THERE'S NO BIG VAN HERE!
BUT LOOK WHAT IS HERE--BURRIS' CAR! IS "BIG JIM" JARREL THE CLIENT WHO WANTS TO BUY THE WAYNE MANSION?
I'VE GOT TO GET POSSESSION OF THE WAYNE PROPERTY, BECAUSE OF THE CAVERN HIDDEN UNDER IT!
THEN THE SECRET OF THE BATCAVE IS KNOWN?
HOW DO YOU KNOW SUCH A CAVERN EXISTS?
THIRTY YEARS AGO, THERE WAS A FLASHY ROBBER IN GOTHAM CITY NAMED WHITEY WEIR! HIS SECRET HIDEOUT WAS NEVER FOUND--THOUGH THE POLICE FINALLY CAPTURED WHITEY AND SENT HIM TO PRISON FOR LIFE!
"BUT IN PRISON, BEFORE HE DIED, WHITEY TOLD ME WHERE THAT HIDEOUT WAS!"
MY HIDEOUT WAS A GREAT CAVE-- I ACCIDENTALLY DISCOVERED IT WHEN I FELL INTO AN UNDERGROUND RIVER THAT CARRIED ME DOWN INTO IT! IT MUST BE STILL UNKNOWN, THOUGH I HEARD THEY BUILT A MANSION THERE YEARS AGO!
I'VE GOT TO HAVE THAT CAVERN! IF WAYNE WON'T SELL, WE'LL RENT A PLACE NEARBY AND TUNNEL TO IT. THEN WE CAN USE THE CAVE UNDER HIS HOUSE WITHOUT WAYNE SUSPECTING IT!
YOU'D BETTER START YOUR BOYS TUNNELING THEN, FOR WAYNE WON'T SELL!
SO THAT'S WHY JARREL WANTED TO BUY YOUR HOME -- HE WANTS THE CAVE UNDER IT! AND IF HE TUNNELS TO IT, HE'LL DISCOVER IT'S THE BAT-CAVE!
YET IF AS BATMAN I STOP HIS TUNNELING, HE'LL SUSPECT MY REASON AND THE BAT-CAVE SECRET WILL BE OUT!
WE'VE GOT TO EVACUATE THE BAT-CAVE, SO THAT IF JARREL TUNNELS INTO IT BEFORE WE GET EVIDENCE TO ARREST HIM, HE'LL FIND ONLY AN EMPTY CAVERN! BUT WHERE WILL WE MOVE OUR EQUIPMENT?
BATMAN-- I'VE AN IDEA! THAT "BATMAN DIME-MUSEUM"?
5

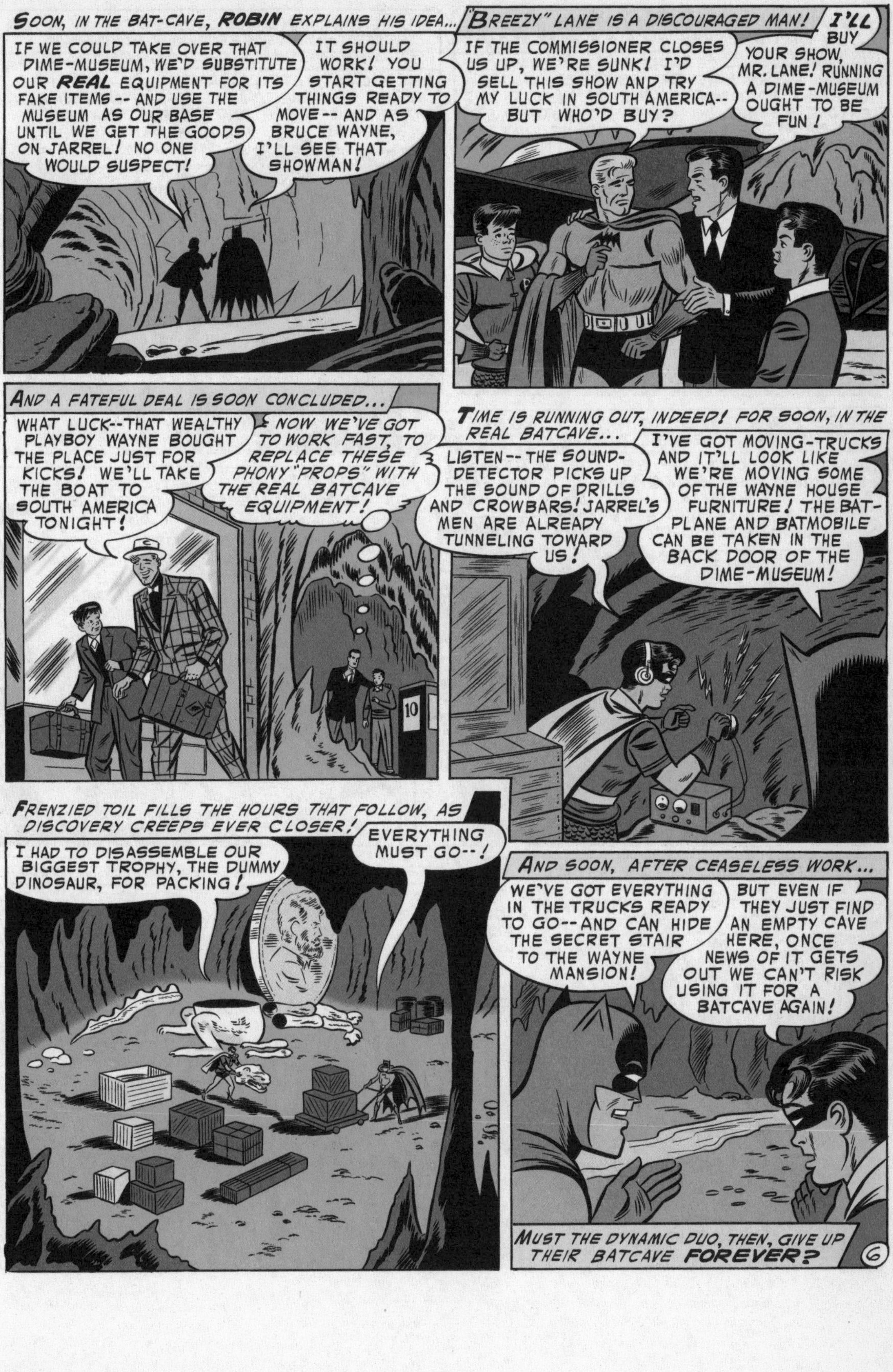
SOON, IN THE BAT-CAVE, ROBIN EXPLAINS HIS IDEA...
IF WE COULD TAKE OVER THAT DIME-MUSEUM, WE'D SUBSTITUTE OUR REAL EQUIPMENT FOR ITS FAKE ITEMS -- AND USE THE MUSEUM AS OUR BASE UNTIL WE GET THE GOODS ON JARREL! NO ONE WOULD SUSPECT!
IT SHOULD WORK! YOU START GETTING THINGS READY TO MOVE -- AND AS BRUCE WAYNE, I'LL SEE THAT SHOWMAN!
"BREEZY" LANE IS A DISCOURAGED MAN!
IF THE COMMISSIONER CLOSES US UP, WE'RE SUNK! I'D SELL THIS SHOW AND TRY MY LUCK IN SOUTH AMERICA-- BUT WHO'D BUY?
I'LL BUY YOUR SHOW, MR. LANE! RUNNING A DIME-MUSEUM OUGHT TO BE FUN!
AND A FATEFUL DEAL IS SOON CONCLUDED...
WHAT LUCK--THAT WEALTHY PLAYBOY WAYNE BOUGHT THE PLACE JUST FOR KICKS! WE'LL TAKE THE BOAT TO SOUTH AMERICA TONIGHT!
NOW WE'VE GOT TO WORK FAST, TO REPLACE THESE PHONY "PROPS" WITH THE REAL BATCAVE EQUIPMENT!
10
TIME IS RUNNING OUT, INDEED! FOR SOON, IN THE REAL BATCAVE...
LISTEN-- THE SOUND-DETECTOR PICKS UP THE SOUND OF DRILLS AND CROWBARS! JARREL'S MEN ARE ALREADY TUNNELING TOWARD US!
I'VE GOT MOVING-TRUCKS AND IT'LL LOOK LIKE WE'RE MOVING SOME OF THE WAYNE HOUSE FURNITURE! THE BAT-PLANE AND BATMOBILE CAN BE TAKEN IN THE BACK DOOR OF THE DIME-MUSEUM!
FRENZIED TOIL FILLS THE HOURS THAT FOLLOW, AS DISCOVERY CREEPS EVER CLOSER!
I HAD TO DISASSEMBLE OUR BIGGEST TROPHY, THE DUMMY DINOSAUR, FOR PACKING!
EVERYTHING MUST GO--!
AND SOON, AFTER CEASELESS WORK...
WE'VE GOT EVERYTHING IN THE TRUCKS READY TO GO--AND CAN HIDE THE SECRET STAIR TO THE WAYNE MANSION!
BUT EVEN IF THEY JUST FIND AN EMPTY CAVE HERE, ONCE NEWS OF IT GETS OUT WE CAN'T RISK USING IT FOR A BATCAVE AGAIN!
MUST THE DYNAMIC DUO, THEN, GIVE UP THEIR BATCAVE FOREVER?
6

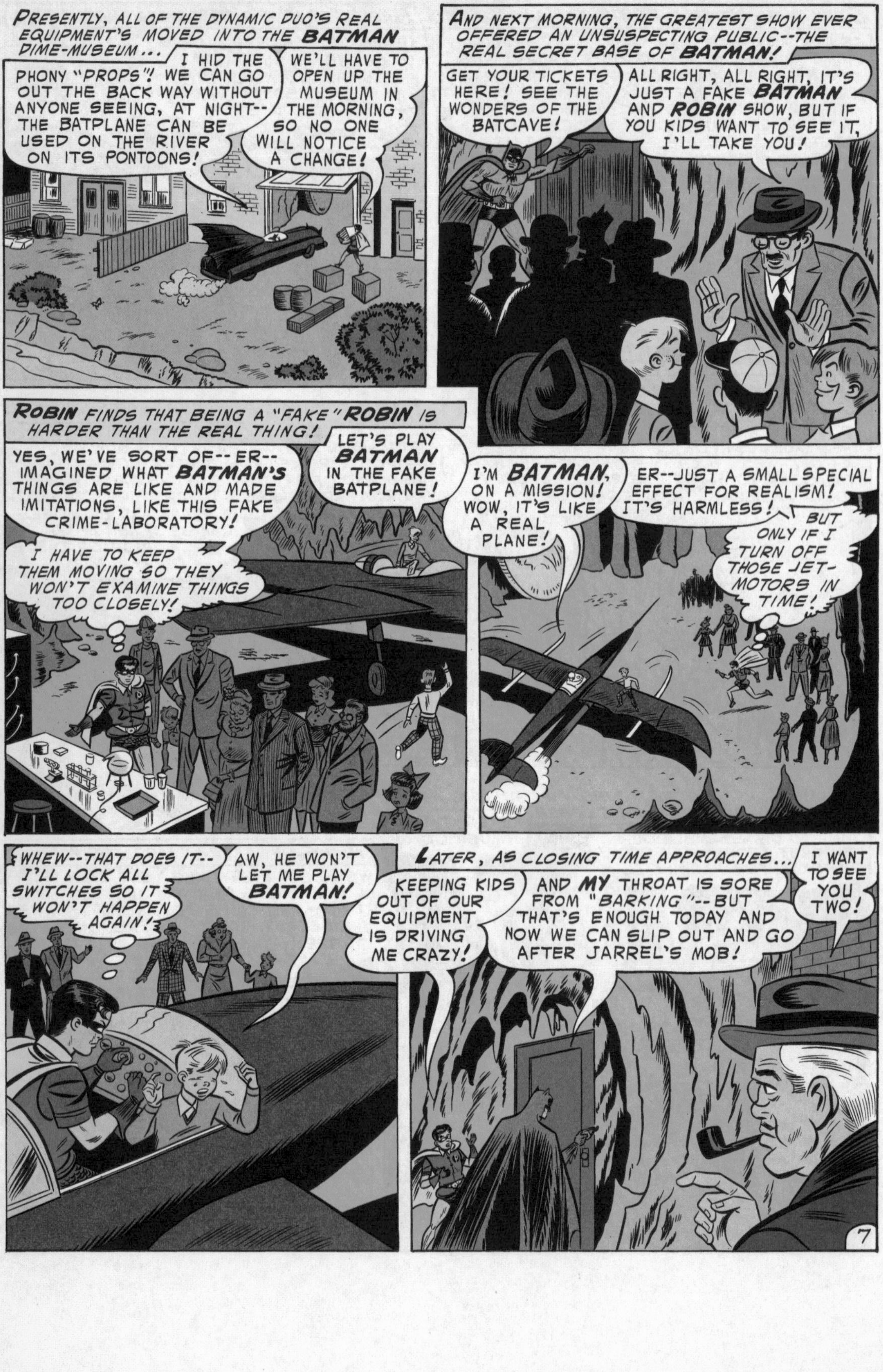

PRESENTLY, ALL OF THE DYNAMIC DUO'S REAL EQUIPMENT'S MOVED INTO THE BATMAN DIME-MUSEUM...
I HID THE PHONY "PROPS"! WE CAN GO OUT THE BACK WAY WITHOUT ANYONE SEEING, AT NIGHT-- THE BATPLANE CAN BE USED ON THE RIVER ON ITS PONTOONS!
WE'LL HAVE TO OPEN UP THE MUSEUM IN THE MORNING, SO NO ONE WILL NOTICE A CHANGE!
AND NEXT MORNING, THE GREATEST SHOW EVER OFFERED AN UNSUSPECTING PUBLIC--THE REAL SECRET BASE OF BATMAN!
GET YOUR TICKETS HERE! SEE THE WONDERS OF THE BATCAVE!
ALL RIGHT, ALL RIGHT, IT'S JUST A FAKE BATMAN AND ROBIN SHOW, BUT IF YOU KIDS WANT TO SEE IT, I'LL TAKE YOU!
ROBIN FINDS THAT BEING A "FAKE" ROBIN IS HARDER THAN THE REAL THING!
YES, WE'VE SORT OF--ER--IMAGINED WHAT BATMAN'S THINGS ARE LIKE AND MADE IMITATIONS, LIKE THIS FAKE CRIME-LABORATORY!
LET'S PLAY BATMAN IN THE FAKE BATPLANE!
I HAVE TO KEEP THEM MOVING SO THEY WON'T EXAMINE THINGS TOO CLOSELY!
I'M BATMAN, ON A MISSION! WOW, IT'S LIKE A REAL PLANE!
ER--JUST A SMALL SPECIAL EFFECT FOR REALISM! IT'S HARMLESS!
BUT ONLY IF I TURN OFF THOSE JET-MOTORS IN TIME!
WHEW--THAT DOES IT-- I'LL LOCK ALL SWITCHES SO IT WON'T HAPPEN AGAIN!
AW, HE WON'T LET ME PLAY BATMAN!
LATER, AS CLOSING TIME APPROACHES...
KEEPING KIDS OUT OF OUR EQUIPMENT IS DRIVING ME CRAZY!
AND MY THROAT IS SORE FROM "BARKING"--BUT THAT'S ENOUGH TODAY AND NOW WE CAN SLIP OUT AND GO AFTER JARREL'S MOB!
I WANT TO SEE YOU TWO!
7

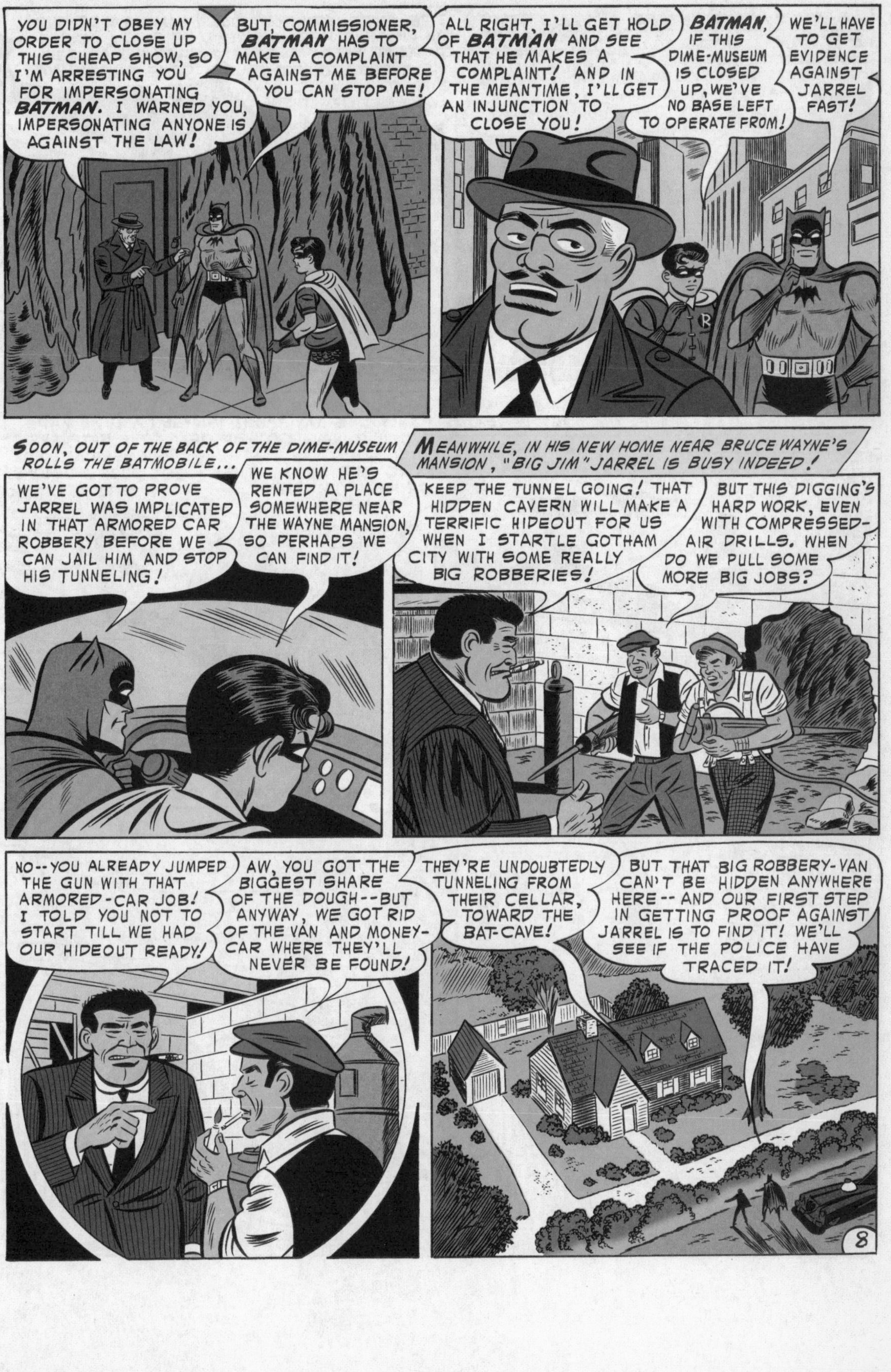
YOU DIDN'T OBEY MY ORDER TO CLOSE UP THIS CHEAP SHOW, SO I'M ARRESTING YOU FOR IMPERSONATING BATMAN. I WARNED YOU, IMPERSONATING ANYONE IS AGAINST THE LAW!
BUT, COMMISSIONER, BATMAN HAS TO MAKE A COMPLAINT AGAINST ME BEFORE YOU CAN STOP ME!
ALL RIGHT, I'LL GET HOLD OF BATMAN AND SEE THAT HE MAKES A COMPLAINT! AND IN THE MEANTIME, I'LL GET AN INJUNCTION TO CLOSE YOU!
BATMAN, IF THIS DIME-MUSEUM IS CLOSED UP, WE'VE NO BASE LEFT TO OPERATE FROM!
WE'LL HAVE TO GET EVIDENCE AGAINST JARREL FAST!
SOON, OUT OF THE BACK OF THE DIME-MUSEUM ROLLS THE BATMOBILE...
WE'VE GOT TO PROVE JARREL WAS IMPLICATED IN THAT ARMORED CAR ROBBERY BEFORE WE CAN JAIL HIM AND STOP HIS TUNNELING!
WE KNOW HE'S RENTED A PLACE SOMEWHERE NEAR THE WAYNE MANSION, SO PERHAPS WE CAN FIND IT!
MEANWHILE, IN HIS NEW HOME NEAR BRUCE WAYNE'S MANSION, "BIG JIM" JARREL IS BUSY INDEED!
KEEP THE TUNNEL GOING! THAT HIDDEN CAVERN WILL MAKE A TERRIFIC HIDEOUT FOR US WHEN I STARTLE GOTHAM CITY WITH SOME REALLY BIG ROBBERIES!
BUT THIS DIGGING'S HARD WORK, EVEN WITH COMPRESSED-AIR DRILLS. WHEN DO WE PULL SOME MORE BIG JOBS?
NO--YOU ALREADY JUMPED THE GUN WITH THAT ARMORED-CAR JOB! I TOLD YOU NOT TO START TILL WE HAD OUR HIDEOUT READY!
AW, YOU GOT THE BIGGEST SHARE OF THE DOUGH--BUT ANYWAY, WE GOT RID OF THE VAN AND MONEY-CAR WHERE THEY'LL NEVER BE FOUND!
THEY'RE UNDOUBTEDLY TUNNELING FROM THEIR CELLAR, TOWARD THE BAT-CAVE!
BUT THAT BIG ROBBERY-VAN CAN'T BE HIDDEN ANYWHERE HERE -- AND OUR FIRST STEP IN GETTING PROOF AGAINST JARREL IS TO FIND IT! WE'LL SEE IF THE POLICE HAVE TRACED IT!
8

Panel 1: AT POLICE HEADQUARTERS... BATMAN, I WANTED TO SEE YOU! IT'S ABOUT THAT CHEAP DIME-MUSEUM THAT'S---

I'LL ATTEND TO THAT LATER, COMMISSIONER! RIGHT NOW I'M ON THE TRAIL OF THAT BIG VAN THE ARMORED-CAR THIEVES USED!

Panel 2: IT'S WEIRD, HOW THAT HUGE VAN DISAPPEARED! WE'VE CHECKED EVERY GARAGE BIG ENOUGH TO HIDE IT, BUT IT SEEMS TO HAVE VANISHED OFF THE EARTH!

HMM, MAYBE IT DID, AT THAT! YOU'VE GIVEN ME AN IDEA-- COME ON, ROBIN!

Panel 3: AND AS NIGHT FALLS, FROM THE DIME-MUSEUM EMERGES THE BATPLANE, THE MOST VERSATILE CRAFT IN EXISTENCE!

BUT, BATMAN, YOU'RE FOLDING THE BATPLANE'S WINGS!

YES, WE'RE GOING TO LOOK FOR THAT VAN--

Panel 4: --UNDERWATER! THERE WAS ONLY ONE WAY THOSE THIEVES COULD HAVE GOT RID OF SUCH A BIG VAN, AFTER TAKING THE MONEY. THEY DROVE IT INTO THE RIVER TO SINK!

NOW I GET IT! AND WE MADE THE BATPLANE SUBMERSIBLE FOR JUST SUCH MISSIONS!

Panel 5: DOWN THE DARK RIVER, DEEP UNDERWATER, CRUISES THE IMPROVISED SUBMARINE IN SEARCH...

SOMETHING BIG LYING ON THE RIVER-BOTTOM CLOSE TO SHORE, BATMAN!

I SEE IT--WE'LL USE OUR AQUA-LUNG EQUIPMENT TO LOOK IT OVER FAST!

Panel 6: TWO STRANGE FIGURES GRIMLY SEARCH IN THE COLD DEPTHS!

9

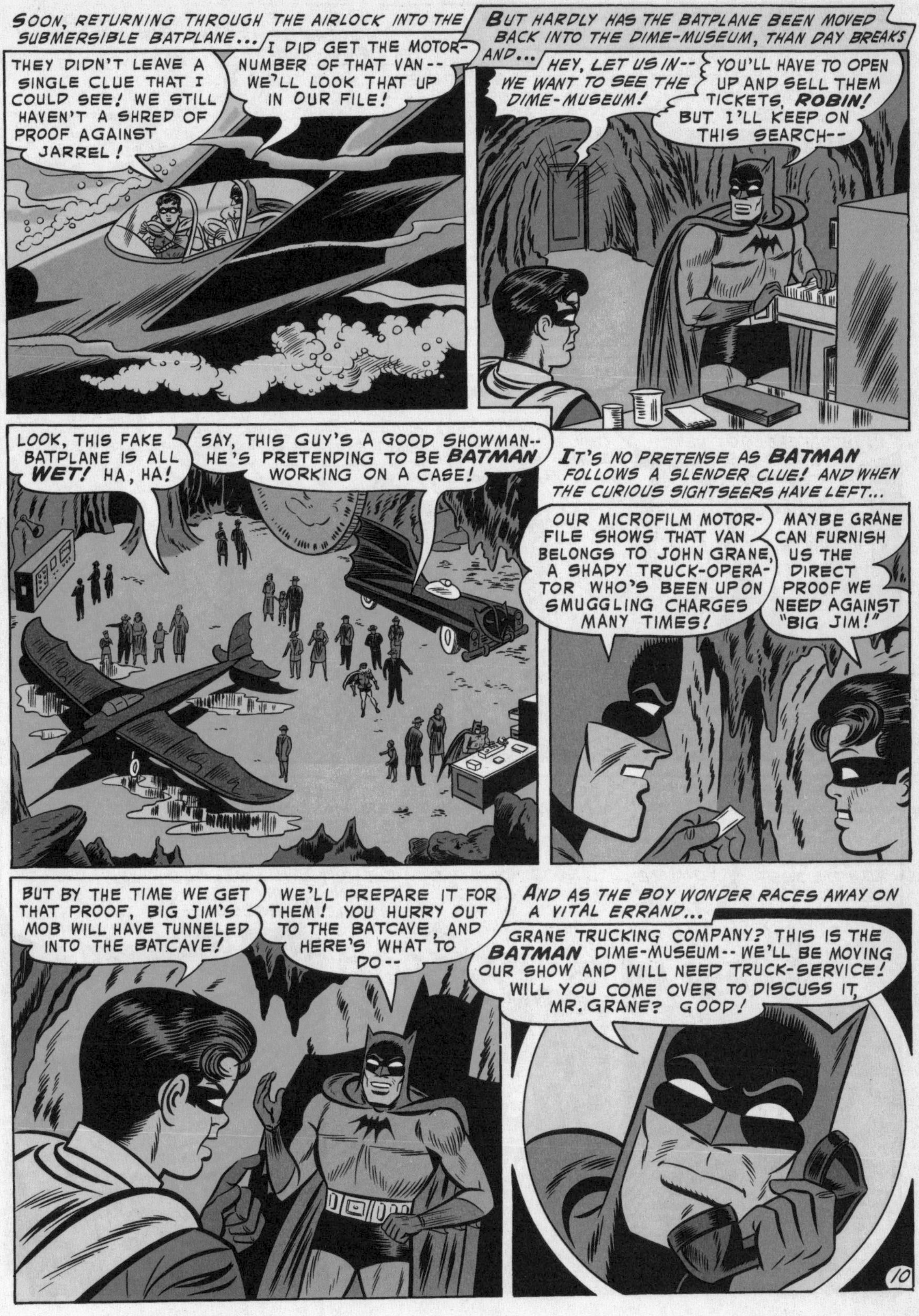
SOON, RETURNING THROUGH THE AIRLOCK INTO THE SUBMERSIBLE BATPLANE...
THEY DIDN'T LEAVE A SINGLE CLUE THAT I COULD SEE! WE STILL HAVEN'T A SHRED OF PROOF AGAINST JARREL!
I DID GET THE MOTOR-NUMBER OF THAT VAN-- WE'LL LOOK THAT UP IN OUR FILE!
BUT HARDLY HAS THE BATPLANE BEEN MOVED BACK INTO THE DIME-MUSEUM, THAN DAY BREAKS AND...
HEY, LET US IN-- WE WANT TO SEE THE DIME-MUSEUM!
YOU'LL HAVE TO OPEN UP AND SELL THEM TICKETS, ROBIN! BUT I'LL KEEP ON THIS SEARCH--
LOOK, THIS FAKE BATPLANE IS ALL WET! HA, HA!
SAY, THIS GUY'S A GOOD SHOWMAN-- HE'S PRETENDING TO BE BATMAN WORKING ON A CASE!
IT'S NO PRETENSE AS BATMAN FOLLOWS A SLENDER CLUE! AND WHEN THE CURIOUS SIGHTSEERS HAVE LEFT...
OUR MICROFILM MOTOR-FILE SHOWS THAT VAN BELONGS TO JOHN GRANE, A SHADY TRUCK-OPERATOR WHO'S BEEN UP ON SMUGGLING CHARGES MANY TIMES!
MAYBE GRANE CAN FURNISH US THE DIRECT PROOF WE NEED AGAINST "BIG JIM!"
BUT BY THE TIME WE GET THAT PROOF, BIG JIM'S MOB WILL HAVE TUNNELED INTO THE BATCAVE!
WE'LL PREPARE IT FOR THEM! YOU HURRY OUT TO THE BATCAVE, AND HERE'S WHAT TO DO--
AND AS THE BOY WONDER RACES AWAY ON A VITAL ERRAND...
GRANE TRUCKING COMPANY? THIS IS THE BATMAN DIME-MUSEUM-- WE'LL BE MOVING OUR SHOW AND WILL NEED TRUCK-SERVICE! WILL YOU COME OVER TO DISCUSS IT, MR. GRANE? GOOD!
10

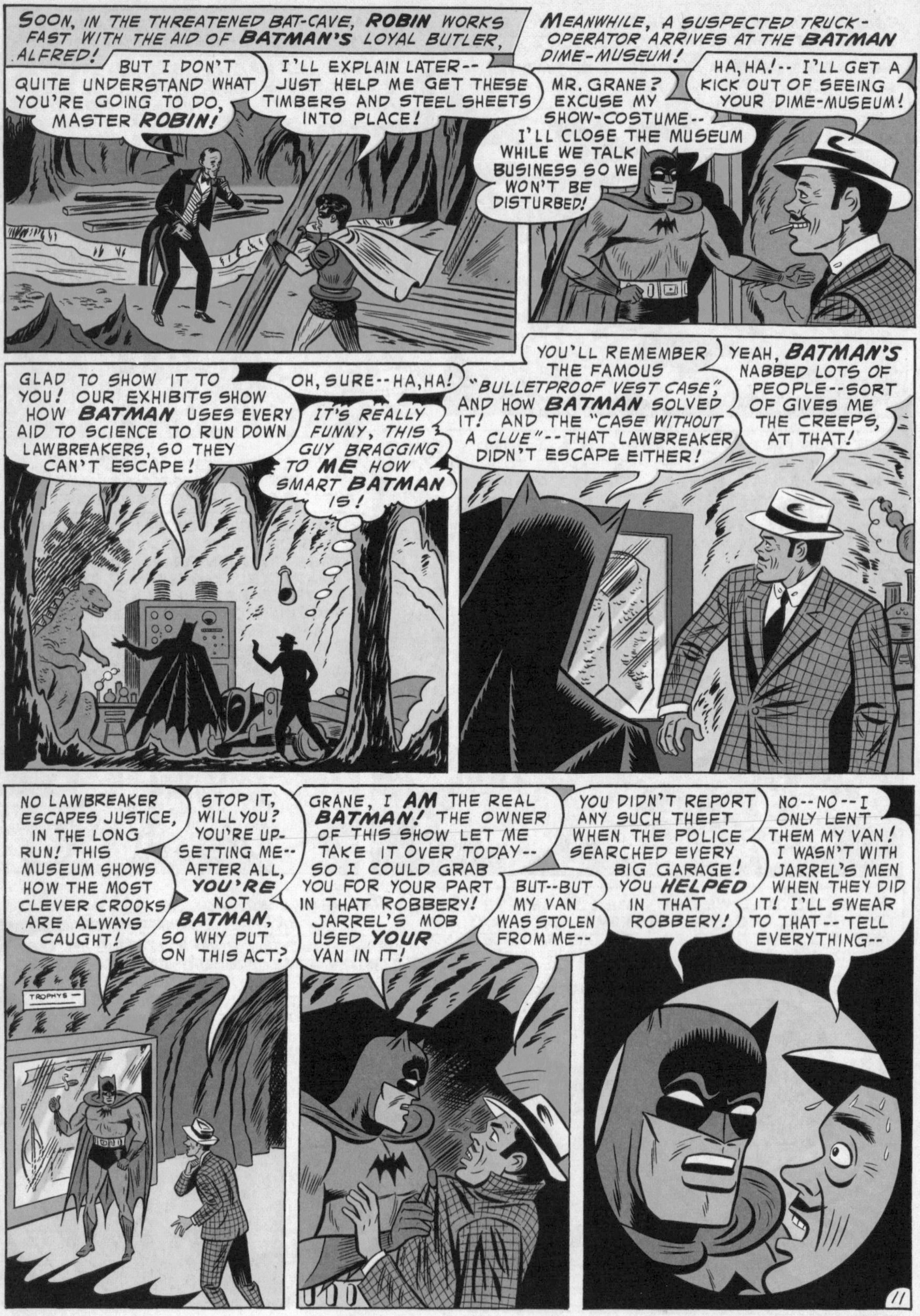

SOON, IN THE THREATENED BAT-CAVE, ROBIN WORKS FAST WITH THE AID OF BATMAN'S LOYAL BUTLER, ALFRED!
BUT I DON'T QUITE UNDERSTAND WHAT YOU'RE GOING TO DO, MASTER ROBIN!
I'LL EXPLAIN LATER-- JUST HELP ME GET THESE TIMBERS AND STEEL SHEETS INTO PLACE!
MEANWHILE, A SUSPECTED TRUCK-OPERATOR ARRIVES AT THE BATMAN DIME-MUSEUM!
HA, HA!-- I'LL GET A KICK OUT OF SEEING YOUR DIME-MUSEUM!
MR. GRANE? EXCUSE MY SHOW-COSTUME-- I'LL CLOSE THE MUSEUM WHILE WE TALK BUSINESS SO WE WON'T BE DISTURBED!
GLAD TO SHOW IT TO YOU! OUR EXHIBITS SHOW HOW BATMAN USES EVERY AID TO SCIENCE TO RUN DOWN LAWBREAKERS, SO THEY CAN'T ESCAPE!
OH, SURE--HA, HA!
IT'S REALLY FUNNY, THIS GUY BRAGGING TO ME HOW SMART BATMAN IS!
YOU'LL REMEMBER THE FAMOUS "BULLETPROOF VEST CASE," AND HOW BATMAN SOLVED IT! AND THE "CASE WITHOUT A CLUE"--THAT LAWBREAKER DIDN'T ESCAPE EITHER!
YEAH, BATMAN'S NABBED LOTS OF PEOPLE--SORT OF GIVES ME THE CREEPS, AT THAT!
NO LAWBREAKER ESCAPES JUSTICE, IN THE LONG RUN! THIS MUSEUM SHOWS HOW THE MOST CLEVER CROOKS ARE ALWAYS CAUGHT!
STOP IT, WILL YOU? YOU'RE UP-SETTING ME-- AFTER ALL, YOU'RE NOT BATMAN, SO WHY PUT ON THIS ACT?
TROPHYS
GRANE, I AM THE REAL BATMAN! THE OWNER OF THIS SHOW LET ME TAKE IT OVER TODAY-- SO I COULD GRAB YOU FOR YOUR PART IN THAT ROBBERY! JARREL'S MOB USED YOUR VAN IN IT!
BUT--BUT MY VAN WAS STOLEN FROM ME--
YOU DIDN'T REPORT ANY SUCH THEFT WHEN THE POLICE SEARCHED EVERY BIG GARAGE! YOU HELPED IN THAT ROBBERY!
NO--NO--I ONLY LENT THEM MY VAN! I WASN'T WITH JARREL'S MEN WHEN THEY DID IT! I'LL SWEAR TO THAT--TELL EVERYTHING--
11

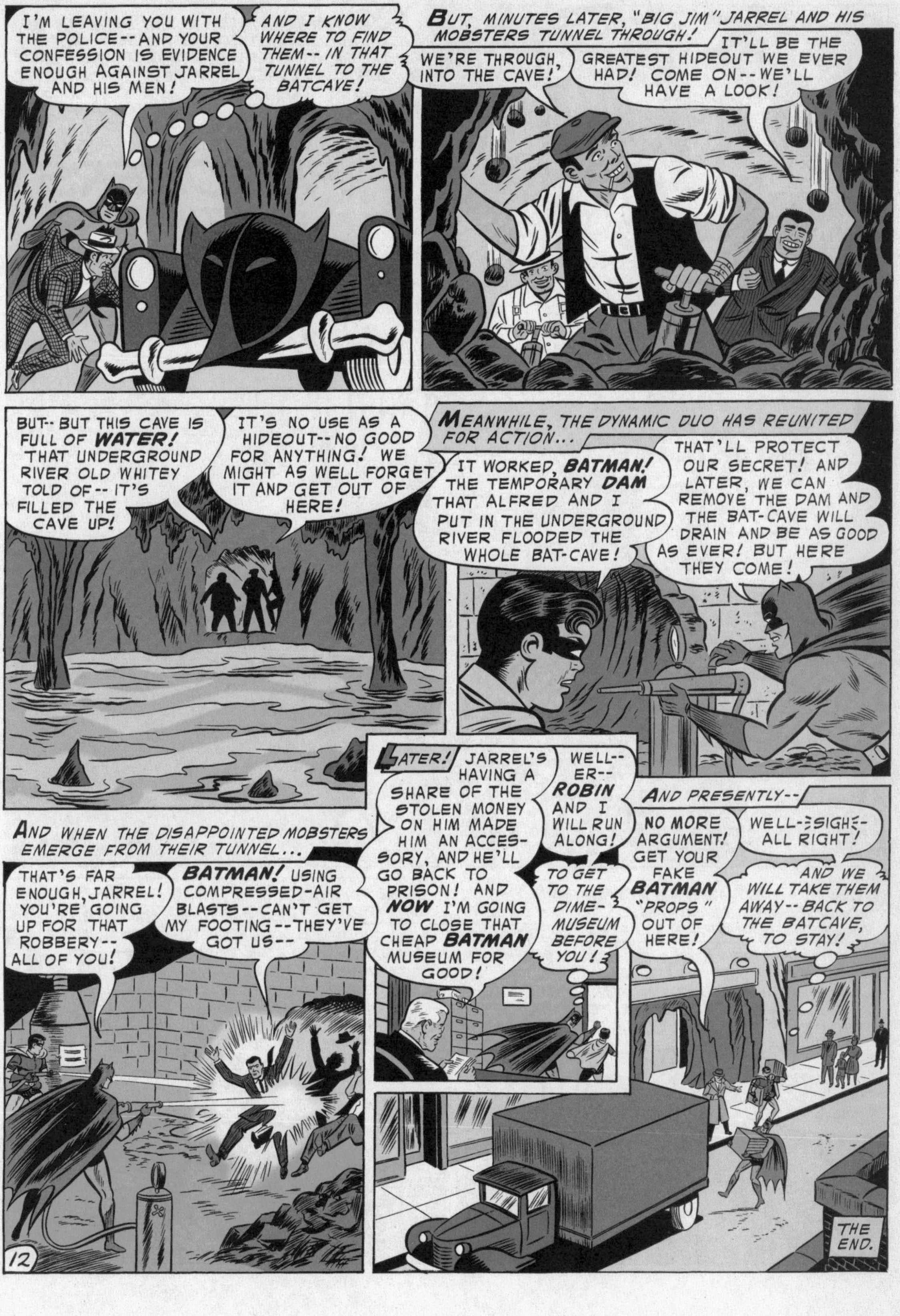
I'M LEAVING YOU WITH THE POLICE--AND YOUR CONFESSION IS EVIDENCE ENOUGH AGAINST JARREL AND HIS MEN!
AND I KNOW WHERE TO FIND THEM--IN THAT TUNNEL TO THE BATCAVE!
BUT, MINUTES LATER, "BIG JIM" JARREL AND HIS MOBSTERS TUNNEL THROUGH!
WE'RE THROUGH, INTO THE CAVE!
IT'LL BE THE GREATEST HIDEOUT WE EVER HAD! COME ON--WE'LL HAVE A LOOK!
BUT--BUT THIS CAVE IS FULL OF WATER! THAT UNDERGROUND RIVER OLD WHITEY TOLD OF--IT'S FILLED THE CAVE UP!
IT'S NO USE AS A HIDEOUT--NO GOOD FOR ANYTHING! WE MIGHT AS WELL FORGET IT AND GET OUT OF HERE!
MEANWHILE, THE DYNAMIC DUO HAS REUNITED FOR ACTION...
IT WORKED, BATMAN! THE TEMPORARY DAM THAT ALFRED AND I PUT IN THE UNDERGROUND RIVER FLOODED THE WHOLE BAT-CAVE!
THAT'LL PROTECT OUR SECRET! AND LATER, WE CAN REMOVE THE DAM AND THE BAT-CAVE WILL DRAIN AND BE AS GOOD AS EVER! BUT HERE THEY COME!
AND WHEN THE DISAPPOINTED MOBSTERS EMERGE FROM THEIR TUNNEL...
THAT'S FAR ENOUGH, JARREL! YOU'RE GOING UP FOR THAT ROBBERY--ALL OF YOU!
BATMAN! USING COMPRESSED-AIR BLASTS--CAN'T GET MY FOOTING--THEY'VE GOT US--
12
LATER! JARREL'S HAVING A SHARE OF THE STOLEN MONEY ON HIM MADE HIM AN ACCESSORY, AND HE'LL GO BACK TO PRISON! AND NOW I'M GOING TO CLOSE THAT CHEAP BATMAN MUSEUM FOR GOOD!
WELL--ER--ROBIN AND I WILL RUN ALONG!
TO GET TO THE DIME-MUSEUM BEFORE YOU!
AND PRESENTLY--
NO MORE ARGUMENT! GET YOUR FAKE BATMAN "PROPS" OUT OF HERE!
WELL--SIGH--ALL RIGHT!
AND WE WILL TAKE THEM AWAY--BACK TO THE BATCAVE, TO STAY!
THE END.

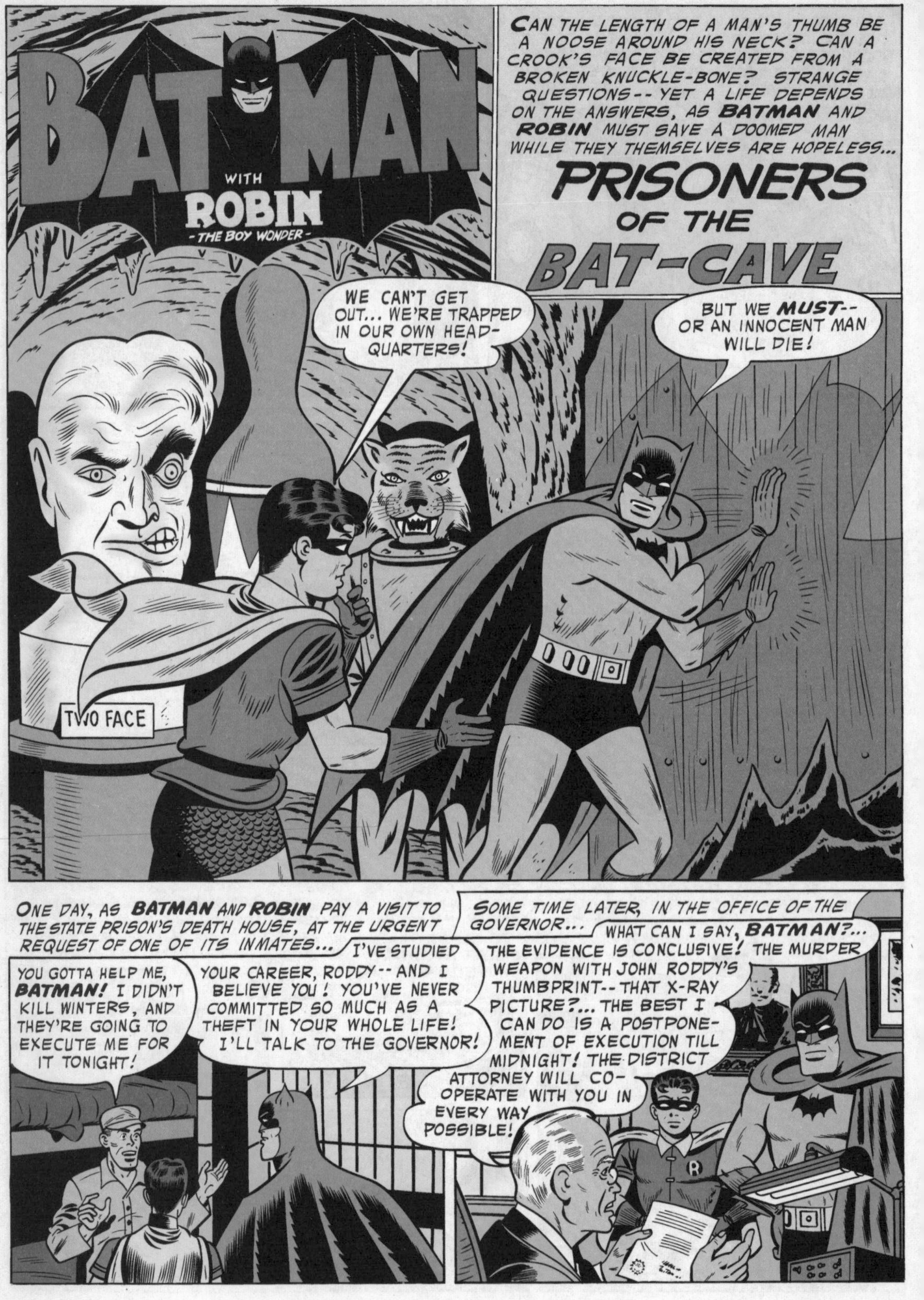
BATMAN
WITH ROBIN -THE BOY WONDER-
CAN THE LENGTH OF A MAN'S THUMB BE A NOOSE AROUND HIS NECK? CAN A CROOK'S FACE BE CREATED FROM A BROKEN KNUCKLE-BONE? STRANGE QUESTIONS-- YET A LIFE DEPENDS ON THE ANSWERS, AS BATMAN AND ROBIN MUST SAVE A DOOMED MAN WHILE THEY THEMSELVES ARE HOPELESS...
PRISONERS OF THE BAT-CAVE
WE CAN'T GET OUT... WE'RE TRAPPED IN OUR OWN HEAD-QUARTERS!
BUT WE MUST-- OR AN INNOCENT MAN WILL DIE!
TWO FACE
ONE DAY, AS BATMAN AND ROBIN PAY A VISIT TO THE STATE PRISON'S DEATH HOUSE, AT THE URGENT REQUEST OF ONE OF ITS INMATES...
YOU GOTTA HELP ME, BATMAN! I DIDN'T KILL WINTERS, AND THEY'RE GOING TO EXECUTE ME FOR IT TONIGHT!
I'VE STUDIED YOUR CAREER, RODDY-- AND I BELIEVE YOU! YOU'VE NEVER COMMITTED SO MUCH AS A THEFT IN YOUR WHOLE LIFE! I'LL TALK TO THE GOVERNOR!
SOME TIME LATER, IN THE OFFICE OF THE GOVERNOR...
WHAT CAN I SAY, BATMAN?... THE EVIDENCE IS CONCLUSIVE! THE MURDER WEAPON WITH JOHN RODDY'S THUMBPRINT-- THAT X-RAY PICTURE?... THE BEST I CAN DO IS A POSTPONE-MENT OF EXECUTION TILL MIDNIGHT! THE DISTRICT ATTORNEY WILL CO-OPERATE WITH YOU IN EVERY WAY POSSIBLE!

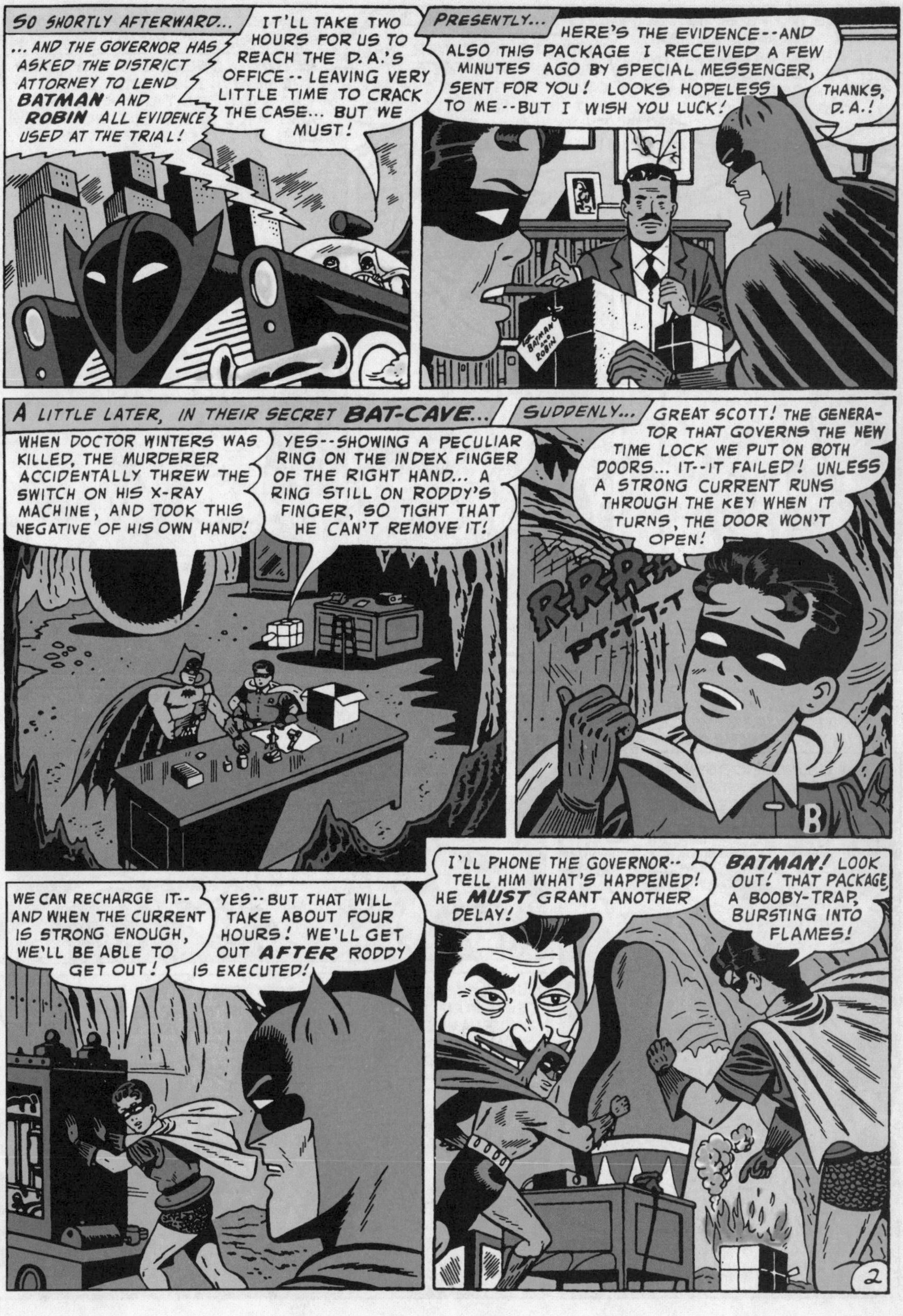
SO SHORTLY AFTERWARD...
... AND THE GOVERNOR HAS ASKED THE DISTRICT ATTORNEY TO LEND BATMAN AND ROBIN ALL EVIDENCE USED AT THE TRIAL!
IT'LL TAKE TWO HOURS FOR US TO REACH THE D.A.'S OFFICE -- LEAVING VERY LITTLE TIME TO CRACK THE CASE... BUT WE MUST!
PRESENTLY...
HERE'S THE EVIDENCE--AND ALSO THIS PACKAGE I RECEIVED A FEW MINUTES AGO BY SPECIAL MESSENGER, SENT FOR YOU! LOOKS HOPELESS TO ME--BUT I WISH YOU LUCK!
THANKS, D.A.!
A LITTLE LATER, IN THEIR SECRET BAT-CAVE...
WHEN DOCTOR WINTERS WAS KILLED, THE MURDERER ACCIDENTALLY THREW THE SWITCH ON HIS X-RAY MACHINE, AND TOOK THIS NEGATIVE OF HIS OWN HAND!
YES--SHOWING A PECULIAR RING ON THE INDEX FINGER OF THE RIGHT HAND... A RING STILL ON RODDY'S FINGER, SO TIGHT THAT HE CAN'T REMOVE IT!
SUDDENLY...
GREAT SCOTT! THE GENERATOR THAT GOVERNS THE NEW TIME LOCK WE PUT ON BOTH DOORS... IT--IT FAILED! UNLESS A STRONG CURRENT RUNS THROUGH THE KEY WHEN IT TURNS, THE DOOR WON'T OPEN!
R-R-R-R
PT-T-T-T
WE CAN RECHARGE IT--AND WHEN THE CURRENT IS STRONG ENOUGH, WE'LL BE ABLE TO GET OUT!
YES--BUT THAT WILL TAKE ABOUT FOUR HOURS! WE'LL GET OUT AFTER RODDY IS EXECUTED!
I'LL PHONE THE GOVERNOR--TELL HIM WHAT'S HAPPENED! HE MUST GRANT ANOTHER DELAY!
BATMAN! LOOK OUT! THAT PACKAGE A BOOBY-TRAP, BURSTING INTO FLAMES!
2

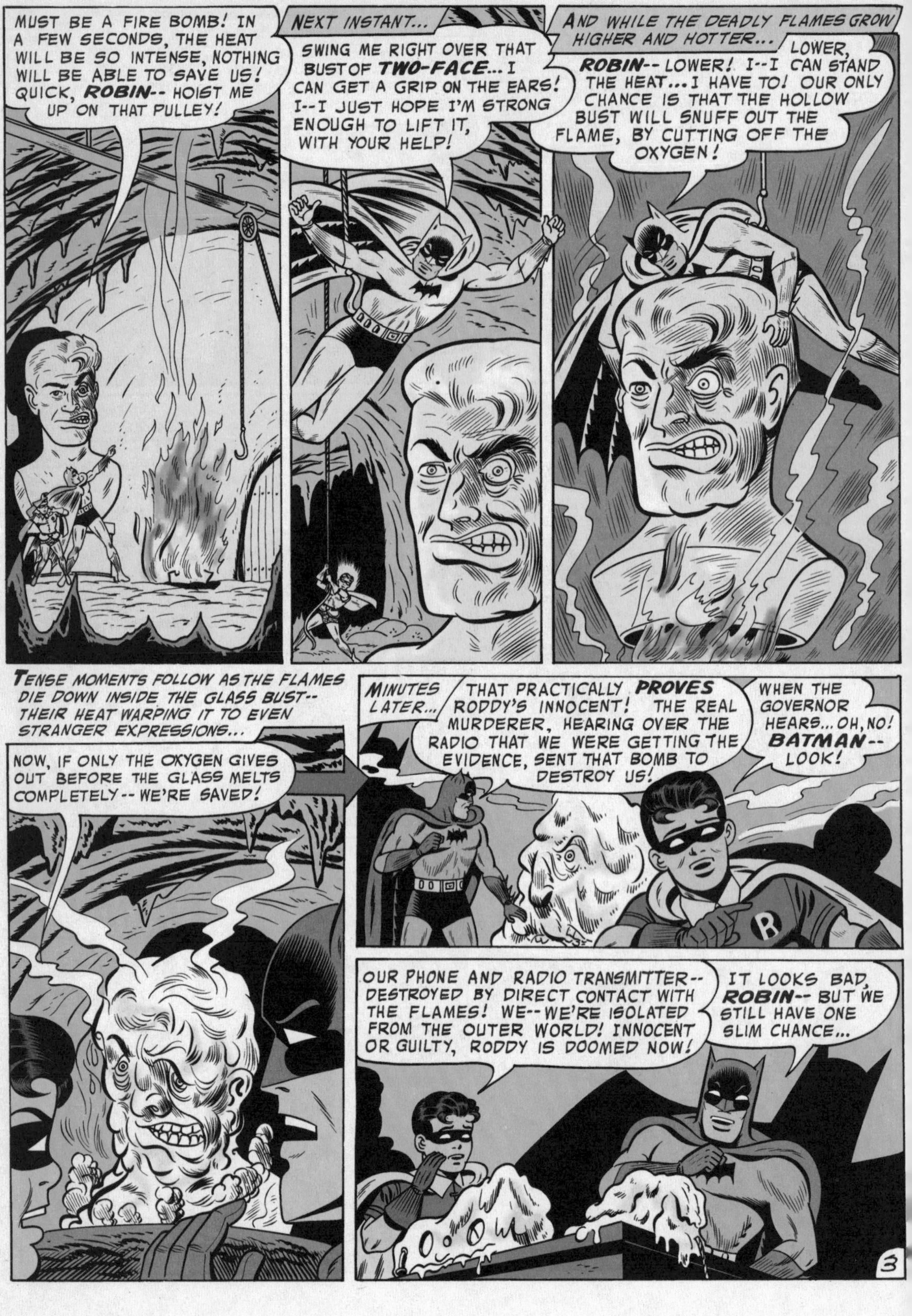
MUST BE A FIRE BOMB! IN A FEW SECONDS, THE HEAT WILL BE SO INTENSE, NOTHING WILL BE ABLE TO SAVE US! QUICK, ROBIN-- HOIST ME UP ON THAT PULLEY!
NEXT INSTANT...
SWING ME RIGHT OVER THAT BUST OF TWO-FACE... I CAN GET A GRIP ON THE EARS! I--I JUST HOPE I'M STRONG ENOUGH TO LIFT IT, WITH YOUR HELP!
AND WHILE THE DEADLY FLAMES GROW HIGHER AND HOTTER...
LOWER, ROBIN-- LOWER! I--I CAN STAND THE HEAT... I HAVE TO! OUR ONLY CHANCE IS THAT THE HOLLOW BUST WILL SNUFF OUT THE FLAME, BY CUTTING OFF THE OXYGEN!
TENSE MOMENTS FOLLOW AS THE FLAMES DIE DOWN INSIDE THE GLASS BUST-- THEIR HEAT WARPING IT TO EVEN STRANGER EXPRESSIONS...
NOW, IF ONLY THE OXYGEN GIVES OUT BEFORE THE GLASS MELTS COMPLETELY-- WE'RE SAVED!
MINUTES LATER...
THAT PRACTICALLY PROVES RODDY'S INNOCENT! THE REAL MURDERER, HEARING OVER THE RADIO THAT WE WERE GETTING THE EVIDENCE, SENT THAT BOMB TO DESTROY US!
WHEN THE GOVERNOR HEARS... OH, NO! BATMAN-- LOOK!
OUR PHONE AND RADIO TRANSMITTER-- DESTROYED BY DIRECT CONTACT WITH THE FLAMES! WE--WE'RE ISOLATED FROM THE OUTER WORLD! INNOCENT OR GUILTY, RODDY IS DOOMED NOW!
IT LOOKS BAD, ROBIN-- BUT WE STILL HAVE ONE SLIM CHANCE...
3

WE MUST FIND THE IDENTITY OF THE REAL MURDERER, USING ONLY OUR BRAINS, OUR FILES, AND THE CRIME-FIGHTING TOOLS WE HAVE HERE! AFTERWARD-- WELL...MAYBE ONE OF US WILL GET AN INSPIRATION ABOUT THAT LOCK!

WE'LL START BY ASSUMING THAT RODDY IS INNOCENT-- BUT SOMEONE FRAMED HIM BY GETTING HIS THUMBPRINT ON THE MURDER WEAPON! IF THAT'S THE CASE, I'M SURE WE CAN FIND OUT! LOOK AT THE SCREEN AND I'LL SHOW YOU WHAT I MEAN...

"WHEN A GUN IS HELD NATURALLY, THE THUMBPRINT ENDS THE SAME NUMBER OF INCHES FROM THE BUTT AS THE LENGTH OF THE MAN'S THUMB.."

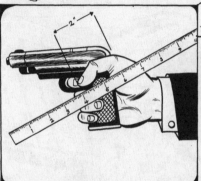

LET'S SEE, NOW...THE MAN WHO FIRED THIS GUN HAD A .THUMB TWO AND 3/4 INCHES LONG-- UNUSUALLY LONG!

THAT'S TERRIFIC! I JUST LOOKED UP RODDY'S RECORD... HIS THUMB IS BARELY TWO INCHES LONG! HE WAS FRAMED!

AND THIS IS HOW IT WAS DONE! THE KILLER GOT AN IMPRESSION OF RODDY'S THUMB, TRANSFERRED IT TO A RUBBER FINGER LIKE THIS--AND WORE IT WHEN HE DID THE KILLING, NOT THINKING THAT HIS OWN THUMB WAS LONGER THAN RODDY'S!

NOW LET'S SEE IF WE CAN PUT A FACE TO THAT THUMB--AND THEN WORRY ABOUT GETTING OUT OF HERE, IMPOSSIBLE AS IT SEEMS! I'LL PROJECT AN ENLARGEMENT OF THAT X-RAY-- AND SEE WHAT WE CAN FIND THERE!

HMM-- THAT DIVING SUIT... SEEMS TO SUGGEST SOMETHING... BUT I CAN'T QUITE PUT MY FINGER ON IT! WELL-- MAYBE IT'LL COME TO ME LATER!

4

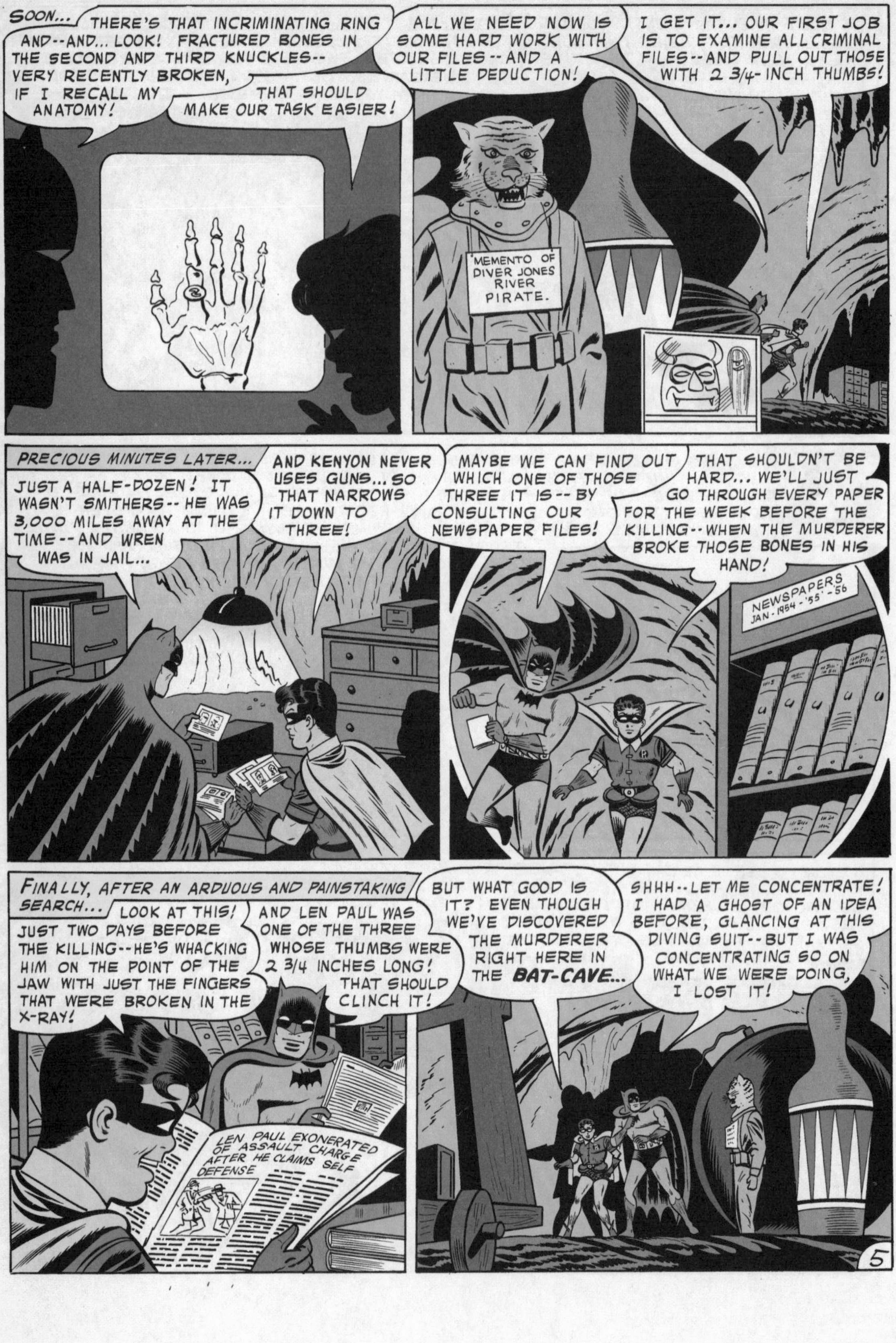
SOON...
THERE'S THAT INCRIMINATING RING AND--AND... LOOK! FRACTURED BONES IN THE SECOND AND THIRD KNUCKLES-- VERY RECENTLY BROKEN, IF I RECALL MY ANATOMY!
THAT SHOULD MAKE OUR TASK EASIER!
ALL WE NEED NOW IS SOME HARD WORK WITH OUR FILES -- AND A LITTLE DEDUCTION!
I GET IT... OUR FIRST JOB IS TO EXAMINE ALL CRIMINAL FILES -- AND PULL OUT THOSE WITH 2 3/4-INCH THUMBS!
MEMENTO OF DIVER JONES RIVER PIRATE.
PRECIOUS MINUTES LATER...
JUST A HALF-DOZEN! IT WASN'T SMITHERS -- HE WAS 3,000 MILES AWAY AT THE TIME -- AND WREN WAS IN JAIL...
AND KENYON NEVER USES GUNS... SO THAT NARROWS IT DOWN TO THREE!
MAYBE WE CAN FIND OUT WHICH ONE OF THOSE THREE IT IS -- BY CONSULTING OUR NEWSPAPER FILES!
THAT SHOULDN'T BE HARD... WE'LL JUST GO THROUGH EVERY PAPER FOR THE WEEK BEFORE THE KILLING -- WHEN THE MURDERER BROKE THOSE BONES IN HIS HAND!
NEWSPAPERS JAN - 1954 - '55' - '56
FINALLY, AFTER AN ARDUOUS AND PAINSTAKING SEARCH...
LOOK AT THIS! JUST TWO DAYS BEFORE THE KILLING -- HE'S WHACKING HIM ON THE POINT OF THE JAW WITH JUST THE FINGERS THAT WERE BROKEN IN THE X-RAY!
AND LEN PAUL WAS ONE OF THE THREE WHOSE THUMBS WERE 2 3/4 INCHES LONG! THAT SHOULD CLINCH IT!
LEN PAUL EXONERATED OF ASSAULT CHARGE AFTER HE CLAIMS SELF DEFENSE
BUT WHAT GOOD IS IT? EVEN THOUGH WE'VE DISCOVERED THE MURDERER RIGHT HERE IN THE **BAT-CAVE**...
SHHH -- LET ME CONCENTRATE! I HAD A GHOST OF AN IDEA BEFORE, GLANCING AT THIS DIVING SUIT -- BUT I WAS CONCENTRATING SO ON WHAT WE WERE DOING, I LOST IT!
5

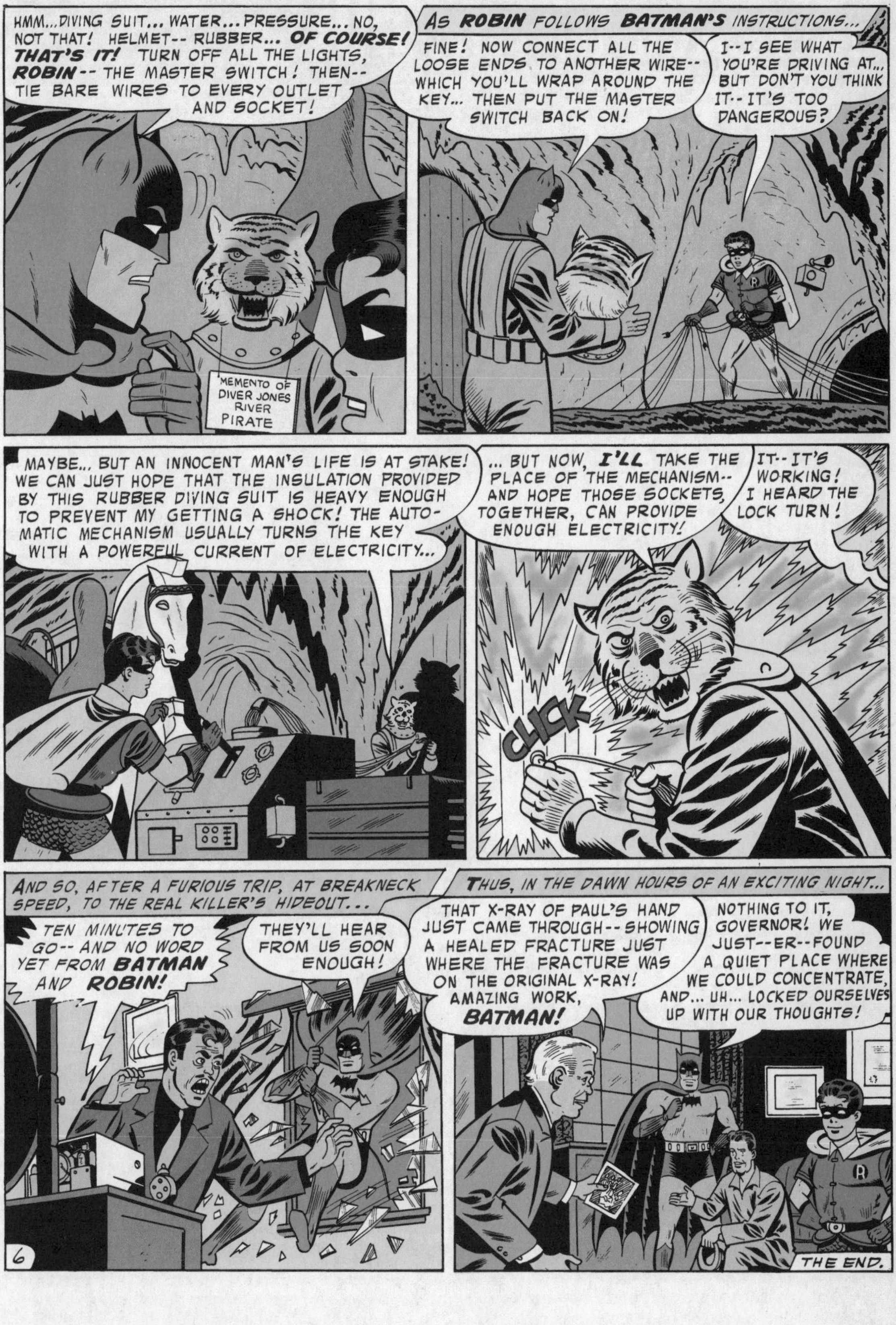
HMM...DIVING SUIT... WATER... PRESSURE... NO, NOT THAT! HELMET-- RUBBER... OF COURSE! THAT'S IT! TURN OFF ALL THE LIGHTS, ROBIN-- THE MASTER SWITCH! THEN-- TIE BARE WIRES TO EVERY OUTLET AND SOCKET!
MEMENTO OF DIVER JONES RIVER PIRATE
AS ROBIN FOLLOWS BATMAN'S INSTRUCTIONS...
FINE! NOW CONNECT ALL THE LOOSE ENDS TO ANOTHER WIRE-- WHICH YOU'LL WRAP AROUND THE KEY... THEN PUT THE MASTER SWITCH BACK ON!
I--I SEE WHAT YOU'RE DRIVING AT... BUT DON'T YOU THINK IT-- IT'S TOO DANGEROUS?
MAYBE... BUT AN INNOCENT MAN'S LIFE IS AT STAKE! WE CAN JUST HOPE THAT THE INSULATION PROVIDED BY THIS RUBBER DIVING SUIT IS HEAVY ENOUGH TO PREVENT MY GETTING A SHOCK! THE AUTOMATIC MECHANISM USUALLY TURNS THE KEY WITH A POWERFUL CURRENT OF ELECTRICITY...
... BUT NOW, I'LL TAKE THE PLACE OF THE MECHANISM-- AND HOPE THOSE SOCKETS, TOGETHER, CAN PROVIDE ENOUGH ELECTRICITY!
IT-- IT'S WORKING! I HEARD THE LOCK TURN!
CLICK
AND SO, AFTER A FURIOUS TRIP, AT BREAKNECK SPEED, TO THE REAL KILLER'S HIDEOUT...
TEN MINUTES TO GO-- AND NO WORD YET FROM BATMAN AND ROBIN!
THEY'LL HEAR FROM US SOON ENOUGH!
6
THUS, IN THE DAWN HOURS OF AN EXCITING NIGHT...
THAT X-RAY OF PAUL'S HAND JUST CAME THROUGH-- SHOWING A HEALED FRACTURE JUST WHERE THE FRACTURE WAS ON THE ORIGINAL X-RAY! AMAZING WORK, BATMAN!
NOTHING TO IT, GOVERNOR! WE JUST--ER--FOUND A QUIET PLACE WHERE WE COULD CONCENTRATE, AND... UH... LOCKED OURSELVES UP WITH OUR THOUGHTS!
THE END.

BATCAVE IN THE 90s

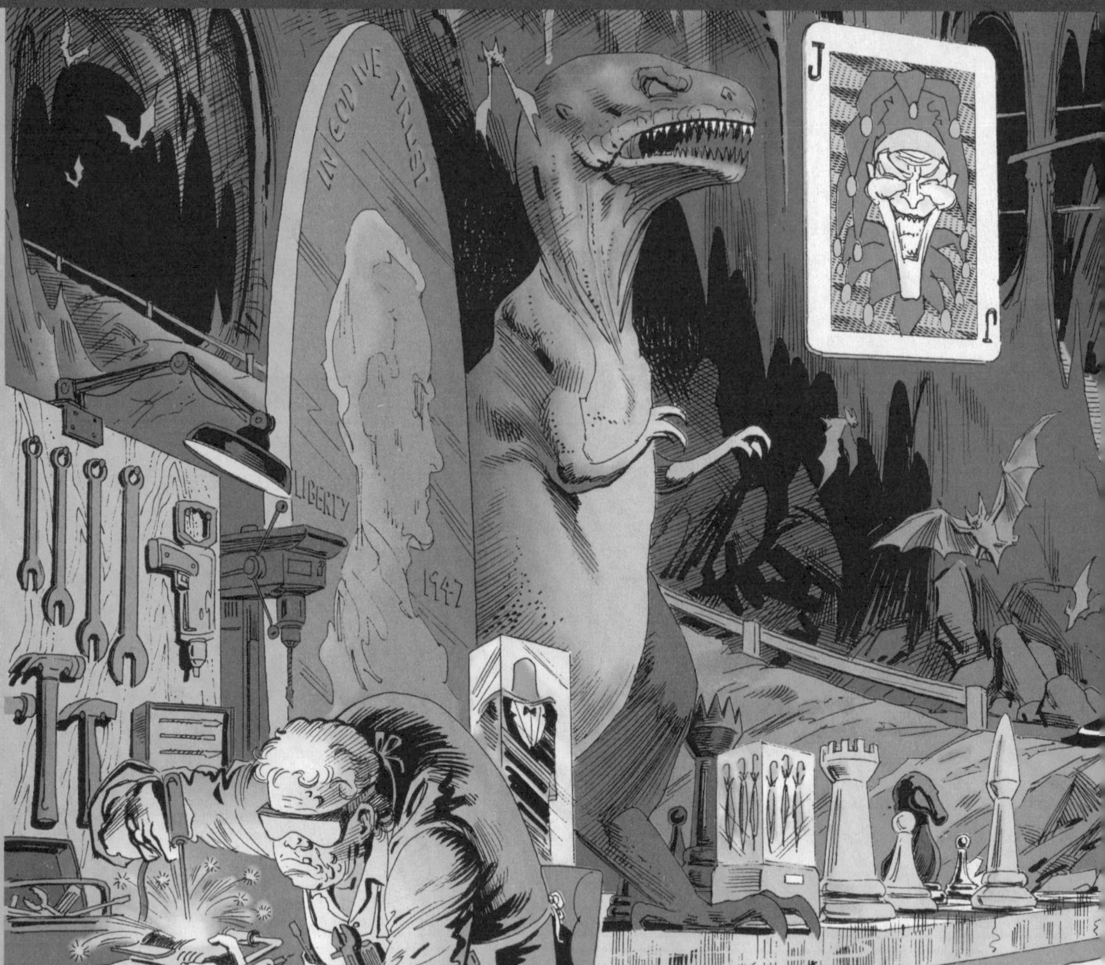
IN GOD WE TRUST
LIBERTY
1947
J

From: **WHO'S WHO IN THE DC UNIVERSE #13** *(1991)*

Text: **MARK WAID** *Art:* **NORM BREYFOGLE**

Situated on the outskirts of Gotham City, beneath Wayne Manor, is the Batcave, the vast nerve center of the Batman's never-ending war on crime. Not only does the Batcave serve to house the Dark Knight's crimefighting equipment, it also provides him a necessary sanctuary in which to formulate his battles against those who would threaten the innocents of Gotham.

Bruce Wayne's first encounter with what was to become the Batcave came years before the brutal murder of his parents. As a four-year-old, Bruce ignored his father's repeated warnings against exploring the Wayne Manor grounds without supervision, and fell into a deep cavern filled with bats. Though unhurt, Bruce was paralyzed with fear and might have died in the cave had not his father followed him down and retrieved him.

Many years later, during the early days of his new career as the Batman, Wayne decided to make use of the bat-filled grotto. With the help of his butler and companion, Alfred, Batman sealed off its tributary tunnels, equipped it with rudimentary power and ventilation systems, and began the long process of turning it into a serviceable headquarters.

There are two main levels to the Batcave. The upper level contains the laboratory, which houses equipment equal in scope and precision to anything used by the FBI, including a DNA/typing spectrograph, an electron microscope, and a ballistic microscope. Nearby is a full machine shop that serves as a vehicle repair area, and a garage for the Batmobile. A two-mile-long tunnel connects the garage to the Batmobile's secret exit: a hidden door located a half-mile from a sparsely traveled segment of the main road to Gotham.

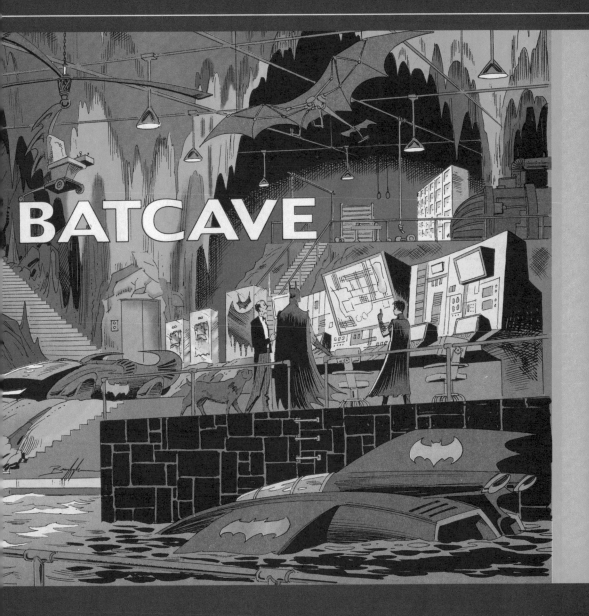

BATCAVE

The Batcave's lower level is home to the Batman's gymnasium, which compromises a full range of Olympic-level training devices. Also on this level is a workshop in which Batman designs and builds his various vehicles and weapons. Next to the workshop is the single most important piece of equipment, an incredibly sophisticated CD-ROM mainframe that contains the world's most comprehensive database on crime and criminals. Periodically, Batman updates the computer's files by secretly tapping into federal and international computer systems. Thanks to advancements in microwave transmission, he can at any time access the computer's database from a terminal in his Batmobile.

The Batcave's lower level also contains the most visually spectacular section of Batman's headquarters: the Trophy Room. Among its more notable features are a huge reproduction of a 1947 penny and a giant robot Tyrannosaurus Rex, both mementos of previous cases; an enormous Joker playing card suspended from the ceiling; and a glass case in which hangs the Robin uniform of Jason Todd, who died in action at the hands of the Joker. Off to the side of the trophy room lies the Batcave's power source, a hydroelectric generator run by a nearby subterranean river.

The only entrance to the Batcave from the inside of Wayne Manor is in Bruce Wayne's study, where a vast spiral staircase leading to the Batcave is hidden behind Wayne's grandfather clock. Only the Batman and his allies know how to access this secret passageway: the hands of the clock must be set to 8:25, the time of his parents' deaths.

Approximately halfway down the tunnel that connects the Batcave to its hidden exit is a seldom-used branch passageway which leads to the secret aircraft hangars built into a nearby hill. These hangars contain the Batcopter and the customized F-4 Phantom jet known as the Batplane. In the past, camouflaged doors and fog-generating equipment allowed these vehicles undetected entry and exit; in recent years, however, as the growing neighborhoods of Gotham have begun encroaching on what was once remote territory, the Batman has for the most part abandoned these modes of travel.

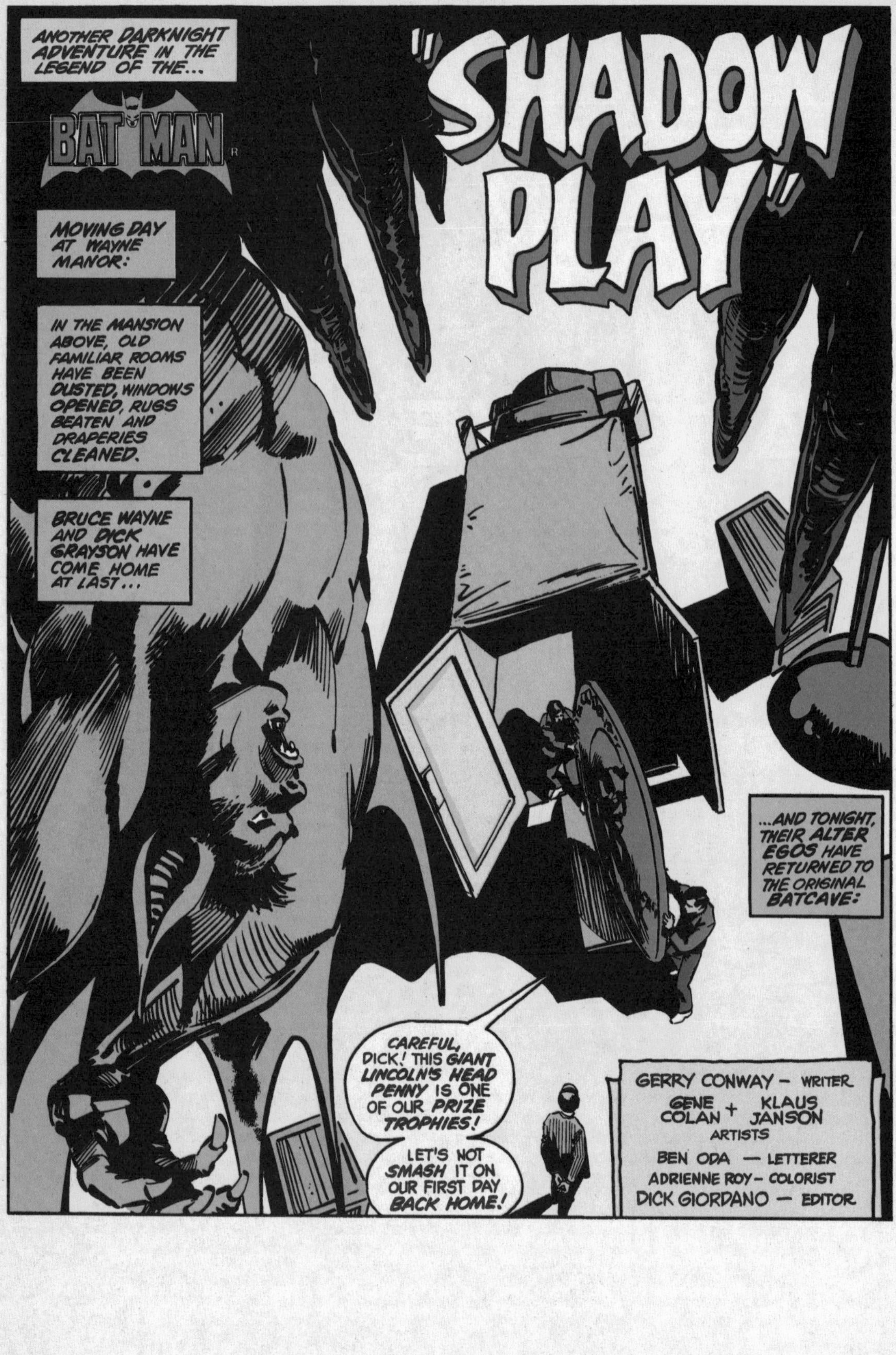
ANOTHER DARKNIGHT ADVENTURE IN THE LEGEND OF THE...
BATMAN
"SHADOW PLAY"
MOVING DAY AT WAYNE MANOR:
IN THE MANSION ABOVE, OLD FAMILIAR ROOMS HAVE BEEN DUSTED, WINDOWS OPENED, RUGS BEATEN AND DRAPERIES CLEANED.
BRUCE WAYNE AND DICK GRAYSON HAVE COME HOME AT LAST...
...AND TONIGHT, THEIR ALTER EGOS HAVE RETURNED TO THE ORIGINAL BATCAVE:
CAREFUL, DICK! THIS GIANT LINCOLN'S HEAD PENNY IS ONE OF OUR PRIZE TROPHIES!
LET'S NOT SMASH IT ON OUR FIRST DAY BACK HOME!
GERRY CONWAY - WRITER
GENE COLAN + KLAUS JANSON ARTISTS
BEN ODA — LETTERER
ADRIENNE ROY - COLORIST
DICK GIORDANO — EDITOR

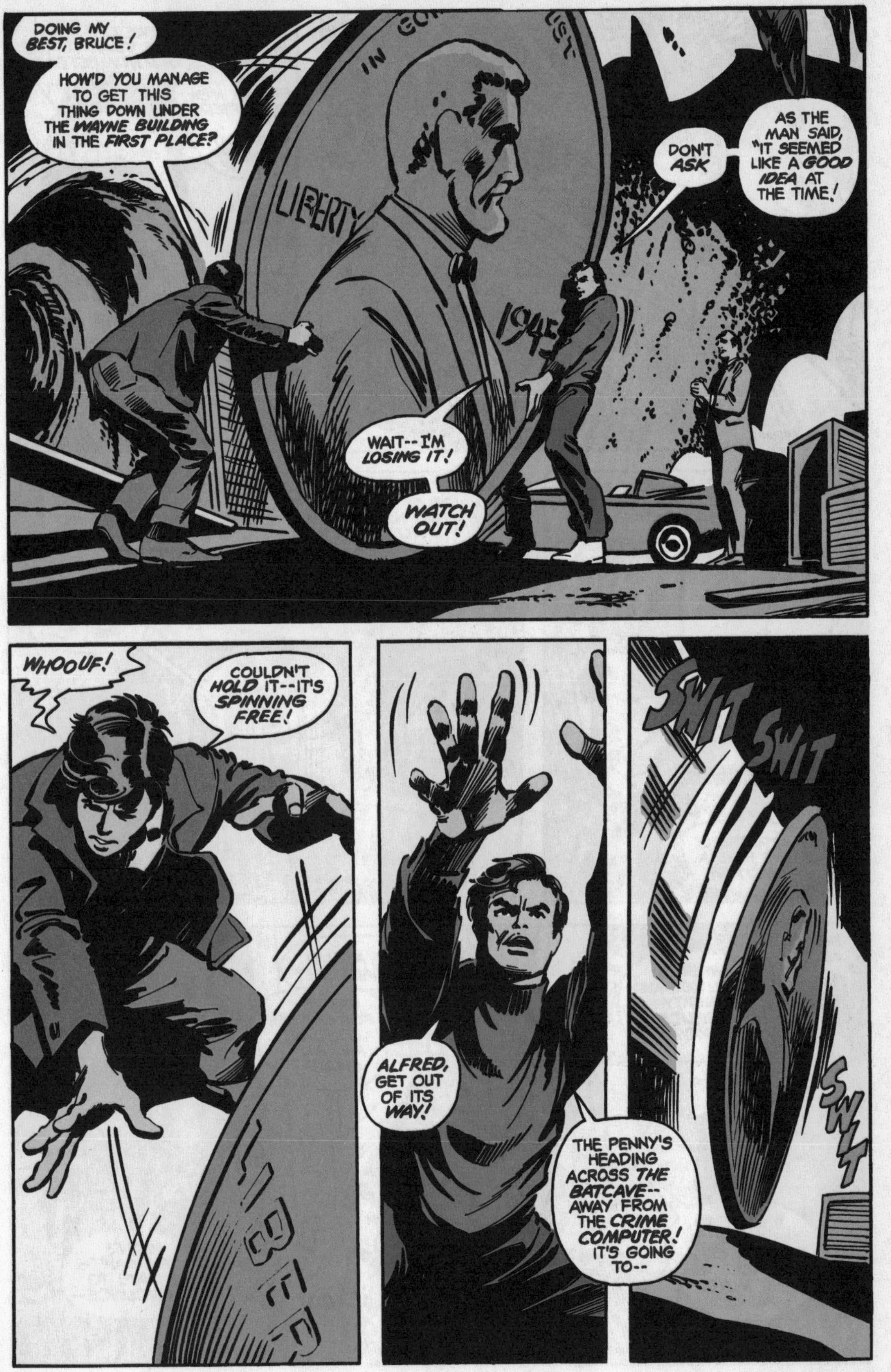
DOING MY BEST, BRUCE!
HOW'D YOU MANAGE TO GET THIS THING DOWN UNDER THE WAYNE BUILDING IN THE FIRST PLACE?
DON'T ASK
AS THE MAN SAID, "IT SEEMED LIKE A GOOD IDEA AT THE TIME!
WAIT--I'M LOSING IT!
WATCH OUT!
WHOOUF!
COULDN'T HOLD IT--IT'S SPINNING FREE!
ALFRED, GET OUT OF ITS WAY!
THE PENNY'S HEADING ACROSS THE BATCAVE--AWAY FROM THE CRIME COMPUTER! IT'S GOING TO--
SWIT SWIT
SWIT

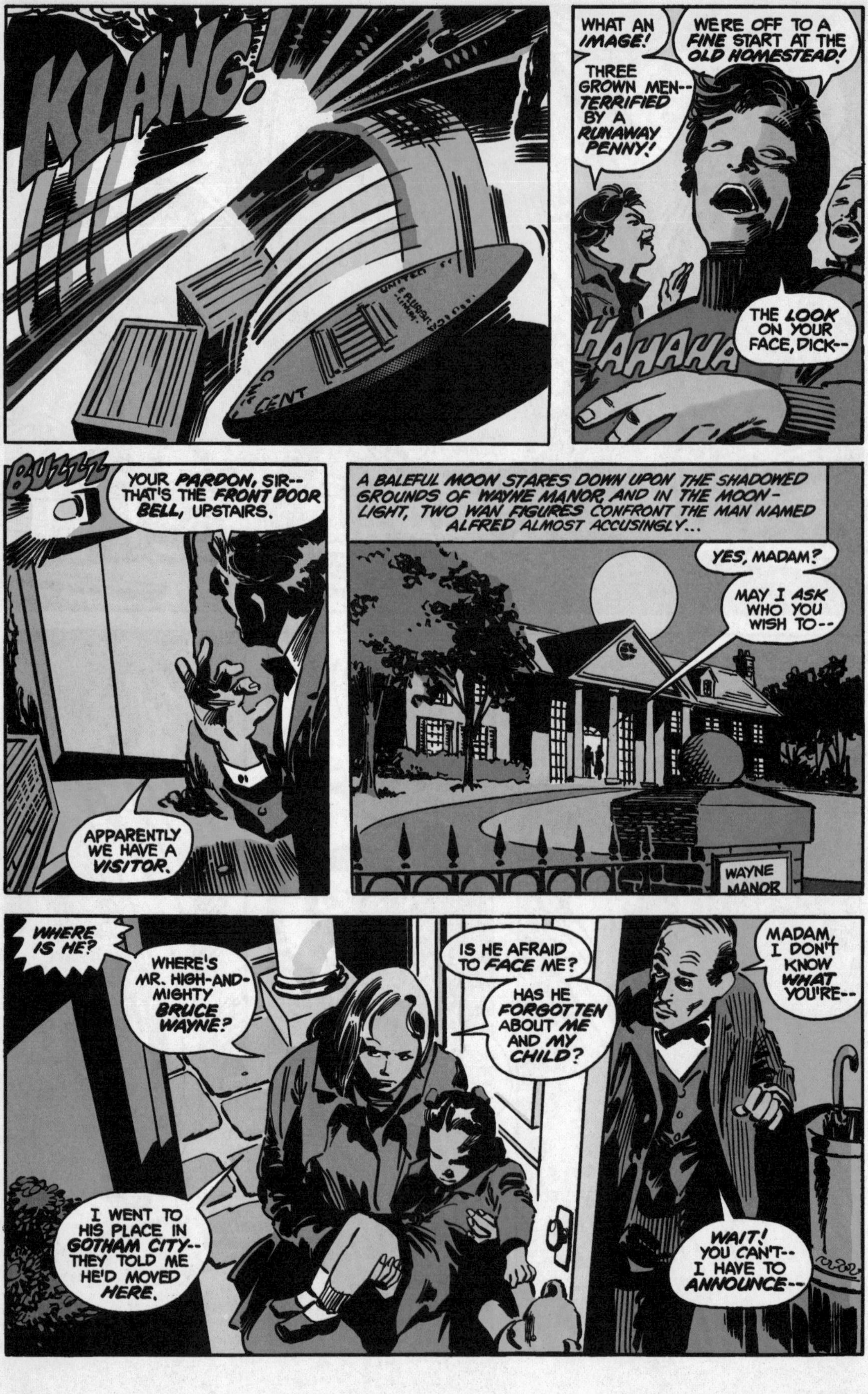
KLANG!
UNITED
E PLURIBUS UNUM
LIBERTY
CENT
WHAT AN IMAGE!
THREE GROWN MEN-- TERRIFIED BY A RUNAWAY PENNY!
WE'RE OFF TO A FINE START AT THE OLD HOMESTEAD!
HAHAHA
THE LOOK ON YOUR FACE, DICK--
BUZZZ
YOUR PARDON, SIR-- THAT'S THE FRONT DOOR BELL, UPSTAIRS.
APPARENTLY WE HAVE A VISITOR.
A BALEFUL MOON STARES DOWN UPON THE SHADOWED GROUNDS OF WAYNE MANOR, AND IN THE MOON-LIGHT, TWO WAN FIGURES CONFRONT THE MAN NAMED ALFRED ALMOST ACCUSINGLY...
YES, MADAM?
MAY I ASK WHO YOU WISH TO--
WAYNE MANOR
WHERE IS HE?
WHERE'S MR. HIGH-AND-MIGHTY BRUCE WAYNE?
I WENT TO HIS PLACE IN GOTHAM CITY-- THEY TOLD ME HE'D MOVED HERE.
IS HE AFRAID TO FACE ME?
HAS HE FORGOTTEN ABOUT ME AND MY CHILD?
MADAM, I DON'T KNOW WHAT YOU'RE--
WAIT! YOU CAN'T-- I HAVE TO ANNOUNCE--

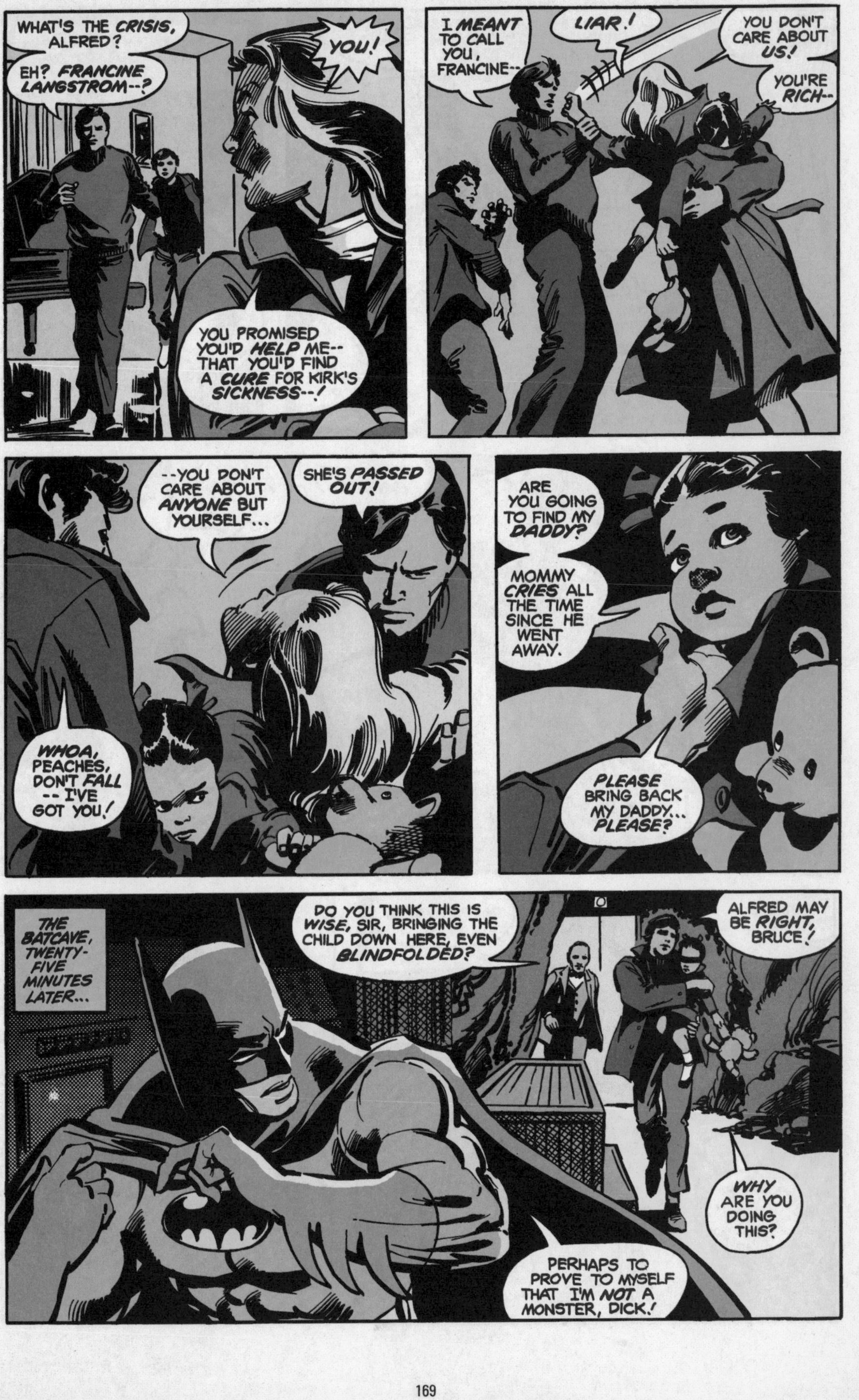
WHAT'S THE CRISIS, ALFRED?
EH? FRANCINE LANGSTROM--?
YOU!
YOU PROMISED YOU'D HELP ME-- THAT YOU'D FIND A CURE FOR KIRK'S SICKNESS--!
I MEANT TO CALL YOU, FRANCINE--
LIAR!
YOU DON'T CARE ABOUT US!
YOU'RE RICH--
--YOU DON'T CARE ABOUT ANYONE BUT YOURSELF...
SHE'S PASSED OUT!
WHOA, PEACHES, DON'T FALL -- I'VE GOT YOU!
ARE YOU GOING TO FIND MY DADDY?
MOMMY CRIES ALL THE TIME SINCE HE WENT AWAY.
PLEASE BRING BACK MY DADDY... PLEASE?
THE BATCAVE, TWENTY-FIVE MINUTES LATER...
DO YOU THINK THIS IS WISE, SIR, BRINGING THE CHILD DOWN HERE, EVEN BLINDFOLDED?
ALFRED MAY BE RIGHT, BRUCE!
WHY ARE YOU DOING THIS?
PERHAPS TO PROVE TO MYSELF THAT I'M NOT A MONSTER, DICK!

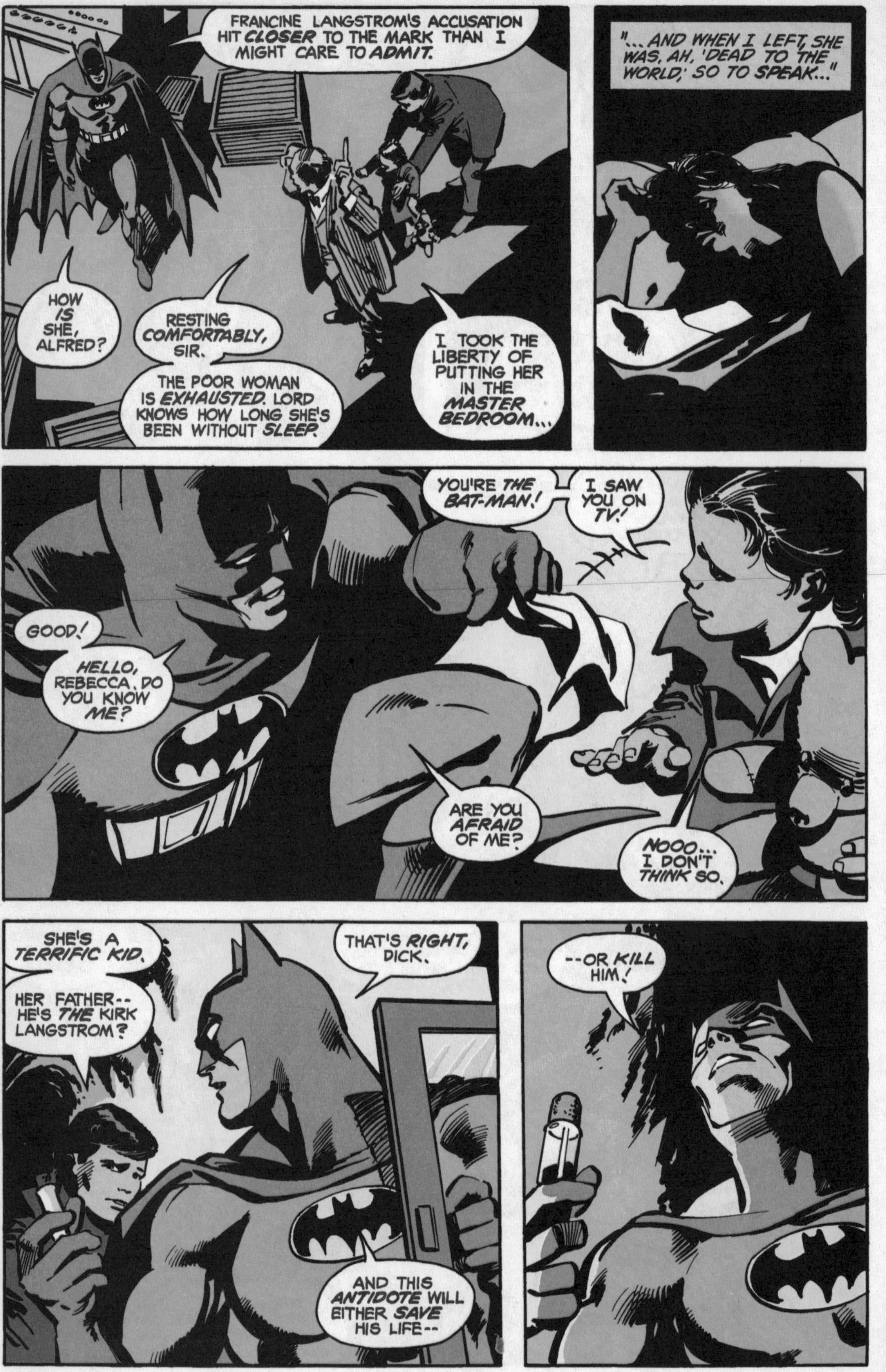
FRANCINE LANGSTROM'S ACCUSATION HIT CLOSER TO THE MARK THAN I MIGHT CARE TO ADMIT.
HOW IS SHE, ALFRED?
RESTING COMFORTABLY, SIR.
THE POOR WOMAN IS EXHAUSTED. LORD KNOWS HOW LONG SHE'S BEEN WITHOUT SLEEP.
I TOOK THE LIBERTY OF PUTTING HER IN THE MASTER BEDROOM...
"...AND WHEN I LEFT, SHE WAS, AH, 'DEAD TO THE WORLD,' SO TO SPEAK..."
YOU'RE THE BAT-MAN!
I SAW YOU ON TV!
GOOD!
HELLO, REBECCA. DO YOU KNOW ME?
ARE YOU AFRAID OF ME?
NOOO... I DON'T THINK SO.
SHE'S A TERRIFIC KID.
HER FATHER-- HE'S THE KIRK LANGSTROM?
THAT'S RIGHT, DICK.
AND THIS ANTIDOTE WILL EITHER SAVE HIS LIFE--
--OR KILL HIM!

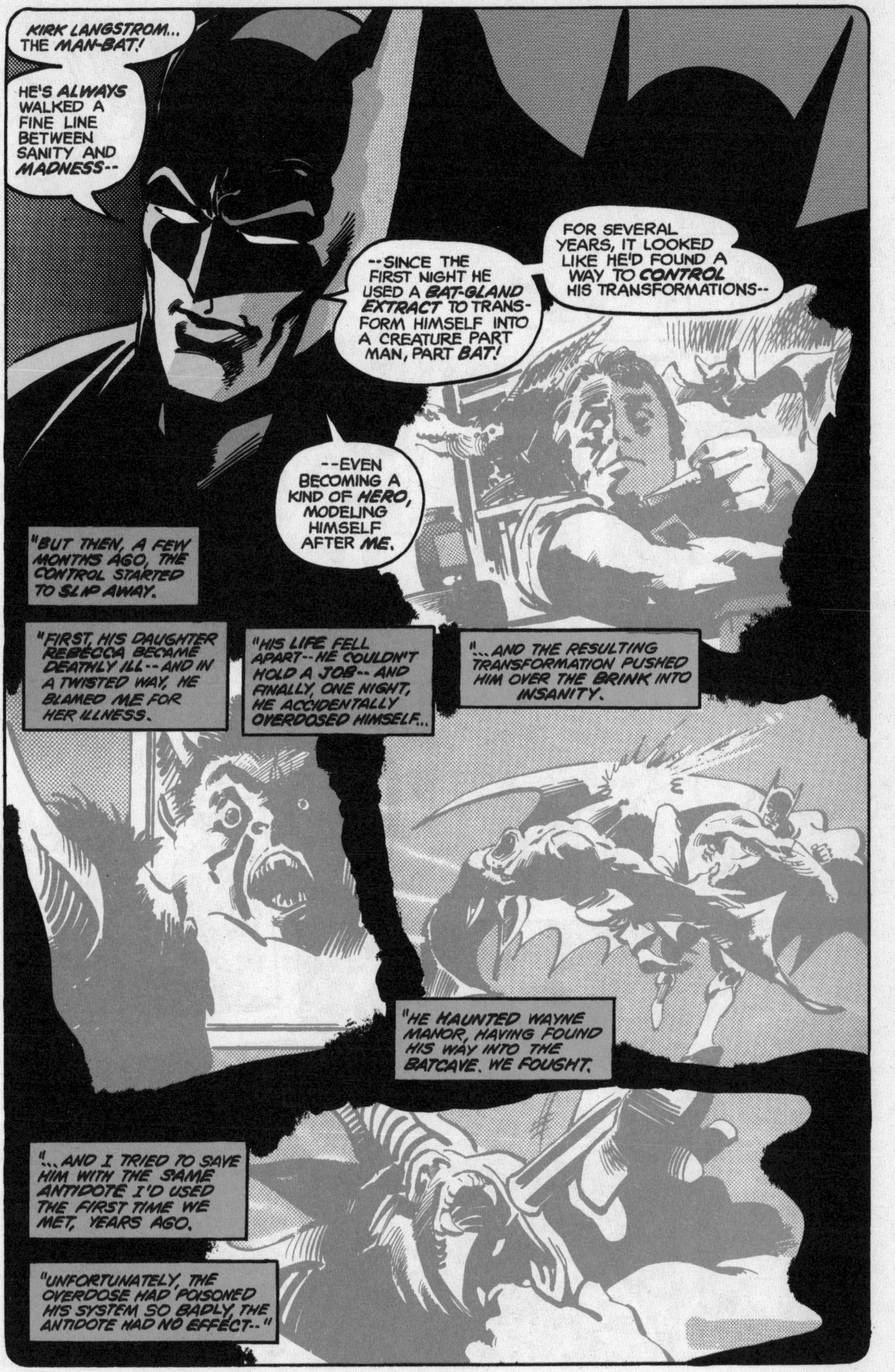
KIRK LANGSTROM... THE MAN-BAT!
HE'S ALWAYS WALKED A FINE LINE BETWEEN SANITY AND MADNESS--
--SINCE THE FIRST NIGHT HE USED A BAT-GLAND EXTRACT TO TRANSFORM HIMSELF INTO A CREATURE PART MAN, PART BAT!
FOR SEVERAL YEARS, IT LOOKED LIKE HE'D FOUND A WAY TO CONTROL HIS TRANSFORMATIONS--
--EVEN BECOMING A KIND OF HERO, MODELING HIMSELF AFTER ME.
"BUT THEN, A FEW MONTHS AGO, THE CONTROL STARTED TO SLIP AWAY.
"FIRST, HIS DAUGHTER REBECCA BECAME DEATHLY ILL--AND IN A TWISTED WAY, HE BLAMED ME FOR HER ILLNESS.
"HIS LIFE FELL APART--HE COULDN'T HOLD A JOB--AND FINALLY, ONE NIGHT, HE ACCIDENTALLY OVERDOSED HIMSELF...
"...AND THE RESULTING TRANSFORMATION PUSHED HIM OVER THE BRINK INTO INSANITY.
"HE HAUNTED WAYNE MANOR, HAVING FOUND HIS WAY INTO THE BATCAVE. WE FOUGHT.
"...AND I TRIED TO SAVE HIM WITH THE SAME ANTIDOTE I'D USED THE FIRST TIME WE MET, YEARS AGO.
"UNFORTUNATELY, THE OVERDOSE HAD POISONED HIS SYSTEM SO BADLY, THE ANTIDOTE HAD NO EFFECT--"

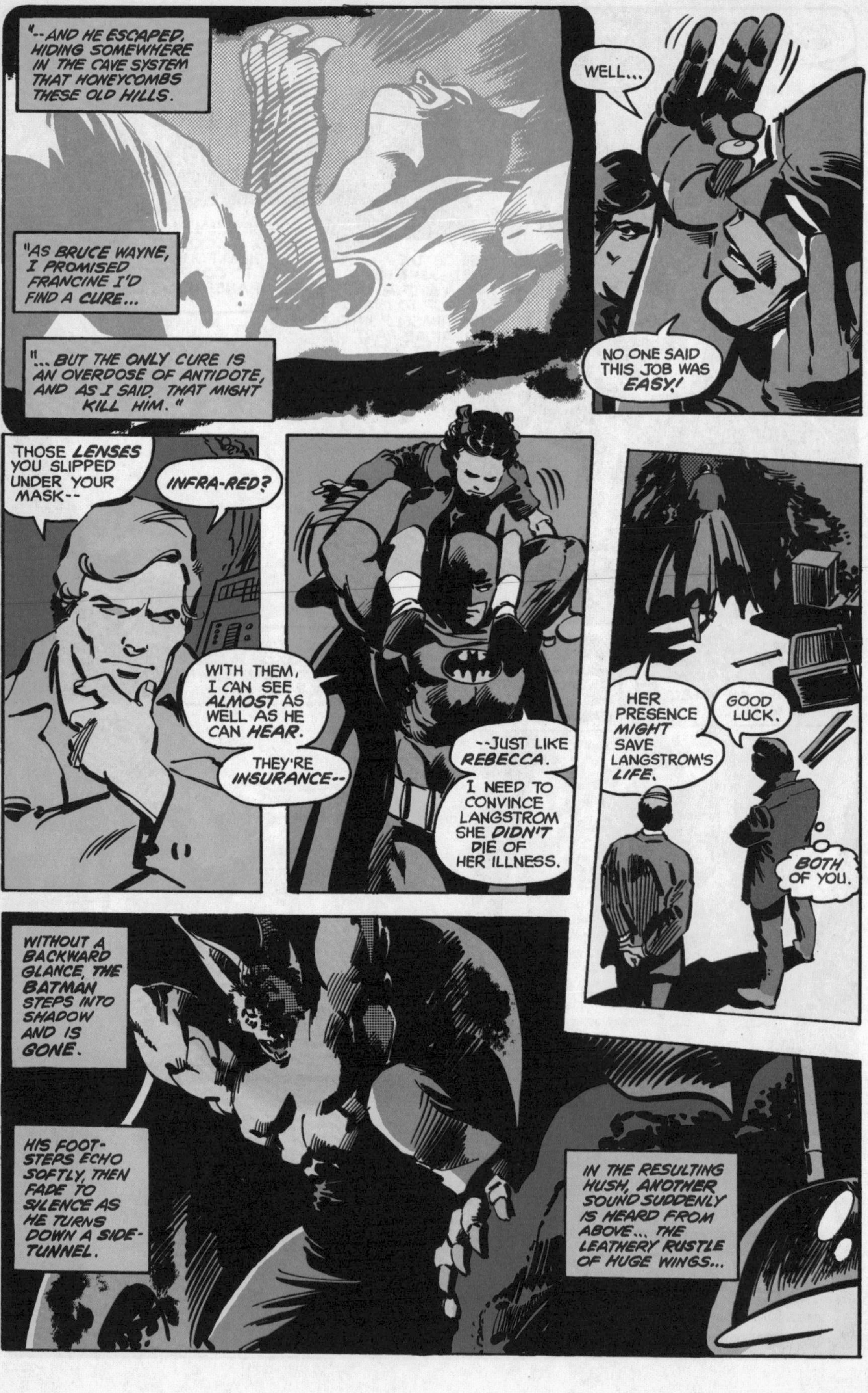
"--AND HE ESCAPED, HIDING SOMEWHERE IN THE CAVE SYSTEM THAT HONEYCOMBS THESE OLD HILLS.
"AS BRUCE WAYNE, I PROMISED FRANCINE I'D FIND A CURE...
"...BUT THE ONLY CURE IS AN OVERDOSE OF ANTIDOTE, AND AS I SAID, THAT MIGHT KILL HIM."
WELL...
NO ONE SAID THIS JOB WAS EASY!
THOSE LENSES YOU SLIPPED UNDER YOUR MASK--
INFRA-RED?
WITH THEM, I CAN SEE ALMOST AS WELL AS HE CAN HEAR.
THEY'RE INSURANCE--
--JUST LIKE REBECCA.
I NEED TO CONVINCE LANGSTROM SHE DIDN'T DIE OF HER ILLNESS.
HER PRESENCE MIGHT SAVE LANGSTROM'S LIFE.
GOOD LUCK.
BOTH OF YOU.
WITHOUT A BACKWARD GLANCE, THE BATMAN STEPS INTO SHADOW AND IS GONE.
HIS FOOT-STEPS ECHO SOFTLY, THEN FADE TO SILENCE AS HE TURNS DOWN A SIDE-TUNNEL.
IN THE RESULTING HUSH, ANOTHER SOUND SUDDENLY IS HEARD FROM ABOVE... THE LEATHERY RUSTLE OF HUGE WINGS...

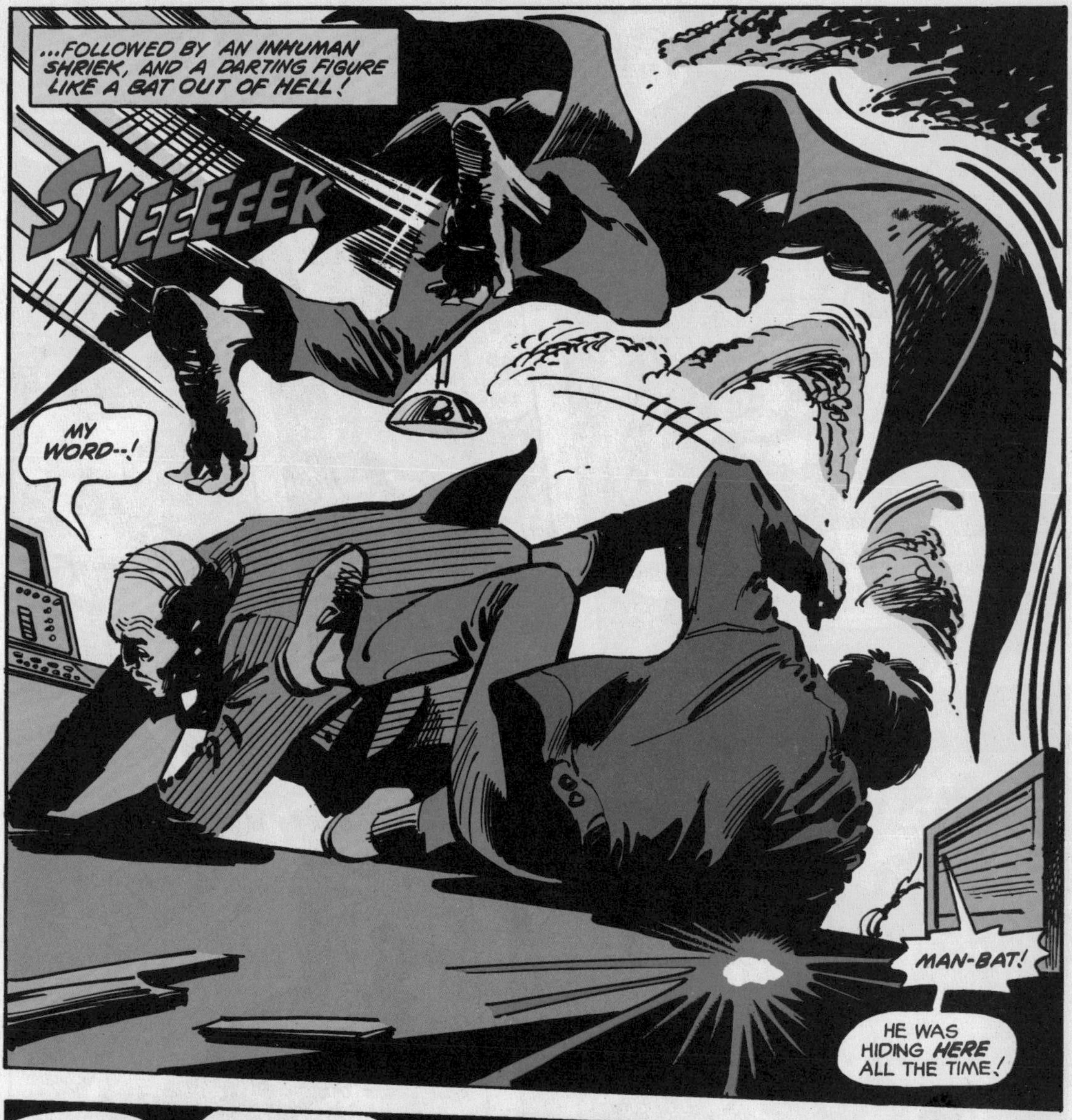
...FOLLOWED BY AN INHUMAN SHRIEK, AND A DARTING FIGURE LIKE A BAT OUT OF HELL!
SKEEEEEK
MY WORD--!
MAN-BAT!
HE WAS HIDING HERE ALL THE TIME!

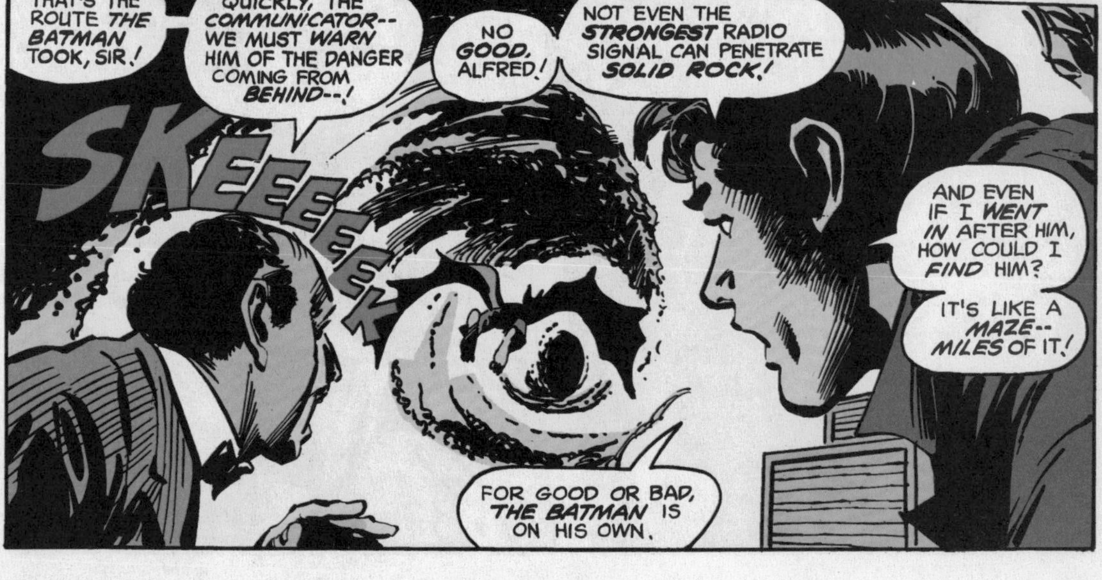
THAT'S THE ROUTE THE BATMAN TOOK, SIR!
QUICKLY, THE COMMUNICATOR-- WE MUST WARN HIM OF THE DANGER COMING FROM BEHIND--!
NO GOOD, ALFRED!
NOT EVEN THE STRONGEST RADIO SIGNAL CAN PENETRATE SOLID ROCK!
SKEEEEEK
AND EVEN IF I WENT IN AFTER HIM, HOW COULD I FIND HIM?
IT'S LIKE A MAZE-- MILES OF IT!
FOR GOOD OR BAD, THE BATMAN IS ON HIS OWN.

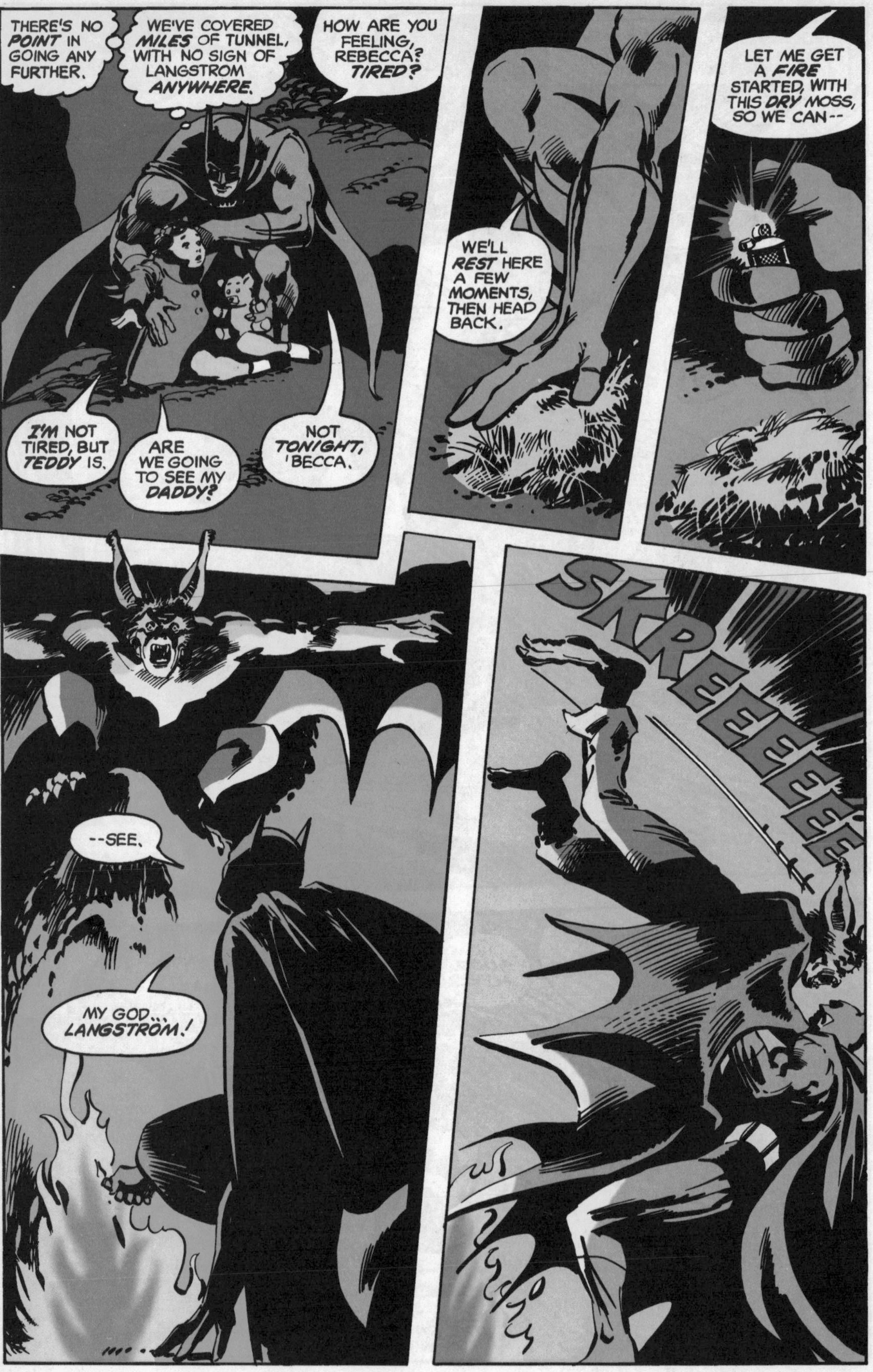
THERE'S NO POINT IN GOING ANY FURTHER.
WE'VE COVERED MILES OF TUNNEL, WITH NO SIGN OF LANGSTROM ANYWHERE.
HOW ARE YOU FEELING, REBECCA? TIRED?
I'M NOT TIRED, BUT TEDDY IS.
ARE WE GOING TO SEE MY DADDY?
NOT TONIGHT, 'BECCA.
WE'LL REST HERE A FEW MOMENTS, THEN HEAD BACK.
LET ME GET A FIRE STARTED, WITH THIS DRY MOSS, SO WE CAN--
--SEE.
MY GOD... LANGSTROM!
SKREEEEEEEE

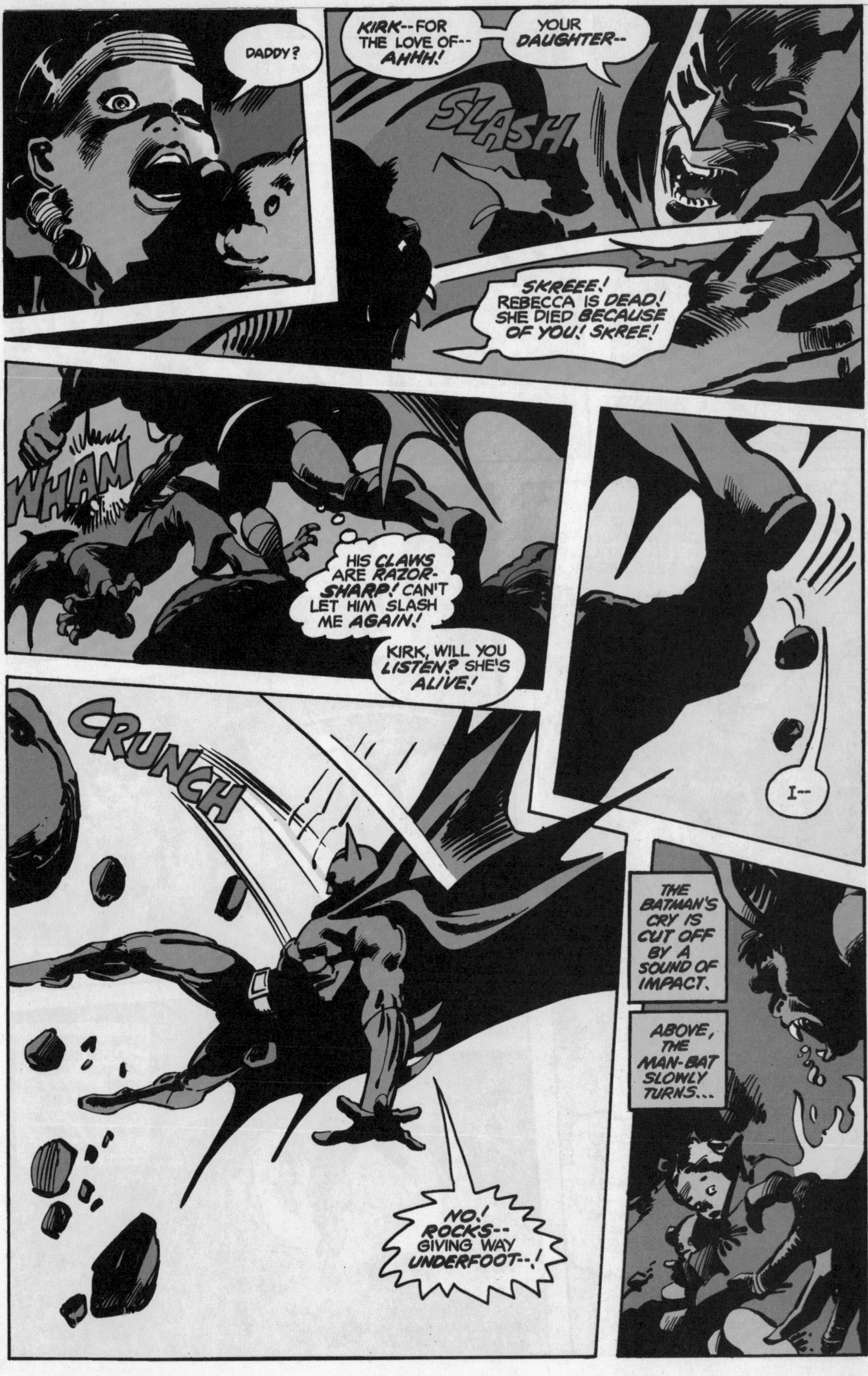
DADDY?
KIRK--FOR THE LOVE OF-- AHHH!
YOUR DAUGHTER--
SLASH
SKREEE! REBECCA IS DEAD! SHE DIED BECAUSE OF YOU! SKREE!
WHAM
HIS CLAWS ARE RAZOR-SHARP! CAN'T LET HIM SLASH ME AGAIN!
KIRK, WILL YOU LISTEN? SHE'S ALIVE!
I--
CRUNCH
NO! ROCKS--GIVING WAY UNDERFOOT--!
THE BATMAN'S CRY IS CUT OFF BY A SOUND OF IMPACT.
ABOVE, THE MAN-BAT SLOWLY TURNS...

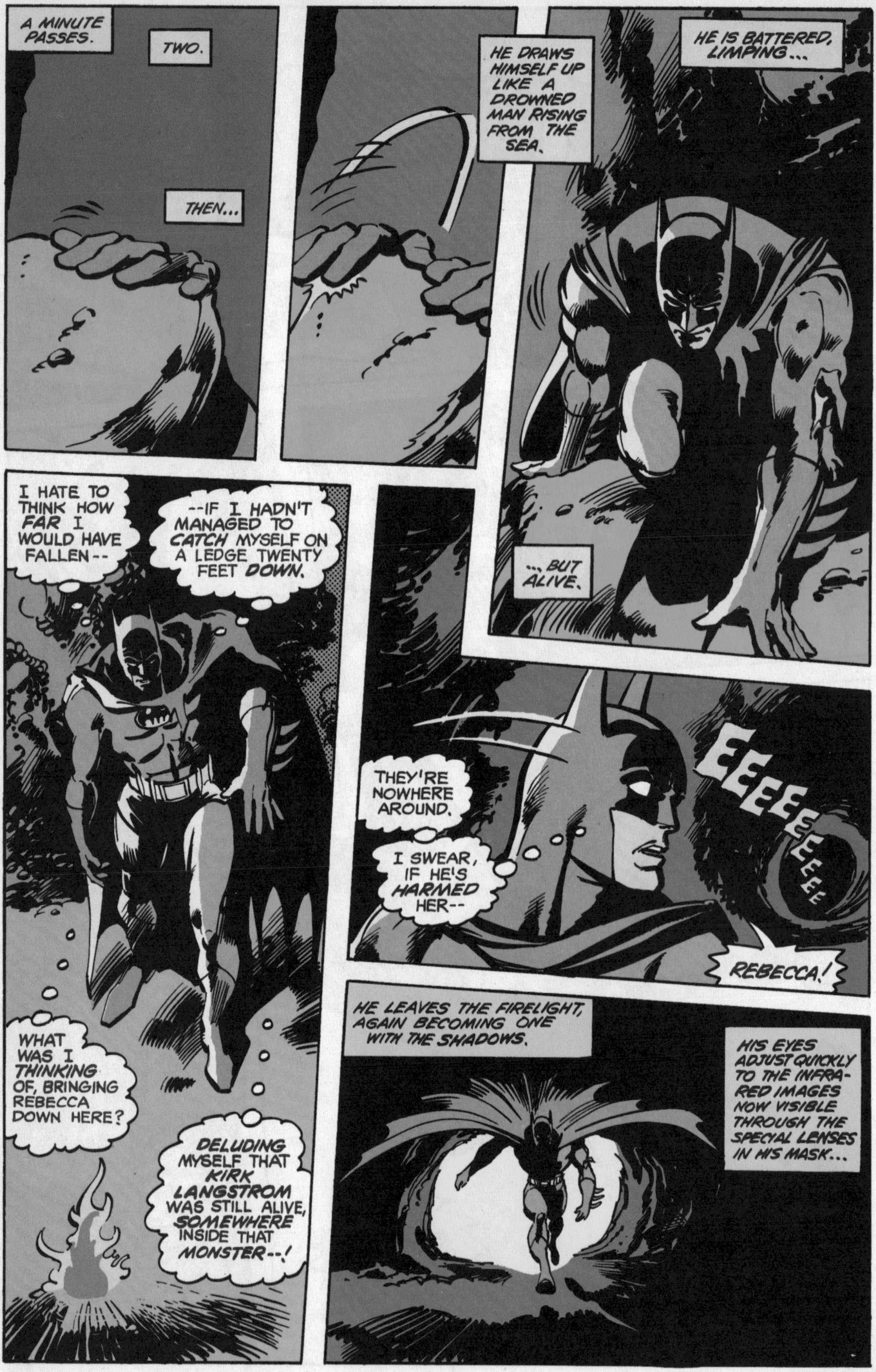

A MINUTE PASSES.
TWO.
THEN...
HE DRAWS HIMSELF UP LIKE A DROWNED MAN RISING FROM THE SEA.
HE IS BATTERED, LIMPING...
...BUT ALIVE.
I HATE TO THINK HOW FAR I WOULD HAVE FALLEN--
--IF I HADN'T MANAGED TO CATCH MYSELF ON A LEDGE TWENTY FEET DOWN.
WHAT WAS I THINKING OF, BRINGING REBECCA DOWN HERE?
DELUDING MYSELF THAT KIRK LANGSTROM WAS STILL ALIVE, SOMEWHERE INSIDE THAT MONSTER--!
THEY'RE NOWHERE AROUND.
I SWEAR, IF HE'S HARMED HER--
EEEEEEEEEE
REBECCA!
HE LEAVES THE FIRELIGHT, AGAIN BECOMING ONE WITH THE SHADOWS.
HIS EYES ADJUST QUICKLY TO THE INFRA-RED IMAGES NOW VISIBLE THROUGH THE SPECIAL LENSES IN HIS MASK...

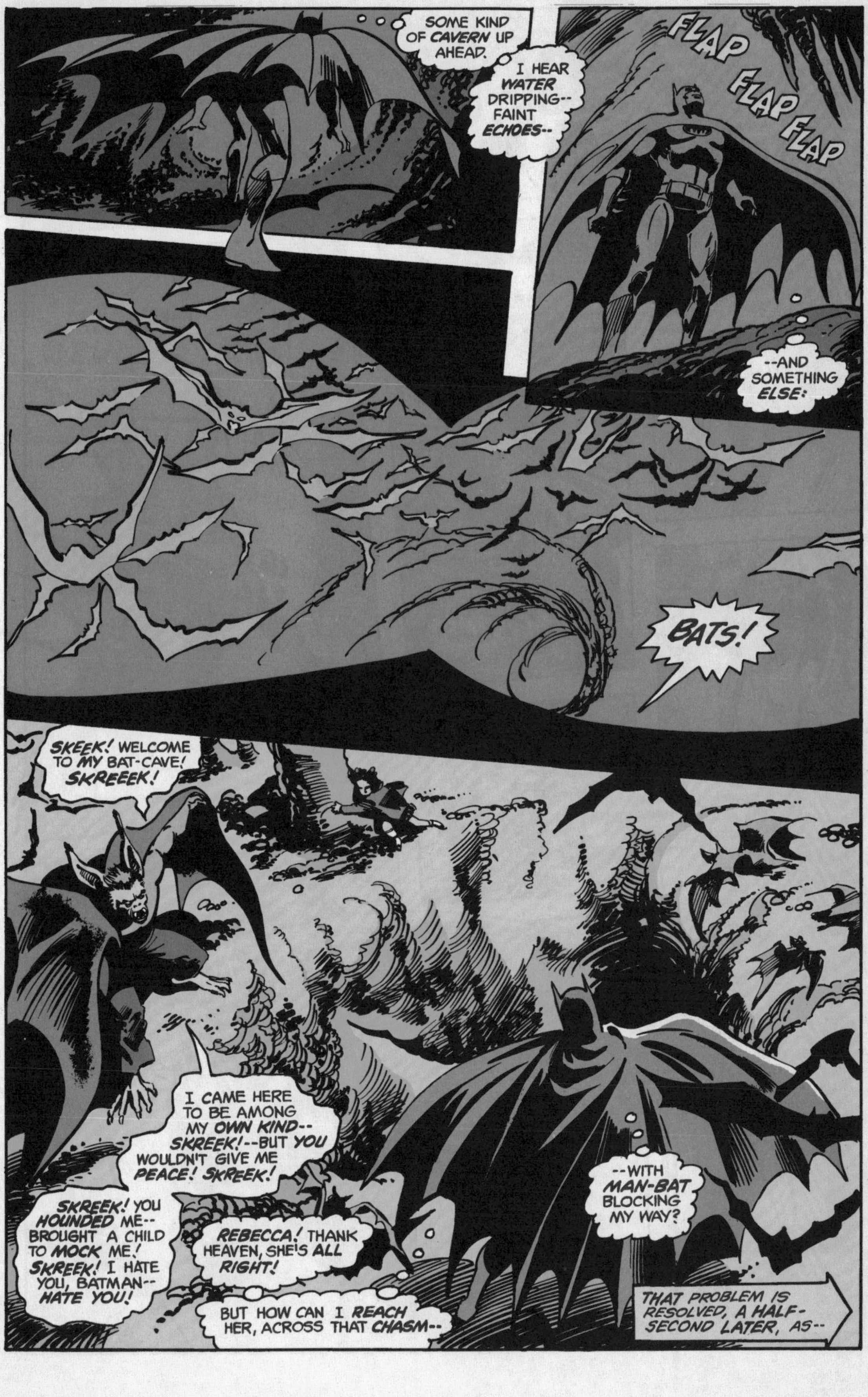
SOME KIND OF CAVERN UP AHEAD.
I HEAR WATER DRIPPING-- FAINT ECHOES--
FLAP FLAP FLAP
--AND SOMETHING ELSE:
BATS!
SKEEK! WELCOME TO MY BAT-CAVE! SKREEEK!
I CAME HERE TO BE AMONG MY OWN KIND-- SKREEK!--BUT YOU WOULDN'T GIVE ME PEACE! SKREEK!
SKREEK! YOU HOUNDED ME-- BROUGHT A CHILD TO MOCK ME! SKREEK! I HATE YOU, BATMAN-- HATE YOU!
REBECCA! THANK HEAVEN, SHE'S ALL RIGHT!
BUT HOW CAN I REACH HER, ACROSS THAT CHASM--
--WITH MAN-BAT BLOCKING MY WAY?
THAT PROBLEM IS RESOLVED, A HALF-SECOND LATER, AS--

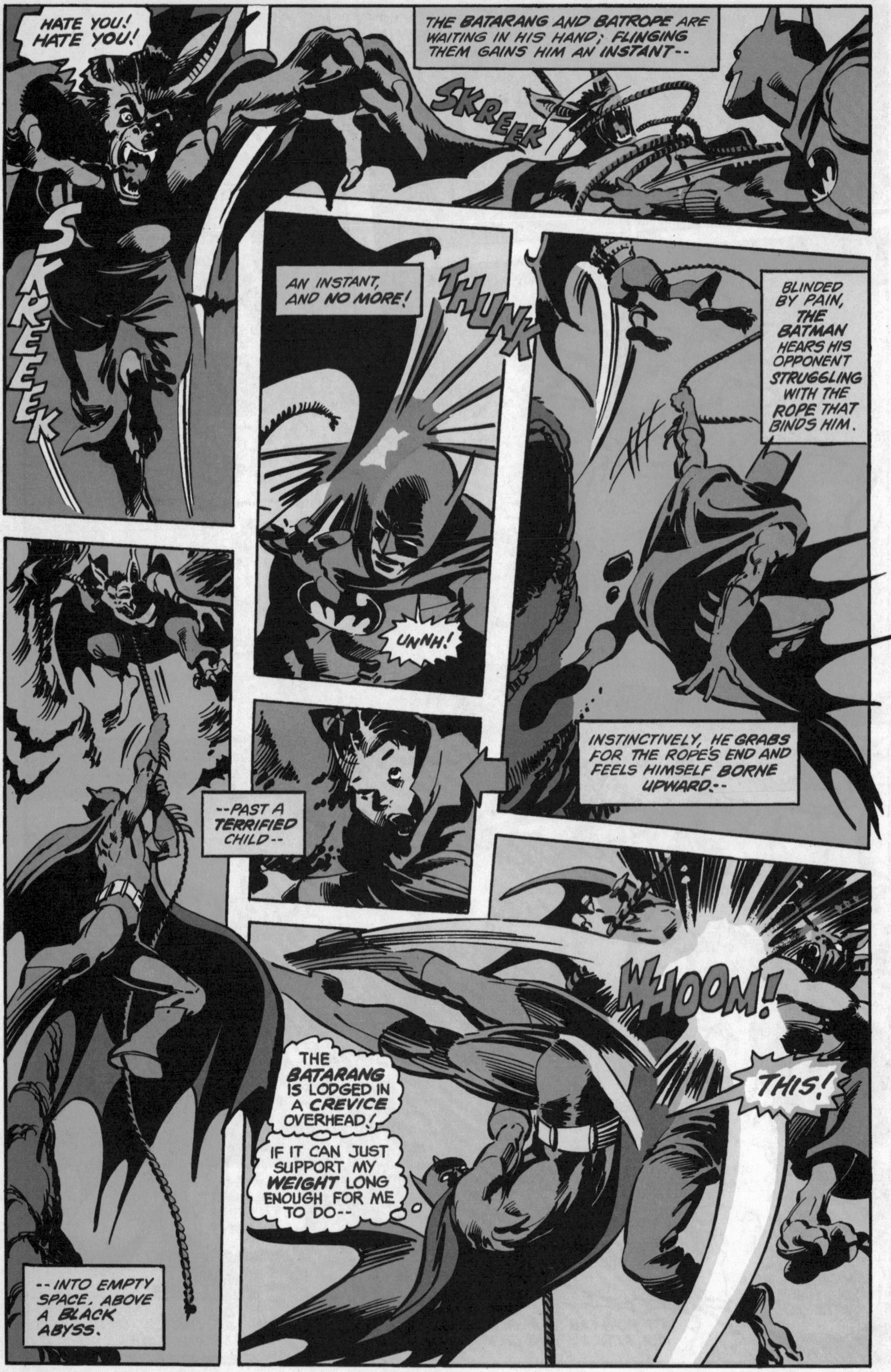
HATE YOU! HATE YOU!
THE BATARANG AND BATROPE ARE WAITING IN HIS HAND; FLINGING THEM GAINS HIM AN INSTANT--
SKREEK
SKREEEEK
AN INSTANT, AND NO MORE!
THUNK
UNNH!
BLINDED BY PAIN, THE BATMAN HEARS HIS OPPONENT STRUGGLING WITH THE ROPE THAT BINDS HIM.
INSTINCTIVELY, HE GRABS FOR THE ROPE'S END AND FEELS HIMSELF BORNE UPWARD--
--PAST A TERRIFIED CHILD--
--INTO EMPTY SPACE, ABOVE A BLACK ABYSS.
THE BATARANG IS LODGED IN A CREVICE OVERHEAD!
IF IT CAN JUST SUPPORT MY WEIGHT LONG ENOUGH FOR ME TO DO--
WHOOM!
THIS!

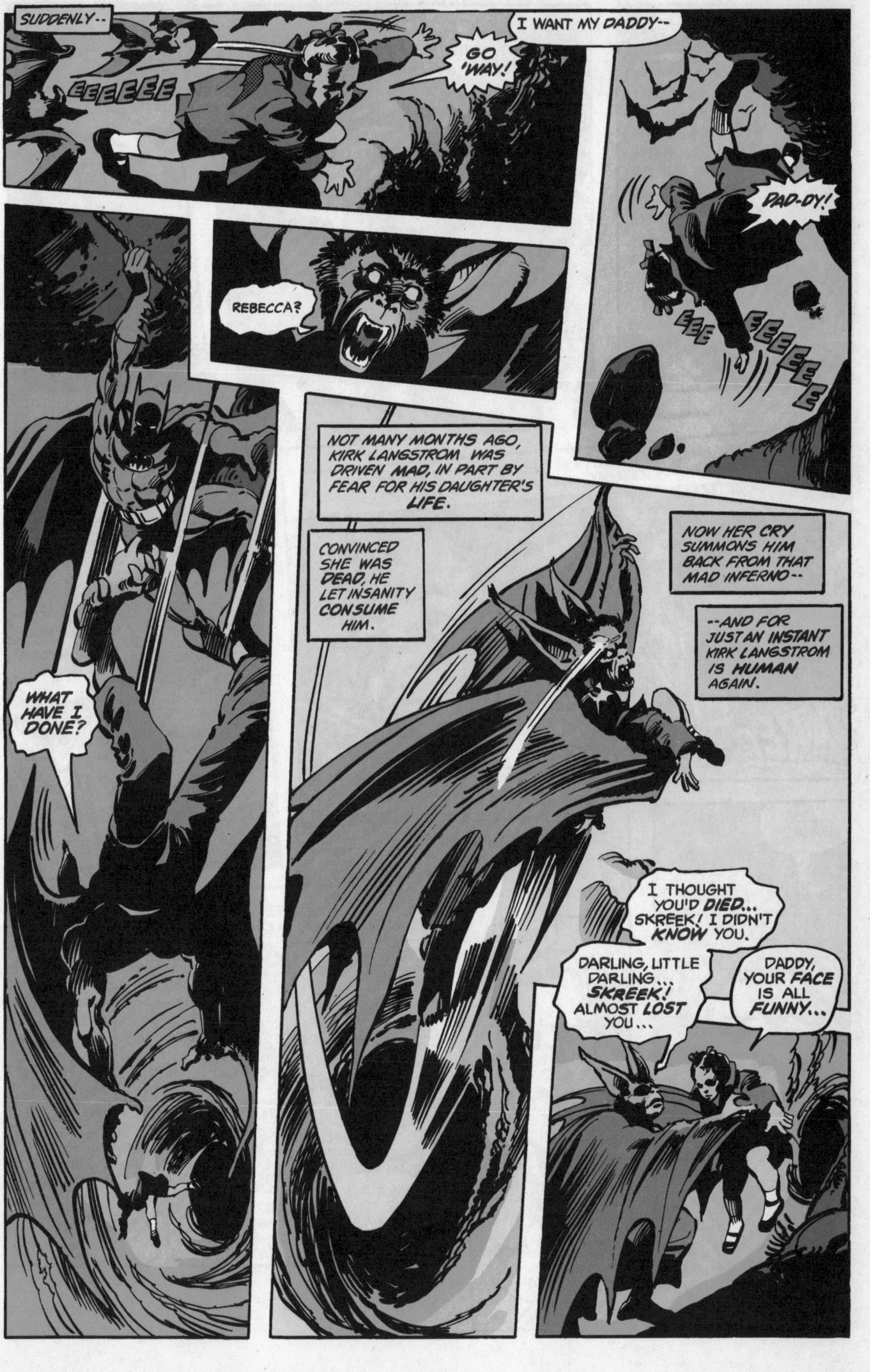
SUDDENLY--
EEEEEE
GO 'WAY!
I WANT MY DADDY--
DAD-DY!
EEE EEEEEE
REBECCA?
NOT MANY MONTHS AGO, KIRK LANGSTROM WAS DRIVEN MAD, IN PART BY FEAR FOR HIS DAUGHTER'S LIFE.
CONVINCED SHE WAS DEAD, HE LET INSANITY CONSUME HIM.
NOW HER CRY SUMMONS HIM BACK FROM THAT MAD INFERNO--
--AND FOR JUST AN INSTANT KIRK LANGSTROM IS HUMAN AGAIN.
WHAT HAVE I DONE?
I THOUGHT YOU'D DIED... SKREEK! I DIDN'T KNOW YOU.
DARLING, LITTLE DARLING... SKREEK! ALMOST LOST YOU...
DADDY, YOUR FACE IS ALL FUNNY...

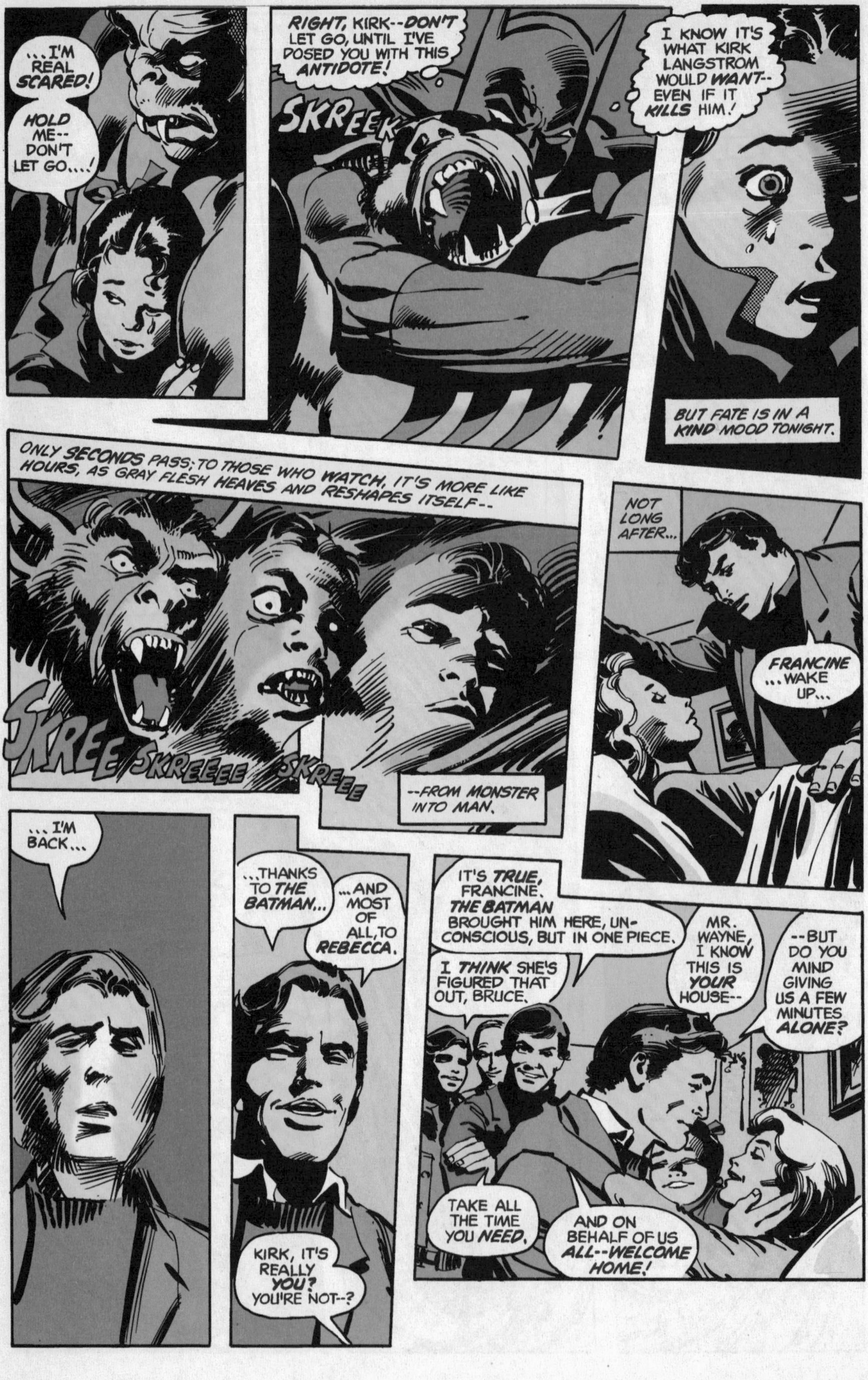
...I'M REAL SCARED!
HOLD ME-- DON'T LET GO....!
RIGHT, KIRK--DON'T LET GO, UNTIL I'VE DOSED YOU WITH THIS ANTIDOTE!
SKREEEK
I KNOW IT'S WHAT KIRK LANGSTROM WOULD WANT-- EVEN IF IT KILLS HIM!
BUT FATE IS IN A KIND MOOD TONIGHT.
ONLY SECONDS PASS; TO THOSE WHO WATCH, IT'S MORE LIKE HOURS, AS GRAY FLESH HEAVES AND RESHAPES ITSELF--
SKREEE SKREEEEE SKREEE
--FROM MONSTER INTO MAN.
NOT LONG AFTER...
FRANCINE ...WAKE UP...
...I'M BACK...
...THANKS TO THE BATMAN...
...AND MOST OF ALL, TO REBECCA.
KIRK, IT'S REALLY YOU? YOU'RE NOT--?
IT'S TRUE, FRANCINE. THE BATMAN BROUGHT HIM HERE, UN-CONSCIOUS, BUT IN ONE PIECE.
I THINK SHE'S FIGURED THAT OUT, BRUCE.
MR. WAYNE, I KNOW THIS IS YOUR HOUSE--
--BUT DO YOU MIND GIVING US A FEW MINUTES ALONE?
TAKE ALL THE TIME YOU NEED.
AND ON BEHALF OF US ALL--WELCOME HOME!

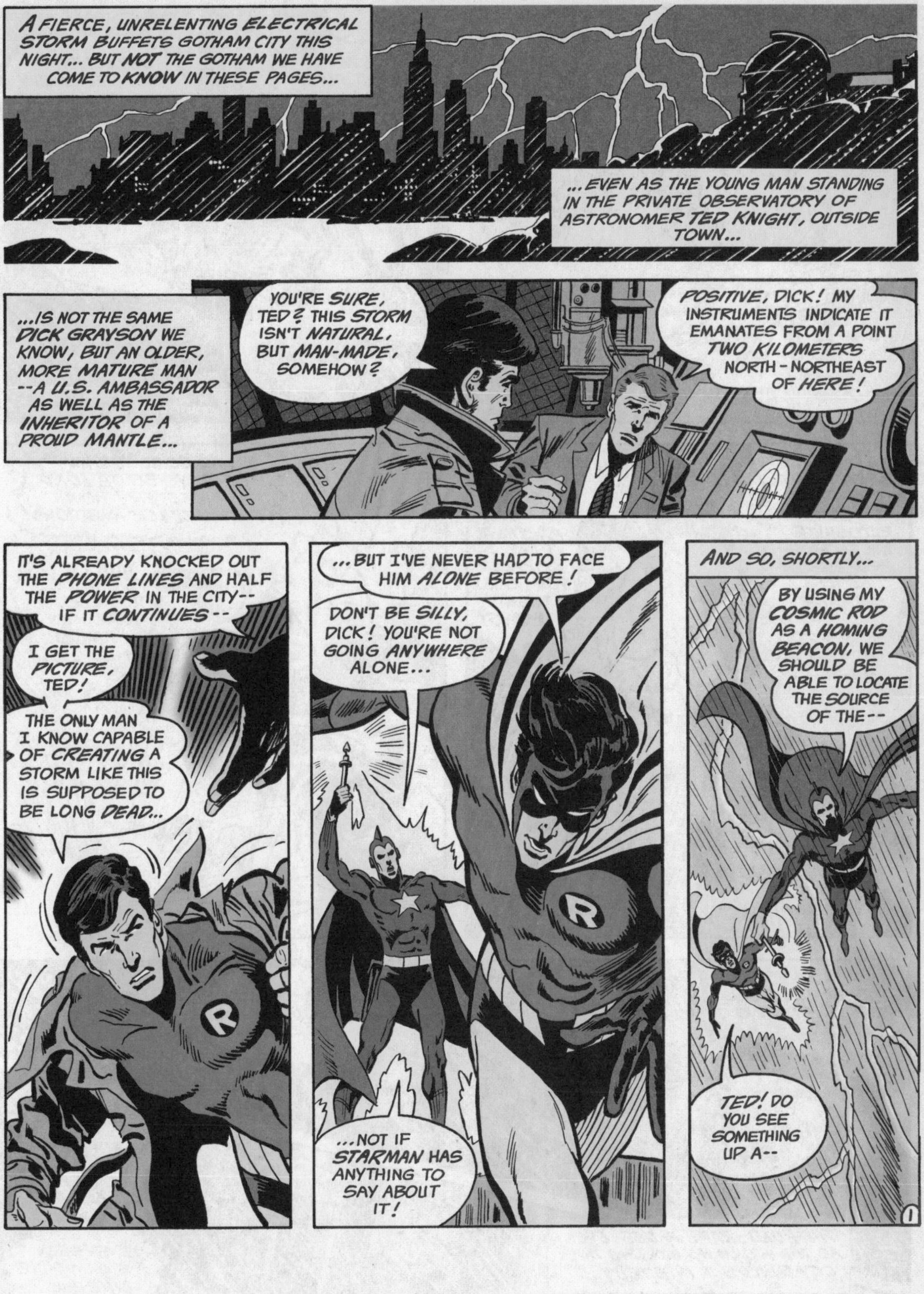
A FIERCE, UNRELENTING ELECTRICAL STORM BUFFETS GOTHAM CITY THIS NIGHT... BUT NOT THE GOTHAM WE HAVE COME TO KNOW IN THESE PAGES...
...EVEN AS THE YOUNG MAN STANDING IN THE PRIVATE OBSERVATORY OF ASTRONOMER TED KNIGHT, OUTSIDE TOWN...
...IS NOT THE SAME DICK GRAYSON WE KNOW, BUT AN OLDER, MORE MATURE MAN --A U.S. AMBASSADOR AS WELL AS THE INHERITOR OF A PROUD MANTLE...
YOU'RE SURE, TED? THIS STORM ISN'T NATURAL, BUT MAN-MADE, SOMEHOW?
POSITIVE, DICK! MY INSTRUMENTS INDICATE IT EMANATES FROM A POINT TWO KILOMETERS NORTH-NORTHEAST OF HERE!
IT'S ALREADY KNOCKED OUT THE PHONE LINES AND HALF THE POWER IN THE CITY-- IF IT CONTINUES --
I GET THE PICTURE, TED!
THE ONLY MAN I KNOW CAPABLE OF CREATING A STORM LIKE THIS IS SUPPOSED TO BE LONG DEAD...
...BUT I'VE NEVER HAD TO FACE HIM ALONE BEFORE!
DON'T BE SILLY, DICK! YOU'RE NOT GOING ANYWHERE ALONE...
...NOT IF STARMAN HAS ANYTHING TO SAY ABOUT IT!
AND SO, SHORTLY...
BY USING MY COSMIC ROD AS A HOMING BEACON, WE SHOULD BE ABLE TO LOCATE THE SOURCE OF THE--
TED! DO YOU SEE SOMETHING UP A--
1

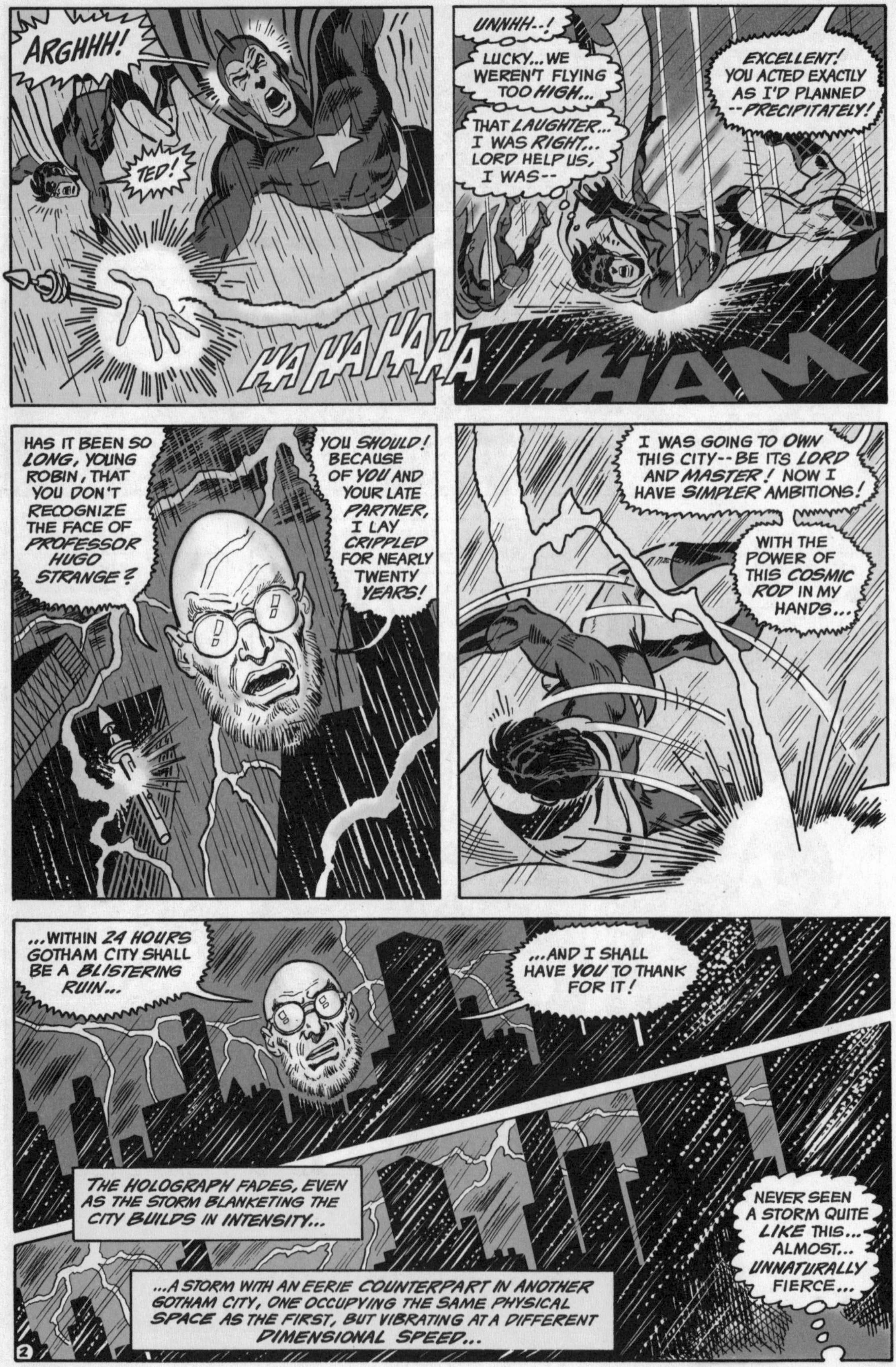
ARGHHH!
TED!
UNNHH..!
LUCKY... WE WEREN'T FLYING TOO HIGH...
THAT LAUGHTER... I WAS RIGHT... LORD HELP US, I WAS--
EXCELLENT! YOU ACTED EXACTLY AS I'D PLANNED --PRECIPITATELY!
HAHAHAHAHA
WHAM
HAS IT BEEN SO LONG, YOUNG ROBIN, THAT YOU DON'T RECOGNIZE THE FACE OF PROFESSOR HUGO STRANGE?
YOU SHOULD! BECAUSE OF YOU AND YOUR LATE PARTNER, I LAY CRIPPLED FOR NEARLY TWENTY YEARS!
I WAS GOING TO OWN THIS CITY--BE ITS LORD AND MASTER! NOW I HAVE SIMPLER AMBITIONS!
WITH THE POWER OF THIS COSMIC ROD IN MY HANDS...
...WITHIN 24 HOURS GOTHAM CITY SHALL BE A BLISTERING RUIN...
...AND I SHALL HAVE YOU TO THANK FOR IT!
THE HOLOGRAPH FADES, EVEN AS THE STORM BLANKETING THE CITY BUILDS IN INTENSITY...
NEVER SEEN A STORM QUITE LIKE THIS... ALMOST... UNNATURALLY FIERCE...
...A STORM WITH AN EERIE COUNTERPART IN ANOTHER GOTHAM CITY, ONE OCCUPYING THE SAME PHYSICAL SPACE AS THE FIRST, BUT VIBRATING AT A DIFFERENT DIMENSIONAL SPEED...
2

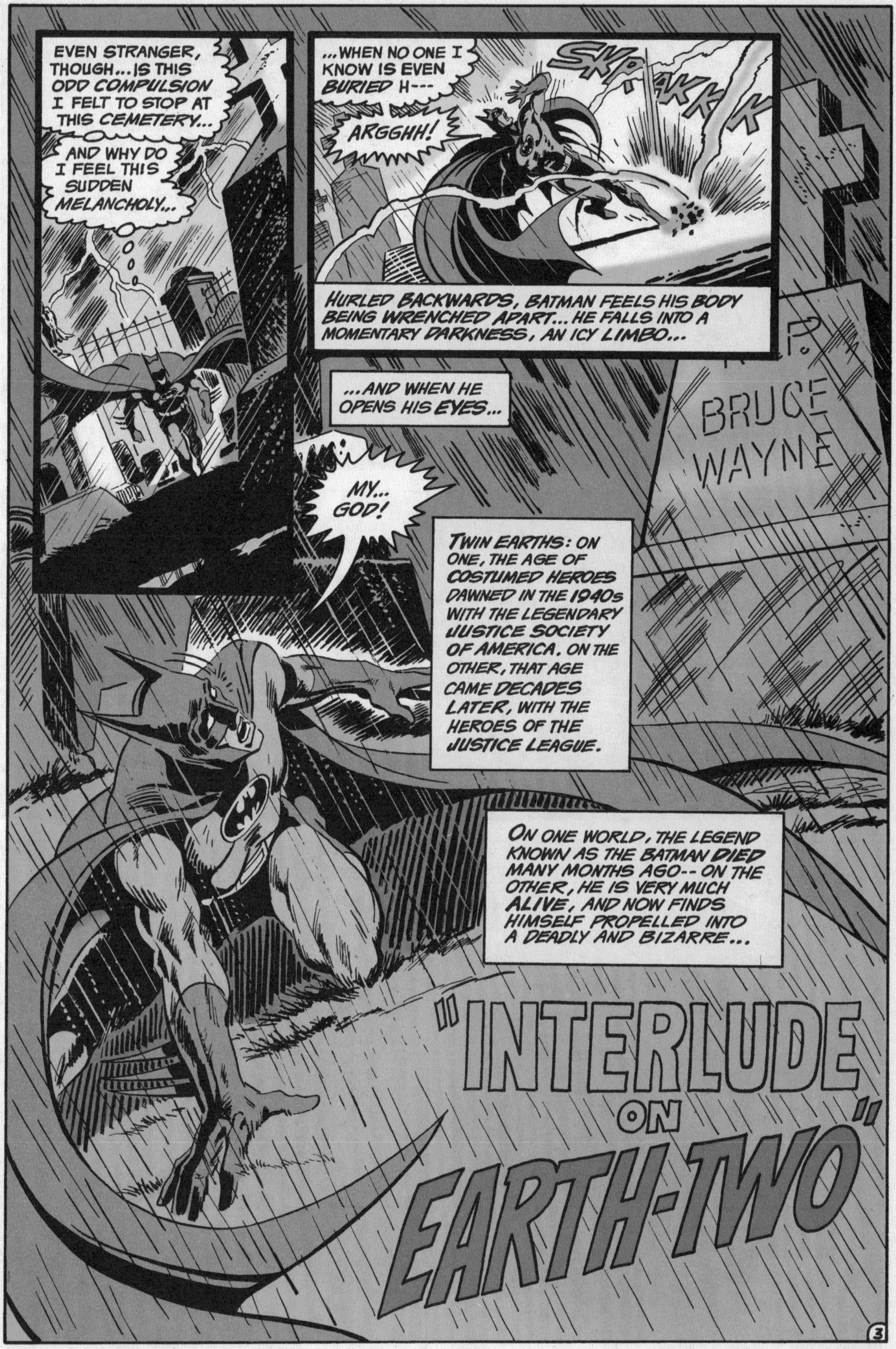
EVEN STRANGER, THOUGH...IS THIS ODD COMPULSION I FELT TO STOP AT THIS CEMETERY...
AND WHY DO I FEEL THIS SUDDEN MELANCHOLY...
...WHEN NO ONE I KNOW IS EVEN BURIED H---
SKPAKKK
ARGGHH!
HURLED BACKWARDS, BATMAN FEELS HIS BODY BEING WRENCHED APART... HE FALLS INTO A MOMENTARY DARKNESS, AN ICY LIMBO...
...AND WHEN HE OPENS HIS EYES...
R.I.P.
BRUCE WAYNE
MY... GOD!
TWIN EARTHS: ON ONE, THE AGE OF COSTUMED HEROES DAWNED IN THE 1940s WITH THE LEGENDARY JUSTICE SOCIETY OF AMERICA. ON THE OTHER, THAT AGE CAME DECADES LATER, WITH THE HEROES OF THE JUSTICE LEAGUE.
ON ONE WORLD, THE LEGEND KNOWN AS THE BATMAN DIED MANY MONTHS AGO-- ON THE OTHER, HE IS VERY MUCH ALIVE, AND NOW FINDS HIMSELF PROPELLED INTO A DEADLY AND BIZARRE...
"INTERLUDE ON EARTH-TWO"
3

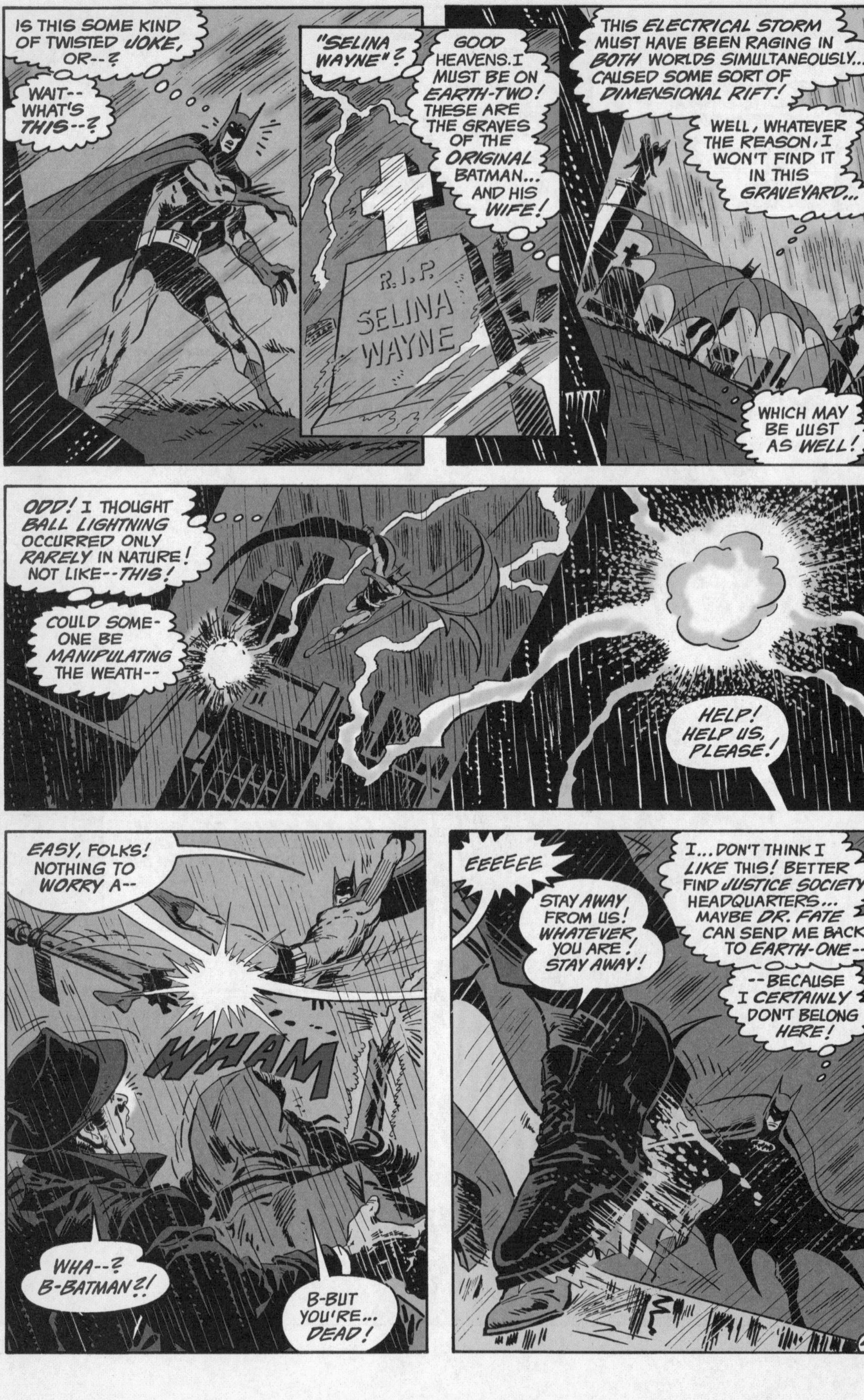
IS THIS SOME KIND OF TWISTED JOKE, OR--?
WAIT-- WHAT'S THIS--?
"SELINA WAYNE"?
GOOD HEAVENS. I MUST BE ON EARTH-TWO! THESE ARE THE GRAVES OF THE ORIGINAL BATMAN... AND HIS WIFE!
R.I.P. SELINA WAYNE
THIS ELECTRICAL STORM MUST HAVE BEEN RAGING IN BOTH WORLDS SIMULTANEOUSLY... CAUSED SOME SORT OF DIMENSIONAL RIFT!
WELL, WHATEVER THE REASON, I WON'T FIND IT IN THIS GRAVEYARD...
WHICH MAY BE JUST AS WELL!
ODD! I THOUGHT BALL LIGHTNING OCCURRED ONLY RARELY IN NATURE! NOT LIKE--THIS!
COULD SOME-ONE BE MANIPULATING THE WEATH--
HELP! HELP US, PLEASE!
EASY, FOLKS! NOTHING TO WORRY A--
WHAM
WHA--? B-BATMAN?!
B-BUT YOU'RE... DEAD!
EEEEEE
STAY AWAY FROM US! WHATEVER YOU ARE! STAY AWAY!
I... DON'T THINK I LIKE THIS! BETTER FIND JUSTICE SOCIETY HEADQUARTERS... MAYBE DR. FATE CAN SEND ME BACK TO EARTH-ONE--
--BECAUSE I CERTAINLY DON'T BELONG HERE!
4

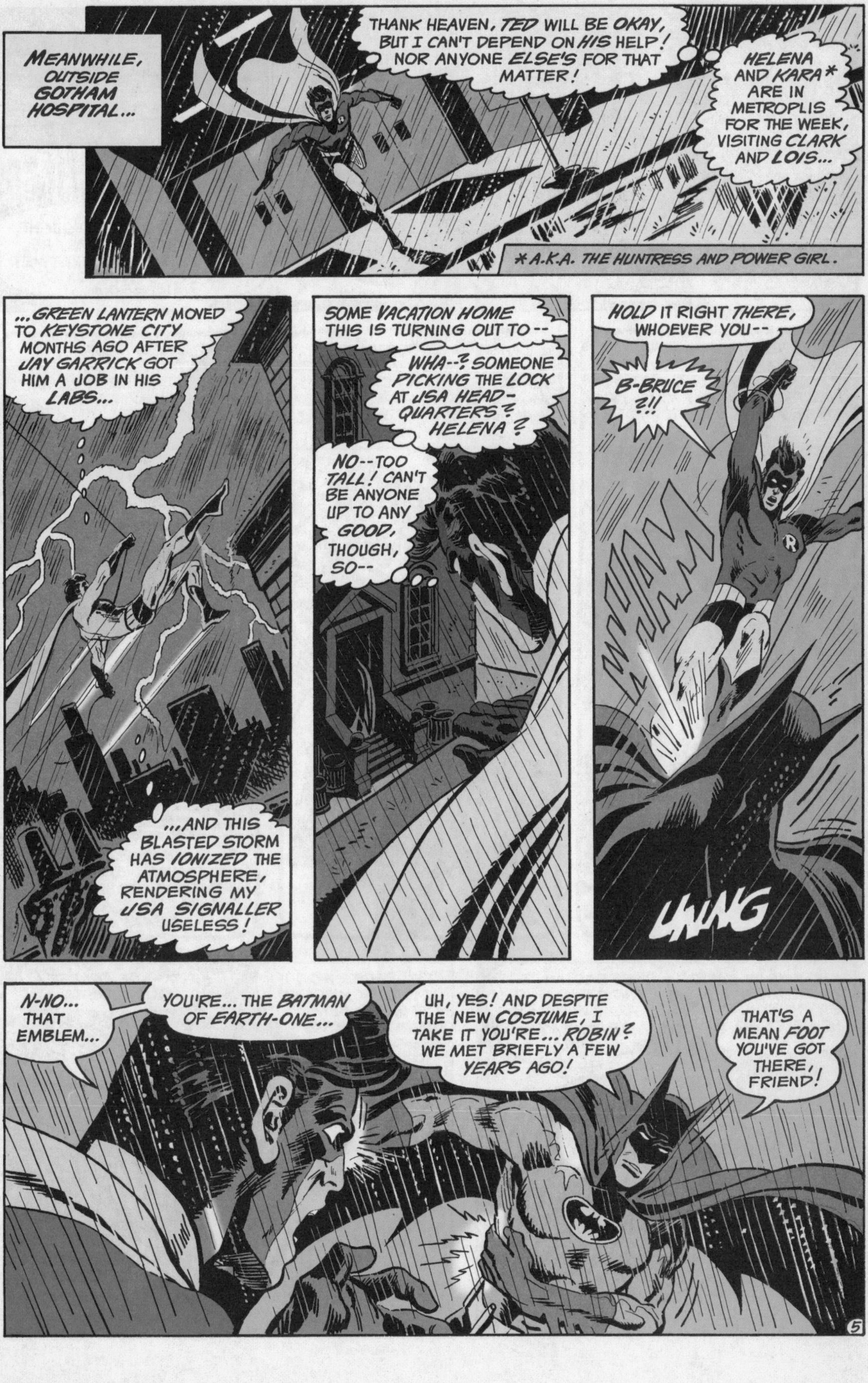
MEANWHILE, OUTSIDE GOTHAM HOSPITAL...
THANK HEAVEN, TED WILL BE OKAY, BUT I CAN'T DEPEND ON HIS HELP! NOR ANYONE ELSE'S FOR THAT MATTER!
HELENA AND KARA* ARE IN METROPLIS FOR THE WEEK, VISITING CLARK AND LOIS...
*A.K.A. THE HUNTRESS AND POWER GIRL.
...GREEN LANTERN MOVED TO KEYSTONE CITY MONTHS AGO AFTER JAY GARRICK GOT HIM A JOB IN HIS LABS...
...AND THIS BLASTED STORM HAS IONIZED THE ATMOSPHERE, RENDERING MY JSA SIGNALLER USELESS!
SOME VACATION HOME THIS IS TURNING OUT TO--
WHA--? SOMEONE PICKING THE LOCK AT JSA HEAD-QUARTERS? HELENA?
NO--TOO TALL! CAN'T BE ANYONE UP TO ANY GOOD, THOUGH, SO--
HOLD IT RIGHT THERE, WHOEVER YOU--
B-BRUCE ?!!
WHAM
UNNG
N-NO... THAT EMBLEM...
YOU'RE... THE BATMAN OF EARTH-ONE...
UH, YES! AND DESPITE THE NEW COSTUME, I TAKE IT YOU'RE... ROBIN? WE MET BRIEFLY A FEW YEARS AGO!
THAT'S A MEAN FOOT YOU'VE GOT THERE, FRIEND!
5

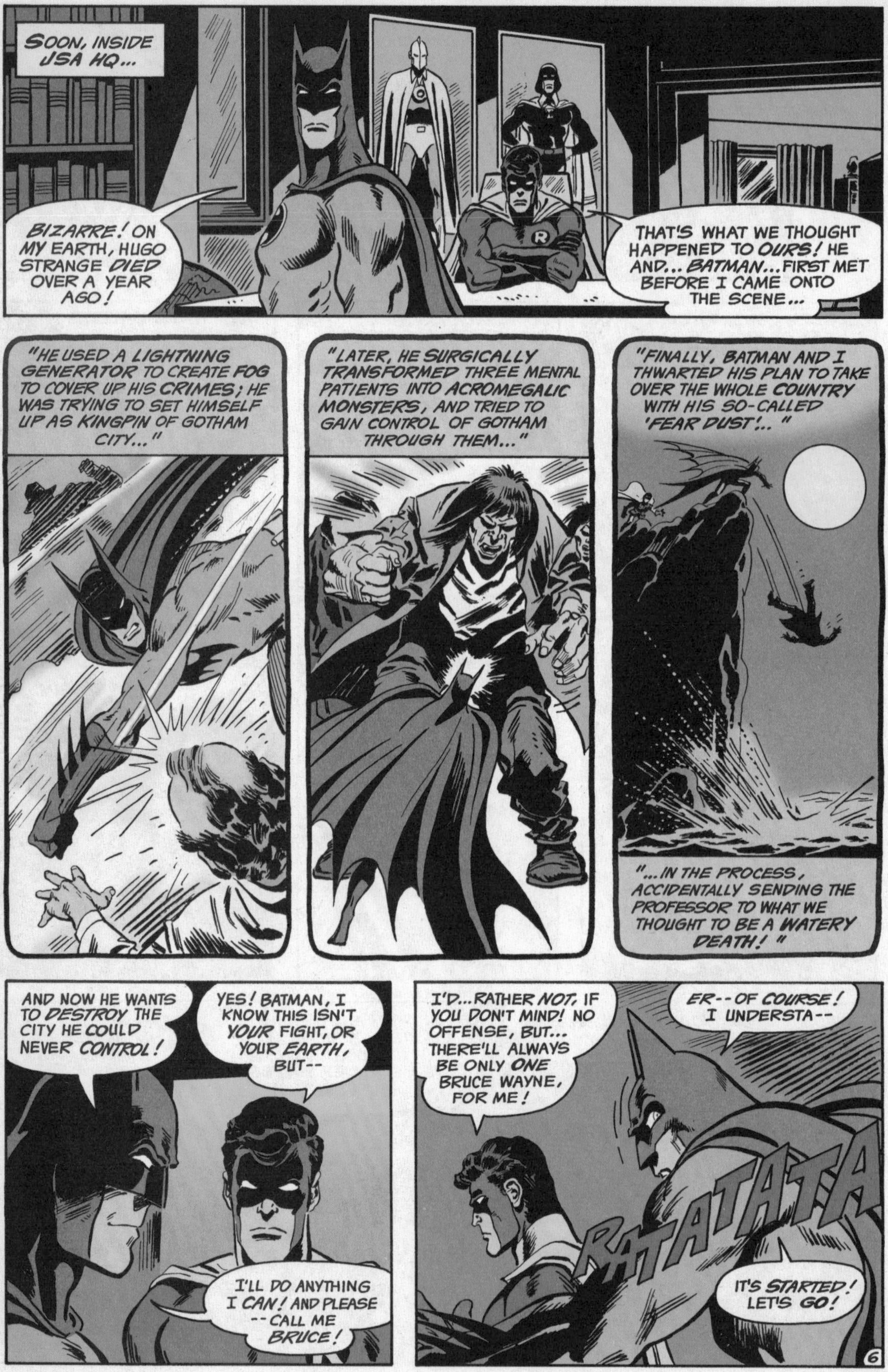
SOON, INSIDE JSA HQ...
BIZARRE! ON MY EARTH, HUGO STRANGE DIED OVER A YEAR AGO!
THAT'S WHAT WE THOUGHT HAPPENED TO OURS! HE AND... BATMAN... FIRST MET BEFORE I CAME ONTO THE SCENE...
"HE USED A LIGHTNING GENERATOR TO CREATE FOG TO COVER UP HIS CRIMES; HE WAS TRYING TO SET HIMSELF UP AS KINGPIN OF GOTHAM CITY..."
"LATER, HE SURGICALLY TRANSFORMED THREE MENTAL PATIENTS INTO ACROMEGALIC MONSTERS, AND TRIED TO GAIN CONTROL OF GOTHAM THROUGH THEM..."
"FINALLY, BATMAN AND I THWARTED HIS PLAN TO TAKE OVER THE WHOLE COUNTRY WITH HIS SO-CALLED 'FEAR DUST'!.."
"...IN THE PROCESS, ACCIDENTALLY SENDING THE PROFESSOR TO WHAT WE THOUGHT TO BE A WATERY DEATH!"
AND NOW HE WANTS TO DESTROY THE CITY HE COULD NEVER CONTROL!
YES! BATMAN, I KNOW THIS ISN'T YOUR FIGHT, OR YOUR EARTH, BUT--
I'LL DO ANYTHING I CAN! AND PLEASE --CALL ME BRUCE!
I'D...RATHER NOT, IF YOU DON'T MIND! NO OFFENSE, BUT... THERE'LL ALWAYS BE ONLY ONE BRUCE WAYNE, FOR ME!
ER--OF COURSE! I UNDERSTA--
RATATATA
IT'S STARTED! LET'S GO!
6

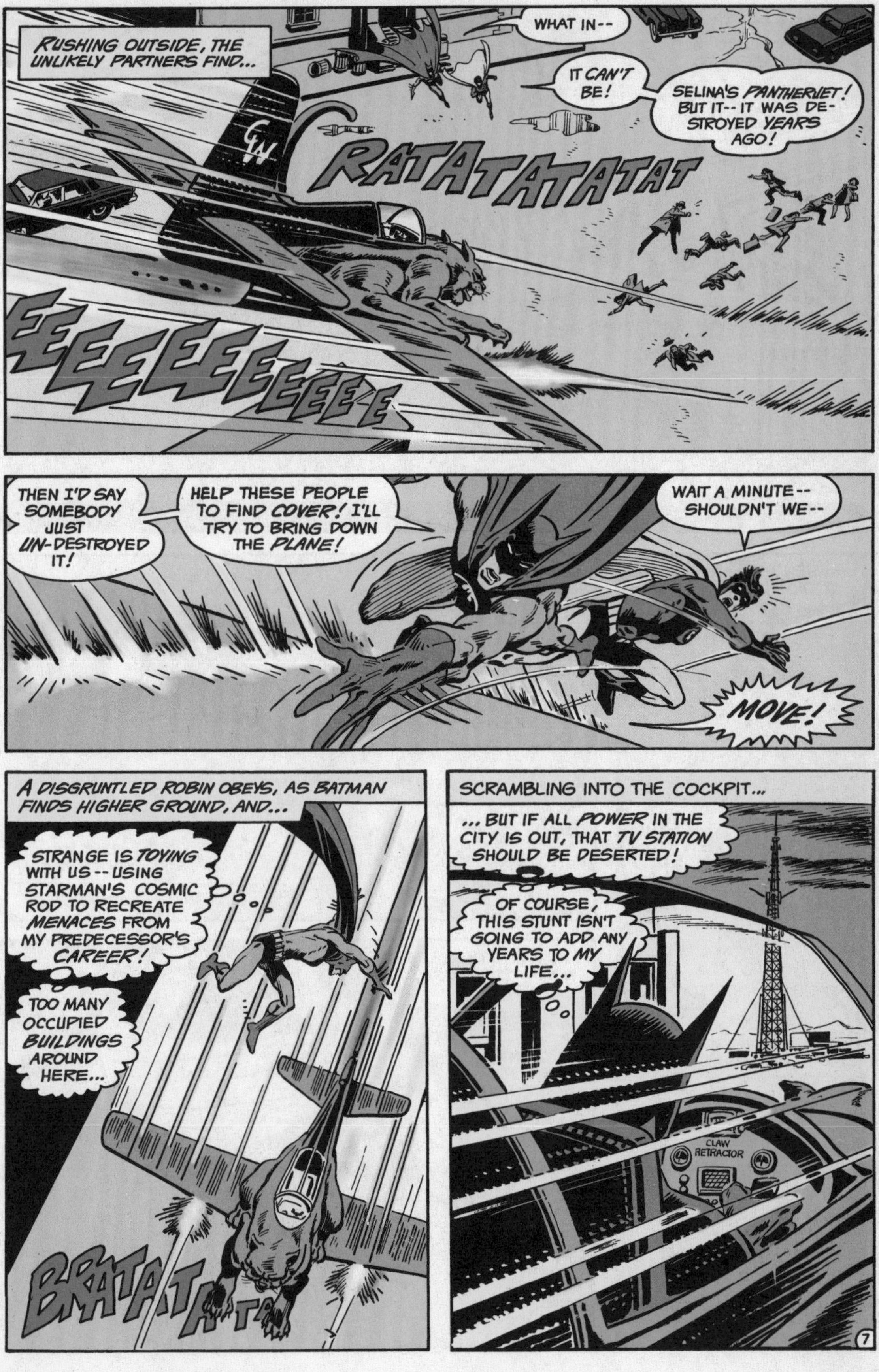
RUSHING OUTSIDE, THE UNLIKELY PARTNERS FIND...
WHAT IN--
IT CAN'T BE!
SELINA'S PANTHERJET! BUT IT-- IT WAS DE-STROYED YEARS AGO!
RATATATATATAT
EEEEEEEEEEE-E
THEN I'D SAY SOMEBODY JUST UN-DESTROYED IT!
HELP THESE PEOPLE TO FIND COVER! I'LL TRY TO BRING DOWN THE PLANE!
WAIT A MINUTE-- SHOULDN'T WE--
MOVE!
A DISGRUNTLED ROBIN OBEYS, AS BATMAN FINDS HIGHER GROUND, AND...
STRANGE IS TOYING WITH US -- USING STARMAN'S COSMIC ROD TO RECREATE MENACES FROM MY PREDECESSOR'S CAREER!
TOO MANY OCCUPIED BUILDINGS AROUND HERE...
BRATATATATA
SCRAMBLING INTO THE COCKPIT...
...BUT IF ALL POWER IN THE CITY IS OUT, THAT TV STATION SHOULD BE DESERTED!
OF COURSE, THIS STUNT ISN'T GOING TO ADD ANY YEARS TO MY LIFE...
CLAW RETRACTOR
7

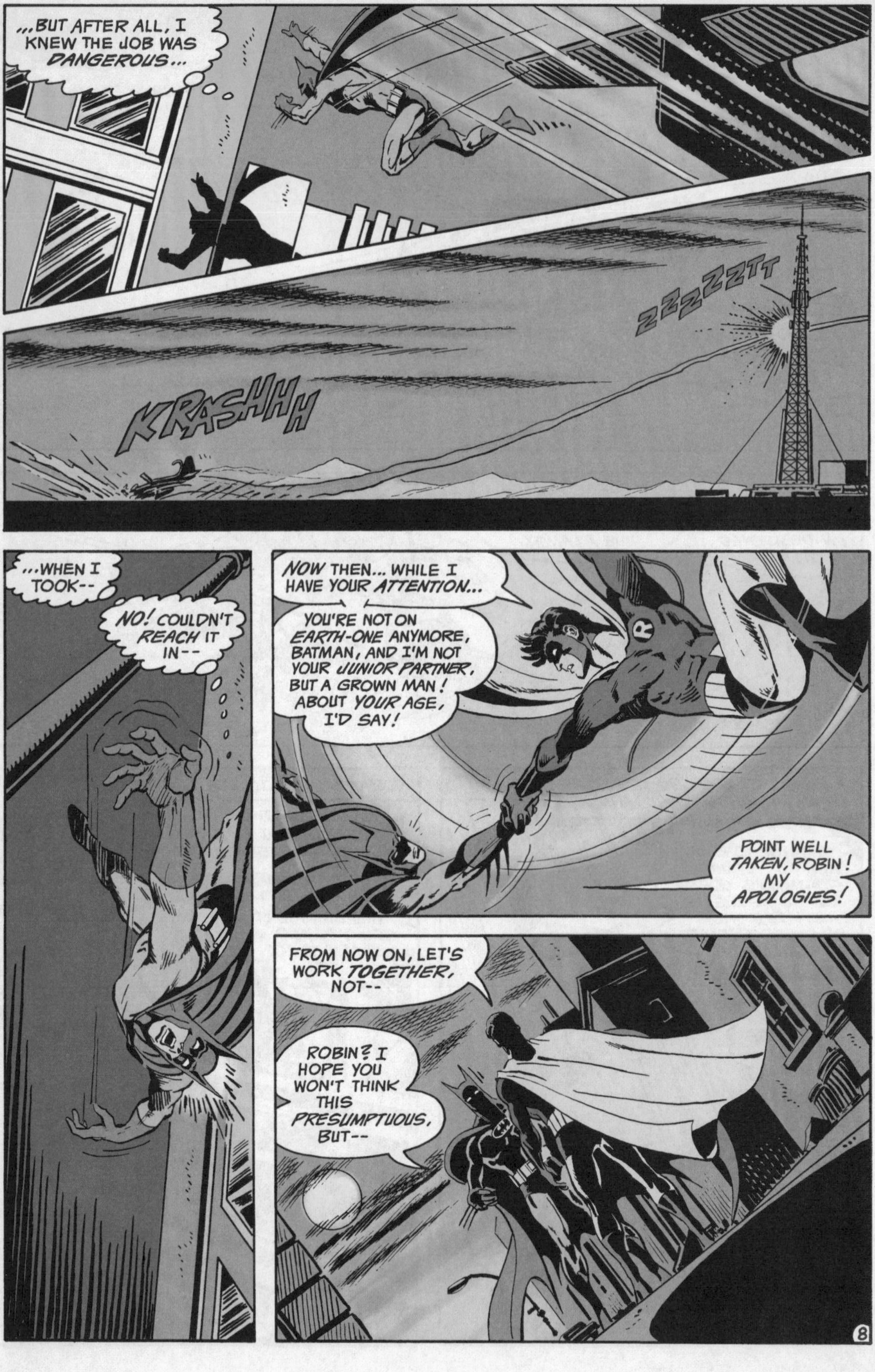

...BUT AFTER ALL, I KNEW THE JOB WAS DANGEROUS...
ZZZZZTTT
KRASHHHH
...WHEN I TOOK--
NO! COULDN'T REACH IT IN--
NOW THEN... WHILE I HAVE YOUR ATTENTION...
YOU'RE NOT ON EARTH-ONE ANYMORE, BATMAN, AND I'M NOT YOUR JUNIOR PARTNER, BUT A GROWN MAN! ABOUT YOUR AGE, I'D SAY!
POINT WELL TAKEN, ROBIN! MY APOLOGIES!
FROM NOW ON, LET'S WORK TOGETHER, NOT--
ROBIN? I HOPE YOU WON'T THINK THIS PRESUMPTUOUS, BUT--
8

KWRRR

MOVE IT OR LOSE IT!

GOOD GRIEF. IT'S ...ONE OF THE *SPINNER'S* OLD WEAPONS!

MAYBE WE CAN USE A *VEHICLE* TO... *PUSH* IT, GUIDE ITS *COURSE*...

Y-YEAH...THAT'S JUST WHAT... *BATMAN* DID...

BEFORE EITHER CAN MAKE A *MOVE*, HOW-EVER, A THIN BUT TENSILE ROPE LASHES OUT FROM *NOWHERE*, AND...

THWAK

WHO ON EARTH COULD'VE DONE--

ROBINSON & SPRANG ART SUPPLIES

KRASH

DEAR *ROBIN!* HOW SOON THEY *FORGET!*

BATWOMAN ?!

I HEARD A NEWS REPORT ABOUT THE *CATWOMAN'S* PLANE, AND RUSHED OVER HERE AS SOON AS I--

9

--COULD...

OH MY *LORD*... WHO--?

UH, KATHY...THIS IS...THE *BATMAN* OF *EARTH-ONE!* YOU MAY REMEMBER ME TELLING YOU ABOUT MY ENCOUNTERS WITH THEIR *JUSTICE LEAGUE*--?

YES...OF *COURSE!* HOW DO YOU DO... *BATMAN?*

PLEASED TO... *MEET* YOU, KATHY!

KATHY...OH LORD, KATHY, ON MY WORLD, YOU *DIED* LAST YEAR! IT'S LIKE...*TOUCHING A GHOST...*

BUT THEN... I GUESS THAT'S WHAT *YOU'RE* FEELING, TOO...

SUDDENLY...

HOW *SWEET*-- A *REUNION!* AND HOW *CONSIDERATE* OF YOU, ROBIN, TO FIND ME ANOTHER *BATMAN* TO KILL!

IT'S ONLY *FITTING*, THEN, THAT THE *INSTRUMENT* OF YOUR *DEATHS...*

...SHOULD BE ONE OF THE *INSTRUMENTS* OF YOUR SO-CALLED *JUSTICE!*

SKREEEEE

BATMAN! WATCH OUT FOR THE *NOSE*-- IT'S RAZOR-SHARP *STEEL!*

NOT UNLIKE ONE OF *MY* EARLY MODELS!

I ONLY HOPE...

RRRROOAR

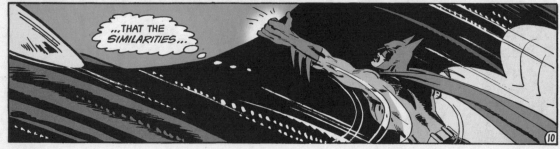

...THAT THE *SIMILARITIES...*

10

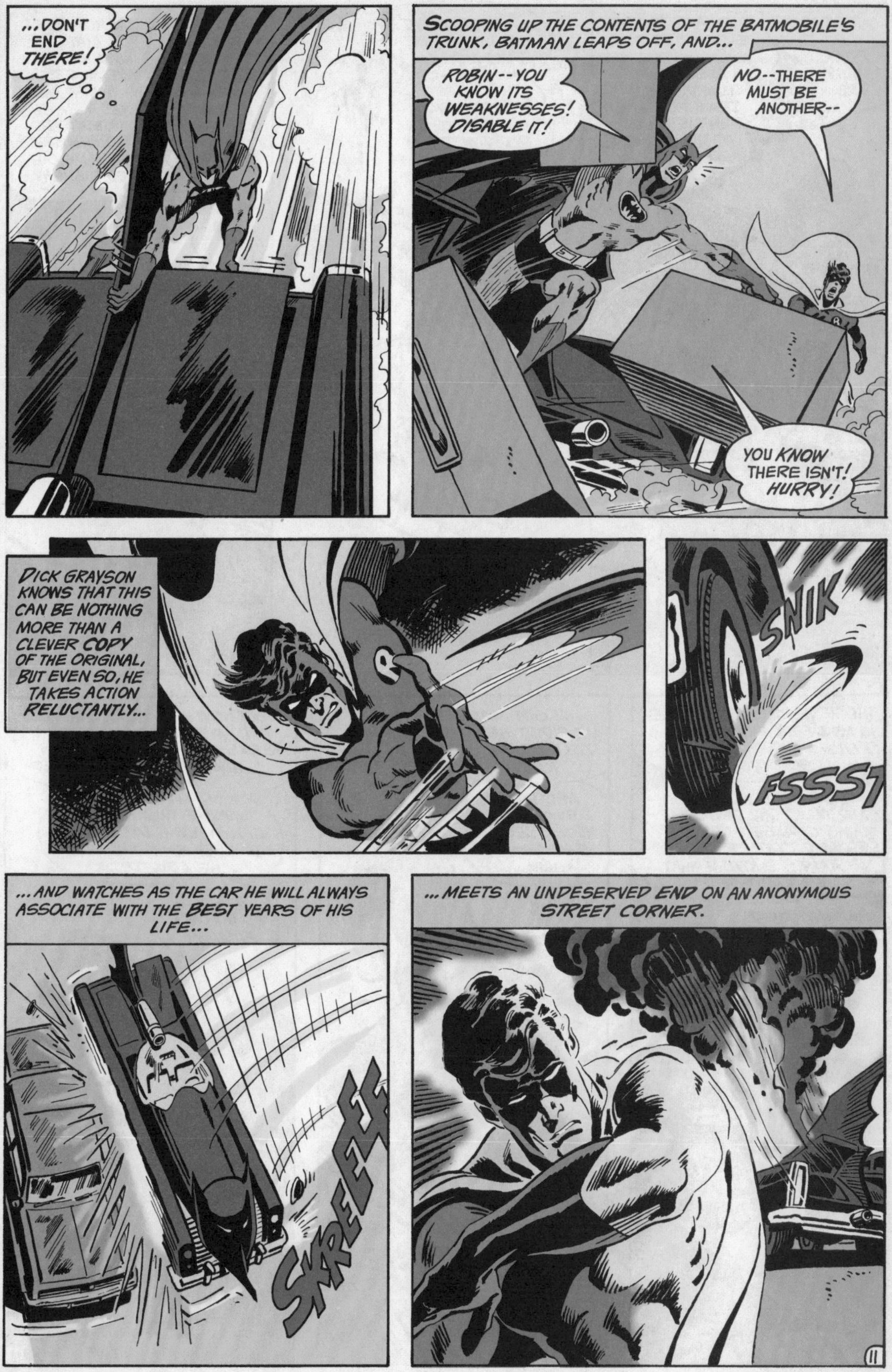
...DON'T END THERE!
SCOOPING UP THE CONTENTS OF THE BATMOBILE'S TRUNK, BATMAN LEAPS OFF, AND...
ROBIN--YOU KNOW ITS WEAKNESSES! DISABLE IT!
NO--THERE MUST BE ANOTHER--
YOU KNOW THERE ISN'T! HURRY!
DICK GRAYSON KNOWS THAT THIS CAN BE NOTHING MORE THAN A CLEVER COPY OF THE ORIGINAL, BUT EVEN SO, HE TAKES ACTION RELUCTANTLY...
SNIK
FSSST
...AND WATCHES AS THE CAR HE WILL ALWAYS ASSOCIATE WITH THE BEST YEARS OF HIS LIFE...
SKREEE
...MEETS AN UNDESERVED END ON AN ANONYMOUS STREET CORNER.
11

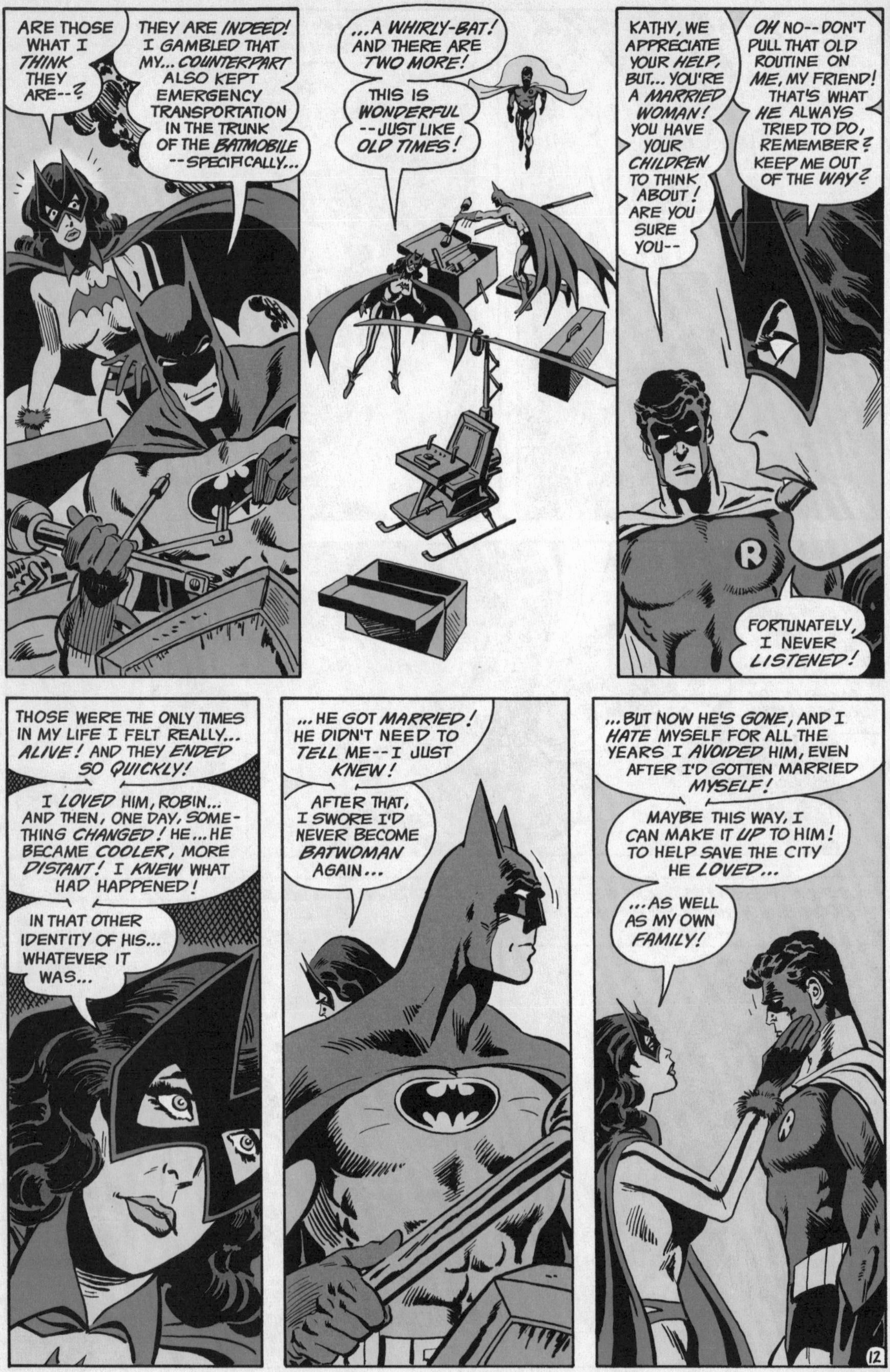

ARE THOSE WHAT I *THINK* THEY ARE--?
THEY ARE *INDEED!* I GAMBLED THAT MY... *COUNTERPART* ALSO KEPT EMERGENCY TRANSPORTATION IN THE TRUNK OF THE *BATMOBILE* --SPECIFICALLY...
...A *WHIRLY-BAT!* AND THERE ARE *TWO MORE!*
THIS IS *WONDERFUL* --JUST LIKE *OLD TIMES!*
KATHY, WE APPRECIATE YOUR *HELP*, BUT... YOU'RE A *MARRIED WOMAN!* YOU HAVE YOUR *CHILDREN* TO THINK ABOUT! ARE YOU SURE YOU--
OH NO--DON'T PULL THAT OLD ROUTINE ON *ME*, MY FRIEND! THAT'S WHAT *HE* ALWAYS TRIED TO DO, REMEMBER? KEEP ME OUT OF THE *WAY?*
FORTUNATELY, I NEVER *LISTENED!*
THOSE WERE THE ONLY TIMES IN MY LIFE I FELT REALLY... *ALIVE!* AND THEY *ENDED* SO *QUICKLY!*
I *LOVED* HIM, ROBIN... AND THEN, ONE DAY, SOME-THING *CHANGED!* HE...HE BECAME *COOLER*, MORE *DISTANT!* I *KNEW* WHAT HAD HAPPENED!
IN THAT OTHER IDENTITY OF HIS... WHATEVER IT WAS...
...HE GOT *MARRIED!* HE DIDN'T NEED TO *TELL* ME--I JUST *KNEW!*
AFTER THAT, I SWORE I'D NEVER BECOME *BATWOMAN* AGAIN...
...BUT NOW HE'S *GONE*, AND I *HATE* MYSELF FOR ALL THE YEARS I *AVOIDED* HIM, EVEN AFTER I'D GOTTEN MARRIED *MYSELF!*
MAYBE THIS WAY, I CAN MAKE IT *UP* TO HIM! TO HELP SAVE THE CITY HE *LOVED*...
...AS WELL AS MY OWN *FAMILY!*
12

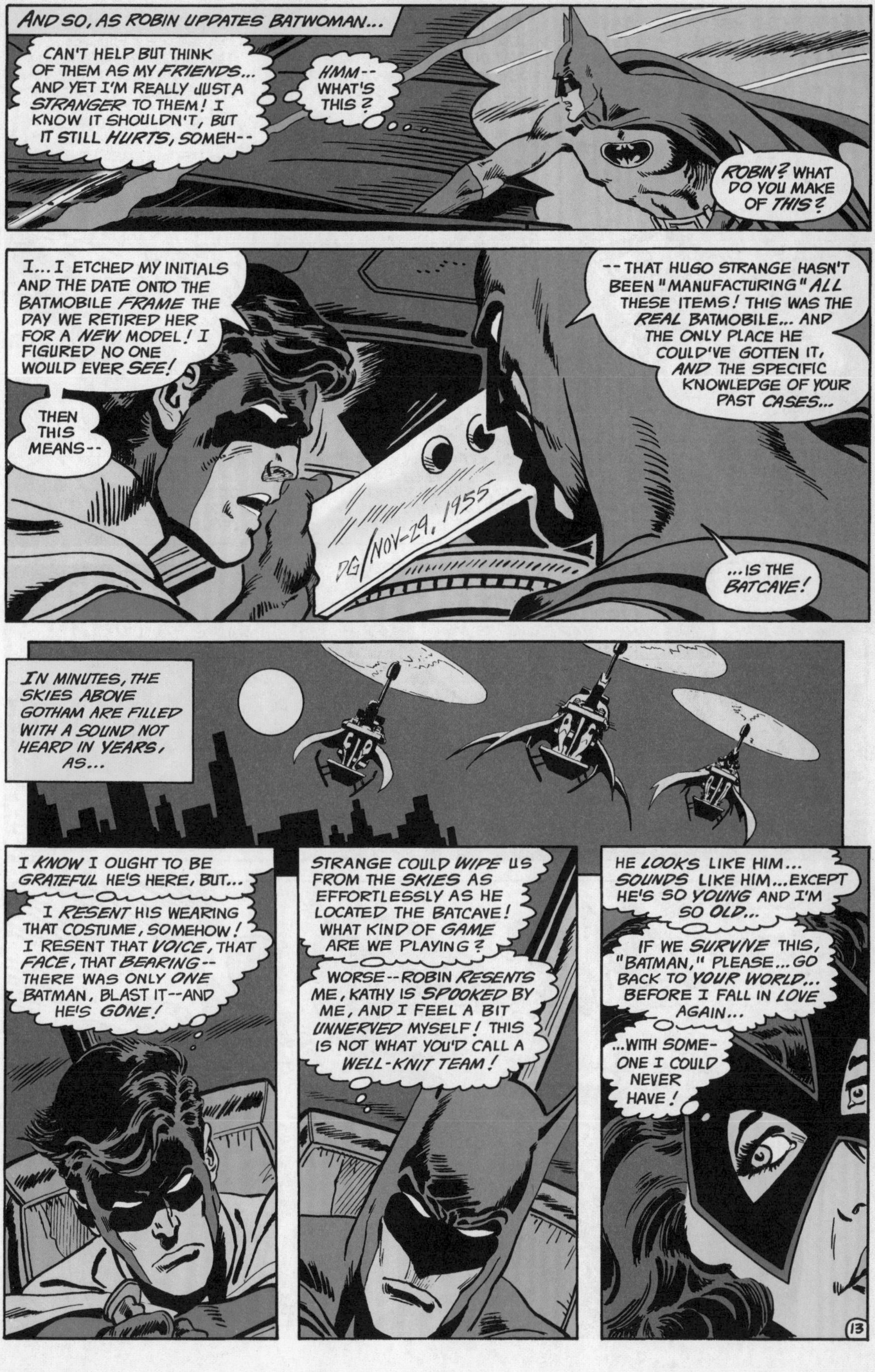
AND SO, AS ROBIN UPDATES BATWOMAN...
CAN'T HELP BUT THINK OF THEM AS MY FRIENDS... AND YET I'M REALLY JUST A STRANGER TO THEM! I KNOW IT SHOULDN'T, BUT IT STILL HURTS, SOMEH--
HMM-- WHAT'S THIS?
ROBIN? WHAT DO YOU MAKE OF THIS?
I... I ETCHED MY INITIALS AND THE DATE ONTO THE BATMOBILE FRAME THE DAY WE RETIRED HER FOR A NEW MODEL! I FIGURED NO ONE WOULD EVER SEE!
THEN THIS MEANS--
--THAT HUGO STRANGE HASN'T BEEN "MANUFACTURING" ALL THESE ITEMS! THIS WAS THE REAL BATMOBILE... AND THE ONLY PLACE HE COULD'VE GOTTEN IT, AND THE SPECIFIC KNOWLEDGE OF YOUR PAST CASES...
DG/NOV-29, 1955
...IS THE BATCAVE!
IN MINUTES, THE SKIES ABOVE GOTHAM ARE FILLED WITH A SOUND NOT HEARD IN YEARS, AS...
I KNOW I OUGHT TO BE GRATEFUL HE'S HERE, BUT...
I RESENT HIS WEARING THAT COSTUME, SOMEHOW! I RESENT THAT VOICE, THAT FACE, THAT BEARING-- THERE WAS ONLY ONE BATMAN, BLAST IT--AND HE'S GONE!
STRANGE COULD WIPE US FROM THE SKIES AS EFFORTLESSLY AS HE LOCATED THE BATCAVE! WHAT KIND OF GAME ARE WE PLAYING?
WORSE--ROBIN RESENTS ME, KATHY IS SPOOKED BY ME, AND I FEEL A BIT UNNERVED MYSELF! THIS IS NOT WHAT YOU'D CALL A WELL-KNIT TEAM!
HE LOOKS LIKE HIM... SOUNDS LIKE HIM... EXCEPT HE'S SO YOUNG AND I'M SO OLD...
IF WE SURVIVE THIS, "BATMAN," PLEASE... GO BACK TO YOUR WORLD... BEFORE I FALL IN LOVE AGAIN...
...WITH SOMEONE I COULD NEVER HAVE!
13

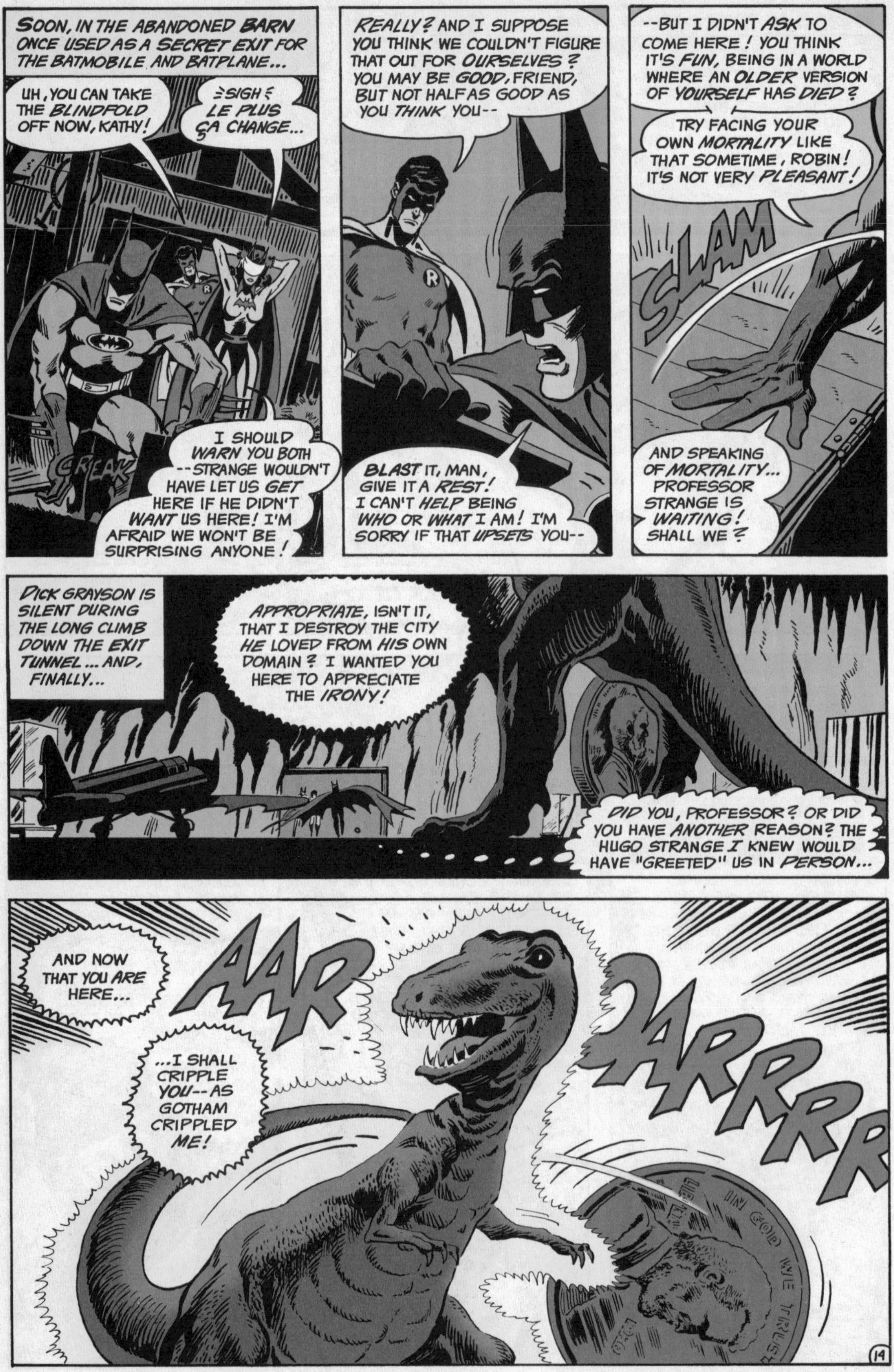
SOON, IN THE ABANDONED BARN ONCE USED AS A SECRET EXIT FOR THE BATMOBILE AND BATPLANE...
UH, YOU CAN TAKE THE BLINDFOLD OFF NOW, KATHY!
≷SIGH≶ LE PLUS ÇA CHANGE...
CREAK
I SHOULD WARN YOU BOTH --STRANGE WOULDN'T HAVE LET US GET HERE IF HE DIDN'T WANT US HERE! I'M AFRAID WE WON'T BE SURPRISING ANYONE!
REALLY? AND I SUPPOSE YOU THINK WE COULDN'T FIGURE THAT OUT FOR OURSELVES? YOU MAY BE GOOD, FRIEND, BUT NOT HALF AS GOOD AS YOU THINK YOU--
BLAST IT, MAN, GIVE IT A REST! I CAN'T HELP BEING WHO OR WHAT I AM! I'M SORRY IF THAT UPSETS YOU--
--BUT I DIDN'T ASK TO COME HERE! YOU THINK IT'S FUN, BEING IN A WORLD WHERE AN OLDER VERSION OF YOURSELF HAS DIED?
TRY FACING YOUR OWN MORTALITY LIKE THAT SOMETIME, ROBIN! IT'S NOT VERY PLEASANT!
SLAM
AND SPEAKING OF MORTALITY... PROFESSOR STRANGE IS WAITING! SHALL WE?
DICK GRAYSON IS SILENT DURING THE LONG CLIMB DOWN THE EXIT TUNNEL... AND, FINALLY...
APPROPRIATE, ISN'T IT, THAT I DESTROY THE CITY HE LOVED FROM HIS OWN DOMAIN? I WANTED YOU HERE TO APPRECIATE THE IRONY!
DID YOU, PROFESSOR? OR DID YOU HAVE ANOTHER REASON? THE HUGO STRANGE I KNEW WOULD HAVE "GREETED" US IN PERSON...
AND NOW THAT YOU ARE HERE...
...I SHALL CRIPPLE YOU--AS GOTHAM CRIPPLED ME!
AAR
RARRRR
14

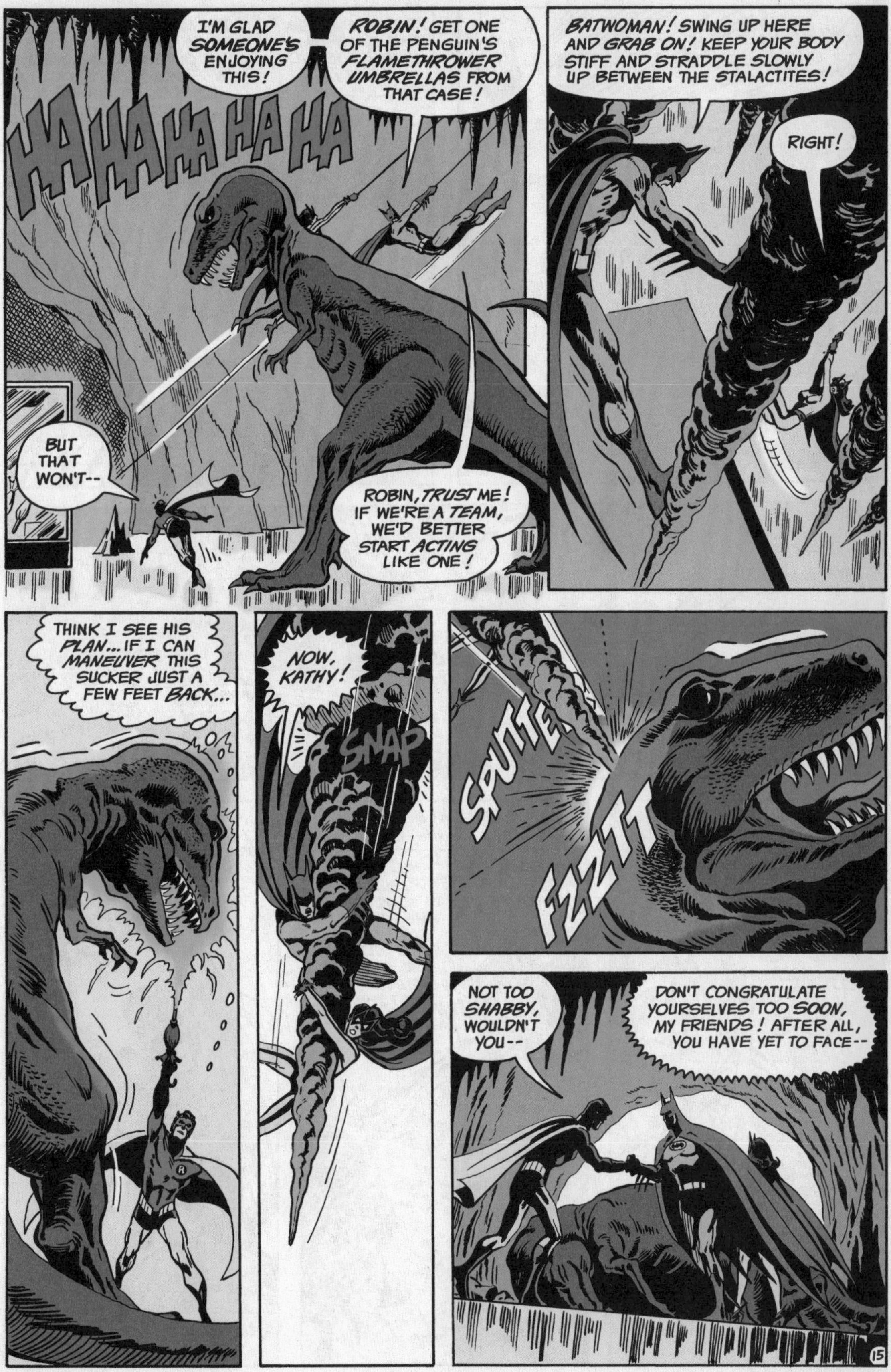
I'M GLAD SOMEONE'S ENJOYING THIS!
ROBIN! GET ONE OF THE PENGUIN'S FLAMETHROWER UMBRELLAS FROM THAT CASE!
HA HA HA HA HA HA
BUT THAT WON'T--
ROBIN, TRUST ME! IF WE'RE A TEAM, WE'D BETTER START ACTING LIKE ONE!
BATWOMAN! SWING UP HERE AND GRAB ON! KEEP YOUR BODY STIFF AND STRADDLE SLOWLY UP BETWEEN THE STALACTITES!
RIGHT!
THINK I SEE HIS PLAN... IF I CAN MANEUVER THIS SUCKER JUST A FEW FEET BACK...
NOW, KATHY!
SNAP
FZZTT
NOT TOO SHABBY, WOULDN'T YOU--
DON'T CONGRATULATE YOURSELVES TOO SOON, MY FRIENDS! AFTER ALL, YOU HAVE YET TO FACE--
15

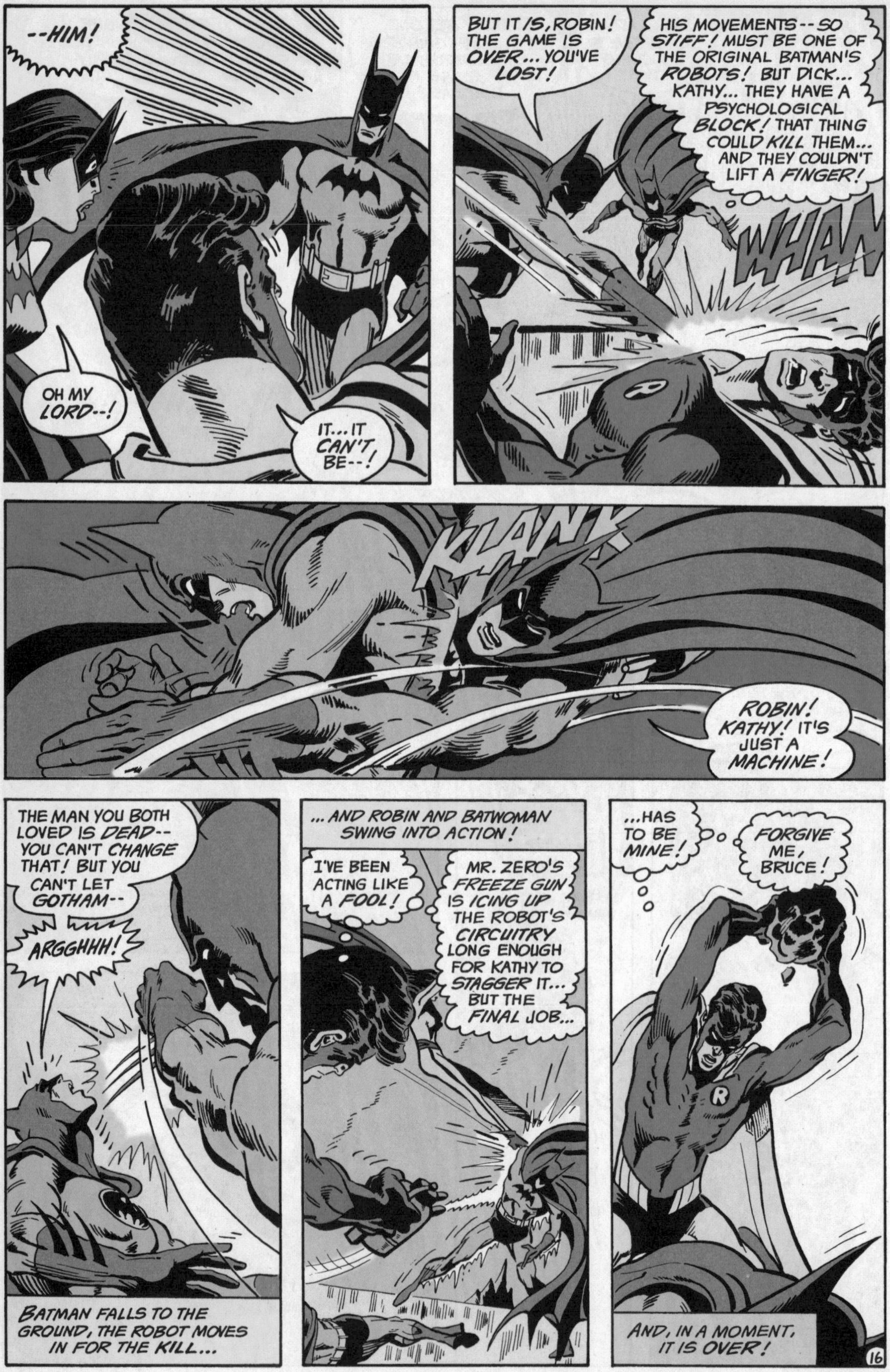
--HIM!
OH MY LORD--!
IT... IT CAN'T BE--!
BUT IT IS, ROBIN! THE GAME IS OVER... YOU'VE LOST!
HIS MOVEMENTS--SO STIFF! MUST BE ONE OF THE ORIGINAL BATMAN'S ROBOTS! BUT DICK... KATHY... THEY HAVE A PSYCHOLOGICAL BLOCK! THAT THING COULD KILL THEM... AND THEY COULDN'T LIFT A FINGER!
WHAM
KLANK!
ROBIN! KATHY! IT'S JUST A MACHINE!
THE MAN YOU BOTH LOVED IS DEAD--YOU CAN'T CHANGE THAT! BUT YOU CAN'T LET GOTHAM--
ARGGHHH!
BATMAN FALLS TO THE GROUND, THE ROBOT MOVES IN FOR THE KILL...
... AND ROBIN AND BATWOMAN SWING INTO ACTION!
I'VE BEEN ACTING LIKE A FOOL!
MR. ZERO'S FREEZE GUN IS ICING UP THE ROBOT'S CIRCUITRY LONG ENOUGH FOR KATHY TO STAGGER IT... BUT THE FINAL JOB...
...HAS TO BE MINE!
FORGIVE ME, BRUCE!
AND, IN A MOMENT, IT IS OVER!
16

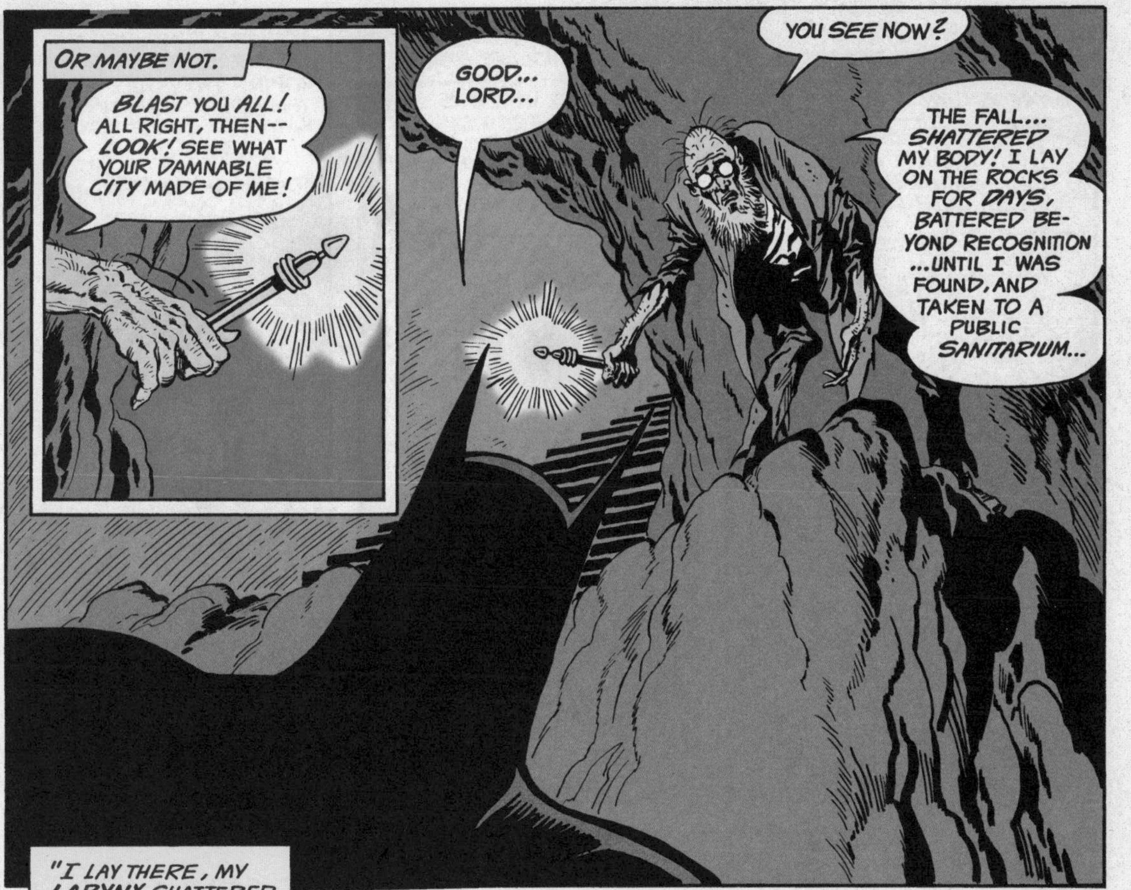
OR MAYBE NOT.
BLAST YOU ALL! ALL RIGHT, THEN-- LOOK! SEE WHAT YOUR DAMNABLE CITY MADE OF ME!
GOOD... LORD...
YOU SEE NOW?
THE FALL... SHATTERED MY BODY! I LAY ON THE ROCKS FOR DAYS, BATTERED BEYOND RECOGNITION ...UNTIL I WAS FOUND, AND TAKEN TO A PUBLIC SANITARIUM...

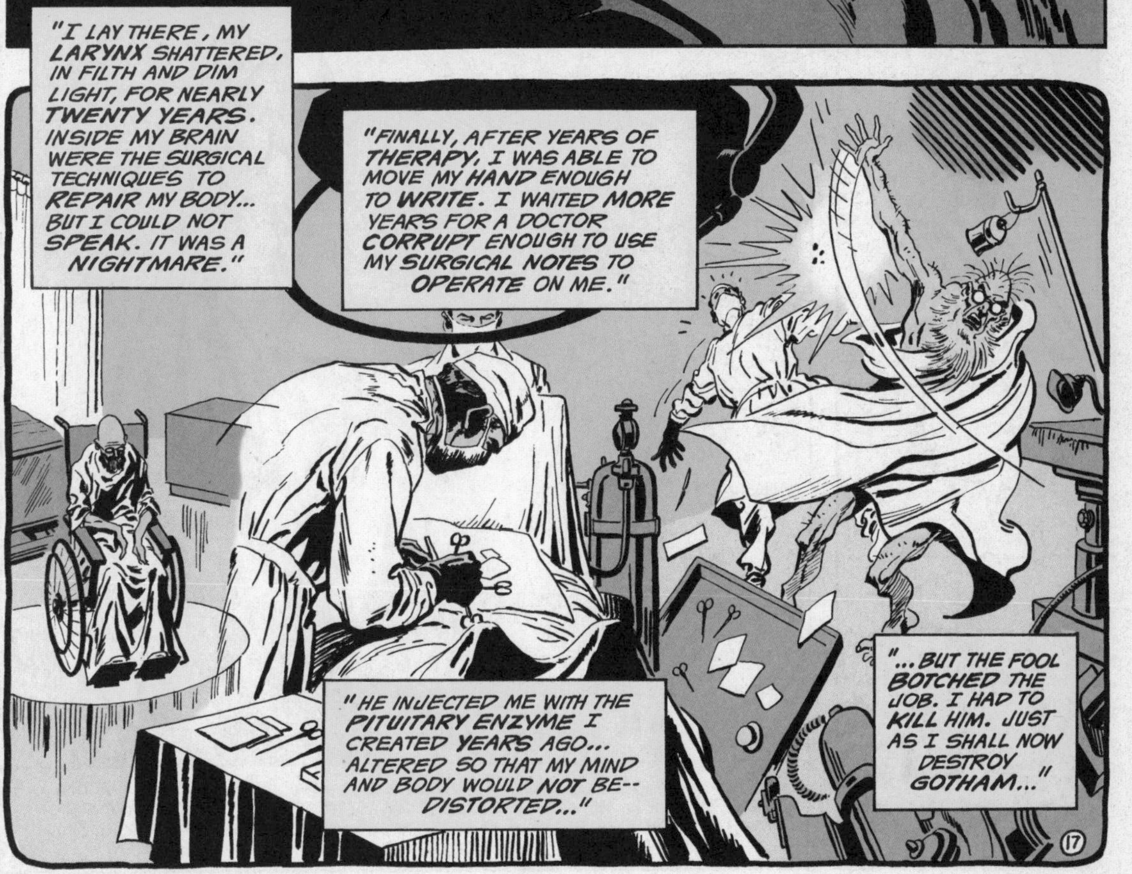
"I LAY THERE, MY LARYNX SHATTERED, IN FILTH AND DIM LIGHT, FOR NEARLY TWENTY YEARS. INSIDE MY BRAIN WERE THE SURGICAL TECHNIQUES TO REPAIR MY BODY... BUT I COULD NOT SPEAK. IT WAS A NIGHTMARE."
"FINALLY, AFTER YEARS OF THERAPY, I WAS ABLE TO MOVE MY HAND ENOUGH TO WRITE. I WAITED MORE YEARS FOR A DOCTOR CORRUPT ENOUGH TO USE MY SURGICAL NOTES TO OPERATE ON ME."
"HE INJECTED ME WITH THE PITUITARY ENZYME I CREATED YEARS AGO... ALTERED SO THAT MY MIND AND BODY WOULD NOT BE-- DISTORTED..."
"...BUT THE FOOL BOTCHED THE JOB. I HAD TO KILL HIM. JUST AS I SHALL NOW DESTROY GOTHAM..."
17

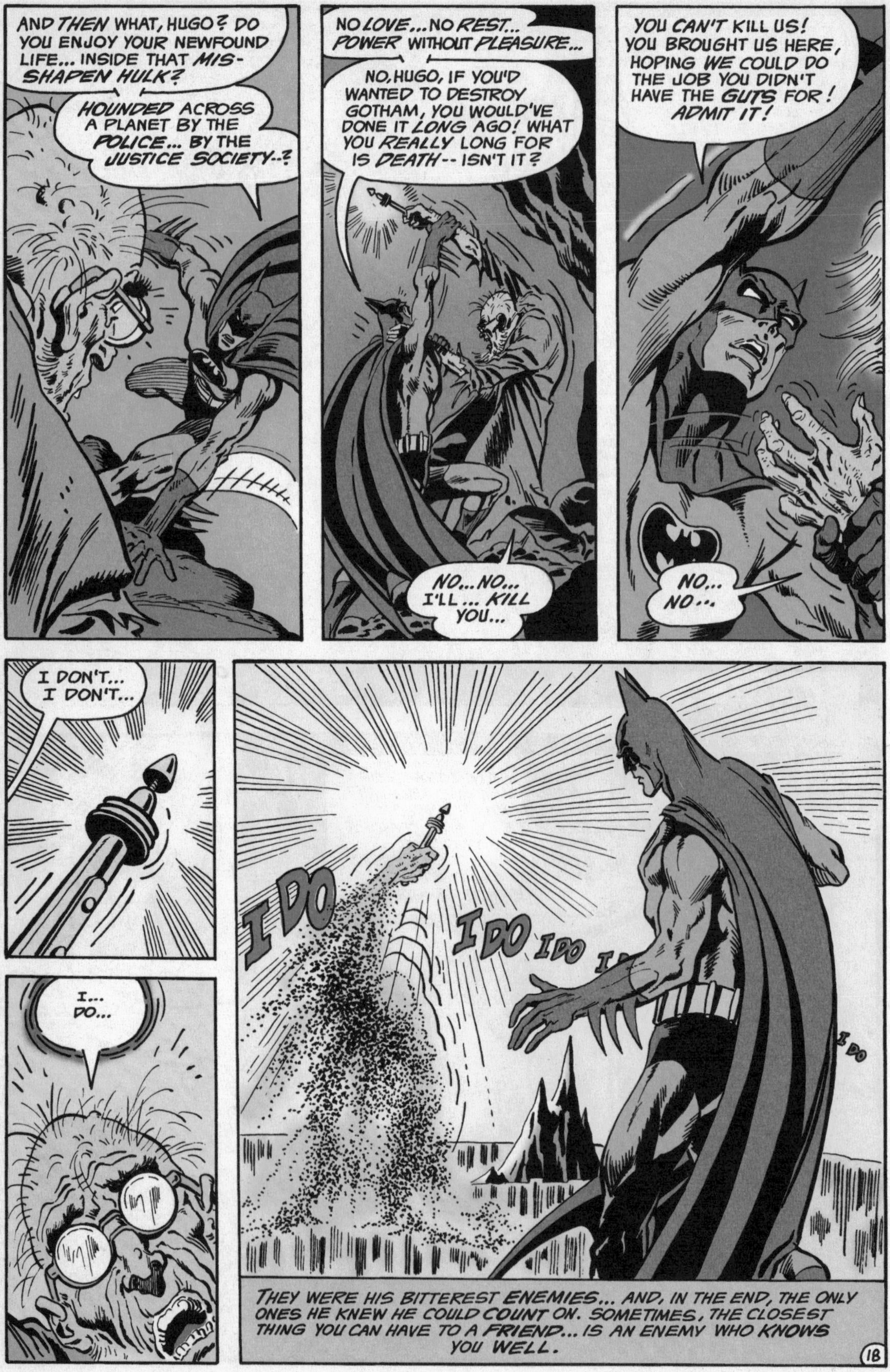
AND THEN WHAT, HUGO? DO YOU ENJOY YOUR NEWFOUND LIFE... INSIDE THAT MIS-SHAPEN HULK?
HOUNDED ACROSS A PLANET BY THE POLICE... BY THE JUSTICE SOCIETY--?
NO LOVE... NO REST... POWER WITHOUT PLEASURE...
NO, HUGO, IF YOU'D WANTED TO DESTROY GOTHAM, YOU WOULD'VE DONE IT LONG AGO! WHAT YOU REALLY LONG FOR IS DEATH -- ISN'T IT?
NO... NO... I'LL... KILL YOU...
YOU CAN'T KILL US! YOU BROUGHT US HERE, HOPING WE COULD DO THE JOB YOU DIDN'T HAVE THE GUTS FOR! ADMIT IT!
NO... NO...
I DON'T... I DON'T...
I... DO...
I DO
I DO I DO
I DO
THEY WERE HIS BITTEREST ENEMIES... AND, IN THE END, THE ONLY ONES HE KNEW HE COULD COUNT ON. SOMETIMES, THE CLOSEST THING YOU CAN HAVE TO A FRIEND... IS AN ENEMY WHO KNOWS YOU WELL.
18

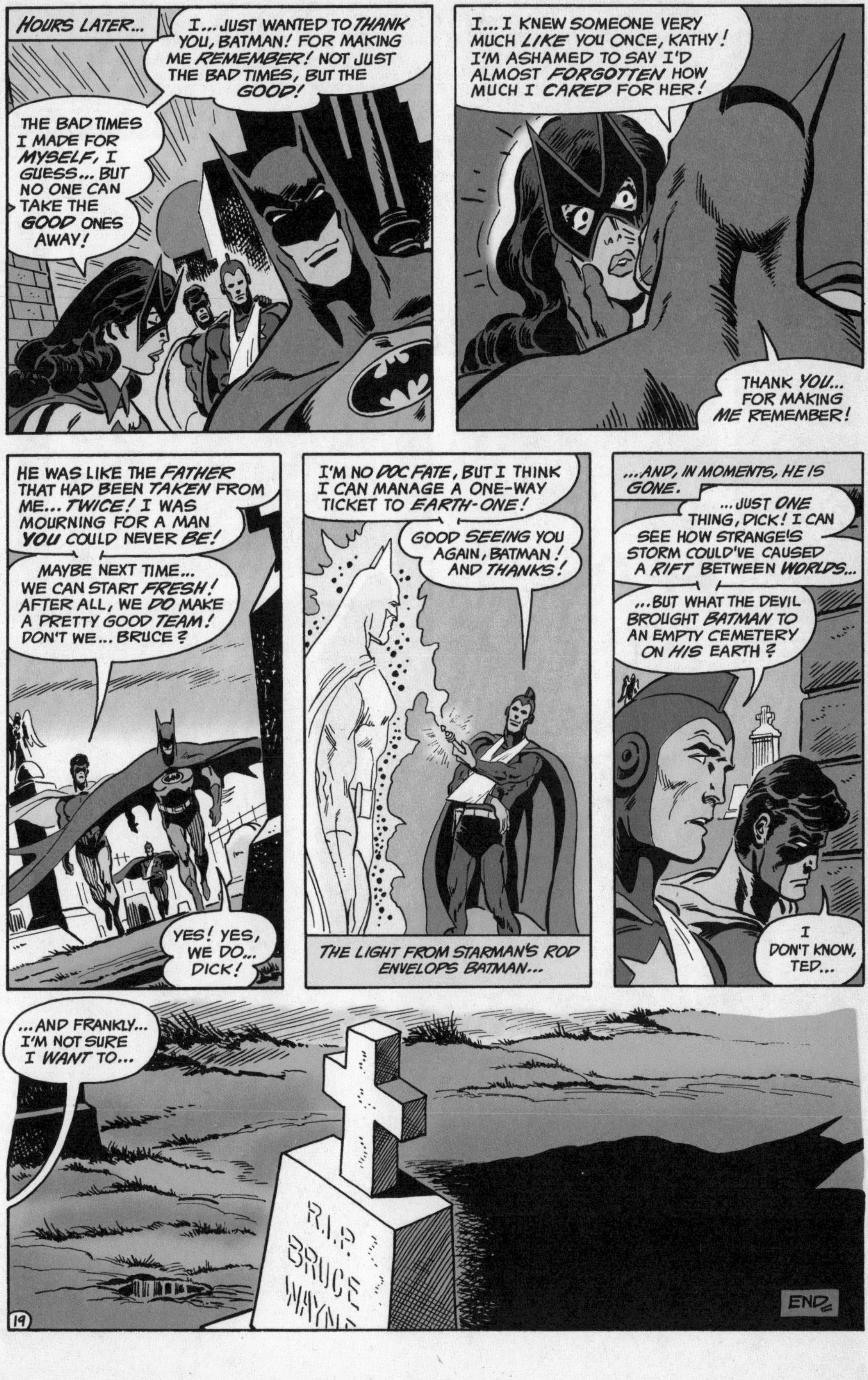

HOURS LATER...
I... JUST WANTED TO THANK YOU, BATMAN! FOR MAKING ME REMEMBER! NOT JUST THE BAD TIMES, BUT THE GOOD!
THE BAD TIMES I MADE FOR MYSELF, I GUESS... BUT NO ONE CAN TAKE THE GOOD ONES AWAY!
I... I KNEW SOMEONE VERY MUCH LIKE YOU ONCE, KATHY! I'M ASHAMED TO SAY I'D ALMOST FORGOTTEN HOW MUCH I CARED FOR HER!
THANK YOU... FOR MAKING ME REMEMBER!
HE WAS LIKE THE FATHER THAT HAD BEEN TAKEN FROM ME... TWICE! I WAS MOURNING FOR A MAN YOU COULD NEVER BE!
MAYBE NEXT TIME... WE CAN START FRESH! AFTER ALL, WE DO MAKE A PRETTY GOOD TEAM! DON'T WE... BRUCE?
YES! YES, WE DO... DICK!
I'M NO DOC FATE, BUT I THINK I CAN MANAGE A ONE-WAY TICKET TO EARTH-ONE!
GOOD SEEING YOU AGAIN, BATMAN! AND THANKS!
THE LIGHT FROM STARMAN'S ROD ENVELOPS BATMAN...
...AND, IN MOMENTS, HE IS GONE.
...JUST ONE THING, DICK! I CAN SEE HOW STRANGE'S STORM COULD'VE CAUSED A RIFT BETWEEN WORLDS...
...BUT WHAT THE DEVIL BROUGHT BATMAN TO AN EMPTY CEMETERY ON HIS EARTH?
I DON'T KNOW, TED...
...AND FRANKLY... I'M NOT SURE I WANT TO...
R.I.P. BRUCE WAYN
19
END

BATCAVE IN THE PRESENT

From: BATMAN: THE ULTIMATE GUIDE TO THE DARK KNIGHT (DK PUBLISHING) *(2005)*
Art: **TOM GRINDBERG**

SATELLITE BATCAVES

LOCATED UNDER VARIOUS PARTS OF GOTHAM CITY
Art: **STAN WOCH**

BATCAVE EAST

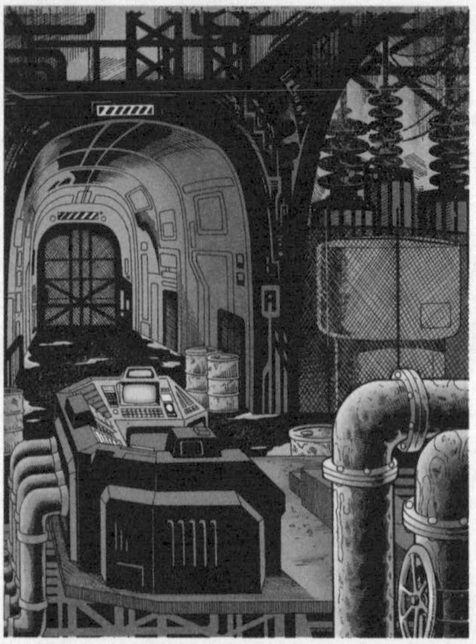

BATCAVE SOUTH

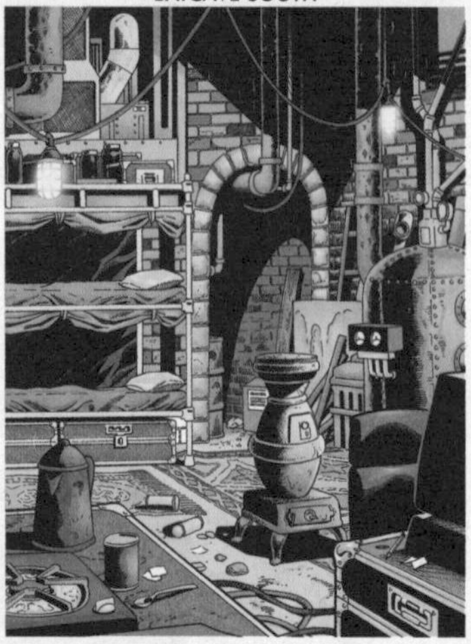

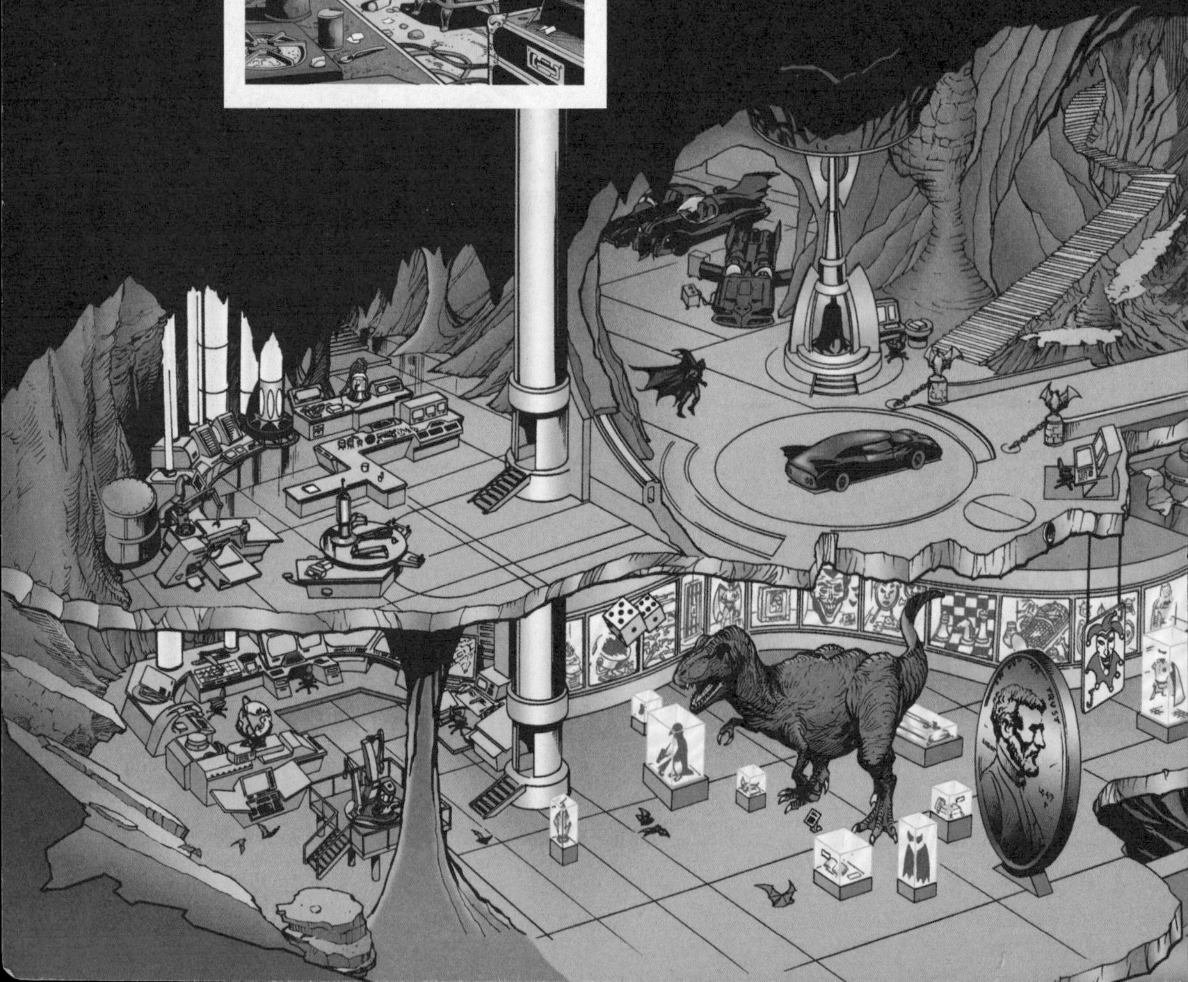

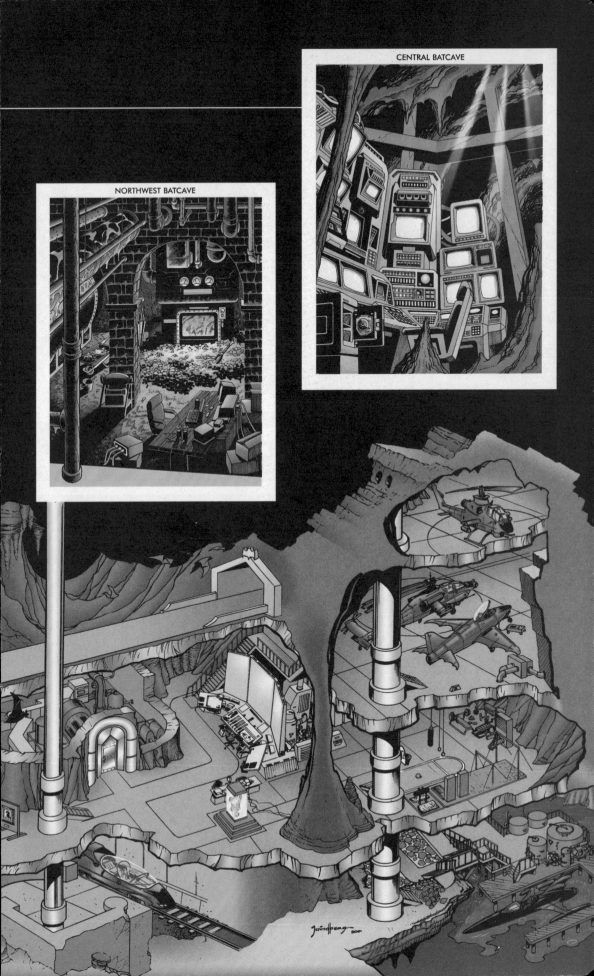

NORTHWEST BATCAVE

CENTRAL BATCAVE

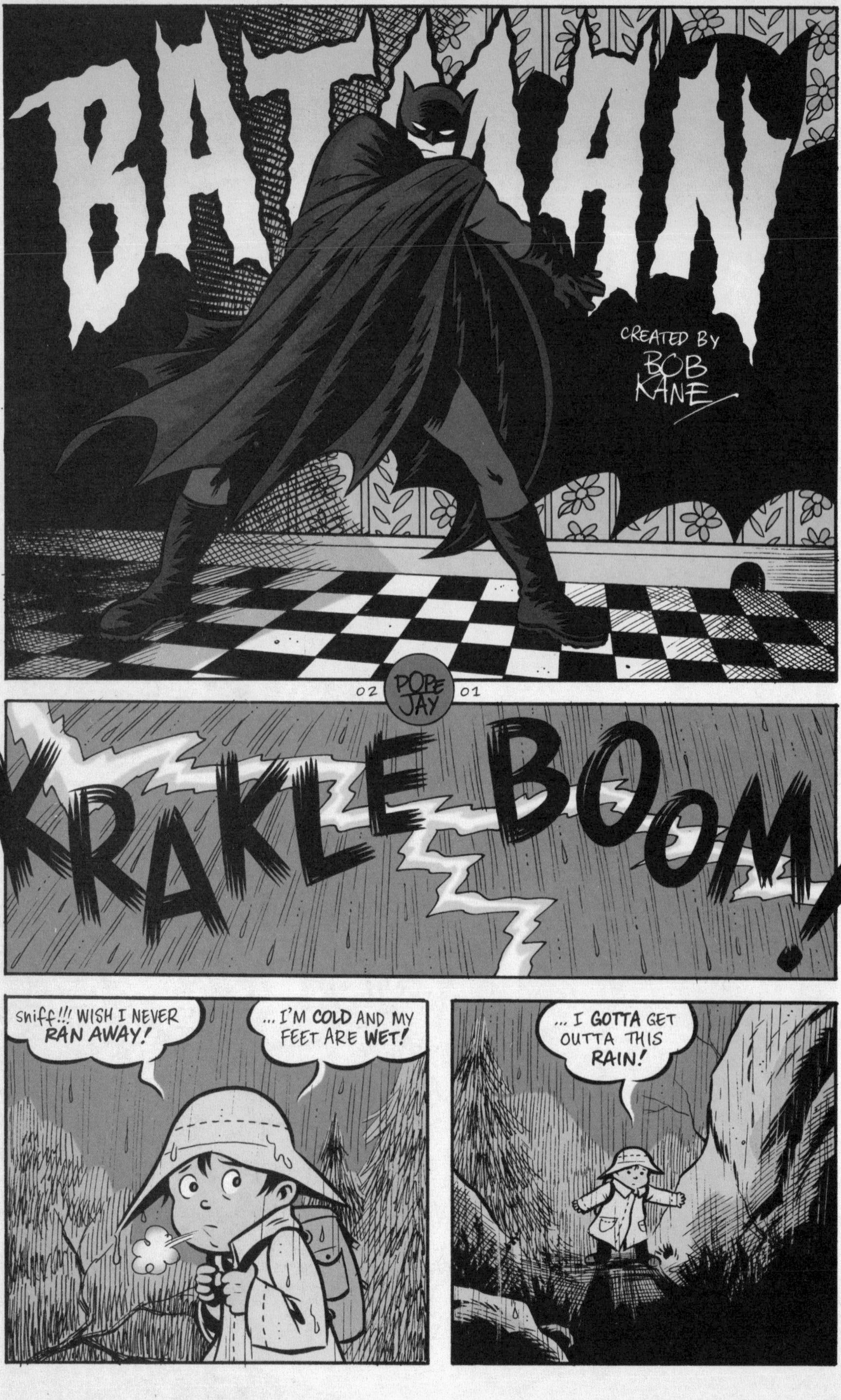
BATMAN
CREATED BY BOB KANE
02 POPE JAY 01
KRAKLE BOOM!
sniff!!! WISH I NEVER RAN AWAY!
... I'M COLD AND MY FEET ARE WET!
... I GOTTA GET OUTTA THIS RAIN!

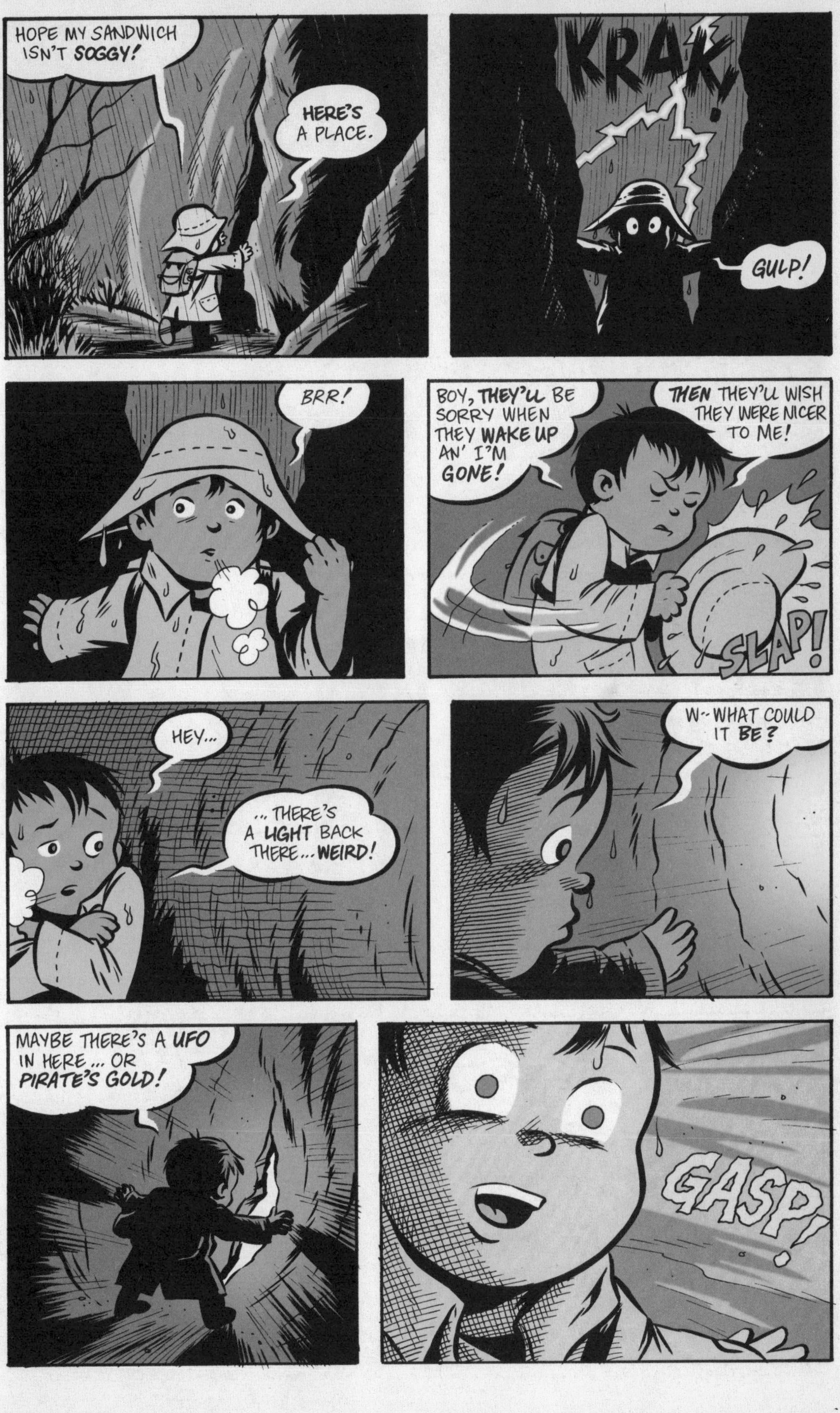
HOPE MY SANDWICH ISN'T **SOGGY!**
HERE'S A PLACE.
KRAK!
GULP!
BRR!
BOY, **THEY'LL** BE SORRY WHEN THEY **WAKE UP** AN' I'M **GONE!**
THEN THEY'LL WISH THEY WERE NICER TO ME!
SLAP!
HEY...
...THERE'S A **LIGHT** BACK THERE... **WEIRD!**
W-- WHAT COULD IT **BE?**
MAYBE THERE'S A **UFO** IN HERE ... OR **PIRATE'S GOLD!**
GASP!

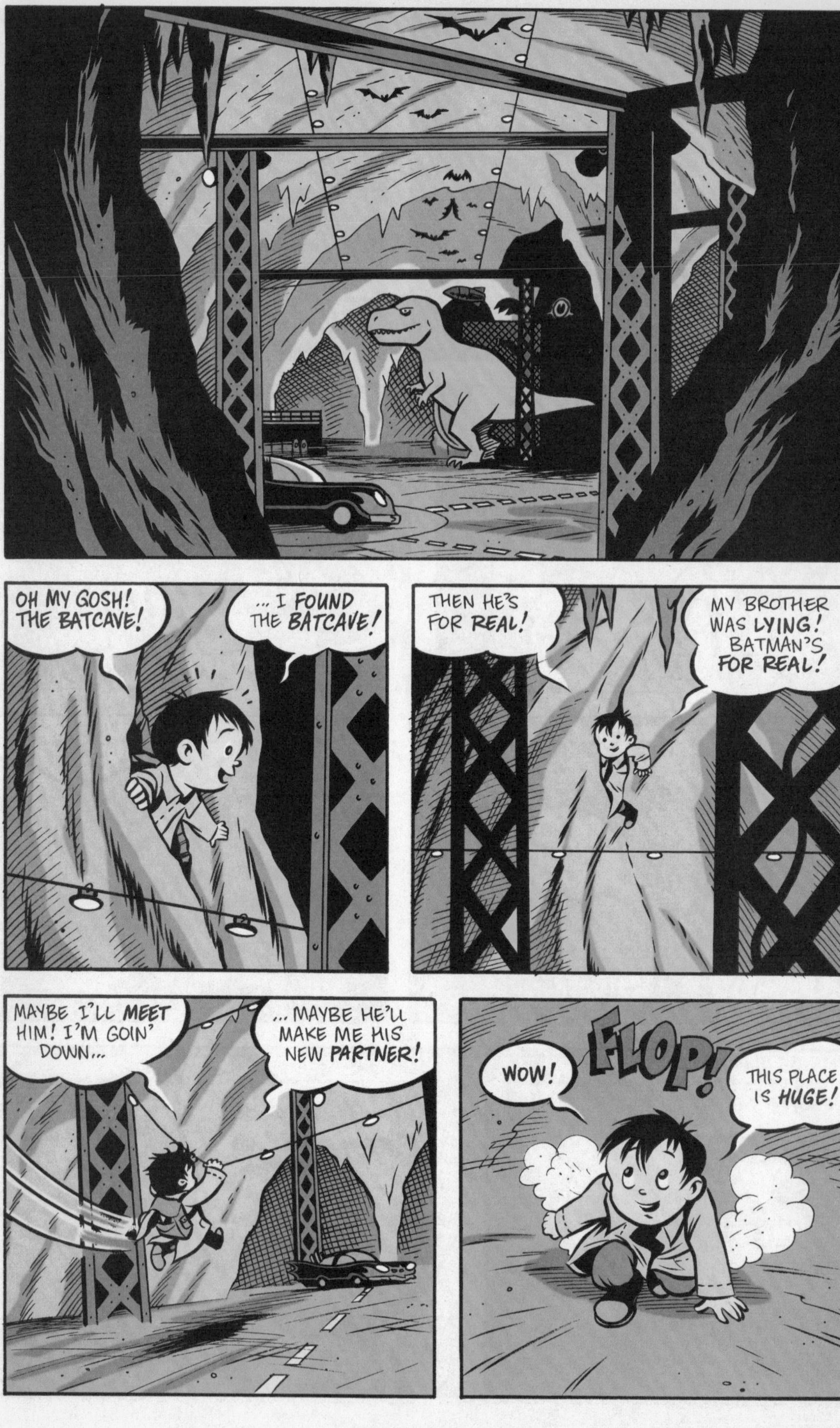
OH MY GOSH! THE BATCAVE!
... I FOUND THE BATCAVE!
THEN HE'S FOR REAL!
MY BROTHER WAS LYING! BATMAN'S FOR REAL!
MAYBE I'LL MEET HIM! I'M GOIN' DOWN...
... MAYBE HE'LL MAKE ME HIS NEW PARTNER!
FLOP!
WOW!
THIS PLACE IS HUGE!

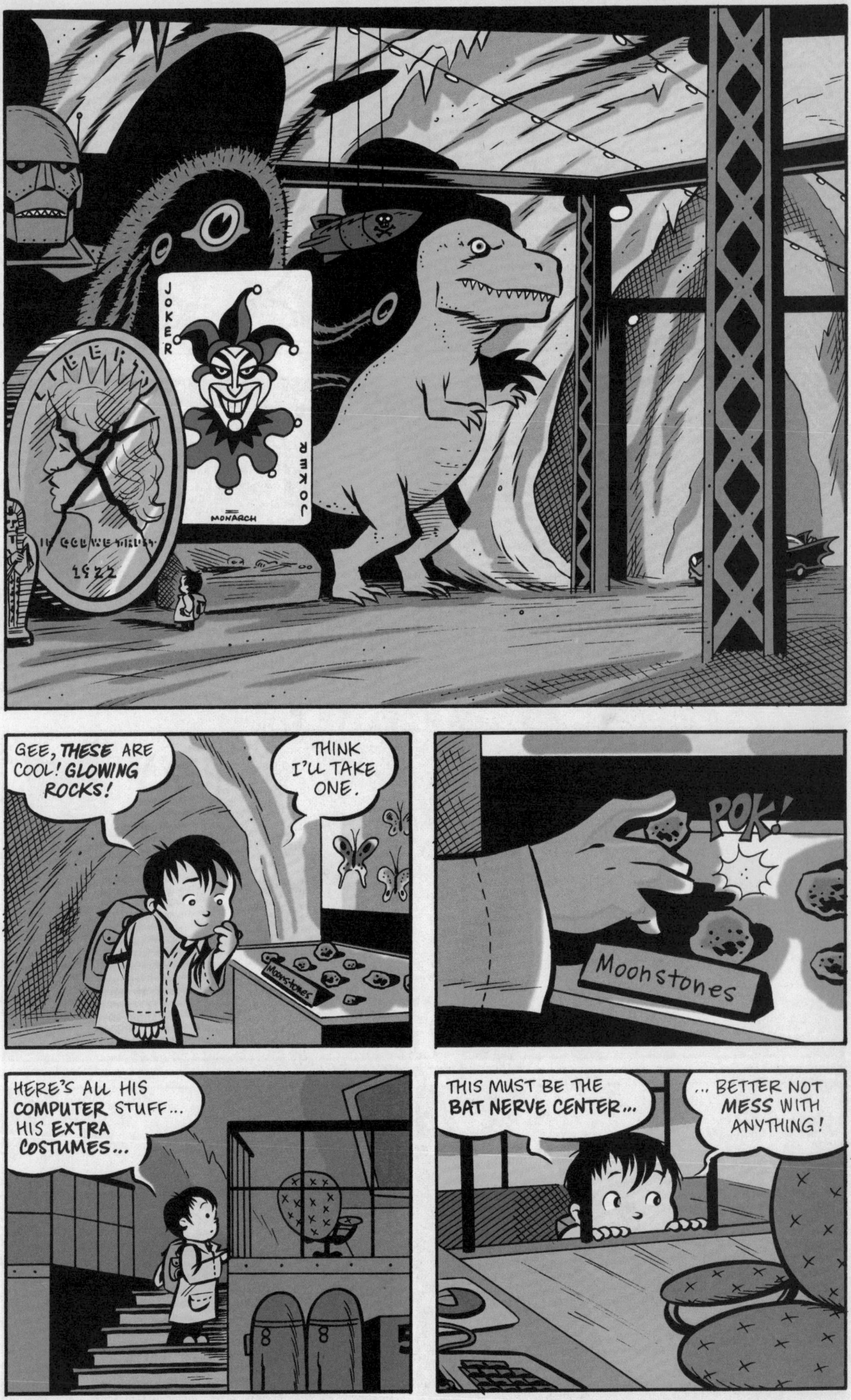
JOKER
MONARCH
LIBERTY
IN GOD WE TRUST
1922
GEE, THESE ARE COOL! GLOWING ROCKS!
THINK I'LL TAKE ONE.
Moonstones
POK!
Moonstones
HERE'S ALL HIS COMPUTER STUFF... HIS EXTRA COSTUMES...
THIS MUST BE THE BAT NERVE CENTER...
... BETTER NOT MESS WITH ANYTHING!

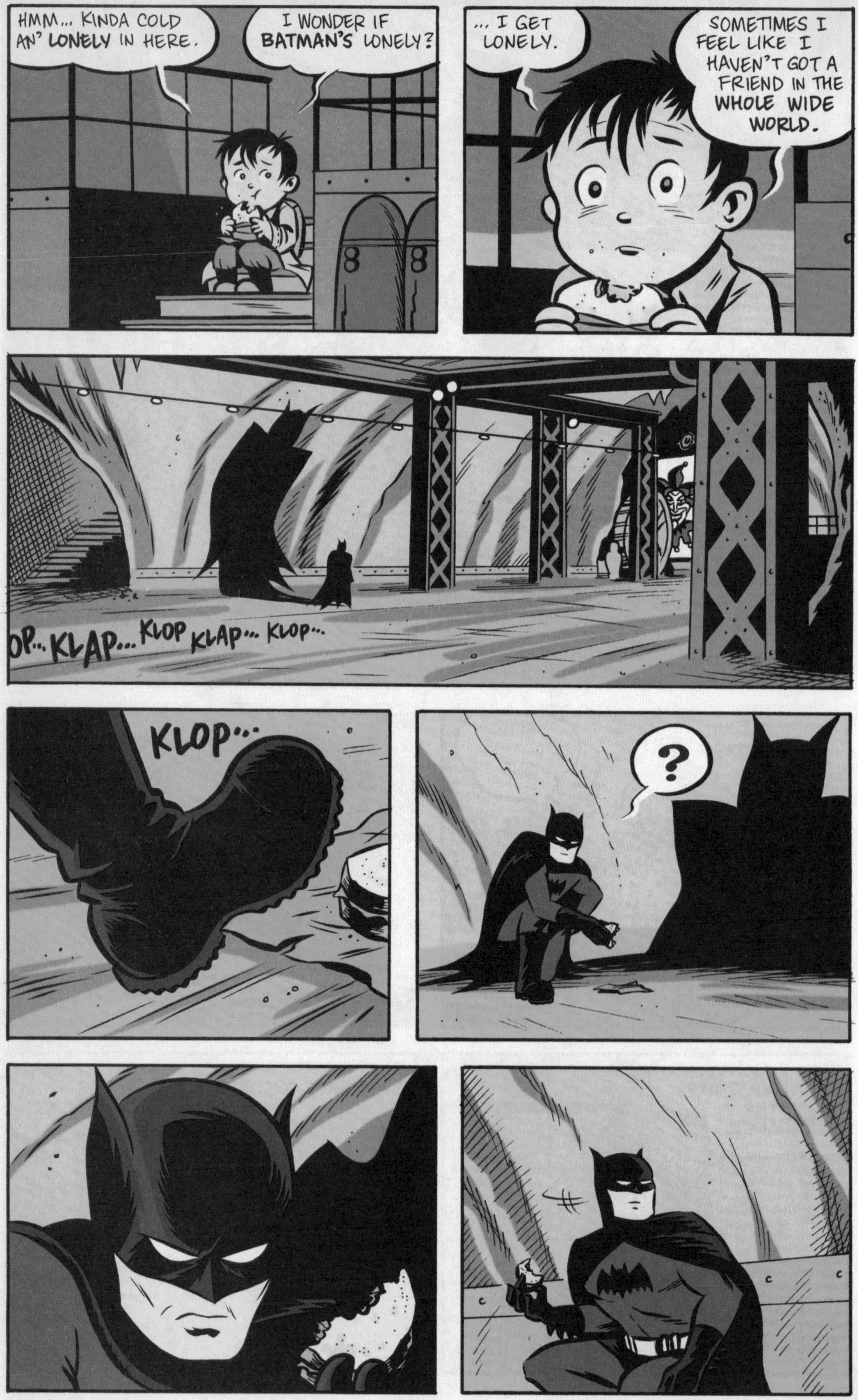
HMM... KINDA COLD AN' LONELY IN HERE.
I WONDER IF BATMAN'S LONELY?
... I GET LONELY.
SOMETIMES I FEEL LIKE I HAVEN'T GOT A FRIEND IN THE WHOLE WIDE WORLD.
OP... KLAP... KLOP KLAP... KLOP...
KLOP...
?

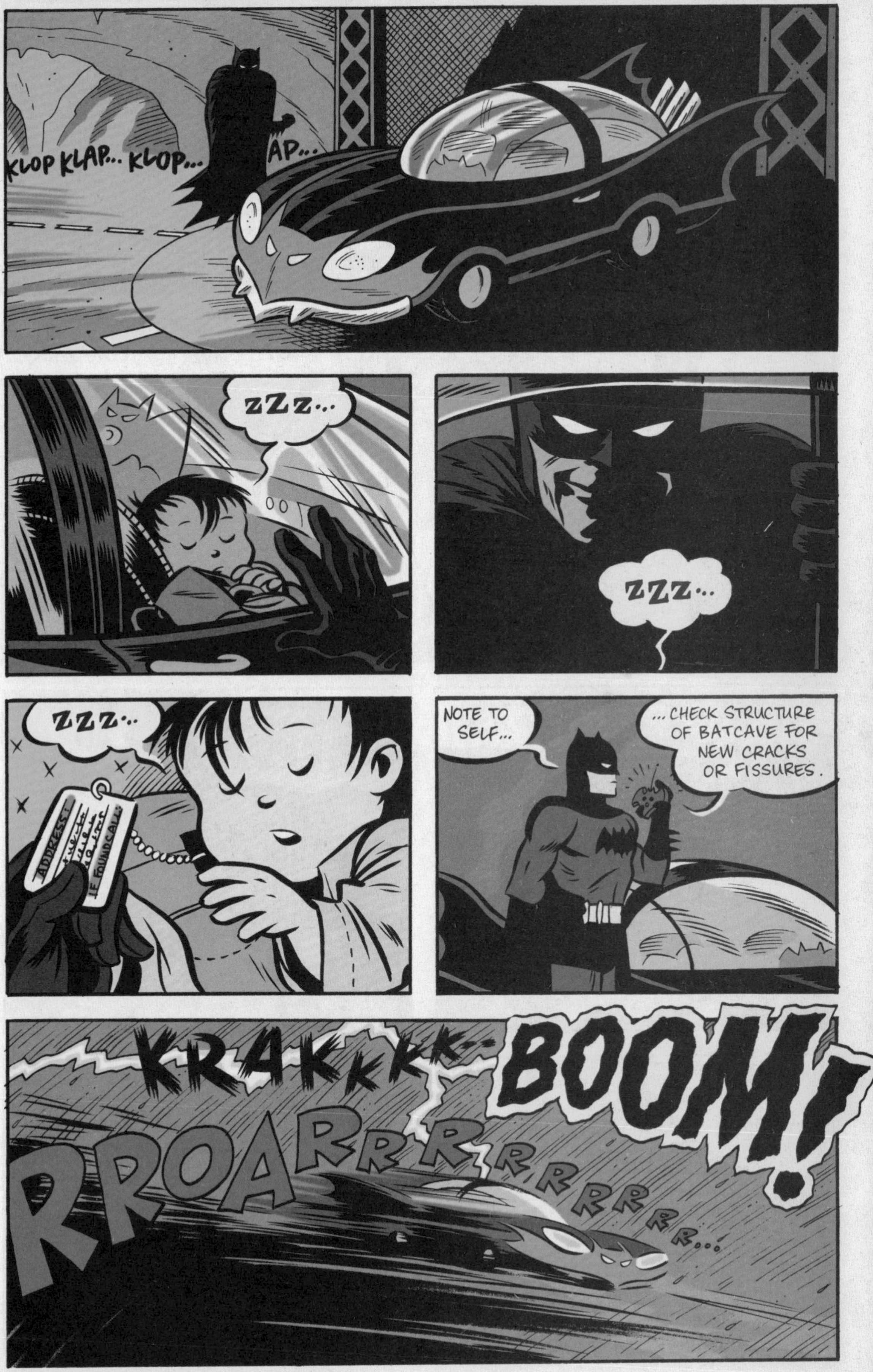
KLOP KLAP... KLOP...
AP...
ZZZ...
ZZZ...
ZZZ...
NOTE TO SELF...
...CHECK STRUCTURE OF BATCAVE FOR NEW CRACKS OR FISSURES.
KRAKKKK-BOOM!
RROARRRRRRRRR...

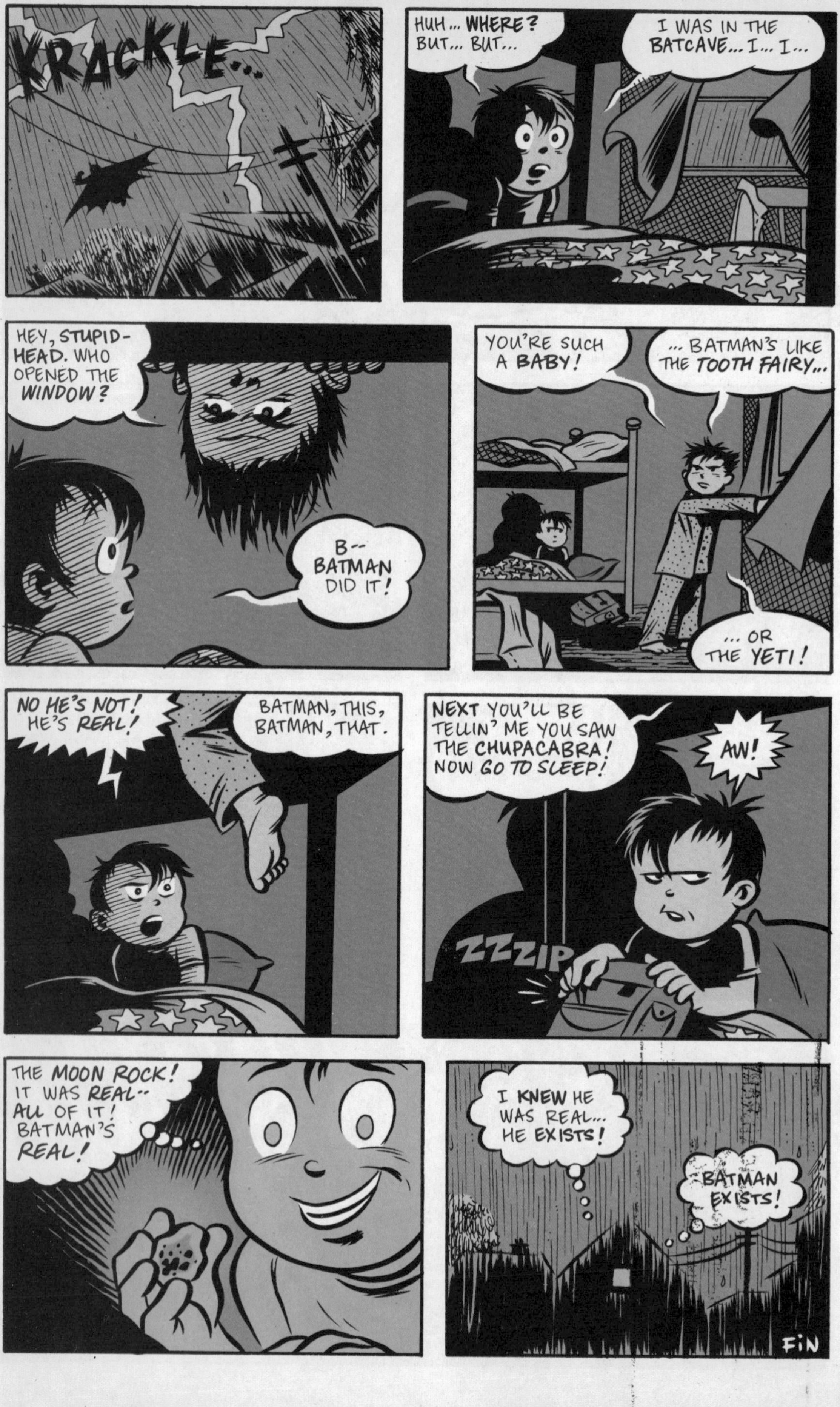
KRACKLE...
HUH... WHERE? BUT... BUT...
I WAS IN THE BATCAVE... I... I...
HEY, STUPID-HEAD. WHO OPENED THE WINDOW?
B-- BATMAN DID IT!
YOU'RE SUCH A BABY!
... BATMAN'S LIKE THE TOOTH FAIRY...
... OR THE YETI!
NO HE'S NOT! HE'S REAL!
BATMAN, THIS, BATMAN, THAT.
NEXT YOU'LL BE TELLIN' ME YOU SAW THE CHUPACABRA! NOW GO TO SLEEP!
AW!
ZZZIP
THE MOON ROCK! IT WAS REAL-- ALL OF IT! BATMAN'S REAL!
I KNEW HE WAS REAL... HE EXISTS!
BATMAN EXISTS!
FIN